BECOMING LOGICAL
An Introduction to Logic

Becoming Logical

☐ AN INTRODUCTION TO LOGIC

ROBERT PAUL CHURCHILL
George Washington University

ST. MARTIN'S PRESS   NEW YORK

Library of Congress Catalog No: 83-61626

Copyright © 1986 by St. Martin's Press, Inc.

All rights reserved.

Manufactured in the United States of America.

09876
fedcba

For information, write:
St. Martin's Press, Inc.
175 Fifth Avenue
New York, NY 10010

cover design: Darby Downey
text design: Betty Binns Graphics/Martin Lubin

ISBN: 0-312-07066-7

PREFACE

An introductory logic text should offer students their first acquaintance with the variety of skills and techniques used to assess arguments. It should offer intensive training in the important and traditional domains of deductive and inductive logic. And it should show students how logical skills have practical consequences in reasoning and can be applied in contexts outside the traditional subject matter of logic. *Becoming Logical* is intended to meet all these objectives.

Part One begins with the skills of informal argument analysis and connects these skills with both the basic concepts of logic and the common linguistic fallacies encountered in daily life. Part Two covers the classical domain of deductive logic from Aristotelian categorical logic through monadic predicate logic. Part Three introduces techniques for evaluating inductive inferences and arguments involving probabilities, showing how logical principles can be applied to scientific reasoning about hypotheses. Part Four emphasizes practical reasoning—by demonstrating how an understanding of the principles of sound reasoning helps us detect and avoid common fallacies, by exploring the principles of legal reasoning, and, finally, by summarizing logical skills and showing how they can be applied to extended arguments.

In writing this text, I have paid as much attention as possible to what students have taught *me* over the past ten years about becoming logical. Each chapter is sensitive to the introductory student's need for explanation. I have attempted to emphasize the purpose of the logical procedures that are introduced and to satisfy, whenever possible, the reader who wants to know why he or she should acquire a certain logical skill. Important concepts are explained carefully and in detail; complex procedures are presented gradually and thoroughly; and special attention has been given to explaining those aspects of deductive reasoning that many introductory students find perplexing. Illustrations and examples have been chosen with care, and the exercises at the end of each section offer students both quick reinforcement and ample opportunity to practice the skills just learned. Students will be able to test their own progress on the exercises by checking the solutions to selected exercises at the end of the text.

Because this text was born of my classroom experiences, in the main it presents tried and true methods of teaching logic. Throughout, I have tried to improve the discussion of standard subjects—such as the discussion of Mill's methods, a notoriously obscure corner of most logic texts. I have also tried to bring the standard areas of logic closer to the skills of practical reasoning and argument analysis. For this reason, in the chapters on deductive reasoning, considerable attention has been given to the practical applications of deductive techniques and to the translation of arguments in natural language either into syllogisms in standard form or into symbolized truth-functional arguments.

The effort to bridge the gap between practical reasoning and the traditional subjects of logic has also led to some important decisions about the content and organization of the text. Although categorical logic can be completely subsumed under predicate logic, *Becoming Logical* offers a thorough coverage of traditional categorical logic. There are two reasons for its retention. First, because categorical logic involves the appraisal of arguments in natural language, studying it makes the transition from informal argument analysis to formal deductive reasoning smoother and more comfortable for students. Second, a careful study of categorical logic, more than the study of any other aspect of deductive logic, seems to help students improve the clarity and organization of their own writing.

I have included tree diagrams (Section 14-2) in Chapter 14 with the analysis of extended arguments. Including them in Chapter 1, as some texts do, would present them before students are sufficiently adept at argument analysis to make proper use of them. In addition, returning to the general techniques of argument analysis in Chapter 14 allows an instructor to pull together all the resources in the book at the end of the course. It also clarifies the purpose of the entire book: to offer students logical skills that can be applied in practical contexts.

I have also decided to discuss informal fallacies at different places in *Becoming Logical* rather than group them together in a single chapter. Fallacies arising from linguistic confusion are discussed in Chapter 4, both because their treatment there is continuous with the discussion of the complexities and pitfalls of language in Chapter 3 and because students are prepared to understand these fallacies without much experience in recognizing sound arguments. The bulk of the informal fallacies, and especially the fallacies of relevance, are presented in Chapter 12 *after* students have been introduced to examples of good reasoning in Chapters 5 through 11. While an instructor may choose to present all the informal fallacies early in a course, I believe they are best learned when they can be contrasted with valid and reliable forms of inference.

Becoming Logical departs from standard logic texts in other important ways. A new feature is the introduction in Chapter 2 of a section on the ethics of argumentation. Students are introduced to principles of responsible, fair, and charitable criticism early in the text so that they can apply these principles throughout their study of logic. A section in Chapter 12—on avoiding fallacies and playing fair—reinforces the orientation toward an ethical analysis of arguments.

Another new feature is Chapter 13, which analyzes arguments made in courtrooms and in judicial opinions. Because it does not presuppose knowledge of the law or of legal process, Chapter 13 is completely accessible to undergraduate students. As a major demonstration of the practical applications of logic, the discussion of reasoning in the law demonstrates the relevance of logic to important contexts in which decisions are made.

In addition to the section on tree diagrams, Chapter 14 contains a six-step summary of argument analysis and a discussion of moral arguments. Although both subjects have appeared in books that emphasize practical reasoning, they are rarely included in comprehensive texts, like this one, that thoroughly cover fundamentals of deductive and inductive logic as well.

Becoming Logical offers a generous assortment of topics, enough even for a course that extends over a full academic year. The breadth of coverage maximizes the instructor's choice of subjects. And instructors who teach a single-semester course will find that the text offers even greater flexibility in the design of a course. The following are five alternative outlines for a one-semester course of about fourteen weeks:

1. A general survey course that introduces inductive reasoning and the informal fallacies while emphasizing deductive reasoning: Chapter 1, Chapter 2, Chapter 5, Chapter 6, Chapter 7, Chapter 8, Chapter 10 (sections 10-1 and 10-2), Chapter 11 (section 11-3), Chapter 12, and Chapter 4 (sections 4-1, 4-2, and 4-3).

2. A course in practical reasoning emphasizing informal argument analysis and especially the linguistic skills involved in argument analysis: Chapter 1, Chapter 2, Chapter 3, Chapter 4, Chapter 5, Chapter 6, Chapter 10 (sections 10-1 and 10-2), Chapter 12, Chapter 14, and, highly recommended, Chapter 7 and Chapter 8 (section 8-1).

3. A course in practical reasoning emphasizing the application of logical principles in science and the law: Chapter 1, Chapter 2, Chapter 7, Chapter 8, Chapter 10, Chapter 11, Chapter 13, and Chapter 14.

4. A course emphasizing deductive reasoning with an introduction to inductive reasoning and some elements of practical reasoning: Chapter 1 (sections 1-1 through 1-4), Chapter 2, Chapter 6 (optional), Chapter 7, Chapter 8, Chapter 9 and Chapter 5 (sections 5-1 through 5-3), Chapter 10, and either Chapter 11 or Chapter 12, and Chapter 4 (sections 4-1 through 4-3), or Chapter 13, or Chapter 14.

5. A general survey course with brief introductions to deductive reasoning, inductive reasoning, and practical reasoning: Chapter 1, Chapter 2, Chapter 3, Chapter 4 (sections 4-1 and 4-2), Chapter 5 (sections 5-1 and 5-2), Chapter 6 (sections 6-1 through 6-3), Chapter 7 (sections 7-1 and 7-2), Chapter 8 (section 8-1), Chapter 10 (sections 10-1 and 10-2), Chapter 11 (sections 11-1 and 11-2), and Chapter 12 (sections 12-1 through 12-4).

Additional suggestions for designing particular courses may be found in the *Instructor's Manual*. In addition, the manual contains remarks designed to help instructors plan their teaching of each chapter. (Further student exercises are available in the separate *Study Guide*.)

The publication of *Becoming Logical* would not have been possible without the efforts and generous assistance of a large number of people. Among the pedagogical pioneers in logic who have influenced my own teaching and to whom I am indebted, several stand out in particular: Morris R. Cohen and Ernest Nagel, whose *Introduction to Logic and Scientific Method* was the progenitor of the comprehensive logic text; Michael Scriven and Stephen N. Thomas, whose work pioneered the development of argument analysis and practical reasoning; Ronald N. Giere, whose *Understanding Scientific Inference* is a major advance in the logic of scientific reasoning and who greatly influenced my own thinking; and Howard Kahane and S. Morris Engel, who have done excellent work on informal fallacies.

Three editors at St. Martin's Press—first Walter Kossmann, and then Michael Weber and Patricia Mansfield—earned my gratitude for their confidence in the project and their nurturing role in bringing it to completion. A large number of professional logicians read and commented on one or more drafts of the text. These philosophers included William R. Brown, Southwest Missouri State University; John Copeland, Drew University; Leland Creer, Central Connecticut State University; Frank Fair, Sam Houston State University; Thomas R. Foster, Ball State University; Emily Grosholz, Pennsylvania State University; Robert Gurland, New York University; Peter Hutcheson, Southwest Texas State University; Al Martinich, University of Texas at Austin; G. J. Mattey, University of California, Davis; Carolyn McMullen, University of Illinois at Chicago Circle; Brooke Moore, California State University, Chico; Herbert Otto, Plymouth State College; and Eric Wefald, New York University. While I found these reviewers to be hard taskmasters, I was continually inspired by their dedication to logic and to improving the standards of public discourse and argumentation. I am grateful to them for helping me avoid a number of pitfalls and for their many helpful suggestions. Whatever errors may remain in the text are, of course, my sole responsibility.

Special thanks go to my colleagues in the Department of Philosophy at George Washington University, all of whom offered continual support and encouragement, especially William B. Griffith; to my wife, Eileen, and my daughter, Rebecca, for their patience and for graciously sharing the burden of completing this project; to Jane Cullen, who did much to improve the clarity and order of the text, both as developmental editor for St. Martin's Press and as a logician in her own right; and finally, to the hundreds of logic students who guided me by their honest questioning, sustained me with their hopes for self-improvement, and shared some of my happiest moments in the classroom.

ROBERT PAUL CHURCHILL

CONTENTS

□   *Part three*
INDUCTIVE REASONING 327

CHAPTER TEN
Generalization, analogy, and probability 329

☐ *Part four*

PRACTICAL REASONING 409

CHAPTER FOURTEEN
The practice of analyzing arguments 498

BECOMING LOGICAL

An Introduction to Logic

INTRODUCTION

A tragic circumstance of our day is the inability of medical science to offer a reliable cure for certain kinds of cancer. Frustration on the part of some cancer victims has led them to seize on treatments that have not been proven effective in standard tests. One such treatment involves the use of the chemical substance known as laetrile, which has numerous advocates among cancer victims, their families, and their friends.

Consider someone who believes that laetrile is an effective cure for cancer and who wants others to share this belief. The statement "Laetrile is an effective cure for cancer" therefore expresses a belief this person communicates to others through speech and writing. But as newspaper reports and other media coverage over the past several years indicate, this belief is highly controversial. Many doctors claim that laetrile is worthless as a cure for cancer. And it is potentially dangerous, because a cancer patient who chooses it may delay or forgo more effective treatment.

The controversial nature of the claims made for laetrile illustrates two further points: (1) there is an important distinction between belief and truth, and (2) in order for our beliefs to be accepted as reasonable by others, especially by those who might initially reject them, there must be justification for them. Uncle Silas believes that laetrile cures cancer, but his believing this cannot make it true.

Many widely believed statements are either of questionable truth or outright false, and many statements are in fact true even though no one believes them. In Christopher Columbus's day, for example, many people believed that the earth was flat, but this does not mean the earth was flat at that time. And until the continent of Australia was explored, Europeans could not have known that "Some swans are black" expresses a true statement. *To have a belief is to accept a given statement as true.* Thus, saying "Uncle Silas believes laetrile cures cancer" is shorthand for saying that Uncle Silas regards the statement "Laetrile is an effective cure for cancer" as true.

What, then, is truth? Answering this question is a tall order; the nature of truth has for centuries been debated by philosophers of all kinds. For our purposes, however, questions about truth will be considered as follows: When

1

I ask whether Uncle Silas's claim about laetrile is true, I am simply asking whether it *corresponds* to the way things are. The statement expressed as "Laetrile is an effective cure for cancer" is true only if the substance called laetrile does cure cancer; otherwise, the statement is false.

At any given time, a statement is either true or false, and not both. Occasionally, you hear someone say that something is "true for me even though it may not be true for anyone else." The only sense we can make of such a remark is that this person believes the statement is true, regardless of what others believe, and perhaps even has a strong feeling that it is true. Nevertheless, a false statement is false no matter how strongly we feel about it or how important we think it is for the statement to be true.

One justifies a statement by showing that there are good *reasons* for asserting that it is true. Uncle Silas is justified in believing that laetrile cures cancer only if it is reasonable to believe that laetrile *does* cure cancer. This point may seem so simple as to be obvious. But the matter is far from simple, for in most important cases it is not at all clear whether it is more reasonable to believe or to doubt a controversial statement. If I want to know whether it is now raining, I can go to the window and check; if I want to know the dimensions of my desk, I can measure it. The evidence in both cases is available, and I know how to go about examining it. But often it is difficult to know what should count as reliable evidence—as illustrated by the debate over the effectiveness of laetrile.

The evidence from tests on cancer patients as well as laboratory animals indicates that laetrile is ineffective as a cure for cancer. How, then, can we account for the large number of people who have taken laetrile and testify to its effectiveness? When studied individually, their case histories are less than persuasive. Some people appear never to have had cancer and to have been the victims of misdiagnosis. Others have mistakenly thought themselves cured of cancer. Still others have attributed a temporary improvement of their symptoms to the use of laetrile, even though cancer patients who have never taken it experience such improvements fairly frequently.

Pro-laetrile groups argue that the evidence against laetrile is not reliable. They claim that the number of case histories examined is too small, that the laboratory tests have been too few, and that experimenters have either followed the wrong procedures in conducting their tests or have misinterpreted their data. They also question the relevance of the data: given the differences between the physiology and metabolism of rats and human beings, they ask whether evidence of the ineffectiveness of laetrile in treating rats really counts as evidence of its probable ineffectiveness in treating humans.

Supporters of laetrile should be able to explain why laetrile is effective, but the two leading explanations have been found to be highly doubtful. It was first claimed that laetrile, which contains traces of the poison cyanide, would destroy tumor cells but not normal cells. Cancerous cells were believed to contain an abnormal amount of an enzyme that triggers the release of cyanide from laetrile, and normal cells were thought to contain a different enzyme that neutralizes the cyanide. However, the enzyme that is supposed to release the cyanide is actually found in smaller amounts in cancer cells than in normal cells; the enzyme that is supposed to neutralize the cyanide in normal cells is found in equal amounts in cancerous cells.

In 1970, advocates of laetrile began describing it as a vitamin—"vitamin B-17"—and suggested that cancer is a result of a vitamin B-17 deficiency. But so far, no scientific evidence supports this view. After extensive experiments at the National Cancer Institute and the Memorial Sloan-Kettering Institute, investigators concluded that laetrile is not a vitamin and that no known disease results from a deficiency of it. Indeed, laetrile has no nutritional value and appears to play no role in cellular metabolism, growth, or development.

The preceding discussion contains arguments that are used to convince people either that laetrile is an effective treatment for cancer or that it is not.

One attempts to justify a statement by exhibiting it as the conclusion of an argument.

The *conclusion* is the statement the person presenting the argument wants us to believe. Other statements, presented by the arguer as reasons for believing the conclusion, are called the *premises*. An argument thus consists of a set of statements: the premises plus the conclusion.

Typically, an arguer claims both (1) that the premises, or reasons offered, are true, and (2) that the premises support the conclusion by making its truth probable as well—or, in the strongest cases, by insuring the truth of the conclusion. The premises justify the conclusion by providing the information needed to make our believing the conclusion reasonable. The premises themselves are accepted as true, and it is assumed by the arguer that the premises transmit their truth to the conclusion, so to speak.

Logic is, in large part, the study of arguments and, in particular, a study of the conditions under which we are justified in believing a conclusion.

The study of arguments begins in Part One. Chapter 1 presents skills needed to recognize arguments—to identify their premises, conclusions, and other important features. Chapter 2 discusses the different ways premises can be connected to a conclusion, while Chapter 3 calls attention to the way language is used to shape thought—an important aspect of analyzing arguments. Chapter 4 thus completes Part One by examining some of the ways language frustrates clear thinking and by introducing techniques for clarifying the meaning of words and statements.

Parts Two and Three examine the conditions under which we are justified in believing the conclusions of arguments. Here, logic is concerned with evaluating arguments to determine whether they are strong or weak, good or bad. Part Two will consider *deductive* arguments—those in which the strength of the reasoning depends upon the connection between the premises and the conclusion. The way in which the premises and conclusion are connected is determined by the *form* of the argument. And if a deductive argument has the proper form, then true premises will ensure that the conclusion is true as well. One who uses such a deductive argument is said to be demonstrating or proving that the conclusion is true.

As an example of a deductive argument, consider the way someone might argue for the conclusion that laetrile is not a vitamin. The completed argument might go like this:

> **If laetrile is a vitamin, then either it has nutritional value and plays a role in cellular metabolism, or a disease results from a deficiency of it.**
>
> **Laetrile has no nutritional value and plays no role in cellular metabolism.**
>
> **No disease results from a deficiency of laetrile.**
>
> **Therefore, laetrile is not a vitamin.**

Because the correctness or *validity* of deductive arguments like this depends on their form, logicians have been able to devise explicit methods for evaluating such arguments. Formal methods for checking the validity of a wide range of arguments are discussed in Chapter 5 through Chapter 9. Chapters 5 and 6 present techniques for evaluating deductive arguments that began with the work of the ancient philosopher Aristotle in the fourth century B.C. As revised and expanded by modern logicians, these techniques greatly assist in evaluating *syllogisms* and related arguments. Chapters 7 through 9 introduce the techniques of elementary symbolic logic, all of which were developed in the late nineteenth and twentieth centuries.

Of course, not all arguments can be regarded as demonstrations or proofs. Arguments that occur frequently in the physical and social sciences are *inductive* arguments. These arguments are employed when we must reach reliable conclusions about probable future experiences based on our past experiences. Consider, for example, the reasoning of someone who is considering whether it will be worthwhile to use laetrile in the struggle against cancer. This person knows that laetrile has been shown to be ineffective as a cure for cancer in laboratory animals. But what reason is there to believe that the results of laboratory tests on animals are relevant to the debate over whether laetrile will be effective as a cure for cancer in humans? The following inductive argument might be offered in answer to this question:

> **The pathogenesis of cancer in humans and laboratory animals is similar; that is, most of the causes of cancer in humans are also causes of cancer in laboratory animals.**
>
> **Malignant tumors develop and metastasize (spread) in humans in much the same way that they develop and metastasize in laboratory animals.**
>
> **Chemical and radiation treatments that check the spread of cancer in humans have also been shown to check the spread of cancer in laboratory animals.**

Laetrile has been shown to be ineffective as a treatment for cancer in laboratory animals.
Therefore, laetrile probably will be ineffective as a treatment for cancer in humans.

Inductive arguments of this kind are *analogies*, and they are among the patterns of reasoning studied in Part Three. Chapter 10 examines generalizations, analogies, and techniques for estimating probabilities. Chapter 11 offers a general examination of the reasoning involved in testing hypotheses, as well as reasoning about cause-and-effect relations.

Although all logical skills have important practical consequences in improving reasoning, the focus on practical reasoning in Part Four has less to do with particular techniques than with the general use or abuse of reasoning. Chapter 12 examines common fallacies or counterfeit arguments that are often mistaken for reasonable, sound arguments. Chapter 13 analyzes the role of argumentation in courts and in judicial opinions—a subject of great interest to many logic students. Finally, in addition to discussing extended arguments and moral reasoning, Chapter 14 presents "The Six Steps of Argument Analysis." These steps summarize many of the techniques introduced in the text and organize them into a convenient strategy for reaching a comprehensive judgment about the merits and demerits of any argument that students might encounter inside or outside the classroom.

☐ *Part one*

LOGIC AND ARGUMENT

CHAPTER ONE

Recognizing arguments

Since the time of the seventeenth-century philosopher René Descartes (1596–1650), the principle that one must examine the method used to study a subject before beginning one's study has been widely accepted. This principle is especially relevant to logic. Our subject matter is argumentation; but to appraise arguments competently, we must first develop an awareness of certain methods indispensable to their analysis. To this end, we shall consider certain features of arguments and of the language in which they are expressed.

☐ 1-1. SENTENCES AND STATEMENTS

An element of everyday language without which argumentation, whether spoken or written, would be impossible is the *sentence*. Whenever you hear someone speak, or when you read a book, a newspaper, or a magazine article, what you hear or read is a series of sentences. Any such series of sentences is also called a *discourse*, so you are at this moment reading a discourse.

Logicians, like grammarians, distinguish between different types of sentences: declarative sentences make claims, or assertions; interrogative sentences ask questions; imperatives issue orders; and exclamations express emotion. *We shall understand a sentence to be a string of words that conforms to grammatical conventions so as to comprise a complete grammatical unit*, and we shall devote particular attention to declarative sentences.

It is important to appreciate the difference between sentences, on the one hand, and *statements*, or *propositions*, on the other hand. For language does not conform exactly to thought. The philosopher Ludwig Wittgenstein (1889–1951) claimed in his work *Tractatus Logico-philosophicus* that natural, or everyday, language obscures thought the way clothes conceal the human body: "Language disguises thought. So much so, that from the outward form of the clothing it is impossible to infer the form of the thought beneath it, because the outward form of the clothing is not designed to reveal the form of the body, but for entirely different purposes." Wittgenstein's position is too extreme: well-constructed sentences do not disguise the thoughts they express.

But just as there is a difference between what is worn and the person who wears it, there is often an important difference between what is thought and how that thought is expressed in language.

It is the statement—the unit of thought conveyed through a sentence—that interests the logician. And not every sentence expresses a statement:

A sentence expresses a statement when it is used to assert or deny something. Only those sentences that could be either true or false express statements.

To understand the distinction between sentences and statements, consider the following:

1. *Two different sentences can express the same statement.* For example:

Raymond fears Bigfoot.
Bigfoot is feared by Raymond.

Any information that would make one of these sentences true or false would make the other true or false as well. But they are different: the second sentence contains five words while the first contains three, and the order of the words is not the same.

2. *While a sentence is always part of a particular language, statements are not peculiar to any of the languages in which they can be expressed.* The Latin sentence *Veritas vos liberabit* conveys the same message as the English sentence "The truth shall make you free." Those who know French, German, Spanish, or Russian can translate the Latin sentence into still other sentences. Yet the sentences all have a single meaning, because they all express the same statement.

3. *Just as more than one sentence can express the same statement, the same sentence can, in different contexts, be used to convey different statements.* Consider the sentence "When you turn in your paper, I shall lose no time in reading it." Ordinarily, this would be taken to mean that the speaker will put other things aside and turn to the paper as quickly as possible. If it were said in an ironic tone of voice, however, the speaker could mean that the paper will probably be so inconsequential that it can be quickly disposed of. A similar ambiguity surrounds the remark "Nothing is too good for her." But it is not only ambiguous remarks that have alternate meanings. As everyone knows, "Aren't you ashamed of yourself?" invariably means what is more directly conveyed by "You should be ashamed of yourself!"

4. *A sentence may be used to express more than one statement.* For example, the compound sentence "Jake whistled a tune while writing his essay, but Erica was glum about her prospects of passing" expresses two statements: "Jake whistled a tune while writing his essay" and "Erica was glum about her prospects of passing." From a grammatical point of view, the compound sentence is a single sentence—a single grammatical unit. But logicians recognize two distinct statements expressed by that one sentence.

Besides having a certain grammatical *form*, sentences have a *function*. As the following examples show, they are used for *informative, directive, evaluative, emotive* (sometimes called *expressive*), and *ceremonial* purposes.

The planet Neptune is now further from the sun than the planet Pluto. (informative)
Print your name legibly, last name first. (directive)
It was wrong of you to withhold the truth about her illness. (evaluative)
Wow, what a super show! (emotive)
How are you today? (ceremonial)

A sentence's function cannot always be determined by examining its grammatical form. Most declarative sentences are informative in function, but the declarative sentence "I love you" is likely to be emotive as well as informative. And other types of sentences can be informative. The kind of interrogative sentence called a rhetorical question is sometimes informative—as, for example, when a shopper asks, "Isn't this price a bit high?" or when a parent asks a child, "Aren't you a good girl to be so helpful?" Often, the intentions of the speaker and the context of the utterance are more dependable than grammatical form as indicators of the function of a sentence.

Statements are usually expressed in declarative sentences. But regardless of its grammatical form, a sentence always expresses a statement if its function is informative. Such a sentence conveys information that is either correct or incorrect—that either corresponds to reality or does not. We may not know now whether the statements expressed by the sentences "Venus is covered by clouds of sulfuric acid" and "The belief that human beings have free will is a delusion" are true or false. But because such sentences are intended to increase our store of knowledge, it is always appropriate to ask whether they could be known to be true or false.

In general, the question of truth or falsity is irrelevant to directive, emotive, and ceremonial discourse. If you say "Hurrah for the Yankees!" or "Please pass the salt," can I sensibly ask, "True or false?" Emotive expressions can be sincere or feigned, deep or superficial; directives can be clear or confusing, explicit or oblique. But neither emotive expressions nor directives are in themselves true or false. The sentence "I said 'Please pass the salt' " expresses a statement that is true or false depending on whether I did or did not request the salt. But "Please pass me the salt" is itself neither true nor false.

The same applies to ceremonial discourse. Sentences like "How are you today?" do not express a statement and are rarely requests for information. Usually, they have only a formal purpose. Someone who asks "How are you today?" does not really want to know how you are feeling—which is why a response like "Fine, thank you" is usually appropriate. The same question can be a genuine request for information—for example, when a doctor is addressing a patient. But then it has more than a ceremonial function.

Sentences that are evaluative in function can be either informative, emotive, or directive—and it is often difficult to know which. When someone makes a moral judgment (for example, "Abortion is wrong") or an aesthetic judgment ("Andrew Wyeth's painting *Christina's World* conveys a sense of loneliness and despair"), is the sentence informative? Is the sentence about abortion a factual claim, or is it instead an emotional expression of dislike or even a directive that can be rephrased as "You ought to oppose abortion"? Such questions about the status of moral judgments have long troubled philosophers. For our purposes, an evaluative sentence expresses a statement when the context makes it clear that the speaker is offering reasons for a judgment.

A sentence is never informative unless it is plausible to assume that the speaker regards it as true or false. Thus, we have a general way of distinguishing sentences that express statements from other kinds of sentences. *We need only ask whether it is sensible to inquire about the truth or falsity of what the speaker says.* Knowing something about the speaker's intentions and the context of the utterance will help us answer this question. So also will knowing about the meanings of the words used in the sentence, the objects referred to by these words, and the ordinary ways in which similar sentences are used.

When considering the distinction between sentences and statements, the main point to remember is that while grammarians and linguists are interested in sentences, logicians are interested in the relationships between the statements, or propositions, that sentences convey. Before an argument can be appraised, the statements that make it up must be identified. It is therefore important to cut through the words and reach the thought embedded in them.

One notices if one will trust one's eyes the shadow cast by language upon truth.
W. H. AUDEN

■ EXERCISE 1-1

■ A. Which of the following sentences would function as informative in most contexts? Which would usually be directive, emotive, evaluative, or ceremonial?

1. How are you feeling today?

2. The pie is moldy.

3. Please listen.

*4. Stop it, if you can.

---

* An asterisk before an exercise indicates that the solution is given in the Solutions to Exercises section at the back of the book.

5. I shall pay you the money tomorrow.

6. See your dentist twice a year.

7. What a glorious sunset!

*8. All material bodies attract in direct proportion to their masses and in inverse proportion to the square of their distances.

9. Ah, the sheer, breathtaking beauty of this scene!

10. No oil painting is as famous as Leonardo da Vinci's *Mona Lisa.*

11. You must make certain beyond a reasonable doubt that the defendant was the owner of the weapon used in the murder on July 13, 1982.

*12. The defendant was not the owner of the weapon in question.

13. Hear ye, hear ye!

14. Nobody in this room knows who the burglar is.

15. God bless America.

*16. Can you believe that?

17. Aren't you feeling just a little guilty about what happened?

18. I advise you to follow your sister's example.

19. Michelangelo's painting of the ceiling of the Sistine Chapel is the greatest work of art ever produced by one artist.

*20. I wish you all a happy new year.

21. In the fifteenth century, Nicholas Copernicus proposed that the planets revolve around the sun.

22. His conviction for grand larceny was unjust.

23. The defendant will rise and face the jury.

*24. Your honor, we find the defendant guilty of the crime as charged.

25. Take my advice and save your money.

■ B. The next list is more challenging. Again decide which sentences can be understood to express statements. For what purposes might the other sentences be used?

1. "Naked came I into the world, and naked I go out."—Miguel de Cervantes

2. If you don't want to be in trouble, I believe you should watch your step.

3. "Love your enemies, do good to them which hate you."—Luke 6:27

*4. Goodbye, we've had a wonderful time.

5. I pronounce you husband and wife.

6. "We are such stuff as dreams are made of . . . ."—Shakespeare, *The Tempest*

7. I prefer ginger ale to cola.

*8. Since you went away, it's been the blues every day.

9. People who live in glass houses shouldn't throw stones.

10. "I am not a crook."—Richard Nixon

11. "War is hell."—General William Sherman

*12. "Unless Thou wert incomprehensible Thou wouldst not be God."—John Cardinal Newman

13. "Moors are all of them cheats, forgers, and schemers."—spoken by Don Quixote in Miguel de Cervantes' *Don Quixote*

14. "Ladies and gentlemen of the court caught sleeping with their boots on will be instantly decapitated."—Peter the Great

15. *Vive la France!*

*__16.** "The best man who ever breathed isn't good enough for the worst woman in the world."—W. C. Fields in *My Little Chickadee*

17. The whole world loves a lover.

18. Do you want to see the United States of America become a pitiful, helpless giant?

19. How kind of you to invite me.

*__20.** Don't forget your papers are due next Thursday.

21. "The rain in Spain falls mainly on the plain."—*My Fair Lady*

22. If I were you, I would take the money and run.

23. It is a pleasure to meet you.

*__24.** "Spanish is the language for lovers, Italian for singers, French for diplomats, German for horses, and English for geese."—Spanish proverb

25. Sunsets over the Pacific Ocean are far more beautiful than they are over the Atlantic Ocean.

26. "If God did not exist, then everything would be permitted."—spoken by Ivan in Fyodor Dostoyevski's *The Brothers Karamazov*

27. "Love God and do as you please."—St. Augustine

*__28.** It was a mistake for President Ronald Reagan to lift the grain embargo against the Soviets.

29. "Tell me not in mournful numbers, / Life is but an empty dream!"—Henry Wadsworth Longfellow

30. "Let's face the music and dance."—Irving Berlin

31. Fire!

*__32.** How clever of you to ask Harry to your party first!

33. I simply love opera, but I detest ballet.

34. Yale is far and away a better university than Princeton.

35. *Che sera, sera.* ∎

☐ 1-2. PREMISES AND CONCLUSIONS

From now on, we shall occasionally simplify the discussion by referring to a sentence that expresses a statement as if it were itself a statement. This will allow us to define an argument in the following way:

An argument consists of a set of statements in which one or more statements are put forward as reasons for accepting another statement as true.

The statements offered as reasons are called the *premises* of the argument. The statement the premises support, or justify, is called the *conclusion* of the argument.

This definition may at first seem wide of the mark, for often when we say people are "having an argument" we mean that in addition to their apparent disagreement over the truth of some statement, they are displaying irritation or anger. Furthermore, among their claims, there may be no recognizable pattern of statements intended to support a conclusion. Although arguing reveals a number of interesting psychological and sociological features of human behavior, these fall outside the scope of logic.

Logic is concerned with the kinds of arguments that involve *reasoning*, and it provides methods by which we can differentiate between correct and incorrect arguments. In reasoning, the aim is to move from already known truths (or statements reasonably believed to be true) to new or previously unrecognized truths, thereby increasing our store of knowledge.

Thus, the logician considers an argument to be any bit of reasoning that presents at least one statement—a premise—as a reason for accepting another statement. No discourse is an argument, however, unless it contains a clearly identifiable conclusion in addition to the supporting premise or premises. The statements that make up an argument must be so related to one another that each premise is plausibly a reason for the conclusion. And in the sense that the premise is offered as support for the conclusion, the relation between the statements is one-directional, or asymmetrical. The goal of an argument is to make the conclusion acceptable to some audience.

Analyzing a few arguments will show how premises and conclusions are related. In *Dialogues Concerning Two Chief World Systems*, Galileo wrote, "Venus and Mercury must revolve around the sun, because of their never moving far away from it, and because of their being seen now beyond it and now on this side of it. . . ." The argument contained in this quotation can be represented as follows:

PREMISE:	Venus and Mercury never move far away from the sun.
PREMISE:	Venus and Mercury have been observed to be on alternate sides of the sun.
CONCLUSION:	Venus and Mercury revolve around the sun.

The argument, as rewritten, is said to be in *logically proper form*, meaning that its component parts have been explicitly identified and the asymmetrical relationship between the premises and the conclusion revealed.

There are other ways of clarifying premises and conclusions when analyzing an argument. Consider the following quotation from Aristotle's *Politics*: "In a democracy the poor have more power than the rich, because there are more of them, and the will of the majority is supreme." This quotation can be analyzed by putting a bracket around the conclusion and labeling it C and underlining the premises and labeling them P:

(C) [In a democracy the poor have more power than the rich], because
(P) <u>there</u> <u>are</u> <u>more</u> <u>of</u> <u>them</u>, and (P) <u>the</u> <u>will</u> <u>of</u> <u>the</u> <u>majority</u> <u>is</u> <u>supreme</u>.

Contrast these examples with the kind of antagonistic conversation that is popularly referred to as an argument. In J. P. Donleavy's novel *A Singular Man*, George Smith trudges two miles through heavy snow to visit the home of his estranged wife Shirley and his children. A mood of animosity is created when George first knocks on the door and his daughter is reluctant to open it. George and Shirley then engage in some ill-humored sparring, part of which goes as follows (Shirley is speaking first):

"You take being a father so seriously. Trudge through the snow with your little presents. Get left on the stoop of your own house. Do we cost too much?"
"Enough."
"We cost too much."
"You're saying it, not me."
"How's business, George?"
"Depressingly full of insult."
"O you poor ruthless thing, let me get something cold to put on your head."
"I think I'll be going. There's no point having you irresponsibly get at me. As regards cost, I'm indifferent."
"So funny how you changed. You must have been the tightest guy I ever met. Remember the time . . ."
"Now shut up."
"Gee."

There is no need to continue; such exchanges are unfortunately all too familiar. However, this example does illustrate that what is casually regarded as "arguing" often doesn't contain what a logician would consider an argument. In the passage above, there is no statement that serves as a reason for another.

People generally quarrel because they cannot argue.
G. K. CHESTERTON

This is not to say that arguments never occur in works of fiction. They can and do. Just before the exchange between George and Shirley, George encounters the locked door and hears the voice of one of his children behind it. George, speaking first, says,

"Whoever it is, open it."
"No."

"Why won't you open it?"

"Because I don't like you."

"Who's speaking in there, is that you Willbur?"

"Stop calling me boys' names."

"Clarissa."

"Smart. How did you guess?"

"What's happened to your voice?"

"None of your business."

"I'm asking you for the last time, Clarissa to open up this door. I'm frozen."

"It's not your house."

"It is my house."

"We live in it and that means we own it and that means I can keep this door shut and you out of here if I want. I guess you understand English, don't you?"

"Call your mother."

The last sentence spoken by Clarissa contains two small arguments. The conclusion of the first is "the house belongs to us," the premise for which is "we live in it." The second can be reworded to read: "This house is our house; therefore, I can keep the door shut and you out if I want." Note that the conclusion of the first argument is a premise for the second one.

The forgoing examples show that we cannot rule out the presence of an argument by relying solely upon the context in which discourse occurs. Whether a set of statements presents an argument depends in part upon the author or speaker's intentions, as indicated by the context. But we must rely mostly upon internal features of the passage—namely, the relationship between an identifiable conclusion and one or more premises—to determine whether an argument is present.

Not all speech and writing is an attempt to present an argument, of course. As an indispensable part of our social existence, language performs a number of other vitally important functions. But in logic the focus is on argument.

Besides distinguishing between arguments and nonarguments, logicians must also distinguish between good arguments and bad arguments. According to our definition, an argument consists of a conclusion and at least one other statement that can plausibly be regarded as a premise supporting that conclusion.

Consider the following example:

Jack deserves an A in this course because his parents have made great sacrifices to send him to college and he will not be admitted to a good law school if he receives a lower grade.

This is an illustration of poor reasoning because the premises offered as grounds for the conclusion that Jack deserves an A in the course are irrelevant. But despite the irrelevance of the premises to the conclusion, the passage has the logical structure characteristic of arguments. So instead of dismissing the passage as failing to present an argument, we say that it presents a *bad* argument—one in which the premises fail to support the conclusion. Such arguments are called *fallacies*, or *fallacious arguments*, because they contain an error.

A fallacy, or fallacious argument, is any argument rendered defective by an error in reasoning.

Sometimes the defects are easy to spot, sometimes they are subtle. Indeed, some fallacious arguments can mislead people into thinking that the reasoning they represent is logically sound. One must therefore resist the temptation to use the term *argument* in an evaluative sense by labeling all examples of fallacious reasoning as nonarguments.

■ **EXERCISE 1-2**

Indicate which of the following passages present arguments. Write out the conclusion of each argument.

1. "Having found the bomb, we have to use it. We have used it against those who attacked us without warning at Pearl Harbor, against those who have starved and beaten and executed American prisoners of war, against those who have abandoned all pretense of obeying international laws of warfare. We have used it in order to shorten the agony of war, in order to save the lives of thousands and thousands of young Americans."—President Harry S Truman, August 9, 1945

2. "I draw the line in the dust and toss the gauntlet before the feet of tyranny, and I say segregation now, segregation tomorrow, segregation forever."—Alabama Governor George C. Wallace, January 1963

3. "We do not hate those who injure us, if they do not at the same time wound our self-love. We can forgive anyone sooner than those who lower us in our own opinion. It is no wonder, therefore, that we as often dislike others for their virtues as for their vices. We naturally hate whatever makes us despise ourselves."—William Hazlitt, *Characteristics*

*****4.** "That [Alexander] Hamilton ever held any considerable sum in securities seems highly improbable, for he was at no time a rich man, and at his death left a small estate."—Charles A. Beard, *An Economic Interpretation of the Constitution of the United States*

5. "Where all other circumstances are equal, wages are generally higher in new than in old trades. When a projector attempts to establish a new manufacture, he must at first entice his workmen from other employments by higher wages than they can either earn in their old trades, or than the nature of his work would otherwise require, and a considerable time must pass away before he can venture to reduce them to the common level."—Adam Smith, *The Wealth of Nations*

6. "For only to the extent that man has fulfilled the concrete meaning of his personal existence will he also have fulfilled himself. . . . The meaning which a being has to fulfill is something beyond himself, it is never just himself."—Viktor E. Frankel, quoted by Milton Mayeroff in *On Caring*

7. "In the evolution of life the first senses must have been those which monitor physical conditions which are immediately important for survival. Touch, taste and temperature senses must have developed before eyes: for visual patterns are only important when interpreted in terms of the world of objects. But this requires an elaborate nervous system . . . if behavior is controlled by belief in what the object is rather than directly by sensory input."—R. L. Gregory, *The Intelligent Eye*

*8. "Nothing is worth my life, not all the goods
They say the well-built city of Ilium contains . . .
A man can capture steers and fatted sheep
But once gone, the soul cannot be captured back."
—Achilles in Homer's *The Iliad*

9. "The death penalty is a warning, just like a lighthouse throwing its beams out to sea. We hear about shipwrecks, but we do not hear about the ships the lighthouse guides safely on their way. We do not have proof of the number of ships it saves, but we do not tear the lighthouse down."—J. Edgar Hoover, *FBI Law Enforcement Bulletin*

10. "Italy is a fundamentally Catholic country where scientific culture was relatively little developed until recent times. Thus it is very probable that altruistic suicides are more frequent there than in France or Germany, since they occur somewhat in inverse ratio to intellectual development."—Emile Durkheim, *Suicide*

11. "If we live, we live to the Lord, and if we die, we die to the Lord; so then, whether we live or whether we die, we are the Lord's."—Romans 14:8

*12. "Man, being the servant and interpreter of Nature, can do and understand so much and so much only as he has observed in fact or in thought of the course of Nature; beyond this he neither knows anything nor can do anything."—Francis Bacon, *Works*

13. "Every important advance in business ethics has been achieved through a long history of pain and protest. The process of change begins when a previously accepted practice arouses misgivings among sensitive observers. Their efforts at moral suasion are usually ignored, however, until changes in economic conditions or new technology make the practice seem increasingly undesirable."—Albert Carr, "Can an Executive Afford a Conscience?" *Harvard Business Review*

14. "Every duty is either rigorous or meritorious. All rigorous duties follow from the Categorical Imperative, and so do all meritorious duties. Thus, all duties follow from the Categorical Imperative."—Immanuel Kant, *Foundations of the Metaphysics of Morals*

15. "If the law consists of the decisions of the judges and if those decisions are based on the judge's hunches, then the way in which the judge gets his hunches is the key to the judicial process. Whatever produces the judge's hunches makes the law."—Jerome Frank, *Law and the Modern Mind*

*16. "Dave Lowry could have escaped," the Lone Ranger said. "There were a number of times when he could have shot me from ambush. He didn't do it, even though he knew that it would mean freedom. And there was a time when I was trapped by a landslide. Dave saved my life. He didn't have to do that. He could have ridden off and left me there to die. But, instead, he saved my life, though he knew I would go on and capture him. Does that sound like the act of a hardened killer?"—Fran Striker, *The Lone Ranger on Powderhorn Trail*

17. "If you were of the world, the world would love its own; but because you are not of the world [but I chose you out of the world]; therefore the world hates you."—John 15:18–19

18. "Perhaps family life itself originated from the need to sleep and to cluster for protection while in this state. Because sleep occurs during the dark hours when man is least able to cope with his environment, and because man asleep is not alert to the dangers of the outer world, sleep is a state of vulnerability. It is necessary to seek a place of refuge in which to sleep. A troop of baboons has its tree, the wolf has its den; primitive man had a cave or his hut, and we have our bedrooms. Having constructed a safe place to sleep, man is able to use the word 'Home.' "—William C. Dement, *Some Must Watch While Some Must Sleep*

19. "The police are the armed guardians of the social order. The blacks are the chief domestic victims of the American social order. A conflict of interest exists, therefore, between the blacks and the police."—Eldridge Cleaver, *Soul on Ice*

*20. "I've always reckoned that looking at the new moon over your left shoulder is one of the carelessest and foolishest things a body can do. Old Hank Bunker done it once, and bragged about it; and in less than two years he got drunk and fell off the shot tower, and spread himself out so that he was just a kind of a layer, as you may say; and they slid him edgewise between two barn doors for a coffin, and buried him so, so they say, but I didn't see it. Pap told me. But anyway it all came of looking at the moon that way, like a fool."—Mark Twain, *The Adventures of Huckleberry Finn*

21. "While the extrovert is sociable, the introvert is *territorial*. That is, he desires space: private places in the mind and private environmental places. Introverts seem to draw their energies from a different source than do extroverts. Pursuing solitary activities, working quietly alone, reading, meditating, participating in activities which involve few or no other people—these seem to charge the batteries of the introvert."—David Keirsey and Marilyn Bates, *Please Understand Me*

22. "Your honor says, I am either a knave or a madman; now, as I'll assure your honor I am no knave, it follows that I must be mad."—Tobias Smollett, *Humphrey Clinker*

23. "[H]uman babies begin to babble at three or four months as a kind of preparation for speech, and the babbling increases until they begin to form understandable words, after which it declines. The intriguing point about babbling is that it is a spontaneous, self-generated activity and not an attempt to imitate adult speech, the proof being that deaf children, too, babble."—Morton Hunt, *The Universe Within*

*24. "Soldiers are conscripted and forced to fight, but conscription by itself does not force them to kill innocent people. Soldiers are attacked and forced to fight, but neither aggression nor enemy onslaught forces them to kill innocent people. Conscription and attack bring them up against serious risks and hard choices. But constricted and frightening as their situation is, we still say that they choose freely and are responsible for what they do. Only a man with a gun at his head is not responsible."—Michael Walzer, *Just and Unjust Wars*

25. "In time I began to recognize that all of these smaller complaints about rigidity, emotional suffocation, the tortured logic of the law were part of a more fundamental phenomenon in the law itself. Law is at war with ambiguity, with uncertainty. In the courtroom, the adversary system—plaintiff against defendant—guarantees that someone will always win, someone lose. No matter if justice is evenly with each side, no matter if the issues are indefinite and obscure, the rule of law will be declared."—Scott Turow, *One L* ∎

☐ 1-3. FEATURES OF ARGUMENTS

Being aware of certain characteristics of arguments will make it easier to recognize them and their component parts.

1. *An entire argument may be expressed in a single sentence.* Consider the following example:

> I know that the number of midshipmen at the Naval Academy is greater than the number of days in the year, thus I conclude with certainty that there are at least two midshipmen who have the same birthday.

In this case, the arguer's conclusion is "There are at least two midshipmen who have the same birthday," and the premise is "The number of midshipmen at the Naval Academy is greater than the number of days in the year." The premise establishes the conclusion with certainty, for if there are more midshipmen than the number of days in the year (365), it is not possible that each midshipman was born on a different day.

2. *The premises and conclusion of an argument can occur in any order.* Ideally, for the purposes of logical analysis, arguments would be expressed so that the premises came first and the conclusion last, as in the example below:

> **The unicorn is a mythical beast.**
> **No mythical beasts inhabit New York City.**
> **Therefore, no unicorn inhabits New York City.**

In ordinary discourse, however, the conclusion may occur anywhere in the passage. Look again at the quotation from Aristotle's *Politics*:

> In a democracy the poor have more power than the rich, because there are more of them, and the will of the majority is supreme.

Here the conclusion is stated first and the premises follow. (Note that this is also an example of an argument expressed in a single sentence.)

The following example is from Dr. Martin Luther King, Jr., "Letter from Birmingham Jail":

> Any law that degrades human personality is unjust. All segregation statutes are unjust because segregation distorts the soul and damages the personality.

Here the conclusion, "All segregation statutes are unjust," is placed between two premises. The premises are "Any law that degrades human personality is unjust" and "Segregation distorts the soul and damages the personality."

3. *Some arguments contain words or phrases that indicate a statement is being used as either a premise or a conclusion.* The words or phrases in the group

below generally signal that what follows them is a reason for another statement in the discourse. In other words, they indicate the premise of an argument.

INDICATOR WORDS FOR PREMISES

all owing	inasmuch as
as	in view of the fact that
as indicated by	is evidence for
as shown by	on the correct supposition that
assuming as we may that	otherwise
because	may be deduced from
for	may be derived from
for the reason that	may be inferred from
given that	since

The words or phrases in the following group generally, but not always, indicate that the statement in which they occur is a conclusion.

INDICATOR WORDS FOR CONCLUSIONS

accordingly	it follows that
allows us to infer that	leads one to believe that
bears out the point that	means that
consequently	points to the conclusion that
demonstrates that	proves that
entails that	so
hence	therefore
I conclude that	thus
implies that	which shows that
in this way one sees that	You see that

Several of these indicator words appear in arguments discussed earlier. *Because* served as an indicator word to introduce premises in the arguments by Galileo, Aristotle, and Dr. Martin Luther King, Jr. And in the argument concerning the birthdates of midshipmen at the Naval Academy, the words *thus* and *conclude . . . that* introduce the conclusion.

As helpful as these indicator words are, they can lead one astray because they are sometimes used in other ways. Frequently, the words *thus* and *so* do not indicate conclusions and *because, since, as, for,* and *otherwise* do not indicate premises. For example, *because* can serve to introduce a causal explanation, and *since* often refers to time.

a. *The word* because *used to relate premise and conclusion:*
"Men do not desire the good because it is good; it is good because men desire it."—Baruch Spinoza

b. *The word* because *used to introduce a causal connection:*
The cooking stove won't work because someone put alcohol in it instead of kerosene.

c. *The word* since *used to relate premise and conclusion:*
Since Smedley is a partner in the most successful law firm in the city, his income is probably high for members of his profession.

d. *The word* since *used to introduce a temporal relationship:*
Since Smedley joined the law firm, an increasing proportion of his work has involved malpractice cases.

Indicator words do not always signal the presence of a premise or conclusion in an argument. They are merely clues that a premise or conclusion may follow.

4. *Some argumentative discourse contains no indicator words.* In an essay on obscenity and pornography, Irving Kristol, a social critic, writes:

> [O]bscenity is not merely about sex, any more than science fiction is about science. Science fiction, as every student of the genre knows, is a peculiar vision of power: what it is really about is politics. And obscenity is a peculiar vision of humanity; what it is really about is ethics and metaphysics.

NEW YORK TIMES MAGAZINE, MARCH 28, 1978

Although there are no indicator words in the passage, Kristol's statement that science fiction is really about power and his comparison between science fiction and obscenity are intended as reasons for the conclusion: "what [obscenity] is really about is ethics and metaphysics." Thus, this passage can be treated as an argument about the real significance of obscenity, even in the absence of indicator words.

5. *Some discourses contain two or more arguments that are entwined.* Two arguments are contained in the following quotation from R. G. Collingwood's *The Idea of Nature*: "Matter is activity, and therefore a body is where it acts; and because every particle of matter acts all over the universe, every body is everywhere."

The arguments are as follows:

FIRST PREMISE:	Matter is activity.
FIRST CONCLUSION:	Therefore, a body is where it acts.
SECOND PREMISE:	Every particle of matter acts all over the universe.
SECOND CONCLUSION:	Every body is everywhere.

In *Concerning Civil Government*, John Locke tells us: "It is not necessary—no, nor so much as convenient that the legislative should be always in being; but absolutely necessary that the executive power should, because there is not always need of new laws to be made, but always need of execution of the laws that are made."

Locke's discourse also contains two arguments:

FIRST PREMISE:	**There is not always need of new laws to be made.**
FIRST CONCLUSION:	**It is not necessary that the legislative body should be in continuous session.**
SECOND PREMISE:	**There is always need of execution of the laws that are made.**
SECOND CONCLUSION:	**It is necessary that the executive power should continue in being.**

As this example shows, the arrangement of words and sentences in a passage may provide little indication of the logical relationship of its parts. To decide whether a discourse contains an argument or arguments, ask the following questions about each statement it contains: Is this a reason for an idea that is being put forth in the passage? If so, which specific idea does it support? A positive response to the first question means that the statement is a premise. The idea it supports will be the conclusion of the argument.

6. *The terms* premise *and* conclusion *are themselves relative, or functional.* In a passage containing more than one argument, the conclusion of one argument can serve as a premise in another:

A statement functions as a premise or as a conclusion depending on how it is being used in a given argument.

In sorting premises from conclusions, remember that the conclusion is an assertion the speaker wants the hearer to accept as true, and the premises are statements offered as reasons for accepting the conclusion.

Read the following passage and pick out the premises and conclusions:

The most valuable of all the soil invertebrates to man is probably the earthworm; these animals break down much of the plant debris reaching the soil and turn over the soil and aerate it. Accordingly pesticide residues in the soil that appreciably reduce the numbers of earthworms are a particularly serious matter.

CLIVE A. EDWARDS, *SCIENTIFIC AMERICAN*

You should have found *two* arguments. The conclusion of the first is the statement that the earthworm is probably the most valuable of all soil invertebrates to man, and its premises are that the earthworm breaks down plant debris in the soil and that the earthworm turns over the soil and aerates it. The conclusion of the first argument is a premise in the second argument: the assertion that earthworms are probably the most valuable of soil invertebrates is itself a reason for the further conclusion that pesticide residues that kill earthworms pose a serious problem.

This discourse contains what is called a *complex*, or *extended*, *argument* because one component is itself an argument. The structure can be revealed by rewriting the passage so that the statement "The earthworm is probably the most valuable of all soil invertebrates to man" appears twice—once as a conclusion and once as a premise.

7. *A discourse that is not itself an argument may quote or paraphrase a discourse that is an argument.* In *The German Mind*, the American philosopher George Santayana writes,

> Nietzsche rebelled at the thought of . . . pervasive mediocrity. . . . When he praised cruelty, it was on the ground that art was cruel, that it made beauty out of suffering. Suffering, therefore, was good, and so was crime, which made life keener. Only crime, he said, raises man high enough for the lightning to strike him. In the hope of sparing some obscure person a few groans or tears, would you deprive the romantic hero of so sublime a death?

Here Santayana is describing (however accurately or inaccurately) an argument made by the nineteenth-century German philosopher Nietzsche. The conclusion of the argument—according to Santayana's paraphrase—is that suffering and crime are (sometimes) good.

8. *Not everything said in the course of an argument counts as either premise or conclusion.* An argument against the misuse of photocopying machines begins,

> The widespread availability of photocopying machines provides another means of stealing—as if there weren't already enough ways to break the eighth commandment. The problem involves the laws of copyright, established to protect the rights of individuals to monetary income for their labors. Writers, composers, and illustrators, for example, support themselves and their families not by creative work itself but by *selling* the product of their creativity.[1]

The editorial goes on to describe in detail the abuses of photocopying and the consequent infringement on the rights of creative people. The conclusion is that the misuse of photocopying machines is immoral.

For the purpose of analyzing this argument, the comment following the dash ("as if there weren't already enough ways to break the eighth commandment") can be put aside because it is not a premise. Often passages that contain arguments also contain expressions of emotion, literary flourishes, parenthetical comments, or other language extraneous to the argument. The ability to judge whether material is an element of the argument or merely an aside

---

[1] "Multiplied Theft," *Christianity Today*, September 10, 1971.

depends upon the ability to judge whether it is a statement and, if so, what its relationships are to other statements in the passage.

■ EXERCISE 1-3

Which of the following passages contain arguments, and which do not? Identify the premises and conclusion of each argument in each passage.

1. "All censorships exist to prevent anyone from challenging current conceptions and existing institutions. All progress is initiated by challenging current conceptions, and executed by supplanting existing institutions. Consequently the first condition of progress is the removal of censorship. There is the whole case against censorship in a nutshell."—George Bernard Shaw, preface to *Mrs. Warren's Profession*

2. "The true distinction between these forms . . . is, that in a democracy, the people meet and exercise the government in person, in a republic, they assemble and administer it by their representatives and agents. A democracy, consequently, must be confined to a small spot. A republic may be extended over a large region."—James Madison, The *Federalist*, no. 14

3. "The fact that for a long time Cubism was not understood and that even today there are people who do not see anything in it means nothing. I do not read English, but this does not mean that the English language does not exist; I cannot blame anyone but myself if I do not appreciate that which I know nothing about."—Pablo Picasso, quoted by Mario Zayus in "Picasso Speaks," *Arts*

*4. "No American young or old, must ever be denied the right to dissent. No minority must be muzzled. Opinion and protest are the life breath of democracy—even when it blows heavy."—President Lyndon B. Johnson

5. "It seems that the will of God is changeable. For the Lord says (Gen. vi.7): *It repenteth Me that I have made man.* But whoever repents of what he has done, has a changeable will. Therefore God has a changeable will."—Thomas Aquinas, *Summa Theologica*

6. "Because intense heat is nothing else but a particular kind of painful sensation; and pain cannot exist but in a perceiving being; it follows that no intense heat can really exist in an unperceiving corporeal substance."—George Berkeley, *Three Dialogues*

7. "Even what a person has produced by his individual toil, unaided by anyone, he cannot keep, unless by permission of society. Not only can society take it from him, but individuals could and would take it from him, if society only remained passive; if it didn't interfere *en masse*, or employ and pay people for the purpose of preventing him from being disturbed in the possession."—John Stuart Mill, *On Liberty*

*8. "If there be righteousness in the heart,
    there will be beauty in the character.
If there be beauty in the character,
    there will be harmony in the home.
If there be harmony in the home,
    there will be order in the nation.
If there be order in the nation,
    there will be peace in the world."
—Confucious, *The Great Learning*

9. "Since morals, therefore, have an influence in the actions and affections, it follows that they cannot be derived from reason; and that because reason alone, as we have already proved, can never have such an influence."—David Hume, *Treatise on Human Nature*

10. "As a challenge to theism, the problem of evil has traditionally been posed in the form of a dilemma; if God is perfectly loving, He must wish to abolish evil; and if He is all-powerful, He must be able to abolish evil. But evil exists; therefore God cannot be both omnipotent and perfectly loving."—John Hick, *Philosophy of Religion*

11. "An interesting point arises in connection with these first two conditions. According to the first, Jews have the lowest rate of intermarriage; according to the second, the religiously more devout also have a lower frequency of mixed religious marriages. Thus, it would logically follow that Jews are more religious than either Protestants or Catholics."—Larry Barnett, "Research in Interreligious Dating and Marriage," *Journal of Marriage and the Family*

*12. "The age of innocent faith in science and technology may be over. We were given a spectacular signal of this change on a night in November 1965. On that night all electric power in an 80,000 square mile area of the northeastern U.S. and Canada failed. The breakdown was a total surprise. For hours engineers and power officials were unable to turn the lights on again; for days no one could explain why they went out; even now no one can promise that it won't happen again."—Barry Commoner, *Science and Survival*

13. "Every state is a community of some kind, and every community is established with a view to some good; for mankind always acts in order to obtain that which it thinks good. But, if all communities aim at some good, the state or political community, which is the highest of all, and which embraces all the rest, aims in a greater degree than any other, at the highest good."—Aristotle, *Politics*

14. "The materials of nature (air, earth, water) that remain untouched by human effort belong to no one and are not property. It follows that a thing can become someone's property only if he works and labors on it to change its natural state. From this I conclude that whatever a man improves by the labor of his hand and brain belongs to him, and to him only."—John Locke, *Second Treatise of Government*

15. "Some have suggested that prenatal genetic screening through amniocentesis may become a routine part of prenatal care—similar to tests on the mother for syphilis, diabetes and high blood pressure—as an effort to detect most fatal diseases and malformations before birth. This possibility seems remote. The problem of creating facilities to evaluate the three million births per year in the U.S. are, of course, immense, and many local and regional centers would have to be established. More important is the probability that there is almost certain to be a risk inherent in amniocentesis greater than the probability of detecting an abnormal fetus in an unselected population."—Theodore Friedmann, "Prenatal Diagnoses of Genetic Disease," *Scientific American*

■

☐ 1-4. ENTHYMEMES: ARGUMENTS WITH MISSING PARTS

One feature of some arguments is so important that it demands special emphasis:

9. *Some arguments are not fully stated; one or more premises or even the conclusion may be left out. Such arguments are called enthymemes.* When an argument is missing one or more premises, logicians say that the argument has a *suppressed premise.* The premise in question may be missing for a number of reasons: the arguer may simply have neglected to include it or may believe it to be so widely known as to need no repetition. Or—more rarely—the arguer may hope that the audience will supply and assume the truth of a questionable premise that is needed to support the conclusion being presented.

An example of an argument with a suppressed premise is a comment made by Jeb Stuart Magruder, a White House aide during Richard Nixon's presidency. Speaking of the Watergate affair, Magruder said of Nixon, "I knew he was involved. Only a guilty person accepts a pardon."[2] The suppressed premise is that, after resigning the presidency, Nixon accepted President Gerald Ford's pardon—a fact widely known at the time Magruder made his argument.

Another example of an enthymeme with a suppressed premise is Jonathan Swift's wry observation, "No man will take counsel, but every man will take money; therefore, money is better than counsel." The additional premise needed to complete this argument can be represented as, "The value of something is to be determined by whether or not people willingly take it."

It may seem odd that the missing part of an argument will sometimes be the conclusion. Ordinarily, the purpose of an argument is to lead someone to accept the conclusion. In some circumstances, however, the arguer finds it preferable to supply the reasons and allow the audience to draw the conclusion on its own. The conclusion then seems more striking or original—and hence more acceptable. Such a device is often used by advertisers, who would like people to believe that they are making up their own minds regarding the quality of the advertised products. Here are two examples from television commercials.

The bigger the burger, the better the burger.
The burgers are bigger at Burger King.

When you're out of Schlitz, you're out of beer!

Enthymemes with unstated conclusions can also be more subtly effective. In 1967, Representative Adam Clayton Powell, who was resisting attempts to impeach him, said in a speech before the House of Representatives: "He who is without sin should cast the first stone. There is no one here who does not have a skeleton in his closet. I know, and I know them by name." The unstated conclusion is that no one in the House of Representatives should, figuratively speaking, cast the first stone.

To identify and judge an enthymeme, it is often necessary to complete it by supplying the unstated premise or conclusion. In doing so, one must be careful to express the author's intentions, as understood from the passage. A

[2] *Miami News,* May 4, 1977.

premise may be supplied if it can truly be said to be implicit in the assumptions of the arguer or the audience—if it is part of the general fund of common knowledge, if the arguer can reasonably believe the audience possesses the information in question, or if the "missing link" comes readily to mind. But if we add too much, we end up replacing the intended argument with a new one of our own. A full-bodied argument should not be invented when only the dimmest shadow of one exists, nor should we supply premises of which the author was unaware. The goal is to be fair, while recognizing that it is the arguer's responsibility to make the audience understand the argument.

■ EXERCISE 1-4

Each of the following passages can be construed as an enthymeme. Supply suppressed premises and unstated conclusions as needed to complete each argument.

1. I am an Idealist, because I believe that all that exists is spiritual.

2. Achilles is brave, so he must be deserving of the fair.

3. "Death is nothing to be feared, else it would have appeared so to Socrates."—Epicurus

*4. "There is no human nature since there is no God to conceive it . . . man is only what he wills himself to be."—Jean-Paul Sartre, *Existentialism and Humanism*

5. "But . . . man wishes to live in society; he must therefore forgo a portion of his private good for the sake of the public good."—Marquis de Sade, *Juliette*

6. "If you're not happy, Lipton's not in business. And we're very much in business!"—television advertisement

7. " 'Well,' said the chief in disgust, 'there's two people I don't never argue with: one's a woman and the other's a damn fool. And you ain't no woman!' "—Charles Finney, *The Circus of Dr. Lao*

*8. "Poetry is finer and more philosophical than history; for poetry expresses the universal and history only the particular."—Aristotle, *Poetics*

9. "It's the plain women who know about love. The beautiful women are too busy being fascinating."—Katharine Hepburn

10. "Beware, for I am fearless, and therefore, powerful."—Mary Shelley, *Frankenstein*

11. "Man tends to increase at a greater rate than his means of subsistence; consequently he is occasionally subject to a severe struggle for existence."—Charles Darwin, *The Descent of Man*

*12. "I earnestly desire tranquility . . . but fear I shall never attain it; for, when unoccupied I grow gloomy, and occupation agitates me to feverishness."—James Boswell, *The Life of Samuel Johnson*

13. "Harvey's used magazines. If we ain't got it, it ain't worth readin'."
"I'm looking for an issue of *Forbes*. The July . . ."
"It ain't worth readin'."
—Roy Hayes, *The Hungarian Game*

14. "The elegant Lord Shaftesbury somewhere objects to telling too much truth;

by which it may be fairly inferred, that, in some cases, to lie is not only excusable, but commendable."—Henry Fielding, *Tom Jones*

15. What did you expect of him? Tom is a freshman, and all freshmen are intimidated by college professors.

*16. "Fiction is truer than history, because it goes beyond the evidence."—E. M. Forster

17. "Is not this great poetry? I think that it is. There is no falsehood here."—Edith Sitwell

18. "Art for art's sake makes no more sense than gin for gin's sake."—Somerset Maugham

19. "Appeasers believe that if you keep on throwing steaks to a tiger, the tiger will become a vegetarian."—Heywood Broun

*20. "Conclusions regarding animal behavior are valid only if confirmed by observations in the wild. Freud's generation knew nothing of the broader patterns of animal instinct, because science of that time confined its observations to captive animals."—Robert Ardry, *African Genesis* ■

☐ 1-5. FINER POINTS OF DETECTING ARGUMENTS

Sometimes statements are so related to one another that they appear to constitute an argument although they are not really functioning as such. This problem was touched upon in Section 1-3, where it was shown that the word *because* can be used to indicate both a premise and a causal relation between two events.

10. *A series of statements can be asserted in such a way that the truth of one depends upon the truth of another without its being an argument.* Consider these examples:

 a. There is water all over the floor because the pipes burst.

 b. Fritz suffers from claustrophobia, so he never rides in elevators.

If we think about the circumstances under which these remarks would be made, we see that they are not arguments. Anyone who asserts *a* is explaining why there is water on the floor. That there is water on the floor is apparent, so there is no need for argument. Similarly, the person who asserts *b* is trying to indicate the cause, or motive, that leads Fritz to walk up the stairs—not to establish that he does so.

Another type of statement that is not an argument but is likely to be mistaken for one is the *conditional*. This is a compound statement that is usually expressed by a sentence of the "If . . . , then . . ." form. The part following *if* is referred to as the *antecedent*, and the part following *then*, the *consequent*.

 c. If you turn the switch to the left, then the fan speed will go down.

 d. If your grade point average is above 3.25, then you qualify for honors in the department.

A conditional statement is wrongly interpreted as an argument by dividing it into what seem to be a premise (for example, "your grade point average is above 3.25") and a conclusion ("you qualify for honors in the department"). It is *not* being asserted that the first component ("your grade point average is above 3.25") is, in fact, true. The only thing being asserted by a conditional statement is that a particular relationship holds between the events described in its two components: if the first component is true, then the second component also will be true.

It will help you to distinguish arguments from other series of statements if you keep in mind two major differences. First, the relationship between the premises and conclusion of an argument is almost always *asymmetrical* in that the premises support the conclusion but not vice versa. Arguments should move from what is clearly known and accepted to what is debatable or controversial. Just the reverse is true when we state a cause or motive. The supposed conclusion of *b*, that Fritz insists on using the stairs, is better known than his motive for the action, so it is not properly regarded as the conclusion of an argument.

Second, under ordinary conditions, the person presenting an argument is committed to the claim that each premise is true. By contrast, someone who asserts a conditional is not committed to believing that either the first component by itself or the second component by itself holds true at the time the assertion is being made.

11. *The conclusions of some arguments are not statements but directives: commands, imperatives, or prescriptions.* For the most part, logicians deal with arguments having as their conclusions statements that are capable of being true. A person who finds such an argument convincing will have reason to believe that its conclusion is true. However, there are also arguments whose conclusions do not resemble the conclusions of standard arguments.

As noted in Section 1-1, we shall treat an evaluative sentence as a statement when the context makes it clear that the speaker is offering reasons in support of it. Thus, a sentence like "Stealing is wrong" can be regarded as the conclusion of an argument, even if (as some philosophers maintain) it seems inappropriate to treat this sentence as expressing a true or false statement in the same way a sentence about cell biology or child psychology does.

Just as there can be arguments whose conclusions are expressed as evaluative sentences, there can also be arguments whose conclusions are expressed as directives. Suppose someone reasons, "You need three credits of science; astronomy would fit into your schedule, the professor is a fantastic lecturer, and the work load isn't heavy. Therefore, sign up for astronomy." Here the conclusion, "Sign up for astronomy," is not a sentence it would make sense to regard as true. Instead, *to accept the conclusion of this argument is to be willing to do something.* If the person to whom the argument is addressed finds it convincing, he or she will be willing to sign up for the course.

Such arguments are called *practical* arguments, and no account of arguments is complete unless it includes them. Everyday reasoning is often designed to persuade others to accept the necessity or desirability of acting in some way. For simplicity, however, most of the discussion in subsequent chapters will concern arguments whose conclusions are sentences expressing statements rather than directives.

12. *Some arguments can be recognized more easily if you paraphrase the premise(s) and/or the conclusion.* The objective in logic is to study the *statements* that are expressed by sentences. So it is permissible, even advisable, to change the wording of a sentence if doing so clarifies what the arguer is actually asserting. But when paraphrasing, be careful to interpret the argument in the way that makes the most sense. And a written work should be understood to mean what a user of the language at the time it was written would have meant.

In a famous brief argument, the ancient philosopher Epicurus asserts: "Accustom thyself to believe that death is nothing to us, for good and evil imply sentience, and death is the privation of all sentience." Here the conclusion is a directive, "Accustom thyself to believe that death is nothing to us." But to understand the argument, we must correctly interpret the premise "good and evil imply sentience." This, in turn, requires us to know the meaning of *sentience*, a word not commonly used today. According to the dictionary, *sentience* means the capacity of higher animals to have sensations and feelings. So when Epicurus says that good and evil imply sentience, he must mean that good and evil can be experienced only by living creatures that are capable of consciousness. The premises and conclusion of the argument can therefore be paraphrased as follows:

PREMISE: Only those who are alive can experience things as good
                        or as evil.

PREMISE: Death (the end of life) makes it impossible to have any
                        experience.

CONCLUSION: Therefore, you should adopt the view that death is
                        neither experienced as good nor as bad.

Paraphrasing arguments is one of the important skills involved in logic. And as with all skills, the more practice one has, the easier it becomes.

13. *The distinction between arguments and nonarguments is not always clear. There are "borderline" cases.* Logic provides no hard-and-fast rules for recognizing arguments. *There simply is no substitute for a sensitive understanding of the language we speak and the ways in which it is used to communicate thought.* Learning to recognize arguments is a matter of developing judgment, and nothing helps to develop judgment more than practice with arguments that occur in the rough-and-ready world outside the logic classroom.

Our discussion will be adequate if it has as much clearness as the subject-matter admits of, for precision is not to be sought for alike in all discussions, any more than in all the products of the crafts. . . . For it is the mark of an educated man to look for precision in each class of things just as far as the nature of the subject admits.

ARISTOTLE

Here are two "borderline" cases to consider.

a. The pure and genuine influence of Christianity may be traced to its beneficial though imperfect effects on the barbarian proselytes of the North. If the decline of the Roman empire was hastened by the conversion of Constantine, his victorious religion broke the violence of the fall and mollified the ferocious temper of the conquerors.

EDWARD GIBBON, *THE DECLINE AND FALL OF THE ROMAN EMPIRE*

Is the second part of the last (conditional) sentence a premise for the first statement in the passage? Perhaps, but it is not at all clear that one thought is being offered as a reason for accepting another thought.

b. It's worth using some cumbersome or even ungrammatical language to avoid sexism, just as it would be to avoid racist or religious slurs. This is surely an important undertaking. Grammatical standards are not as important as the avoidance of sex-role stereotyping. . . .[3]

When they first see this passage, many people want to treat it as an argument. They usually reconstruct it, after paraphrasing, in somewhat the following manner:

PREMISE:	Grammatical standards are not as important as the avoidance of sex-role stereotyping.
CONCLUSION:	It's worth using some cumbersome or even ungrammatical language to avoid sexist expressions in language.

An equal number of people are reluctant to see this as an argument, however. The problem, they point out, is that the premise and conclusion (as exhibited in the reconstruction above) amount to about the same thing; they do not convey different thoughts. Thus, it would be unfair to the speaker to claim that he or she was presenting an argument, since this would amount to a charge of weak or ineffective reasoning.

Another approach would be to treat the clause "just as it would be to avoid racist or religious slurs" as an additional premise asserting, "It is as important to avoid sexist slurs as it is to avoid racist and religious slurs." It then appears more plausible to claim that we have an argument.

[3] Adapted from Michael Scriven, *Reasoning* (Englewood Cliffs, N.J.: Prentice-Hall, 1978).

PREMISE:	Grammatical standards are not as important as the avoidance of sex-role stereotyping.
PREMISE:	It is as important to avoid sexist slurs as it is to avoid racist and religious slurs.
CONCLUSION:	It's worth using some cumbersome or even ungrammatical language to avoid sexist expressions in language.

But even this additional premise seems too close in meaning to the conclusion to be independent of it. In fairness to the speaker, we should deny that the passage expresses an argument.

To say that sample *b* is not an argument is not to say that it expresses an unimportant idea. If we consider an idea important enough to be defended by the use of reasoned argument, then it is our responsibility to strengthen or help others strengthen weak reasoning offered in its support. But it would be irresponsible to take the view that a discourse is an argument just because it presents a point of view we want others to accept. And the consequences of trying to find an argument in a passage where none is intended can be unfortunate. Reinterpreting such a passage as a loosely constructed argument creates the false impression that the author's thinking is muddled, and the real significance of the assertion is missed.

14. *Arguments can be good or bad, valid or invalid, sound or unsound.* At times, you may be tempted to say, "That can't really be an argument, because the statement that would count as the conclusion is clearly false and no one would seriously argue that it's true," or "This can't be an argument, because the supposed premises don't give any support to the statement we are expected to accept as the conclusion." But just because the intended conclusion is false or the premises are insufficient to establish the conclusion does not mean that there is no argument. As indicated in Section 1-2, there are *bad* arguments as well as *good* arguments.

The process of identifying an argument differs from the process of judging it. So far, our major concern has been to sharpen our ability to recognize arguments for what they are. In Chapter 2, we shall consider the concepts of *validity* and *soundness*, which will enable us to judge how well an argument justifies the belief presented as its conclusion.

■ **EXERCISE 1-5**

■ A. Identify the passages that are arguments. Which, if any, are statements of causal or temporal relations, and which are conditionals?

1. "Two things fill the mind with ever new and increasing admiration and awe, the starry heavens above and the moral law within."—Immanuel Kant, *Foundations of the Metaphysics of Morals*

2. "The more deeply I understand the central role of caring in my own life, the more I realize it to be central to the human condition."—Milton Mayeroff, *On Caring*

3. Since Christians are theists and Bernard is a Christian, Bernard is a theist.

*4. In 1699, King Charles refused to conciliate with Parliament, and consequently, he was overthrown and beheaded.

5. All the vegetarians I know don't drink alcohol, and Cecile, who is a vegetarian, is therefore also likely to abstain from alcohol.

6. The roof of the church collapsed because green timber had been used for the beams.

7. The best way to learn a foreign language is the way native speakers do—by conversing with someone who speaks the language fluently.

*8. If the Soviets invade Iran to establish the Republic of Baluchistan, then we may be fighting on the side of Iran, as paradoxical as this may seem in light of the 1979–1981 hostage crisis.

9. "Advocates of death point out, with a lamentable degree of truth, that reason is a very feeble force in human affairs."—Bertrand Russell

10. "If a nation expects to be ignorant and free, in a state of civilization, it expects what never was and never will be."—Thomas Jefferson

11. If we don't loosen up the penalties for cocaine use and sale, then we're just going to repeat the savagery and alienation caused by the pot laws.

*12. Hang gliders quite often crash for reasons that are never determined.

13. "A really sensible person wouldn't have a jester. So anyone who has a jester is not sensible."—Denis Diderot, *Rameau's Nephew*

14. If a good hotel can give you a beautiful room for seventy-five dollars a day, make a profit, and pay taxes, then a tax-exempt hospital shouldn't operate in the red for one-hundred-and-fifty dollars a day.

15. "I can only fulfill myself by serving someone or something apart from myself, and if I am unable to care for anyone or anything separate from me, I am unable to care for myself."—Milton Mayeroff, *On Caring*

■ B. Rewrite the arguments expressed in the following passages. Paraphrase the premises and conclusions as needed, and add any obvious and intended missing premises or unstated conclusions.

1. "As Augustine says, *that which is not just seems to be no law at all.* Hence the force of a law depends upon the extent of its justice. Now in human affairs a thing is said to be just from being right, according to the rule of reason. But the first rule of reason is the law of nature . . . consequently, every human law has just so much of the nature of law as it is derived from the law of nature. But if in any point it departs from the law of nature, it is no longer a law but a perversion of law."—Thomas Aquinas, *Summa Theologica*

2. "Judging by the usual analogy of nature, no form can continue, when transferred to a condition of life very different from the original one, in which it was placed. Trees perish in water, fishes in the air, animals in the earth. Even so small a difference as that of climate is often fatal. What reason then to imagine, that an immense alteration, such as is made on the soul by the dissolution of its body, and all its organs of thought and sensation, can be effected without the dissolution of the whole?"—David Hume, *Dialogues Concerning Natural Religion*

3. "The decision to use the atomic bomb against Japan, for example, judged by the knowledge we have today of Japan's military potential in the summer of 1945, was probably a mistake. But even if the employment of the bomb spared the allies an invasion and a bloody campaign in the main islands of Japan, a country claiming to defend the cause of freedom and the ultimate dignity of the individual human being cannot justify such a step on the ground of military strategy alone. One cannot accept the argument that the shortening of a war is the supreme end without at the same time abandoning all moral constraints on the conduct of hostilities. . . ."—Guenter Lewy, "Superior Orders, Nuclear Warfare, and the Dictates of Conscience," *American Political Science Review* 55 (1961)

*4. "But were the hostages really heroes? . . . as a group should they be thought of as heroes?

"No, according to social-psychiatrist [Willard] Gaylin, who says 'there has been entirely too much fuss and too much craziness go on [*sic*] about this.'

" 'I find the use of the word "heroism" peculiar at best. It is not only wrong, it is mischievous. I think it places another unfair burden on these people. . . . Heroism implies choice and action. These people didn't have any choice. Yes, they were victims, maybe even martyrs. But this was a situation the opposite of heroism, a situation that involves humiliation, impotence and abandonment of responsibility.' "—*The Washington Post*, January 31, 1981

5. "The more the worker exerts himself, the more powerful becomes the alien objective world which he fashions against himself, the poorer he and his inner world become, the less there is that belongs to him. It is the same in religion. The more man attributes to God, the less he retains in himself. The worker puts his life into the object; then it no longer belongs to him but to the object. . . . The *externalization* of the worker in his product means not only that his work becomes an object, an *external* existence, but also that it exists *outside him* independently, alien; an autonomous power, opposed to him. The life he has given to the object confronts him as hostile and alien."—Karl Marx, *Philosophic and Economic Manuscripts*

■ C. Which of the following passages contain arguments? Which do not? Which are "borderline" cases? Provide a brief justification for each answer (some passages may require paraphrasing).

1. "When we regard a man as morally responsible for an act, we regard him as a legitimate object of moral praise or blame in respect of it. But it seems plain that a man cannot be a legitimate object of moral praise or blame for an act unless in willing the act he's in some important sense a 'free' agent. Evidently free will, in some sense, therefore, is a precondition of moral responsibility."—C. A. Campbell, *In Defense of Free Will*

2. "Look around this universe. What an immense profusion of beings, animated and organized, sensible and active! You admire this prodigious variety and fecundity. But inspect a little more narrowly these living existences, the only beings worth regarding. How hostile and destructive to each other! How insufficient all of them for their own happiness! How contemptible and odious to the spectator! The whole presents nothing but the idea of a blind nature, impregnated by a great vivifying principle, and pouring forth from her lap, without discernment or prenatal care, her maimed and abortive children."—David Hume, *Dialogues Concerning Natural Religion*

3. "The dawn of genetic engineering is troubled. In part, this is the spirit of the time—the very idea of progress through science is in question. People seriously wonder if through our cleverness we may not blunder into worse dilemmas than we seek to

solve. They are concerned not only for the vagrant lethal virus or the escaped mutant deadly microbe, but also for the awful potential that we might inadvertently so arm the anarchic in our society as to shatter its bonds or conversely so arm the tyrannical in our society as to forever imprison liberty."—Robert Sinsheimer, "Troubled Dawn of Genetic Engineering," *New Scientist*

*4. "Now the reason why man is more of a political animal than bees or any other gregarious animals is evident. Nature, as we often say, makes nothing in vain, and man is the only animal whom she has endowed with the gift of speech. And whereas mere sound is but an indication of pleasure or pain, and is therefore found in other animals . . . the power of speech is intended to set forth the expedient and inexpedient, and likewise the just and the unjust. And it is a characteristic of man that he alone has any sense of good and evil, of just and unjust, and the association of living beings who have this sense makes a family and a state."—Aristotle, *Politics*

5. "The only freedom which deserves the name is that of pursuing our own good in our own way, so long as we do not attempt to deprive others of theirs, or impede their efforts to obtain it. Each is the proper guardian of his own health, whether bodily, or mental and spiritual. Mankind are great gainers by suffering each other to live as seems good to themselves, rather than by compelling each to live as seems good to the rest."—John Stuart Mill, *On Liberty*

6. "It is not surprising that there are many adults who do not like children much, if at all. But they feel they ought to like them, have a duty to like them, and try to discharge this duty by acting, particularly by talking, as if they liked them. Hence the continual and meaningless use of words like *honey, dearie,* etc. Hence, the dreadful syrupy voice that so many adults use when they speak to children."—John Holt, *How Children Fail*

7. "It is time to stop giving lip service to the idea that there are no battles left to be fought for women in America, that women's rights have already been won. It is ridiculous to tell girls to keep quiet when they enter a new field or an old one, so the men will not notice they are there. In almost every professional field, in business and in the arts and sciences, women are still treated as second-class citizens. It would be a great service to tell girls who plan to work in society to expect this subtle, uncomfortable discrimination—tell them not to be quiet, and hope it will go away, but fight it. A girl should not expect special privileges because of her sex, but neither should she 'adjust' to prejudices and discrimination."—Betty Friedan, *The Feminine Mystique*

*8. " 'Spirit? Well, maybe,' he said. 'But there is one thing not clear to me. There was an echo. Now, no man ever seen a spirit with a shadow; well, then, what's he doing with an echo to him, I should like to know? That ain't in nature, surely?' "—Robert Louis Stevenson, *Treasure Island*

9. "Schools and colleges are not intended to foster genius and to bring it out. Genius is a nuisance, and it is the duty of schools and colleges to abate it by setting genius-traps in the way. They are as the artificial obstructions in a hurdle race, tests of skill and endurance, but in themselves useless. Still, so necessary is it that genius and originality should be abated that, did not academics exist, we should have to invent them."—Samuel Butler

10. "The professor knows that even his fragment of the student's time must be competitively protected. If he does not make tangible, time-consuming demands, the student diverts time to courses which do make such demands. It becomes almost impossible to set a reflective, contemplative, deliberate pace in a single course. The ten-

dency is to overassign work, with the expectation that it will probably not be all done. The cumulative effect on the student is brutal. To survive he must learn how not to do his work; he is forced into the adoption of the strategies of studentship; he learns to read too fast, to write and speak with mere plausibility."—Joseph Tussman, *Experiment at Berkeley*

11. "It is better to be a human being dissatisfied than a pig satisfied; better to be Socrates dissatisfied than a fool satisfied. And if the fool, or the pig, are of a different opinion, it is because they only know their own side of the question. The other party to the comparison knows both sides."—J. S. Mill, *Utilitarianism*

*12. "[E]ven if we admit that societies often hold different ethical principles, this does not mean that there are no correct or true principles. To take a parallel case, we know that societies and cultures frequently hold different beliefs about the nature of the world and the things that are on it. This does not mean that the different beliefs are all correct or that the choice among them is arbitrary or due to upbringing."— Ronald Munson, *Intervention and Reflection: Basic Issues in Medical Ethics*

13. "The essential characteristic of philosophy, which makes it a study distinct from science, is *criticism*. It examines critically the principles employed in science and in daily life; it searches out any inconsistencies there may be in these principles, and it only accepts them when, as the result of a critical inquiry, no reason for rejecting them has appeared."—Bertrand Russell

14. "If the body brought a suit against the soul, for all the pains it had endured throughout life, and the ill treatment, and I were to be the judge of the suit, I would gladly condemn the soul, in that it had partly ruined the body by its neglect and dissolved it with bouts of drunkenness, and partly destroyed it, and torn it to pieces with its passion for pleasure—as if, when a tool or a vessel were in bad condition, I blamed the man who was using it carelessly."—Democritus, *Fragments on Ethics*

15. "Aquinas accepted the death penalty for heretics on the ground that it is a far graver matter to corrupt the faith, which is the life of the soul, than to falsify money, which sustains life. So, if it is just to put to death forgers and other criminals, heretics may *a fortiori* be so dealt with. But the premises on which Aquinas relies cannot be established by the methods of common sense. It is a matter of dogma that faith, as the Roman Church defines it, is the life of the soul and that the suppression of heresy— that is, departures from orthodoxy in defiance of ecclesiastical authority—is necessary for the safety of souls."—John Rawls, "Constitutional Liberty and the Concept of Justice," *Nomos IV: Justice*, ed. Carl Friedrich and John Chapman.

*16. "If a great number of countries come to have an arsenal of nuclear weapons, then I'm glad I'm not a young man and I'm sorry for my grandchildren."—David E. Lilienthal, quoted by Louis René Beres, *Apocalypse*

17. "As good almost kill a man as kill a good book. Who kills a man kills a reasonable creature, God's image; but he who destroys a good book kills reason itself."— John Milton, *Areopagitica*

18. "Suppose your doctor, nurse,
          fireman, trashman,
        bus driver and policeman
            had the
            FLU."
—From a pamphlet produced for the National Influenza Immunization Program by the Virginia Department of Health

19. "One of the arguments in the Movement against our attacking Marriage has been that most women are married. This has always seemed strange to me as it is like saying we should not come out against oppression because all women are oppressed. Clearly, of all the oppressive institutions, Marriage is the one that affects the most women. It is logical, then, that if we are interested in building a mass movement of women, this is where we should begin."—Sheila Cronan, "Marriage," in *Radical Feminism*, ed. Anne Koedt, Ellen Levine, and Anita Rapone

*20. "The power of speech over the constitution of the soul can be compared with the effect of drugs on the bodily state; just as the drugs by driving out different humours from the body can put an end either to disease or to life, so with speech: different words can induce grief, pleasure or fear; or again, by means of a harmful kind of persuasion, words can drug and bewitch the soul."—Gorgias the Sophist, *Encomium on Helen*

■

□ CHAPTER TWO

Analyzing arguments

As pointed out in Chapter 1, when considering an argument from a logical point of view, we temporarily suspend interest in what its statements actually mean and focus exclusively on the relationship between the premises and the conclusion. That is, we distinguish the *form* of the argument—the connection between its parts—from its *content*. To increase our ability to understand and evaluate arguments, we must further investigate their formal properties. In addition, we must develop a clearer understanding of what counts as a "good" argument in logic. Particularly, we must consider the concepts of *deduction* and *induction* and *validity* and *soundness* as they apply to argumentation.

□ 2-1. DEDUCTION AND INDUCTION

Logicians divide arguments into two basic types: *deductive* and *nondeductive*. This division marks a significant difference in the way we analyze and evaluate arguments. By far the largest number of nondeductive arguments are of a type called *inductive*, and an understanding of inductive reasoning is indispensable to an analysis of other nondeductive arguments. So this discussion will concern the kinds of arguing called *deduction* and *induction*.

In a deductive argument, the premises are intended to supply all the information needed to support the conclusion. The conclusion makes *explicit* a bit of information already *implicit* in the premises when they are brought together; it is said to be "contained in" the premises. Thus, one who presents a deductive argument believes the truth of the premises will guarantee the truth of the conclusion. Thus,

> A deductive argument is one that would be justified by claiming that if the premises are true, they necessarily establish the truth of the conclusion.

The premises of an inductive argument may supply good reasons for accepting the conclusion; they may even make its truth highly probable. But the truth of the premises cannot *insure* that the conclusion will be true as well.

The conclusion of an inductive argument "goes beyond" the premises: it expresses a conjecture that can definitely be known to be true (or false) only after further observation—if ever.

> An inductive argument is one in which the premises provide evidence for believing the conclusion is true, but not conclusive evidence.

In accepting the conclusion of an argument, one is said to be making an inference.

> An inference is a mental act by which one comes to believe a conclusion because it is supported by premises that are accepted as true.

Depending on whether the argument under consideration is deductive or inductive, one is said to be making a *deductive inference* or an *inductive inference*. Deductive inference involves the rearranging of information; one starts with statements assumed to be true to see what other statements can be logically derived from them. But inductive inference is an information-extending process; one starts with a set of particular observations and infers from them some conclusion about an entity or event that has not yet been experienced. While deductive inference extracts the implications of what is already known, inductive inference moves from the known to the unknown. The following hypothetical case history contains examples of both deductive and inductive inferences.

Imagine that your life's ambition has been to become a first-rate entomologist, a scientist who studies insects. As a child, you had a prize-winning butterfly collection that was the pride of the neighborhood; in high school, you won a science-fair award for the breeding of praying mantises in captivity; and your enthusiasm has just seen you through four arduous years as a zoology major.

On your last exam as a senior you came across the following true-or-false statement:

Some scorpions have antennae.

Given your knowledge of insects and related species, you quickly checked off "false" as the answer to the question. Your reasoning would have gone something like this:

All scorpions are arachnids.
No arachnids have antennae.
Therefore, no scorpions have antennae.

Now on a vacation in Arizona, you notice what appears to be a new species of spider. Deciding to observe these spiders to see if they will spin webs, you reason as follows:

> All the spiders I have observed in their natural habitats have spun webs.
>
> All the kinds of spiders studied in college zoology spin webs.
>
> All species of spiders so far discovered in the southwestern United States have been web spinners.
>
> Therefore, it is highly probable that this new species of spider spins webs.

Your expectations are fulfilled; the spiders are fine web spinners.

You include the news of the discovery in a letter to an acquaintance who works at the Smithsonian Institution in Washington, D.C. Soon your friend sends you an announcement of an opening for an assistant curator at the Smithsonian's "bug museum"—the entomology division of the Museum of Natural History.

You drive your car to Washington, approach the museum, and search for a parking space. The only empty space is next to a fire hydrant. Should you park your car there? Quickly thinking over your past experience, you recall getting two traffic tickets—one in Chicago and one in Pittsburgh—for parking next to fire hydrants. You know someone in St. Louis who also got a ticket for parking next to a fire hydrant. So you decide to pass up this space.

After having safely parked your car in a pay lot, you hurry into the museum's employment office. There, while you fill out an application, you are told that the museum has adopted a new rule for zoologists seeking employment. To qualify for an appointment, an applicant must have either a B.S. and three years of experience, or a B.S. awarded in the last three years and a cumulative grade point average of 3.25 or better. You breathe a sigh of relief. You are fresh out of college with no employment record; you have a B.S.; and you graduated with a 3.57 average. "Wish me luck," you whisper softly to the mounted and displayed skeleton of a brontosaurus as you are ushered into the director's office for an interview.

This hypothetical case contains two illustrations each of deduction and induction. The reasoning that led you to conclude that no scorpions have antennae is an example of deductive inference. You realize this is true simply by seeing how the premises relate arachnids, scorpions, and the characteristic of having antennae. The reasoning concerning employment qualifications is a second example of deductive inference. Here again, the inference—that you meet the job requirements for an assistant curator of entomology—is based solely upon an understanding of the logical relations between the premises. The rule specifies *alternative* conditions for an appointment, and your own qualifications match one of those alternatives.

The two inductive inferences are the assumptions that the new species of spider will be web spinners and that it would be unwise to park near a fire hydrant. Your past experience of spiders—all that you have read about them and directly observed—leads you to infer that members of the new species, which you have not yet studied, will probably spin webs. Likewise, you reason from your past experiences of parking next to fire hydrants and from the experience of a friend who once did so that parking beside this fire hydrant will result in your being ticketed.

Besides occurring within the same discussion, deductive and inductive arguments can be interrelated. The conclusion of an inductive argument can be used as a premise of a deductive argument, and vice versa. Suppose, for example, that a long examination of every known species of spider in the Arizona deserts confirms that they all spin webs. This evidence would be the premise of an inductive argument that concluded "All spiders indigenous to the Arizona deserts are web spinners." This conclusion, in turn, can be used as a premise in a deductive argument:

All spiders indigenous to the Arizona deserts are web spinners.
This spider was found living naturally in the Arizona deserts.
Therefore, this spider is a web spinner.

Deductive and inductive inferences can be distinguished from each other according to the kind of claim being made. If the arguer believes that, given the truth of the premises, the conclusion is established beyond any reasonable doubt, then the argument is intended to be deductive. The arguer justifies the argument by claiming that someone who accepts the premises as true *must* also accept the conclusion as true. Someone, for example, who believes that all scorpions are arachnids and that no arachnids have antennae would be inconsistent in denying that no scorpions have antennae. To do so would be saying that it is both true and false that no scorpions have antennae. And a museum personnel director who accepts a B.S. and a grade point average of 3.25 or above as qualifying an applicant for consideration would be inconsistent in claiming that with a B.S. and a 3.57 average you do not satisfy the specified requirements.

While the premises of an inductive argument may provide very strong support for the conclusion, there would be no inconsistency in accepting the premises but rejecting the conclusion. For example, it could be the case that all species of spiders hitherto observed have been web spinners but still possible (although not probable) that the newly discovered species does not spin webs. Similarly, it is possible (although not probable) that cars parked next to fire hydrants in Washington, D.C., will not be ticketed, even though they have been ticketed in all other American cities and towns in which you have had any experience.

A clue to whether an argument is deductive or inductive can sometimes be found in its wording. If the speaker or writer says that the conclusion "must" follow or "necessarily" follows, then the argument is to be considered deductive. If the conclusion is referred to as "probable" or "likely," or in words to that effect, then the argument is intended to be inductive. It is often impossible to tell from the wording, though, whether an argument is intended to be deductive or inductive. In such cases, we must decide whether the argument makes better sense if interpreted as deductive or as inductive.

Another difference between deduction and induction concerns the kind of information contained in their premises and conclusions. Deduction often involves reasoning from the general to the specific—for example, from characteristics of the whole biological class of arachnids to those of one species— scorpions. And induction often involves making generalizations on the basis of particular instances. An example of such reasoning is as follows:

The new species of spiders discovered in Arizona spin webs.
The spiders I observed at college spin webs.
The spiders my roommate saw in Minnesota spin webs.
Therefore, probably all spiders spin webs.

By no means is all deduction reasoning from the general to the specific, however, nor is induction always from particular instances to a general rule. Here, for example, is a deductive argument in which the distinction between the "general" and "specific" does not even arise:

If the Flying Wallendas have no more accidents, they will revive the public's interest in circus acrobatics.
The Flying Wallendas will have no more accidents.
Therefore, the Flying Wallendas will revive the public's interest in circus acrobatics.

The inductive reasoning involving the parking tickets was an argument from experience of traffic regulations in two specific cities to a conjecture about traffic regulations in another specific city. It did not proceed to a generalization about traffic regulations throughout the world. Here is another inductive argument that does not proceed from specific instances to a general rule:

The wool suit I bought from the local tailor was poorly sewn.
The corduroy suit I bought from the local tailor was poorly sewn.
Therefore, the next suit I buy from the local tailor will be poorly sewn.

In common parlance *deduction* is used to mean almost any kind of inference, though often what is being referred to is an inductive argument. Dr. Watson, Sherlock Holmes's faithful companion, was given to describing Holmes's inferences as "brilliant deductions." However, many of those inferences were inductive, not deductive. For example, in "The Red-Headed League," Holmes "deduces" that a client has been in China by observing that a tattoo on the man's arm has a design peculiar to Chinese tattooers. But Holmes's reasoning is really inductive, for the evidence of the design does not guarantee that the man was in China. The design might have been made by a Chinese tattooer in London or even by a European tattooer copying a Chinese original.

■ **EXERCISE 2-1**

Determine whether each of the following arguments is deductive or inductive. Remember that the argument does not have to be good to qualify as an argument.

1. Since Christians are theists and Arabella is a Christian, she is a theist.

2. Since footsteps were heard outside the house, it is unlikely that a resident was the culprit.

3. Vegetarians are always teetotalers. So Mahatma Gandhi, who was a vegetarian, must have been a teetotaler.

*4. All the vegetarians I know are teetotalers, so Gandhi, who was a vegetarian, was probably a teetotaler.

5. Many fall warblers have yellowish breasts, so that bird is most likely a fall warbler.

6. All poisonous snakes native to the United States have brown and white markings, so that snake you saw in the Poconos, if it was solid black as you say, was not poisonous.

7. The city can't qualify for federal financial assistance unless it reorganizes its social services and pension plans. And you know that won't happen, so the city will continue its deficit spending.

*8. Since $a^2 + b^2 = c^2$ for all right triangles and since $a = 2$ and $b = 4$, $c^2 = 20$ and $c = \sqrt{20}$.

9. The lights were all out and the car was gone, so we concluded that nobody was home.

10. Most major-league baseball players who play the outfield consistently have batting averages over .250. Since Ken Singleton played centerfield for the Orioles for three consecutive years, he must have been batting over .250 when he was traded.

11. Statistics show that 86 percent of people with throat infections who are treated with penicillin recover. Alicia had a throat infection and was treated with penicillin, so she probably will recover.

*12. Because the smog is now worse in Denver than it is in Los Angeles, and the smog is worse in Los Angeles than it is in Phoenix, we may conclude that the quality of the air is better in Phoenix than it is in Denver.

13. Jack fed his puppy limburger cheese and the puppy got sick; he fed the puppy chili and the puppy got sick; he fed the puppy rum cake and the puppy got sick. Then he fed the puppy chicken soup, and it was not sick. Jack concluded that his puppy could tolerate only liquid food.

14. Uncle Silas had been visiting a doctor whose business card identifies him as an oncologist; therefore, Aunt Sarah probably suspects that Uncle Silas has cancer.

15. "One may go so far as to say that if there were no lack or stint of food, then those animals that are now afraid of people or are wild by nature would be tame and familiar with them, and in like manner with one another. This is shown by the way animals are treated in Egypt, for owing to the fact that food is constantly supplied to them the very fiercest creatures live peaceably together. The fact is that they are tamed by kindness, and in some places crocodiles are tame to their priestly keepers from being fed by them. And elsewhere also the same phenomenon is to be observed."—Aristotle, *History of Animals*

*16. "The life of every civilized community is governed by rules. Neither peace of mind for the present nor intelligent planning for the future is possible for people who either live without rules or cannot abide by the rules they have. Making rules for the community, and enforcing them, is the job of the government. No community can be truly civilized, therefore, without an effective and reasonably stable government."—Carl Cohen, *Civil Disobedience*

17. "I do know this pencil exists, but I could not know this if Hume's principles were true; therefore, Hume's principles, one or both of them, are false."—G. E. Moore, *Some Main Problems of Philosophy*

18. "Why then should the education of apes be impossible? Why might the apes, by dint of great pains, at least imitate after the manner of deaf mutes, the motions necessary for pronunciation? I do not dare decide whether the ape's organs of speech, however trained, would be incapable of articulation. But because of the great analogy between ape and man and because there is no known animal whose external and internal organs so strikingly resemble man's, it would surprise me if speech were absolutely impossible to the ape."—Julien de La Mettrie, *L'homme machine*

19. "Now the President may be right in how he reads the Constitution. But he may also be wrong. And if he is wrong, who is there to tell him so? And if there is no one, then the President, of course, is free to pursue his course of erroneous interpretations. What then becomes of our constitutional form of government?"—Leon Jaworski, quoted in the *New York Times*, July 9, 1974

*20. "In the western United States there are two contiguous states that enjoy about the same levels of income and medical care and are alike in many other respects, but their levels of health differ enormously. The inhabitants of Utah are among the healthiest individuals in the United States, while the residents of Nevada are at the opposite end of the spectrum. . . .

"The two states are very much alike with respect to income, schooling, degree of urbanization, climate, and many other variables that are frequently thought to be the cause of variations in mortality. (In fact, average family income is actually higher in Nevada than in Utah.) The numbers of physicians and of hospital beds per capita are also similar in the two states.

"What, then, explains these huge differences in death rates? The answer almost surely lies in the different life-styles of the residents of the two states. Utah is inhabited primarily by Mormons, whose influence is strong throughout the state. Devout Mormons do not use tobacco or alcohol and in general lead stable, quiet lives. Nevada, on the other hand, is a state with high rates of cigarette and alcohol consumption and very high indexes of marital and geographical instability. The contrast with Utah in these respects is extraordinary."—Victor R. Fuchs, *Who Shall Live?*

■

☐ 2-2. VALIDITY, SOUNDNESS, AND RELIABLE INDUCTIVE INFERENCE

In the previous section, we made a distinction between deductive arguments and inductive arguments. We shall now see what it means for each kind of argument to be "good." In deduction, the acceptability of the conclusion depends entirely on the *form* of the argument. In induction, the conclusion is acceptable only if the premises provide sufficient *evidence* to make its truth probable.

To consider deductive arguments first, what, then, is the difference between form and content? And how are the form and content of an argument related to its *validity* and *soundness*—the qualities that make it a good argument?

□ *Form and content*

As we saw in Chapter 1, whether statements about people, things, or events are true or not usually has to do with their relationship to factual situations. Thus, the statement "Ospreys inhabit the Chesapeake Bay" is true, while the statement "Wild orchids grow in Iceland" is false. Ospreys can indeed be found living wild in the tidewater inlets of Chesapeake Bay, but orchids cannot be found growing naturally in the countryside of Iceland. What is true or false, then, is the statement's *content*.

Form is that which remains the same throughout changes in content. It can be likened to the federal income-tax form, which is the same for everyone, even though the information written on it differs depending upon which taxpayer fills it out. The point is illustrated by comparing two statements:

New York City is smaller than Atlanta.

Atlanta is smaller than Chicago.

The first statement is false, the second true. The content of the first statement is different from the content of the second. But both have the same form, as can be seen by substituting letters—known as *variables*, because they have no fixed meaning—for the names of cities:

X is smaller than Y.

Although the truth or falsity of a statement usually depends upon its content, there are exceptions to this general rule. Some sentences express truthful statements just because of the meaning or the logical relationships of the words included in them. "It is either raining or it is not raining" belongs to this group. Regardless of the weather, this sentence will be true because its truth is a consequence of its form.

While truth is a property of statements, *validity and soundness are properties of an argument as a whole*. Premises and conclusions, being statements, are said to be true or false. But in evaluating an argument, we must consider the relationship, or connection, between its parts. Our purpose is to see whether it is possible to move from the truth of the premises to the truth or probable truth of the conclusion.

The speaker or writer who presents an argument is in effect claiming (1) that the premises are true, and (2) that because the premises are true, the conclusion is also true. Thus, two kinds of error can be made when advancing an argument. One can make a *factual error* by being mistaken in claiming that the premises are all true. Or one can make a *logical error* by misinterpreting the logical relation between the premises and the conclusion. If the error has to do with the logical relation between its parts, then the argument has an inadequate form and is said to be *invalid*. If one or more of the premises (and/or the conclusion) are false, the argument is said to be *unsound*. In either case, the argument is fallacious.

□ *Validity*

The concept of validity concerns the form of an argument. If the premises are linked to the conclusion in such a way that their truth would guarantee the truth of the conclusion, then the argument is called *valid*. Validity, therefore, pertains only to deductive arguments. For as shown in Section 2-1, in a deductive argument the conclusion makes explicit information that is implicit in the premises.

> A valid argument is a deductive argument such that, if the premises were all true, the conclusion would have to be true.

A standard example of a valid deductive argument is the following:

All human beings are mortal.
Socrates is a human being.
Therefore, Socrates is mortal.

Now, if all human beings are in the group of mortal beings, and if Socrates is a human being, Socrates must be in the group of mortal beings. The truth of the premises guarantees the truth of the conclusion.

This argument is valid in virtue of its form; it really does not matter what the content of the argument is. To say that it has a *valid form* means that any argument with exactly the same form will also be valid. Thus, a valid argument will still result if the name *Ronald Reagan* is substituted for *Socrates* in the original. In fact, one can substitute different words for all the terms in the original argument and still have a valid argument. For example, the argument

All cetaceans are marine mammals.
A dolphin is a cetacean.
Therefore, a dolphin is a marine mammal.

has the same form as our argument about Socrates' mortality. Both have the form

All *X* are *Y*.

Z is an X.
Therefore, Z is Y.

The validity of an argument depends entirely upon the formal relationship between the premises and conclusion or between the terms (for example, dolphins, cetaceans, marine animals) linked by the premises and conclusion. An argument, whose form is valid can guarantee the *truth* of a conclusion only when the premises are all true. Thus, it is possible to have a valid argument with a false conclusion. The following is one example:

All aquatic creatures have gills.
A whale is an aquatic creature.
Therefore, a whale has gills.

Here we have an argument with the same valid form as the arguments about Socrates and dolphins. We saw that a valid deductive argument cannot have all true premises and a false conclusion. In the argument immediately preceding, the conclusion is false, *but so is the first premise.* This demonstrates that questions about the truth of the premises must be answered independently of questions about the validity of the argument.

Can an *invalid* argument have a true conclusion? Look at this example:

All cetaceans have fins.
All dolphins have fins.
Therefore, all dolphins are cetaceans.

Here the premises are all true, and so is the conclusion. But the premises don't guarantee the conclusion, any more than the premises that all Swedes are Scandinavians and that all Norwegians are Scandinavians can guarantee that all Norwegians are Swedes.

The form of this argument is as follows:

All X are Y.
All Z are Y.
Therefore, all Z are X.

As further evidence that this form is invalid, we can substitute one or more terms to produce an argument with exactly the same form that has true premises and a false conclusion. Let's substitute *fish* for *dolphins:*

All cetaceans have fins.
All fish have fins.
Therefore, all fish are cetaceans.

An argument form cannot be valid if it allows us to deduce a false conclusion from true premises. The conclusion of the previous example, "All dolphins are cetaceans," happens to be true, but not because the premises insure its truth.

□ Soundness

At the beginning of this discussion it was stated that someone who presents a deductive argument is ordinarily claiming (1) that the premises are true, and (2) that because the premises are true, the conclusion is also true. In considering validity, we have been discussing the second point.

To accept a conclusion as justified, we need to know not only that the inference is *valid* but also that the premises are true. Premises are the foundations of an argument; any argument built on unreliable or shaky premises, like the proverbial house built upon sand, cannot be expected to stand.

If an argument is valid and also has true premises, then it is said to be *sound*.

> **A sound argument is a deductive argument that is justified because it is valid and has true premises.**

While valid arguments can be either sound or unsound, all sound arguments are valid. Table 2-1 summarizes these relations.

You might wonder whether anyone would be interested in deductive arguments that are unsound. Sometimes the subject of an argument is so important that adjusting the argument to make it sound is worthwhile. Suppose, for example, that the person presenting the argument has the facts right (true premises) but has reached the conclusion through faulty inference (invalid form). Here it is important to see whether the faulty inference can be replaced by a correct one or whether a conclusion with a similar impact can be reached. Suppose, on the other hand, that the inference is valid but the argument is unsound because the premises are in doubt. In this case, if you are inclined to reject the conclusion, you will want to show why at least one of the premises is false. But if you are inclined to accept the conclusion, you will want to obtain additional information to show that the premises are true.

TABLE 2-1 *Conditions of validity and soundness for deductive arguments*

IF THE PREMISES ARE:	AND THE REASONING IS:	THEN THE ARGUMENT IS:
true	valid	sound
true	invalid	unsound
false	valid	unsound
false	invalid	unsound

The table shows that of the four possible combinations, only one yields an argument that is sound— that is, whose conclusion is justified. Such an argument has both valid form and true premises.

Sometimes we cannot determine whether premises are true. In this case, being able validly to infer the consequences that would follow from such premises if they were true can help us judge whether they are in fact true. If, by a *deductive* inference, we arrive at a conclusion that we know is false, then we can be sure that at least one of the premises is false, because a false conclusion cannot validly be *deduced* from true premises.

Examples of this use of valid inference can be found in the history of science. Up until the eighteenth century, for example, many scientists believed in the existence of phlogiston. Phlogiston was thought to be a constituent of all combustible substances, and it was supposedly released as a flame during combustion. The French chemist Antoine Lavoisier (1743–1794) reasoned that if phlogiston escapes from a substance during combustion, then the product remaining after the combustion process would have less weight than the original substance. However, Lavoisier's experiments on the combustion of metals showed that the end product of the combustion process has *greater* weight than the original metal. This served to show that the initial assumption that combustible substances contain phlogiston was false.

☐ *Reliable inductive inference*

The premises of an inductive argument can never guarantee the truth of the conclusion. As we saw in Section 2-1, no inconsistency is involved in accepting the truth of the premises but denying the truth of the conclusion. Strictly speaking, all inductive arguments are invalid if by valid we mean deductively valid. But to call inductive arguments invalid would be to misunderstand the spirit of inductive inference.

The concept of validity simply does not apply to induction because the purpose of inductive reasoning differs from that of deductive reasoning. Deductive reasoning depends upon the forms by which we move from statements taken to be true to other statements that must therefore also be true. Inductive reasoning takes over when these formal relations cannot be established—when we must reason from statements, or propositions, we take to be true to conclusions that go beyond the range of our present knowledge. Consequently, even good inductive arguments can never be sound in the strict sense in which a valid deductive argument can be sound. They cannot fulfill all the requirements for soundness.

That inductive arguments are not strictly sound does *not* mean that we are never justified in accepting the conclusion of such an argument. But whether an inductive argument can be considered justified—or reliable—depends on both the amount and kind of evidence available to support the conclusion and on the extent to which we intend to rely on the conclusion. Thus, in analyzing inductive arguments, we must discover the *degree* to which the weight and relevance of the evidence warrants belief in the conclusion.

The conclusion of an inductive argument is properly stated in terms of some degree of probability. A conclusion that is claimed to be "highly probable" requires weightier and more pertinent evidence than one that is asserted to be only "probable" or "likely" or "possible." In evaluating the argument, one must determine whether the evidence presented in the premises is sufficient to the probability claimed of the conclusion. If the evidence in the relevant premises is sufficient for the degree of probability claimed for the conclusion, then the conclusion can be accepted as justified—even though we can never be sure it will not be proved false in the long run. Thus, while inductive arguments cannot be valid or sound in the same way that deductive inferences can be valid and sound, we can certainly tell the difference between good and bad, reliable and unreliable, inductive arguments.

■ **EXERCISE 2-2**

The following are intended to be deductive arguments. Indicate in each case whether the argument is valid. Also indicate whether each valid argument is sound: Are its premises all true? Is its conclusion true?

1. All dogs are animals, and all apes are animals. Therefore, all apes are dogs.

2. All dogs are animals and all malamutes are animals. Therefore, all malamutes are dogs.

3. All dogs are animals, and all Siberian huskies are dogs. Therefore, all Siberian huskies are animals.

*4. All mammals are quadrupeds, and all whales are mammals. Therefore, all whales are quadrupeds.

5. All tigers are carnivorous animals, and all jaguars are tigers. Therefore, all jaguars are carnivorous animals.

6. All parts of Canada are west of the Rocky Mountains, and all parts of California are west of the Rocky Mountains. Therefore, California is part of Canada.

7. All birds are quadrupeds, and all crows are quadrupeds. Therefore, all crows are birds. ■

☐ 2-3. NECESSARY AND EMPIRICAL, OR CONTINGENT, STATEMENTS

Some statements can be known to be true or false just by understanding the meaning of the words used to convey them. Examples are the statements expressed by the sentences "A bachelor is an unmarried male" and "A vixen is a female fox." That it would not be correct to call anyone a bachelor unless this person were an unmarried male shows that it is because of the meaning of *bachelor* that "A bachelor is an unmarried male" can be known to be true. Conversely, to say that a married male is a bachelor is to say something that can be known to be false from the meaning of the words involved. In the same way, it is because *vixen* means "female fox" that the sentence, "A vixen is a female fox," expresses a necessarily true statement and "A vixen is a male fox" expresses a necessarily false statement.

To say that one of these examples is *necessarily* true while the other is *necessarily* false is simply to say that its truth or falsity is determined by the meaning of the words and is not open to confirmation or disconfirmation through experience. We would not need to survey, study, or otherwise observe bachelors or vixens to know whether these sentences express true or false statements. Necessary statements can be known to be true or false without empirical evidence—that is, information obtained from observation or sense perception.

In some cases, the truth or falsity of a necessary statement depends on the logical form of the words used to express it as well as on the meaning of the words themselves. A necessarily true statement is expressed by "Roses are red or they are not red" because the terms *are red* and *are not red* are related by *or* to establish exhaustive categories. Likewise, "Roses are red and they are not red" is self-contradictory because the terms are joined by *and*. In these instances, we say that the statement is necessarily true or necessarily false because of its logical form.

A necessary statement is one that can be known to be true or false either by understanding the meanings of the words used to express it, or by understanding its logical form.

In this section, we shall concentrate on necessary statements whose truth or falsity depends on the meanings of the words used to express them. (Chapter 8 will consider statements that are necessarily true or necessarily false because of their logical form.) But whether the truth or falsity of a statement depends on the meanings of its words or on its form, a necessary statement can be known to be true or false without evidence supplied by observation.

By contrast, statements that are called *empirical*—a word derived from the Latin for "experience"—can be known to be true or false only with reference to the kind of evidence acquired through perception—sensory evidence regarding what has been seen or heard or felt or smelled or tasted. This evidence might consist of direct perceptions of one's own, or it might be indirect, consisting, for example, of what one has heard or read concerning the perceptions of others. Much of history and of the sciences consists of empirical information.

Empirical statements are also called *contingent* statements to emphasize that our knowledge of their truth or falsity is dependent, or contingent, on sensory experience. Thus, for instance, "Oranges are grown in southern California" cannot be known to be true just from a knowledge of the meaning of *oranges* and *southern California* or by understanding the relation indicated by the word *in*. We know it is true because oranges are seen to grow there.

This is not to deny that one can believe that an empirical statement—for example, "Laetrile cures cancer"—is true without having reliable evidence to support the belief. But one cannot know that such a statement is true (or entertain a reasonable belief in its truth) without having (or expecting to have) such evidence.

To some extent, experience is needed to know anything. We cannot even know that "If John is a bachelor, then he is unmarried" is necessarily true unless we have had the experience of learning the meanings of the words in the sentence. But this is a weak sense of "having experience." To say that empirical statements are based on experience means that they can be known to be true or false *only if* they are based on direct or indirect evidence obtained by use of the *senses*.

In addition, there are "borderline" cases in which the distinction between necessary and empirical statements is not clear. Some statements do not seem to belong in either category. Consider this example:

If you eat a well-balanced diet, you will get all the vitamins your body needs.

Does this example express a necessarily true statement? It is tempting to say that it does, because a *well-balanced diet* is by definition one that provides the needed vitamins. We cannot be completely confident of this response, however, because *well-balanced diet* is indefinite in meaning. Suppose biochemists discover that the common cold can be prevented only by ingesting massive doses of vitamin C—larger doses than can be acquired by a normal adult through the consumption of natural food. Should we then expand the meaning of *well-balanced diet* to include massive doses of vitamin C provided by pharmaceutical companies? Or should we decide that, under those hypothetical conditions, the statement would be empirical and false?

Although some statements cannot be definitely classified as either necessary or empirical, the distinction is still important. Many statements *do* fit into one category or the other. And with statements that do not fit neatly into either category, it is often useful to ask how they could be understood to be empirical and how they could be understood to be necessary. Answering these questions can bring about a fuller understanding of the meaning of a statement. And insofar as the statement can be understood to be empirical, the analysis can reveal the sort of evidence needed to show that it is true or false.

■ **EXERCISE 2-3**

■ A. Determine whether each of the following statements should be treated as empirical or necessary and, if necessary, whether it is necessarily true or necessarily false. Interpret each statement as you believe it would be ordinarily understood by speakers of English.

1. Water is wet.

2. Oculists treat eyes.

3. Puppies are young.

*4. The only experts in physics are those who hold Ph.D.'s in physics.

5. Small children require little attention.

6. Every right triangle has one and only one angle of ninety degrees.

7. Every dog that is a mangy cur is a dog.

*8. Every intellectual giant is a giant.

9. Every woman who is now married has a spouse.

10. *Webster's Dictionary* is a big book.

11. None but the ugly have been put on the rack.

*12. Canada has several more metropolitan areas than the United States.

13. The knife entered the corpse, mortally wounding it.

14. Competition is a necessity for a free society.

15. Every circle has a center.

*16. Democracy is the best form of government.

17. All declared wars are morally justified wars.

18. Stealing is taking property that does not belong to you.

19. Communism is dangerous.

*20. All red glass is colored.

21. An average human lifetime has a duration of approximately 10^9 seconds.

22. At the Battle of Waterloo, which ended in Napoleon's defeat, an irresistible force met an immovable object.

23. Few Buddhists live in Ohio.

*24. Anyone who is a mother is a woman.

25. The winner emerged victorious.

26. There are dolphins that are not mammals.

27. Either Egbert is my friend or Egbert is not my friend.

*28. Either Egbert is my friend or Egbert is my enemy.

29. Every expectant mother is a mother.

30. Every effect has a cause.

31. An attitude of undue morbidity is unhealthy.

*32. The future now lies beckoning before us.

33. I'm just not as young as I used to be.

34. The Republicans are sure to win the next election, provided they gain sufficient votes.

35. The Democrats are sure to win the next election, if they gain sufficient votes.

*36. John is Jake's half brother, and Jake is John's half brother.

37. If John is Jake's half brother, then Jake is John's half brother.

38. Any two people who have exactly the same grandparents are first cousins.

39. John's siblings are all males.

*40. All ruminant animals are carnivores.

■ B. Decide whether each of the following passages should be treated as expressing (a) an empirical statement, (b) a necessarily true statement, or (c) a necessarily false statement.

1. "When people are out of work, unemployment results."—Calvin Coolidge

2. "Our past has gone into history."—William McKinley

3. "You can fool all of the people some of the time, but you can't fool all of the people all of the time."—Abraham Lincoln

*4. There is a rule that everything good is fattening and there is another rule that every rule has an exception.—television commercial for a diet aid

5. "Winning isn't everything. It's the only thing."—Vince Lombardi

6. "It's quite possible, Octavian, that when you die, you will die without ever having been alive."—Mark Antony

7. "I want to live forever—or die in the attempt."—Yossarian in Joseph Heller's *Catch-22*

*8. "No one is so wrong as the man who knows all the answers."—Thomas Merton

9. "The unexamined life is not worth living."—Socrates

10. "It is a poor sort of memory that only works backwards."—Lewis Carroll

11. "What experience and history teach us is this—that people and governments have never learned anything from history, or acted on principles deduced from it."—Hegel

*12. "The nobles are to be considered in two different manners; that is, they are either to be ruled so as to make them entirely dependent on your fortunes, or else not."—Machiavelli

13. "The world's biggest problems today are really infinitesimal: the atom, the ovum, and a bit of pigment."—Herb Caen

14. "The defendant is entitled to a fair trial before I hang him."—"Hanging Judge" Jeffreys

15. "The best way to get a bad law repealed is to enforce it strictly."—Abraham Lincoln

*16. "Anyone who is popular is bound to be disliked."—Yogi Berra

17. "Growing old isn't so bad when you consider the alternative."—Maurice Chevalier

18. "Only a mediocre person is always at his best."—Somerset Maugham

19. "There has been a lot of progress during my lifetime, but I am afraid it's heading in the wrong direction."—Ogden Nash

*20. "Government is too big and important to be left to the politicians."—Chester Bowles

21. "I am free of all prejudice. I hate everyone equally."—W. C. Fields

22. "Don't worry about your heart, it will last you all of your life."—Dr. Alfred Bach

23. "He who praises everybody praises nobody."—Samuel Johnson

*24. "Nothing is enough to him for whom enough is too little."—Epicurus

25. "Success has made failures of many men."—Charles Adams

26. "We are overpaying him but he is worth it."—Samuel Goldwyn

27. "Generalizations are generally wrong."—Mary Montagu

*28. "The trouble with our time is that the future is not what it used to be."—Paul Valery

29. You always find something in the last place you look for it.

30. "There is nothing in the world constant, but inconsistency."—Jonathan Swift

31. "To rule is easy, to govern difficult."—Goethe

*32. "A woman has to be twice as good as a man to go half as far."—Fannie Hurst

33. "When everyone is somebody, then no one is anybody."—Sir William Gilbert

34. "When a foreign diplomat asked his opposite number in the Chinese Foreign Ministry about prostitution, the Chinese official said, 'There is no prostitution in China. However, we do have some women who make love for money.' "—*The Washington Post*, October 9, 1979

35. "Reflecting on his political philosophy, the man who was once considered the most ardent conservative in America admitted: 'I think I'm kind of moderate.' Though, he added, 'Maybe one can overdo moderation.' "—Ronald Reagan, as quoted by *Time*

*36. " 'There's no use trying,' said Alice: 'we can't believe impossible things.'
" 'I dare say you haven't had much practice,' said the Queen. 'When I was your age I always did it for half an hour a day. Why sometimes I've believed as many as six impossible things before breakfast.' "—Lewis Carroll, *Through the Looking Glass* ■

☐ 2-4. ARGUMENTATION AND ETHICS

As you become more adept at analyzing arguments, *your standards for reasonable and acceptable thinking will rise.* You will expect clearer and more consistent thought of yourself as well as of others. And when you find youself in a debate over some compelling issue—say, abortion, the nuclear arms freeze, the Equal Rights Amendment, the reinstitution of the draft—you will find that you can help raise the level of the discussion by applying your logical skills. You may even begin to feel some responsibility for doing so. And insofar as clear and consistent thinking is generally conducive to finding the best solutions to problems, such contributions will not only be logical but also *ethical.*

What makes the use of logic ethical is not dissimilar to what makes the use of other kinds of special knowledge ethical. Those with special skills have a moral responsibility to use them in certain situations. Someone familiar with lifesaving techniques, for example, has a moral responsibility to use this knowledge to help a person who is drowning. Similarly, if you should voluntarily become involved in a disagreement over a matter that could have serious consequences, you in a sense have an obligation—a kind of *noblesse oblige*—to do what you can to make the dispute more rational.

The ethics of logical analysis can be formulated as four simple principles—the principles of *responsible expertise, fair play, charity,* and *tolerance.*

☐ The principle of responsible expertise

The responsibility, discussed above, to do what one can to raise the level of rational debate and to expose faulty reasoning is the *Principle of Responsible*

Expertise. Having the skill to analyze and evaluate reasoning involves a moral obligation to apply that skill when one willingly engages in a dispute of some importance.

No logician has an obligation to interfere in a matter that is not of at least indirect concern. But once you have decided that you can and should contribute to a discussion, you have an obligation to reason as effectively as you can.

☐ *The principle of fair play*

The *Principle of Fair Play* stipulates that you avoid taking unfair advantage of an adversary in a debate by using chicanery, sophistry, or other "underhanded" techniques. Fallacious reasoning was mentioned in Section 1-3, and you will learn to identify many kinds of fallacies as you study logic further. The objective of learning to detect fallacies is not only to avoid being victimized oneself. Equally important is to avoid fallacies in your own argumentation. It is far better to lose a dispute fairly than to win dishonorably.

The Principle of Fair Play is no ironclad rule, however. There may be times when the consequences of a dispute are so trivial that it does not matter whether one resorts to fallacious reasoning—and doing so may at least be entertaining.

☐ *The principle of charity*

Several allusions were made in Chapter 1 to the *Principle of Charity*. This principle requires that we try to make the best possible interpretation of the discourse being evaluated, whether we are trying to decide if an argument occurs in a passage, looking for the main point of an argument, attempting to clarify the meaning of questionable words or phrases, or formulating missing premises. The aim is to give the benefit of the doubt to the speaker or author. Rather than ridiculing someone for a remark that doesn't follow from what was said earlier or that isn't strictly true, it is more reasonable and responsible to try to reinterpret the passage so that it will make more sense.

It would frustrate attempts to communicate ideas and justify beliefs if arguments had to be perfectly expressed before they could be considered. So be charitable when what the speaker or writer intended requires some guesswork. But being charitable doesn't mean going to extremes to save defective arguments. Reject an argument when there are good reasons for doing so. The Principle of Charity is a reminder to attend to the main thrust of an argument and deal with it fairly.

The Principle of Charity also offers sound practical advice by telling us to avoid setting up a "straw man"—a weak imitation of the argument we are considering. It may be easy to break down a "straw man," but it will also be easy for an adversary to rebut an attack by reformulating the argument slightly to meet your objections. The arguer will simply claim, correctly, that you have misinterpreted the argument by making it seem weaker than it really is.

□ *The principle of tolerance*

The *Principle of Tolerance* is closely related to the Principle of Charity and the Principle of Fair Play, but it pertains more to your general outlook or frame of mind. In logic, to be tolerant is to recognize the fact that there are times and places when argument analysis just doesn't come into play.

Unfortunately, some people have the idea that the goal of logic is to score points over "opponents." They lose sight of its true purpose—to identify sound and reliable arguments—and they go out of their way to look for errors and to correct others. Sometimes called "logic-choppers," such people try to interpret most conversations as argumentative discourse. But language has many uses, only one of which is to convey information and justify beliefs. And there is an important difference between knowledge and wisdom: to be wise is to possess the understanding and skill to make mature judgments about the use of human knowledge in the context of daily life. We should not try to make an argument out of everything.

Life is not an argument.
NIETZSCHE

□ CHAPTER THREE

Language

In everyday life, the thoughts we express to others are embodied in words, which are part of a system called language. We cannot assess the significance of another's communications without understanding the language of the speaker—or writer. And we cannot determine the validity and soundness of someone's reasoning without awareness of the ways words can be used and misused. The focus of this chapter is, therefore, the relationship between language and thought.

Natural language—the everyday language in which arguments are expressed—has five characteristics that are relevant to the analysis of reasoning:

1. *A language is a system of meaningful symbols.* It is a union of sound and sense that permits language users to express thoughts and feelings, evoke responses, provide information, and do many other things.

2. *Language is an intricate system.* Units of sound (called *phonemes*), which are represented by written symbols, are combined to form larger units—words—which in turn are combined in various ways according to the syntax, or grammar, of the language. None of the particular sounds or symbols could be what they are independent of the system as a whole. The set of symbols, or letters, that make up a word are meaningful only in relation to other words and their role in the system.

3. *Language is a social activity.* The system of symbols requires learned behavior on the part of those who use it. And speech takes place in a social setting; its use presupposes a context of shared experience and expected responses.

4. *Language is an institution of a community.* It is governed by rules and conventions that members of the community follow. The meanings of words can be understood because they are used according to these rules.

5. *Language is constantly changing.* Although it persists through time and from speaker to speaker, language adapts to fit new circumstances. Words appear, others drop out of use, and still others acquire additional meanings.

Some scholars claim that thought itself would be impossible without language. The possibility has also been raised that language and thought are so intimately connected that clarity and order in one cannot be attained without

"*I want you to draft the bill with all your usual precision and flair. Explain its purposes, justify its expenditures, emphasize how it fits the broad aims of democratic progress. And one other thing: Can you make it sound like a tax cut?*"

©1979, *The New Yorker Magazine, Inc. Reprinted by permission.*

a corresponding clarity and order in the other. In any case, the abilities to think clearly and to express thoughts effectively are both of great importance to the study of logic.

Men imagine that their minds have the command of language, but it often happens that language bears rule over their minds.
FRANCIS BACON

□ 3-1. LANGUAGE AND THOUGHT

To what extent is thinking verbal? Does it take place exclusively in words, or do we sometimes know what we think before finding words to express it? Philosopher Hannah Arendt argued that thought without speech is inconceivable and that our mental activities are conceived in speech even before being communicated.

Yet the linguist Benjamin Whorf maintains not only that thought is dependent upon the use of language but that it may also be *shaped* by the particular language of the thinker. Whorf studied the language of the Hopi, a tribe of Pueblo Indians living in Arizona, and concluded that the Hopi language creates a world view quite different from that created by English and other Indo-European languages. In particular, the Hopi conceptions of time and space are strikingly different from our "quantitative" conceptions of time and space. Thus, Whorf concluded that the Hopi and English languages not only *describe* the world differently, but they also lead native speakers to *perceive* the world differently.

> When linguists became able to examine, critically and scientifically, a large number of languages of widely different patterns, their base of reference was expanded; . . . and a whole new order of significances came into their ken. It was found that the background linguistic system (in other words, the grammar) of each language is not merely a reproducing instrument for voicing ideas but rather is itself the shaper of ideas. . . . We cut nature up, organize it into concepts, ascribe significances as we do, largely because we are parties to an agreement that holds throughout our speech community and is codified in the patterns of our language.[1]

Much evidence appears to support the Whorfian hypothesis that thought is shaped by the language in which it is organized, recorded, and communicated. For example, the Hanunöö of the Philippine Islands have names for ninety-two varieties of rice, which is a staple of their diet and therefore of great importance to them. Eskimos have names for nine different types of snow. These illustrations suggest that a group of people perceive what is important to them to have greater detail and variety than do other groups, and their language reflects this perception.

In other cases, thought and language are mutually limited. The Zulus have words for "white cow" and "red cow" but no word for "cow" as such. And lacking the word, they appear to lack the concept of the species as well. The Tasaday, a people of the Philippines, share a communal life remarkable for the absence of violent actions and hostile feelings; and there are no words in their language for violence, hatred, or aggression.

The dependence of thought upon language seems most dramatically supported by differences in the way language groups identify colors. English parcels out the visual spectrum into six segments: purple, blue, green, yellow, orange, and red. However, in Basa (a language of Liberia), there is a single major division: *lui* refers to the blue-green end of the spectrum, and *ziza* refers

[1] John B. Carroll, ed., *Language, Thought and Reality* (Cambridge, Mass.: M.I.T. Press, 1964), pp. 212f.

to the red-orange end. Shona (a language of Zimbabwe) groups together the reds and purples and recognizes two other groups that are approximately the blues and the greens-plus-yellows. In Zuni (a language of North America), orange and yellow are combined into a single range, *lupz inna*.

Some experiments on color recognition have tested perceptual differences based on language. In one experiment, Zunis were presented with a small set of different colors—including some for which their language has no names— and then asked after a brief period to pick out the ones previously seen from a much larger collection of color samples. They are reported to have had trouble recognizing the colors for which they lacked names.[2]

Not all studies of color recognition support the view that color perception is dependent upon language. It has been shown, for instance, that while the Dani of New Guinea have only two color terms—*mili* ("dark") and *mola* ("light")—they seem to perceive colors as we do. Research shows that they remember primary colors—blue, green, yellow, and red—better than non-primary colors, just as English-speaking people do, and their ability to judge the similarity of color samples is comparable.[3]

In fact, many psycholinguists reject the view that our minds are in the grip of the language we speak, denying that thinking is dependent on linguistic ability or activity. Psychologist Roger N. Shepard of Stanford University claims that human beings think nonverbally much of the time—that thinking in spatial images precedes the symbolic representation necessary for verbal thought. And according to the Swiss psychologist Jean Piaget, children form conceptions of objects before they have the capacity to express these conceptions in words. They do so entirely by manipulating objects and observing the effects.

Studies such as Piaget's suggest that some key concepts are not a product of linguistic or other social experiences but reflect the nature of the physical world. Yet evidence also shows that thought cannot develop much ahead of a language that expresses it. Deaf children who have not been taught sign language and children deprived of language experience through extreme isolation seem to think in only the simplest terms, as if arrested at the stage of a two- or three-year-old. Normal mental development requires the capacity for mental organization that characterizes the use of language. Moreover, mental processes indispensable to adult thinking, such as the power of abstraction, appear to be directly related to the development of linguistic proficiency. While words may not be needed to think, probably little thinking can occur without them.

Although the controversy over language and thought remains unresolved, there can be no doubt that at least some forms of reflection—especially those related to attitudes and outlooks—are perpetuated by language. The influence of linguistic usage on our perception of the world and ourselves is at times

[2] Dwight Bolinger, *Aspects of Language* (New York: Harcourt, Brace and World, 1968), p. 256.
[3] E. R. Heider, "Universals in Color Naming and Memory," *Journal of Experimental Psychology* 93 (1972).

indirect, subtle, and only partially under conscious control. It is easy to be amused by the slang or jargon of an "in" or "out" group—such as the "beat generation" or "hippies" of a few decades ago and today's "valley girls." But such colorful vocabularies can perpetuate or even generate stereotypes and prejudices. For example, generations of white Southerners, who identified adult black males as "boys," may have felt that this identification was "just the way people talk." But if members of a group use a demeaning term consistently and accept it as "natural," it is probable that the expression is a clue to the way they think.

The following "case study" gives reason for reflection.

In 1978, a student at a prestigious American university on the East Coast conducted a survey of slang current among undergraduates. The university

---

A Lexicon of College Slang

billies	local youths who do not attend the university, but may be seen at bars, sporting events, etc.
dweab	any anonymous person
an egg	an undesirable person, e.g., an undesirable potential fraternity brother
an atomic egg	an extremely undesirable person
a flame	one who is annoying, offensive; also a verb, as in "they're really flaming now"
geek	a person
ghoul	a person who studies to excess and haunts the library
Tensor ghoul	one who studies secretly after everyone else is asleep (from "Tensor lamp")
gork	a person
lunchmeat	any disagreeable, undesirable person
nerd	undesirable person; also a verb, to study while others are relaxing, as in "they're nerding out"
throat	a student who studies to excess, from *cutthroat*; also a verb, as in "to throat for an exam"
townies	students who commute from home
turkey	undesirable person
woodwork	formerly enthusiastic person who becomes apathetic and figuratively crawls into the woodwork
wot or W.O.T.	from "a waste of time" as applied to a date who has been disappointing
yucks	lower-class whites who live near but do not attend the university

Parts of this lexicon were adapted from John J. Perrotta, "A Hopkins Argot," Johns Hopkins Magazine, January 1978.

has high admission standards, and the large percentage of students with plans for postgraduate study in medicine or law intensifies the competition for academic distinction. One finding of the survey was a large number of pejorative terms used to label and describe persons, as indicated by the partial "lexicon" shown in the accompanying box. (Some of these terms—for example, *nerd* and *turkey*—were current in the 1970s, but others seem to have been "native" to that particular campus.) Even many students who had heard these terms used on different occasions were surprised by the number and variety of insults. ·

It is no accident that such an acerbic vocabulary thrives in an intensely competitive atmosphere. And it would not be surprising to learn that college students who are called *ghouls*, *nerds*, *gorks*, and *throats* feel unaccepted and resentful and try more intensely to do better than their detractors.

There has been much concern over the extent to which daily discourse reinforces sexist beliefs and attitudes. A comment on this follows:

I think that it should be clear that in our language—since proper nouns and pronouns reflect sex rather than age, race, parentage, social status, religion, etc.—we believe that one of the most important things we can know about a person is that person's sex. (And, indeed, this is the first thing one seeks to determine about a newborn babe—our first question is almost invariably "Is it a boy or a girl?") Moreover, we would not reflect this important difference pronominally did we not believe that statements frequently mean something when applied to males, and something else when applied to females. Perhaps the most striking aspect of the conceptual discrimination reflected in our language is that man is, as it were, essentially human, whereas woman is only accidentally so.

This charge may seem rather extreme, but consider the following synonyms (which are readily confirmed by any dictionary). "Humanity" is synonymous with "mankind" but not with "womankind." "Man" can be substituted for "humanity" or "mankind" in any sentence in which the terms "mankind" or "humanity" occur without changing the meaning of the sentence, but significantly, "woman" cannot. Thus, the following expressions are all synonymous with each other: "humanity's great achievements"; "mankind's great achievements"; "man's great achievements." "Woman's great achievements" is not synonymous with any of these. . . .

Humanity, it would seem, is a male prerogative. Women are not (and, indeed, until recently, were not legally) human, but only biological mechanisms by which mankind reproduced itself. . . . And hence, just as one of the political goals of feminism is the removal of legal barriers which impose upon women a less than human status, one of the conceptual goals of women's liberation is to alter our conceptual structure so that some day "mankind" will be regarded as an improper and vestigial ellipsis for "humankind" and "man" will have no special privileges in relation to "human being" that "woman" does not have.[4]

[4] " 'Pricks' and 'Chicks': A Plea for 'Persons,' " by Robert Baker, in Richard Wasserstrom, ed., *Today's Moral Problems* (New York: Macmillan, 1975).

Whether or not one agrees with the various arguments contained in this excerpt, it is a dramatic commentary on the relationship between language and thought. Certainly some people carefully refrain from thinking of women in a stereotypical manner even though the language they use continues to support inflexible and inaccurate images. But many other people unwittingly support these and similar stereotypes because they do not reflect on the language they use. The logician's objective is to avoid such errors and accidents by analyzing the way the medium of language can affect the content of thought.

■ **EXERCISE 3-1**

◗ A. With which of the following are you inclined to agree, and why? With which do you disagree? Why?

1. ". . . if we spoke a different language, we would perceive a somewhat different world."—Ludwig Wittgenstein

2. "The fish trap exists because of the fish: once you've gotten the fish, you can forget the trap. . . . [W]ords exist because of meanings: once you've gotten the meanings, you can forget the words."—Chang-Tzu

3. "Words have no meaning. Only people have meaning."—Red Cross Radio Commercial

*4. "If the only tool you have is a hammer, you tend to treat everything as if it were a nail."—Abraham Maslow

5. "A French politician once wrote that it was a peculiarity of the French language that in it words occur in the order in which one thinks them."—Ludwig Wittgenstein

6. "Human language is like a cracked kettle on which we beat out tunes for bears to dance to, when all the time we are trying to move the stars to pity."—Gustave Flaubert

7. "We are all children in a vast kindergarten trying to spell God's name with the wrong alphabet blocks."—Tennessee Williams

*8. "Every term directs a beam of light onto the screen of experience, but whatever it is we wish to illuminate, something else must be left in the shadow."—Abraham Kaplan

9. "We must treat language with respect, for to use it at all (like driving a car) is to take on a considerable responsibility."—Monroe Beardsley

10. "Who is this that darkeneth counsel by words without knowledge?"—Job 38:2

11. "If your language is confusion, your intellect, if not your whole character, will almost certainly correspond."—Arthur Quiller-Couch

*12. "Words are the legs of the mind; they bear it about, carry it from point to point, bed it down at night and keep it off the ground and out of marsh and mists."—Richard Eder

13. "Until we label an out-group it does not clearly exist in our minds."—Gordon Allport

14. "Many broadcasters are fighting, not for *free* speech, but for *profitable* speech."—Nicholas Johnson

15. "If I were an anthropological linguist making observations about a strange and primitive tribe, I would duly note on my tape recorder that I had found linguistic evidence to show that in the areas of sex and marriage the female appears to be more important than the male, but in all other areas of culture, it seems that the reverse is true."—Alleen Pace Nilsen

*16. "Is it not possible that there is a direct correlation between a growing sense of powerlessness and futility in our lives and the jazzed-up language we use?"—Arthur Berger

17. "The art of politics is to find new names for institutions which under old names, have become odious to the people."—attributed to Tallyrand.

■ **B.** Explain what connection, if any, there is between the "message" of each of the following passages and the subject of this section. Be as specific as possible.

1. "While *we* hear a dog's bark as 'bow-wow,' the French hear it as 'oua-oua.' The Spanish further complicate matters by using the words 'guau-guau' to represent a dog's bark; the Rumanians hear it as 'ham-ham,' the Russians as 'vas-vas,' the Italians as 'bu-bu,' the Turks as 'hov-hov,' and the Chinese as 'wang-wang.' It's even worse when it comes to pigs. What we hear as 'oink-oink,' the Russians hear as 'khru-khru,' the Rumanians as 'guits-guits,' and the French as 'oui-oui,' which suggests that in French the pig is a cooperative beast."—Donna Woolfolk Cross, *Word Abuse* (1979)

2. "The Arabs have some six thousand words for 'camel,' including about fifty for pregnant camels. If you find this multiplicity startling, look at *Webster's New International:* it lists a thousand words for 'grass.' "—Ruben Abel, *Man Is the Measure*

3. "A young farmer who had been converted at one of the revivals went before the next conference and asked for a license to be a preacher. 'I know I am born to preach the Word,' said the applicant, 'for I have had three visions all the same, and it has made a lasting impression on me.' 'What was your vision?' asked a bishop. 'Wal, I saw a big, round, blue ring in the sky, and inside, in great gold letters, were "P.C." It meant, "Preach Christ," and I want to join the conference.'

"The argument was about to carry when an old pastor stood up in the back part of the hall and said, 'Young man, we don't doubt your intentions, nor do we doubt that you saw the vision with the golden "P.C."; but I am of the opinion that the "P.C." meant "Plough Corn." '

"The convert is still a farmer."—Robert B. Thomas, *The (Old) Farmer's Almanack* (1895)

*4. "Not all languages have dirty words for sex. Most American Indian languages don't, nor do Malayan or Polynesian. The Trobrianders find all the words for sex and sex organs perfectly acceptable and proper. But it would be a grievous social error to ask a Trobriander girl out to dinner. She would find your invitation scandalously obscene. That's because their dirty words have to do with chewing and swallowing food."—Donna Woolfolk Cross, *Word Abuse* (1979)

5. "A study published by the Institute of Mental Health gives the following popular terms for marijuana: 'weed,' 'hemp,' 'locoweed,' 'giggle grass,' 'reefers,' 'Mary Jane,' 'Mary Wanna,' 'Tea Brand Sticks,' 'boo,' 'Swinging Mother's Trip Kit,' and 'Acapulco Gold.' Another study published by the Drug Awareness Committee adds the following popular terms: 'pot,' 'grass,' 'tea,' 'gage,' 'hash,' and 'hashish.' "—Mario Pei, *Double-Speak in America*

6. "A man is undergoing a major operation when, abruptly, his heart fails. For several minutes, there are no life functions, and he is declared to be dead. But then a famous surgeon rushes in, and using a new experimental procedure, he brings the man back to life. When he returns to consciousness, everyone of course wants to know what he experienced as he lay dead.

" 'I looked into the very face of God,' the man says, awestruck.

" 'What is He like?' the people ask.

"The man answers, 'Well, first of all, *she's* black.' "—Donna Woolfolk Cross, *Word Abuse* (1979) ∎

□ 3-2. LEVELS OF MEANING

"When *I* use a word," Humpty Dumpty said, in rather a scornful tone, "it means just what I choose it to mean—neither more nor less."

"The question is," said Alice, "whether you *can* make words mean so many different things."

"The question is," said Humpty Dumpty, "which is to be master—that's all."

LEWIS CARROLL, *THROUGH THE LOOKING-GLASS*

One consequence of the interdependence of language and thought is that words acquire different levels of meaning. On one level, the language used by a speaker may communicate information while on another level the same words are communicating an attitude or emotional reaction. Thus, the sentences expressing an argument can serve a number of functions simultaneously. In analyzing arguments, it is therefore necessary to distinguish the informative, or cognitive, content of sentences from other levels of meaning.

What do we look for when we investigate the meaning of a word? Many philosophers claim that the meaning of a word lies in its representative function, that is, that words derive their meaning from the objects, actions, or events they represent. According to one such view, the *referential theory*, the meaning of a word is the object, or entity, the word designates. According to another view, the *ideational theory*, its meaning is the idea with which it is associated—the image that is evoked when the word is spoken, read, or heard. Finally, the *behavioral theory* maintains that the meaning of a word consists in the kinds of activities that tend to evoke its utterance and in the range of responses one ordinarily expects of the hearer.

Despite their differences, these three theories share the assumption that the meaning of a word lies outside of the language itself. Words mean what they *stand for*, whether what they stand for are objects, ideas, images, or behavioral responses.

However, there is a second way of investigating meaning that is quite unlike the first. Advocates of this second view claim that the meaning of a

"Take this, Ferguson, and hype it up threefold."

©1979, *The New Yorker Magazine, Inc. Reprinted by permission.*

word is a function of what members of the linguistic community *do* with it— how the particular expression fits into the broader pattern of speech-related behavior.

In the eighteenth century, the philosopher George Berkeley (1685–1753) called attention to the many different uses of language: ". . . the communicating of ideas . . . is not the chief and only end of language as is commonly supposed. There are other ends, as the raising of some passion, the exciting to or deterring from an action, the putting the mind in some particular disposition; to which the former is in many cases barely subservient, and sometimes entirely omitted, when these can be obtained without it, as I think does not infrequently happen in the familiar use of language."[5]

But the twentieth-century philosopher Ludwig Wittgenstein has probably done the most to encourage the view that the meaning of a word is to be understood by examining how it is used. Wittgenstein emphasized the need to examine language within the broader context of human behavior and the purposes and intentions of speakers. Language is thus inseparable from other aspects of human life. Words are significant not so much as symbols but as a means of carrying out intentions and affecting the behavior of others. Therefore, words do not all function the same way; and even the same word can mean different things in different circumstances.

Let us not forget that a word hasn't got a meaning given to it, as it were, by a power independent of us, so that there could be a kind of scientific investigation of what the word *really* means. A word has the meaning someone has given to it.
LUDWIG WITTGENSTEIN

---

[5] *Treatise Concerning the Principles of Human Knowledge* (1710).

> Whenever two or more human beings can communicate with each other, they can, by agreement, make anything stand for anything.
>
> S. I. HAYAKAWA

This way of investigating meaning encourages the classification of linguistic expressions according to the functions they serve. For example, in Section 1-1 the informative function of sentences was distinguished from their directive, emotive, evaluative, and ceremonial uses. Such classifications are helpful to the study of logic because they further understanding of the differences between the argumentative use of language and its other functions.

In addition to its other functions, language can be *performative*. The term *performative utterance* designates circumstances in which *saying* something amounts actually to *doing* it.

A performative utterance is a locution that, when spoken in appropriate circumstances, accomplishes the action it reports.

Thus, if I say, "I suggest you wait a little longer," I have by saying it made a suggestion. And if I say, "I advise you to read the report," I have thereby given advice. Performative utterances, like the examples given, are usually expressed in the first person, and the verbs for such actions are called *performative verbs*. Besides *advise* and *suggest*, other common performative verbs are *accept, apologize, baptize, bid, concede, congratulate, greet, promise, pronounce, thank,* and *warn*. In its performatory function, language is often combined with nonverbal behavior: for example, the handshake, the military salute, the obscene gesture, the notary public's seal on a document, and the signals of the auctioneer and the baseball umpire.

Since linguistic expressions rarely have just one use, it is impossible to designate sentences as exclusively ceremonial, directive, emotive, evaluative, informative, or performative in function. Meaning depends on the context and on the intentions of the speaker. But even if a speaker intends an expression to have a single use, the associations it creates for the hearers may lead them to attach other meanings to it—to mistake one function for another. For example, a doctor encountering a patient on the street might use the ceremonial greeting "How are you?" The patient might, understandably, misinterpret the question as a request for detailed information.

Much of the time effective communication requires an expression to serve multiple functions. For instance, while ceremonial locutions serve primarily to facilitate social exchange, they can also be informative. When someone says, "How nice of you to come," in the right tone of voice and with a smile, the ceremonial words are to be taken literally. The informative sentence "I thank you in advance for your attention to this problem" is intended to serve a directive purpose as well as to report the writer's disposition. And while the exclamation "I'd rather do it myself!" expresses emotion, it simultaneously issues a command and informs hearers of the speaker's preferences.

Excellent examples of discourse with multiple layers of meaning occur frequently in classrooms. Much of the humor of J. Timothy Petersik's observations in "What the Professor Really Means" (see accompanying box) results from the familiarity, to all college students, of certain stock phrases, plus the ulterior messages these phrases *seem* to convey.

What the Professor Really Means

What he or she said	*What it means*
You'll be using one of the leading textbooks in this field.	I used it as a grad student.
If you follow these few simple rules, you'll do fine in this course.	If you don't need any sleep, you'll do fine in the course.
The *gist* of what the author is saying is what's most important.	I don't understand the details either.
Various authorities agree that . . .	My hunch is that . . .
The answer to your question is beyond the scope of this class.	I don't know.
You'll have to see me during my office hours for a thorough answer to your question.	I don't know.
In answer to your question, you must recognize that there are several disparate points of view.	I *really* don't know.
Today we are going to discuss a most important topic.	Today we are going to discuss my dissertation.
Unfortunately, we haven't had the time to consider all the people who made contributions to this field.	I disagree with what roughly half of the people in this field have said.
We can continue this discussion outside of class.	1. I'm tired of this—let's quit. 2. You're winning the argument—let's quit.
Today we'll let a member of the class lead the discussion. It will be a good educational experience.	I stayed out too late last night and didn't have time to prepare a lecture.
Any questions?	I'm ready to let you go.

Box continued.

What the Professor Really Means

The implications of this study are clear.	I don't know what it means, either, but there'll be a question about it on the test.
The test will be a 50-question multiple choice.	The test will be a 60-question multiple guess, plus three short-answer questions (1,000 words or more) and no one will score above 75 percent.
The test scores were generally good.	Some of you managed a *B*.
The test scores were a little below my expectations.	Where was the party last night?
Some of you could have done better.	Everyone flunked.
Before we begin the lecture for today, are there any questions about the previous material?	Has anyone opened the book yet?
According to my sources . . .	According to the guy who taught this class last year . . .
It's been very rewarding to teach this class.	I hope they find someone else to teach it next year.

From J. Timothy Petersik, What the Professor Really Means. *J. Timothy Petersik is Assistant Professor of Psychology at Ripon College, Ripon, Wisconsin. This first appeared in* The Chronicle of Higher Education, *April 27, 1981. It is reprinted by permission.*

A kind of communication on more than one level that adds to the effectiveness of much great poetry and other writing is *metaphor*. An expression is metaphorical when it is used in none of its established senses but is nevertheless intelligible.

A metaphor is a figure of speech that is both literally absurd and nonliterally intelligible.

Consider:

The fog comes
on little cat feet

CARL SANDBURG, "FOG"

In the midst of winter, I finally learned that there was in me an invincible summer.

ALBERT CAMUS, *ACTUELLES*

It makes no sense to think of fog—an amorphous mass—as having "feet," whether of a cat or otherwise. Nor is there a literal sense in which "summer" can be inside the person of Albert Camus. In using a metaphor, one is using a word or phrase in a way that is different from—though related to—its established sense.

Now consider the following passage from Shakespeare's *Macbeth*:

Macbeth:
Methought I heard a voice cry "Sleep no more!
Macbeth does murder sleep," the innocent sleep,
Sleep that knits up the ravell'd sleave of care,
The death of each day's life, sore labour's bath.
Balm of hurt minds, great nature's second course,
Chief nourisher in life's feast. . . .[6]

It is because of a similarity between the healing quality that Shakespeare is attributing to sleep in the third line of the quotation above and what happens when one mends a torn sweater that the reader can understand what is being said, even though the words *knit* and *sleave* are not being used in their everyday senses. And it is because one can understand sentences like "I knitted up the ravelled sleeve of that sweater" that one can understand Shakespeare's metaphor. A metaphor is dependent for its effect upon the established senses of words, but it works *through* these senses to provide a new insight.[7]

Metaphors create new meanings and, in so doing, enlarge the capacity of language. English is full of meaningful phrases that developed from metaphorical uses of words—"fork in the road," "leg of a table," "leaf of a book," and "stem of a glass," to mention only a few.

How exactly does metaphorical use shade over into established usage? The answer, in accordance with the theory that meaning depends at least partly on use, is *gradually and by degrees*. If language is thought of as a continuum, striking examples of metaphor, such as "Sleep knits up the ravelled sleeve of care," are at one end, and literal, well-established usages, such as, "I am knitting a sweater," are at the other. In between are commonplace metaphors, such as "he knit his brows" and "she blew her top," which are used so frequently that they sometimes become dictionary entries.

Because a word can have more than one meaning, the logician must consider not only the way it is generally used but also its function in a particular

---

[6] Act II, Scene 2.
[7] William P. Alston, *Philosophy of Language* (Englewood Cliffs, New Jersey: Prentice-Hall, 1964), p. 98.

case. One must consider the interrelation of three factors: the *intent* of the speaker, the ordinary *effect* of the particular expression upon hearers, and the *social context* in which the expression occurs.

■ EXERCISE 3-2

■ A. Reread the sentences in Exercise 1-1A. From among them, select any five that can be understood to function in at least two different ways (informative, directive, emotive, evaluative, or ceremonial), depending on context. Briefly describe different contexts that would permit alternate interpretations of the sentences you select.

■ B. For each of the following animal terms, present at least one connotation in addition to the central, or literal, meaning of the word.

(a) dog	(k) vulture
(b) dove	*(l) kitten
(c) chick	(m) snake
*(d) bird	(n) pigeon
(e) worm	(o) weasel
(f) fox	*(p) owl
(g) tiger	(q) bat
*(h) lamb	(r) crab
(i) wolf	(s) cow
(j) turkey	*(t) ape

■ C. The author Henry James mentioned "blotting-paper voices" in his description of a desultory conversation. William Faulkner referred at one point to the "viciousness of stamped steel." Find five metaphors that interest you. Explain the insight each metaphor conveys, and how this new meaning is connected to the literal meaning of the words used.

■ D. Below are a number of terms frequently used to describe persons. Determine what each word or phrase means and whether its use is generally commendatory, condemnatory, or neutral. Explain why you think the term "caught on" as a description.

ace	*green thumb
acid head	hot dog
beach bum	John Doe
*cornball	lame duck
dark horse	*lone wolf
diamond in the rough	longhair
egghead	shrink
*fair-haired boy	spring chicken
top banana	*fair-weather friend
flash-in-the-pan	triple threat
grease monkey	wet blanket

☐ 3-3. PITFALLS OF LANGUAGE

Metaphors allow us to go from one level of meaning to another. In their capacity to provide new insights, they provide the most dramatic examples of figurative speech. However, many expressions are figurative to some degree; that is, they suggest nuances of meaning or stimulate associations with other ideas. *Puns, double-entendres* (words or phrases with two meanings, one of which may be indelicate), and *innuendoes* (discussed below) are kinds of figurative speech. In fact, almost every word or phrase occupying a key position in a discourse carries with it a range of connotations, or related ideas, that can make it potentially misleading.

Words or phrases with identical cognitive, or literal, meaning can differ greatly in their emotive meaning—in the attitude they suggest. This is illustrated by the facetious definition of an optimist as someone who says a glass is half full and of a pessimist as someone who says a glass is half empty. The same fact—that the beverage takes up half the capacity of the glass—seems encouraging or discouraging, depending on how it is expressed. It is alleged that when he was president of American Motors, George Romney coined the term *compact car* to replace *small car* because *small* as applied to an automobile was thought to have undesirable connotations. And the philosopher Bertrand Russell contrasted literal and emotive meaning by "conjugating" this "irregular verb": "I am firm; you are obstinate; he is a pig-headed fool."

A locution with pleasing connotations that is substituted for one with disagreeable connotations is called a *euphemism*. Thus, an overweight person is said to be "husky" or to have a "full figure." A maid becomes a "housekeeper," vagrants become "street people," and physical-education majors are said to be majoring in "health care and leisure studies." Table 3-1 presents groups of terms that have more or less the same cognitive meaning but vary widely in their emotive meaning.

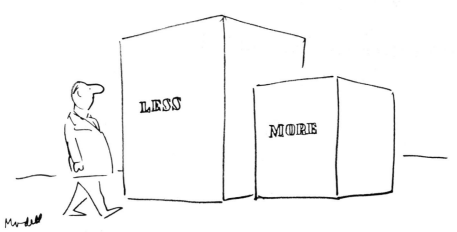

TABLE 3-1 *Positive and negative connotations of terms with approximately the same descriptive content*

POSITIVE (FAVORABLE)	NEUTRAL	NEGATIVE (UNFAVORABLE)
public servant	government official	bureaucrat
street people	vagrants	bums
thrifty	cost-conscious	cheap, tight
aide, right hand	administrative assistant	lackey, bootlicker
attorney, barrister	lawyer	shyster
intercede	intervene	interfere
progress	change	degeneration
modern, progressive	new	newfangled
conciliation	negotiation	appeasement
patriotism	nationalism	chauvinism, jingoism
imaginative	daydreamer	escapist
peace officer	police officer	cop, fuzz, pig
aroma, fragrance	odor	smell, stench
emerging nation	undeveloped country	backward country
associates	partners, coworkers	accomplices, co-conspirators
mortician	funeral director	undertaker
resolute	firm	rigid
speech, address	talk	lecture
upright, righteous	modest, proper	prudish, prissy
innocent, childlike	unwitting, unknowing	naive, childish
slim, slender	thin	scrawny

Tell me what's wrong
With the words or with you
That the thing is all right,
But the word is taboo!
D. H. LAWRENCE

The ability of language simultaneously to express different meanings requires the logician to separate the informative content of a word from the attitude, judgment, or point of view it suggests. To think logically about a problem, we must consider the *reasons* for believing that a statement is true or sufficiently warranted to be given support; and we must avoid being misled by language whose purpose is other than informative. In particular, the pitfalls created by *slanting, hypostatization,* and *con-artistry* must be avoided.

☐ *Slanting*

Slanting occurs when a speaker or writer uses terms with positive or negative connotations to create an impression about a subject that is not warranted by the informative content of the discourse. This device is used intentionally when an arguer advances a point of view that cannot be supported. But slanting can also result from carelessness, which can prevent the arguer from seeing the difference between the explicit meaning of his or her words—the information they literally convey—and their implicit, suggested meaning.

☐ ASSURING

A device that has legitimate use in argumentation but that can be misused to produce slanting is what one logician calls *assuring*.[8] To justify the conclusion of any argument, premises are offered that support it. But this activity depends upon a shared set of beliefs and a certain amount of trust; otherwise, every premise would have to be proved through the introduction of further premises that are also in need of proof, and so on indefinitely. So an arguer is likely to refer to shared beliefs with such assuring phrases as "It goes without saying," "Everyone agrees that," and "As we all know." And an arguer who believes that support for a conclusion is available but who is unaware of how widely known this support is will sometimes indicate that it can be produced on demand. This kind of assuring takes the form of reference to authorities without actually citing them: "According to an informed source," "Doctors agree that," "Recent studies have shown."

Although assuring remarks can serve as an economical means of establishing the reliability of premises, they often mask the weakest parts of an argument. If someone says, "It needs no comment," the audience might well wonder why not. The expression "in fact" should sometimes be taken to mean "in my opinion." When someone says something is "uncontroversial" or "indisputable," the chances are good that it is not. And the expressions "doubtless," "undoubtedly," and "beyond the shadow of a doubt" should evoke skepticism rather than providing assurance. So, too, should "obviously" and "of course."

☐ HEDGING

In contrast to assuring, *hedging* occurs when the arguer so limits the scope of a claim that it is unlikely to be challenged. This can be done by using *most* instead of *all*, *some* instead of *most*, *sometimes* instead of *always*, and *occa-*

---

[8] Robert J. Fogelin, *Understanding Arguments* (New York: Harcourt Brace Jovanovich, 1978), p. 41.

sionally instead of *sometimes*. Probability phrases, such as "it is likely that," "it is arguable that," and "it is conceivably the case that" serve the same purpose.

As innocuous as hedging may appear, it can be used illicitly to insinuate things that are not explicitly stated for lack of evidence. For example, saying "Perhaps he is on the verge of a nervous breakdown" introduces a statement while allowing the speaker to escape responsibility for having directly said it. The breakdown is, after all, only suggested. And often an arguer will introduce a statement in a guarded form and later go on to speak as if it were taken for granted.

☐ INNUENDO

Slanting frequently is accomplished through *innuendo*. An innuendo is an indirect—and often derogatory—intimation about a person or thing. Often innuendo occurs when a statement is placed in a context that serves to distort its meaning, as illustrated by the "Tale of the Old Shipmasters of Salem" (see accompanying box).

A Tale of the Old Shipmasters of Salem

Captain L— had a first mate who was at times addicted to the use of strong drink, and occasionally, as the slang has it, "got full." The ship was lying in port in China, and the mate had been on shore and had there indulged rather freely in some of the vile compounds common in Chinese ports. He came on board, "drunk as a lord," and thought he had a mortgage on the whole world. The captain, who rarely ever touched liquors himself, was greatly disturbed by the disgraceful conduct of his officer, particularly as the crew had all observed his condition. One of the duties of the first officer is to write up the "log" each day, but as that worthy was not able to do it, the captain made the proper entry, but added: "The mate was drunk all day." The ship left port the next day and the mate got "sobered off." He attended to his writing at the proper time, but was appalled when he saw what the captain had done. He went on deck and soon after the following colloquy took place:

"Cap'n, why did you write in the log yesterday that I was drunk all day?"

"It was true, wasn't it?"

"Yes, but what will the owners say if they see it? 'T will hurt me with them."

But the mate could get nothing more from the captain than "It was true, wasn't it?"

The next day, when the captain was examining the book, he found at the bottom of the mate's entry of observation, course, winds, and tides: "The captain was sober all day."

Charles E. Trow, The Old Shipmasters of Salem *(New York: P. Putnam's Sons, 1905).*

Innuendo can also be produced by *irony, understatement,* and *overstatement*. Irony is illustrated by Mark Antony's address to the mob in Shakespeare's *Julius Caesar*. When Antony says, "For Brutus is an honorable man," he is using *honorable* ironically. Throughout the scene it is clear that far from praising Brutus, Antony is trying to rouse the mob against him and Caesar's other assassins.

In *overstatement,* the meaning conveyed is opposite to the one literally expressed. For example, someone who says "I understand why you forgot; you had *so much* to do today" may be criticizing the person for forgetting when actually he or she had little to do.

Sometimes overstatement and euphemism are combined to make the commonplace seem scientific and technical—a popular device of governmental bureaucracies. In publications of the Department of Defense, a parachute has been called an "aerodynamic personnel decelerator," a tin can becomes a "metal cylinder storage container," and a shovel becomes a "combat emplacement evacuator."

Understatement can serve various purposes. It, too, can convey a meaning that is almost opposite to what is literally stated. A student who says "Some of the professors at this university are not bores" is actually suggesting that most of the professors *are* bores. Understatement can also suggest that something is less important than it really is. Thus, President Nixon's press secretary, Ronald Ziegler, called the Watergate break-in "a third-rate burglary attempt"; and others in the administration referred to it as "the Watergate caper" or "the Watergate incident."

☐ DISCOUNTING

One final kind of slanting is *discounting,* the objective of which is to ward off criticism by anticipating it. Sometimes, for effect, contradictory terms are joined together to form what is called an *oxymoron,* as in "frightfully nice," "disgustingly beautiful," "relentlessly charming," and (from advertising) "authentic replica" and "plastic silverware." Discounting similarly involves juxtaposing words or phrases that ordinarily convey inconsistent messages. More specifically, discounting involves the use of certain *conjunctions—but, although, however, nevertheless, still, yet,* and *nonetheless*—to bind together diverging but not necessarily contradictory expressions. The word *but* usually discounts the statement that precedes it in favor of the statement that follows. The word *although* operates in reverse fashion, discounting the statement immediately following it. Here are some examples of discounting:

The situation is critical, but not hopeless.

Brenda is intelligent, but rather lazy.

Fred has a keen imagination, but little respect for the facts.

Although John uses unconventional methods to get ahead, he is no cheater.

Now consider these two statements:

Chalmers is an honest politician, but he is reticent and secretive.
Chalmers is reticent and secretive, but he is an honest politician.

While the statements present the same facts, one sounds critical and the other does not. The first assertion seems to give greater weight to Chalmers's reticence and secretiveness, while the second statement acknowledges these faults but overrides them by pointing out that Chalmers is honest. The statements would be used for different purposes—the first, perhaps, to argue against reelecting Chalmers; the second to argue for reelection.

☐ *Hypostatization*

Figurative speech that introduces poetry to ordinary discourse can be misleading when used in arguments. *Hypostatization* occurs when an abstraction is treated as if it had existence. Hypostatization is called *reification* when the abstraction is thought to exist because the words used to designate it function as ordinary nouns.

Consider the ease with which we say, and accept, statements such as the following:

John saw his duty and he did it.
Sarah did it for Peter's sake.
Sylvester has a lot of luck at the races.
It was Miriam's destiny to be an architect.

Reification would occur if John's *duty*, Peter's *sake*, Sylvester's *luck*, and Miriam's *destiny* were thought to designate particular objects, just as *Aunt Sophie's apron* and *Uncle Silas's pipe* designate particular objects. The question "What is Peter's sake?" can be understood only as a question about how the word *sake* is used in our language (for example, "What do people mean when they say things like, 'She did it for Peter's sake'?"). It would be foolish to treat the question as an inquiry about a mysterious object named by *sake*.

☐ PERSONIFICATION

Personification occurs when abstractions are referred to in terms that apply to human beings and when human activities and intentions are attributed to them. For example, when someone speaks about the "judgment of history" and when it is said that "science makes progress," history and science are being personified. But only persons, not history, make judgments; and scientists, not science make progress.

The following quotations contain examples of personification:

> The State is the divine idea as it exists today. . . . It is the absolute power on earth; it is its own end and object. It is the ultimate end which has the highest right against the individual.[9]

[9] W. H. F. Hegel, quoted by Ward Fearnside and William B. Holther, *Fallacy: The Counterfeit of Argument* (Englewood Cliffs, N.J.: Prentice-Hall, 1959), p. 48.

Language 81

... this world will still be subject to the fiercest fights for the existence of mankind. In the end, only the urge of self-preservation will eternally succeed. Under its pressure so-called "humanity" as the expression of a mixture of stupidity, cowardice, and an imaginary superior intelligence, will melt like snow under the March sun. Mankind has grown strong in eternal struggles and it will only perish through eternal peace.[10]

Both passages illustrate the dramatic effects that can be achieved by such treatment of abstractions. In the first quotation, the state is pictured as having

---

The tyranny of war is often described as if war itself were the tyrant, a natural force like flood or famine or, personified, a brutal giant stalking his human prey, as in these lines from a poem by Thomas Sackville:

> Lastly stood War, in glittering arms y-clad,
> With visage grim, stern looks, and blackly hued;
> In his right hand a naked sword he had
> That to the hilts was all with blood embrued,
> And in his left (that kings and kingdoms rued)
> Famine and fire he held, and therewithal
> He razed towns, and threw down towers and all.

Here is the Grim Reaper in uniform, armed with a sword instead of a scythe. The poetic image enters also into moral and political thought, but only, I think, as a kind of ideology, obscuring our critical judgment. For it is a piece of mystification to represent tyrannical power as an abstract Force. In battle as in politics, tyranny is always a relation among persons or groups of persons. The tyranny of war is a peculiarly complex relation because coercion is common on both sides. Sometimes, however, it is possible to distinguish the sides and to identify the statesmen and soldiers who first took the naked sword to hand. Wars are not self-starting. They may "break out," like an accidental fire, under conditions difficult to analyze and where the attribution of responsibility seems impossible. But usually they are more like arson than accident: war has human agents as well as human victims.

Michael Walzer, Just and Unjust Wars *(New York: Basic Books, 1977), pp. 30–31. The interior quote is from Thomas Sackville, "The Induction," Works, ed. R. W. Sackville-West (London, 1859), p. 115.*

---

[10] Adolf Hitler, *Mein Kampf,* selection reprinted in John Somerville and Ronald E. Santoni, eds., *Social and Political Philosophy* (Garden City, N.Y.: Doubleday, 1963), pp. 458–459.

purpose and is alleged to possess rights. In the second quotation, self-preservation is characterized as succeeding, and humankind is characterized as growing and perishing. The second quotation was intended to legitimize war; it obscures a value judgment about a particular policy by making it seem to be the result of processes that—like Darwinian "natural selection"—are not under human control.

The danger that by personifying an abstraction human beings can avoid accepting responsibility for their actions is brought out in Michael Walzer's comments on war (see box on p. 81).

□ *Con-artistry*

Con-artistry encompasses a host of techniques used to control information and influence attitudes. These techniques range from crude attempts to shape thought to the sophisticated devices of advertising agencies and propagandists. Some of the cruder ruses involve the selection of certain facts and the omission of others, the distortion of information by arranging facts to suggest relationships that do not really exist, name-calling (for example, "bleeding-heart liberals"), the oversimplification of complex issues ("America, love it or leave it"), lifting statements out of context, and distraction by the interjection into an argument of inappropriate humor or wholly irrelevant considerations (so-called red herrings). Some forms of fallacious reasoning employ these or similar techniques and succeed in mimicking valid arguments.

□ DOUBLESPEAK

The practice that has come to be called *doublespeak* is a type of con-artistry that is generally so subtle and so easily absorbed into our language that the perspective or attitude it generates may become a natural and accepted response. Doublespeak involves the selection or invention of emotively neutral—often technical-sounding—terms to dull the force of what is being said and thus make acceptable what otherwise might be unacceptable. The press secretaries and news agencies of modern bureaucracies generate a wealth of doublespeak. During the era of the United States military involvement in Vietnam, the terms and phrases shown below were employed in Department of Defense press releases and by newspapers that carried stories about the war.[11]

DOUBLESPEAK	EQUIVALENT
a case of terminological inexactitude	a lie
adjustment center	solitary-confinement cell
air support	bombing
anomaly	mistake

[11] The term *doublespeak* was introduced by the English author, George Orwell (1903–1950), whose novel *1984*, written in 1949, is a nightmare projection of a future police state, ruled by "Big Brother," where "War is Peace" and all values are transvalued. Many of the terms given in the list here appeared in Howard Kahane, *Logic and Contemporary Rhetoric* (Belmont, CA: Wadsworth Publishing, 1971).

DOUBLESPEAK	EQUIVALENT
civilian irregular defense soldier	mercenary
confrontation management	riot control
containment of information	withholding of information
correctional facility	prison
destabilize	overthrow (as in "destabilize the government")
friendly fire	accidentally shelling friendly villages or troops
free-fire zone	geographical area the bombing of which represents no military objective
incursion	invasion ("Cambodian incursion")
incontinent ordnance	off-target bombs
interdiction	bombing
mobile maneuvering	retreat
new life hamlet	refugee camp
pacification center	concentration camp
protective reaction strike	bombing
redeployment or replacement	troop withdrawal or pullout
resources control program	defoliation
returnee	deserter or defector
security coordinator	bodyguard
selected out	fired, removed from office
selective ordnance	napalm
strategic retrograde action	retreat
surgical strike	precision bombing
termination	killing
termination with prejudice	assassination
search and clear	search and destroy

You always write it's bombing, bombing, bombing. It's *not* bombing! It's air support.
COL. DAVID OPFER, USAF PRESS OFFICER IN CAMBODIA, 1973

Political language . . . is designed to make lies sound truthful, and murder respectable, and to give an appearance of solidity to pure wind.
GEORGE ORWELL

The deceit of doublespeak is double-edged: not only do neutral or technical-sounding terms offset the emotional reaction that would be produced by words that were directly descriptive, they also disguise what is actually going on. And as noted in the discussion of college slang and sexist language in Section 3-1, the words people use to describe and discuss a subject can influence their attitude toward it—another hazard of doublespeak.

■ EXERCISE 3-3

■ A. Explain what connection, if any, there is between the message or point of each of the following passages and the subject matter of this chapter. Be as specific as possible.

　　1. According to a story by the Associated Press, the following incident took place in India.

　　　　A big wild animal of the antelope family and known as the "Nehil Goe" was causing extensive damage to crops in the field. But the farmers would not harm it because "Nehil Goe" means "Blue Cow," and the cow is sacred to the Hindu. So the Indian Government has changed the name to "Nehil Goa" which means "Blue Horse."

　　2. "I never give them hell. I just tell the truth, and they think it is hell."—President Harry S Truman

　　3. "To call someone 'poor,' in the modern way of thinking, is to speak perjoratively of his condition, while the substitution of 'disadvantaged' or 'underprivileged' indicates that poverty wasn't his fault. Indeed, says linguist Mario Pei, by using 'underprivileged,' we are 'made to feel that it is all our fault.' "—"Telling It Like It Isn't," *Time* (September 19, 1969)

　　*4. "A lawyer who said, 'My client feels you made a mistake,' would be derelict in that he may have implied that no one else has that feeling, and, worse, that there was only one mistake. The assertion would be more lawyerlike (a favorite word among lawyers) if put: 'My client, among others, feels that you made a mistake, among others.' It would be an error to put an 'among others' after 'you' because that might imply that others too, made mistakes, opening the door to a defense that those other mistakes were the legally significant ones, if any. The proper retort is, 'Your client, if any, is wrong, and my client's mistake, if any, caused no damage, if any occurred.' Once the lawyers have thus made their positions clear, the chances of a lengthy lawsuit are excellent."—Edward B. Packard, Jr. (intending to be facetious), *Columbia University Forum*, Spring 1967

　　5. In 1839, the British Earl of Durham recommended self-government for the British colony of Canada, which had grown self-reliant "through many years of benign neglect by the British." In recent years, the phrase "benign neglect" has been resurrected by Senator Daniel Patrick Moynihan of New York to be applied to racial minorities.

　　6. "It [force] is unreliable not so much because someone else may possess or produce a superior force in opposition to your own, but because force contains within itself the elements of its own destruction. Force is not murdered; it commits suicide. It kills itself directly in the ancient sense that all power corrupts and absolute power corrupts absolutely, and it kills itself indirectly in the sense that it begets its own assassins."—Roy Pearson, "The Dilemma of Force," *Saturday Review*, February 10, 1968.

7. " 'Voters are basically lazy, basically uninterested in making an *effort* to understand what we're talking about. . . .' Gavin wrote. 'Reason requires a high degree of discipline, of concentration; impression is easier. Reason pushes the viewer back, it assaults him, it demands that he agree or disagree; impression can envelop him, invite him in, without making an intellectual demand. . . . When we argue with him we demand that he make the effort of replying. We seek to engage his intellect, and for most people this is the most difficult work of all. The emotions are more easily roused, closer to the surface, more malleable. . . .' "—Joe McGinnis, *The Selling of the President*

*8. "Like Sorel [Frantz Fanon] argues that violence invests the revolutionary character with 'positive and creative qualities,' since 'each individual forms a violent link in the great chain, a part of the great organism of violence which has surged upward in reaction to the settler's violence in the beginning.' The emerging nation is bound together by a cement which has been mixed with blood and anger."—Grundy and Weinstein, *Ideologies of Violence*, quoting Frantz Fanon, *The Wretched of the Earth*

9. "In correcting a small child, an English, Italian, or Greek speaker will often say, 'Be good.' A French speaker will say, 'Be wise'; a Scandinavian, 'Be friendly'; a German, 'Be in line'; and a Hopi Indian, 'That is not the Hopi way.' Would these societies be encouraging a value in the child? What value? What are the long-range implications of associating behavior with this value?"—Vincent Barry, *Practical Logic*

10. "The labor, time, and ingenuity that go into the coining of suitable (i.e., selling) brand names are unbelievable. Computers as well as foreign language experts are put to work to make sure the name under consideration will not convey unpleasant, ridiculous, or obscene connotations in the language of any of the countries where the product is to be marketed. 'Con' Edison always sends French visitors into stitches. And an American tourist recently came back from France laughing about an orange drink produced there called 'Pshit.' The 'P,' of course, is silent. . . . It has been statistically determined that the favorite component word for brand names is 'magic' ('Magic Moment,' 'Hidden Magic,' 'Deep Magic,' 'Soft Magic,' 'Blue Magic,' 'Magic Flash') with 'king' as the runner-up ('King Vitamin'). The favorite suffix seems to be 'plus' ('Platinum Plus Blades,' 'Orange Plus,' 'Flavor Plus Dog food')."—Mario Pei, *Double-Speak in America*

11. " 'Then you should say what you mean,' the March Hare went on.

" 'I do,' Alice hastily replied, 'at least—at least I mean what I say—that's the same thing, you know.'

" 'Not the same thing a bit!' said the Hatter. 'Why you might as well say that "I see what I eat" is the same thing as "I eat what I see!" '

" 'You might just as well say,' added the March Hare, 'that "I like what I get" is the same thing as "I get what I like!" '—Lewis Carroll, *Alice in Wonderland*

*12. "Say sources and the eyes sparkle. Say documents and a hush falls. Say intelligence and people gasp in awe. . . . Yet intelligence is only information or misinformation. Documents are only papers, sometimes classified, or overclassified. A source is only somebody who told you something, possibly for his own purposes, and possibly incorrect.

"No practice in Washington is more beloved than that of attributing statements to sources who cannot be named. . . . There is nothing like the Richter scale that measures earthquakes on which to rate sources; but well placed is a step below highly placed, reliable means the source has been used before, and usually reliable is a hedge. Acquainted with, in a position to know, close to, familiar with, are only variations on informed, but may sound better in stories about trials and investigations."—Edwin Newman, *Strictly Speaking*

13. "The war is the Father of all things, also our Father; war has forged us, marked us, formed us and hardened us, to make us what we are now. And always, as long as life's whirling wheel will rotate us, this war will be the very axis around which it will turn."—Ernst Junger, *Storm of Steel* (1929)

14. "In South Africa, 'redundant' urbanized Africans were 'endorsed out' of white areas and returned, almost always against their wishes, to tribal 'homelands' they never really knew."—C. Desmond, *The Discarded People*

15. "Most people are quick to accept praise, but slow to accept blame. . . . A good example of these twin characteristics is the way many students speak of their grades: they'll say '*I got a B*,' but '*He gave me a D*.' "—Vincent Ruggiero, *Beyond Feelings*

*****16.** "In the German language men never die in battle. They *fall*. The term is exact for the expression of self-sacrifice when it is motivated by the feeling of comradeship. I may fall, but I do not die, for that which is real in me goes forward and lives on in the comrades for whom I gave up my physical life."—J. Glenn Gray, *The Warriors: Reflections on Men in Battle*

■ B. On the left is a list of terms generally thought to have negative or undesirable connotations. Supply the commonly accepted euphemism for each term from the list on the right.

1. a liar	economy class
2. neutron bomb	Defense Department
3. socialized medicine	sanitation workers
*4. poor	antipersonnel devices
5. junk food	downturn
6. federal handouts to business	underachiever
7. military personnel	advisers
*8. television reruns	recession
9. graveyard	overdependence on drugs
10. second class	resection
11. War Department	sexual reassignment
*12. sex-change operation	sunshine law
13. target cities with nuclear bombs	Social Security
14. cutout	credibility gap
15. fat	inoperative statement
*16. drug addiction	mature
17. garbage collectors	Medicare
18. drunk	cemetery
19. guaranteed income	low-income
*20. uneducated	encore telecasts
21. lazy	convenience foods
22. chronic lying	*nom de plume*
23. spying	family assistance
*24. alias	careless with the truth

25. false statement	radiation enhancement weapon
26. old-age insurance	subsidized business enterprises
27. depression	inebriated
*28. recession	surveillance
29. antisecrecy legislation	culturally deprived
30. weapons to kill infantrymen	countervalue strategy

■ C. Is there any difference in the *information* conveyed by each of the following paired sentences? Is there any difference in the *impressions* conveyed by each of the paired sentences? Explain the differences, if any.

1. Scholl failed to show up.
   Scholl did not show up.

2. Now you pay only $2.39 for Bright detergent in the extra-large size!
   Now you pay only $2.39 for Bright detergent in a size slightly larger than the large size!

3. Sheila ingratiated herself with her boss.
   Sheila won her boss's approval.

*4. Pam's date sat mute the whole evening.
   Pam's date sat silently the whole evening.

5. The student's paper was 750 words long.
   The student's paper was a mere 750 words long.

6. Does she have any hobbies?
   Does she have any avocational pursuits outside of the occupational sphere?

7. Her speech continued for an hour.
   Her speech ran on for an hour.

*8. She says that she was at the meeting.
   She admits that she was at the meeting.

9. He is a disadvantaged youth from a high-density neighborhood.
   He is a poor youth from the ghetto.

10. The car spun out of control and struck a padded drum at the exit ramp of the beltway.
    The car spun out of control and struck an impact-attenuation device at the exit ramp of the beltway.

■ D. Construct two examples of sentences containing assuring terms, two containing hedging terms, and two containing discounting terms.

■ E. Bring to class examples of slanting and euphemism that you find in newspapers, magazines, or textbooks. Cite at least two examples of doublespeak or other aspects of con-artistry from newspaper, magazine, or television advertising. ■

CHAPTER FOUR

Clarifying meaning

Since arguments are expressed in language, argument analysis must involve the clarification of the meaning of words. This chapter discusses techniques for clarifying meaning and for overcoming the hazards of ambiguity and vagueness. The first two sections extend the treatment of the pitfalls of language begun in Chapter 3 by examining the sources of ambiguity and vagueness and exposing their role in fallacious thinking. Section 4-3 shows how knowledge of the different levels of meaning will help defuse some disagreements and assist in finding the real issue in others. The next two sections survey different techniques for clarifying and controlling the meaning of words: definitions are discussed and appraised in Section 4-4; special techniques for making terms precise are examined in Section 4-5. Finally, Section 4-6, on persuasive and revelatory definitions, again reminds us that fresh insights are gained but misunderstanding risked when the cognitive and emotive dimensions of meaning are combined.

□ 4-1. THE HAZARDS OF AMBIGUITY

When in a certain context a word can be understood in more than one way, that word or the phrase or sentence in which it appears is said to be *ambiguous*. Having two or more distinct meanings does not in itself make a word ambiguous; in fact, most words have more than one meaning. The words *fine, fire, fix,* and *frame,* for example, all have different meanings in different contexts (consider "I feel fine"; "Pay the library fine for that overdue book"), although they are not often ambiguous. The cause of ambiguity is therefore not so much that the meaning is variable as that the context allows for more than one interpretation.

A word or phrase is ambiguous if it has more than one meaning and the context in which it is being used does not make the intended meaning explicit.

A sentence can be ambiguous for two reasons. *Syntactical,* or *grammat-*

ical, ambiguity occurs when the construction of a sentence suggests more than one way of construing its meaning. *Semantical ambiguity* occurs when a grammatically correct sentence lends itself to more than one interpretation.

□ Amphiboly

A common type of *syntactical ambiguity* is called *amphiboly*.

An amphiboly is a sentence that can be interpreted in more than one way because the words are arranged in a careless or awkward manner.

In the following sentence, for example, the position of the verb *compose* causes the ambiguity:

The wife of the famous tunesmith was too unhappy to compose herself.

Does the speaker mean the woman was unable to compose music as her husband did or that she was unable to regain her composure?
   In this classified advertisement, a modifying phrase is misplaced:

Wanted: a chair for a child with a cane seat.

Which is wanted—a cane-seated child or a cane-seated chair?
   And awkward arrangement of clauses turns the following invitation into an insult:

Bring your spouse or come stag and enjoy a pleasant evening.

The recipient could understandably ask, "What makes you think my spouse is a killjoy?" If "enjoy a pleasant evening" were placed at the beginning of the sentence or if a comma were inserted after "stag," such a question would not arise.
   Sometimes the misuse of connectives such as *and* and *or* creates a problem, as in this advertisement:

The dress pictured comes in blue, green, red, and yellow.

Here the word *and* suggests that the advertised dress is multicolored. Because it is more likely that the dress is available in each of the four solid colors indicated, *or* should have been used to connect the series.

□ Accent

Shortly after taking office, President Gerald Ford asserted, "The code of ethics that will be followed by those in my administration will be the example I set." Presumably, he meant that he would lead the members of his administration by setting an example of ethical behavior for them to follow. However, the statement was also open to the interpretation that the example Ford was to set for the country would be a code of ethics developed by personnel in his administration. This statement is an illustration of *semantical ambiguity*.

As in this instance, semantical ambiguity often occurs when the proper placement of accent, or emphasis, is unclear. The same sentence can express different meanings, depending on where the stress should fall or what tone of voice is intended. Two other examples of such ambiguity were given in Section 1-1: "Nothing is too good for her" and "When you turn in your paper, I shall lose no time in reading it." Ambiguities of this kind occur most frequently in writing because there are no vocal or gestural clues to the attitude of the writer.

The above examples of amphiboly and accent are not arguments, so they cannot be considered fallacies. As defined in Section 1-2, *a fallacy, or fallacious argument, is any argument rendered defective by an error in reasoning.* It is easy to see, though, how ambiguous sentences contribute to the sort of mis-understanding that leads to fallacious reasoning. For example, because of the syntactical or semantical ambiguity of an expression, one might accept as the premise of an argument a statement other than the one the speaker or writer intended. One might then reach a wrong conclusion based on this mistaken premise.

To see how such a problem could arise, consider the famous words of the Declaration of Independence: "all men are created equal." Most historians have interpreted Thomas Jefferson to mean that "all men are created *equal*"— that is, born with the same inalienable rights and therefore deserving of equal treatment before the law. However, someone who interpreted Jefferson as meaning that "all men are *created* equal" might agree with Nathaniel Ames, who observed that

All men are created equal,
But differ greatly in the sequel.[1]

Putting the stress on *created* rather than on *equal* conveys the idea that each person is created in the same *way*. This might lead one to conclude that social inequality was not inconsistent with Jefferson's intent in writing the Declaration of Independence.

□ *Equivocation*

Ambiguous words or phrases can also occur in sentences that are intended to express complete arguments. Sometimes these arguments are fallacious because of ambiguity in the way the same word is used in different premises or in the conclusion of the argument.

---

[1] Quoted by David H. Fischer in *Historian's Fallacies* (New York: Harper Torchbooks, 1970), p. 273.

Equivocation is the use of a key word or phrase in more than one sense in the course of an argument.

The person advancing such an argument (or taken in by it) *equivocates* by drawing an inference based on the shift of meaning of the word or phrase. Here is an example:

A person ought to do what is right.
I have a right to overeat.
Therefore, I ought to overeat.

This argument depends on ambiguous use of the word *right*. There is an important difference between doing *what is right* (as, for instance, in doing what a moral rule requires) and *a right* (that is, a privilege or liberty, such as the right to vote). The bizarre conclusion of the argument is possible only if the author is allowed to trade on the ambiguity of this key word.

Because it is a rich source of verbal nonsense, examples of equivocation are often found in humorous literature. For example:

"Who did you pass on the road," the King went on, holding out his hand to the Messenger for some hay.

"Nobody," said the Messenger.

"Quite right," said the King, "this lady saw him too. So of course Nobody walks slower than you."

"I do my best," the Messenger said in a sullen tone. "I'm sure nobody walks much faster than I do!"

"He can't do that," said the King, "or else he'd have been here first."[2]

Fallacies of equivocation sometimes appear to be plausible arguments because their premises are unobjectionable when considered independently of one another. Here is a well-known example:

Only man is rational.
No woman is a man.
Therefore, no woman is rational.

This argument is fallacious because in the first premise the term *man* is used to denote the species *homo sapiens*, whereas in the second premise it is used to denote the male sex. However, each of the premises *taken singly* can be said to be true. According to most definitions of *rationality*, *homo sapiens* is the only rational species, and *woman*, by definition, is a human being of the female sex.

Equivocation is a constant danger for the unwary because so many words

---

[2] Lewis Carroll, *Through the Looking Glass*, Chapter 7.

have more than one meaning. And unlike the sharp contrast of meaning apparent in the above examples, the shift from one meaning to another in a long passage can occur gradually as the author provides background support or embellishments of the premises. The only safeguard against such equivocation is to insist that any recurring term be given the *same* meaning each time it is used. If, when reading, you suspect that the meaning of a key term has shifted, reread the passage, keeping the meaning of the suspect term uniform. If the discourse has been spoken, point out the alternative meanings, and ask the speaker for a clarification of the term.

Such careful analysis will often reveal either an absurd premise or an absurd conclusion. Thus, if we read through the argument above using the term *homo sapiens* each time *man* occurs, we see that the second premise ("No woman is a man") is false. When we read through the argument replacing *man* with *human being of the male sex* each time it occurs, we see that the first premise ("Only man is rational") is false.

Words with variant, or indeterminate, meanings are often responsible for equivocation. This is particularly true of terms used to make comparisons, especially where rough estimates of quantity or quality are given. *Large, small, long, short*, and *more*, for example, are notoriously vague. If the owner of a pet hamster should argue

> All hamsters are animals.
> Hector is a white hamster.
> Therefore, Hector is a white animal.

no one would object. However, imagine the argument

> All hamsters are animals.
> Hector is a large hamster.
> Hector is a large animal.

This argument will not work because the adjective *large*—unlike *white* in the previous argument—implicitly involves a comparison. Whether an object is large or not depends on the *class* in question. A large hamster is large compared with other hamsters, but not in comparison with dogs, horses, elephants, or whales. (If Hector were in fact a monster hamster, according to a science-fiction scenario, then the conclusion would be true, but not because the premises guarantee its truth.)

The following anonymous popular jingle also exploits the vagueness of comparative terms.

> The more you study, the more you know.
> The more you know, the more you forget,
> The more you forget, the less you know,
> So why study?

Here the use of *more* indicates comparison, but the quantity being compared does not remain the same. The second line may be true: Einstein may have forgotten more about physics than you or I will ever know about that subject. But the number of facts Einstein may have forgotten would be in proportion to his vast knowledge of facts after extensive research—*not* in proportion to what he knew before starting to study. Thus, the second line is intelligible if it means the increase of forgotten facts relative to the increase of total learned facts. By the third line, however, the base of comparison has been shifted from the total number of learned facts to the total number of facts known *before you began to forget*.

I love you
Therefore I am a lover;
All the world loves a lover
You are all the world to me—
Consequently
You love me.

J. G. VIVIAN

■ EXERCISE 4-1

■ A. The following are all amphibolies. Analyze each one to determine (a) what ambiguity is involved; (b) how the ambiguity has arisen; and (c) how the passage could be rewritten to convey what you believe to be the intended meaning.

1. "A fourteen-year-old youth helped pull a drowning woman to shore, and to his dismay, discovered it was his mother."—*Wilmington* [N.C.] *Morning Star*

2. "The Town of Durham owes a debt of gratitude to Malcolm J. Chase, who recently announced that he would not run for reelection to the Board of Selectmen, on which he served from 1952 to 1955 and from 1969 to 1978."—The 1977 Annual Report of Durham, New Hampshire

3. "The OSU research failed to find any significant differences between people who survive a heart attack and those who die from one."—*Columbus* [Ohio] *Dispatch*

*4. "Each year at this time, fruit growers have to make special efforts to control mice in orchards, to prevent them from serious injury."—*Hudson* [N.Y.] *Register-Star*

5. "Enraged, Achilles Hector shall subdue."—*The Iliad*

6. "The author takes a stand against a tree while waiting for a black bear with a black powder rifle."—*The American Hunter*

7. $1.00 Off
      On Any Ice
   Cream Cake In
      Stock
   Since 1934
Carvel—Advertisement in the *Harrison* [N.Y.] *Independent*

*8. "The Emperor Penguin is about 4 ft. tall and during the 2 months of incubating its young does not eat."—Ripley's *Believe It or Not*

9. "Traditionally, Potomac has represented a haven for the wealthy, who live in custom-built homes nestled in the countryside behind white clapboard fences that are worth in some cases between $300,000 to $500,000."—*The Washington Post*

10. "All Utah Condemned to Face Firing Squad"—Story headline, *The Washington Post*, March 9, 1980

11. "John Veitch did not recoil. He has the open-air suntan, the breeziness of an outdoorsman. If eyes may be described as 'candid,' his are. They are dark and set between a nose that suggests a slight ridge."—*The Daily Racing Form*

*12. "Then she realized that as usual she was being unfair to him, that neither he nor any of the children was the least bit concerned over his white sweater and well-tailored gray flannel pants, that they simply liked him because he didn't press them but waited for them to come to him and then gave them his full attention when they did."—Judith Rossner, *Looking for Mr. Goodbar*

13. "One nineteen-year-old woman escaped from a Volkswagen of a man who abducted and handcuffed her after identifying himself to her as a policeman."—*The New York Times*

14. "The Greenville Woman's Club will hold its annual Christmas Tea on December 15 at 1:30 P.M. at the home of Mrs. Robert Taft.

"Mrs. Theodore Thomas of Peterborough will once again be the special guest, and she will talk on "Let's make a Merry Christmas" by making beautiful season arrangements. She was not enjoyed by the members last year."—*The Peterborough* (N.H.) *Monadnock Ledger*

■ B. The following arguments are examples of the fallacy of equivocation. Read each argument carefully and identify both the word or phrase that has shifted meaning and the alternative meanings involved.

1. The rich are superior to you and me, since we are not rich. Furthermore, since superior persons should rule the country, it is obvious that our government should be an oligarchy of the rich.

2. We are told that it is wrong to discriminate against women in employment. Yet we must discriminate. After all, we discriminate when we select men over women for construction work and work as dockworkers. Most women lack the necessary strength for these jobs. Hence, it makes no sense to say that discrimination against women is wrong.

3. A person who lies or tells the truth by compulsion or by necessity cannot truly be regarded as a free agent. But everyone must either lie or tell the truth. Therefore, insofar as telling the truth or lying is concerned, no one is really a free agent.

*4. No legal system is sound if it ignores the facts of life. Sexual relations are facts of life we all must come to discover and regulate. Thus, our legal system is not sound unless it provides laws to regulate the sexual relations between people.

5. Individual rights should be protected by law. It is right for individuals to be charitable. Charitable behavior should therefore be protected by law.

6. All fraternity members are unintellectual partygoers. John is a member of Phi Beta Kappa. The honor society called Phi Beta Kappa is a fraternity. Therefore, John is an unintellectual partygoer.

7. The existence of a Creator is implied by scientific terminology, because the

phrase "law of nature" is constantly used in science, and whenever there is a law, there must be a lawgiver.

*8. Freedom of speech is the very heart and soul of democracy. Six-year-old Louis should therefore have perfect freedom to say what he pleases. This follows from your own admission that every member of a democracy should have freedom of speech.

9. Mr. Peabody was mad when he heard that his property taxes would increase. He was mad when the neighbor's son broke his window, and mad again when he was overcharged at the supermarket. In fact, Mr. Peabody has been mad most of the time lately, and mad people should be institutionalized for their own good. Therefore, Mr. Peabody should be put in an institution for his own good.

10. It's hard to accept, but pain is really desirable. After all, the only proof that something is desirable is that people actually desire it. And it must be admitted that there are some people called masochists who desire pain.

11. Nothing is better than good health and happiness. But a life of sorrow and toil is better than nothing. Therefore, a life of sorrow and toil is better than good health and happiness.

*12. Everyone will admit that it is honorable to try to become an expert in one field. The individual sought by the FBI was trying to become an expert thief and forger. Hence, what the individual was trying to do was honorable.

13. All laws should be respected and obeyed. The formula $E = mc^2$ is a law. Therefore, the formula $E = mc^2$ should be respected and obeyed.

14. God is love, and love is an emotion. Therefore, God is an emotion. ■

☐ 4-2. EXPLOITING VAGUENESS

Vagueness is a consequence of the necessary flexibility of language. Not only do many words have different meanings depending on the context in which they are used, but some words and phrases are imprecise. Examples include *a moment, not long,* and *a few minutes* (in connection with units of time); *a bunch, a lot,* and *a great deal* (in connection with quantity); and *pretty hard, fairly good,* and *not bad* (in connection with quality).

A word or phrase is vague if its meaning is indeterminate in the context in which it is used.

Although a certain amount of imprecision is both acceptable and un-avoidable, vague words are sometimes deliberately chosen to make a conclusion seem more reasonable than it really is. One such use of vagueness is called the *slippery-slope fallacy*, or the *fallacy of the continuum*.

If my wife calls me at the office to say we are having company for dinner and asks me to pick up a pound of thinly sliced imported salami, nothing much happens if I eat one slice on the way home. But if, after it is too late to get any more, I eat almost half a pound on the way home (as I have), I am going to catch hell.

So somewhere between eating two slices and eating half a pound there is a critical point. It cannot be precisely defined. If I say it is six slices, and you then ask me if I couldn't eat seven slices and still not catch hell, I'd have to agree. Then you ask me about eight, and then nine. Finally I say, "Stop. You are playing the salami game. I granted you six slices from the original pound, but I'm going to draw the line there."
JOHN D. ARNOLD, *MAKE UP YOUR MIND!*

Whenever a distinction is made between things that can be placed on a continuum (for example, the cutoff point between a grade of A and a grade of B), someone can object that the distinction is unwarranted because the difference is "just a matter of degree." The person who commits this fallacy asserts (or grants) that one small difference is unimportant and that we will therefore find ourselves "slipping down the slope" to the next little difference, and so on, until we reach an outcome (stated in the conclusion) that everyone recognizes as horrible. The fallacy involves the unwarranted assumption that making definite distinctions between things on a continuum is impossible.

The many common names for this fallacy present graphic images: "the camel's back" (from the expression "the straw that broke the camel's back"), the "wedge argument" (once you get the thin edge of a wedge in the door, nothing will stop it until the door is completely open), the "bald man argu-ment," and "the argument of the beard." The last two names come from the ancient practice of debating such questions as "how many hairs must a man have to have a beard?"

The argument of the beard and the bald man argument were debators' tricks used to convince the unwary that there really was no difference between a man's having a beard and being clean-shaven, or between a man's having a full head of hair and being bald. To see that they have the same form as the slippery slope argument, consider the following. Suppose someone tells you that you do not really know the difference between being bald and having a full head of hair. You protest that the difference is obvious. The questioner then leads you to agree that the difference depends on the number of hairs on a man's head: a perfectly bald man has no hairs on his head at all. You are then asked how many hairs a man with a full head of hair has. You probably make a rough guess, after which the arguer subtracts hairs one by one. Eventually, the number of remaining hairs is in a gray area between being bald and not-bald, and a precise dividing line cannot be established. At this point, the arguer will claim triumphantly that because you can't tell when the dividing line is crossed, you do not know the difference after all.

Once an audience becomes susceptible to this kind of argument regarding trivial matters, the same pattern of argumentation can be used for significant purposes—for example, to deny the difference between sanity and insanity, health and sickness, education and propaganda, amateur athletics and professional athletics, police interrogation and police brutality, coercion and terrorism, or smoking marijuana and using heroin. The following quotation is a full-blown example of the fallacy.

> **The Human Life Amendment (and that is no euphemism) was introduced in response to the Supreme Court's unbelievable pronouncement that it is the law of the United States that unborn babies may be freely killed because they are incapable of "meaningful life."**
>
> **We do not know at this time whether the Court plans to pursue this reasoning to include paralyzed people, very old people, retarded people, or deformed people. But all such citizens might be described as being incapable of "meaningful life."**
>
> FROM EDWIN A ROBERTS, "AN AMENDMENT ABOUT LIFE," *THE NATIONAL OBSERVER*

Attempts to justify the "Americanization" of the Vietnam War frequently relied on the slippery-slope fallacy. A version of it was presented by the comedian Bob Hope: "Everybody I talked to there [Vietnam] wants to know why they can't go in and finish it, and don't let anybody kid you about why we're there. If we weren't, those Commies would have the whole thing, and it wouldn't be long until we'd be looking off the coast of Santa Monica [California]."[3] Hope's argument is based on the so-called domino theory about Communist intentions and strategies—that if one country is taken over by Communists, others, like falling dominoes, will follow. But just because it is not immediately apparent where the sliding can be stopped, once the first step down the slope has been taken or the first country has fallen, does not mean that one event will inevitably lead to the next.

The slippery-slope fallacy involves linguistic confusion—the use, deliberate or not, of vague words as key terms in an argument. *Clean-shaven, wealthy, poor, middle-aged, middle-class,* and *good-looking,* for example, are

[3] *The New York Times Magazine,* October 4, 1970.

vague because we are often uncertain which things can be described by these terms. Other words—such as *democracy, socialism, freedom,* and *rights*—are vague because they have been used in reference to many different things. One cannot know exactly where to draw the line between a more-or-less democratic government and a more-or-less authoritarian government, between being rich and being poor, or between a clean-shaven man and a man with a beard. Does a man with five o'clock shadow have a beard? Three days' stubble? A week's growth?

Yet, even though borderline cases can be troublesome, it is usually possible to tell the difference between extreme cases. The fact that some male chins cannot be decisively labeled bearded or clean-shaven does not prevent us from telling the difference generally between one and the other. And just because certain things are ranked on a continuum does not mean that differences between them are unimportant. It is rational to make distinctions, *provided* that these distinctions are supported by *reasons*. Attention should be focused on the strength or weakness of the reasons given for making a distinction where one is recommended, and *not* on the gray area between similar cases.

■ **EXERCISE 4-2**

The following passages illustrate the slippery-slope fallacy. For each example identify the vague or ambiguous words that result in fallacious reasoning.

1. JOE: If we legalize marijuana, we could hardly avoid legalizing cocaine and then heroin, which only differ in degree with respect to addictiveness and the dangers of excessive use.
BILL: But how can people oppose the legalization of marijuana? After all, doctors prescribe Valium to help the anxiety-ridden and other drugs to give depressed patients a lift, while society condones the consumption of alcohol during "happy hours." The use of these drugs differs only in degree from the use of marijuana.

2. We should legalize gambling because we cannot stop it. It is an integral part of living; investors gamble everyday on the stock market, and anyone gambles who crosses a busy street, orders dinner in an expensive restaurant, or gets married.

3. If we are going to give free medical care to all people, as the senator proposes, why not provide them with free transportation, food, housing, and clothing, all at the expense of the taxpayer? Socialization is just a question of degree, and we cannot move much farther in that direction unless we want to have a completely Socialist state.

*4. FIRST CUSTOMER: The sign says to take a free sample. That doesn't entitle people to take as many as they want.
SECOND CUSTOMER: It can't hurt if I take an extra sample. What's the difference between one and two?
FIRST CUSTOMER: Or three and four? Or five and six?

5. There are important reasons why there should not be an Equal Rights Amendment to the United States Constitution. Sexual equality would make sexual differences an invalid ground for different legal classifications. Thus, if the ERA becomes the law of the land, the consequences would be bisexual restrooms, female combat troops, and

even the invalidating of statutes creating sex crimes or of those specifying the amount of weight a woman could be required to lift on a job.

6.

© 1979, *United Features Syndicate, Inc. Reprinted by permission.*

7. "In rationalizing South African police suppression of student demonstrations in 1972, Prime Minister [Balthazar] Vorster quoted 'an unnamed American authority' as saying that peaceful demonstrations led to nuisance demonstrations, then to scattered violence, explosive terror, personal terror, and finally general terror."—*The Guardian*, June 15, 1972

*8. A refugee is a refugee—they all need our help. Thus, if we are going to provide sanctuary for impoverished Cuban refugees, then we ought to go ahead and provide it for the thousands of poor Haitians, and the boat people of Indochina. In fact, we might just as well throw the doors open to all the oppressed and downtrodden people of the earth. If we start to accept any of them, we'll have to make room for the hundreds of thousands to follow.

9. "As a marine biologist, I must take exception to the concept of treating animals as 'equals.' If this reasoning is followed to a logical end, we must not only treat all birds and animals as equals, but also all of the lower animals (snakes and lizards, fishes, insects, and spiders, and then even the single-celled protozoans, many of which are parasites).

"Any taxonomist knows that all living organisms form a continuum. If it is wrong to poison squirrels or bats, then it would also be wrong to poison snails and ants. Likewise, if we find it wrong to kill snails and ants, then we must stop the wholesale murder of minute organisms when we chlorinate our drinking water. Are these small animals not entitled to equality simply because a microscope must be used to see them?"—Letter to the editor, *The National Observer*, June 9, 1973

10. "A person apparently hopelessly ill may be allowed to take his own life. Then he may be permitted to deputize others to do it for him should he be no longer able to act. The judgment of others then becomes the ruling factor. Already at this point euthanasia is not personal and voluntary, for others are acting 'in behalf of' the patient as they see fit. This may well incline them to act on behalf of other patients who have not authorized them to exercise their judgment. It is only a short step, then, from voluntary euthanasia (self-inflicted or authorized), to direct euthanasia administered to a patient who has given no authorization, to involuntary euthanasia conducted as part of a social policy."—J. Gay-Williams, "The Wrongfulness of Euthanasia" in R. Munson, ed., *Intervention and Reflection*

11. "Until recently the laws of all Western societies sanctioned and reinforced tabus against an unlimited sexual freedom that, if actively sought, could be destructive of organized society.

"Thus, a first experiment of this kind just might be the last experiment ever. Goaded on by the predatory forces of commercial opportunism, expectations of carnal gratification—aroused by increasingly salacious spectacles, and increasing facilities for new sexual perversions—would soar beyond the physical limits of attainment. In the unrelenting search for the uttermost in orgiastic experience, cruel passions might be unleashed, impelling humanity into regions beyond barbarism. One has only to recall the fantastic sadistic barbarities of the Nazi era . . . to accept this conjecture as neither far fetched nor fanciful, and to recognize that civilization is indeed but skin-deep. . . ."—Edward J. Mishan, "Making the World Safe for Pornography," *Encounter*, March 1972

*12. In an argument about the Falklands War of 1982, Noel Annan discusses an argument (not his own) presented to justify the British invasion:

"The argument runs as follows. If you do not show that you oppose injustice now, and awaken your fellow citizens to share that view, you may not be able to awaken them if danger ever threatens their own shores for their independence; and you will not have done what could be done to inhibit the invasions across borders that other dictators will be contemplating in the years ahead. Give in to every threat so long as it is not crucial . . . and you may find that the will of the nation is not to be counted on when the crucial moment comes. . . ."—Noel Annan, "Mrs. Thatcher's Case," *The New York Review of Books*, July 15, 1982 ■

□ 4-3. TYPES OF DISPUTE AND DISAGREEMENT

□ *Factual disputes and disagreements in attitude*

People often find themselves in disagreement over facts: one party believes that something is true, while another party believes it is false. For instance, Uncle Silas believes laetrile cures cancer; Doctor Walpole believes that laetrile does not cure cancer.

A factual dispute is a disagreement over the truth or falsity of one or more statements.

Disputes of this kind can be settled by recourse to the evidence: observation, reports by witnesses, statistics, documents, historical records, and the like. Not all the evidence needed to resolve a particular factual dispute may be available, but *in principle* such disputes can be resolved by appealing to the facts.

However, some kinds of disputes cannot be settled by appeal to the facts. Sometimes people agree that an object has certain properties or that an event has actually occurred and yet find themselves strongly diverging in their attitudes toward it. In such a case, there is agreement at one level of meaning—the factual, or cognitive—but disagreement on a different level—the emotive. Here we have what the philosopher Charles L. Stevenson has called a disagreement in attitude.[4]

---

[4] Charles L. Stevenson, *Ethics and Language* (New Haven: Yale University Press, 1944).

A disagreement in attitude is a difference in viewpoint on how one should feel about a factual situation.

Each party in such a dispute is likely to describe the situation in a way that suggests approval or disapproval. For example, suppose that at a dinner party young Gretchen Quick tries to entertain the company by talking volubly. Aunt Julie later describes Gretchen as a fluent conversationalist, while Mrs. Bash says Gretchen is a terrible chatterbox. Both Aunt Julie and Mrs. Bash agree that Gretchen talked a great deal. But the words they choose demonstrate that language functions emotively and evaluatively as well as informatively.

It is also possible for parties (1) to agree in both belief and attitude, (2) to agree in attitude despite disagreeing in belief, and (3) to disagree in both belief and attitude. To give an example of the third possibility, consider young Slim Yeager, who is also a witness to Gretchen's performance at the dinner table. Slim agrees with Aunt Julie that Gretchen is an impressive conversationalist. But Slim, who has not been to many dinner parties, is unaware that older adults like to dominate the conversation at such affairs, and he does not believe that Gretchen talked a great deal. In fact, young Slim says he remembers that both Mrs. Bash and Aunt Julie were more voluble than Gretchen.

Often, it is difficult to determine whether divergent descriptions reveal differences in attitude or in belief. Suppose, for example, we both read Agatha Christie mystery novels. I say that Agatha Christie has a marvelous imagination. You say that she has no respect for the facts. Is this a factual dispute or a disagreement in attitude? The answer is probably attitude. But, perhaps Agatha Christie is somewhat inconsistent regarding details, and perhaps the events she describes are sometimes improbable—and perhaps you noticed this evidence and I did not. Instances of this kind remind us of the close connection between language and thought and between language and emotion.

It is impossible to expect anything approaching mathematical precision in our attempts to tell whether disagreement reflects a factual dispute, a disagreement in attitude, or some combination of both. There will be times, however, when you will be called upon to help resolve a disagreement. You will then have to determine the nature of the disagreement, for the method appropriate to the resolution of one kind of disagreement is generally irrelevant to the other. Disagreements in attitude are more likely to be resolved by changing the way people *feel* and *react* toward events, whereas disagreements in belief can be settled most aptly by gathering more information and bringing it to the attention of others.

□ *Verbal disputes*

A second kind of disagreement that cannot be settled by appeal to the facts has been called the *verbal dispute*.

A verbal dispute is a disagreement caused by a difference of opinion over the meaning of certain words or concepts.

The adversaries in such a dispute believe there is a controversy over the truth or falsity of a single statement. But because they are attaching different meanings to the same sentence, they are actually asserting the truth or falsity of different statements.[5] In such cases, the disputants argue at cross-purposes.

A report by the philosopher William James of a verbal dispute is often retold. While on a camping trip with friends, James left the group for a solitary ramble. When he returned to the campsite, he found the others engaged in a debate concerning a squirrel clinging to the trunk of a tree. As someone walked around the tree, the squirrel edged sideways around the trunk, always keeping the trunk between itself and the moving person. No one doubted that the person went around the tree. But James's friends could not seem to agree on whether or not the person went around the squirrel. Here is how James dealt with the dispute:

> "Which party is right," I said, depends on what you *practically* mean by 'going around' the squirrel. If you mean passing from the north of him to the east, then to the south, then to the west, and then to the north again, obviously the man does go around him, for he occupies these successive positions. But if on the contrary you mean being first in front of him, then on the right of him, then behind him, then on his left, and finally in front again, it is quite obvious that the man fails to go round him, for by the compensating movements the squirrel makes, he keeps his belly turned towards the man all the time, and his back turned away. Make the distinction, and there is no occasion for any further dispute.[6]

In the context described by James, the phrase *going around* is ambiguous, which explains why some of the campers believed the statement "The camper went around the squirrel" was true while other campers believed it was false. But the campers who believed it was true that the man went around the squirrel accepted *going around* in the sense of "passing from the north of him to the east, then to the south, then to the west, and then to the north again." The campers who believed it was false that the man went around the squirrel were rejecting this as a correct definition of *going around*. So, while some campers were maintaining, based on the facts of the case, that one proposition was true (the man went around the squirrel), the other group was maintaining that *another* proposition was false.

Did James's distinction settle the matter? He reports: "Although one or two of the hotter disputants called my speech a shuffling evasion, saying they wanted no quibbling or scholastic hair-splitting, but meant just plain honest English "round," the majority seemed to think that the distinction had assuaged the dispute."[7]

---

[5] This point is well made by Morris S. Engel, *With Good Reason*, 2d ed. (New York: St. Martin's Press, 1976), p. 40.
[6] William James, *Essays in Pragmatism* (New York: Hafner, 1948), p. 141.
[7] James, *Essays in Pragmatism*, p. 141.

The sort of verbal dispute illustrated by this story can be interminable unless the trouble is located in some undefined and ambiguously used word or phrase. Imagine the potential for a verbal dispute arising from a discussion of the following questions:

Is there a right to health care?
Is a liberal-arts education worthwhile?
Has humanity progressed in the last 100 years?
Is religion meaningless in an age of science?

Not all disputes involving the meaning of terms or concepts can be settled by showing that a particular disagreement is "merely verbal." Verbal disputes can be symptoms of other disagreements. Sometimes those engaged in the dispute will not realize that they are arguing over different statements because there is one real difference between them—a difference of attitude. Or two persons may disagree over a general subject, such as the safety of nuclear energy plants, without realizing that their dispute over a specific aspect of that subject—for example, whether or not emissions of radioactive air from the Three Mile Island reactor were "hazardous"—is a verbal dispute. In that case, settling the verbal dispute would leave the factual dispute unresolved.

■ **EXERCISE 4-3**

■ A. Indicate whether each of the following conversations is a factual dispute or a disagreement in attitude. Do any involve both types of disagreement? Be prepared to defend your answers.
   1. SILAS: We do not know yet whether laetrile cures cancer, since the experiments on this issue lead to confusing results.
LOUISE: Laetrile is no cure for cancer, as many experiments conclusively show.
   2. TOM: The bribe-taking of congressmen as exposed through the FBI's ABSCAM investigation is a shocking development and is sure to destroy the confidence of the public in Congress.
TERRY: There is nothing new in the kinds of financial deals made by members of Congress. We have survived public scandals in the past, and we shall continue to do so.
   3. ALICE: This is an unbearably bitter winter.
BARRY: The average temperature is about normal for winters in this part of the country.
   *4. LAWYER A: The autopsy report places the time of Lee Loud's death at approximately midnight. And we know the defendant has been positively identified by a witness, Pat Smith, as the person who got into Lee Loud's car between 11:30 and 11:40 P.M. at the intersection of Georgia Avenue and Seaton Lane.
LAWYER B: Pat Smith's testimony is unreliable. As you know, Pat Smith has admitted to drinking on the night in question, and he is unable to tell us why he was driving in the vicinity of Georgia and Seaton at that time of night.
   5. WARREN: Belief in the existence of God is as groundless as it is useless. Nothing good at all comes from believing in God. The world will never be happy until atheism is universal.

JEROME: That can't be true. Atheists don't take any interest in the welfare of their fellow humans. Do you know of any hospitals, orphanages, or relief societies dedicated to the principles of atheism?

■ B. Indicate for each of the following conversations whether the dispute should be regarded as factual or verbal. Be prepared to defend your answers.

1. SCOTT: Harry and Carrie are so materialistic—they talk of nothing but money, and they enjoy nothing more than showing off their new clothes and driving around in their expensive car.

KATHY: I don't much care for Harry and Carrie either, but you're mistaken about their being materialistic. I happen to know that they attend church regularly, and they believe in the resurrection of souls. They once defended Plato's view of the immortality of the soul in a philosophy class I was in.

2. SAM: I don't think the Sharpes are decent parents. They're so concerned with "doing their own thing" that they don't really listen to their kids or try to understand their problems.

MAURY: No, the Sharpes are doing just fine as parents. They both work, and yet they find plenty of time to do things with their children. They all go shopping together, and the parents always prepare nutritious, homemade meals.

3. CHRISTINE: Whatever the Supreme Court says, I think preferential admissions policies for minority students are unjust. If our objective is a genuinely nondiscriminatory society, then we cannot favor anyone, even Chicanos or blacks, on the basis of race or ethnic heritage. To do so is inconsistent with the principle of equality.

GRETCHEN: I can't agree. The principle of equality sometimes requires that we give minority applicants special consideration. If we are really going to treat one another as equals, then we must take steps to bring those who are disadvantaged up to the same place as others. We do a disservice to the principle of equality if we try to apply the same inflexible rules to everyone alike.

*4. MR. PRIM: Mr. Chase lied when he wrote this check and said that he had enough money in his checking account to cover it. I think we should close our charge account with him.

MS. PROPER: Chase didn't lie. It's true that what he said was false at the time, but lying always involves the intent to deceive, and Chase intended to get right back to his bank and deposit enough cash to cover the check.

MR. PRIM: Ha! Even on your own definition, Mr. Chase lied. He intended to deceive us, didn't he? He wanted us to believe the check was good at the time it was written. What other proof do you need of his intentions?

MS. PROPER: He only said the check was good because the salesperson, who doesn't know him, was reluctant to take it. He was in a hurry, and he didn't have his driver's license with him. Look, he's been a customer for years; he knows that we usually don't deposit checks we've received for a week or so. He couldn't have anticipated that you'd change that. If you put his actions back into context, you'll agree that his intentions weren't bad.

■ C. The following conversations can be regarded as disputes. Indicate whether each is mainly a factual, verbal, or attitudinal disagreement. Try to decide what sorts of additional considerations would solve the dispute in each case.

1. PROF. WHITE: This student is quiet and reserved in class.
PROF. GRAY: The student you have in mind is shy and rather timid.

2. PROF. BLACK: The student is an independent and original thinker.
PROF. GRAY: The student you are referring to never agrees with anybody.

3. PROF. BLACK: This student is really an independent and original thinker, even if you don't care for so much freedom in your classroom.
PROF. GRAY: How can you say she's an independent thinker? Her papers consist of nothing but strings of quotations taken out of the standard authorities on the subject.

*4. PROF. GRAY: As far as I'm concerned, she just doesn't make a good impression in class.
PROF. WHITE: I'm surprised you're not more observant. She's always punctual, she looks fresh and ready for work, and her appearance is always neat and tidy.

5. PROF. BLACK: It's true that some of her research papers are not very original—at least the papers she's written for you—but it's clear from her participation in class that she is able to gain important insights on her own.
PROF. GRAY: That's not original thinking—that's just having a creative imagination.

6. PROF. WHITE: I believe, and I am sure Professor Black will agree, that we should nominate her for departmental honors. She is clearly qualified on the basis of her work.
PROF. GRAY: I'm afraid you're mistaken. She does have a 3.67 in her major, but the college regulations say that an honors student must have maintained, at minimum, a 3.25 average in each of the last four semesters. While this student's work in the department never fell below 3.4, her overall average for the last half of the junior year was 3.20.

7. PUFF: Professor Towertop is one of the best teachers at the university. The enrollments in his classes are greater than they are for any other course, they keep increasing, and attendance at his lectures is always high.
HUFF: Professor Towertop is not really a good teacher. He never challenges his students to think on their own; the work he assigns is usually irrelevant to the objectives of his courses; and he is far too lenient in grading. Students take his courses because they know they can get through them easily.

*8. PUFF: Professor Towertop is one of the best teachers at the university. Enrollments in his classes are greater than they are for any other course, they keep increasing, and attendance at his lectures is always high.
GRUFF: Good teacher, you say? Towertop does have huge enrollments, and he holds his students' interest. But isn't that what any professor worthy of the title is supposed to do? I don't think Towertop is better than any other professor at this dump, and I don't think we should hand out laurel leaves for mediocre performances.

9. PUFF: Professor Towertop is one of the best teachers at the university. The enrollments in his classes are greater than they are for any other course, they keep increasing, and attendance at his lectures is always high.
ENUFF: Well, if what you say were true, I'd admit Towertop's the best on our faculty. It's a weird notion of good teaching, anyway. The student government has made the teaching award a kind of popularity contest. It's their award; I guess they're entitled to define good teaching any way they like. But Towertop has problems. The enrollment in his Human Sexuality Course is down over the last two semesters, and some of my friends in his class say he's stopped taking the roll because the attendance has gotten so bad.

10. JACK: Professor Blowdermint shouldn't be nominated for the best teacher award. Students evaluate her classes negatively, and she is said to be very severe in class.

JILL: She is very serious in class, but I don't call a professor who expects work to be completed on time "severe." Besides, she is an excellent teacher. She is always producing new ideas and getting her students to think on their own. Her students have great respect for her, and more of her students go on to graduate school than do any other group of students in the department.

JACK: Professor Blowdermint may be an excellent researcher, as you suggest, but we need to nominate a good teacher. And, in any case, a good teacher has to be able to give something to all her students, not just those cut out for graduate-level work.

JILL: If you'll do a little history, you'll see that not one of the past recipients of the teaching award has been cited for popularity. Student evaluation forms have never played a significant role in the judging, but letters of recommendation from past students have always been important. I'm going to nominate Dr. Blowdermint, whatever you may think of it. ■

□ 4-4. DEFINING TERMS

Because many words have indeterminate meanings or can be used ambiguously, an arguer often encounters the challenge, "Define your terms." In ordinary language, the word *definition* refers to a number of different ways of clarifying meaning. Two such everyday kinds of definition are called *ostensive* and *denotative*. Both consist of giving examples.

□ *Ostensive and denotative definitions*

The word *ostensive*, which comes from the Latin word *ostens* for "display," applies to giving examples either nonverbally—by pointing or gesturing—or through a combination of verbal and nonverbal behavior: "This is a pomegranate [holding it up]"; "That's a peacock [pointing]"; "When I mentioned parallel lines, I meant lines like this [drawing them on the blackboard]"; "Now this is the polka [performing the dance]." This kind of definition is limited because it does not provide a way of paraphrasing sentences containing the word in question (*pomegranate, peacock, parallel, polka*) with equivalent sentences in which the word does not occur.

Denotative definition consists of giving examples verbally. Thus, if someone asks, "What is a deciduous tree?" one might respond by saying, "Well, maples, oaks, sycamores, poplars, and birches are all deciduous trees." Or a tourist from abroad might ask, "What do you mean by 'national holiday' in your country?" to which might be replied that New Year's Day, Washington's Birthday, Memorial Day, the Fourth of July, and Labor Day are all national holidays. Information of this kind specifies what is called the *extension* of the term being defined—the class of objects to which it can correctly be said to apply.

A limitation of this kind of definition is that the list of objects in the extension of a term cannot be substituted for that term without changing the meaning of the sentence in which it occurs. For example, squares, rectangles, pentagons, and octagons are all polygons—that is, closed plane figures having three or more angles and sides. But try to substitute a denotative definition of *polygon* for that word in the following sentence without changing its meaning: "Only one polygon has five sides." Similarly, no list of individual bachelors is equivalent in meaning to the word *bachelor*.

Ostensive and denotative definitions are both of limited usefulness for reasons other than those already noted. They cannot be employed for words that have no extension, such as *centaur*, *warlock*, and *unicorn*. Nor are they useful when examples (such as *snow* for Bedouins in the Sahara Desert) are not readily available. They are also inadequate for clarifying words whose meanings are not directly related to physical objects—the concepts *liberty*, *justice*, *equality*, *beauty*, *evolution*, *relativity*, *nationalism*, and *romanticism*, to mention only a few.

Another drawback of ostensive and denotative definitions is that objects falling within the extension of any one term frequently fall within the extension of other terms as well. Suppose, for example, I try to explain what a chair is to a man from Mars by pointing to chairs in my home. All my chairs happen to be made of wood. What will the Martian think when he sees people sitting in chairs made of metal and plastic? Will he refuse to call these *chairs*? If I tell him that they are chairs too because people are sitting on them, what will he think if he sees people sitting on tabletops, doorsteps, footstools, and log stumps?

It is also impossible through ostensive or denotative definition to explain what is called the *intension* of a term—the collection of attributes shared by all the objects referred to by that word. Suppose several foreign visitors, newly arrived at Dulles Airport, have heard fellow passengers talk excitedly about visiting the national monuments in Washington, D.C. I take the visitors to see the Lincoln Memorial next to the Reflecting Pool, the Jefferson Memorial at the Tidal Basin, the Washington Monument on the Mall, and the statue in Arlington Cemetery of marines raising the flag over Iwo Jima. After this sightseeing, they ask what all these things called national monuments have in common. "Do all your monuments commemorate heroic men and women?" they ask. "Are they all maintained by your National Park Service? Must they be designated a shrine by an act of Congress and financed through public taxation?" The kind of clarification requested by the visitors cannot be accomplished merely by citing instances of the appropriate use of the term *national monument*.

For the purposes of logic, the main drawback of both ostensive and denotative definitions is that neither tells how to substitute clear and more familiar words for words that are unfamiliar, ambiguous, or confusing. To require this is to assign to the word *definition* a precise meaning that it is not typically understood to have in more ordinary contexts.

> In logic, the word *definition* means "a rule that tells how to transform sentences containing unknown words or phrases into equivalent sentences containing other, more clearly understood, locutions."

□ *Analytical, or connotative, definitions*

The kind of definition used in logic is called *analytical*, or *connotative*. Such a definition clarifies meaning by explaining the intension of the term being defined—by drawing attention to attributes shared by all the things to which the word applies.

> **An analytical, or connotative, definition clarifies the meaning of a word by describing the characteristics shared by all the particular objects—whether physical or mental—to which the word applies.**

The objects that form the extension of the term are thus analyzed into their attributes, or properties—some of which they share with other objects. The word being defined is then said to *connote* the properties these objects have in common, which is why such definitions are sometimes called *connotative*. But as explained in Section 3-2, a given term can have many connotations, some of which are either emotive or accidental (formed by association with other words) and which do not refer to properties of all the objects to which the term applies.

In logic, the expression being defined is called the *definiendum*, and the expression given as equivalent to it in meaning is called the *definiens*. And in an analytical definition, the definiens is declared to be a *replacement* for the definiendum.

To show that the definition is a report about the meaning of a term, the definiendum is italicized (and frequently quotation marks are placed around the definiens). Thus, *bachelor* is being explicitly defined in this line:

Bachelor is "an unmarried male."

but not in this line:

A bachelor is an unmarried male.

The second sentence has the appearance of a factual assertion. And sometimes in the absence of quotation marks it is impossible to tell whether the sentence is a definition or the statement of a fact. For example:

An osprey is a large hawk that feeds on fish.

Is this a definition of *osprey*, or is it an assertion of the same type as "An osprey has a wingspread of four and one-half feet"? The use of italics would make it clear that the sentence is telling us the meaning of the word *osprey*.

□ *Lexical definitions*

The dictionary definition, or *lexical definition*, of a word is a report of its current meaning in the natural language of which it is a part. Such highly regarded dictionaries as the *Oxford English Dictionary* and *Webster's Third International Dictionary* are often considered final authorities on correct English usage.

Since dictionaries are primarily intended to report word usage, it is proper to regard the definitions they contain as expressing true or false statements about correct current usage. (In many cases, reports of usage are supported by quotations from primary sources.) However, reports of word usage only partially illuminate the intensional, or connotative, meaning of words.

In addition, a major disadvantage of many dictionaries, especially abridged and bilingual ones, is that they often provide only *synonymous definitions*: they explicate the meaning of a word by replacing it with a more familiar synonym. Examples include using *vagrant* for *vagabond*, *tramp* for *hobo*, *sugar* for *glucose*, and *blockhead* for *dolt*. This kind of definition is helpful as a quick way of expanding one's vocabulary, but its usefulness is limited. Since synonyms have roughly the same connotations, someone in doubt about the connotative meaning of a word will not be greatly enlightened by hearing its synonym. Furthermore, insofar as synonyms are only roughly equivalent in meaning, the suggested connotations of a word will change depending on which other words are offered as synonyms.

Because of the limited usefulness of lexical definitions, logicians concentrate on definitions that attempt to clarify the intensional meaning of a word by delineating classes, or categories, of objects and attributes.

□ Definition by genus and species

One kind of analytical definition is what logicians—borrowing terms from biology—call *definition by genus and species*. The usefulness of this version follows from the fact that many terms apply to complex things that can be analyzed into attributes related by class and subclass.

> **Definition by genus and species clarifies the meaning of a term by describing a class, or category, to which objects named by the term belong and by explaining how these particular objects differ from others belonging to the same class.**

Here is an example of a definition by genus and species:

DEFINIENDUM		DEFINIENS	
Thermometer	means	"an instrument	used to measure temperature."
		GENUS	SPECIES

In such definitions, the *genus* is the class of entities that have some common characteristic. The *species* is the subclass. In the example, *instrument* designates the genus or class—all the items that share the characteristic of being a mechanical device made and used by human beings to accomplish some specific purpose. The definition tells us that a thermometer is in this category. But because there are many different kinds of instruments—a surgeon's instruments, musical instruments, and so forth—the words "used to measure temperature" are needed to subdivide the genus into the appropriate species, or subclass. The species tells how thermometers differ from other entities in the genus designated by "instrument."

Here are some other examples of definition by genus and species:

The word *acorn* means "the fruit of the oak tree."

In geometry the word *square* means "a plane figure having four equal sides and four right angles."

Kitchen means "a room in which food is prepared for consumption."

Logicians have developed four rules for constructing or evaluating definitions by genus and species. Although the rules alone will not ensure the construction of good definitions, they are reliable guides in appraising definitions.

Rule 1. The definiens should be neither too broad nor too narrow.

There are three ways in which the definiens can be too broad:

1. *The genus may include too many different kinds of species.* For example, "man-made" embraces so many different kinds of things that it is not very useful in defining *vest*. It would be better to include *vest* in "clothing" or "garments." Similarly, *terrier* should be included in "dog," rather than in "animal"; and *pliers* should be included in "tool," rather than "metallic object."

2. *The definition may present only a genus and no species.* Pneumonia is not adequately defined as "a disease of the lungs" because there are a number of other diseases of the lungs.

3. *The genus may be expressed in negative terms.* A definition of *wolverine* as "not a wolf and not a bear" would be far too broad, since many other nonwolverines—such as cats, dogs, and cows—are also neither wolves nor bears. A definition should not be expressed in negative terms when it can be given affirmatively. Some words, though—*orphan, widow, bald, blind, deaf,* and *mute,* for example—require definition in negative terms.

The genus can also be too narrow. *Chair* should not be put in the genus of "wooden furniture" because some chairs are made of materials other than wood. To say that *kitchen* means "a room in a house in which food is prepared for consumption" is to overlook the fact that kitchens are also found in such places as restaurants, churches, and recreation vehicles.

Finally, the species included in the definiens can be either too broad or too narrow, thereby failing to identify the subcategory adequately. The definition of *painting* as "color applied to a surface" would be too broad, because both artists and house painters apply color to surfaces. But, in the definition of *painting* as "a design drawn on canvas with a brush," the species is too narrow, because paintings can be made on surfaces other than canvas—such as wood or the ceiling of the Sistine Chapel—and they can be executed with an instrument other than a brush—for example, with a spatula.

Rule 2. The definiens should state the most important attributes of the species.

This rule is related to the first rule. According to a story from antiquity, the philosophers who succeeded Plato at the Academy in Athens expended much mental effort in defining *man*. They finally declared with satisfaction that *man* meant "featherless biped." But their composure was soon shattered when a prankster (legend says it was the historian Diogenes) tossed a plucked chicken over the wall into the Academy. Here was a featherless biped that was clearly not a man. The genus and species—biped and featherless, respectively—were, as the prank demonstrated, too broad. After additional thought, the academics added the phrase "with broad nails" to their definiens. But somehow they completely ignored the essential attribute of human beings—their rationality. The capacity to use reason, rather than the presence or absence of feathers and broad nails, is the species' most outstanding feature. Thus, the definition, "*Man* means 'the rational animal'" is superior, even though the definiens is still too broad (there may be other rational animals).

When the genus is too broad or the species too narrow, the definiens often will fail to state the most important characteristics of the objects included in the extension of the term. In the sentence "*Parent* means 'one's immediate biological ancestor,'" both Rule 1 and Rule 2 have been violated. The genus is too narrow, for parents can also have adopted children. And because parents in these instances are protectors and guardians rather than biological progenitors, the definiens has not stated the essential characteristics.

Here is a definition that clearly violates Rule 2.

Pollen is "the yellow, powderlike substance from the stamen of a flower."

Although no substance other than pollen can accurately be described by this definiens, a crucial factor is omitted—namely, the role of pollen as male sex cells in the fertilization of plants.

Rule 3. A definition must not be circular.

A definition is circular if the definiens repeats the word to be defined or uses a variant of it. The following are examples of circularity:

Student means "one who studies."
A *fatalist* means "a believer in fatalism."

But a definition can be circular even if the word being defined or a variant of it does not appear in the definiens. In the following example, the description in the definiens is synonymous with the definiendum:

By "sleep-inducing drug" we can understand "a drug that has soporific powers."

Although offering a synonym can help explain a word to someone who is more familiar with the synonym, the result is not a definition by genus and species. The purpose of such a definition is to show how the things in connection with which the term is used are related to other classes of similar entities. Synonyms do not do this; they just trade one name for another.

Rule 4. The definiens should be clear enough to be understood by ordinary users of the language.

A definition should not be presented in obscure, ambiguous, or figurative language. Perhaps you have heard an *economist* defined as "someone who knows the price of everything and the value of nothing," or a *lawyer* as "someone in whom ignorance of the law is not punished." Such quips can be insightful as well as humorous, but they are not really definitions.

Definitions that use a special vocabulary (jargon) or require specialized knowledge are unsatisfactory when offered as definitions for the nonspecialist. A well-known example is Dr. Samuel Johnson's definition of a net as "anything made with interstitial vacuities." Contemporary examples include the definition of *battle fatigue* as "acute environmental reaction" and *space suit* as "a pressure garment assembly." And the philosopher John Dewey's definition of *inquiry* is of little practical use outside scholarly literature. He called it, "the controlled or directed transformation of an immediate situation into one that is so determinate in its constituent distinctions and relations as to convert the elements of the original situation into a unified whole."

Definition by genus and species is successful only when the term to be defined can be included in some classes and excluded from others. Some words that cannot be defined this way are *being, entity, object, substance,* and *thing.* The extension of each is so broad that it cannot be restricted to any category; it is a universal attribute or ultimate category. (Everything that exists is, in some sense, an entity or an object; and into what genus can *substance* be put?) However, the number of terms that cannot be defined by genus and species is small compared with the number that can be so defined.

A more serious problem is created by the many words that lack an accepted central meaning. The use of a term may be so varied or controversial that it is difficult to tell what is central to its meaning and what falls within the gray area of meaning that is accepted but not central. *Civil disobedience, due process, equality, freedom, justice, legality, privacy, rights,* and *violence* are all terms of this kind.

☐ *Defining by limiting conditions*

Another type of analytical definition, *definition by limiting conditions,* can be used to clarify indefinite terms such as those just mentioned.

Definition by limiting conditions consists of listing the conditions for the proper use of a term.

The purpose of this kind of definition is to clarify the meaning of a term by contrasting the circumstances under which it is correctly applied and those under which its meaning is skewed or distorted. One begins the definition by listing conditions that characterize the circumstances under which the term is ordinarily used. This list then serves as a basis of comparison when the term is used in other circumstances.

For example, a physician conducting an extensive survey of reports on the treatment of a disease finds the word *syndrome* used frequently. The word seems to be significant in the reports, but it is also used somewhat inconsistently by different researchers. To clarify the term, the doctor specifies the following conditions for its use:

It refers to a group or cluster of symptoms.

These symptoms occur predictably together.

They relate to abnormal organic conditions.

They occur in cases of a specific disease or abnormality.

They occur in typical cases of the disease or abnormality.

Is each of these conditions necessary for the correct use of *syndrome?* Are there other conditions related to ordinary uses of *syndrome* that should be added? The physician may not be able to say, but forming this list has been an important step in clarifying the meaning of the term. The physician's understanding of the term can now be explained to other investigators, and the physician has reason to complain that its meaning is being stretched if it is used in reference to cases in which one or more of these conditions are absent. And anyone who believes the physician's understanding of the term to be incorrect has only to demonstrate that one or more of the listed conditions does not in fact apply.

Ideally, a definition by limiting conditions, when complete, would provide a list of the *necessary and sufficient conditions* for the use of the term. Saying that the list of conditions is necessary means that the term cannot be correctly applied unless these conditions are present. Saying that the list of conditions is sufficient means that the presence of these conditions is all that is required for the term to apply correctly. But the advantage of this procedure is that— by inviting comparisons and contrasts between different circumstances in which the term is used—it clarifies meaning before a definition is widely accepted.

As another illustration, here is a list of conditions for the term *profession*:

Provides an essential or highly valued service.

Requires specialized skill or knowledge.

Requires a long period of training and is difficult to enter.

Allows extensive autonomy and self-regulation.

Emphasizes service rather than monetary gain.

Expects its individual members to accept personal responsibility for their actions.

This list works well for the traditional professions: physicians, lawyers, professors, and priests. The conditions seem to be necessary and, when taken together, complete. But what about *professional* athletes? Referring to highly paid athletes as members of a *profession* violates the fifth condition, which pertains to service rather than personal gain. But is this condition really necessary? After all, some doctors and lawyers also enter their chosen fields primarily for monetary gain or personal prestige. We may not be able to say whether the fifth condition or any one on the list is really necessary. But thinking about these conditions helps us understand what it means to be a member of a *profession*.

A list of necessary and sufficient conditions cannot be obtained for many terms. Suppose we are able to draw up a list of eight conditions for a term that has numerous common uses. One accepted usage of the word might meet Conditions 1, 2, 3, and 5; another accepted usage might meet Conditions 2, 3, 5, and 8; still another might satisfy Conditions 3, 4, 7, and 8. Yet, each use of the term may be correct.

The philosopher Ludwig Wittgenstein drew an analogy between this feature of meaning and *family resemblances* among human beings. The members of a family can resemble each other in a variety of ways: facial features (blue eyes, cleft chin, dimpled cheeks, ruddy complexion), height, hair color, voice, way of laughing, gestures when talking, gait, and so on. Yet, in a family of, say, eight members, not all these features will be present in each individual. And possibly the members of the family will have no single distinguishing feature in common. Nevertheless, they could all be unmistakably members of the same family.

This notion of family resemblances is illustrated by the following passage in which Wittgenstein analyzes the meaning of the word *games*:

> Consider for example the proceedings that we call "games." I mean board games, card games, ball games, Olympic games, and so on. What is common to them all?—Don't say, "there *must* be something common, or they would not be called 'games'"—but *look and see* whether there is anything common to them all.—For if you look at them you will not see something that is common to *all*, but similarities, relationships, and a whole series of them at that. To repeat: don't think, but look!—Look for example at board games with their multifarious relationships. Now pass to card games; here you find many correspondences with the first group, but many common features drop out, and others appear. When we pass next to ball games, much that is common is retained, but much is lost—Are they all "amusing"? Compare chess with noughts or crosses. Or is there always winning and losing, or competition between players? Think of patience. In ball games there is winning and losing, but when a child throws his ball at the wall and catches it again, this feature has disappeared. Look at the parts played by skill and luck; at the differences between skill in chess and skill in tennis. Think now of games like ring-a-ring-a-roses:

Here is the element of amusement, but how many other characteristic features have disappeared! And we can go through the many, many other groups of games in the same way; we can see how similarities crop up and disappear.

And the result of this examination is: we see a complicated network of similarities overlapping and criss-crossing: sometimes overall similarities, sometimes similarities of detail.[8]

□ *Definitions and counterexamples*

A strategy for criticizing a definition by genus and species is to think of a counterexample: something that would fall into the definiens but not the definiendum, or vice versa. If the definition is correct—if what it reports is true about current usage—then one should be able to replace the definiendum with the definiens in any sentence without changing the meaning of the sentence.

But this is an ideal test: only an exact synonym can satisfy it. And synonyms are generally unenlightening because they tell nothing further about the use of the term. The test will therefore be more valuable if it is adjusted in the following way:

In an analytical definition, anything in the extension of the definiendum must also be in the extension of the definiens.

That is, anything correctly described by the left-hand side of the "equation" must be something that is correctly described by the right-hand side, and vice versa. It would be a contradiction if something could be described by the term on the left-hand side and by the negation of the phrase on the right-hand side.

This procedure must be modified when testing a definition by limiting conditions, for in these cases, the definiens is never expressed by a simple sentence. In fact, the special advantage of definition by limiting conditions is that it increases exactness without producing an equivalent definiens. However, it is still appropriate to ask whether an example—such as *professional athlete*—reflects the proper meaning of the term although it does not seem to fulfill one or more of the conditions listed. While exceptions, or counterexamples, do not show that this second kind of analytical definition is mistaken, they do show what conditions need to be added or modified to handle the examples.

■ **EXERCISE 4-4**

Evaluate the following definitions according to the rules for definition by genus and species. In addition, rewrite a definition where necessary to make it explicit.

[8] *Philosophical Investigations*, trans. G. E. M. Anscombe (London: Macmillan, 1953), p. 66.

1. *Satisfaction* means "the state of not having unfulfilled desires."

2. A hazard is anything that is dangerous.

3. *Language* means "the tool of thought."

*4. Rationality is the opposite of insanity.

5. *Bus* means "a device for public transportation."

6. A totem pole is a pole or post carved and painted with sacred or revered figures, and erected by Indians of the Northwestern Coast of North America.

7. A mineral is any substance that is neither vegetable nor animal.

*8. *Clock* means "an instrument for keeping time."

9. Biology is the science that studies the biological nature of things.

10. A light-year is the unit of distance light travels in a year at 186,000 miles per second.

11. *Mammal* by definition means "four-legged land animal that suckles its young."

*12. *Bread* is the staff of life.

13. *Cube* means a "regular solid, each of whose faces is square."

14. Heat is a form of energy produced by the accelerated vibration of molecules.

15. War is a breach of a state of peace, and peace means an absence of war.

*16. *Pusillanimous* means "fainthearted."

17. A good teacher is one that is not just average or poor.

18. "Habit" means "a practice that is hard to break or end."

19. A carburetor is part of an internal combustion engine.

*20. *Lie* means "a locution deliberately antithetical to a verity apprehended by the intellect." ■

☐ 4-5. DEFINITIONS FOR SPECIAL PURPOSES

The meaning of a word is sometimes made precise for use in a specific context. These assigned meanings are definitions only in a weak sense because they are not rules for transforming a sentence into an equivalent sentence or group of sentences. Such meanings are sometimes called *precising definitions*. The three main kinds are technical, operational, and stipulative definitions.

Technical definitions make the meaning of a word more precise by placing restrictions on its use in some special context. This is usually done by specifying characteristics associated with the use of the word. For example, the meaning of *head of household* as used in ordinary language is vague. However, the Internal Revenue Service provides a technical definition of the term for its purposes. In tax guides, *head of household* means "a person who both maintains a household and contributes over half the cost of maintaining the household, who is unmarried on the last day of the tax year, and who has at least one relative using the household as his or her principal residence for the entire year." Technical definitions are important in the sciences. For example, physicists define the words *mass, force, field, stress,* and *strain* in ways understood primarily by serious students in the subject area and not by the average person.

Operational definitions are also used in the experimental sciences. An operational definition states the meaning of a term by connecting its proper use to some observable condition or behavioral disposition. Only if this condition or disposition is present is the word being used correctly. For instance, a psychologist may specify the meaning of an *aggressive act* as "some type of physical attack upon other persons or their property, or verbal abuse of other people." This operational definition would allow the psychologist to design experimental situations to test the occurrence of such behavior and to distinguish it from behavioral dispositions or traits such as assertiveness and dominance. The psychologist's study of what are thus defined as *aggressive acts* may or may not contribute significantly to what the nonspecialist considers the central problems associated with aggressiveness and social interaction. But unless the psychologist claims to be defining what is commonly understood by the word *aggression*, it would not be appropriate to appraise the operational definition as true or false. Operational definitions are not expected to explain *all* we may mean by the use of a word.

The true meaning of a term is to be found by observing what a man does with it, not by what he says about it.
P. L. BRIDGEMAN

A *stipulative definition* represents an explicit decision to use a word in a given way. Stipulative definitions have the form, "Let us use the word *w* to mean . . . ." Since these definitions represent proposals to use a word in a certain way, they can be judged to be useful or not useful, clear or obscure, but not true or false. However, once a stipulative definition comes to be accepted by users, it becomes lexical; that is, another usage of the word is reported.

Table 4-1 presents a number of stipulative definitions—in these cases terms that entered our language in association with some notable personage, either real or fictional. Some were added to the language by choice; others came into use through a general but unexpressed consensus that they were appropriate and filled what had been a gap in the language.

Stipulative definition can add new dimensions of meaning to familiar words and can even change established meanings. It would be unwise, though, to attempt to change the meaning of a word through a stipulative definition unless there was a strongly held belief among speakers of the language that a change was needed. As we saw in Section 3-3, verbal disputes occur when disputants attach different meanings to the same term. Arbitrarily changing the meaning of a word to suit one's purposes is therefore likely to invite verbal dispute.

TABLE 4-1

boycott	To avoid having dealings with someone; after Captain Charles Cunningham Boycott (1832–1897), a tax agent for estates on County Mayo, Ireland, and a victim of the treatment that assumed his name.
chauvinism	A blind enthusiasm for military glory; from Nicholas Chauvin of Rochefort, a much-wounded veteran of the First Republic who became an idolator of Napoleon.
dunce	A term that came to be applied by sixteenth-century humanists to apparently dim-witted enemies of learning and progress; named after Dunce, Scotland, birthplace of John Duns Scotus, whose followers' views fell out of favor during the Renaissance.
gerrymander	As governor of Massachusetts, Elbridge Gerry (1744–1814) enacted a law that divided the territory into new senatorial voting districts. The fresh boundaries were so irregular and elongated that, according to tradition, an observer remarked that they looked like a salamander. To this the astute governor retorted, "Gerry mander, rather." Gerry was elected vice president of the United States in 1812.
malapropism	The ludicrous misuse of a word in place of one it resembles. This was the failing of Mrs. Malaprop, a character in Richard Sheridan's *The Rivals*, originally acted at Covent Garden Theatre in 1775.
martinet	A punctilious disciplinarian; after Jean Martinet, Inspector General of Infantry in the reign of Louis XIV of France. Martinet was an autocratic disciplinarian and drillmaster. He was killed at the siege of Duisberg in 1672 when he was accidently shot by his own artillery while leading an infantry assault.
sandwich	Derived from John Montagu, the fourth Earl of Sandwich (1718–1792), who is said to have once spent twenty-four hours at the gaming table, subsisting only on thick slices of meat placed between slices of toast.
spoonerism	A transposition of letters or sounds in a word or sentence. Such a slip of the tongue is technically known as *metathesis*, but came to be called a *spoonerism* after the unfortunate Rev. W. A. Spooner (1844–1930), Warden of New College, Oxford. Spooner was famous for slips such as "our queer old dean" (for "our dear old queen") and "half-warmed fishes" (for "half-formed wishes"). Some other examples for which Spooner was responsible include: "The Lord is a shoving leopard," "You are occupewing my pie," and "Ladies, may I sew you to your sheets?"

There are some notable exceptions to this general rule, however. For example, at one time the word *cybernetics* meant "the art of steering ships." The physicist André-Marie Ampère stipulated a meaning for the term when he used it to refer to the science of social control. And later, in 1948, the mathematician Norbert Wiener stipulated another meaning for *cybernetics* as a science of communication that compares the functioning of the human nervous system with complex electronic calculating machines. In recent decades, this meaning has been extended. Today, the study of cybernetics includes an analysis and evaluation of the ways communication can be used to control living organisms as well as mechanistic devices and organizations.[9]

■ **EXERCISE 4-5**

Decide whether each of the following passages should be treated as a technical, operational, or stipulative definition. In each case, give the reason for your choice.

1. A relation *R* is transitive if for all objects *a*, *b*, *c*, if *R* holds between *a* and *b* and between *b* and *c*, then it holds between *a* and *c*.

2. For our purpose, we shall understand a marathon to be a footrace of twenty-six miles and 385 yards, run over an open course.

3. By *full employment*, we mean a jobless rate of 5 percent or less.

*4. "Capital is that part of the wealth of a country which is employed in production, and consists of food, clothing, tools, raw materials, machinery, etc., necessary to give effect to labour."—David Ricardo

5. A galaxy is a grouping of millions of stars together with gases and dust in a gravitational system with a disklike shape, whose diameter approaches 90,000 light-years, and whose thickness approaches 15,000 light-years.

6. To say that one substance is harder than another means that if we rub two unscarred objects, *A* and *B*, against one another and *B* is scarred and *A* is not, then *A* is harder than *B*.

7. If a solution is acidic, it will turn litmus paper red.

*8. "Law is a rule and measure of acts, whereby man is induced to act or is restrained from acting. . . ."—Saint Thomas Aquinas

9. "The Christian holds that we can know there is a God; the atheist, that we can know there is not. The agnostic suspends judgment, saying that there are not sufficient grounds either for affirmation or denial."—Bertrand Russell, *What Is an Agnostic?*

10. "When we call anything a person's right, we mean that he has a valid claim on society to protect him in the possession of it, either by force of law, or by that of education and opinion. . . . To have a right, then, is, to have something which society ought to defend me in the possession of."—John Stuart Mill, *Utilitarianism* ■

□ 4-6. PERSUASIVE AND REVELATORY DEFINITIONS

A discussion of definitions would be incomplete without considering problems presented by the multiple functions of language, especially its emotive func-

[9] William J. Kilgore, *An Introductory Logic*, 2d ed. (New York: Holt, Rinehart and Winston, 1979), p. 82.

tion. Some discussion of the problems resulting from ambiguity and variable meaning appeared in Chapter 3 and in earlier sections of this chapter. We now need to consider methods that are used to influence attitudes and actions and that are often mistaken for definitions. People who use these methods generally say either that they are presenting a definition or that they are just trying to clarify the meaning of a word. But their primary concern is to alter the point of view or a belief of the reader or listener. Two such methods are *persuasive definition* and *revelatory definition*.

The difference between defining words as such and using sentences that *look like* definitions but serve other purposes is illustrated by the following examples. Suppose someone asks for a definition of a *conservative* and the class wag pipes up, "A conservative is a man who is too cowardly to fight and too fat to run." And consider the poet e. e. cummings's definition of a *politician* as "an arse upon which everyone has sat except a man." Such "definitions" are sometimes intended only as humorous jibes. Sometimes, however, they are intended to convey a negative attitude about the subject (for example, politicians) and to influence others to adopt that attitude. In accomplishing this latter purpose, they function persuasively.

Any sentence phrased as a definition and used to express emotion and thereby influence attitudes is a *persuasive definition*. But these only look like definitions: their job is to persuade, not to describe the meaning of words.

An illuminating example of a persuasive definition is the World Health Organization (WHO) "definition" of the word *health*. According to the WHO, "Health is a state of complete physical, mental and social well-being and is not merely the absence of disease or infirmity." But surely the social problems of inflation, job discrimination, unemployment, inadequate education, and inadequate transportation facilities, among others, that adversely affect social well-being are not health problems. They are related to health problems in a variety of complex ways, but these problems are not the *same as* health problems. The WHO definition attempts to make us think about social problems *as if* they were also health problems. This may be because the emotive connotations of *health* are always positive; politicians or world leaders never speak out against improvements in health. Thus, if we think of social reforms as

© 1980, *Jefferson Communications, Inc. Reprinted by permission of* The Chicago Tribune–New York News Syndicate, Inc.

matters of health policy, we may be influenced to support these programs with greater enthusiasm.

For purposes of comparison, here are two further definitions of *health* taken from the work of commentators on health issues.

Health can be regarded as an expression of fitness to the environment, as a state of adaptedness.
RENE DUBOIS

Health is a state of physical well-being which need not be complete but is at least without significant impairment of function.
DANIEL CALLAHAN

And a definition of *health* by genus and species would give us the following "formula":

> *Health* means "the optimal functioning of an organism with freedom from disease and abnormality."

Sometimes a sentence that looks like a definition will use a metaphor to communicate a vital new insight. For example, a nineteenth-century writer defined *architecture* as "frozen music." He was not trying to describe how the word *architecture* was used in the language, nor was he stipulating a new definition. Instead, he was suggesting a unique way of looking at architecture by comparing the relationship between the parts of a building with the relationship between the parts of a musical composition. Such a revealing and insightful metaphor is called a *revelatory definition*,[10] even though it is not really a definition but only has the form of one.

Revelatory definitions, which convey insight, also serve to influence attitudes. Ambrose Bierce gave us a relevatory definition when he said that "a bore is a person who talks when you want him to listen." Bierce was pointing out not merely that a bore is someone who talks too much, but also that *we* consider him a bore because *we* don't want him to talk so much. The "definition" of *bore*, if enlightening, also inclines us toward tolerance.

---

[10] Stephen Barker, *The Elements of Logic*, 2d ed. (New York: McGraw-Hill, 1974), p. 213.

■ **EXERCISE 4-6**

■ A. Discuss each of the following attempts at definition and indicate which should be regarded as persuasive definitions. Which, if any, offer revelatory insights?

1. *Woman* means "a person who has not developed her intelligence because of a repressive male-dominated society."

2. "By euthanasia is meant the slaying of helpless invalids and people in incurable pain."—Knights of Columbus, "The Sacredness of Life"

3. A decision is a deliberate choice made in response to some problematic situation.

*4. "Family" means "people related by heterosexual marriage, blood or adoption."—White House Conference on the Family

5. "What is moral is what you feel good after."—Ernest Hemingway

6. "A bureaucrat is a Democrat who holds some office that a Republican wants."—Alben W. Barkley

7. A conservative is a person who wants to live in the past.

*8. "*Bride:* A woman with a fine prospect of happiness behind her."—Ambrose Bierce

9. An amphiboly is an ambiguous sentence that results from faulty grammatical structure.

10. "The only unnatural sex act is one which you cannot perform."—Alfred Kinsey

11. "Family" means "two or more persons who share resources, responsibilities for decisions, values and goals and have commitment to one another over time."—White House Conference on the Family, Minority Report

*12. "A conclusion is the place where you got tired thinking."—Martin H. Fischer

■ B. The following passages can be regarded as revelatory definitions. Briefly describe the insight conveyed by each expression.

1. "Man is the only animal that blushes. Or needs to."—Mark Twain

2. "Home is the place where, when you have to go there, they have to take you in."—Robert Frost

3. "A baby is God's opinion that the world should go on."—Carl Sandburg

*4. "Experience is a comb life gives you after you lose your hair."—Judith Stern

5. Poetry is "the impish attempt to paint the color of the wind."—Maxwell Bodenheim

6. A yawn is "a silent shout."—G. K. Chesterton

7. "Art is a lie that makes us realize the truth."—Pablo Picasso

*8. "Man. A biodegradable but non-recyclable animal blessed with opposable thumbs-capable of grasping at straws."—Bernard Rosenberg

9. "A man with a new idea is a crank until the idea succeeds."—Mark Twain

10. "My definition of a free society is a society where it is safe to be unpopular."—Adlai Stevenson   ■

□ *Part two*

DEDUCTIVE REASONING

☐ CHAPTER FIVE

Categorical statements

The premises and conclusions of many arguments are categorical statements—that is, they concern class relationships:

A categorical statement is an assertion or a denial that all or some members of the subject class are included in the predicate class.

The following argument consists entirely of categorical statements.

All marsupials are mammals.
All wallabies are marsupials.
Therefore, all wallabies are mammals.

The first premise is a claim that all members of the subject class—marsupials—are included in the predicate class—mammals. The second premise is the claim that all members of the class wallabies are included in the class marsupials. And the conclusion is the claim that all members of the class wallabies are included in the class mammals.

The verb *are*, which links the subject and predicate classes in a categorical statement, is called a *copula*. The word *all* or *some*, which precedes the subject class, is called a *quantifier*. The way the quantifier and the copula relate the subject and predicate classes determines what is called the *categorical form* of the statement.

Chapter 6 will present methods of determining the validity or invalidity of arguments made up of categorical statements. This chapter analyzes categorical statements themselves.

☐ 5-1. QUANTITY, QUALITY, AND CATEGORICAL FORM

Each categorical statement possesses a certain *quantity*, the characteristic of asserting something about some or all members of the subject class. Categorical statements that refer to all members of the subject class are said to be *universal* in quantity. Thus, "All astronauts are healthy individuals" and "No legumes are fruits" express universal statements. Categorical statements that make assertions about some members of the subject class are *particular* in quantity. Thus, "Some astronauts are women" and "Some vegetables are not legumes" express particular statements.

In addition, each categorical statement possesses a certain *quality*. When it is asserted that all or part of the subject class are included in the predicate class, the statement is *affirmative* in quality. Both "All astronauts are healthy individuals" and "Some astronauts are women" express affirmative statements. Categorical statements asserting that all or part of the subject class are excluded from the predicate class are *negative* in quality. Both "No legumes are fruits," and "Some vegetables are not legumes" express negative statements. The *no* in "no legumes are fruits" serves as a universal quantifier and also indicates a relation of exclusion between the subject and predicate classes—so it determines both quantity and quality.

The various combinations of quantity and quality produce four *categorical forms: universal affirmative, universal negative, particular affirmative*, and *particular negative*. These relationships are summarized in Table 5-1.

Because all categorical statements have the same order of parts, the letters S and P are used as variables for the subject and predicate terms, respectively. The use of these letters is a reminder that the logician is interested in the formal properties of the statement—the relationship between classes—and not its content.

During the Middle Ages, logicians gave the four categorical forms the special names of A, E, I, and O. These four letters came from the first two vowels in the Latin word "*affirmo*" ("I affirm") and the vowels in the Latin "*nego*" ("I deny"). It will be convenient to retain these names as a shorthand way of discussing the form of a specific statement. Table 5-2 sums up what has been presented so far.

□ *Translating sentences into standard form*

To permit categorical statements to be analyzed, the sentences that express them must be written in what is called standard categorical form, or standard form. The quantifier, the *subject term*—that is, a word or phrase designating the subject class—the copula, and the *predicate term*—that is, a word or phrase

TABLE 5-1

		QUALITY	
		AFFIRMATIVE	NEGATIVE
QUANTITY	UNIVERSAL	**All *S* are *P***	**No *S* are *P***
	PARTICULAR	**Some *S* are *P***	**Some *S* are not *P***

TABLE 5-2

CATEGORICAL FORM	NAME	EXAMPLE
All *S* are *P*. (Universal Affirmative)	*A*	All astronauts are healthy individuals.
No *S* are *P*. (Universal Negative)	*E*	No legumes are fruits.
Some *S* are *P*. (Particular Affirmative)	*I*	Some astronauts are women.
Some *S* are not *P*. (Particular Negative)	*O*	Some vegetables are not legumes.

designating the predicate class—must all be explicitly displayed, and in a certain order.

SUBJECT TERM   PREDICATE TERM

All citizens of Boston   are   fans of the Celtics.

QUANTIFIER   COPULA

In the following discussion, the names A, E, I, and O will be used to refer to sentences in standard form as well as to the statements they express. For example, "Some citizens of Boston are not fans of the Celtics" is in O form, meaning that (1) the categorical statement expressed by the sentence is particular negative and (2) the sentence is in corresponding standard form.

Even though there are only four categorical forms, a large number of different sentences can be translated into standard form.[1] Here, for example, are two sentences that appear to be unlikely candidates:

Spiders have eight legs.
Uncle Scrooge hoards money.

The sentence "Spiders have eight legs" presents three difficulties. First, it has no explicit quantifier. Second, it has no copula. Third, *eight legs* cannot be regarded as the name for a predicate class. "Uncle Scrooge hoards money" presents the same kinds of problems and introduces a fourth one: *Uncle Scrooge* is not a general term that names a class. Let us consider each of these difficulties in turn.

---

[1] Indeed, some philosophers, such as Gottfried Leibniz (1646–1716), have argued that every sentence that expresses a statement can be translated into standard form. Other philosophers, such as Bertrand Russell (1872–1970), have argued that sentences expressing relational statements, such as "Socrates was the teacher of Plato" and "Denver is to the west of Chicago," must be analyzed differently. Nevertheless, all agree that a very large number of sentences can be translated into standard form.

☐ QUANTIFYING THE SUBJECT CLASS

When no quantifier for the subject term is given, one must be supplied from the context or from general knowledge of relevant facts. Someone who says "Spiders have eight legs" undoubtedly means that *all* spiders have eight legs, so the universal quantifier applies. Similarly, "Reptiles are not warm-blooded animals" would be understood as "No reptiles are warm-blooded animals." Common knowledge about the characteristics of spiders and reptiles as classes permits us to identify these assertions as universal propositions.

If someone says "Dogs chase cars," however, the intended quantifier is not so clear. Should we interpret the speaker as meaning that *all* dogs chase cars, even though it would be easy to present counterexamples to such a claim? Some people have a way of making sweeping statements for emphasis, even when they know them to be literally false. If there is evidence that the speaker really did intend to make a broad universal statement, "Dogs chase cars" should be treated as being in A form—as universal affirmative. Otherwise, it should be treated as being in *I* form—an affirmative statement about *some* dogs.

> In general, when the context provides no clues, one should quantify the subject term as *some* rather than *all*.

Statements in which the subject class is preceded by such expressions as *at least one, most, many, nearly all, lots,* and *a few,* are interpreted as particular propositions. The quantifier *some* is used as a translation for these expressions.

Note that the words replaced by *some* are vague. Is a person who says "A few actors attended the fund-raiser" claiming that there were at least two actors at the fund-raiser? Exactly three? More than four? Such questions usually have no answer, for the words are not meant to be precise. Logicians must find ways to overcome this vagueness.

> For the purposes of logic *some* is always interpreted to mean "at least one."

And logicians impose no limit on the number that can be encompassed by the word *some*. For instance, a speaker who says "Some of my neighbors are veterans" is not committed to believing that some neighbors are nonveterans. Interpreting the statement as the claim that *at least one* neighbor is a veteran leaves open the possibility that *all* the neighbors are veterans:

> The use of *some* does not exclude the possibility that the subject of the statement may refer to the entire class.

Avoid reading more into a statement than was intended by the speaker. Someone who says "Some politicians are honest" may be suggesting that some politicians are *not* honest, depending upon the context and the speaker's tone of voice. In general, however, "Some S are P" does not mean what "Some S are not P" expresses.

In addition, the decision to translate quantifying expressions such as *most, many,* and *nearly all* as *some* occasionally means that the categorical reformulation will express something weaker than the original sentence. For example, when "Nearly all New Yorkers are gregarious" is understood as "At least one New Yorker is a gregarious person," some of the force of the original sentence is lost. *At least one* would ordinarily be considered an inadequate phrase to use in a generalization about many millions of people. But in applying the methods of categorical logic, we do not need to distinguish between particular sentences of varying strength. If the assertion is about all or none of the subject class, the expression is universal; otherwise, it is particular.

☐ SUPPLYING THE COPULA

In sentences such as "Dogs chase cars," "Cats eat fish," and "Hens lay eggs," which do not contain the verb *are* functioning as a copula, standard form requires that a copula be supplied. When adding the copula, the predicate must be restated in a way that preserves the sense of the original while maintaining a grammatical sentence. Thus, "Cats eat fish" becomes "All cats are fish-eaters"; "Hens lay eggs" becomes "All hens are egg-laying animals"; and "Dogs chase cars" becomes "Some dogs are car-chasers." As these examples illustrate, sentences that have main verbs other than *are* can be put into standard form by transforming the original verb into a noun or a part of a noun phrase.

The copula is always understood as the present tense of the verb *to be.* Sentences containing the verb *to be* in the past tense or the future tense are put into standard form by introducing the verb *to be* in the present tense and making the original verb part of the predicate term. Thus, "Some Puritans were stern advocates of chastity" becomes "Some Puritans are people who were stern advocates of chastity." And "No racists will be elected to Congress" becomes "No racists are persons who will be elected to Congress."

Finally, for the sake of neatness and consistency, a sentence is not regarded as *strictly* categorical unless the copula is the plural *are.* Consequently, "No logic student is a lazy person" becomes "No logic students are lazy persons."

☐ NAMING THE PREDICATE CLASS

Because both the subject and predicate terms of a categorical statement refer to classes, the predicate term must be a substantive, or nounlike, expression, rather than an adjective. "Steelworkers are muscular" thus becomes "All steelworkers are muscular persons." In the sentence "Frogs like to eat flies" the predicate term becomes the class of animals that like to eat flies, and the sentence is rewritten as "All frogs are animals that like to eat flies."

Be careful not to reword the predicate term so it names a class that is either too broad or too narrow. For example, "Textbooks are expensive" should become "All textbooks are expensive books." It would be misleading to use the translation "All textbooks are expensive things" because the predicate class would be too broad. Textbooks are expensive when compared with small paperbacks but not when compared with sports cars, rare coins, gemstones, and holidays in Hawaii. "Quite a few New Yorkers are loquacious" should become "Some New Yorkers are loquacious persons" and not "Some New Yorkers are loquacious New Yorkers." The predicate class in the second translation is too narrow because the speaker was undoubtedly referring to loquacious New Yorkers as human beings of a certain kind, rather than as New Yorkers of a certain kind.

As some of the above examples demonstrate, the subject or predicate term occasionally contains a verb. The sentence must then be carefully interpreted to distinguish this verb from the copula. For example, in "Some scientists who are biophysicists are geneticists," the *S* term is the entire phrase *scientists who are biophysicists*. But in "All skydivers are athletes who are poor insurance risks," the *S* term is only the word *skydivers*. The *P* term in the second sentence is *athletes who are poor insurance risks*.

☐ TRANSLATING SINGULAR TERMS

A sentence with a singular term as the subject—for example, "June flies an airplane," "Alphonse is not a graduate student," and "The city of Frederick is northwest of Washington, D.C."—does not express a statement about the relation of two classes. Rather, it expresses a *singular statement*: an assertion that an individual or an object has, or does not have, a certain property, or is, or is not, a member of a certain class.

Any statement about an individual can be treated as a universal statement, however. This is done by treating the statement as if it were about a single-member class. According to this convention, to refer to an individual is to refer to *all* members (each and every member) of a class that has only *one* member. The sentence "June flies an airplane" thus becomes "All persons identical with June are persons who fly airplanes" and "Alphonse is not a graduate student" becomes "No persons identical with Alphonse are graduate students." The sentence "The city of Frederick is northwest of Washington, D.C." becomes "All places identical with the city of Frederick are places northwest of Washington, D.C."

The greater the number of sentences we can translate into standard form, the greater our ability to recognize arguments that assert or deny class relationships. And recognizing an argument is a necessary step toward determining whether it is valid and sound.

■ EXERCISE 5-1

◨ A. State the standard form (A, E, I, or O) of each of the following sentences, and identify the subject and predicate terms.
   1. Bats are mammals.
   2. A bat is not a bird.
   3. The dodo is extinct.
   *4. These apples are red.

5. Many students were not in class yesterday.

6. Movies are entertaining.

7. Cockroaches are unwelcome visitors in the kitchen.

*8. Almost 60 percent of the students are over twenty years of age.

9. All American voters believe in democracy.

10. There are nonwhite swans.

11. Cats are all carnivores.

*12. Some habits of thought do not improve decision making.

13. Every case of infection is accompanied by fever.

14. Many technical books are not widely read.

15. Obese people aren't always jolly people.

*16. Any athlete who receives payments for a performance is not an amateur.

17. Each party goer is a fun-loving person.

18. Nothing that is a vegetable is a mineral.

19. Vegetarians never eat meat.

*20. There are women among those sent into outer space.

■ B. Put each of the following sentences into standard form.

1. Good scholars are not always interesting lecturers.

2. Every book he owns has his initials in it.

3. Some people will be angry about the Supreme Court decisions on privacy.

*4. No one who comes on time will be sent away empty-handed.

5. Income-tax deductions for gambling losses are never allowed.

6. Some cars still being driven on our highways do not have pollution-control devices.

7. All prospective stockholders were invited to the business meeting.

*8. Those who do not complete this exercise are inattentive students.

9. Everyone he loves loves him in return.

10. Anything that is beautiful is rare.   ■

□ 5-2. VENN DIAGRAMS AND THE DISTRIBUTION OF TERMS

One way to analyze a categorical statement is by means of a diagram. And the most frequently used method for doing this is the *Venn diagram technique*, named for John Venn (1834–1923), the British logician who developed it.

As shown in Figure 5-1, two overlapping circles are used—one to represent the class of things referred to by the subject term, S, and one to represent the class of things referred to by the predicate term, P. The circles representing the subject and predicate classes are placed within a rectangle, which stands for the *universe of discourse*. For our purposes, the universe of discourse in-

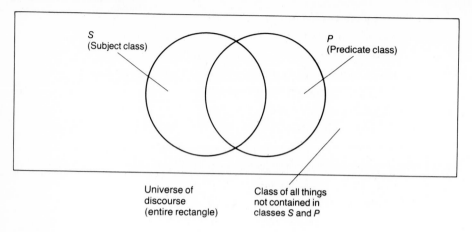

Universe of
discourse
(entire rectangle)

Class of all things
not contained in
classes *S* and *P*

FIGURE 5-1
Venn diagram

cludes everything that can be named or described, whether physical or non-physical. The area inside the rectangle and outside both circles represents the class of all things not contained in either of the classes represented by the subject and predicate terms.

As an example, consider a statement in which *Danes* is the name of the subject class and *redheads* is the name of the predicate class. Thus, the circle on the left, marked *S*, represents the class of Danes; and the circle on the right, marked *P*, represents the class of redheads. The area common to both circles represents the class of things that are both Danes and redheads. The area outside both circles but within the rectangle represents everything that is neither a Dane nor a redhead.

The subject and predicate terms of a categorical statement are said to be either *distributed* or *undistributed*. A term preceded by a universal quantifier (*all* or *no*) is *distributed*, meaning that every member of the class is included. A term preceded by the particular quantifier (*some*) is *undistributed*; not every member of the class is included.

Let us now see how the Venn diagram can be used to exhibit the form of each categorical statement in which the terms in the example can appear. The following sentences express the four possible forms:

A: All Danes are redheads.
E: No Danes are redheads.
I: Some Danes are redheads.
O: Some Danes are not redheads.

The A-form sentence, "All Danes are redheads," expresses the claim that each and every member of the class of Danes is contained in the class of redheads. Thus, in Figure 5-2, all Danes are represented by the area where

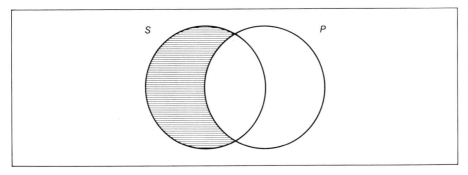

FIGURE 5-2
Venn diagram for A-form statement

the S and P circles overlap. *We show this by crossing out the remainder of the S circle to indicate that it is empty:* there are no Danes that are not contained in the class of redheads. We do *not* cross out any of the P circle because the sentence says nothing about all redheads.

The subject term for any sentence in A form is distributed because the statement is about all members of the class—in the example, all Danes. The predicate term is undistributed in A form. As Figure 5-2 shows, no part of the circle representing redheads is crossed out. This means that not all members of the class of redheads are referred to—there may be other redheads (say, Swedish or English) in addition to those who are Danish.

Now examine Figure 5-3, the Venn diagram for the E-form statement expressed as "No Danes are redheads." In this case, the area common to both circles is crossed out to indicate that there are no members of the S class, Danes, that are also members of the P class, redheads.

Both the S and P terms are distributed in the E form: any statement in this form asserts a relationship of total exclusion between the class designated by the subject term and the class designated by the predicate term. In the

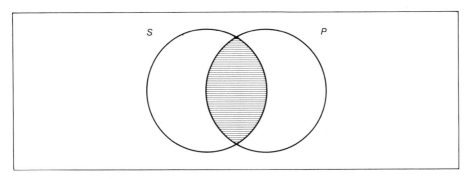

FIGURE 5-3
Venn diagram for E-form statement

example, no matter what other attributes the members of the subject class may have, the quality of being a Dane is sufficient to exclude one from the class of redheads. In this sense, all Danes are accounted for as well as all redheads: all Danes are non-redheads; all redheads are non-Danes.

Now consider Figure 5-4, which illustrates the *I*-form statement expressed as "Some Danes are redheads." Because *some* is understood to mean "at least one," the statement is a claim that at least one member of the subject class, Danes, will be found in the area common to both circles in the figure—the area populated by Danes who are also redheads. We place an asterisk in this area to indicate that there is at least one Dane who is a redhead.

No other marking appears in the diagram because a statement in *I* form says nothing about *all* members of the subject class or *all* members of the predicate class. There may or may not be Danes who are not redheads, and there may or may not be redheads who are not Danes; the outer sections of the circles remain open to represent these possibilities. Thus, both the subject and predicate terms of *I* form are undistributed. Neither term accounts for all possible members of the class it designates.

The sentence "Some Danes are not redheads," an O-form statement, expresses the fourth possibility. Again, *some* means "at least one." In Figure 5-5, we place an asterisk in the part of the *S* circle that is *outside* of the circle representing the predicate class, redheads. This indicates that at least one member of the class of Danes is excluded from the class of redheads: that is, at least one Dane is not a redhead.

The subject term of an O-form statement is undistributed.

The O-form example says nothing about all Danes. There may or may not be members of the class represented by the subject term that are also members of the class represented by the predicate term; that is, there may or may not be Danes who are also redheads.

The situation is different with respect to the predicate term, however.

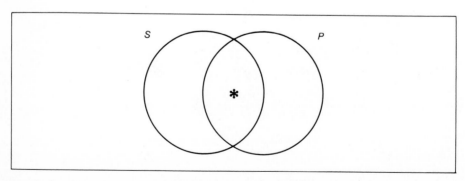

FIGURE 5-4
Venn diagram for I-form statement

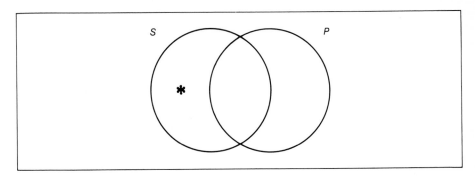

FIGURE 5-5
Venn diagram for O-form statement

Something is asserted about all members of the class represented by the predicate, redheads—namely, that they are all excluded from the subject class of at least one Dane. Thus, the predicate term of an O-form statement is distributed. If something (at least one Dane) is excluded from the class designated by the predicate term (redheads), it must be excluded from each and every part of the class. No redhead can be among the one or more Danes who are non-redheads.

TABLE 5-3 *Distribution of terms*

FORM	SUBJECT TERM	PREDICATE TERM
A	Distributed	Undistributed
E	Distributed	Distributed
I	Undistributed	Undistributed
O	Undistributed	Distributed

A listing of categorical statements and the combinations of distributed and undistributed terms appears in Table 5-3. This information will be used later to show why some arguments expressed in categorical statements are valid and others are invalid.

■ **EXERCISE 5-2**

■ A. Use a Venn diagram to illustrate the categorical form of each statement expressed below.
    1. All lifeguards are virtuous persons.
    2. No lifeguards are virtuous persons.
    3. Some lifeguards are virtuous persons.

*4. Some lifeguards are not virtuous persons.

5. No members of the Little League are girls.

6. Some members of the Little League are girls.

7. All charming persons are flirts.

*8. No charming persons are flirts.

9. Some speed limits are reasonable regulations.

10. Some speed limits are not reasonable regulations.

■ B. Determine the categorical form of each sentence below, and indicate whether the subject and predicate terms are distributed or undistributed.

1. Most children aren't naughty.

2. Orchids are always fragrant flowers.

3. Heavily salted broth is usually unappetizing.

*4. Rattlesnakes are pit vipers.

5. Neurotics are never happy.

6. Clark Gable was the male lead in *Gone with the Wind*.

7. The star of *High Noon* was Gary Cooper.

*8. Most ideals can't be realized in practice.

9. Dogs can be found that do not bark.

10. Unscrupulous people never listen to their consciences.   ■

□ 5-3. THE TRADITIONAL SQUARE OF OPPOSITION

In the previous section, Venn diagrams were used to illustrate the logical relations between the subject and predicate classes of single categorical statements. In this section, we will consider the logical relations between different categorical statements having identical subjects and identical predicates. If one knows, for example, that an A-form statement is true, what, if anything, can be known about the *truth values*—that is, the truth or falsity—of E, I, and O statements with identical S classes and identical P classes? Assuming that for each form the subject class contains at least one member,[2] the logical relations between the four forms can be represented by what is called the *traditional square of opposition*.

---

[2] In other words, the subject of the categorical statement is assumed to be something that exists. Categorical statements about imaginary or doubtful entities—such as fictional characters, centaurs, and ghosts—will be interpreted under the hypothetical viewpoint (to be discussed later in this chapter under "The Hypothetical Viewpoint") and treated differently.

□ *Contradictories*

To begin the analysis of the relationships between the different kinds of categorical statements, look at the Venn diagrams for the A form and the O
form—reproduced in Figure 5-6. As the upper left diagram shows, the A form
asserts that all members of the S class are in the area where the S and P circles
overlap. But this is just what the O form denies. The asterisk in the Venn
diagram for the O form indicates that not all members of the S class are in
the area of overlap between the S and P circles.

Now look at the Venn diagrams for E-form and I-form statements. The
area of overlap between the S and P circles in the Venn diagram for the E
form is crossed out, indicating that this area is empty. But in the Venn diagram
for the I form, the asterisk in the same area indicates that this region is *not*
empty. Thus, I form denies what E form asserts, and vice versa.

We can conclude the following. The logical relationship between A-form
and O-form statements having the same S and P terms is one of *contradiction*.
The logical relationship between E-form and I-form statements having the
same S and P terms is also one of *contradiction*. Contradictory statements

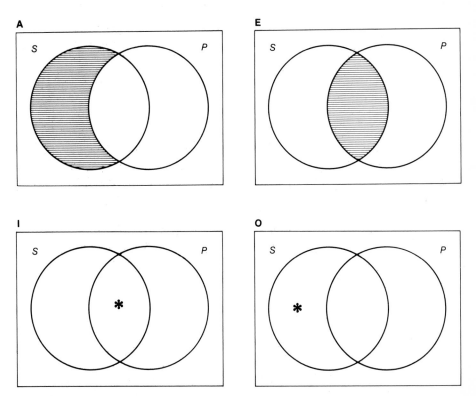

FIGURE 5-6

Relationships between different kinds of categorical statements

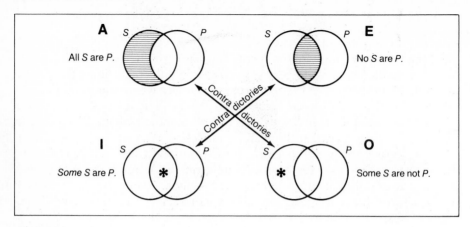

FIGURE 5-7
Relationship between contradictories

cannot both be true at the same time, nor can they both be false at the same time.

> **Contradictory statements are categorical statements related in such a way that if one is true, the other must be false, and if one is false, the other must be true.**

To illustrate the relationship of contradiction, consider the A-form statement "All lifeguards are collegians." If it is true, then the O-form statement, "Some lifeguards are collegians" must be false.[3] And if the A statement is false, then the O statement must be true. Likewise, given the truth of the O statement "Some lifeguards are not collegians," the A statement "All lifeguards are collegians" must be false. And if the O statement is false, then the A statement must be true.

The same relationship holds between the E and I statements. If the E statement "No lifeguards are collegians" is true, then the I statement "Some lifeguards are collegians" is false. And if the E statement is false, then the I statement must be true. In addition, if the I statement is true, the E statement must be false; and if the I statement is false, the E statement must be true.

The relationship between contradictories is illustrated in Figure 5-7. Double-headed arrows are used to indicate that the inference works in both directions: the truth of one statement makes the other statement false, and vice versa.

☐ *Contraries*

A-form and E-form statements are related by *contrariety*. To see this, look first at the Venn diagrams for A form and E form. In the diagram for E form, the

---

[3] For the sake of convenience, we shall continue to refer to a sentence expressing a statement, such as "All lifeguards are collegians," as if it were itself a statement.

area of overlap between the S and P circles is crossed out to indicate that it is an empty region. But this is exactly the same region containing all members of the subject class if the A statement is correct. So if, for example, the A statement "All accountants are mathematicians" is true, the E statement "No accountants are mathematicians" must be false. Likewise, if the E statement "No accountants are mathematicians" is true, the A statement must be false. For if the overlapping area of the S and P circles is empty, then it cannot be the case that all accountants are in this area. Both the A and E statements cannot be true at the same time.

Now suppose that the A statement "All accountants are mathematicians" is *false*. Its being false means that there is at least one accountant who is not a mathematician. (The O statement is true.) But there may or may not be some other accountants who *are* mathematicians. Thus, the truth or falsity of the E statement—"No accountants are mathematicians"—cannot be determined by knowing that the A statement is false.

Similarly, if the E statement is false, then at least one accountant is a mathematician. (The I statement is true.) But we cannot tell whether the A statement is true or false because we do not know whether all the accountants that might exist are in the area where the S and P circles overlap. Thus, if the E statement is false, the truth or falsity of the A statement cannot be determined.

These facts about the A and E statements provide a definition of *contrariety*.

> Two categorical statements are contraries if they are related in such a way that both cannot be true at the same time, but both can be false.

All A and E statements with identical S and identical P terms are contraries.

□ Subcontraries

I and O statements can be related as *subcontraries*. Consider the Venn diagrams in Figure 5-6 for the statements in I form and O form. The Venn diagram for the I statement "Some comedians are neurotic persons" signifies that at least one comedian is in the class of neurotic persons: the area common to both the S and the P circles contains an asterisk. And the Venn diagram for the O statement "Some comedians are not neurotic persons" signifies that at least one comedian is not in the class of neurotic persons: the area outside the P circle contains an asterisk. However, in neither Venn diagram is an area that contains an asterisk shaded. Thus, it is possible for both I and O statements with identical S and identical P terms to be true. Knowing only that some members of the class of comedians are members of the class of neurotic persons, we cannot tell whether some comedians are excluded from the class of neurotic persons; it may be that all comedians are neurotic. In the same vein, knowing only that "Some comedians are not neurotic persons" is true, we cannot tell anything about the truth or falsity of the I statement "Some co-

medians are neurotic persons"; it is still possible that no comedians are neurotic.

Both of the *I*-form and *O*-form examples can be true, but both cannot be false. Given our assumption that at least one comedian exists, if the *I* statement "Some comedians are neurotic persons" is false, then the *O* statement "Some comedians are not neurotic persons" must be true; and if the *O* statement is false, then the *I* statement must be true. Such pairs of statements are called *subcontraries*.

> **Two categorical statements are subcontraries if both cannot be false at the same time but both can be true.**

All *I* and *O* statements with identical *S* and *P* terms are subcontraries.

☐ *Subimplication*

One kind of relationship between *A* and *I* statements and between *E* and *O* statements is called *subimplication*.

> **Subimplication is the process by which the truth of a particular statement is inferred from the truth of its corresponding universal statement.**

Thus, given the assumption that at least one logician exists, if the *A* statement "All logicians are philosophers" is true, then the *I* statement "Some logicians are philosophers" must also be true. Likewise, if the *E* statement "No logicians are philosophers" is true, then the *O* statement "Some logicians are not philosophers" is also true.

However, if the *A* statement "All logicians are philosophers" is false, we cannot determine whether the corresponding *I* statement is true or false: some logicians may be philosophers, or none may be philosophers. And if the *E* statement "No logicians are philosophers" is false, it is impossible to determine the truth value of the corresponding *O* statement: if only some logicians are philosophers, the *O* statement is true; but if all logicians are philosophers, it is false. In subimplication, only the truth of the particular categorical statement can be inferred from the truth of the corresponding universal statement.

☐ *Superimplication*

Another relationship between *I* and *A* statements and between *O* and *E* statements is called *superimplication*.

> **Superimplication is the process by which the falsity of a universal statement is inferred from the falsity of its corresponding particular statement.**

If the *I* statement "Some logicians are philosophers" is false, one can infer that the corresponding *A* statement "All logicians are philosophers" is false.

For if it is false that even one member of the class of logicians is contained in the class of philosophers, it is surely false that every member of the class of logicians is contained in the class of philosophers. Similarly, if the O statement "Some logicians are not philosophers" is false, then some logicians must be philosophers and the E statement "No logicians are philosophers" must also be false.

If one knows only that the I statement "Some logicians are philosophers" is true, however, the truth value of the corresponding A statement is undetermined. All members of the class of logicians may be in the class of philosophers, or only some may be in the class of philosophers. For the same reason, if the O statement "Some logicians are not philosophers" is true, the truth value of the corresponding E statement is also undetermined. In superimplication, only the falsity of the universal statement can be inferred from the falsity of the corresponding particular statement.

The traditional square of opposition that was begun in Figure 5-7 can now be completed. All the possible logical relationships between categorical statements that have identical subject terms and identical predicate terms are represented in Figure 5-8.

The arrows in Figure 5-8 symbolize the inferences that can be based on the four kinds of categorical statements, and the letters T and F stand for true and false. The first letter in each pair stands for the known truth value of one member of a pair of statements, and the second letter indicates what can therefore be inferred about the truth value of the second statement. Thus, if the A statement "All militarists are fanatics" is true, then by contradiction the O statement "Some militarists are not fanatics" is false; by contrariety the E

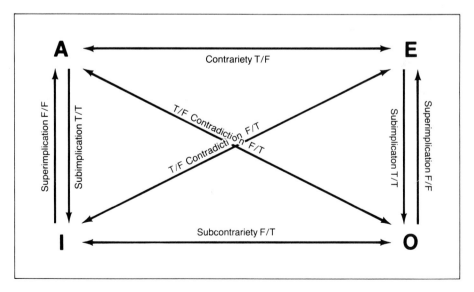

FIGURE 5-8
Traditional square of opposition

TABLE 5-4 *Inferences from the traditional square of opposition*

RELATIONSHIP	INFERENCE
Contradiction $A \longleftrightarrow O$ $E \longleftrightarrow I$	Whatever the known truth value of one statement in a pair, the truth value of the second can be inferred to be exactly opposite to it.
Contrariety $A \longrightarrow E$ $E \longrightarrow A$	If one universal statement is known to be true, the second universal statement can be inferred to be false.
Subcontrariety $I \longrightarrow O$ $O \longrightarrow I$	If a particular statement is known to be false, the second particular statement can be inferred to be true.
Subimplication $A \longrightarrow I$ $E \longrightarrow O$	If a universal statement is known to be true, the corresponding particular statement can be inferred to be true as well.
Superimplication $I \longrightarrow A$ $O \longrightarrow E$	If a particular statement is known to be false, the corresponding universal statement can be inferred to be false as well.

statement "No militarists are fanatics" is false; and by subimplication the *I* statement "Some militarists are fanatics" is true.

If there is only one pair of letters, it means that only one kind of inference can be made. If the A statement is false, then its contradictory "Some militarists are not fanatics" is true; the truth or falsity of its contrary "No militarists are fanatics" is undetermined; and the truth value of its subimplicant "Some militarists are fanatics" is also undetermined.

Table 5-4 contains a summary of the logical relationships illustrated in the traditional square of opposition.

□ *The hypothetical viewpoint*

The logical system considered thus far requires the *existential viewpoint*—the assumption, already mentioned, that the class of things referred to by the subject term of each categorical statement contains at least one member that exists. Use of the traditional square of opposition must be limited when the statements to be analyzed contain subject terms that refer to what are called *empty classes*—classes whose members are fictitious or whose existence is in doubt. For example, the statements "All dragons are fire-breathing serpents," "The present czar of Russia is bald," and "El Dorado is a city of gold" all contain S terms that refer to empty classes. There are no dragons; Russia at present does not have a czar; a city of gold named El Dorado does not exist.

In everyday discourse, we sometimes encounter statements in which the subject terms may or may not refer to empty classes. Suppose, for instance, that a shopkeeper hangs up a sign that says "Shoplifters will be prosecuted to the full extent of the law." It would be unwise to regard this statement from the existential viewpoint because the person who asserts it by posting the sign is surely considering the possibility that the subject class designated in the statement will remain empty. The shopkeeper hopes, by taking a precautionary measure, to avoid the necessity for legal action. The warning should be understood as the assertion that *if* there are shoplifters, then they will be prosecuted to the full extent of the law. This interpretation does not presuppose the existence of at least one member of the class designated by the S term. Indeed, if the existential presupposition is made, the meaning of the statement is distorted.

From the existential viewpoint, if we know the truth of a universal statement we are logically committed to the truth of the corresponding particular statement as well. In this case, the A statement, put into standard form, is "All shoplifters are persons who will be prosecuted to the full extent of the law." But the shopkeeper need not believe in the truth of the I statement "Some shoplifters are persons who will be prosecuted to the full extent of the law." If the sign is effective, there will not be any shoplifters to prosecute.

Now, suppose that we insist on applying the logical relations represented by the traditional square of opposition and there are no shoplifters—that is, the I statement is false. If the I statement is false, then by superimplication the corresponding A statement is false as well. So it must be false that all shoplifters will be prosecuted to the full extent of the law. But this result is unacceptable, because it is still possible that *if* there are shoplifters (in the future), then they will be prosecuted.

In general, when the S class may be empty, A statements are understood to mean "*If* there are any S's, *then* they are P's." Similarly, the E statement "No S are P" is understood as "*If* there are any S's, *then* they are not P's." The need for this interpretation of universal statements in certain contexts was emphasized by the English logician, George Boole (1815–1864). The interpretation is known as the *hypothetical viewpoint*.

The hypothetical viewpoint does not presuppose that the subject classes of universal A and E statements have members, but the interpretation of particular I and O statements always requires that the subject class have at least one member. Consider, for example, the statement "Some shoplifters will be prosecuted." Now suppose there have been no shoplifters whatsoever. Here one would say that the statement is false, because its assertion presupposes that there actually were some shoplifters. In other words, in asserting that at least one S is P, one is saying that *there is* at least one S such that it is P. Similar considerations apply to O form: to say "Some S are not P" is to assert that there is at least one S such that it is not a P.

There is no formal procedure for determining whether statements in A form or E form are best interpreted from the existential or the hypothetical viewpoint. The decision must be made by considering both the context in which the statement is made and general background knowledge. Sometimes the decision depends on whether a statement makes more sense from the hypothetical viewpoint or the existential viewpoint. However, if the hypothetical viewpoint is appropriate, use of the traditional square of opposition is greatly limited.

Not all of the logical relationships in the traditional square of opposition can be maintained from the hypothetical viewpoint.

Indeed, few of the relationships in the square of opposition in Figure 5-8 apply if one adopts the hypothetical viewpoint. Forms A and O, and forms E and I, remain contradictories. However, if there is nothing that is S, the I and O statements, "Some S are P" and "Some S are not P," are both *false*. And since A is the contradictory of O and E is the contradictory of I, "All S are P" and "No S are P" must both be *true*. Thus, from the hypothetical viewpoint, I and O are not subcontraries and A and E are not contraries.

Furthermore, neither subimplication nor superimplication is possible from the hypothetical viewpoint. I and O are both false, so the truth of I cannot be inferred from the truth of A, nor the truth of O from the truth of E. And given that S refers to an empty class, one cannot infer the falsity of either A or E from the falsity of I or O. A and E statements remain true because their contradictories are false.

Thus, in analyzing statements from the hypothetical viewpoint, only the limited version of the square of opposition that appears in Figure 5-7 applies. From this viewpoint, knowing the truth value of a categorical statement allows one to infer only the truth value of its contradictory.

© 1981, *Universal Press Syndicate. Reprinted by permission.*

■ **EXERCISE 5-3**

■ A. Complete the following sentences using the traditional square of opposition (existential viewpoint).

1. Given that *O* is true, *A* is _____, *E* is undetermined, and *I* is _____.
2. Given that *A* is true, *E* is _____, *I* is true, and *O* is _____.
3. Given that *E* is true, *A* is _____, *I* is _____, and *O* is true.
*4. Given that *I* is true, *E* is false, *A* is _____, and *O* is _____.
5. Given that *A* is false, *O* is _____, *E* is _____, and *I* is undetermined.
6. Given that *E* is false, *I* is true, *A* is _____, and *O* is _____.
7. Given that *I* is false, *A* is _____, *E* is true, and *O* is _____.
*8. Given that *O* is false, *E* is _____, *A* is true, and *I* is _____.
9. Given that both *A* and *I* are false, *E* is _____, and *O* is _____.
10. Given that both *A* and *E* are false, *I* is _____, and *O* is _____.

■ B. Using the existential viewpoint, (a) identify the relationship that exists between each pair of categorical statements below. (b) Assuming that the first statement of each pair is true, what can be inferred about the truth value of the second statement? (c) Assuming that the first statement is false, what can be inferred about the truth value of the second statement?

1. All successful businesswomen are assertive persons.
   Some successful businesswomen are assertive persons.
2. Some politicians are not dreamers.
   All politicians are dreamers.
3. Some rock stars are flamboyant persons.
   Some rock stars are not flamboyant persons.
*4. No skunks are household pets.
   Some skunks are household pets.
5. All Preakness winners are colts bred in Maryland.
   No Preakness winners are colts bred in Maryland.
6. Some cases of cancer are not terminal illnesses.
   Some cases of cancer are terminal illnesses.
7. Some professional football players are not sentimental persons.
   No professional football players are sentimental persons.
*8. No desserts are fattening foods.
   All desserts are fattening foods.
9. Some Toyotas are cars made in the United States.
   Some Toyotas are not cars made in the United States.
10. Some persons called "Englishmen" are women.
   No persons called "Englishmen" are women.

■ C. Determine whether the existential viewpoint or the hypothetical viewpoint would be more appropriate for the interpretation of each of the following statements.

1. All Greek gods are the offspring of Zeus.
2. All of Beatrice's children are in school.
3. All bodies freely falling near the surface of the earth fall at 32 feet per second squared.
*4. No conscientious objector will be required to serve in the armed forces of the United States.
5. Poltergeists can be detected by people with extrasensory perception.
6. All of her jewels are emeralds and rubies.
7. World War III will not be won by nuclear armaments.
*8. All bodies cooled to absolute zero will conduct electricity.
9. None of the Old Testament prophets were women.
10. All mountain peaks in the United States higher than 14,000 feet are in Alaska. ■

☐ 5-4. IMMEDIATE INFERENCE

The inferences discussed so far have been concerned only with statements that contain identical subjects and identical predicates. One can also make an inference from a categorical statement to one that does not have exactly the same subject and predicate, assuming that the categorical statements are *logically equivalent*.

> Two categorical statements are logically equivalent if and only if they both necessarily have the same truth value.

Having the same truth value means that if one statement is true, it follows that the other statement is true, and that if one statement is false, it follows that the other is false.
The process of inferring directly from one categorical statement to another is called *immediate inference*.

> Immediate inference is the assumption, without intervening—or "mediating"—premises, that because one categorical statement is true (or false), a logically equivalent categorical statement must also be true (or false).

Two categorical statements are logically equivalent and the inference from one to another is valid only if correctly drawn Venn diagrams for both statements look *exactly* alike. The diagrams show that there are various ways of changing the logical form of a statement without changing its truth value. The procedures for rewriting logically equivalent statements are *conversion, obversion, contraposition,* and *conversion by limitation*. The difference between the existential and hypothetical viewpoints is of importance only in conversion by limitation.

□ *Conversion*

One of the simplest ways to transform a categorical statement is to change it to its *converse* through the process called *conversion*.

Conversion is the switching of the subject and predicate terms of a categorical statement.

Only the converses of *E* and *I* statements are logically equivalent to the original statements. To see that this is so, consider first the *E* statement "No soldiers are police officers." When subject and predicate change places, we have the converse "No police officers are soldiers." The diagrams are exactly the same, confirming that the *E* statement and its converse are equivalent (see Figure 5-9).

The *I* statement "Some soldiers are police officers" has as its converse the statement "Some police officers are soldiers." Again, the Venn diagrams (Figure 5-10) show that conversion leaves the meaning of the statement unchanged. Consequently, both the original *I* statement and its converse have the same truth value.

However, switching the subject and predicate of an *A* statement produces a new statement that is *not* equivalent to the original statement. For example, the *A* statement "All soldiers are police officers" becomes "All police officers are soldiers," which, as Figure 5-11 shows, completely changes the meaning of the original *A* statement. The converse of an *A* statement is an independent statement entirely different from the original.

By converting the *O* statement "Some soldiers are not police officers" we obtain "Some police officers are not soldiers." This, too, is an independent statement. Figure 5-12 shows that an *O* statement and its converse are not logically equivalent.

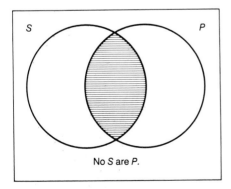

No S are P.

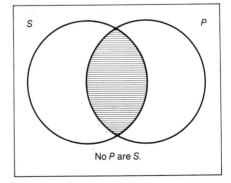

No P are S.

FIGURE 5-9
Conversion of E *form*

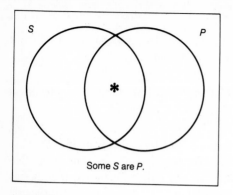 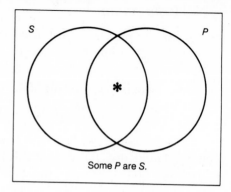

Some S are P.   Some P are S.

FIGURE 5-10
Conversion of I *form*

☐ Obversion

Another way to transform a categorical statement into a new statement that is logically equivalent is through *obversion*.

> **In obversion, the quality of both the statement and the predicate term is changed.**

The obverted form is called the *obverse* of the original statement. The obverse of each of the four forms of categorical statement is logically equivalent to the original statement.

Let us start with the A statement "All senators are patriots." This is a universal affirmative statement, so its obverse is a universal negative statement. Thus, "All senators are . . ." becomes "No senators are . . ." We also negate

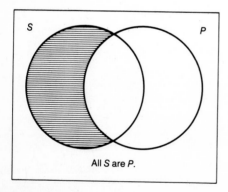 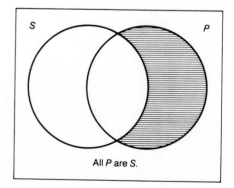

All S are P.   All P are S.

FIGURE 5-11
Conversion of A *form*

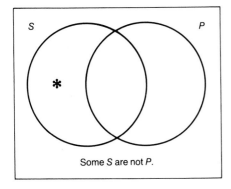 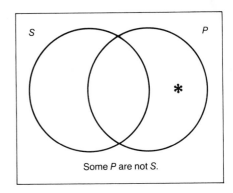

FIGURE 5-12
Conversion of O form

the predicate term, replacing it with its *class complement*—a term that refers to all the things *not* belonging to the original class. The class complement of *patriots* is *nonpatriots*. The quantity of the predicate term, and the subject term, remains unchanged.

The Venn diagrams in Figure 5-13 show that the universal affirmative "All senators are patriots" and its obverse statement "No senators are nonpatriots" are logically equivalent. The diagram for the A statement shows that all S are in the P circle, and the diagram for the E statement *shows the same thing*. In other words, there are no S outside the P circle.[4]

If we start with the E statement "No senators are patriots," we form its obverse by changing its quality from negative to affirmative and, again, by negating the predicate. The result is "All senators are nonpatriots." Here, as before, it can be seen from the Venn diagrams—Figure 5-14—that the original statement and its obverse are equivalent. The diagram on the right shows that all S are outside the P circle—that is, that no S are in the P circle.

Turning to the *I* statement "Some senators are patriots," we form its obverse by changing it from particular affirmative to particular negative and negating the predicate. This produces "Some senators are not nonpatriots," which can be seen in Figure 5-15 to be equivalent to the original statement. The new statement says that some S are not outside the P circle, which is the same thing as saying that some S are inside the P circle.

Finally, turning to the O statement "Some senators are not patriots," we change the statement from particular negative to particular affirmative by changing "Some senators are not . . ." to "Some senators are . . . ." Then, negating the predicate term, we obtain "Some senators are nonpatriots." The

---

[4] It may not seem at first that Venn diagrams can illustrate the relationship between S and non-P. However, since all P are in the circle marked P, non-P is represented as anything outside the P circle. Similarly non-S would be anything outside the S circle.

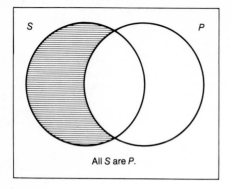

FIGURE 5-13
Obversion of A *form*

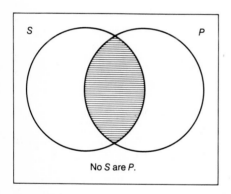

FIGURE 5-14
Obversion of E *form*

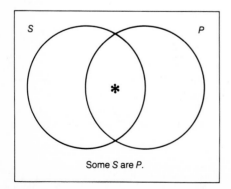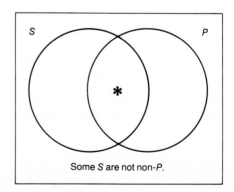

FIGURE 5-15
Obversion of I *form*

Venn diagrams in Figure 5-16 show that the new *I* statement is logically equivalent to the original *O* statement.

Note that the original *O* statement has the negation as part of its copula (the statement as a whole is negative), while the new *I* statement has the negation as part of its predicate term. To help distinguish the two kinds of negation when obverting statements, *non-* is being used to express the negation of the predicate term and *not* is being reserved to express class exclusion (a negative statement).

□ *Contraposition*

Logically equivalent statements can also be obtained through successive operations of obversion and conversion. For example, the *A* statement "All sonnets are poems" can be obverted to "No sonnets are non-poems." That statement can, in turn, be converted to "No non-poems are sonnets," which can in its turn, be obverted to "All non-poems are non-sonnets." Each step in this transformation produces a statement that is logically equivalent to the previous statement, and the final result is called the *contrapositive* of the original statement.

> **In contraposition, the subject and predicate of the original statement trade places, and each is negated.**

The Venn diagrams in Figure 5-17 show that the contrapositive of an *A* statement is logically equivalent to the original.

If we start with the *O* statement "Some sonnets are not poems," obvert it, then convert it, then obvert it again, we arrive at the statement "Some non-poems are not non-sonnets." This, too, is logically equivalent to the original (see Figure 5-18).

Contraposition preserves the meaning of *A* and *O* statements, but not that of *E* and *I* statements. The obverse of the *E* statement "No S are P" is "All S

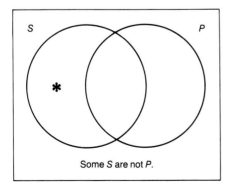

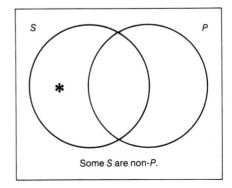

FIGURE 5-16
Obversion of O form

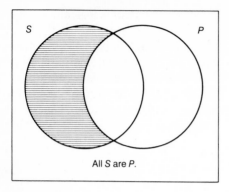

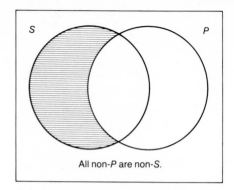

FIGURE 5-17
Contraposition of A *form*

are non-P," which is an A statement, and as we have seen, an A statement is not equivalent to its converse. So the second step, conversion, would produce a statement that was not logically equivalent to the original. Likewise with the I form: in this case the second step involves converting an O statement, and an O statement is not equivalent to its converse. Figures 5-19 and 5-20 show that the contrapositives of E and I statements are entirely independent of the original statements.

□ *Conversion by limitation*

Although the converse of an A statement is not logically equivalent to the original, it is possible through what is called *conversion by limitation* to validly derive an I statement from an A statement.

Conversion by limitation is a process by which an I statement is obtained from

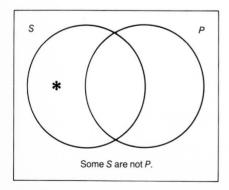

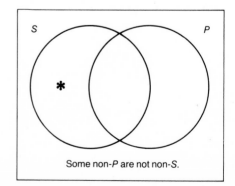

FIGURE 5-18
Contraposition of O *form*

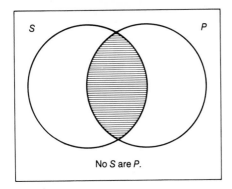

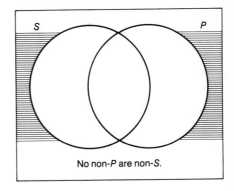

FIGURE 5-19
Contraposition of E *form*

an A statement by switching the S and P terms and changing the quantity of the statement.

From "All saxophonists are performers," we can validly derive "Some performers are saxophonists," as indicated by Figure 5-21. However, this operation is not really an immediate inference: the converse by limitation is not logically equivalent to the original statement but merely implied by it. This is demonstrated by the fact that the Venn diagrams in Figure 5-21 do not look exactly alike. In addition, conversion by limitation is legitimate only from the existential point of view, because at least one member of the S class (saxophonists in this case) must be presupposed.

□ *Characteristics of immediate inference*

The essential aspects of the immediate inferences of conversion, obversion, contraposition, and conversion by limitation are summarized in Table 5-5. But

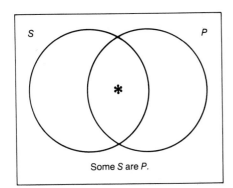

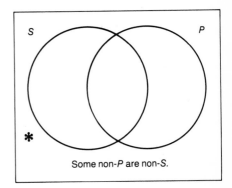

FIGURE 5-20
Contraposition of I *form*

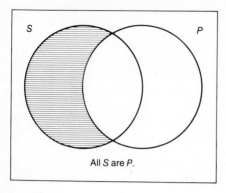
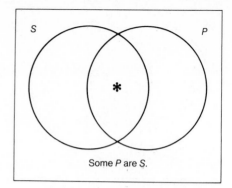

All S are P.   Some P are S.

FIGURE 5-21
Conversion by limitation

when examining the table and when working on the exercises for this section, keep in mind the following points about the various procedures.

1. *The operations of conversion, obversion, and contraposition all involve symmetrical relations between statements.* In other words, if statement *r* is the converse of statement *q*, then *q* is the converse of *r*. Similarly, if *r* is the obverse of *q*, *q* is the obverse of *r*. The symmetry of these relations can be demonstrated by taking the converse, obverse, or contrapositive of a statement and subjecting it to the same operation of immediate inference by which it was obtained in the first place.

Note, however, that the relation between an *A* statement and its converse by limitation is *asymmetrical*. If *r* is the converse by limitation of *q*, then *q* never is the converse by limitation of *r*. One could not validly derive the *A* statement "All saxophonists are performers" from the *I* statement "Some performers are saxophonists."

2. *A double negative can be changed to a positive, provided both negatives*

TABLE 5-5 *Operations of immediate inference*

OPERATION	PROCESS	VALID INFERENCE
Conversion	Switch *S* and *P* terms	*E* converted *I* converted
Obversion	Change quality and negate *P* term	*A* obverted to *E* *E* obverted to *A* *I* obverted to *O* *O* obverted to *I*
Contraposition	Switch and negate both *S* and *P* terms	*A* contraposed *O* contraposed
Conversion by Limitation	Change quantity and switch *S* and *P* terms	*A* converted to *I*

modify the same form. If we have "No S are non-*P*," for example, and we obvert this statement to "All S are non–non-*P*," we are then justified in canceling the double negation in the predicate and writing "All S are *P*." By contrast, the negatives in "No non-S are *P*" do not cancel because *non-* qualifies the subject term while *no* qualifies the whole statement. "No non-S are *P*" is *not* equivalent to "All S are *P*."

3. *Changing the quality of a categorical statement by obversion is not the same thing as negating the statement.* Obversion changes a statement into another that is logically equivalent, thereby preserving its initial truth value. Thus, if "All S are *P*" is true, its obverse, "No S are non-*P*," must also be true. However, negating a statement without also changing the quality of the predicate term changes its truth value. Thus, to negate "All S are *P*" is not to obvert it but to say, "It is not the case that all S are *P*," or to say (what amounts to the same thing) that its contradictory, "Some S are not *P*" (O form), is true.

4. *When obverting or contraposing a statement, one must always replace the negated term with its class complement, or contradictory.* Thus, to obtain the obverse of "Some contestants are winners," one must replace *winners* with a term referring to the class containing everything except winners. The complement of *winners* is *nonwinners*, not *losers*; for although not everyone or everything is either a winner or a loser, absolutely everything is either a winner or a nonwinner.

Many pairs of terms—for example, *moral* and *immoral*, *courageous* and *cowardly*, *gentle* and *harsh*, *generous* and *stingy*, *loyal* and *disloyal*, and *noble* and *base*—are not contradictories, or complements, but contraries. No one is both generous and stingy (at the same time and with respect to the same action), but this does not mean that the terms are contradictories. Not everyone, and certainly not everything, is either one or the other. For this reason, *nongenerous* rather than *stingy* is the complement of *generous*.

In addition, care must be exercised in negating subject and predicate terms that refer to classes of indefinite scope and size—that is, when it is not clear how restrictive the class term was intended to be. In obverting, "No philosophy majors are lazy students," for instance, we would negate the predicate term, *lazy students*, as a whole. But what exactly is the class complement of the predicate term? Is it *nonlazy students*—that is, students who are not lazy— or *everything that is not a lazy student*, including *lazy nonstudents*? Of these two possibilities, *nonlazy students* seems more probable because the subject term, *philosophy majors*, picks out a subclass of students. It is unlikely that the original statement was meant to imply that philosophy majors are nonstudents. Thus, "All philosophy majors are nonlazy students" seems to be the correct obversion, rather than "All philosophy majors are lazy nonstudents."

■ **EXERCISE 5-4**

■ A. Write the converses of 1 through 5, the obverses of statements 6 through 15, and the contrapositives of statements 16 through 20.

1. Some sports enthusiasts are college professors.

2. Some sailors are pirates.

3. No professional generals are philosophers.

*4. Some nonsmokers are nondrinkers.

5. No nonresidents are voters.

6. Some screen stars are pessimists.

7. Some vegetarians are pacifists.

*8. No belligerents are noncombatants.

9. All radicals are revolutionaries.

10. No scientists are existentialists.

11. All foreigners are non-Americans.

*12. Some basketball players are not tall guards.

13. No diplomats are unskillful amateurs.

14. Some acts of war are infamous crimes.

15. No impressionist painters are unrecognized masters.

*16. All schizophrenics are psychotics.

17. Some journalists are not reporters.

18. Some nonaddicts are not nonsmokers.

19. All unadulterated meats are poisonous foods.

*20. Some nonhumans are not unintelligent beings.

■ B. If the statements *a* through *e* below are all true, what, if anything, can be determined about the truth or falsity of each of the subsequent statements? (Answer *true, false,* or *nothing.*) Justify each answer.

(a) No puritans are witches.

(b) Some martyrs are nonsaints.

(c) No women are witches.

(d) All persons burned at the stake are scapegoats.

(e) Some scapegoats are martyrs.

1. No witches are puritans.

2. Some martyrs are not saints.

3. Some nonmartyrs are nonscapegoats.

*4. All scapegoats are persons burned at the stake.

5. Some nonsaints are not nonmartyrs.

6. Some saints are not martyrs.

7. All puritans are nonwitches.

*8. Some martyrs are scapegoats.

9. No nonwitches are nonwomen.

10. No witches are women.

11. Some scapegoats are persons burned at the stake.

*12. Some saints are puritans.

13. All women are nonwitches.

14. No nonsaints are women.

15. No nonwitches are nonpuritans.   ∎

□ 5-5. PRACTICAL APPLICATIONS

Understanding the logical properties of categorical statements makes it possible to test the validity of the large number of arguments called *categorical syllogisms*. Such arguments, which will be discussed in detail in Chapter 6, consist of two categorical statements as premises and a third categorical statement as the derived conclusion. The ability to test the validity of categorical syllogisms will be an important advance in argument analysis.

In addition, other benefits accrue from the study of categorical statements, especially from understanding the square of opposition and the process of immediate inference. One benefit is the increased capacity to understand information formulated in terms of class relations and to communicate such information with precision. Another is an increased ability to resolve disputes arising from misunderstanding of the logical relations between categorical statements.

Although not every statement can be translated into one or another of the four categorical forms (*A*, *E*, *I*, and *O*), a large number can be translated. But any assertion about class inclusion or exclusion, even if it does not appear as part of a categorical syllogism, should be translated, at least mentally, into one of the standard forms. Doing so will clarify the meaning of the statement by making the class relationships it presents clearer and more straightforward. It should also help determine whether the statement is necessary or empirical and, if empirical, what sort of evidence would be needed to support it.

□ *Further aspects of translation*

Certain common grammatical constructions can actually obscure the quantity or quality of the categorical statements that the sentences express. Knowing the proper interpretations of these familiar but bothersome constructions will facilitate translating sentences into standard form.

□ "ALL . . . ARE NOT" AND "NOT ALL"

Statements that employ the expressions "All . . . are not" and "Not all" are negative in quality but are ambiguous in quantity. Usually, such statements are correctly translated into *O* form. Thus, someone who says "Not all sports fans love baseball" probably means "Some sports fans are not people who love baseball." It is improbable that the speaker means to say that *no* sports fans love baseball, which would be expressed in *E* form. Similarly, someone who says "All students are not going to the game" probably does not mean that none are going ("No *S* are *P*") but rather that some are not going ("Some *S* are not *P*"). The function of the *not* in this statement is to *contradict* the universal affirmative statement, "All students are going to the game."

The context or background information, however, may make it clear that *E* is the appropriate categorical form. Given what is known about reptiles, for example, "All reptiles are not warm-blooded animals" should become the *E* statement "No reptiles are warm-blooded animals." Likewise, "All members of the Rockefeller family are not on welfare" is best interpreted as *E* form: "No members of the Rockefeller family are persons on welfare."

☐ "FEW" AND "A FEW"

A sentence like "Few men are truly honest" may at first seem to be expressing partial inclusion (*I* form), but what it really means is that "Most men are not truly honest," or partial exclusion (*O* form). Similarly, "Few man are not truly honest" is meant to convey the idea that "Most men are truly honest," or partial inclusion (*I* form). Therefore, when translating statements containing *few*, rewrite the sentence using the particular quantifier (*some*) and changing the quality of the relationship between the subject and predicate terms. Thus, "Few children smoke" becomes "Some children are not persons who smoke," and "Few adults do not drive automobiles" becomes "Some adults are persons who drive automobiles."

The expression *a few* differs in meaning from *few*, for it simply indicates the quantifier *some*. Hence, statements containing *a few* are translated by using the particular quantifier *some* and keeping the original relationship between the terms, as shown in the following examples:

A few professors are short-tempered
Some professors are short-tempered persons.
A few professors are not pusillanimous
Some professors are not pusillanimous persons.

☐ RADICAL TRANSLATION

Some statements that look quite unlike categorical statements can still be translated into one of the four categorical forms by adding references to time, place, occasion, or circumstance. For example, "Whenever it rains, it pours" does not appear to be categorical. But if we think of it as expressing a statement about times, it can become "All times when it rains are times when it pours." Similarly, "The buses don't run on time when it snows" becomes "All occasions on which it snows are occasions on which the buses don't run on time." The statement "Dishonesty is reprehensible" can become "All cases of dishonesty are cases of reprehensible behavior."

☐ "NONE BUT," "NONE EXCEPT," AND "ALONE"

Statements constructed with the expressions "None but," "None except," and "alone" are *exclusive* statements. For example, *none but* in "None but students may attend the game" indicates that the predicate applies exclusively to the subject. This statement is properly translated as "All persons who may attend the game are students." The same translation applies to the following two statements:

> None except students may attend the game.
> Students alone may attend the game.

This shows that the *grammatical* subject is really the *logical* predicate, and the order of the class names must be changed in putting the expression into standard form.

☐ "ONLY"

"Only," like "none but" and "none except," usually serves to make a statement exclusive. Thus, "Only students may attend the game" has the same meaning as "None but students may attend the game," and it should be translated in the same way.

But one must be careful not to assume more than the statement actually says. For example, a sign "Employees Only" on a door no doubt means something like "Only employees may enter this room"—in categorical form, "All persons who may enter this room are employees." But would it also be correct to interpret the sign as "All employees are people who may enter this room"? In this somewhat special case, it would be correct. But usually it is not permissible to interpret "Only S are P" as "All S are P." For example, the sentence "Only state residents will receive financial aid" conveys the information that all who receive financial aid are state residents, but it does *not* say that all state residents will receive financial aid.

There are two cases in which the word *only* does not function to make a statement exclusive. The expression *the only* simply introduces the subject term. So one does not translate the statement "The only people who were invited to my party are friends" by reversing the subject and predicate terms. In addition, a sentence in which the word *some* follows *only* requires both an *I* and an *O* statement for the rendering of its complete meaning. Thus, "Only some women pledge sororities" becomes "Some women are persons who pledge sororities" *and* "Some women are not persons who pledge sororities."

☐ "ALL EXCEPT," "ALL BUT," AND "UNLESS"

The expressions "All . . . except," "All but," and "unless" signify a *negative* subject term. Sentences containing them are translated as "All non-S are P." Examples of such sentences are

> All except aliens are eligible to vote.
> All but aliens are eligible to vote.
> Anyone is eligible to vote unless he or she is an alien.

All of these are translated as "All nonaliens are persons eligible to vote."

Sentences such as these *suggest* more than they actually express. It is tempting to translate the examples as "No aliens are eligible to vote," but this would be incorrect, for although the examples specify that nonaliens are in the class of eligible voters, they do *not* say that aliens are excluded from this class. (It should not be assumed that eligibility to vote pertains to political office.) Similarly, it is tempting to assume that the sentence "Everyone in the class except Carol preferred to postpone the test" conveys the information that Carol preferred not to postpone the test. However, it is possible that Carol was the only member absent at the time the class's opinion was determined and that she would have voted for postponement had she been present. Logically speaking, no information about the eligibility of aliens or about Carol's preferences is conveyed by the sentences above.

Note that the position of the word *unless* does not affect the meaning of a sentence. For example, "Unless excused, every student must attend class" and "Every student must attend class unless excused" express exactly the same statement and are translated as "All unexcused students are students who must attend class." Generally, the word or words immediately following *unless* express the first term of the categorical statement—the subject term—and must be negated.

Also note that *all except* and *all but* have a different meaning from *none except* and *none but*. This is illustrated by the following pairs of sentences:

All except students are eligible players.
All but students are eligible players.
None except students are eligible players.
None but students are eligible players.

The second pair, but not the first pair, translate into "All eligible players are students."

□ *Disputes over categorical statements*

Understanding the logic of categorical statements permits us to resolve disputes over the meanings of such assertions and their logical implications—disputes that are as vexing as they are common. For example, suppose you overhear the following dispute between two people, Joe and Fran:

JOE: Passions always interfere with reason. Hence, everything that interferes with reason is a passion.

FRAN: No, that can't be right. Even if it's true that passions always interfere with reason, the most you are entitled to infer is that some things that interfere with reason are passions. Other things may also hinder clear thinking.

Joe and Fran disagree over the meaning of Joe's first utterance, "Passions always interfere with reason." But underlying this disagreement is a logical error on Joe's part. To see this, translate his first assertion into standard A form: "All passions are things that interfere with reason." Once Joe's second assertion is also translated—"All things that interfere with reason are passions"—it can be seen that he has attempted to convert the original A statement, apparently believing that the assertions are equivalent. But as shown in Section 5-4, the conversion of A form is not valid immediate inference.

Fran is on the right track. She recognizes that if Joe switches the subject and predicate terms, he can infer only an *I* statement from the original A form. Using conversion by limitation, Joe can obtain a statement that will be true if the original claim is true.

■ EXERCISE 5-5

■ A. The following are examples of disputes involving mistakes over the logic of categorical statements. Answer the questions that appear at the end of each dialogue.

1. JOE: No utopian conception of a state provides a practical plan for action.
FRED: It follows, therefore, that since some utopian conceptions of a state are not practical, some other utopian conceptions are practical plans for action.
JANE: Fred is wrong because what Joe says is true, and therefore, all utopian conceptions of a state are impractical.
In your judgment, which of the three speakers has reasoned illogically? Why?

2. MAY: Some of the social reforms that we desire have no chance of being realized. Therefore, some things that have a chance of being realized are not the social reforms that we desire.
TED: Well, I think your conclusion is probably true, but it's not supported by the fact that some of the social reforms we desire have no chance of being realized.
Is Ted correct or incorrect? Why?

3. TED: Socialists do advocate a planned economy, and Brett advocates a planned economy, but that doesn't mean Brett is a Socialist.
LUCY: Brett must be a Socialist since it's true that Socialists advocate a planned economy and therefore that all persons who advocate a planned economy are Socialists.
Whose view is correct? Why?

*4. SUE: Can you believe Fred? He said that since death comes to all who wait, those who do not wait will not die. But that's nonsense, so Fred must have made a mistake.
LOU: You shouldn't be so quick to discard Fred's insight. He reached his conclusion through a correct operation of immediate inference. Thus, what he says must be true even if it is hard to understand. I think we should study more philosophy to discover how one can avoid waiting—the march of time—you know, get "outside" of time somehow. Therein lies the secret of immortality.
Which of these two positions is more reasonable? Why?

5. SAM: It's true that all humans are living beings entitled to relief from pain and suffering. But it follows from this that all nonhumans are living beings who are not entitled to relief from pain and suffering. What's the point, then, of your animal-rights crusade?
JANE: For Pete's sake, Sam, try to avoid gross logical errors! I certainly agree that all humans are living beings entitled to relief from pain and suffering. But this truth allows

you to deduce only that all nonliving beings not entitled to relief from pain and suffering are nonhumans. No one would doubt that we don't think of inanimate objects such as rocks and stars as having rights to humane treatment. But there are also nonhuman living beings who are entitled to relief from pain and suffering, namely, animals.

Whose reasoning is more logical, Sam's or Jane's? Why?

6. CUSTOMS OFFICER: Customs clearance is not taking as long as it may seem. All of the passengers whose passports have been checked for landing are already waiting in the lounge area of the promenade deck.

CAPTAIN: Thank goodness! My stewards have swept all passenger areas and have had every passenger go to the promenade deck lounge. And since, as you say, all the passengers there have had their passports cleared, we can proceed to have them disembark at once. We'll make that noon sailing deadline after all!

CUSTOMS OFFICER: But there are some in the lounge who haven't been examined yet.

CAPTAIN: Confound it, man, don't you even know what you are talking about?

Who is being more logical, the captain or the customs officer? Why?

■ B. Interpreting each of the following statements in the way most likely to be intended, translate it into proper categorical form.

1. Only wise individuals tell no lies.
2. A few latecomers missed the excitement.
3. He who hesitates is lost.
*4. Few professors wear beards.
5. All who have fame and fortune are not happy.
6. Only rats and humans will kill members of their own species.
7. Wherever they go, I go too.
*8. Whenever one is angry, one's adrenaline production increases.
9. Wellington defeated Napoleon at Waterloo.
10. Foolish are they who reason from false premises.
11. Thinking that is not creative is not effective.
*12. The only survivors were young children.
13. Blessed is the peacemaker.
14. They always arrive on time.
15. The sincere and trustful alone are to be respected.
*16. Nobody would speak that way, unless he or she were a boor.
17. Everyone at the party except Sally danced the tango.
18. Sheep only produce wool.
19. Wills signed by two witnesses but not notarized are not enforceable instruments of the law.
*20. Those who have not been told that they have a terminal illness cannot imagine how terrifying that news can be.
21. Mortally wounded lay General "Stonewall" Jackson.
22. Some tasty foods are not fattening.
23. The woman seen in the trench coat was not a spy.

*24. A Trinity graduate does not associate with thieves.

25. Only some college students are gentlefolk.

■ C. Rewrite each of the following arguments so that (a) the premises and conclusion are all expressed as categorical statements, and (b) the premises are followed by the conclusion. (*Hint:* To find the proper subject and predicate terms for the premises, first translate the conclusion.)

1. Most lifeguards are good swimmers; skindivers are sometimes lifeguards, so there are skindivers who are good swimmers.

2. A beach enthusiast is never uncomfortable in the sun because sun-worshipers are generally beach enthusiasts and only those who are comfortable in the sun are sun-worshipers.

3. Nothing is worthwhile unless it is moral, and there are worthwhile causes; and hence there are moral causes.

*4. It follows that some Americans are coffee lovers from the fact that no tea lovers are coffee lovers and some Americans are not tea lovers.

5. All lawyers are logicians, so no engineers are logicians, because you will not find an engineer who is also a lawyer.

6. Plagiarism is dishonest because whatever involves deliberate misrepresentation is dishonest and plagiarism involves a deliberate misrepresentation.

7. Not all existentialists are atheists. Marcel is an existentialist; thus Marcel is not an atheist.

*8. Only gullible people are fans of the book *Chariots of the Gods?* Therefore, fans of the book *Chariots of the Gods?* are people who believe in astronaut-gods, since only gullible people believe in astronaut-gods.

9. Misogynists dislike women; hence, they are neurotic.

10. Every textbook is a book intended for careful study. A few reference books are textbooks. Therefore, a few reference books are books intended for careful study. ■

Categorical syllogisms

Immediate inference based on the traditional square of opposition, explained in Chapter 5, involves inference from one categorical statement to an equivalent categorical statement. Together, the statements form a simple argument—one that consists of a conclusion and a single premise.

We now consider arguments consisting of three categorical statements: a conclusion and two premises. Such an argument is called a *categorical syllogism*.

> **A categorical syllogism is a deductive argument that consists of three categorical statements containing three terms in all, each term appearing in two different statements.**

In a categorical syllogism, the conclusion is drawn from the two premises by means of a "mediating" third, or middle, term that appears in both premises. The subject class of the conclusion is asserted to be included in or excluded from the predicate class, depending upon the relations of both S and P classes to a third class designated by the middle, or M, term.

☐ 6-1. MOOD AND FIGURE

To identify and evaluate the inference from premises to conclusion in a categorical syllogism, one must put the syllogism into standard categorical form. Each statement must, if necessary, be rephrased in standard form. The next step is to identify the conclusion.

As an illustration, consider the following argument:

All utopians are social reformers, and since no social reformers are pacifists, it follows that no utopians are pacifists.

The conclusion, written in standard form, is "No utopians are pacifists." The term appearing as the predicate of the conclusion (*pacifists*) is called the *major term* of the syllogism, and the premise containing the major term is called the *major premise*. The term appearing as the subject of the conclusion (*utopians*) is the *minor term*, and the premise containing this term is the *minor premise*. The third term (*social reformers*), which appears in both premises but not the conclusion, is called the *middle term.*

Presented in standard form, with the major premise first, the minor premise second, and the conclusion last, the argument is as follows:

> **No social reformers are pacifists.**
> **All utopians are social reformers.**
> _____
> **No utopians are pacifists.**

The line preceding the third statement serves to identify it as the conclusion. Often in logic the conclusion is preceded by the mathematical symbol ∴ or by the word *therefore*.

Note that the major premise of the argument is an *E* statement, its minor premise is an *A* statement, and its conclusion is an *E* statement. The three letters, listed in the order of the statements they represent—in this case, *EAE*—make up what is called the *mood* of the syllogism.

> **The mood of a syllogism is the combination of categorical forms of its statements when the statements are arranged in standard order (major premise, minor premise, conclusion).**

Allowing the letter *P* to stand for the major term (predicate of the conclusion), *S* for the minor term (subject of the conclusion), and *M* for the middle term (term occurring in both premises), we can represent the above syllogism schematically as follows:

> **No *M* are *P.***
> **All *S* are *M.***
> _____
> **No *S* are *P.***

The arrangement of the three terms within the statements in which they occur forms a pattern called the *figure* of the syllogism.

> **The figure of a syllogism is the arrangement of the middle term in the premises.**

There are four possible arrangements of the middle term, or four different figures, as shown in Table 6-1. You will see from the table that the sample syllogism is in the figure on p. 166. An amusing way to remember which figure is which is to think of the middle terms as outlining the front of a shirt collar.

The validity of a categorical syllogism depends on its logical form, and some combinations of mood and figure are known to be valid forms. So iden-

TABLE 6-1 *The four figures*

FIGURE 1		FIGURE 2		FIGURE 3		FIGURE 4	
M	*P*	*P*	*M*	*M*	*P*	*P*	*M*
S	*M*	*S*	*M*	*M*	*S*	*M*	*S*
S	*P*	*S*	*P*	*S*	*P*	*S*	*P*

tifying the mood and figure of a syllogism is a step toward determining its validity—*if* one already knows which forms are valid.

There are 256 syllogistic forms in all: four possible types of statement (A, E, I, O) for each of the two premises and the conclusion (4 × 4 × 4 = 64), and four possible arrangements of the terms within the statements (64 × 4 = 256). Through the ages, various procedures have been followed in determining which of the 256 forms are valid.

The least efficient of these procedures was the first one developed. Ancient and medieval logicians examined each of the 256 possible forms to see whether a specific argument could be construed that would have true premises and a false conclusion. Because (as discussed in Section 2-2) it is not possible for a valid deductive argument to have true premises and a false conclusion, a logical form was known to be invalid if it was possible to produce a single argument of that form having true premises and a false conclusion. Logicians were able to produce such counterexamples for all of the 256 forms except the 24 in Table 6-2. So they concluded that only syllogisms in these 24 forms were valid.

In early discussions of the syllogism, an existential viewpoint was always adopted, for the importance of the distinction between the existential and hypothetical viewpoints was not recognized by philosophers. From the hypothetical viewpoint, however, only 15 forms are valid. Those identified by asterisks in the table require that the existential viewpoint be taken.

As an aid in memorizing the valid forms, medieval logicians assigned them names, the vowels in the name indicating the mood of the form. Thus, AAA in the first figure was called *Barbara*, EAE in the second figure was called

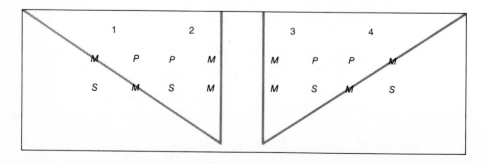

TABLE 6-2 *Moods and figures of valid syllogisms*

FIGURE 1	FIGURE 2	FIGURE 3	FIGURE 4
AAA	*EAE*	*AAI**	*AAI**
EAE	*AEE*	*IAI*	*AEE*
AII	*EIO*	*AII*	*IAI*
EIO	*AOO*	*EAO**	*EAO**
AAI*	*AEO**	*OAO*	*EIO*
EAO*	*EAO**	*EIO*	*AEO**

* A valid form only if the existential viewpoint is assumed.

Cesare, and so on. The names were woven into a Latin verse,[1] which students learned to recite:

> Barbara, Celarent, Darii, Ferioque *prioris*;
> Cesare, Camestres, Testino, Baroco *secundae*;
> *Tertia* Darapti, Disamis, Datisi, Felapton,
> Bocardo, Ferison, *habet*; *quarta in super addit*
> Bramantip, Camenes, Dimaris, Fesapo, Fresison.

One could memorize these lines of verse or keep Table 6-2 handy and check actual arguments against the list to see whether they matched any of the valid forms. But while these procedures are colorful, they are also cumbersome. It is both more efficient and more enlightening to adopt a procedure for checking validity that explains *why* a particular argument is valid or invalid. One such alternative procedure involves using Venn diagrams.

■ **EXERCISE 6-1**

The following examples require the construction of valid syllogisms.

   1. Construct a valid syllogism in mood *EAE*, figure 2, using the terms *bronco-busters, vegetarians,* and *pacifists.*

   2. Construct a valid syllogism in mood *EIO*, figure 2, using the terms *captains of industry, people who hold Ph.D.'s,* and *millionaires.*

---

[1] The verse omits *AAI* and *EAO* in the first figure, *AEO* and *EAO* in the second, and *AEO* in the fourth. Although medieval logicians recognized these five forms as valid, they regarded them as "weakened" forms. In each of the five cases, a particular conclusion is drawn from premises from which a universal conclusion can validly be derived. The logicians thought it pointless to derive a particular conclusion when the "stronger" universal conclusion could be derived instead.

3. Construct a valid syllogism in mood *EIO*, figure 1, using the terms *college professors, members of Reverend Moon's church*, and *deluded spiritualists.*

***4.** Construct a valid syllogism in mood *AII*, figure 1, using the terms *professional basketball players, people who are overpaid for their talents*, and *people who are greatly admired.*

5. Construct a valid syllogism in mood *OAO*, figure 3, using the terms *college freshmen, persons prepared for college*, and *persons who have made a major investment in their future.*

6. Construct a valid syllogism in mood *IAI*, figure 3, using the terms *criminals, persons who were unloved children*, and *people who cannot form intimate personal relationships.*

7. Construct a valid syllogism in mood *EIO*, figure 4, using the terms *rock-star groupies, people with musical ability*, and *jazz musicians.*

***8.** Construct a valid syllogism in mood *AOO*, figure 2, using the terms *Christian Scientists, believers in the power of prayer*, and *social scientists.*

9. Construct a valid syllogism in mood *IAI*, figure 4, using the terms *marines, stoics*, and *people who believe emotion is a sign of weakness.*

10. Construct a valid syllogism in mood *AAA*, figure 1, using the terms *logic students, persons who can use symbols*, and *persons capable of abstract reasoning.* ■

□ 6-2. THE VENN-DIAGRAM TEST FOR VALIDITY

The Venn diagrams studied in Chapter 5 illustrate the relations between two terms, so they contain only two overlapping circles. In a categorical syllogism, the statements contain a total of three different terms (*S, P,* and *M*), so three overlapping circles are needed (see Figure 6-1).

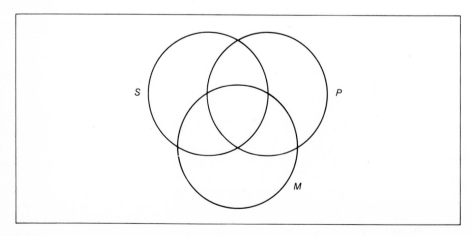

FIGURE 6-1

Venn diagram for a categorical syllogism

To test the validity of a syllogism, we mark the diagram to illustrate the statements in the premises. If the diagram is drawn correctly and the argument is valid, the diagram will exactly represent the conclusion. If the argument is invalid, the diagram will not represent the conclusion. Since only the premises are diagrammed, it may seem odd that the completed diagram should picture the conclusion. But remember that we are working with *deductive* arguments, and deduction does not go beyond the evidence provided in the premises to new information. Deductive arguments make relations that are *implicit* in the premises *explicit* in the conclusion—they show what also must be true if the premises of the argument are true.

Let us first diagram the argument given as an example in Section 6-1:

No social reformers are pacifists.
All utopians are social reformers.

No utopians are pacifists.

As shown by Figure 6-2, drawing three overlapping circles produces a diagram that has eight subdivisions, or regions. These represent all possible subclasses formed by the three classes involved. Thus, region 1 is reserved for utopians who are not pacifists and not social reformers. Region 2 contains utopians who are pacifists but not social reformers. Region 3 contains pacifists who are not utopians and not social reformers. In region 4 are found utopians who are social reformers but not pacifists. Region 5 is the location of social reformers who are both utopians and pacifists. Region 6 contains social reformers who are pacifists but not utopians. In region 7 social reformers who are neither utopians nor pacifists are found. Finally, region 8 is the location of those who are neither social reformers nor utopians nor pacifists.

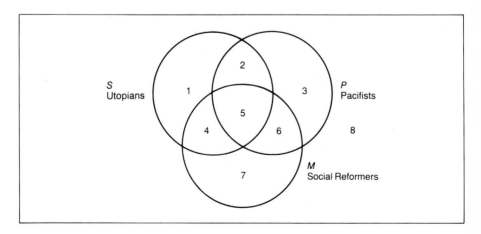

FIGURE 6-2
Eight regions of a Venn diagram for a categorical syllogism

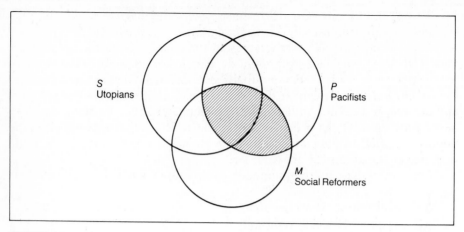

FIGURE 6-3

The major premise of the syllogism is the assertion that no social reformers are pacifists. This means that none who are in the social-reformer circle are in the pacifist circle. To show this on the diagram, we cross out regions 5 and 6 (Figure 6-3). The minor premise is that all utopians are social reformers, which means that all those who are in the utopian circle are in the social reformer circle as well. Consequently, regions 1 and 2 must be crossed out to indicate that these areas are also empty.

The resulting diagram (Figure 6-4) is a "picture" of the assertion that no utopians are pacifists. Region 2 and region 5—the only regions in which both utopians and pacifists could be included—have been crossed out to indicate that they are empty. So, the conclusion has been shown to follow validly from the premises: the diagram is an accurate representation of the conclusion.

To save time and avoid error when using Venn diagrams to test syllogisms,

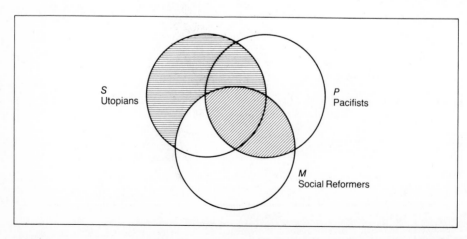

FIGURE 6-4

one should follow a uniform procedure. As mentioned at the beginning of this section, the first steps are to identify the premises and the conclusion and to put the syllogism into standard form. It is important to identify the premises and conclusion correctly because mistaking the conclusion for a premise will produce the diagram for an argument that is entirely different from the one to be tested.

The same circles should always be used for the subject, predicate, and middle terms, and the arrangement shown in Figure 6-1 will be used throughout this book. Thus, the circle on the upper left represents the class named by the subject term (remember that the *S* term is identified as the subject, or minor term, of the conclusion). The circle on the upper right is for the *P* class (identified as the predicate, or the major term, of the conclusion). And the third circle, at the bottom, represents the class named by the middle term (which occurs in both premises but not in the conclusion). Always draw the three circles—creating eight distinct regions—*before* beginning to shade or add other marks to the circles.

Let us now apply the Venn-diagram test to another argument:

> Some women who vote for liberal Democrats are not supporters of the Equal Rights Amendment because no women who describe themselves as housewives are supporters of the Equal Rights Amendment, and some women who describe themselves as housewives vote for liberal Democrats.

Here the conclusion of the argument is the very first statement. And when the argument is put into standard form, it turns out to be in mood *EIO*, figure 3:

> **No women who describe themselves as housewives are supporters of the Equal Rights Amendment.** No *M* are *P*. *E* form
>
> **Some women who describe themselves as housewives are women who vote for liberal Democrats.** Some *M* are *S*. *I* form
>
> ---
>
> **Some women who vote for liberal Democrats are not supporters of the Equal Rights Amendent.** Some *S* are not *P*. *O* form

The major premise tells us that the overlap between the circle for women who describe themselves as housewives and the circle for supporters of the Equal Rights Amendment is empty. So we cross out this region of the diagram (Figure 6-5). The minor premise tells us that there is at least one woman who describes herself as a housewife and who votes for liberal Democrats. To show this, we place an asterisk in the part of the overlap between the housewives and voters circles that was not crossed out. The result (Figure 6-6) exactly represents the conclusion, which means that the argument is valid.

When a particular statement is to be diagramed, it is sometimes unclear into which of the eight regions an asterisk should be placed. One way to indicate the uncertainty is by drawing a bar through the regions in question.

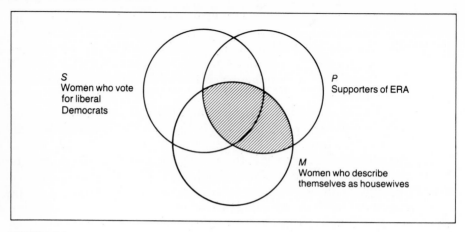

FIGURE 6-5

Consider, for example, the following argument:

Some rodeo stars are women.

All rodeo stars are people who yearn for the days when the West was wild.

Therefore, some people who yearn for the days when the West was wild are women.

This syllogism is in mood *IAI*, figure 3. The major premise ("Some rodeo stars are women") is a particular statement, which means that an asterisk should go somewhere in the part of the rodeo-star circle that overlaps the circle for women. But this area contains two regions, 5 and 6, and the asterisk could

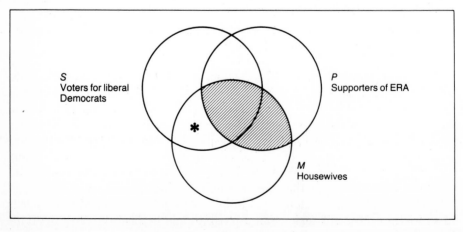

FIGURE 6-6

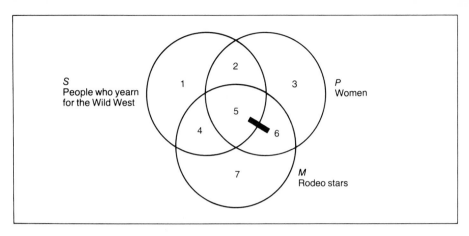

FIGURE 6-7

belong in either one. So instead of using an asterisk to diagram this premise, we draw a bar through regions 5 and 6 (Figure 6-7). The bar indicates that one or the other region contains one or more female rodeo stars.

When the minor premise ("All rodeo stars are people who yearn for the days when the West was wild") is diagramed, all of the circle for rodeo stars must be crossed out except the part that is also in the circle for people who yearn for the days when the West was wild. This eliminates region 6 as the possible location for rodeo stars who are women. The completed diagram (Figure 6-8) correctly represents the conclusion, so the argument is valid.

Let us now apply the Venn-diagram test to a syllogism that, according to Table 6-2, is invalid:

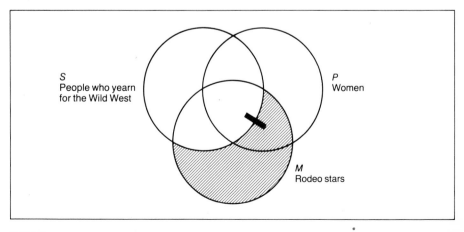

FIGURE 6-8

All registered voters are legal residents.
Some Hispanics are not registered voters.

Therefore, some Hispanics are not legal residents.

This argument is in mood AOO, figure 1. A bar must again be used, this time to diagram the minor premise "Some Hispanics are not registered voters" (Figure 6-9). The bar entering both region 1 and region 2 indicates that the one or more Hispanics who are not registered voters cannot be definitely placed in either region. Thus, the premises cannot guarantee the conclusion that at least one Hispanic is not a legal resident.

The difference between the hypothetical and existential viewpoints, discussed in Section 6-1, affects the validity of some syllogisms:

Syllogisms having two universal premises and a particular conclusion can be valid only from the existential viewpoint.

As indicated by Table 6-2, nine combinations of mood and figure (those marked by asterisks) produce syllogisms that are valid only if existential assumptions are made. The existential viewpoint is required to make these syllogisms valid because particular statements, unlike universal statements, assert the existence of at least one entity. Since in a valid syllogism true premises guarantee a true conclusion, a syllogism with two universal premises and a particular conclusion can be valid only if the existential presupposition involved in the argument is also warranted. The problem does not arise when one of the premises is particular—for example, in *AII*, figure 1, or *EIO*, figure 2—because, in these cases, a premise makes the existential claim and, for the sake of checking validity, the premises are assumed to be true.

Consider the following argument, which has two universal premises and

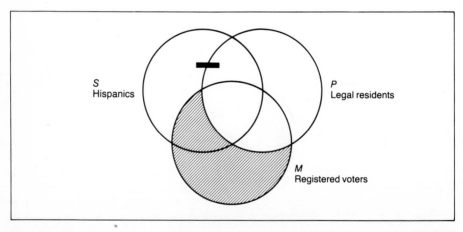

FIGURE 6-9

has a particular statement as the conclusion (mood *AAI*, figure 1):

All persons who believe in the possibility of extraterrestrial visitation are persons with extrasensory perception.   (All *M* are *P*.)
All persons taken aboard ships from outer space are persons who believe in the possibility of extraterrestrial visitation.   (All *S* are *M*.)

Therefore, some persons who have been taken aboard ships from outer space are persons who have extrasensory perception.   (Some *S* are *P*.)

If we diagram the premises without presupposing the existence of persons who have been taken aboard ships from outer space, the argument is invalid— as shown by Figure 6-10. No information supplied by the premises entitles us to put an asterisk in region 5, the only part of the *S* circle not crossed out. If we could assume the existence of such persons, however, we could then add an asterisk. As this example shows, a syllogism in mood *AAI*, figure 1, is valid provided that we presuppose the existence of at least one member of the class referred to by the *S* term (Figure 6-11).

The syllogisms that are valid only from the existential viewpoint and the terms that require assumptions about members of the classes named by the terms are indicated in Table 6-3.

No hard-and-fast rules dictate when the existential viewpoint rather than the hypothetical viewpoint should be employed, but selecting the proper viewpoint is never a matter of mere convenience or personal preference. One can usually provide reasons why one viewpoint is more appropriate than the other. Thus, for example, given the absence of reliably objective means of verifying the reports of those who claim to have been taken aboard spacecraft by extraterrestrial beings, it is unreasonable to adopt anything other than the hypothetical viewpoint in considering the sample argument about persons who have had this experience.

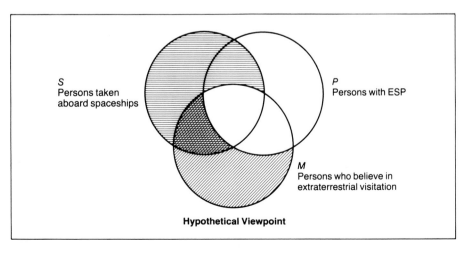

S
Persons taken
aboard spaceships

P
Persons with ESP

M
Persons who believe in
extraterrestrial visitation

Hypothetical Viewpoint

FIGURE 6-10

TABLE 6-3 *Categorical syllogisms valid only from the existential viewpoint*

PRESUPPOSITION REQUIRED	FIGURE 1	FIGURE 2	FIGURE 3	FIGURE 4
One or more members of	*AAI*	*AEO*		
S exist	*EAO*	*EAO*		*AEO*
One or more members of			*AAI*	*EAO*
M exist			*EAO*	
One or more members of				
P exist				*AAI*

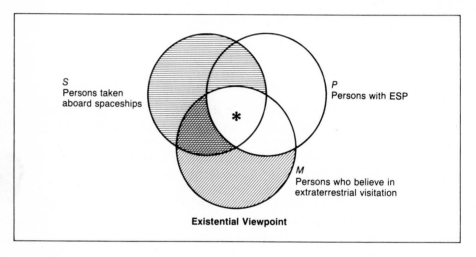

FIGURE 6-11

■ **EXERCISE 6-2**

Using the Venn-diagram method, determine whether each of the following syllogisms is valid or invalid.

   1. All artists are persons who appeal to our emotions. All propagandists are persons who appeal to our emotions. Therefore, all propagandists are artists.

   2. No admirers of Phyllis Schlafly are admirers of Bella Abzug. Some members of the New Right are admirers of Phyllis Schlafly. Therefore, no members of the New Right are admirers of Bella Abzug.

   3. Some draft evaders are conscientious objectors. Some conscientious objectors are pacifists. Therefore, some pacifists are draft evaders.

   *4. All wealthy tax evaders are unethical persons. Some lawyers are wealthy tax evaders. Therefore, some lawyers are unethical persons.

5. Some cigarette smokers are marijuana smokers. No teetotalers are cigarette smokers. Therefore, no teetotalers are marijuana smokers.

6. No Republicans are liberals. Some liberals are libertarians. Therefore, no libertarians are Republicans.

7. No R-rated movies are films for children. Some Home Box Office programs are R-rated movies. Therefore, some Home Box Office programs are not films for children.

*8. All logicians are professional philosophers. No professional philosophers are welfare recipients. Therefore, no welfare recipients are logicians.

9. All students now reading this argument are persons studying the logic of categorical syllogism. All persons studying the logic of categorical syllogism are students who have learned from Aristotle. Therefore, all students now reading this argument are students who have learned from Aristotle.

10. Some boxing champions are Black Muslims. Some racists are boxing champions. Therefore, some racists are Black Muslims.

11. All innovative programs are financial risks. Some creative programs are innovative programs. Therefore, some creative programs are financial risks.

*12. All persons who believe in extraterrestrial visitation are persons who believe in parapsychology. No experimental psychologists are people who believe in parapsychology. Therefore, no experimental psychologists are people who believe in extraterrestrial visitation.

13. All delegates who side with Arab terrorists are persons who argue that Israel must relinquish the West Bank. All Egyptian delegates are persons who argue that Israel must relinquish the West Bank. Therefore, all Egyptian delegates are delegates who side with Arab terrorists.

14. All entertainers are people who thrive on the adulation of the public. No Shakespeare scholars are people who thrive on the adulation of the public. Therefore, no Shakespeare scholars are entertainers.

15. All democracies are states in which the will of the people is supreme. No dictatorships are democracies. Therefore, no dictatorships are states in which the will of the people is supreme. ∎

☐ 6-3. RULES OF THE SYLLOGISM

Studying the Venn diagrams for valid syllogisms permits two generalizations about how the diagram must look.

1. No valid syllogism will have a Venn diagram that contains exactly three crossed-out regions.

2. No syllogism is valid if its Venn diagram contains a bar that touches more than one region that is not crossed out; for the syllogism to be valid, all but one segment of the bar must be in a region that is crossed out.

A study of valid syllogisms in standard form also allows generalizations about the relations of quality and quantity and about all the patterns of distribution that were discussed in Section 5-2. These generalizations, in turn,

© 1981, Sidney Harris. Reprinted by permission.

serve as criteria for validity—the set of rules for valid categorical syllogisms listed below. Applying these rules to syllogisms is an efficient and conclusive way of checking validity. If a syllogism satisfies all the rules, it is valid. If it violates even one rule, it is invalid.

The accuracy of the rules can be confirmed by checking the results of their application against the list of valid forms in Table 6-2 or by drawing Venn diagrams. No syllogism that satisfies all the rules will be invalid because of mood and figure; nor can a Venn diagram show an argument to be valid if it violates any of the rules.

The Rules for Valid Categorical Syllogisms

1. In a valid syllogism, the middle term must be distributed at least once.

2. In a valid syllogism, every term distributed in the conclusion must be distributed in the premises.

3. In a valid syllogism, there must be either no negative statements or exactly two, one of which must be in the conclusion.

4. No syllogism valid from the hypothetical viewpoint has two universal premises and a particular conclusion.

A categorical syllogism is like a complete, unbroken chain, and the rules are means of checking the links of the chain. Because, in a valid deductive argument, the truth of the premises guarantees the truth of the conclusion, it must be possible to show that the class relations claimed by the conclusion can be substantiated, or accounted for, by the relations of inclusion or exclusion asserted in the premises.

To see how the rules are applied, consider the following syllogism:

All persons who promise more than they can deliver are persons who overestimate their own abilities.

All presidential candidates are persons who promise more than they can deliver.

All presidential candidates are persons who overestimate their own abilities.

Using the abbreviations S for the subject or minor term, P for the predicate or major term, and M for the middle term, we can represent the syllogism as follows:

All M are P.

All S are M.

All S are P.

Each of these statements is in A form, which means that the subject term is distributed and the predicate term is undistributed (see Table 5-3). This pattern of distribution is shown by drawing circles around each of the distributed terms.

All $\widehat{M}$ are P.

All $\widehat{S}$ are M.

All $\widehat{S}$ are P.

We are now ready to apply the rules. The syllogism satisfies the *first* rule because the middle term, M, is distributed in the major premise. The middle term, M, links the classes P and S as surely as a college campus is linked to a state because it is in a city located in that state. The major premise tells us that all M are in the P class, and the minor premise tells us that all S are in the M class. The conclusion completes this link by indicating that all S are in the P class.

The sample argument satisfies the *second* rule because the term S, which is distributed in the conclusion, is also distributed in the minor premise. This means that all members of the S class have been accounted for: there is no possibility that there are some S which are not M. Furthermore, since M is distributed in the major premise, there is no possibility that there are some M

that are not *P*. Consequently, there is no possibility that there are some *S* that are not *P*, which is exactly what the conclusion indicates.

The syllogism satisfies the *third* rule because it contains no negative statements. And it satisfies the *fourth* rule both because the conclusion is a universal statement and because the existential viewpoint is warranted. Because this example satisfies all four of the rules for valid categorical syllogisms, it is a valid syllogism. Every valid syllogism must satisfy each of the four rules.

□ *The fallacy of undistributed middle*

A syllogism that is invalid because it violates the first rule is called a *fallacy of undistributed middle*. In such a syllogism, the link between the terms of the premises and conclusion is broken. Suppose, for example, you do poorly on an economics exam and the instructor who hands back the papers makes this unattractive argument:

> **Those who didn't study did poorly on the exam.**
> **You did poorly on the exam.**
>
> ---
> **You didn't study.**

This argument can be represented as a categorical syllogism with the subject term rephrased as *persons identical to you*, the predicate term rephrased as *persons who did not study*, and the middle term rephrased as *persons who did poorly on the exam*. When the abbreviations for the distributed terms are circled, the argument can be represented as follows:

> All Ⓟare *M*.
> All Ⓢare *M*.
>
> ---
> All Ⓢare *P*.

Note that the middle term, *M*, is not distributed in either premise. This means that because all members of the class designated by *M* have not been accounted for, the category of those who did poorly on the exam may well be broader than the category of those who didn't study. The argument attempts to place you in the class of those who didn't study by identifying you as one who did poorly on the exam. But there is a gap in this reasoning—the class of those who did poorly on the exam can include you as well as those who didn't study without requiring us to think of you as *among* those who didn't study. Thus, proving that you did poorly does not prove that you didn't study, just as living on a certain continent does not prove that you live in a certain country (provided that the continent contains more than one country).

A syllogism is invalid unless the middle term is distributed at least once. If in the major premise you refer to *some* part of the class named by the middle term and in the minor premise you also refer to *some* part of it, there is no way of being sure that in both cases you are speaking of the *same* part of it.

□ *The fallacy of illicit distribution*

According to the second rule for valid categorical syllogisms, one cannot validly include more of a class in the conclusion than is referred to in the premises. An argument that violates this rule is called a *fallacy of illicit distribution.*
Here is an example:

> **All stupid people are people who become the victims of deceit and propaganda.**
> **No logic students are stupid people.**
> _____
> **No logic students are people who become the victims of deceit and propaganda.**

This argument is in mood *AEE*. Represented symbolically with M standing for *stupid people*, P for *people who become the victims of deceit and propaganda*, and S for *logic students*, and with the distributed terms encircled, the argument is:

> **All (M) are P.**
> **No (S) are (M.)**
> _____
> **No (S) are (P.)**

The middle term, *M*, is distributed; so Rule 1 is satisfied. The minor term, *S*, which is distributed in the conclusion, is also distributed in the premise in which it occurs. But while the major term, *P*, is distributed in the conclusion, it is undistributed in the major premise; so Rule 2 has been violated.

To understand why this example is invalid and why a valid syllogism must satisfy Rule 2, remember that in a valid deductive argument, the conclusion never goes beyond the evidence stated in the premises. The conclusion cannot validly claim more than the premises warrant. Yet, the conclusion of this example states that 100 percent of those who become victims of deceit and propaganda are excluded from the category of logic students (both *S* and *P* are distributed). This claim is unwarranted because the major premise accounts for *only some* of those who become the victims of deceit and propaganda. Because the class of victims is undistributed in the major premise, the possibility is left open that stupid people are only some of the people who are victimized by dishonesty and chicanery. It is possible that some victims are not stupid and even that some victims are logic students.

□ *The fallacy of faulty exclusion*

Categorical syllogisms that violate Rule 3 are called *fallacies of faulty exclusion.* Three kinds of arguments are invalid because of this error. First consider the following:

No male chauvinists are just administrators.
No men who support the Equal Rights Amendment are male chauvinists.

All men who support the Equal Rights Amendment are just administrators.

This argument is in mood *EEA*. With *male chauvinists* symbolized as *M*, *just administrators* as *P*, and *men who support the Equal Rights Amendment* as *S*, and with the distributed terms encircled, the argument becomes:

No Ⓜare Ⓟ
No Ⓢare Ⓜ
All Ⓢare *P*.

This syllogism violates Rule 4 because both negative statements, or exclusions, are premises. The conclusion attempts to relate the term *S* (*men who support the Equal Rights Amendment*) to the term *P* (*just administrators*). But this relationship cannot be shown to follow from premises that do no more than deny the existence of relationships.

In the second kind of fallacy of faulty exclusion, all three statements are negative, as in the following example, in mood *EEE*:

No insects are birds.
No birds are mammals.

No insects are mammals.

Although the conclusioin of this argument is true, one is not justified in asserting it on the basis of the premises. Nothing can be validly inferred from premises that both assert only relations of exclusion. To attempt such an inference is like arguing that a city is not on a certain continent because the city is not in a certain country and the country is not on the continent.

As further illustration that a syllogism consisting of three negative statements is invalid, consider the following argument, which has true premises and a false conclusion:

No men are women.
No women are major-league baseball players.

Therefore, no men are major-league baseball players.

A syllogism with only one negative statement is the third kind of fallacy of faulty exclusion. Here is one in mood *EAA*:

No assertive women are opponents of the Equal Rights Amendment.
All women in business are assertive women.

All women in business are opponents of the Equal Rights Amendment.

In this argument, there is a link between *women in business* and *assertive women*, but, because of the negative premise, the chain is broken between *assertive women* and *opponents of the Equal Rights Amendment*. Thus, the class inclusion claimed by the conclusion is unwarranted. The premises, if true, actually prove the contrary of the stated conclusion: they prove that no women in business are opponents of the Equal Rights Amendment.

□ *Fallacies of unwarranted existential assertion*

A syllogism that has a particular statement as its conclusion cannot be valid if the existence of persons or objects designated by one or more of the terms in the argument is uncertain. Thus, if the hypothetical viewpoint must be taken, then syllogisms in moods *AAI*, *AEO*, and *EAO* are invalid, as are those in *AAO*, *EEI*, and *EEO*—which also violate Rule 3. The reason for this rule is that, unlike universal categorical statements, particular categorical statements require the assumption that at least one member of each class named in the statement exists. If Rule 4 were not applied, a particular statement asserting the existence of some person or object is supposedly guaranteed by two universal statements that actually provide no evidence that such a person or object exists. An invalid syllogism of this kind is as follows:

All fire-breathing dragons are beasts slain by knights.
All beasts slain by knights are beasts of prey.

Some beasts of prey are fire-breathing dragons.

Logicians have no commonly accepted name for syllogisms that violate Rule 4. But as a convenient device for remembering why such arguments are invalid, they can be thought of as *fallacies of unwarranted existential assertion*.

A step-by-step guide for checking the validity of syllogistic arguments follows. Note that the four rules for checking validity need not be applied in the order in which they have been discussed. In fact, it is easiest to apply Rule 3 before applying Rules 1 and 2 because the number of negative statements and their role in the argument can be determined before checking the distribution of the terms involved. And remember that the four rules apply only to syllogisms that are—or have been translated into—standard categorical form.

Some arguments that appear to violate one or more of the four rules can actually be transformed into valid syllogisms. How such arguments can be identified and transformed will be discussed in the next section.

A Guide for Checking the Validity of a Categorical Syllogism

1. Make sure the argument is indeed a categorical syllogism: it must have just three categorical statements and three different terms in all, each term occurring in exactly two statements.

2. Find the conclusion. It will tell you what the major premise is (the premise that contains the predicate term of the conclusion).

3. Rewrite the argument in standard form.

4. Check the quality of each categorical statement. There must be either no negative statements or exactly two; and if there are two negative statements, one of them must be the conclusion.

If the argument does not conform to these requirements, it violates Rule 3 and is *invalid*—so you may stop. If it does not violate the rule, proceed.

5. Determine the distribution of each term every time it occurs in the argument.

6. Find the middle term, and check to see that it is distributed at least once.

If it is not, the argument violates Rule 1 and is *invalid*—so you may stop. If the middle term is distributed at least once, proceed.

7. Check to see whether every term distributed in the conclusion is distributed in the premise in which it occurs.

If not, the syllogism violates Rule 2 and is *invalid*—so you may stop. If the syllogism conforms to the rule, proceed.

8. Check the quantity of the premises and conclusion.

If all statements are universal and steps 1 to 7 have been completed, the argument is *valid.*

If one premise is particular and steps 1 to 7 have been completed, the argument is *valid.*

If both premises are universal but the conclusion is particular, proceed to step 9.

9. Reread both premises carefully, and determine whether both *could* be true on the presupposition that entities named by the class terms *do* exist.

If so, the syllogism can be regarded from the existential viewpoint and is *valid.*

If not, the syllogism must be regarded from the hypothetical viewpoint and is *invalid.*

■ **EXERCISE 6-3**

■ A. Put each of the following syllogisms into standard form and use the four rules for valid syllogisms to determine whether each is valid or invalid. Name the fallacy committed by each invalid syllogism.

1. All poets are creative thinkers. Some scientists are not poets. Therefore, no scientists are creative thinkers.

2. Some jazz musicians are oboists. Some oboists are not concert artists. Therefore, some jazz musicians are not concert artists.

3. All large towns are towns with ghettos. Some manufacturing towns are large towns. Thus, some manufacturing towns are towns with ghettos.

*4. All mammals are animals that have four-chambered hearts. Some animals found in Borneo are animals that have four-chambered hearts. Therefore, some animals found in Borneo are mammals.

5. All screen stars are vain people. No screen stars are humble people. Therefore, no vain people are humble people.

6. No monks are ascetics. Some Buddhists are not monks. Therefore, some Buddhists are ascetics.

7. No Americans are fluent speakers of Urdu. Some speakers of Sanskrit are fluent speakers of Urdu. Therefore, some speakers of Sanskrit are not Americans.

*8. All Socialists are advocates of Medicare. Some liberals are advocates of Medicare. Therefore, some liberals are Socialists.

9. All professors are persons who are myopic. No professors are persons who wear hearing aids. Thus, no persons who wear hearing aids are persons who are myopic.

10. No immoral businesses are respectable businesses. All businesses involving drug peddling are immoral businesses. Therefore, no businesses involving drug peddling are respectable businesses.

*11. All missionaries are altruists. Some altruists are women. Therefore, some missionaries are women.

*12. No pit vipers are household pets. All mambas are pit vipers. Therefore, no mambas are household pets.

13. No marijuana smokers are law-abiding citizens. All compulsive gamblers are marijuana smokers. Therefore, no compulsive gamblers are law-abiding citizens.

14. All charming persons are persons who put others at ease. Some charming persons are not flirts. Therefore, no persons who put others at ease are flirts.

15. Some philosophers are adventurers. All soldiers of fortune are adventurers. Therefore, some soldiers of fortune are philosophers.

*16. No common stocks are good investments. All bonds are common stocks. Therefore, some bonds are good investments.

17. No edible things are toadstools. Some edible things are mushrooms. Therefore, some mushrooms are not toadstools.

18. All circus performers are entertainers. Some lion tamers are not circus performers. Therefore, some lion tamers are not entertainers.

19. No belligerent players are good sports. Some hockey players are belligerent players. Therefore, some hockey players are not good sports.

*20. No engineers are logicians. No lawyers are engineers. Therefore, all lawyers are logicians.

■ B. Translate each of the following syllogistic arguments into standard form. Then determine the validity of each argument on the basis of its mood and figure, a Venn diagram, or the four rules for valid categorical syllogisms.

1. All good teachers are good counselors, because most compassionate individuals make good counselors and every good teacher is compassionate.

2. At least some of the doctors at the clinic are not alcoholics, for no alcoholics are happy women and some of the doctors at the clinic are not happy women.

3. All horses are quadrupeds; so, because some horses are faster runners than human beings, some quadrupeds are faster runners than human beings.

*4. We can be sure that many people who are impressed by *Worlds in Collision* are gullible because most people impressed by that book are fans of *Chariots of the Gods?*, and all fans of the latter book are gullible.

5. Some long-haired youths have been mistaken for deadbeat troublemakers, and anyone mistaken for a troublemaker is a victim of prejudice. It follows then that some long-haired youths are victims of prejudice.

6. All students who get everything right on the test will receive an A. No students who have IQs of less than 140 will get everything right. So some students who will get an A on the test do not have IQs of less than 140.

7. There must be a fire at City Hall, because I saw a fire engine there. And you find fire engines only at fires.

*8. Gossiping is always irresponsible since it reinforces prejudices; and whatever reinforces prejudices is irresponsible.

9. Ronald Reagan is not the president of the United States; the president of the United States was never a movie star. Thus, Ronald Reagan was never a movie star.

10. To grade fairly, one must grade according to a student's performance; to grade fairly, one must judge dispassionately; hence, a grade based on a student's performance is the result of dispassionate judgment.

11. Some sky divers deny the reality of death. Stunt artists are sometimes sky divers, so there are stunt artists who also deny the reality of death.

*12. Because no biologist who believes in Darwinian evolution is a literal interpreter of Genesis, no literal interpreter of Genesis is a college graduate, for all biologists who believe in Darwinian evolution are college graduates.

13. No deterrent to crime takes the form of capital punishment. Thus, because all true deterrents are penalties worth preserving, no form of capital punishment is a penalty worth preserving.

14. No trains that stop at Charlottesville stop at Petersburg, because all trains that stop at Petersburg stop at Norfolk and no trains that stop at Charlottesville stop at Norfolk.

15. Vitlovska is obviously to be Premier Neshkov's successor, for Vitlovska was given a standing ovation at the annual meeting of the Communist Party, and anyone given such an accolade must be the chosen successor. ■

☐ 6-4. PRACTICAL APPLICATIONS

A major objective of the study of logic is to be able to apply methods and skills learned in the classroom to the solution of practical problems. As noted in Section 2-4, a knowledge of logic increases one's capacity to evaluate the soundness of the arguments encountered in daily life and to contribute constructively to discussions of important issues. Familiarity with logic affords confidence that reasoning can be applied to problems that might otherwise be avoided as too abstruse or complicated. In addition, applying the principles of logical reasoning to one's own thoughts makes one's beliefs and world view increasingly clear and consistent.

Although many arguments encountered in the rough-and-ready world outside the classroom can be interpreted as categorical syllogisms, they are rarely expressed in standard form. Therefore, it is crucial to recognize that, despite appearances, many arguments can be evaluated according to the methods explained in this chapter.

There are four respects in which an argument that lends itself to syllogistic reasoning can fall short of standard form.

1. The argument may contain statements that are not categorical statements.
2. The argument may appear to contain more than three different terms.
3. The argument may have fewer than the three categorical statements requisite for categorical syllogisms.
4. The argument may have more than three categorical statements.

Item 1 was discussed extensively in Sections 5-1 and 5-5. The statements of an argument that is to be interpreted as a categorical syllogism can be rephrased as necessary according to the principles explained in those sections. Let us look in turn at each of the three remaining trouble spots—items 2, 3, and 4.

☐ *Reducing the number of terms*

Arguments that are made up of just three statements and appear to be about just three different classes may be unlike syllogisms in that some of their terms are negations of other terms. The following argument is an example.

> **All city employees are literate persons.**
> **Some sanitation workers are illiterate persons.**
> ___
> **Some sanitation workers are not city employees.**

This argument, as it stands, has four terms: *city employees, literate persons, sanitation workers,* and *illiterate persons.* Since *literate persons* and *illiterate persons* are contradictory, or complementary, terms, however (see Section 5-

4), we can use immediate inference to reword the argument and reduce the number of terms to three. Thus, the major premise—"All city employees are literate persons"—can be obverted to "No city employees are illiterate persons." This change produces a syllogism in mood *EIO*, figure 2, which is valid.

Reducing the number of terms cannot always be accomplished so simply. At times, more than one operation of immediate inference is required—conversion and then obversion, for example. Or immediate inference may need to be applied to more than one statement.

Sometimes, there is more than one way by which the total number of terms can be reduced to three. Consider this argument:

> No computer scientists are untrained in logic.
> Some mathematicians are untrained in logic.
> ___
> Some persons who are not computer scientists are mathematicians.

As it stands, the argument has four terms: *computer scientists, persons who are untrained in logic, mathematicians,* and *persons who are not computer scientists.* One way to put the argument into standard form would be to convert the first statement to "No persons untrained in logic are computer scientists" and then obvert it to obtain "All persons untrained in logic are persons who are not computer scientists." Doing this would eliminate *computer scientists,* leaving only the required three terms.

Alternatively, the conclusion could be converted to "Some mathematicians are persons who are not computer scientists" and then obverted to obtain (when shortened) "Some mathematicians are not computer scientists." The first procedure would yield a syllogism in mood *AII*, figure 1; the second, a syllogism in mood *EIO*, figure 2. Both are valid forms.

If operations of immediate inference are needed to reduce the number of terms, they *must* be completed before applying the four rules for valid syllogisms. For example, the following argument appears to violate Rule 3, because all of its statements are negative:

> No diabetics are Olympic-record holders.
> No persons who take insulin are nondiabetic.
> ___
> Therefore, no persons who take insulin are Olympic-record holders.

But obverting the second premise to "All persons who take insulin are diabetic" eliminates persons who are nondiabetic and produces an argument that can be symbolized as:

> No *M* are *P*.
> All *S* are *M*.
> ___
> No *S* are *P*.

This syllogism is in mood *EAE*, figure 1, which is a valid form and satisfies all the rules.

□ *The fallacy of four terms*

Some arguments that appear to have just three terms actually have four. In these cases, one term is ambiguous, having different meanings in different statements. The shift in meaning produces what is called the *fallacy of four terms* or—as it was called in Section 4-1—the *fallacy of equivocation*.

Here is an example of such an argument:

Whatever is right is useful.
Only one of my hands is right.

Therefore, only one of my hands is useful.

The shift in the meaning of *right* results in an argument with four terms: *whatever is right* in the sense of *correct*; *that which is useful*; *one of my hands*; and *that which is on my right side*.

Now consider the following:

All actions subject to law are subject to a lawgiver.
All movements of the planets are subject to law.

Therefore, all movements of the planets are subject to a lawgiver.

In this example, the shift in meaning involves the term *subject to law*. In the first statement (which is the major premise), the term connotes behavior in conformity with decrees or enactments of legislators. Law is understood as prescribing a code of conduct with penalties for infractions of the code. In the second statement (the minor premise), *law* connotes observed regularities that describe uniformities among natural events. In the first sense, but not the second, laws are made and enforced by willful agents with purposes.

Both examples must be regarded as containing four different terms rather than three. So besides being fallacious arguments, they are not genuine syllogisms.

□ *Enthymemes*

An argument with fewer than three categorical statements can be evaluated by the methods of categorical logic if it is an *enthymeme*—an argument that has an unexpressed premise or conclusion (see Section 4-4). So, before deciding that an argument cannot be treated as a syllogism because it lacks the required three statements, determine whether it can plausibly be amended by making an implicit statement explicit.

Here is an example of such an argument:

Only students who are good at analytical thinking are admitted to law school, since only they receive high scores on the LSAT.

This can be treated as a categorical syllogism once the unstated premise, "All students admitted to law school are students who receive high scores on the LSAT," is added.

As noted in Chapter 1, the difficulty posed by enthymemes lies in knowing how far to go in providing the missing parts. Two guidelines apply to every situation:

1. In fairness to the author of the argument, *add only what you confidently believe to express the arguer's thought.* This means the added statement must be one that the arguer would be likely to consider true, that it must not make the argument into one the arguer would have been unlikely to use, and that it must not weaken the argument—for example, by creating an inconsistency that the author would have noticed and avoided.

2. *Feel no obligation to add information that falls outside the range of common knowledge or experience.* It is the responsibility of the arguer to make explicit all statements that critical readers or listeners cannot readily provide for themselves.

□ Sorites

Arguments that contain more than three categorical statements appear to consist of incomplete syllogisms mixed together. In fact, the Greek term for these arguments, *sorites*, literally means "piles" or "heaps." For example:

Terrorists are illogical.
Nobody who can memorize Shakespeare's plays is uneducated.
Illogical persons are uneducated.

No terrorists can memorize Shakespeare's plays.

The basic approach in analyzing and evaluating a sorites is to divide it into multiple syllogisms, applying to each the methods used on a single syllogism: rephrasing sentences in standard form, identifying suppressed premises and conclusions, applying the operations of immediate inference, and using one of the tests for validity. The first step in the procedure is to pair off two premises that have a common term and state the conclusion that is presumably to be drawn from these premises. This conclusion should have a term in common with one of the remaining premises and should, in turn, be treated as one premise of a second pair. A conclusion is then drawn from the second pair, and so on, until all the premises have been employed. The resulting conclusion will be the conclusion of the whole sorites.

In the preceding example, "All terrorists are illogical persons" (i.e., standard form of the first premise) can be paired with "All illogical persons are uneducated persons" to obtain the conclusion "All terrorists are uneducated persons." That conclusion is then treated as a suppressed premise and paired with "No persons who can memorize Shakespeare's plays are uneducated persons." These two premises yield the final conclusion: "No terrorists are persons who can memorize Shakespeare's plays."

Sorites can be valid or invalid:

The validity of any sorites can be determined by treating it as a chain of syllogisms and checking the validity of each syllogism. If a single syllogism is invalid, the sorites as a whole is invalid.

To verify that the argument above is valid, for example, check each syllogism of the reconstructed chain by referring to the lists of valid mood and figure combinations in Table 6-2, by using the Venn-diagram test, or by applying the four rules for valid syllogisms discussed in Section 6-3.

Some valid forms of sorites have been identified by logicians, the best known being the Aristotelian Sorites. The latter is a chain argument in which all of the conclusions are suppressed except the last. In addition, the predicate of each premise functions as the subject of the subsequent premise, and while the subject of the conclusion is the subject of the original premise, the predicate of the conclusion is the predicate of the premise immediately preceding it.

Here is an example of an Aristotelian Sorites, with the suppressed conclusions in parentheses:

FIRST SYLLOGISM	**All wheat farmers in Clayton County are advocates of farm subsidies.**
	All advocates of farm subsidies are supporters of the Farm Bureau.
SECOND SYLLOGISM	**(All wheat farmers in Clayton County are supporters of the Farm Bureau.)**
	All supporters of the Farm Bureau are registered Republicans.
THIRD SYLLOGISM	**(All wheat farmers in Clayton County are registered Republicans.)**
	All registered Republicans are advocates of a grain sale to Russia.

All wheat farmers in Clayton County are advocates of a grain sale to Russia.

Represented symbolically, and with the suppressed conclusions omitted, the argument is as follows:

$$
\begin{array}{|l}
\text{All } A \text{ are } B. \\
\text{All } B \text{ are } C. \\
\text{All } C \text{ are } D. \\
\text{All } D \text{ are } E. \\
\hline
\text{All } A \text{ are } E.
\end{array}
$$

A quick way of telling whether a sorites is *invalid* is to test it according to the following two rules:

1. Only one of the original set of premises may be negative.
2. Only one of the original set of premises may be particular.

If either rule is broken, a syllogism somewhere in the completed chain will have two negative premises or two particular premises. A syllogism with one of these combinations is invalid, and its presence in the chain makes the sorites invalid.

While the violation of one of these rules is sufficient to make a sorites invalid, however, nonviolation is not sufficient to insure that a sorites is valid. Sorites that conform to these two rules must be checked for validity by the methods explained above.

■ EXERCISE 6-4

■ A. Translate each of the following arguments into standard form, reducing the number of terms to three where necessary. Determine whether the arguments are valid or invalid by means of Venn diagrams or the rules for valid syllogisms.

1. Some party members must be nonvoters, since all officers are party members and some officers are not voters.

2. All tax assessors are incompetent, and all bank examiners are competent. Therefore, no tax assessors are bank examiners.

3. No drinks made from cola nuts are nutritional foods, because no drinks containing caffeine are nutritional, and no decaffeinated drinks are drinks made from cola nuts.

*4. Some honest persons are charged with cheating. But all cheaters are dishonest. Thus, some cheaters are not charged with cheating.

5. Some socialists are pacifists. All socialists are nonanarchists. Therefore, some pacifists are not anarchists.

6. Some dissatisfied employees are illiterate workers, for all literate workers are unsupervised, and some supervised employees are not satisfied employees.

7. No irresponsible people are careful drivers. No mature teenagers are careless drivers. Hence, all irresponsible people are immature teenagers.

*8. Only the strong survive, for none but victors in the struggle for life are strong, and all survivors are victors in the struggle for life.

9. It is now impossible for the senator to win the presidential election, for any

successful candidate must not fail to carry either California or New York, and both California and New York have gone to the senator's opponent.

10. It follows that many Americans are unconcerned about energy problems from the fact that many Americans continue to drive gas-guzzling cars, and no one who drives a gas-guzzler is concerned about energy shortages.

11. Some unauthorized reports reveal the truth about foreign affairs. All authorized reports are untrustworthy. Therefore, some reports that reveal the truth about foreign affairs are not trustworthy.

*12. A business executive argues: Those who can, do. Those who can't, teach. Therefore, teachers aren't doers.

■ B. Complete each of the following enthymemes by supplying the missing premise or the unstated conclusion you believe the speaker was assuming. Determine whether each argument, once completed, is valid or invalid.

1. Coca-Cola is addicting; it contains caffeine.

2. The company's hiring practices are discriminatory, for women are given preference over equally qualified men.

3. The news of foreign affairs you hear is all superficial and inaccurate because you get all your news from television news programs.

*4. He is a freshman, so he cannot be expected to be good at calculus.

5. Some women are good legislators, and no good legislator is intimidated by conservative pressure groups.

6. No Greek gods had human mothers, because all beings born of women are mortal.

7. No poisonous snakes native to North America are solid in color, and the snakes John saw in the woods were all black or dark green.

*8. Salespeople will do whatever is most likely to sell their products. That is why they so often lie.

9. It was announced at the beginning of this course that no late papers would be accepted, and it is now three days past the paper deadline.

10. Capital punishment should be abolished, for all executions mutilate people.

11. Whatever has the potential for meaningful life has the right to life. A fetus has the potential for meaningful life.

*12. A majority of Americans are opposed to homosexuality. That is why homosexuality should be illegal.

13. Sex acts among consenting adults are victimless crimes. There's the reason for legalizing consensual homosexuality.

14. The deployment of MX missiles destabilizes the balance of deterrence between the United States and Russia. Whatever destabilizes the balance of deterrence greatly increases the risk of nuclear war.

15. As the saying goes, "When in Rome, do as the Romans do"; and for all practical purposes, this *is* "Rome."

■ C. Identify any arguments below that commit the fallacy of four terms. Translate the remaining arguments into either categorical syllogisms or sorites, and determine, by means of the rules for valid syllogisms, whether each is valid or invalid.

1. Only aroused and vigilant citizens are loyal. No one asleep or relaxing is an aroused and vigilant citizen. Therefore, no one is a loyal citizen when that person sleeps or relaxes.

2. All capitalists believe in the free-enterprise system, because only those who oppose a state-controlled economy are supporters of open competition, and all supporters of open competition are capitalists.

3. The soul cannot die, because only things made up of component parts die; and since it is a spirit, the soul has no component parts.

*4. No laws supported by ethical women are laws that discriminate against women. All laws inconsistent with ERA are sexist laws. Therefore, no laws supported by moral women are laws inconsistent with ERA.

5. Elise has a heart of gold. Gold is heavy. Hence, Elise is heavyhearted.

6. Every senator who has a good voting record is endorsed by the Conservative Caucus. Every senator endorsed by the Liberals for Social Action has a good voting record. Thus, all senators endorsed by the Liberals for Social Action are endorsed by the Conservative Caucus.

7. Some soap-opera personalities are Hollywood stars. All Hollywood stars influence popular culture. No one who influences popular culture is an original thinker. Therefore, some soap-opera personalities are not original thinkers.

*8. All Middle Eastern countries that approve of United States foreign policy will continue to supply the United States with crude oil. No Middle Eastern country influenced by Iran approves of United States foreign policy. All Middle Eastern countries that continue to supply the United States with crude oil will become targets of increased Soviet hostility. Therefore, no Middle Eastern country influenced by Iran will become a target of increased Soviet hostility.

9. All unteachable persons are unresponsive. All philosophy students are responsive. No teachable persons are unintelligent persons. No intelligent persons are happy persons. Therefore, some philosophy students are not happy persons.

10. No polite person ever swears in public. But American presidents swear in public when they take the oath of office. Hence, no American president is a polite person. ■

CHAPTER SEVEN

Truth functions

In Chapter 6, we saw how to test the validity of a categorical syllogism by discovering the basic classes named by its general terms and the relations of quantity and quality between these classes. This chapter introduces a system of deductive logic designed to test arguments in which whole statements, rather than general terms, function as the basic units. And instead of looking for the logical relations between classes, we shall examine the ways in which symbols called *logical operators* connect entire statements with one another.

Consider this argument:

You will take the midterm exam or you will write a paper.
It is not the case that you will take the midterm exam.

Therefore, you will write a paper.

Its basic elements consist of *simple statements* and the connecting words, or *connectives*, that indicate the relationships between the statements. The first premise, "You will take the midterm exam or you will write a paper," expresses a *compound statement* whose components are two simple statements: "You will take the midterm exam" and "You will write a paper." These simple statements are connected by the word *or*. The second premise also expresses a compound statement: it is the denial, or negation, of the first simple statement of the first premise, "You will take the midterm exam." The conclusion repeats the second component of the first premise. If this argument is valid (and, as will be shown in Chapter 8, it is), its validity depends entirely upon the way in which the simple statements are arranged through the use of connectives.

The logic of truth functions is the study of the patterns, or arrangements, of simple statements that produce valid arguments. Chapter 8 presents techniques for evaluating truth-functional arguments. This chapter explains the basic concepts of *compound statement*, *truth function*, and *logical operator*.

☐ 7-1. TRUTH-FUNCTIONAL COMPOUNDS

The logic of truth functions is concerned with statements, as expressed by sentences like the following:

   1. The dog chased the cat and the cat knocked over the vase.

Every sentence used as an example in this chapter will therefore express a statement. Sentences that do not express statements fall outside the scope of the logic of truth functions.[1] While we are studying the logical properties of the statements expressed by sentences, it will be convenient, as in earlier discussions, to refer to sentences like (1) as if they were themselves statements.

   All statements are either simple or compound. Examples (2) through (5) are all simple statements.

   2. The bugler played reveille.
   3. The soldiers fell in line.
   4. I will do better on the next quiz.
   5. I will have to speak to the professor.

Example (1) above and examples (6) and (7) are compound statements.

   6. The bugler played reveille and the soldiers fell in line.
   7. Either I will do better on the next quiz or I will have to speak to the professor.

Comparing (2) through (5) with (6) and (7) shows the difference between compound and simple statements:

   A compound statement is a statement that has one or more simple statements as its component parts.

   The simple statements contained in compound statements can be identified by placing parentheses around them, as in (7a) and (8).

   7a. Either (I will do better on the next quiz) or (I will have to speak to the professor).
   8. If (I outline this chapter), then (I will do better on the next quiz).

   In the next example, a compound statement contains a component that is itself compound:

   9. If the New York Yankees lose two of their last three games and the Baltimore Orioles win all of their remaining games, then the Orioles will finish first in the Eastern Division of the American League.

The statement taken as a whole has two components, which are identified in (9a) by brackets:

---

[1] The distinction between sentences and statements is discussed in Section 1-1.

9a. If [the New York Yankees lose two of their last three games and the Baltimore Orioles win all of their remaining games], then [the Orioles will finish first in the Eastern Division of the American League].

To show that the first component is also a compound statement, the simple statements it contains are identified by parentheses in (9b).

9b. If [(the New York Yankees lose two of their last three games) and (the Baltimore Orioles win all of their remaining games)], then [the Orioles will finish first in the Eastern Division of the American League].

Each and every statement has a truth value: it is either true or false, and it cannot be both true and false. Thus, compound statements, as well as simple statements, must have truth values.

A component statement can be true or false independently of the remainder of the statement in which it occurs. For example, the simple statements that are components of (6)—"The bugler played reveille" and "The soldiers fell in line"—have separate truth values. We might know it is false that the bugler played reveille (he or she played taps instead) without knowing whether it is true or false that the soldiers fell in line.

But the truth value of a compound statement cannot be determined independently of the truth values of its simple components. We can know whether (2) is true by obtaining information about what the bugler actually played, but we cannot know whether (6) is true without knowing the truth values of *both* (2) and (3). Because the truth value of a compound statement is thus a function of the truth values of its simple components, statements such as (6) through (9) are called *truth-functional compounds* or *truth functions*.

> **A truth function is a compound statement whose truth value is completely determined by the truth values of its component parts.**

To know whether examples (6) through (9) are true or false, it is also necessary to know *how* the simple statements they contain have been combined into truth functions. Note that in examples (7a), (8), (9a), and (9b) the words *either, or, and, if,* and *then* are not included within the parentheses or brackets as parts of the simple statements. Instead, these words precede or follow simple statements, uniting them into truth functions. Such words, which are called *connectives,* are the English equivalents of *logical operators*—symbols that indicate how simple statements have been combined to form a compound statement.

> **A logical operator is a symbol that, when connected to a statement or pair of statements, produces a truth function.**

There are five different logical operators: the *tilde* ($\sim$), the *ampersand* (&), the *wedge* ($\vee$), the *horseshoe* ($\supset$), and the *triple bar* ($\equiv$). These symbols are

TABLE 7-1 *Logical operators*

SYMBOL	SYMBOL NAME	COMMON ENGLISH CONNECTIVES	TRUTH FUNCTION
~	tilde	*not; it is not the case that; it is false that*	negation
&	ampersand	*and; but*	conjunction
V	wedge	*or; either . . . or*	disjunction
⊃	horseshoe	*if . . . then*	conditional
≡	triple bar	*if and only if*	biconditional

displayed in Table 7-1 along with equivalent English connectives.[2] The column on the far right contains the name of the truth function that is produced when the corresponding logical operator is attached to component statements. As Table 7-1 shows, each logical operator produces a different truth function. In addition, each logical operator can be thought of as a rule: given the truth values of the component statements, the logical operator determines the truth value of the resulting truth function.

☐ Negation

As Table 7-1 shows, a number of English words and phrases are equivalent to the tilde, the symbol for *negation* (~). For instance, sentences (10), (10a), and (10b) all express the denial of the simple statement, "Thelma likes to study Spanish."

    10. Thelma does not like to study Spanish.
    10a. It is not the case that Thelma likes to study Spanish.
    10b. It is false that Thelma likes to study Spanish.

And the three sentences are expressed symbolically in the same way. A single capital letter is selected to stand for the component being negated—preferably the initial letter of some key word—say, "S" for *Spanish*. The tilde is then placed immediately to the left of that letter, as in (10c).

    10c. ~S

    The tilde in (10c) means that the truth value of "~S" is exactly opposite to the truth value of its component, "S." If "S" is true, "~S" is false, and if "S" is false, "~S" is true.

---

[2] The symbols for the logical operators are chosen by convention. Other widely used symbols are the *dot* (·) in place of the ampersand, the *arrow* (→) in place of the horseshoe, and the *double arrow* (↔) in place of the triple bar.

□ Conjunction

Whenever the logical operator "&" is placed between two symbolized statements, the result is a *conjunction*. Each component in a conjunction is called a *conjunct*.

The statement

11. Thelma likes peaches and she likes apricots.

can be symbolized as

11a. *P & A*

where "*P*" stands for the conjunct "Thelma likes peaches" and "*A*" stands for the conjunct "She likes apricots."

A conjunction is true only if both of its components are true. This means that the conjunction "*P & A*" is true only if both "*P*" and "*A*" are true. If either "*P*" or "*A*" is false, or if both are false, then "*P & A*" is false.

In addition to *and,* equivalent English expressions for conjunction include *but, both . . . and, although, whereas,* and *however.* Thus, each of the following compound statements can be treated as a truth-functional conjunction:

12. Thelma likes peaches, but she is allergic to fresh pears.
13. Lee is both a basketball player and an outstanding student.
14. Sabina was prepared to lead the class discussion, although she arrived a few minutes late.
15. Fred elected to take the midterm exam, whereas Susan decided to write the paper.
16. He spoke rapidly; however, his views were clearly presented.

□ Disjunction

When the logical operator "∨"—the wedge—is placed between two symbolized statements, the result is a *disjunction*. Each component of a disjunction is called a *disjunct*.

If one or both of the components are true, the disjunction itself is true. Thus, the statement

17. Either Phyllis is going to Dallas or she is going to San Francisco.

symbolized as

17a. *D ∨ S*

will be false only if Phyllis is not going to at least one of the two cities—that is, only if the disjuncts "*D*" and "*S*" are both false.

Like the tilde and the ampersand, the wedge has a number of equivalent English expressions, including *or else, or, alternatively, otherwise*, and, as in (17), *either . . . or*. But whatever words it represents, the wedge is always meant to be *inclusive*—that is, it includes the possibility that one or both of the disjuncts is true. And the compound is true if *one or both* of its *disjuncts* are true.

The disjunction symbolized by the wedge differs from *exclusive* uses of words expressing disjunction. In such cases, a compound is true only if *one* component is true. Otherwise—including cases where both components are true—the disjunction is false.

An example of an exclusive conjunction would be the statement that one is willing to go to a dance or to a movie, *but not to both*. This would be asserted as

18. I will either go to a dance or to a movie, but not to both.

Another way to express the same statement would be

18a. I will go to a dance or to a movie, but I will not go to both a dance and a movie.

Both (18) and (18a) are symbolized by (18b):

18b. $(D \lor M) \mathbin{\&} \mathord{\sim}(D \mathbin{\&} M)$

This is different, indeed, from

19. I will either go to a dance or to a movie.

which, in our symbolic language, looks like this:

19a. $D \lor M$

Unless the wording, punctuation, or context clearly indicate that a statement should be understood as a disjunction in the exclusive sense, all disjunctions will be considered inclusive and will be symbolized by the wedge.

☐ Dominant operators

A truth function often contains components that are themselves compound statements. For example, an analysis of (18) shows that it contains the compond statements "I will go to a dance or to a movie" and "I will not go to both a dance and a movie."

The statement as symbolized by (18b) is seen to be a conjunction, with "$(D \lor M)$" as one conjunct and "$\mathord{\sim}(D \mathbin{\&} M)$" as another conjunct. The ampersand that joins these two symbolized statements is called the *dominant operator* because it applies to the compound *as a whole.*

In symbolizing statements, parentheses serve as a type of logical punctuation. They eliminate ambiguity and make it clear which operator is the dominant one. Without parentheses, (18b) would appear as

18c. $D \vee M \& \sim D \& M$

From (18c), it is not possible to tell whether the tilde is connected with the conjunction "$(D \& M)$" or with "D" alone. It is also not possible to know whether the compound as a whole is the conjunction shown in (18b) or the disjunction shown in (19b).

19b. $D \vee (M \& \sim(D \& M))$

When, as in (19b), double sets of parentheses are needed to identify the components of a compound, brackets are substituted for the outer set:

19c. $D \vee [M \& \sim(D \& M)]$

The brackets in (19c) indicate that everything to the right of the wedge is a single disjunct. And the parentheses inside the brackets indicate that the tilde attaches to the conjunction "$D \& M$."

Complex compounds sometimes require the equivalent of triple sets of parentheses for their symbolization. Braces are then used to symbolize the outermost set: { }. Parentheses are used first, to identify the smallest units in the symbolized statement, and they are followed by brackets and then braces to indicate components of increasing complexity.

The dominant operator, which determines the truth-functional form of the whole compound, *dominates* any operators that occur in components of the compounds. These other operators are said to *fall within the scope* of the dominant operator. For example, consider (20) below:

20. $(S \& T) \vee [\sim(P \& C) \& K]$

The wedge between the disjunct "$(S \& T)$" and the disjunct "$[\sim(P \& C) \& K]$" dominates the entire compound. It dominates three ampersands and one tilde.

The logical operators that apply to compound components are also said to dominate the operators that fall within their scope. For example, in (20) the tilde in "$\sim(P \& C)$" dominates the ampersand in "$(P \& C)$." Furthermore, since the conjunct "$\sim(P \& C)$" is itself one component of a conjunction—"$[\sim(P \& C) \& K]$"—the ampersand immediately in front of "K" dominates the tilde.

So far, (20) does not have any content, because the simple statements that the capital letters symbolize have not been specified. But if, for instance, we let "S" stand for "You'll study hard," "T" for "You'll take better notes," "P" for

"You will pass physics," "*C*" for "You will pass chemistry," and "*K*" for "You'll regret you became premed," then (20) will symbolize the following compound statement:

> **20a.** Either you'll study hard and take better notes, or else you won't pass both physics and chemistry and you'll regret you became premed.

As can be seen from this example, the words *or else*, which replace the dominant operator—the wedge—in the symbolized statement, determine the logical form of (20a).

Identifying the dominant operators of compounds helps one to see that compound statements that at first look equivalent may not in fact be so. For example, consider (21) and (22):

> **21.** Either Harold speaks French, or Marie speaks French and Kurt speaks German.
> **22.** Harold speaks French, and either Marie speaks French or Kurt speaks German.

Statement (21) is a disjunction with a conjunction—"Marie speaks French and Kurt speaks German"—as a component. But (22) is a conjunction with a disjunction—"Either Marie speaks French or Kurt speaks German"—as a component. The symbolized versions are shown in (21a) and (22a).

> **21a.** $H \vee (M \mathrel{\&} K)$
> **22a.** $H \mathrel{\&} (M \vee K)$

Note that (21) and (21a) can still be true if Harold does not speak French, but (22) and (22a) must be false if he does not speak French.

□ *The conditional*

A compound formed by the operator "⊃" or by the words *if . . . then* is called a *conditional*. (See Section 1-5.) The component that precedes the horseshoe in a symbolized statement or that occurs between *if* and *then* in an English statement is called the *antecedent*. The component following the horseshoe or occurring after the word *then* is called the *consequent*.

In (23), the antecedent is the statement "Patricia passes the bar exam," and the consequent is "She will join the law firm of Smedley, Portoe, and Popper."

> **23.** If Patricia passes the bar exam, then she will join the firm of Smedley, Portoe, and Popper.

Statement (23) is symbolized as

> **23a.** $P \supset J$

where "*P*" stands for the antecedent and "*J*" stands for the consequent.

The effect of combining two statements to form a conditional compound is to assert that if the antecedent is true, then so is the consequent. Thus, to assert (23) is to claim that if the antecedent "Patricia passed the bar exam" is true, then the consequent "Patricia will join Smedley, Portoe, and Popper" is true as well. And the horseshoe in (23a) means that if "*P*" is true, then "*J*" will also be true. A conditional is the claim that we cannot have both a true antecedent and a false consequent.[3]

Note that a conditional claims only that *if* the antecedent is true, the consequent is true as well. A conditional does *not* claim that the antecedent *is* true. Example (23) is not false if the antecedent turns out to be false—that is, if Patricia fails the bar exam. The statement gives no information about what will happen if the antecedent turns out to be false. Patricia may still join the law firm, perhaps as a consultant until she passes the bar exam the next time around, in which case the antecedent will be false and the consequent true. Or she may fail the exam and not join the law firm; then, both the antecedent and the consequent will be false. In either case, the conditional statement itself will be true.

A conditional statement is false under only one circumstance: if the antecedent is true and the consequent is false. This means that a conditional whose antecedent is false will be true no matter what the truth value of its consequent and that a conditional whose consequent is true will be true no matter what the truth value of its antecedent.

Why it is reasonable and appropriate to designate a conditional true except when its antecedent is true and its consequent false will be discussed in Section 7-4. For the present, the question will be treated like one that might arise in the game of chess: "Why does the knight move orthogonally—one square to the side and two squares forward?" Knowing the answer to this question will increase one's knowledge of chess, but not knowing the answer should not interfere with playing the game. In logic, one needs first to know what "moves" are permissible, that is, what the rules are. Thus, for present purposes, we *stipulate* that a conditional with a false antecedent or a true consequent is to be regarded as true.

☐ *The biconditional*

The biconditional operator "≡" placed between two symbolized statements produces a compound that is called a *biconditional*. The most common English equivalent for the biconditional operator is *if and only if*. So the statement

24. Litmus paper turns red if and only if it comes into contact with acid.

---

[3] As we shall see in Section 7-3, "*P* ⊃ *J*" and "~(*P* & ~*J*)" are equivalent—that is, whenever the first is true, the second is true as well, and whenever the first is false, the second is false as well—provided that *P* and *J* stand for the same simple statements in both compounds.

is symbolized as

24a. $R \equiv A$

where "R" stands for "Litmus paper turns red" and "A" stands for "It comes into contact with acid."

The biconditional is a compound that is true only if its components have the same truth value. Thus, the statement "$R \equiv A$" will be true if both "R" and "A" are true or if both "R" and "A" are false (taking *or* in the exclusive sense). And it will be false if "R" is true and "A" is false or if "R" is false and "A" is true.

A biconditional can be thought of as the conjunction of two conditionals, one of which is the reversal of the other. For instance, (24) and (24a) are equivalent to

25. If litmus paper turns red, then it has come into contact with acid; and
  if it has come into contact with acid, then litmus paper turns red.

which can be alternatively symbolized as

25a. $(R \supset A) \ \& \ (A \supset R)$

The need for the biconditional could therefore be offset by treating such a statement as the conjunction of two conditionals. However, including the biconditional as a truth-functional compound permits one to avoid unnecessarily cumbersome statements.

English equivalents of the biconditional operator seldom occur in ordinary discourse. Phrases besides *if and only if* that often express the biconditional are:

exactly when
is equivalent to
is both necessary and sufficient for
is a necessary and sufficient condition for
just in case
just insofar as

☐ *Variables and statement forms*

So far, examples of truth-functional compounds have been symbolized using logical operators and capital letters that stand for particular statements. For instance, "$P \supset J$" symbolizes statement (23): "If Patricia passes the bar exam, then she will join the firm of Smedley, Portoe, and Popper." However, a great many statements—indeed, all conditionals—have the same form as statement (23). It is therefore possible to symbolize the *form* of the conditional independently of any particular conditional statement. For this purpose, we use low-

TABLE 7-2 *Statement forms and substitution instances of truth-functional compounds*

TRUTH FUNCTION	STATEMENT FORM	EXAMPLE OF SUBSTITUTION INSTANCE
Negation	$\sim p$	$\sim S$ (10c)
Conjunction	$p \& q$	$P \& A$ (11a)
Disjunction	$p \vee q$	$D \vee S$ (17a)
Conditional	$p \supset q$	$P \supset J$ (23a)
Biconditional	$p \equiv q$	$R \equiv A$ (24a)

ercase letters from the middle of the alphabet such as p, q, r, and s. Whereas the capital letters P and J stand for particular statements, the symbols p and q are *variables*: they are used to stand for any statement whatsoever.

When "P" and "J" in (23a) are replaced with variables, the result—"$p \supset q$"—symbolizes not just that statement but every conditional. Because it represents the form of the conditional, "$p \supset q$" is called a *statement form*. Any particular compound statement having this form is a *substitution instance* of "$p \supset q$."

As Table 7-2 indicates, the form of every truth-functional compound can be symbolized by a statement form, and the substitution instance results from replacing variables with symbols representing particular statements.

Unless otherwise indicated, truth-functional compounds will be symbolized by their corresponding statement forms in the remainder of this chapter. This will be a reminder that it is the form of a truth-functional compound that interests the logician, not its content or subject matter.

■ **EXERCISE 7-1**

■ A. Follow the directions for each exercise below.

1. Rewrite "$\sim A \& B \& C$" to show that the dominant operator is an ampersand and that one conjunct is the conjunction of B and C.

2. Rewrite "$\sim A \& B \& C$" to show that the dominant operator is an ampersand and that one conjunct is the negation of a conjunction.

3. Rewrite "$A \supset \sim B \vee C$" to show that the dominant operator is the wedge and that one disjunct is a conditional.

*****4.** Rewrite "$A \supset \sim B \vee C$" to show that the dominant operator is the horseshoe and that the consequent is the negation of a disjunction.

5. Rewrite "$A \vee B \supset \sim C \equiv D$" to show that the dominant operator is the horseshoe and that the antecedent is a disjunction and the consequent is a biconditional.

6. Rewrite "$A \vee B \supset \sim C \equiv D$" to show that the dominant operator is the triple bar and that one side of the biconditional is a conditional with a disjunction as its antecedent.

7. Rewrite "$A \lor B \supset {\sim}C \equiv D$" to show that the dominant operator is the triple bar and that one side of the biconditional is a disjunction with a conditional as a disjunct.

*8. Rewrite "$A \lor B \supset {\sim}C \equiv D$" to show that the dominant operator is the wedge and that one disjunct is a biconditional with a conditional as its antecedent.

9. Rewrite "$A \lor B \supset {\sim}C \equiv D$" to show that the dominant operator is the wedge and that one disjunct is a conditional with a biconditional as a consequent.

10. Rewrite "${\sim}A \& B \lor C \supset D$" to show that the dominant operator is the tilde and that the compound negated by the tilde is a disjunction.

■ B. Symbolize the following statements using variables and logical punctuation as needed.

1. It is false that Tim can't drive.

2. Sheila has signed up for either calculus or physics.

3. They asked me to speak at the rally, and I spoke about anarchism.

*4. The book fell behind your desk.

5. The earth is not flat.

6. If it snows tonight, then we will go skiing tomorrow.

7. We'll go skiing tomorrow if it snows tonight.

*8. We won't go skiing tomorrow if it doesn't snow tonight.

9. If it didn't snow last night, then we'll still go skiing tomorrow.

10. The speech made Thelma excited and anxious.

11. If either I get paid today or Fred repays me the money he borrowed, then I'll go out to dinner tonight.

*12. If both Greg and Sabina have joined the opposition, then we are sure to lose the election.

13. Harriet no longer lives at that address.

14. If it's raining and not snowing, then we won't go skiing and we'll be stuck at home playing gin rummy or watching soaps on television. (*Hint:* Use five variables.)

15. You'll be elected to the honor society if and only if you have both a high grade-point average and very favorable recommendations from your professors.

■ C. Match each numbered statement of the first group below with the equivalent symbolized compound from among the lettered statements that follow. (Each has exactly one mate.) Let "W" stand for "The wine keeps flowing," "B" for "The balalaika players keep playing," "L" for "The lights are dimmed," "D" for "The dancing stops," and "P" for "The party will be a success."

1. If the wine keeps flowing and the balalaika players keep playing, then the party will be a success.

2. If the wine keeps flowing and the balalaika players keep playing, then the party will be a success and the dancing won't stop.

3. If the party is a flop, then either the wine has stopped flowing or the dancing has stopped.

*4. The dancing will stop if and only if the balalaika players stop playing and the lights are dimmed.

5. The party will be a flop if and only if the wine stops flowing.

6. If the lights are dimmed and the wine keeps flowing, then the balalaika players can stop playing and the party will still be a success.

7. It's not the case both that the wine will stop flowing and the balalaika players will stop playing.

*8. The balalaika players will stop playing and the party will be a flop if and only if the wine stops flowing.

9. Either the wine will run out or the balalaika players will leave, but the party will not be a flop.

10. The party will be a success if the wine flows, the balalaika players play, and the dancing continues.

11. That the dancing stops if the lights dim is not the case.

*12. If the lights are dimmed, the dancing will stop; and the balalaika players will leave.

13. It is not the case that the balalaika players play if and only if the wine flows.

14. It is not true that the dancing will stop if the balalaika players leave and the lights are dimmed.

15. The wine will stop flowing and the balalaika players will leave, but the party will be a success if the lights are turned down and the dancing doesn't stop.

*16. The balalaika players have left, but the party is still a success.

17. If the party is a success, then the balalaika players will leave and the lights will be dimmed.

18. If the dancing hasn't stopped, then either the balalaika players are still going at it or the wine is still flowing.

19. Either the dancing will not stop or the party will be a flop.

*20. Either the party will be a flop or the dancing must not stop; and if the dancing is not to stop, then the balalaika players must keep playing and the lights must be dimmed.

a. $\sim D \vee \sim P$

b. $\sim P \equiv \sim W$

c. $\sim B \;\&\; P$

d. $\sim (B \equiv W)$

e. $\sim D \supset (B \vee W)$

f. $P \supset (\sim B \;\&\; L)$

g. $D \equiv (\sim B \;\&\; L)$

h. $(W \;\&\; B) \supset P$

i. $\sim P \supset (\sim W \vee D)$

j. $\sim (\sim W \;\&\; \sim B)$

k. $(\sim B \;\&\; \sim P) \equiv \sim W$

l. $(\sim W \vee \sim B) \;\&\; \sim P$

m. $\sim (L \supset D)$

n. $(L \supset D) \;\&\; \sim B$

o. $(W \;\&\; B) \supset (P \;\&\; \sim D)$

p. $(L \;\&\; W) \supset (\sim B \;\&\; P)$

q. $[(W \;\&\; B) \;\&\; \sim D] \supset P$

r. $(\sim W \;\&\; \sim B) \;\&\; [(L \;\&\; \sim D) \supset P]$

s. $\sim [(\sim B \;\&\; L) \supset D]$

t. $(\sim P \vee \sim D) \;\&\; [\sim D \supset (B \;\&\; L)]$

■ D. Determine the truth value of each of the following compounds, where "*H*" stands for "Harvard was founded before Massachusetts became a state," "*S*" stands for "Stanford is in California," "*O*" stands for "Oxford is an American university," and "*P*" stands for "Princeton University is in Texas."

1. ~H

2. H & P

3. ~(~O)

*4. S ∨ O

5. H & (P & S)

6. ~H ∨ ~S

7. ~S & O

*8. ~(O ∨ P)

9. H ⊃ P

10. ~(O & ~H)

11. ~H ⊃ P

*12. H ⊃ S

13. S ⊃ ~O

14. H ≡ O

15. ~P ≡ ~O

*16. P ∨ (O ∨ H)

17. (S & O) ≡ (P ∨ ~H)

18. (S ≡ O) ⊃ ~P

19. (H & S) ⊃ (O ∨ P)

*20. (O ⊃ H) ≡ (H ⊃ O) ∎

☐ 7-2. TRUTH TABLES

Section 7-1 presented rules for determining the truth value of each of the five basic truth-functional compounds: negation, conjunction, disjunction, the conditional, and the biconditional. The rules also define the roles of the logical operators by telling how these operators can combine simple statements into true compound statements.

The circumstances under which the logical operators combine components to produce true compound statements can also be shown by constructing a table that displays all possible combinations of truth values for the components of a truth-functional compound. Such a *truth table*, as it is called, shows how the truth values of the component parts affect the truth value of the compound as a whole.

A truth table lists all possible combinations of truth values of a given set of simple statements, showing how each combination affects the truth value of a compound having those statements as components.

The first step in constructing a truth table is to list all possible truth values for the variables that represent the components of a given compound statement. Since "p" and "q," for example, can each be either true or false but not both at the same time, there are four possible combinations of truth values for these variables. Each vertical column lists the ways in which they can be true or false in relation to each other, and each horizontal row represents one of these combinations.

p	q
T	T
F	T
T	F
F	F

The table shows that "*p*" and "*q*" can both be true; "*q*" can be true but "*p*" false; "*q*" can be false but "*p*" true; and both "*p*" and "*q*" can be false.

We next add the conjunction of "*p*" and "*q*" to the table. The vertical line is used to separate the *base columns*—the columns displaying the possible truth values of the variables—from the column for the truth-functional compound that includes the variables.

p	*q*	*p* & *q*
T	T	
F	T	
T	F	
F	F	

According to the rule for conjunction, a compound formed with the ampersand is true only if both components are true; otherwise, it is false. Thus, by looking at each row of truth values under "*p*" and "*q*," we see that "*p* & *q*" is true only under the conditions shown in the first row. The conjunction is false under the conditions shown in the remaining three rows. The column under "*p* & *q*" is therefore filled in as follows:

p	*q*	*p* & *q*
T	T	T
F	T	F
T	F	F
F	F	F

The truth table can display the truth conditions of every truth-functional compound. A new column is generated for a compound by applying the rule for the logical operator. For example, a compound formed by disjunction is true if one or both components is true. So we add to the table a column for disjunction by placing a T in each row in which either "*p*" or "*q*" is true or both are true and by entering an F where this is not the case.

p	*q*	*p* & *q*	*p* ∨ *q*
T	T	T	T
F	T	F	T
T	F	F	T
F	F	F	F

By applying the rules for the conditional and the biconditional, the truth table expands to include six columns.

p	q	p & q	p ∨ q	p ⊃ q	p ≡ q
T	T	T	T	T	T
F	T	F	T	T	F
T	F	F	T	F	F
F	F	F	F	T	T

Because negation involves only one component statement, only two rows are needed in the truth table for this truth-functional compound.

p	~p
T	F
F	T

Since a truth table shows the conditions under which each of the five basic compounds will be true or false, it will indicate the truth conditions for any compound. No matter what actual statements "*p*" and "*q*" may stand for, a compound formed by conjoining them can be true only when both components are true; a compound formed by disjunction will be true if only one component is true; and so on.

No matter how complex a statement, a truth table can be used to show the conditions under which it would be true and those under which it would be false. This can be illustrated by constructing a truth table for the following statement: "If Charles isn't invited to dinner, then Hilary won't come; and if Hilary doesn't come, then Jack will be unhappy." The statement is symbolized as (~p ⊃ ~q) & (~q ⊃ ~r) where "*p*" stands for "Charles is invited to dinner," "*q*" for "Hilary comes to dinner," and "*r*" for "Jack will be happy."

We begin the truth table by constructing the base columns for the variables. The base columns always appear on the far left of the table, and they display all possible combinations of truth values of the simple statements symbolized by the variables. Because the symbolized statement in the example contains three variables, the table will have three base columns. And, as is customary, the variables will be listed in alphabetical order.

The number of rows in a truth table depends on the number of variables. The tables with two variables had four possible combinations of truth value. But because each additional variable could be either true or false, the number of rows in a truth table must double every time another variable is added. Because there are three variables—"*p*," "*q*," and "*r*"—in our example, the base columns for the table must have eight rows. (For four variables, sixteen rows would be needed; for five variables, thirty-two rows; and so on.) To insure that no possible combinations of truth or falsity are overlooked, we follow a simple rule in constructing the base columns: The first column is made up of alternating T's and F's (T F T F . . .); in the second column, the T's and F's are doubled (T T F F . . .); and in the third column, the T's and F's are quadrupled (T T T T F F F F . . .). (If there were a fourth variable, the fourth column would consist of eight T's followed by eight F's.) The base columns for the present table are as follows:

p	q	r
T	T	T
F	T	T
T	F	T
F	F	T
T	T	F
F	T	F
T	F	F
F	F	F

The next step is to draw a vertical line to separate the base columns from the remainder of the truth table to be generated. In addition, the horizontal line below the abbreviations for the variables is extended to the right, making it sufficiently long to accommodate all of the columns to be generated. We also place the statement form for the compound, "$(\sim p \supset \sim q) \& (\sim q \supset \sim r)$," at the far right. It belongs on the far right because its truth value will be the last to be determined.

p	q	r		$(\sim p \supset \sim q) \& (\sim q \supset \sim r)$
T	T	T		
F	T	T		
T	F	T		
F	F	T		
T	T	F		
F	T	F		
T	F	F		
F	F	F		

An inspection of the statement form at the far right of the table shows that its dominant operator is the ampersand and its conjuncts are "$\sim p \supset \sim q$" and "$\sim q \supset \sim r$." To determine the truth value of this conjunction, we need to know the truth value of each of its conjuncts. Accordingly, we enter columns in the table for "$\sim p \supset \sim q$" and "$\sim q \supset \sim r$." But note that "$\sim p \supset \sim q$" and "$\sim q \supset \sim r$" are also conditionals that contain compounds: the negations of the variables "p," "q," and "r." A column is therefore needed for each negation. The truth table now appears as shown at the top of p. 212.

The compounds above the horizontal line are arranged from left to right in order of increasing dominance. We do this because in constructing the columns to the right, we will need to depend upon information in the columns

p q r	~*p*	~*q*	~*r*	~*p* ⊃ ~*q*	~*q* ⊃ ~*r*	(~*p* ⊃ ~*q*) & (~*q* ⊃ ~*r*)
T T T						
F T T						
T F T						
F F T						
T T F						
F T F						
T F F						
F F F						

to the left. In constructing the column for "~*p* ⊃ ~*q*," for example, the combinations of truth values for "~*p*" and "~*q*" will have to be considered, rather than those for "*p*" and "*q*," since the components of "~*p* ⊃ ~*q*" are the negations "~*p*" and "~*q*."

The truth table is filled out according to the rule for the logical operator contained in each compound statement. The column for "~*p*" will have T's and F's exactly opposite to those in the column for "*p*"; likewise for "~*q*" and "*q*," and "~*r*" and "*r*."

p q r	~*p*	~*q*	~*r*	~*p* ⊃ ~*q*	~*q* ⊃ ~*r*	(~*p* ⊃ ~*q*) & (~*q* ⊃ ~*r*)
T T T	F	F	F			
F T T	T	F	F			
T F T	F	T	F			
F F T	T	T	F			
T T F	F	F	T			
F T F	T	F	T			
T F F	F	T	T			
F F F	T	T	T			

According to the rule for the conditional, "~*p* ⊃ ~*q*" will be false when the antecedent "~*p*" is true and the consequent "~*q*" is false. So check the columns for "~*p*" and "~*q*" and enter F in the column for "~*p* ⊃ ~*q*" in the second and sixth rows. Place T's in all other rows, because the conditional will be true under these possible combinations of the truth and falsity of the antecedent and consequent.

Construct the column for "~*q* ⊃ ~*r*" by examining the columns for "~*q*" and "~*r*" and again applying the rule for the conditional. Place an F in the third and fourth rows and T's in all other rows. The table now appears as follows:

p *q* *r*	~*p*	~*q*	~*r*	~*p* ⊃ ~*q*	~*q* ⊃ ~*r*	(~*p* ⊃ ~*q*) & (~*q* ⊃ ~*r*)
T T T	F	F	F	T	T	
F T T	T	F	F	F	T	
T F T	F	T	F	T	F	
F F T	T	T	F	T	F	
T T F	F	F	T	T	T	
F T F	T	F	T	F	T	
T F F	F	T	T	T	T	
F F F	T	T	T	T	T	

Because the columns for the conjuncts "~*p* ⊃ ~*q*" and "~*q* ⊃ ~*r*" are now complete, we need refer only to them to construct the column for "(~*p* ⊃ ~*q*) & (~*q* ⊃ ~*r*)." And because a conjunction is true only when both components are true, "(~*p* ⊃ ~*q*) & (~*q* ⊃ ~*r*)" will be true only when its conjuncts have the truth values assigned in the first, fifth, seventh, and eighth rows. The completed truth table appears in Table 7-3.

It is important to understand exactly what Table 7-3 shows and what it does not show. It displays all possible combinations of truth values for the variables "*p*," "*q*," and "*r*" that would make the conjunction "(~*p* ⊃ ~*q*) & (~*q* ⊃ ~*r*)" true. However, *the truth table does not tell whether "(~*p* ⊃ ~*q*) & (~*q* ⊃ ~*r*)" is in fact true or false. It does not indicate which combination of truth values of the variables actually obtain.*

Nevertheless, the table is a valuable aid in determining the truth or falsity of substitution instances. For example, if we know that the statement substituted for "*p*" is true while the statements substituted for "*q*" and "*r*" are false, we know that that particular conjunction is true. In this case, the truth values of the variables would be represented by the seventh row in the base columns of the table in Table 7-3. As the table shows, given this combination of truth

TABLE 7-3

p *q* *r*	~*p*	~*q*	~*r*	~*p* ⊃ ~*q*	~*q* ⊃ ~*r*	(~*p* ⊃ ~*q*) & (~*q* ⊃ ~*r*)
T T T	F	F	F	T	T	T
F T T	T	F	F	F	T	F
T F T	F	T	F	T	F	F
F F T	T	T	F	T	F	F
T T F	F	F	T	T	T	T
F T F	T	F	T	F	T	F
T F F	F	T	T	T	T	T
F F F	T	T	T	T	T	T

values for "*p*," "*q*," and "*r*," the conjunction "(~*p* ⊃ ~*q*) & (~*q* ⊃ ~*r*)" will be true. Thus, because the compound statement "If Charles isn't invited to dinner, then Hilary won't come; and if Hilary doesn't come, then Jack will be unhappy" is a substitution instance of "(~*p* ⊃ ~*q*) & (~*q* ⊃ ~*r*)," that compound statement will be true under this assignment of truth values.

■ **EXERCISE 7-2**

■ A. Construct a truth table for each of the following compounds.
 1. (*p* & *q*) ∨ *r*
 2. *p* & (*q* ∨ *r*)
 3. *p* ⊃ (*q* & *r*)
 *4. *p* ⊃ (*q* ∨ ~*r*)
 5. *p* ⊃ (*q* ⊃ *r*)
 6. ~*p* ⊃ ~*q*
 7. ~*q* ≡ (~*q* ⊃ *r*)
 *8. (*p* & *q*) ⊃ (*r* ∨ ~*q*)
 9. ~*p* ∨ (*q* & ~*r*)
 10. (~*p* ∨ *q*) ≡ (*p* ⊃ *q*)

■ B. Use truth tables to determine whether the compounds in each exercise below would be true under the same truth conditions for the variables "*p*" and "*q*."
 1. *p* ⊃ *q* and ~*q* ⊃ ~*p*
 2. *p* ≡ *q* and (*p* ⊃ *q*) & (*q* ⊃ *p*)
 3. *p* ⊃ *q* and ~*p* ∨ *q*
 *4. *q* ⊃ *p* and *q* ∨ ~*p*
 5. *p* ≡ *q* and ~*q* ≡ ~*p*
 6. ~(*p* ⊃ *q*) and *p* ∨ ~*q*
 7. ~(~*p* ∨ ~*q*) and *p* ∨ *q*
 *8. ~(~*p* & ~*q*) and *p* & *q*
 9. ~(*p* & *q*) and ~*p* ∨ ~*q*
 10. ~(*p* ∨ *q*) and ~*p* & ~*q*   ■

☐ **7-3. TRUTH-FUNCTIONAL EQUIVALENCE**

If two statements are true and false under exactly the same conditions, they are *logically equivalent*. Truth-functional compounds that are logically equivalent are *truth-functionally equivalent*.

Because truth tables display the entire set of truth conditions for a compound statement, a truth table can be used to determine whether two statements are truth-functionally equivalent. For example, consider the compound statements

1. If nuclear proliferation continues, then the risk of nuclear war will increase.
2. Either nuclear proliferation will not continue or the risk of nuclear war will increase.

In symbolic form, with their components represented by the variables "p" and "q" and with the appropriate logical operators, the statements appear as in (1a) and (2a).

1a. $p \supset q$
2a. $\sim p \vee q$

Because the statements contain two variables, the table will have two base columns, each containing four rows. Because one of the statements contains a negation—"$\sim p$"—a column must be included to show the truth values of that component. The truth values for the conditional "$p \supset q$" and the disjunction "$\sim p \vee q$" are then entered in the table, following the rules for their logical operators. The completed truth table is shown below.

p	q	$\sim p$	$p \supset q$	$\sim p \vee q$
T	T	F	T	T
F	T	T	T	T
T	F	F	F	F
F	F	T	T	T

Now inspect the columns under the dominant operators of each compound, row by row. If the columns are *exactly alike*, the statement forms are truth-functionally equivalent. But if they differ in any way—if in any row one column has T and the other has F—then the statement forms are *not* truth-functionally equivalent. As the truth table demonstrates, any statements with the forms "$p \supset q$" and "$\sim p \vee q$" have exactly the same columns and are therefore truth-functionally equivalent. Whatever substitution instances we select for "$p \supset q$" and "$\sim p \vee q$" will have the same truth value, as long as the variables "p" and "q" symbolize the same simple statements.

Thus, (1) and (2) are truth-functionally equivalent.

In addition, (1) and (2) are truth-functionally equivalent to

3. It is not the case both that nuclear proliferation will continue and the risk of nuclear war will not increase.

Statement (3) will be false only when the truth value of "p" is T and the truth value of "q" is F, and this is the only condition under which both "$p \supset q$" and "$\sim p \vee q$" will be false. The truth-functional equivalence of these three statement forms is demonstrated in Table 7-4.

TABLE 7-4

p q	~p	~q	p ⊃ q	~p ∨ q	p & ~q	~(p & ~q)
T T	F	F	T	T	F	T
F T	T	F	T	T	F	T
T F	F	T	F	F	T	F
F F	T	T	T	T	F	T

☐ *Transformation rules*

A claim that one statement form is truth-functionally equivalent to another statement form is called a *transformation rule*. An example of such a rule is as follows:

> **4.** The statement form "*p* ⊃ *q*" is equivalent to the statement form "~*p* ∨ *q*."

The transformation rule is a way of saying that, wherever a statement of one form appears as a component, it can be replaced by a statement of the other form.

For example, in (5), "*p* ⊃ *q*" occurs as a disjunct in the left-hand component of the conjunction.

> **5.** [*r* ∨ (*p* ⊃ *q*)] & [(*r* ⊃ *p*) & *q*]

According to the transformation rule given in (4), this disjunct can be replaced by "~*p* ∨ *q*" without changing the truth conditions of the entire conjunction. In other words, (5) can be transformed into (6) by replacing the component "*p* ⊃ *q*" with "~*p* ∨ *q*":

> **6.** [*r* ∨ (~*p* ∨ *q*)] & [(*r* ⊃ *p*) & *q*]

Similarly, since "~*p* ∨ *q*" and "~(*p* & ~*q*)" are equivalent, (6) can be transformed into (7).

> **7.** [*r* ∨ ~(*p* & ~*q*)] & [(*r* ⊃ *p*) & *q*]

Statements (5), (6), and (7), then, are truth-functionally equivalent. This means that substitution instances of these statement forms will be logically equivalent, assuming the same three simple statements are substituted for the respective variables "*p*," "*q*," and "*r*." Moreover, if a substitution instance of (5) is known to be true, then substitution instances of (6) and (7) are true as well—again, provided that each statement substituted for a variable in (5) replaces the same variable in both (6) and (7).

Knowing that (5), (6), and (7) are truth-functionally equivalent permits one validly to infer a substitution instance of (6) or (7) from a substitution instance of (5). Thus, the transformation rules also tell which inferences from one truth-functional compound to another are valid.

Transformation rules can be completely symbolized by replacing the phrase "is equivalent to" with the triple bar ($\equiv$). Thus, (4) can be written as

4a. $(p \supset q) \equiv (\sim p \lor q)$

Because the components to the right and the left of the triple bar are equivalent, the truth conditions for the biconditional are satisfied and the use of the triple bar is justified.

There is an important difference between (4a) as a transformation rule and the rule for the biconditional, however. As the logical operator representing the biconditional, the triple bar means that the compound formed by it can be true only if both of its components have the same truth value. The biconditional is therefore a rule for the formation of a true truth-functional compound. By contrast, a transformation rule is a rule that tells how to preserve the truth value of a truth-functional compound by replacing a component of the compound statement with an equivalent component.

Twelve transformation rules are recognized in truth-functional logic. These are listed in Table 7-5. As the table shows, several rules provide equivalences for more than one pair of statement forms.

Each of the transformation rules in Table 7-5 can be justified by using a truth table. To do this, construct a truth table with a column for the statement form appearing on each side of the triple bar; then check the columns of T's and F's to verify that they are exactly alike. The truth table in Table 7-6, for example, justifies both contraposition and divergence.

A transformation rule can also be justified by considering what the rules for the truth-functional compounds require. Consider, for example, the rule for absorption:

$[p \supset (p \ \& \ q)] \supset (p \supset q)$

Absorption is a transformation by which a conjunction that is the consequent of a conditional is permitted to "absorb" a conjunct that is the same as the antecedent of the conditional. According to the rule for conjunction, the consequent "$p \ \& \ q$" of the conditional "$p \supset (p \ \& \ q)$" can be true only when both "p" and "q" are true. But if "p" is true, then the antecedent of the conditional "$p \supset (p \ \& \ q)$" must be true; and by the rule for the conditional, so is the conditional itself.

Now if "p" is false, "$p \ \& \ q$" is false and the antecedent of "$p \supset (p \ \& \ q)$" is also false. But then the conditional "$p \supset (p \ \& \ q)$" is *still* true, since the conditional is false only when the antecedent is true and the consequent is false. Thus, whatever the values of "p" and "q," the truth conditions for "$p \supset (p \ \& \ q)$" will always be the same as the truth conditions for the conditional "$p \supset q$."

TABLE 7-5 *Transformation rules*

Duplication:	$p \equiv (p \ \& \ p)$
	$p \equiv (p \lor p)$
Double Negation:	$p \equiv (\sim\sim p)$
Commutation:	$(p \lor q) \equiv (q \lor p)$
	$(p \ \& \ q) \equiv (q \ \& \ p)$
	$(p \equiv q) \equiv (q \equiv p)$
Association:	$[p \lor (q \lor r)] \equiv [(p \lor q) \lor r]$
	$[p \ \& \ (q \ \& \ r)] \equiv [(p \ \& \ q) \ \& \ r]$
Conditional Exchange:	$(p \supset q) \equiv (\sim p \lor q)$
	$(p \supset q) \equiv [\sim(p \ \& \ \sim q)]$
Biconditional Exchange:	$(p \equiv q) \equiv [(p \supset q) \ \& \ (q \supset p)]$
Contraposition:	$(p \supset q) \equiv (\sim q \supset \sim p)$
	$(p \equiv q) \equiv (\sim q \equiv \sim p)$
Divergence:	$[\sim(p \equiv q)] \equiv (p \equiv \sim q)$
Absorption:	$[p \supset (p \ \& \ q)] \equiv (p \supset q)$
De Morgan's laws:	$[\sim(p \lor q)] \equiv (\sim p \ \& \ \sim q)$
	$[\sim(p \ \& \ q)] \equiv (\sim p \lor \sim q)$
Distribution:	$[p \ \& \ (q \lor r)] \equiv [(p \ \& \ q) \lor (p \ \& \ r)]$
	$[p \lor (q \ \& \ r)] \equiv [(p \lor q) \ \& \ (p \lor r)]$
Exportation:	$[(p \ \& \ q) \supset r] \equiv [p \supset (q \supset r)]$

De Morgan's laws, named for the logician Augustus De Morgan (1806–1871), include two different though similar transformations. These transformations are possible only when a tilde negates an entire disjunction or an entire conjunction.

The first of De Morgan's laws involves transforming a negated disjunction into a conjunction of negations: $[\sim(p \lor q)] \equiv [\sim p \ \& \ \sim q]$. The transformation

TABLE 7-6 *Proofs of transformation rules for contraposition and divergence*

				CONTRAPOSITION		CONTRAPOSITION		DIVERGENCE	
p	q	$\sim p$	$\sim q$	$p \supset q$	$\sim q \supset \sim p$	$p \equiv q$	$\sim q \equiv \sim p$	$\sim(p \equiv q)$	$p \equiv \sim q$
T	T	F	F	T	T	T	T	F	F
F	T	T	F	T	T	F	F	T	T
T	F	F	T	F	F	F	F	T	T
F	F	T	T	T	T	T	T	F	F

is permissible because if we know a disjunction is false, then we also know that both components are false. According to the rule for disjunction, if either component of the disjunction "$p \lor q$" is true, the disjunction as a whole is true. Thus, "$p \lor q$" can be false only if both "p" and "q" are false. This is the same as saying that if "$\sim(p \lor q)$" is true, then "$\sim p \,\&\, \sim q$" must also be true, and if "$\sim(p \lor q)$" is false, "$\sim p \,\&\, \sim q$" must also be false.

The second De Morgan transformation consists of turning a negated conjunction into a disjunction of negations: $[\sim(p \,\&\, q)] \equiv [\sim p \lor \sim q]$. If a conjunction is false—that is, if "$\sim(p \,\&\, q)$" is true, then we know from the truth-table definition of conjunction that one or both of the components must be false—in other words, that "$\sim p \lor \sim q$" is true.

Table 7-5 is a reference resource that can be used much as a dictionary or table of weights and measures would be used. Truth-functional compounds that you suspect to be equivalent to each other can be checked against the transformation rules. But if you find yourself without access to this table, you can still determine whether any two truth-functional compounds are equivalent by constructing a truth table that contains them both.

■ **EXERCISE 7-3**

■ A. Provide truth-functionally equivalent statement forms for each of the following.

　1. It's not the case that Bill won't see his doctor about his chest pains.

　2. If the board of trustees has the long-term interests of the college in mind, it will approve the increase in scholarship aid.

　3. If the professors aren't in their offices by 8:00 A.M., they won't be prepared for their nine o'clock classes.

　*4. It's not the case that Fred will both pass the midterm exam and drop the course.

　5. Sabina will receive her M.D. in June, and either she'll do her residency in Boston or she'll do it in New York.

　6. If Sabina receives her M.D. in June and moves to New York, she'll do her residency in New York.

　7. We can't buy a new car this year and we can't vacation in the Rockies.

　*8. Either Harold will enroll in law school, or he will work and study political science in the evening division of the graduate school.

　9. It's not true that you will be expelled from college if and only if you cheat on a final exam.

　10. If you preregister for the course, then you are sure to get a seat in the class; and if you do get a seat, then it's because you preregistered.

■ B. Replace each of the following with a truth-functionally equivalent statement form. State the transformation rule used in each case.

　1. (A & B) & (A & B)

　2. $\sim[\sim(A \,\&\, B)]$

　3. A

*4. $\sim A \lor B$
5. $C \supset (A \supset B)$
6. $\sim A \equiv B$
7. $(A \& B) \supset C$
*8. $(B \& A) \lor (B \& C)$
9. $C \lor (B \& A)$
10. $A \supset (A \& B)$
11. $(S \supset R) \& (R \supset S)$
*12. $\sim(S \lor R)$
13. $S \lor (R \lor T)$
14. $\sim[(S \supset T) \lor (R \supset T)]$
15. $\sim(S \& R)$
*16. $\sim[(S \& T) \& (S \& R)]$
17. $R \& (S \& T)$
18. $\sim(S \equiv T)$
19. $(A \& B) \& (S \& T)$
*20. $(S \lor T) \supset (A \supset B)$ ∎

☐ 7-4. TRANSLATING FROM ENGLISH INTO SYMBOLIC LOGIC

In addition to the English connectives discussed in previous sections, a number of other English words and locutions commonly serve to express the operations of conjunction, disjunction, the conditional, and the biconditional. These same connectives also occur in simple statements and in compounds that are not truth functional. Familiarity with the English equivalents of the logical operators sharpens one's ability to recognize truth-functional statements and to translate them accurately into the symbolic language of truth-functional logic.

This section will help you refine these translation skills. Special attention will be given to English connectives associated with the conditional, and the discussion will return to the question of justifying the truth values logicians assign to the conditional.

☐ *Conjunctive connectives*

As noted in Section 7-1, the logical operator for conjunction has many English equivalents. Each of the following can be represented by the statement form for conjunction:

The dollar declines *and* the pound declines.
The dollar declines *but* the mark increases.

The dollar declines, *whereas* the ruble increases.
The dollar declines; *however,* the yen increases.
The dollar declines; *moreover,* the lira declines.
The dollar declines, *although* the franc increases.
The dollar declines, *as* it depends on the price of gold.
The dollar declines, *yet* the peso declines more rapidly.
The dollar declines, *even though* oil prices remain stable.

The underlined expressions are not entirely synonymous, but there is a common factor in their meaning that justifies their being symbolized by the ampersand. Under ordinary circumstances, a person who asserts a compound statement formed by any of these English connectives is committed to accepting both of the constituent simple statements as true. And as we saw in the previous section, these are exactly the truth conditions for the conjunction.

The mere presence of English connectives in a statement does not insure that it is a truth-functional compound, however. These connectives may also be used in simple statements. This distinction is illustrated by the following:

1. Herman Melville's *Moby Dick* is a great work of literature and philosophy.
2. General George Patton and the Third Army defeated the Germans at the Battle of the Bulge.

Statement (1) is a shorthand way of saying "Herman Melville's *Moby Dick* is a great work of literature and Herman Melville's *Moby Dick* is a great work of philosophy." However, (2) cannot be treated as the truth-functional conjunction "General George Patton defeated the Germans at the Battle of the Bulge and the Third Army defeated the Germans at the Battle of the Bulge," because that wording does not capture the sense that the general and the Third Army did this *together* and at the same time. Thus, while (1) is a truth-functional compound, (2) is a *simple* statement with a compound subject.

Note that the truth of any substitution instance of the conjunction "p & q" is independent of the order of its components. The statement forms "p & q" and "q & p" are logically equivalent. Thus, a statement is not a truth-functional conjunction if the order of its components affects its truth. The following examples show the difference between a conjunction that is truth-functional and one that is not:

3. While Janice works hard, she lacks experience.
4. Janice and Michael got married and they had twins.

The truth value of (3) is not affected by reversing the order of its components; (3) is logically equivalent to (5):

5. While Janice lacks experience, she works hard.

However, (4) is *not* equivalent to (6):

6. Janice and Michael had twins and they got married.

Statement (4) could be true and (6) false. Statement (4) asserts a temporal order between two events; the conjunction *and* means "and then" and is not adequately represented by the ampersand.

In addition to the words *and, but, whereas, however, moreover, although, as, yet, even though,* and *while*—which have been illustrated—the following can also be used to express conjunction:

Both . . . and:	Both Franklin D. Roosevelt and John F. Kennedy were Democrats.
Besides:	Besides Adele, George is applying to graduate school.
As well as:	College texts as well as high-school history books may convey impressions of racial superiority.
In addition to:	Joachim in addition to Alice signed the petition.
But even so:	I know he was upset; but even so, he should have held his tongue.
Inasmuch as:	You may keep the book as long as you like, inasmuch as you find it so interesting.
Nevertheless:	We have had a record snowfall; nevertheless, class will be held as usual.

It would be impossible to draw up a comprehensive list of connectives that are always equivalent to the conjunctive operator because language is far too versatile. Words that are equivalent to the conjunctive operator on some occasions do "double duty" and have other meanings in other contexts. For instance, some connectives double as *temporal indicators* to specify a time sequence between the events mentioned in each clause (see Section 1-3). The following words in this group include *while, yet, as,* and even *and*—as shown by example (4). There are two different uses of *as*:

The word as *used to express conjunction:* You need to reread the assignment, as you are not ready for the test.
The word as *used to express a temporal relationship:* Ramona flew out the front door as the car pulled up to her house.

Other connectives perform different functions when they occur as adverbs; this is especially true for *nevertheless, yet, however, moreover,* and *besides.* The following are illustrations.

The word nevertheless *used as an adverb:* He will be present nevertheless.
The word yet *used as an adverb:* She has not yet graduated from Harvard Law School.

The word however *used as an adverb to mean "in whatever manner"*: However hard he tried, Luis could not solve the problem.

Two connectives that are both correctly translated as conjunctive operators can have subtle differences in meaning. For example, consider the words *whereas* and *although* as used in statements (7) and (8):

7. Gloria came to the dance, whereas Harry did not.
8. Gloria came to the dance, although Harry did not.

Insofar as we are concerned with the truth-functional compounds formed by connecting simple statements with *whereas* and *although*, we regard both words as signifying the same operation of conjunction. However, the choice of one connective over another can convey extralogical shades of meaning. Statement (7) appears simply to state that Gloria came to the dance and Harry did not. But (8) appears to suggest something more: that if Gloria came to the dance, Harry might have been expected to come too. The hint conveyed by (8) is due primarily to the discounting brought about by the use of *although*. (See the discussion of discounting in Section 3-3.)

Despite the different shades of meaning between (7) and (8), both statements have the same truth conditions. For (7) and (8) to be true, it is necessary only for Gloria to have been at the dance and Harry absent. Thus, for the purposes of logic, (7) and (8) are treated as truth-functionally equivalent, and both are symbolized as "G & ~H."

As shown by this discussion—and, earlier, in Section 1-1—the same words can be used to express different statements. Whether to treat a connective as equivalent to the conjunctive operator must be decided on a case-by-case basis.

□ Negation and conjunction

English connectives for negation that cause no difficulty on their own can be misleading when they occur in compound statements with connectives for conjunction. One such expression is *not both . . . and*, which must be translated as the negation of a conjunction and not as the conjunction of two negations. This is shown by the following example:

9. The Declaration of Independence was not written by both Thomas Jefferson and Abraham Lincoln.

The correct paraphrase of (9) is

10. It is not the case that both Thomas Jefferson wrote the Declaration of Independence and Abraham Lincoln wrote the Declaration of Independence.

This can be abbreviated and symbolized as

11. ~(J & L)

It is important not to regard (9) as asserting "~*J* & ~*L*." This translation denies the possibility that one of the two famous men wrote the Declaration of Independence, a possibility that we must presume the user of *not both . . . and* intended to leave open.

Expressions that generally signify conjunction plus negation are *instead of, rather than,* and *without.* So statements in which they occur should be paraphrased in such a way that the expression is replaced by *and not* or *but not.* For example, (12), (13), and (14) should be paraphrased, respectively, as (12a), (13a), and (14a).

> **12.** They went to the zoo instead of the Washington Monument.
>
> **13.** Denise was elected class president rather than Jerome.
>
> **14.** He made up his mind without waiting for her explanation.
>
> **12a.** They went to the zoo but not to the Washington Monument.
>
> **13a.** Denise was elected class president and not Jerome.
>
> **14a.** He made up his mind, and it is not the case that he waited for her explanation.

□ *Disjunctive connectives*

The number of English words and phrases that can be used to express disjunction is relatively small. The most common disjunctive connectives are the following:

> or
> either . . . or
> or else
> or, alternatively
> otherwise
> with the alternative that
> unless

Four points about disjunctive operators are important to remember.

1. *The word* or *is sometimes used, not to express the disjunctive operator, but instead as a synonym for the phrase "that is to say."* For instance, the botanist who says

> **15.** The African violet, or *Saintpaulia ionantha,* requires well-drained soil.

is not claiming that either the African violet or the *Saintpaulia ionantha* requires well-drained soil. Instead, the Latin expression is being used as a different name for the same species. Thus, (15) is properly regarded in truth-functional logic as a simple statement, not as a truth-functional compound.[4]

---

[4] Translating *or* as a wedge in such cases will be harmless, however, since the resulting disjunction—"*p* ∨ *p*"—will have the same truth value as the original statement—"*p*."

2. *A truth-functional disjunction is nonexclusive.* As we have seen, a disjunction is true if one or both of its components are true. The exclusive sense of disjunction is regarded as a disjunction plus the negation of the conjunction of the disjunct: that is, as "$(p \lor q)$ & $\sim(p$ & $q)$." If it is unclear from the context whether a disjunction is meant in the exclusive or nonexclusive sense, the best policy is to treat it as nonexclusive unless there is a strong reason to believe it is intended as exclusive. A remark should be interpreted in the most plausible way—the way that is most likely to be true—and a nonexclusive disjunction has a better chance than an exclusive disjunction of being true. Thus, for instance, if the weather forecaster says

16. Monday will bring us precipitation in the form of sleet or freezing rain.

we will not regard the statement as false if both sleet and freezing rain fall on Monday.

3. The expression *neither . . . nor* translates as the denial of a disjunction, not as the disjunction of two denials. Thus,

17. Neither the Falcons nor the Buccaneers have won the Super Bowl.

is translated as "$\sim(F \lor B)$," and not as "$\sim F \lor \sim B$." Only "$\sim(F \lor B)$" is the denial of "$F \lor B$" and will be true only when "$F \lor B$" as a whole is false.

4. *The word* unless *expresses nonexclusive disjunction.* This is illustrated by the following assertion, made by an instructor:

18. You will fail the course, unless you rewrite this paper.

One might be tempted to regard this comment as excluding the possibility that you will both rewrite the paper and fail the course. However, this possibility has not been excluded. The instructor has asserted that you would definitely fail the course if the paper was not rewritten—*not* that you would receive a passing grade if you rewrote the paper, *no matter what else might happen.* The possibility remains open that you will rewrite the paper and fail the course anyway, perhaps because you fail the final exam or because you do not attend the remaining class meetings. Thus, (18) is *not* to be interpreted as "If you do rewrite the paper, then you will not fail the course"—or "If p, then not q."

Statement (18) is correctly interpreted as a conditional with a negative antecedent: "$\sim p \supset q$." It can be rewritten as

18a. If you do not rewrite this paper, then you will fail the course.

However, the statement form "$\sim p \supset q$" is truth-functionally equivalent to "$p \lor q$," as a truth table will demonstrate. Thus, the easiest course is to translate *unless* using the wedge except when there is clear reason to regard it as signifying exclusive disjunction. In other words, translate *unless* as you would *either . . . or.*

□ *Conditional connectives*

In this part of our translation guide, we have three objectives:

1. To be able to identify English equivalents of the conditional.

2. To distinguish truth-functional conditionals from simple statements called *subjunctive conditionals* or *counterfactual conditionals*.

3. To continue the discussion begun in Section 7-1 of the truth values logicians assign to the conditional by considering additional reasons for accepting this assignment of truth values.

□ SYMBOLIZING CONDITIONALS

In symbolizing truth-functional conditionals, one must be sure to put the antecedent and consequent in the proper order. Generally, the clause immediately following the word *if* is the antecedent, except when *if* is preceded by *only*. The clause immediately following *only if* is always the consequent. Thus,

> If Anna arrives, then Boris will sing.
> If Anna arrives, Boris will sing.
> Boris will sing if Anna arrives.

can be symbolized as "$A \supset B$" where "A" stands for "Anna arrives" and "B" for "Boris sings." However,

> Boris will sing, only if Anna arrives.
> Only if Anna arrives, will Boris sing.

must both be symbolized as "$B \supset A$" because "Anna arrives" is the consequent in both cases.

The reason the addition of *only* brings about such an important change is that the conditionals in the second set of statements—unlike those in the first set—assert that Anna's arrival is the only condition under which Boris will sing. Thus, it is not the case that Boris will sing if Anna doesn't arrive ("$\sim A \supset \sim B$"); and this combination of truth values is possible only when "Anna arrives" is the consequent. If we intend to use "Anna arrives" as the antecedent, we must recognize that "Boris sings" can still be true, depending upon other conditions—for example, the unexpected arrival of someone else whom Boris admires.

A large number of English words and phrases serve to express the conditional operator. For example,

> Given that Anna arrives, Boris will sing.
> Boris will sing provided that Anna arrives.
> Boris sings whenever Anna arrives.

are all truth-functional conditionals that can be symbolized as "$A \supset B$."

The best procedure in translating from English into symbolic language is to disregard the grammatical order of the clauses and to identify the antecedent and the consequent by the "indicator" words that precede them. Once either the antecedent or the consequent is identified, one will know how to symbolize the compound statement. Table 7-7 contains partial lists of such indicator words.

Precautions similar to those taken in identifying and translating conjunctions must be taken in identifying conditionals. When it occurs in a statement without *then*, the word *if* may not express a logical operator. In each of the following examples, the clause introduced by *if* is either polite or rhetorical and does not express the antecedent of a truth-functional conditional.

I'll stay until ten o'clock, if I won't be in your way.
He's slow on the uptake, if you catch my drift.
Pick up some beer on your way home, if you can remember.

Finally, as curious as it may seem, the word *and* sometimes functions as a conditional operator. This oddity occurs when the clause preceding *and* is an imperative and the clause following it is a declarative sentence. For instance,

Stop shouting and I'll listen to you.
Let her be more independent, and her attitude will improve.

can be regarded, respectively, as the following conditionals:

If you stop shouting, then I'll listen to you.
If you let her be more independent, then her attitude will improve.

TABLE 7-7 *Indicator words for components of conditionals*

WORDS THAT PRECEDE THE ANTECEDENT	WORDS THAT PRECEDE THE CONSEQUENT
if	then
given that	only if
insofar as	it follows that
provided that	implies
so long as	leads to
follows from	means that
is implied by	is a sufficient condition for
whenever	
to the extent that	
is a necessary condition for	

In the event that both clauses are imperatives, though, the sentence cannot be treated as a conditional. Consider

Stop shouting and listen to me!

Because this is a conjunction of imperatives, neither component expresses a statement. The sentence therefore falls outside the scope of truth-functional logic.

☐ SUBJUNCTIVE, OR COUNTERFACTUAL, CONDITIONALS

Some sentences have the grammatical structure of conditionals but do not express truth-functional conditionals. Consider these examples:

If I were Jane, I would see Professor Hilbert today.
You wouldn't be so bold if you had more intelligence.
He would be miserable if he hadn't passed calculus.
If I were skiing in Aspen, I'd be having a good time.
If President Carter had gotten the hostages out of Iran sooner, he would have been reelected.
The South would still have slavery today if Robert E. Lee had won at Gettysburg.

English connectives frequently used to express the conditional connect the clauses in each of these examples. However, the sentences are distinguished from truth-functional conditionals by what grammarians call their subjunctive mood: an attitude of speculation. Each example is a speculation about what should or would have happened or about what would or would not be the case today if something else—such as Lee's winning at Gettysburg—had happened. This speculative attitude is frequently indicated by the occurrence of the word *would* as part of the verb phrase in the consequent. Subjunctive conditionals are sometimes called *counterfactual conditionals* because the antecedent clause (for example, "Lee had won at Gettysburg") often expresses a statement that is the opposite of a known fact.

While the truth or falsity of a truth-functional conditional is wholly dependent upon the truth conditions of its component parts, this is usually not the case with subjunctive conditionals. For example, suppose I assert, "If I were skiing in Aspen, I would be having a good time," when *in fact* I am now in Washington, D.C. One might be tempted to regard the clauses of this subjunctive conditional as roughly equivalent to the statements "I am skiing in Aspen" and "I am having a good time." This would mean that the entire conditional must be regarded as true, since the antecedent ("I am skiing in Aspen") is false. (Recall the truth conditions for the conditional.) But the fact that I am now in the District of Columbia is irrelevant to the question of what my mental state *would be* if I *were* in Colorado. If it is meaningful to regard the subjunctive conditional I asserted as true or false, then its truth must be based on psychological facts—whether skiing really gives me pleasure, whether I dislike large crowds or the commercial atmosphere of Aspen, and so forth, and not merely on the truth or falsity of its components.[5]

Because subjunctive conditionals cannot be treated as truth-functional conditionals (at least not in any straightforward way), it is standard practice in truth-functional logic to regard them as *simple* statements. This practice will be followed throughout the book.

☐ Further justification of the conditional

The truth table below is a reminder that a truth-functional conditional is false under only one set of conditions. Those are the conditions shown in row 3, where the antecedent is true and the consequent is false.

p	q	$p \supset q$
T	T	T
F	T	T
T	F	F
F	F	T

While the truth values in rows 1 and 3 can be seen to be reasonable by considering ordinary linguistic usage, the decision to regard the conditional as true in rows 2 and 4 cannot so easily be supported by appealing to natural discourse. Logicians have simply stipulated—that is, decided by convention—that under the truth conditions of "p" and "q" in rows 2 and 4, the conditional will be true. These logical conventions are justified by good reasons involving the consistency and usefulness of the methods of truth-functional logic.

Consider the following statement, which is true under the truth conditions specified by row 4 (antecedent false, consequent false).

19. If Susan has accepted the job, then she will leave Washington.

Statement (19) is truth-functionally equivalent to statement (20)

20. If Susan has not left Washington, then she has not accepted the job.

because both are substitution instances of truth-functionally equivalent statement forms. As Table 7-5 (in Section 7-3) indicates, "$p \supset q$," the statement form of (19), and "$\sim q \supset \sim p$," the statement form of (20), are equivalent by contraposition.

Thus, the truth value for the conditional shown in row 4 of the truth table

---

[5] Some logicians argue that it is dubious whether these conditional sentences even express statements. See Bangs L. Tapscott, *Elementary Applied Symbolic Logic* (Englewood Cliffs, N.J.: Prentice-Hall, 1976), p. 47.

is justified. A conditional with both a false antecedent and a false consequent must be true because it is merely the contrapositive of a conditional with a true consequent and a true antecedent. If the truth conditions for "*p*" and "*q*" are both false and both "~*q*" and "~*p*" are therefore true—as designated in row 4—then "*p* ⊃ *q*" is simply the contrapositive of "~*q* ⊃ ~*p*." The truth table below presents this situation.

p *q*	~*p*	~*q*	*p* ⊃ *q*	~*q* ⊃ ~*p*
T T	F	F	T	T
F T	T	F	T	T
T F	F	T	F	F
F F	T	T	T	T

The *internal consistency* of the system therefore guarantees that a conditional with both a false antecedent and a false consequent will be true. We accept the conditional as true under the truth values assigned to its components in row 4 because we accept it as true under the assignments in row 1 and because "*p* ⊃ *q*" and "~*q* ⊃ ~*p*" are logically equivalent statement forms.

The character of truth-functional logic also justifies our accepting the conditional as true in row 2. It would be possible to manage without the conditional, for all truth-functional conditional statements can be translated into truth-functional disjunctive compounds by using the wedge and the tilde as logical operators. (In Section 7-3 a truth table was used to demonstrate the truth-functional equivalence of "*p* ⊃ *q*" and "~*p* ∨ *q*.") But as will be shown in Chapter 8, it is extremely convenient to be able to symbolize statements as conditionals when using the methods of formal deduction to check the validity of extended arguments.

The comparison of the truth values for the conditional and the biconditional in the following truth table shows that the assignment of the truth value T to the conditional in row 2 is also required to establish the conditional as a distinct truth-functional compound. If we were to regard cases in which the antecedent is false and the consequent is true as cases in which the conditional is false, we would eliminate the distinction between the conditional and the biconditional.

p *q*	*p* ⊃ *q*	*p* ≡ *q*
T T	T	T
F T	T	F
T F	F	F
F F	T	T

It might be objected that the point of translation is to represent the truth conditions of actual compound statements and that we should not accept logical conventions—such as the assignment of truth values to the conditional in rows 2 and 4 of the truth table—if they misrepresent our use of natural language. But these decisions do not conflict with ordinary usage. Rows 2 and 4 represent uses of the conditional that go well beyond its uses in ordinary discourse. They serve instead the purposes of deductive logic. We therefore accept the logical conventions when the reasons for them are sufficient.

As this section indicates, there can be no formal rules for translation. We must make use of every skill we have that helps us understand the meaning of a statement: information about the context, past experience with similar statements, common sense, and our intuitive "feel" for the language, as well as logical procedures. In addition, since there are no hard-and-fast rules, we must expect to find cases over which reasonable persons may disagree.

■ EXERCISE 7-4

■ A. Symbolize the statements that are truth-functional compounds. Explain why each of the statements you do not symbolize is not a truth-functional compound.

1. Camus and Sartre were French philosophers.

2. Oswald and Marie are siblings.

3. The Panthers did not win although they gained more than three hundred yards rushing in the football game.

*4. I know she was cross, but even so, she shouldn't belittle her friends.

5. Vesalius's *De Fabrica*, which was published in 1543, was a great work of art as well as a major advance in the study of human anatomy.

6. While the organization of ideas in his written work is clear, his papers are ungrammatical.

7. While you are dong your logic exercises I will be listening to Bruce Springsteen.

*8. If I were President Reagan, I'd cut military spending.

9. The United States is headed for a depression unless the rate of inflation decreases.

10. Pete won't believe Diane unless she supports her claim with facts.

11. The professor is complaining of poor attendance in addition to disruptive laughter in class.

*12. The American hostages in Iran were freed as President Reagan was inaugurated.

13. Erica is not yet qualified for this position.

14. He is eager to take the job; however, he is not ready to assume so much responsibility.

15. Not only your income but also your withholding taxes will increase.

*16. The price of natural gas is rising, even though the price of oil is also rising.

17. James counted fifty-six votes for the motion, whereas Sally counted only fifty-five.

18. The president was elected on the promise to cut government red tape, yet federal regulations continue to proliferate.

19. You cannot visit her in the hospital, however much you may want to.

*20. Stuart got dressed and left his apartment.

21. Since Harold has been accepted at Harvard Law School, it's impossible for him to talk about anything else.

22. Eat arsenic and you will die.

23. Ask him for a date and he'll accept.

*24. Perkins is caught between a rock and a hard place.

25. Nietzsche admired Socrates and Leonardo da Vinci.

26. Doreen leaned too far over the edge and fell in.

27. Gavin finished his project; however, Deborah did not finish hers.

*28. there is many a slip between the cup and the lip.

29. Insult her and she will never speak to you again.

30. This animal is a common toad, or *bufo vulgaris*.

31. He won't be admitted to the theater, even though he is first in line.

*32. Percy called Dr. Sprague a charlatan, or quack.

33. I'm happy even though I am tired.

34. You will win the award just insofar as you meet all the qualifications.

35. Alison was elected treasurer instead of Michelle.

*36. Jake made his choice without deliberating over his options.

37. Rachel came without her friends.

38. Neither Matisse nor Seurat were Cubists.

39. Both Faulkner and Fitzgerald were not from the South.

*40. If Tom is Jack's cousin, then Jack is Tom's cousin.

■ B. Which of the following compounds are logically equivalent to the conditional, "If Anna attends, then Ivan will sing"?

1. Ivan will sing, only if Anna attends.

2. Only if Anna attends will Ivan sing.

3. Provided that Anna attends, Ivan will sing.

*4. Whenever Ivan sings, Anna attends.

5. Anna's attending is implied by Ivan's singing.

6. If Anna attends, Ivan sings.

7. Only if Ivan sings will Anna attend.

*8. Ivan will sing, given that Anna attends.

9. Insofar as Ivan sings, Anna attends.

10. Ivan's singing follows from Anna's attending.

11. If Anna attends, it follows that Ivan will sing.

*12. Anna's attending is a sufficient condition for Ivan's singing.

13. Ivan's singing is a necessary condition for Anna's attending.

14. Inasmuch as Anna is attending, Ivan will sing.

15. Anna's attending is a necessary condition for Ivan's singing.
*16. Anna will attend provided that Ivan will sing.
17. Ivan's singing leads to Anna's attending.
18. Anna will attend only in the event that Ivan sings.
19. Ivan's singing is a necessary and sufficient condition for Anna's attending.
*20. Ivan will sing but Anna won't attend.　■

□ CHAPTER EIGHT

Evaluating truth-functional arguments

Arguments made up of truth-functional compounds are either valid or invalid because of their form. This chapter extends the methods that were introduced in Chapter 7 to the evaluation of such arguments. It presents three ways of demonstrating that an argument has a valid truth-functional form and is therefore valid: truth tables; formal deductions, or derivations; and indirect proof. The role in argument evaluation of tautologies—statements that are necessarily true because of their truth-functional form—and contradictions—statements that are necessarily false because of their truth-functional form—is explained. Also shown is the way in which abbreviated truth tables can be used to demonstrate the invalidity of a truth-functional argument form and, correspondingly, of an argument in that form.

□ 8-1. TRUTH TABLES AND VALID ARGUMENT FORMS

Truth tables were used in Chapter 7 to present definitions of the logical operators and to show how the truth value of a truth-functional compound is determined by the truth values of its component parts. We shall now see that truth tables have an additional use: if an argument can be translated adequately into the symbolic language of truth-functional logic, a truth table will show whether it is valid or invalid.

The claim made for deductive validity is very strong: it is not possible for a valid deductive argument to have all true premises and a false conclusion. This means that when a valid deductive argument is tested by a truth table, no combinations of truth values for the variables symbolizing simple statements will make all the premises true and the conclusion false. Every combination of truth values that makes all the premises true also makes the conclusion true.

The first step in using the truth-table method of testing validity is to replace the premises and conclusion of the argument with the statement forms for which they are substitution instances. Consider, for example, argument (1):

1. **You will take the midterm exam or you will write a paper.**
   You are not going to take the midterm exam.

   Therefore, you will write a paper.

With the logical symbol for *therefore* preceding the conclusion, this is symbolized as

1a. $p \lor q$
    $\sim p$
    $\therefore q$

Since (1a) presents the statement forms of the premises and conclusion, it represents the *argument form* for (1), and (1) is a substitution instance of this argument form.

The truth table is constructed according to the method explained in Chapter 7. It must have a base column for every variable, and the number of rows will depend on the number of variables. The table must contain a column for the conclusion and one for each premise. It must also have columns for any components of the conclusion or premises that may be truth functions. Because the conclusion of (1a) consists of one of the variables—"q"—one of the base columns can, in this case, represent the truth values of the conclusion.

	CONCLUSION	PREMISE	PREMISE
p	q	$\sim p$	$p \lor q$

The columns are derived by listing the possible combinations of truth and falsity for the variables and applying the rules for truth-functional compounds:

	CONCLUSION	PREMISE	PREMISE
p	q	$\sim p$	$p \lor q$
T	T	F	T
F	T	T	T
T	F	F	T
F	F	T	F

We now inspect the table to see whether there is any row in which a T appears in the column for each of the premises and an F appears in the column for the conclusion. If in a single row *all* the premises turn out to have T's while the conclusion has an F, we will have found an *invalidating row*. One such row is sufficient to show that it is *possible* for all the premises to be true and the conclusion false simultaneously, and any argument form with such a row cannot be valid. This, in turn, means that any substitution instance of an argument in that form will be invalid.

If the truth table contains no invalidating rows, the argument form being tested is a *valid argument form*. This means that any substitution instance of this form will be a valid argument. If (1a) is a valid argument form, then argument (1), as well as any other argument with the same form, is valid.

In checking the truth table for (1a), we find that there are no invalidating rows. Although the conclusion is false in both row 3 and row 4, these do not count as invalidating rows since a premise is also false in each of these rows. In row 2, where both premises have the value T, the conclusion has a T as well.

Since the truth table has no invalidating rows, it demonstrates that (1a) is a valid argument form. Whenever the premises are both true, the conclusion will be true as well.

Even if a truth table has rows in which the premises and the conclusion all come out T, a single invalidating row is sufficient to show that the argument form is invalid. As an illustration, consider this argument:

2. If you know how to construct a truth table,
   then you've studied Section 7-2.
   You don't know how to construct a truth table.
   _____
   Therefore, you haven't studied Section 7-2.

This has the following argument form:

2a. $p \supset q$
   $\sim p$
   $\therefore \sim q$

As shown by the following truth table, this argument form is invalid. Despite the fact that the conclusion and both premises are all T in row 4, row 2 is an invalidating row: it shows that a substitution instance of (2a) *could* have true premises and a false conclusion. And this means that the form of the argument cannot guarantee that if the premises are true, the conclusion will be true as well.

p	q	PREMISE $\sim p$	CONCLUSION $\sim q$	PREMISE $p \supset q$
T	T	F	F	T
F	T	T	F	T
T	F	F	T	F
F	F	T	T	T

Being familiar with common valid argument forms permits one to recognize some valid arguments even before they are exhibited in truth tables. This applies not only to arguments in these forms but also to complex truth-functional arguments constructed from simple forms. By recognizing one of the elementary forms when it occurs in a longer argument, one is halfway toward determining whether the longer argument is valid or invalid.

Eleven valid argument forms are listed in Table 8-1. The conventional name for each form is followed by its representation in symbolic language. Below the name of each form is a substitution instance—an example in English of an argument having this particular form—plus a brief explanation of why this argument form is valid. The validity of any of these forms can be confirmed by constructing a truth table. The validity of the form called disjunctive argument, for example, is confirmed by the truth table for (1a).

☐ *Rules of inference*

The eleven valid argument forms in Table 8-1 serve as *rules of inference* that can be stated alternatively in English and in the symbolic language of truth-functional logic. For example, the statements "Given two premises, we can infer their conjunction" and "'*p*'; '*q*'; therefore, '*p* & *q*'" are both equivalent to the rule of inference called *adjunction*.

Each rule of inference describes a set of premises—that is, one or more statement forms—and describes what validly can be inferred from this set. If a set of statements can be described in the same way as the premises in one of the rules of inference, one is entitled to deduce a conclusion according to the rule.

Consider these statements:

It is not the case both that Gabrielle will be elected to the student council and travel to France for her junior year abroad.
Gabrielle has been elected to the student council.

Presented symbolically, the statements are as follows:

$\sim(p \ \& \ q)$
$\therefore p$

As shown by Table 8-1, the statement forms appear as premises in the inference rule for *conjunctive argument*. And since the rule of inference entitles us to infer "$\sim q$" from these premises, we can also infer from the statements about Gabrielle that

Therefore, Gabrielle will not travel to France for her junior year abroad.

Because the rules of inference present valid argument forms, a particular argument is known to be valid if its statement forms can be completely described by a rule of inference. Applying the rules therefore represents a stride forward in terms of efficiency. It is often much easier to show that an argument is valid by showing that a rule of inference justifies the deduction than by

TABLE 8-1 *Valid argument forms*

Conjunctive Simplification	$p \;\&\; q$	$p \;\&\; q$
	$\therefore p$	$\therefore q$
Example:	Inflation will continue and unemployment will increase.	
	Therefore, inflation will continue.	
Explanation:	Because both components of a conjunctive argument are true, it is permissible to infer that either of its conjuncts is true.	
Adjunction	p	
	q	
	$\therefore p \;\&\; q$	
Example:	They bought a Toyota.	
	They drove to Ohio.	
	Therefore, they bought a Toyota and they drove to Ohio.	
Explanation:	Because both premises are presumed true, we can infer their conjunction.	
Conjunctive Argument	$\sim(p \;\&\; q)$	$\sim(p \;\&\; q)$
	p	q
	$\therefore \sim q$	$\therefore \sim p$
Example:	He will not take both Latin and Greek.	
	He is taking Latin.	
	Therefore, he will not take Greek.	
Explanation:	Because the first premise says that at least one of the conjuncts is false and the second premise identifies a true conjunct, we can infer that the other conjunct is false.	
Disjunctive Argument	$p \lor q$	$p \lor q$
	$\sim p$	$\sim q$
	$\therefore q$	$\therefore p$
Example:	Either the New York Yankees will win the pennant or the Baltimore Orioles will.	
	The Yankees will not win the pennant.	
	Therefore, the Orioles will win the pennant.	
Explanation:	Because at least one disjunct must be true, by knowing one is false we can infer that the other is true.	

TABLE 8-1 *(Continued)*

Disjunctive Addition	p
	$\therefore p \vee q$
Example:	It is snowing.
	Therefore, either it is snowing or it is raining.
Explanation:	Given that a statement is true, we can infer that a disjunction comprised by it and any other statement is true, because only one disjunct needs to be true for the disjunctive compound to be true.

Modus Ponens, or Affirming the Antecedent

$$p \supset q$$
$$p$$
$$\therefore q$$

Example:	If it snows Saturday, then we will ski on Sunday.
	It will snow Saturday.
	Therefore, we will ski on Sunday.
Explanation:	Given the conditional claim that the consequent is true if the antecedent is true, and given that the antecedent is true, we can infer the consequent.

Modus Tollens, or Denying the Consequent

$$p \supset q$$
$$\sim q$$
$$\therefore \sim p$$

Example:	If it snows Saturday, then we will ski on Sunday.
	It is not the case that we will ski on Sunday.
	Therefore, it is not the case that it will snow Saturday.
Explanation:	Given the conditional claim that the consequent is true if the antecedent is true, and given that the consequent is false, we can infer that the antecedent is also false.

Chain Argument	$p \supset q$
	$q \supset r$
	$\therefore p \supset r$
Example:	If her project on Norse folklore is approved, then she will be a Fulbright Scholar to Norway.
	If she is a Fulbright Scholar to Norway, she will become an expert in ethnomusicology.

TABLE 8-1   *(Continued)*

	Therefore, if her project in Norse folklore is approved, she will become an expert in ethnomusicology.
Explanation:	Given two conditionals such that the antecedent of the second is the consequent of the first, we can infer a conditional such that its antecedent is the same as the antecedent of the first premise and its consequent is the same as the consequent of the second premise.
Biconditional Argument	$p \equiv q$ $p \equiv q$ $p \equiv q$ $p \equiv q$ p q $\sim p$ $\sim q$ $\therefore q$ $\therefore p$ $\therefore \sim q$ $\therefore \sim p$
Example:	The Panthers will win if and only if Bruce plays for them. Bruce will play for the Panthers. Therefore, the Panthers will win.
Explanation:	Given a biconditional and given that the truth value of one side is known, we can infer that the other side has exactly the same truth value.
Constructive Dilemma	$p \supset q$ $p \supset q$ $r \supset s$ $r \supset q$ $p \lor r$ $p \lor r$ $\therefore q \lor s$ $\therefore q$ (Equivalent to $q \lor q$)
Example:	If John works harder on his courses, then he will be admitted to the MBA program. If John works harder on his job, then he will be retained by the firm. John will either work harder on his courses or work harder on his job. Therefore, either John will be admitted to the MBA program or he will be retained by the firm.
Explanation:	Given two conditionals, and given the disjunction of their antecedents, we can infer the disjunction of their consequents.
Destructive Dilemma	$p \supset q$ $p \supset q$ $r \supset s$ $p \supset r$ $\sim q \lor \sim s$ $\sim q \lor \sim r$ $\therefore \sim p \lor \sim r$ $\therefore \sim p$ (Equivalent to $\sim p \lor \sim p$)

TABLE 8-1 *(Continued)*

Example:	If it snows, then we will go skiing.
	If it rains, then we will go to the movies.
	Either we will not go skiing or we will not go to the movies.
	Therefore, either it will not snow or it will not rain.
Explanation:	Given two conditionals, and given the disjunction of the negation of their consequents, we can infer the disjunction of the negation of their antecedents.

constructing a truth table. Arguments in the form of the constructive dilemma, for example, have four different variables and therefore require truth tables with sixteen rows.

An argument is not necessarily invalid because it does not satisfy a known rule of inference, however. Some valid arguments do not have one of the simple valid argument forms described by the rules. But the truth-table technique can always be depended on to provide a conclusive answer. A truth table will show whether any truth-functional argument is valid or invalid.

□ *Formal fallacies*

Not infrequently, invalid arguments are mistaken for valid ones. In particular, two invalid forms of argument are common enough to have earned names as formal fallacies:

A formal fallacy is one that arises over an error concerning the form or logical properties of an argument.

The *fallacy of denying the antecedent* is a formal fallacy involving the mistaken belief that the following is a valid argument form:

$p \supset q$
$\sim p$
$\therefore \sim q$

But this argument form is the same as (2a), which was shown by a truth table to be invalid.

This error involves a misunderstanding of the truth-functional definition of the conditional. Remember that when the antecedent "p" is false, the conditional will be true whether the consequent "q" is true or false. Thus, given the truth of "$p \supset q$" and "$\sim p$," we *cannot* validly infer "$\sim q$." It would be possible for "q" to be either true or false.

The *fallacy of affirming the consequent*, which involves the mistaken belief that

$$p \supset q$$
$$q$$
$$\therefore p$$

is a valid argument form also arises from misunderstanding the truth conditions for the conditional. As we know, if the consequent is true, then the conditional is true whether the antecedent is true or false. Thus, given "$p \supset q$" and "q" we *cannot* validly infer "p" because "$\sim p$" could also be true. A truth table for this argument form, too, will show it to be invalid.

□ *Recognizing valid argument forms*

In deciding whether an argument has a valid form, the crucial consideration is the pattern created by the *dominant operators* of the premises and conclusion. One must discern and focus upon the relationships between the variables in the argument form.

Consider the argument forms for conjunctive argument (3) and chain argument (4):

3. $\sim (p \,\&\, q)$
  p
  $\therefore \sim q$

4. $p \supset q$
  $q \supset r$
  $\therefore p \supset r$

Each argument form can be represented abstractly by substituting a rectangle for the first variable, a circle for the second, and a star for the third:

3a. $\sim (\square \,\&\, \bigcirc)$
  $\square$
  $\therefore \sim\bigcirc$

4a. $\square \supset \bigcirc$
  $\bigcirc \supset \star$
  $\therefore \square \supset \star$

The rectangles, circles, and stars serve as reminders that the variables are merely placeholders. In identifying the *form* of the argument, we do not concern ourselves with what is "inside" the rectangle or the other symbols—that is, we do not consider the *content* of the statements. The geometrical symbols in (3a) and (4a) can be replaced by simple statements, or they can be replaced by truth-functional compounds. Whatever statements are substituted for the symbols, the result will be an argument of the same form, as long as the substitutions are consistent—that is, as long as the same simple or compound statement is substituted each time a given symbol occurs in the argument.

Thus, argument (5) exhibits the same argument form as (3), although one of the components of (5)—what has replaced the rectangle—is itself a compound. Furthermore, argument (6) has the same valid argument form as (4), although each of the variables in (4) has been replaced by a compound.

5. $\sim[(p \lor r) \, \& \, q]$

$\quad p \lor r$

$\quad \therefore \sim q$

6. $(p \supset s) \supset (q \, \& \, u)$

$\quad (q \, \& \, u) \supset (r \lor t)$

$\quad \therefore (p \supset s) \supset (r \lor t)$

Because the dominant operators for (3) and (5) are the same, they are treated as having the same argument form, and likewise with (4) and (6). This principle can be generalized to apply to all the rules of inference.

Whatever valid inference follows from a set of statement forms will follow from any set of statement forms having compounds with dominant operators that exactly match the dominant operators of the initial set of statement forms.

■ **EXERCISE 8-1**

■ A. Symbolize each of the following arguments using the suggested letters. Indicate which arguments are valid and which are invalid. Name the argument form exhibited by each valid argument.

  1. Erica has been trained in pediatrics. Therefore, Erica has been trained in either pediatrics or gerontology. (P, G)

  2. Jarvis will pass logic only if he does the exercises. But Jarvis never does exercises. Therefore, Jarvis will not pass. (P, E)

  3. If the dean has the long-range interest of the college in mind, the dean will approve Professor Quine's recommendation for tenure. The dean does have the long-range interest of the college in mind. Therefore, the dean will approve Professor Quine's recommendation for tenure. (I, A)

  *4. William Faulkner didn't write both *Light in August* and *The Sun Also Rises*. He did write *Light in August*. So we know he didn't write *The Sun Also Rises*. (L, S)

  5. If smoking cigarettes is not a cause of lung cancer, then smokers should not have a greater incidence of lung cancer than nonsmokers. Lung cancer is far more

prevalent among smokers. Therefore, smoking cigarettes is a cause of lung cancer. (*C, I*)

6. If the dean has the long-range interest of the philosophy department in mind, he will recommend Professor Quine for tenure. The dean has recommended Professor Quine for tenure. Therefore, the dean does have the long-range interest of the philosophy department in mind. (*I, R*)

7. William Faulkner didn't write both *Tender Is the Night* and *Gone with the Wind*. It is certain that he didn't write *Gone with the Wind*. Therefore, he must be the author of *Tender Is the Night*. (*T, G*)

*8. If Mount St. Helens is in the Cascade Mountains, then it is near the San Andreas fault. If Mount St. Helens is near the San Andreas fault, then earthquake tremors will precede volcanic eruptions. Thus, if Mount St. Helens is in the Cascade Mountains, earthquake tremors will precede volcanic eruptions. (*C, S, E*)

9. The United States must depend on oil from either Saudi Arabia or Venezuela. Our country doesn't need to depend on oil from Venezuela. Thus, it must depend on oil from Saudi Arabia. (*S, V*)

10. Lillian will pass the course if and only if she passes the final exam. She has received a grade of C on the final exam. Therefore, she has passed the course. (*C, F*)

11. If Sherlock Holmes's inference is correct, then Moriarity is the murderer. If Watson's pearl-handled pistol is missing, then Moriarity is the murderer. So, if Watson's pearl-handled pistol is missing, Sherlock Holmes's inference is correct. (*I, M, P*)

*12. If no scientist can disprove astrology, then astrologers are worth listening to. There is a scientist who can disprove astrology. So astrologers are not worth listening to. (*D, W*)

13. If Lee becomes a lawyer, Lee will be successful, and if Lee joins the diplomatic corps, Lee will be successful. It is not the case that Lee will become neither a lawyer nor a diplomat. So Lee will be successful. (*L, S, D*)

14. Either the flag of Indonesia flies over New Guinea or the flag of Australia does. The flag of Indonesia does fly over New Guinea. Therefore, the flag of Australia does not fly over New Guinea. (*I, A*)

15. If the Soviet Union continues to increase the accuracy of its intercontinental ballistic missiles, then the United States will invest heavily in antisatellite weapons. If the United States and the Soviet Union negotiate a new strategic arms limitation treaty, then both sides will reduce the number of intercontinental ballistic missiles. Either both sides won't reduce the number of intercontinental ballistic missiles, or the United States won't invest heavily in antisatellite weapons. Therefore, either the Soviet Union won't continue to increase the accuracy of its intercontinental ballistic missiles, or the United States and the Soviet Union won't negotiate a new strategic arms limitation treaty. (*I, A, N, R*)

■ **B.** Construct truth tables to determine whether each of the following arguments is valid or invalid.

1. Either the birthrate in Mexico will decline, or Mexico will face an economic crisis. So it is not the case that either the birthrate in Mexico won't decline or that Mexico won't face an economic crisis.

2. It is not true that both the price of gold is fixed and that people speculate on the price. People do speculate on the price of gold. Consequently, it is not fixed.

3. Either Shirley will get her degree in May, or she will drop out of school and take a job with her mother. If I know her, she will not drop out of school. Consequently, she will get her degree.

*4. If grade inflation is to cease, grade anxiety among students must decrease. If grade inflation ceases, then standardized test scores will become less important in law-school admissions. Thus, if grade anxiety among students decreases, standardized test scores will become less important in law-school admissions.

5. If the testimony of the witness was correct, the defendant was guilty. The defendant was indeed guilty. So the testimony of the witness must have been correct.

6. If there is an indictment, then if he is brought to trial he will be convicted. But he won't be brought to trial. So, either there will be an indictment or he will be convicted.

7. Either the maid is guilty or the governess is lying. If the maid is guilty, Lady Poultney was murdered for her diamond tiara. The governess is not lying. Therefore, Lady Poultney was murdered for her diamond tiara.

*8. If the economic theory of Adam Smith is unsound, then so is that of Thomas Malthus. If the economics of David Ricardo is unsound, then so is that of Smith. So if the economic theory of Malthus is sound, that of Ricardo is also sound.

9. If Sam got an A in Spanish, he must have worked hard and paid attention in class. But it is false that he worked hard and paid attention in class. So he didn't get an A in Spanish.

10. If the high-pressure system has moved in, the weather back home is clear and the temperatures are warm. But because the system has not moved in, the weather must be either cloudy or cool.

11. Either the president is happy and the college has been accredited, or the president is happy and the endowment was increased. The president is happy. The endowment was not increased. Therefore, the college was accredited.

*12. Stephanie is a lawyer only if she hasn't been disbarred. It's not the case that she hasn't been disbarred. So Stephanie isn't a lawyer.

13. If he passed the bar exam, he has graduated from law school. He is a lawyer if and only if he passed the bar exam and graduated from law school. So either he isn't a lawyer, or he passed the bar exam.

14. If the drought continues, then the crops will fail. If the crops fail, the farmers will be ruined. But if the state is declared a disaster area, the farmers will not be ruined. The drought will continue and the state will be declared a disaster area. Therefore, the farmers will not be ruined.

15. If East Germany develops closer ties with West Germany, then the Polish people will demand greater liberalization within their own country. If the Polish people demand greater liberalization, then the Soviet Union will risk social unrest by increasing its military presence in Poland. But the Soviet Union won't risk social unrest by increasing its military presence in Poland. Therefore, East Germany won't develop closer ties with West Germany.

■ C. Determine by means of truth tables whether each of the following arguments is valid or invalid.

1. $A \supset B$
   $\therefore A \supset (A \& B)$

2. $\sim(A \& B)$
   A
   $\therefore \sim B$

3. $A \lor B$
   $C \supset A$
   $\therefore C \supset B$

*4. $A \supset B$
$C \mathbin{\&} A$
$\therefore B \lor C$

5. $\sim(A \lor B)$
$\sim A \supset C$
$\therefore C$

6. $C \supset (D \mathbin{\&} E)$
$\sim D \lor \sim E$
$\therefore \sim C$

7. $C \supset (D \lor E)$
C
$\therefore D$

*8. $\sim D \lor E$
$E \supset F$
$\therefore \sim F \supset \sim D$

9. $G \supset \sim H$
$(H \mathbin{\&} J) \lor G$
$\therefore \sim H$

10. $\sim(H \mathbin{\&} I)$
$I \lor J$
$\therefore H \supset J$

11. $\sim(J \mathbin{\&} \sim K)$
$K \lor \sim L$
$\sim L$
$\therefore J$

*12. $(J \supset K) \mathbin{\&} (L \supset M)$
$\sim M \lor \sim K$
$\sim J$
$\therefore \sim L$

13. $M \supset N$
$O \supset M$
$\therefore N \lor O$

14. $P \supset (Q \supset R)$
$Q \supset (P \supset R)$
$\therefore (P \lor Q) \supset R$

15. $(Q \mathbin{\&} R) \supset (Q \lor S)$
$Q \lor R$
$\therefore Q \mathbin{\&} R$ ■

□ 8-2. TAUTOLOGIES AND CONTRADICTIONS

It is possible to produce truth-functional compounds that will be true whatever the truth values of their components. An example is the compound "$p \lor \sim p$." As the truth table shows,

p	$\sim p$	$p \lor \sim p$
T	F	T
F	T	T

whatever the truth values of "p" and "$\sim p$," "$p \lor \sim p$" must be true.

The compound "$p \lor \sim p$" is a special kind of necessarily true statement[1] called a *tautology*.

A tautology is a truth-functional compound that is necessarily true because of its truth-functional form.

Only a tautology will have a T in every row of its truth table. Some additional examples of tautologies are

$\sim(p \mathbin{\&} \sim p)$

$p \supset p$

$p \equiv p$

These and "$p \lor \sim p$" have been given names. The compound "$p \lor \sim p$" is called the *law of excluded middle* because it reflects the fact that any given

---

[1] These are statements that we know to be true without needing to make empirical observations. See Section 2-3.

MISS PEACH   By Mell Lazarus

Miss Peach by Mel Lazarus. © *1983 Field Enterprises, Inc. Reprinted by permission.*

statement must be either true or false—there being no third, or middle, alternative. The compounds "$p \supset p$" and "$p \equiv p$" are known as *laws of identity* because they concern relationships between identical statements. The compound "$\sim(p \,\&\, \sim p)$" is called the *law of noncontradiction* because it reflects the fact that a statement cannot be both true and false.

The transformation rules discussed in Section 7-3 are all tautologies. If, for example, a truth table is constructed for the rule for conditional exchange—"$(p \supset q) \equiv (\sim p \lor q)$"—the column for this biconditional will consist entirely of T's because its components, "$p \supset q$" and "$\sim p \lor q$," will have identical columns. All the other transformation rules can also be shown by truth tables to be tautologies.

It is possible, too, to produce truth-functional compounds that will be *false* whatever the truth values of their components. As shown below, the compound "$p \,\&\, \sim p$" has an F in every row of its truth table.

p	$\sim p$	$p \,\&\, \sim p$
T	F	F
F	T	F

This compound is an example of a *contradiction:*[2]

> A contradiction is a truth-functional compound that is necessarily false because of its truth-functional form.

Only a contradiction will have an F in every row of its truth table. Other

---

[2] It is important to appreciate the difference between a *contradiction* (a necessarily false statement); *contradictories* (pairs of statements that have opposite truth values, the one being a negation of the other); and *contraries* (statements that cannot both be true but that can both be false). Contradictories and contraries are discussed in Section 5-3.

examples of contradictions are:

$p \equiv {\sim}p$

${\sim}(p \vee {\sim}p)$

Substitution instances of statement forms that are necessarily true or necessarily false are themselves referred to as tautologies or contradictions. And like their corresponding statement forms, the substitution instances are always either necessarily true or necessarily false.

A substitution instance of a compound that is neither a tautology nor a contradiction is said to be *contingent*.

> **A contingent statement is one whose truth table shows it to have both T's and F's in its column.**

It is always *logically* possible for a contingent statement to be either true or false (but not both). That is, a contingent statement that turns out to be factually true could have been false without violating any logical rule; and one that turns out to be false could have been true without violating any logical rule.

☐ *Tautologies and valid argument forms*

There is a tautology corresponding to every valid truth-functional argument. The tautology is a conditional statement whose antecedent is the conjunction of the premises of the argument and whose consequent is the conclusion of the argument. For instance, the conditional "$[{\sim}(p \& q) \& p] \supset {\sim}q$" is a tautology that corresponds to conjunctive argument (see Table 8-1), and the conditional "$[(p \supset q) \& p] \supset q$" is a tautology that corresponds to *modus ponens*.

To say that an argument is valid is to say that if all of its premises are true, then its conclusion must be true. Under such circumstances, the corresponding conditional cannot have a true antecedent and a false consequent, and so it will be necessarily true—a tautology. Thus, another way of defining truth-functional validity is as follows:

> **A truth-functional argument is valid if and only if its premises, when conjoined as the antecedent of a conditional, and its conclusion, when written as the consequent of the same conditional, result in a tautology.**

All truth-functional arguments could be tested for validity by constructing a truth table for the conditional formed in this way. However, this procedure would be no less time-consuming than the more traditional truth-table method.

□ *The paradoxes of entailment*

When tautologies and contradictions occur as parts of arguments, they can have peculiar results, which are called *paradoxes of entailment*. There are two such paradoxes. The first involves an argument whose conclusion is a tautology, and the second involves an argument that has a contradiction as one of its premises.

1. *Given the definition of validity, any argument whose conclusion is a tautology will necessarily be valid.* Since the conclusion of such an argument can only be true, it is impossible for its truth table to exhibit a row in which the premises are all true and the conclusion is false.

Consider this example:

Ronald Reagan is the president of the United States.

Therefore, either Poland is a European country or Poland is not a European country.

Even though the premise and the conclusion bear no relation to each other, this argument is valid. A tautology can validly be deduced from any statement whatsoever. But because intuitively it seems impossible for such an argument to be valid, its validity is called a *paradox*.

The escape from this paradox requires that a distinction be made between what the definitions and procedures of truth-functional logic permit, on the one hand, and what one succeeds in *proving* by such an argument on the other hand. Truth-functional logic allows tautologous statements to be constructed. Furthermore, the concept of validity allows a tautology to be derived from any premise or premises. But such arguments are always *trivial*. Because the conclusion, as a tautology, is necessarily true on its own, the premises never succeed in establishing its truth. Where the premises are irrelevant to the truth of the conclusion, the argument, whether formally valid or not, is fallacious. Such arguments are all *non sequiturs* (see Sections 12-3 and 12-4).

2. *Given the definition of validity, any argument with a contradiction as a premise will necessarily be valid.* This is not as peculiar as it may at first appear when one considers the requirements for a valid argument. A valid argument cannot have all true premises and a false conclusion. Now, if one of the premises of an argument is a contradiction—that is, necessarily false—then all its premises cannot be true and the conclusion false. Therefore, the following argument is valid:

King Kong is the world's largest ape, and King Kong is not the world's largest ape.

Therefore, the world's largest ape is in the Tokyo Zoo.

The same result obtains when an argument has two or more premises that contradict each other. If it is logically impossible for a set of premises both to be true at the same time, the premises are said to be *inconsistent*. And any argument with an inconsistent set of premises must be valid: all the premises cannot be true and the conclusion false. Because any statement whatsoever can validly be deduced from inconsistent premises, the following is a valid argument:

> **Ronald Reagan was a competent governor.**
>
> **It's not the case that Ronald Reagan was a competent governor.**
> _____
> **Therefore, the Lone Ranger is the czar of Russia.**

However, although such arguments are valid, they can never be *sound*. A sound argument guarantees the truth of its conclusion only if the premises are all true, but in arguments of this type *one premise is necessarily false*. Furthermore, it is peculiar even to speak about proving a conclusion by arguing from inconsistent premises. In everyday language, *proving* means to "establish the truth of" a statement, and because it is possible to deduce *any* conclusion from inconsistent premises, such premises cannot support any particular conclusion. An argument with inconsistent premises is a fallacious argument (see Section 12-1).

■ **EXERCISE 8-2**

■ A. Identify the statement forms listed below that are equivalent to "$p \lor q$." Also identify the statement forms that are contradictories of "$p \lor q$"—that is, the ones having exactly opposite truth values.

    1. $\sim q \supset p$

    2. $\sim p \ \& \ \sim q$

    3. $\sim(\sim p \supset q)$

  *4. $\sim(\sim q \ \& \ \sim p)$

    5. $\sim p \ \& \ \sim(\sim p \supset q)$

■ B. Indicate which of the following statement forms are tautologies, which are contradictions, and which are contingent.

    1. $\sim p \lor \sim(q \ \& \ \sim r)$

    2. $\sim p \ \& \ (\sim q \lor p)$

    3. $\sim p \ \& \ (\sim q \ \& \ r)$

  *4. $(p \ \& \ q) \lor (\sim p \ \& \ \sim q)$

    5. $(p \lor q) \ \& \ (\sim p \lor \sim q)$

    6. $(p \ \& \ q) \supset (p \lor q)$

    7. $(\sim p \supset p) \ \& \ (p \supset \sim p)$

  *8. $(p \lor q) \supset (p \ \& \ q)$

    9. $p \supset (q \supset p)$

10. $\sim[p \,\&\, \sim(p \lor q)] \supset [q \,\&\, \sim(q \lor p)]$
11. $(q \,\&\, r) \supset [(q \lor p) \,\&\, (r \lor \sim p)]$
*12. $[(p \supset q) \,\&\, (q \supset r)] \supset (p \supset r)$
13. $[(p \lor q) \,\&\, (p \,\&\, q)] \supset p$
14. $[(p \lor q) \,\&\, \sim p] \supset \sim q$
15. $[(p \lor q) \supset r] \equiv [(p \supset r) \,\&\, (q \supset r)]$

■ C. Demonstrate that the following are tautologies.
1. $(p \supset \sim p) \equiv \sim p$
2. $[(p \lor q) \,\&\, (r \lor s)] \equiv [(p \,\&\, r) \lor (q \,\&\, r) \lor (p \,\&\, s) \lor (q \,\&\, s)]$
3. $[(p \,\&\, q) \lor (r \,\&\, s)] \equiv [(p \lor r) \,\&\, (q \lor r) \,\&\, (p \lor s) \,\&\, (q \lor s)]$
*4. $[p \,\&\, (p \lor q)] \equiv [p \lor (p \,\&\, q)]$
5. $[p \,\&\, (q \lor \sim q)] \equiv p$

■ D. Demonstrate that the following are equivalencies.
1. $[p \lor (q \,\&\, \sim q)] \equiv p$
2. $[p \supset (q \supset r)] \equiv [q \supset (p \supset r)]$
3. $[(p \supset q) \,\&\, (p \supset r)] \equiv [p \supset (q \,\&\, r)]$
*4. $[(p \supset r) \,\&\, (q \supset r)] \equiv [(p \lor q) \supset r]$
5. $[(p \supset q) \lor (p \supset r)] \equiv [p \supset (q \lor r)]$ ■

□ 8-3. FORMAL DEDUCTIONS, OR DERIVATIONS

You and a friend are discussing an acquaintance, Margaret, who is anxiously waiting to hear that she has passed the bar exam. Two firms, O'Rourke & Springer and Fisher & Walsh, have made job offers to Margaret contingent upon her becoming a member of the bar; and Margaret has made it clear that she will accept employment with one firm or the other. In addition, she has been told by each firm that, if everything goes well, she can expect to become a partner in five years. However, your friend points out that it will not be possible for Margaret to attain this goal and remain chairperson of the state's Democratic Party Central Committee. In the midst of your conversation, Margaret telephones to say that she has passed the bar exam. "Well," your friend says with a sigh, "good-bye to the best organizer the Democratic Party has ever had in this state." Is your friend right in concluding that Margaret will give up her office?

Your friend's reasoning could be represented as an argument to the conclusion that Margaret will resign from her position in the Democratic party. By allowing "B" to stand for "Margaret passes the bar exam," "O" for "Margaret joins the O'Rourke Firm," "F" for "Margaret joins the Fisher Firm," "P" for "Margaret will become a partner in five years," and "C" for "Margaret remains chairperson of the state's Democratic Party Central Committee," the argument can be represented symbolically as follows:

$B \supset (O \vee F)$
$(O \vee F) \supset P$
$\sim(P \,\&\, C)$
B
$\therefore \sim C$

Assuming for purposes of this discussion that all the premises are true, we can evaluate the validity of the argument—but doing so will require a different method from those explained so far. Because the argument involves five simple statements—"B," "O," "F," "P," and "C"—a truth table for the argument form would require 32 rows. Furthermore, the argument is too long to treat as an instance of one of the valid argument forms listed in Table 8-1. There are too many premises, and they do not match the premises described by any one of the rules of inference.

A method that does permit the evaluation of long and involved arguments consists of combining and recombining premises in such a way that one moves in a continuous series of steps from the premises to the conclusion. This process is known as *performing a formal deduction* or *constructing a derivation.* When a formal deduction succeeds in showing an argument to be valid, it constitutes a *demonstration,* or *proof,* of validity.

Look again at the argument about Margaret. The key problem is to determine whether the conclusion, "$\sim C$," can validly be derived from the premises. To do this by means of formal deduction, one sets down the premises, and then, based on those premises, one adds a series of intermediate statements that are designed to lead to the conclusion. Each intermediate statement is justified through the application of a rule of inference or a transformation rule. If the conclusion can be shown to follow validly from the original premises and the intermediate statements, the argument is valid.

1. $B \supset (O \vee F)$ ⎫
2. $(O \vee F) \supset P$ ⎬ **INITIAL PREMISES**
3. $\sim(P \,\&\, C)$
4. B ⎭
5.   ⎫
6.
.   ⎬ **INTERMEDIATE STATEMENTS**
.
.   ⎭
$n \sim C$ ⎬ **CONCLUSION**

One begins constructing a formal deduction by symbolizing the statements in the argument with abbreviations rather than variables. This is because the formal deduction is a proof of the validity of a particular argument and not a demonstration that a general argument form is a valid form. So, for example, the first premise of the argument under consideration is symbolized as "B ⊃ (O ∨ F)" rather than as "*p* ⊃ (*q* ∨ *r*)."

The next step is to list and number the premises.

1. B ⊃ (O ∨ F)
2. (O ∨ F) ⊃ P
3. ~(P & C)
4. B

Next, if we concentrate only on the first two lines and remember the rule of inference for chain argument ("'*p* ⊃ *q*'; '*q* ⊃ *r*'; therefore, '*p* ⊃ *r*'"), we see that the premises in these lines have the same form as the premises in a chain argument. We are thus justified in adding the conclusion "B ⊃ P" as a new line:

5. B ⊃ P   From (1) and (2) by chain argument

Now we see that, together, lines 5 and 4 form the premise conditions for *modus ponens*. This permits us to derive as a further line the conclusion "P."

6. P   From (5) and (4) by *modus ponens*

Finally, lines 3 and 6 together satisfy the rule of inference for conjunctive argument. Therefore, from these lines we derive

7. ~C   From (3) and (6) by conjunctive argument

And since "~C" is also the conclusion of the original argument, the initial argument has been shown to be valid.

When the lines in the formal deduction are arranged as a continuous series, it appears this way:

1. B ⊃ (O ∨ F)   Premise
2. (O ∨ F) ⊃ P   Premise
3. ~(P & C)   Premise
4. B   /∴ ~C   Premise/Conclusion
5. B ⊃ P   From (1) and (2) by chain argument
6. P   From (5) and (4) by *modus ponens*
7. ~C   From (3) and (6) by conjunctive argument

Note that the conclusion of the argument being tested is placed on the same line (line 4) as the last premise and separated from it by a diagonal line, or solidus. This avoids the possibility of mistaking the conclusion for a premise, and it also marks the end of the original premises and the beginning of the intermediate statements, or derived lines. Numbering the lines facilitates checking the validity of the chain because each derived line can be justified by citing the numbers of the lines from which it is derived, along with the name of the rule used to derive it.

Various rules of inference can be applied and reapplied to generate intermediate statements and reach the desired conclusion. Indeed, there is no such thing as *the* correct formal deduction, or derivation. Any series of valid steps constitutes a proof of the argument, and there may be an indefinite number of possible proofs.

For example, we might have begun the deduction for the above argument by combining lines 1 and 4 and applying the rule of *modus ponens* to obtain

5'. $O \lor F$ From (1) and (4) by *modus ponens*

We might then have combined lines 2 and 5', again applying *modus ponens*, to obtain

6'. P From (2) and (5) by *modus ponens*

From lines 3 and 6', "$\sim C$" could then have been derived by conjunctive argument, as before:

7'. $\sim C$ From (3) and (6') by conjunctive argument

Although only rules of inference were applied in the deductions performed so far, new lines can also be generated by applying transformation rules. And the rules can be used in combination with each other: a new line can be added if it either follows from earlier lines by the rules of inference or can be shown by a transformation rule to be equivalent to some preceding line.

Suppose, for instance, that we wish to prove that "$K \supset N$" follows validly from the premises "$M \equiv N$," "$K \supset J$," and "$\sim M \supset \sim J$." As before, the premises are listed and numbered, and the conclusion is placed to the right of the last premise:

1. $M \equiv N$
2. $K \supset J$
3. $\sim M \supset \sim J$ /∴ $K \supset N$

At first, we fail to recognize valid patterns of inference; there seem to be no combinations of premises that will yield new lines by applying the rules of inference. But by applying the transformation rule for contraposition to line

3, we obtain

    4. $J \supset M$ From (3) by contraposition

And now, by chain argument, lines 2 and 4 yield

    5. $K \supset M$ From (2) and (4) by chain argument

Again by a transformation rule, biconditional exchange, we obtain

    6. $(M \supset N) \mathbin{\&} (N \supset M)$ From (1) by biconditional exchange

Conjunctive simplification now permits the derivation from line 6 of

    7. $M \supset N$ From (6) by conjunctive simplification

And finally, the conclusion is obtained by again applying a rule of inference:

    8. $K \supset N$ From (5) and (7) by chain argument

There is an important difference in the way the rules of inference and transformation rules can be applied, however:

Inference rules are to be used in a deduction only for deriving whole lines from other whole lines, not from parts of lines.

For example, from

1. p
2. $p \supset q$

we can derive "q" by *modus ponens*. But it would be a misuse of the rule to attempt to derive "q" from

1. p
2. $p \supset (q \lor r)$

because the consequent of line 2 is "$q \lor r$" and not "q" alone. To take another example, "p" can be derived by conjunctive simplification from "$p \mathbin{\&} q \mathbin{\&} r$" but not from "$(p \mathbin{\&} q) \lor r$" because the dominant operator of the latter is the wedge rather than the ampersand.

Greater flexibility is allowed in the use of transformation rules:

Transformation rules may be applied in a deduction either to whole lines or to parts of lines.

TABLE 8-2 *Truth-functional rules for use in formal deduction*

RULES OF INFERENCE

Adjunction (Adj.)	p, q; therefore $p \,\&\, q$
Biconditional Argument (Bicon. Arg.)	$p \equiv q, p$; therefore q
	$p \equiv q, q$; therefore p
	$p \equiv q, \sim p$; therefore $\sim q$
	$p \equiv q, \sim q$; therefore $\sim p$
Chain Argument (Chain)	$p \supset q, q \supset r$; therefore $p \supset r$
Conjunctive Argument (Conj. Arg.)	$\sim(p \,\&\, q), p$; therefore $\sim q$
	$\sim(p \,\&\, q), q$; therefore $\sim p$
Conjunctive Simplification (Conj. Simp.)	$p \,\&\, q$; therefore p
	$p \,\&\, q$; therefore q
Constructive Dilemma (C.D.)	$p \supset q, r \supset s, p \lor r$; therefore, $q \lor s$
	$p \supset q, r \supset q, p \lor r$; therefore, q
Destructive Dilemma (D.D.)	$p \supset q, r \supset s, \sim q \lor \sim s$; therefore, $\sim p \lor \sim r$
	$p \supset q, p \supset r, \sim q \lor \sim r$; therefore, $\sim p$
Disjunctive Addition (Disj. Add.)	p; therefore, $p \lor q$
Disjunctive Argument (Disj. Arg.)	$p \lor q, \sim p$; therefore, q
	$p \lor q, \sim q$; therefore, p
Modus Ponens (M.P.)	$p \supset q, p$; therefore, q
Modus Tollens (M.T.)	$p \supset q, \sim q$; therefore $\sim p$

TRANSFORMATION RULES

Absorption (Abs.)	$[p \supset (p \,\&\, q)] \equiv (p \supset q)$
Association (Assoc.)	$[p \lor (q \lor r)] \equiv [(p \lor q) \lor r]$
	$[p \,\&\, (q \,\&\, r)] \equiv [(p \,\&\, q) \,\&\, r]$
Biconditional Exchange (Bicon. Exch.)	$(p \equiv q) \equiv [(p \supset q) \,\&\, (q \supset p)]$
Commutation (Com.)	$(p \lor q) \equiv (q \lor p)$
	$(p \,\&\, q) \equiv (q \,\&\, p)$
	$(p \equiv q) \equiv (q \equiv p)$
Conditional Exchange (Con. Exch.)	$(p \supset q) \equiv (\sim p \lor q)$
	$(p \supset q) \equiv [\sim(p \,\&\, \sim q)]$
Contraposition (Contrapos.)	$(p \supset q) \equiv (\sim q \supset \sim p)$
	$(p \equiv q) \equiv (\sim q \equiv \sim p)$

TABLE 8-2 *(Continued)*

De Morgan's laws (De M.)	$[\sim(p \lor q)] \equiv (\sim p \ \& \sim q)$ $[\sim(p \ \& \ q)] \equiv (\sim p \lor \sim q)$
Distribution (Dist.)	$[p \ \& \ (q \lor r)] \equiv [(p \ \& \ q) \lor (p \ \& \ r)]$ $[p \lor (q \ \& \ r)] \equiv [(p \lor q) \ \& \ (p \lor r)]$
Divergence (Div.)	$[\sim(p \equiv q)] \equiv (p \equiv \sim q)$
Double Negation (D.N.)	$p \equiv (\sim\sim p)$
Duplication (Dup.)	$p \equiv (p \ \& \ p)$ $p \equiv (p \lor p)$
Exportation (Exp.)	$[(p \ \& \ q) \supset r] \equiv [p \supset (q \supset r)]$

Thus, if a deduction has as one line "$(p \supset q) \ \& \ (r \lor s)$," one can add "$(\sim p \lor q) \ \& \ (r \lor s)$" as a new line, since "$p \supset q$" and "$\sim p \lor q$" are equivalent by conditional exchange. The equivalence of the parts to each other guarantees that the whole of the new line will be equivalent to the whole of the preceding line.

Just as the same rules may be used and reused in a deduction, the same line may be used more than once. In fact, a line may be used as often as one likes. In addition, the same statement may occupy more than one place in a new line if this outcome is justified by a rule. For instance, from "$(\sim A \lor C) \lor \sim(A \ \& \sim C)$," the new line "$(A \supset C) \lor (A \supset C)$" can be obtained, because each side of the original disjunction is equivalent to the conditional "$A \supset C$." Likewise, the rule for chain argument ("$p \supset q$', '$q \supset r$; therefore, '$p \supset r$'") entitles one to derive "$(A \ \& \ B) \supset (A \ \& \ B)$" from the lines "$(A \ \& \ B) \supset (C \lor D)$" and "$(C \lor D) \supset (A \ \& \ B)$." In this second case, the conjunction "$A \ \& \ B$" replaces both the "p" and the "r" in the rule of inference.

For convenient reference in performing deductions, the rules of inference and the transformation rules are summarized in Table 8-2, along with their common abbreviations. Together, the rules provide what is called a *complete set*. This means that any truth-functional argument that can be shown to be *valid* using truth tables can be proven to be valid using the truth-functional rules of formal deduction.

☐ *Strategies for constructing deductions*

Because there are no mechanical procedures that automatically tell which steps to take in moving from premises to conclusion, constructing a deduction is a matter of solving a problem step-by-step. A deduction can proceed in any number of ways; there is no "proper order." One simply starts by looking for combinations of premises that satisfy any of the rules of inference or that can be replaced by equivalent statements according to the transformation rules. It does not matter how many lines are needed to reach the conclusion.[3] And if a series of steps leads to a dead end, one simply starts over using different rules and different combinations of lines. There is only one way to go wrong when performing a deduction: by adding a new line that is not justified by a rule.

Once one becomes familiar with the rules of inference and the transformation rules, many possibilities suggest themselves in the course of a deduction. It becomes increasingly easy to note combinations of lines that will produce new lines.

In addition, here are some tactics that can be of help:

1. *Try working backward from the conclusion.* You will want the completed deduction to consist of a coherent series of steps leading from the premises to the conclusion. But in *planning* your moves, it may help to look at the symbols used in the conclusion and find these symbols in the premises. Then try to determine what must be done to elicit this combination of symbols from the premises.

2. *Look for rules of inference that are easiest to identify.* In particular, be alert for instances of *modus ponens, modus tollens,* and chain argument.

3. *Consider breaking up conjunctions by conjunctive simplification.* Simplifying lines in the deduction will make it easier to tell which rules are applicable to those lines.

4. *Remember the rule of inference for disjunctive addition.* This rule will account for the presence in the conclusion of a symbol that is not present in the initial premises.

5. *If lines appear as negations, changing these to their equivalents can make a rule of inference easier to recognize.* De Morgan's laws can be used to replace negative disjunctions and negative conjunctions. And a negative conditional can be rewritten as a conjunction. (The negative conditional "$\sim(p \supset q)$" is equivalent to "$\sim[\sim(p \;\&\; \sim q)]$" by conditional exchange, and hence to "$p \;\&\; \sim q$" by double negation.)

6. *Look at the conclusion and think of alternative statements with which it is equivalent.* Sometimes, mentally replacing the conclusion with an equivalency will help one find the steps needed to move from the premises to the conclusion. For example, it is difficult to see how to derive the conclusion "$\sim J \supset (\sim J \;\&\; S)$" from the single premise "$J \lor S$."

1. $J \lor S \quad /\therefore \sim J \supset (\sim J \;\&\; S)$

However, according to the transformation rule for absorption—"$p \supset (p \;\&\; q)$" is equivalent to "$p \supset q$"—the conclusion is equivalent to "$\sim J \supset S$."

---

[3] The more adept one becomes at constructing proofs, the greater the interest in comparing alternate deductions for what logicians call "elegance": the fewer the lines, the more "elegant" the proof. But elegance is a matter of aesthetic appreciation that has no bearing on the correctness or incorrectness of a proof.

Recognizing this permits one to move to the conclusion in three easy steps:

2. $\sim(\sim J) \vee S$ From (1) by double negation
3. $\sim J \supset S$ From (2) by conditional exchange
4. $\sim J \supset (\sim J \mathbin{\&} S)$ From (3) by absorption

☐ *Adding tautologies*

Another useful tactic is to add a tautology as an intermediate statement. Adding a tautology cannot affect the logical relationship between the premises and the conclusion of an argument: whatever conclusions follow from the original set of premises will still follow after the tautology is added, and no new conclusions not implied by the original premises will be implied by these premises plus the tautology.[4] But this device can be helpful when it is difficult to think of appropriate inference rules and transformation rules to apply.

For example, suppose one intends to show that "$\sim(J \mathbin{\&} K)$" validly follows from "$J \equiv (L \vee M)$," "$\sim(L \vee M)$," and "$M \supset (L \mathbin{\&} K)$." As usual, the premises are listed and numbered, and the conclusion is written on the line with the last premise:

1. $J \equiv (L \vee M)$ Premise
2. $\sim(L \vee M)$ Premise
3. $M \supset (L \mathbin{\&} K)$ $/\therefore \sim(J \mathbin{\&} K)$ Premise/Conclusion

A large number of intermediate lines can be generated by applying rules—for example:

4. $[J \supset (L \vee M)] \mathbin{\&} [(L \vee M) \supset J]$ From (1) by biconditional exchange
5. $J \supset (L \vee M)$ From (4) by conjunctive simplification
6. $\sim J$ From (2) and (5) by *modus tollens*
7. $\sim L \mathbin{\&} \sim M$ From (2) by De Morgan's laws
8. $\sim M$ From (7) by conjunctive simplification

---

[4] Adding a tautology cannot make an otherwise valid argument invalid, nor can it change an invalid argument into a valid one. As a truth table shows, an argument is invalid only if there is a possible combination of truth values that would make the conclusion come out F and all premises come out T. But adding a tautology—a column to the table with T in every line—neither increases nor diminishes the chance of there being such a combination.

9. $\sim M \lor (L \mathbin{\&} K)$	From (3) by conditional exchange
10. $(\sim M \lor L) \mathbin{\&} (\sim M \lor K)$	From (9) by distribution
11. $\sim M \lor K$	From (10) by conjunctive simplification
12. $M \supset K$	From (11) by conditional exchange

Despite these steps, the goal of moving from "$M \supset K$" to "$\sim(J \mathbin{\&} K)$" remains elusive.

If, instead of adding the intermediate lines shown, a new line is added by using the rule for disjunctive addition, the deduction can be completed in just three steps (starting over with a new line 4):

4. $\sim J$	From (1) and (2) by biconditional argument
5. $\sim J \lor \sim K$	From (4) by disjunctive addition
6. $\sim(J \mathbin{\&} K)$	From (5) by De Morgan's laws

It is often difficult to see when a single rule such as disjunctive addition should be used, and in such cases it can help to add a tautology to the premise set. If we add the tautology "$(J \mathbin{\&} K) \supset J$" to the original premise set of the above argument, the conclusion can be deduced as follows:

4. $(J \mathbin{\&} K) \supset J$	Tautology
5. $\sim J$	From (1) and (2) by biconditional argument
6. $\sim(J \mathbin{\&} K)$	From (4) and (5) by *modus tollens*

Although it may appear from this example that adding a tautology is an easy way to complete any deduction, the method has two main drawbacks. First, the usefulness of a tautology generally cannot be recognized until one has already tried to continue by applying the rules. Second, unless the added line

TABLE 8-3 *Tautologies for use in constructing deductions*

$$p \lor \sim p$$
$$p \equiv p$$
$$\sim(p \mathbin{\&} \sim p)$$
$$p \supset p$$
$$p \supset (p \lor q)$$
$$(p \mathbin{\&} q) \supset p$$
$$(p \mathbin{\&} q) \supset (p \lor q)$$

is already known to be a tautology, it must be justified through the construction of a truth table—a task that can be more laborious than completing the deduction without relying on a tautology. The device is best reserved for occasions when one has become stalemated.

A few known tautologies are listed in Table 8-3.

■ **EXERCISE 8-3**

■ A. For the following deductions, indicate how each line following the premises was derived, and name the rule that justifies it.

(1) 1. $(A \lor B) \supset C$ Premise
   2. $\sim B \supset D$ Premise
   3. $\sim D$ /∴ C Premise/Conclusion
   4. $\sim(\sim B)$
   5. B
   6. $B \lor A$
   7. $A \lor B$
   8. C

(2) 1. $(A \,\&\, B) \supset C$ Premise
   2. $D \supset A$ Premise
   3. $A \supset (B \supset C)$ /∴ $(D \,\&\, B) \supset C$ Premise/Conclusion
   4. $D \supset (B \supset C)$
   5. $(D \,\&\, B) \supset C$

(3) 1. $P \,\&\, Q$ Premise
   2. $\sim(P \,\&\, R)$ Premise
   3. $(\sim R \lor S) \supset T$ /∴ T Premise/Conclusion
   4. P
   5. $\sim R$
   6. $\sim R \lor S$
   7. T

*(4) 1. $\sim P \lor Q$ Premise
   2. $\sim(Q \,\&\, \sim S)$ /∴ $P \supset S$ Premise/Conclusion
   3. $P \supset Q$
   4. $Q \supset S$
   5. $P \supset S$

(5) 1. $A \lor (B \,\&\, C)$ Premise
   2. $(A \lor B) \supset D$ /∴ D Premise/Conclusion
   3. $(A \lor B) \,\&\, (A \lor C)$
   4. $A \lor B$
   5. D

(6) 1. $(P \lor Q) \lor R$ Premise
   2. $\sim P$ Premise
   3. $(Q \lor R) \supset (S \,\&\, T)$ /∴ T Premise/Conclusion
   4. $P \lor (Q \lor R)$
   5. $Q \lor R$
   6. $S \,\&\, T$
   7. T

(7) 1. $S \supset T$ Premise
     2. $(S \& T) \supset U$ Premise
     3. $\sim(S \& U)$ /∴ $\sim S$ Premise/Conclusion
     4. $S \supset (S \& T)$
     5. $S \supset U$
     6. $S \supset (S \& U)$
     7. $\sim S$

*(8) 1. $(P \vee \sim Q) \vee R$ Premise
      2. $\sim P \vee (Q \& \sim P)$ /∴ $Q \supset R$ Premise/Conclusion
      3. $(\sim P \vee Q) \& (\sim P \vee \sim P)$
      4. $\sim P \vee \sim P$
      5. $\sim P$
      6. $P \vee (\sim Q \vee R)$
      7. $\sim Q \vee R$
      8. $Q \supset R$

(9) 1. $(H \supset I) \supset (\sim J \supset K)$ Premise
     2. $\sim I \supset K$ Premise
     3. $H \supset \sim K$ /∴ $J \vee K$ Premise/Conclusion
     4. $\sim(\sim K) \supset \sim H$
     5. $K \supset \sim H$
     6. $\sim I \supset \sim H$
     7. $H \supset I$
     8. $\sim J \supset K$
     9. $\sim(\sim J) \vee K$
    10. $J \vee K$

(10) 1. $L \supset (M \& N)$ Premise
      2. $O \supset P$ Premise
      3. $M \supset \sim L$ Premise
      4. $\sim O \supset L$ Premise
      5. $\sim P \vee [Q \vee (L \vee R)]$ Premise
      6. $Q \supset \sim P$ /∴ R Premise/Conclusion
      7. $\sim L \vee (M \& N)$
      8. $(\sim L \vee M) \& (\sim L \vee N)$
      9. $\sim L \vee M$
     10. $L \supset M$
     11. $L \supset \sim L$
     12. $\sim L \vee \sim L$
     13. $\sim L$
     14. $\sim(\sim O)$
     15. O
     16. P
     17. $\sim(\sim P)$
     18. $Q \vee (L \vee R)$
     19. $(Q \vee L) \vee R$
     20. $\sim Q$
     21. $\sim Q \& \sim L$
     22. $\sim(Q \vee L)$
     23. R

■ B. Prove that the following arguments are valid.

(1) (A & B) ⊃ C
    ~A ∨ B
    A
    ∴ C

(2) A ⊃ B
    C ⊃ D
    ~A ⊃ F
    ~F
    ∴ B ∨ D

(3) (C & D) ⊃ F
    G ⊃ C
    ∴ (G & D) ⊃ F

*(4) (C ⊃ D) & (F ⊃ G)
    C ∨ F
    (D ∨ G) ⊃ H
    ∴ H

(5) (P ⊃ Q) ⊃ (R & S)
    (R & S) ⊃ (T ≡ W)
    ~(T ≡ W)
    ∴ ~(P ⊃ Q)

(6) P ≡ Q
    Q ⊃ R
    ∴ (~P ∨ R) & (~Q ∨ P)

(7) A ∨ (B & C)
    (A ⊃ B) & (C ⊃ D)
    ~D & ~E
    ∴ B

*(8) (A ⊃ B) & (A ∨ C)
    (C ⊃ D) & (C ∨ A)
    ∴ B ∨ D

(9) D ⊃ C
    E ⊃ F
    (C ∨ F) ⊃ G
    ~G
    ∴ ~(D ∨ E)

(10) ~(P & Q)
    Q ∨ (R ⊃ S)
    P & ~S
    ∴ R ⊃ (R & D)

(11) R & S
    (R ∨ T) ⊃ (R ⊃ U)
    S ⊃ V
    ∴ U & V

*(12) L ⊃ M
    (N ∨ O) ⊃ L
    (~L ∨ M) ⊃ O
    ∴ M

(13) L
    ~M
    [(L ∨ N) & ~M] ⊃ (N & ~O)
    P ⊃ O
    N ∨ P
    ∴ N & ~P

(14) ~(Q ⊃ R)
    Q ⊃ S
    T ⊃ R
    ∴ ~(S ⊃ T)

(15) S ∨ (~S & T)
    S ⊃ V
    ∴ (V & S) ≡ S

■ C. Symbolize the following arguments, and prove that each is valid by the method of formal deduction.

1. If Gail takes either precalculus or business mathematics, then she will have met the requirements for graduation. So, if she takes business mathematics, she will have met the requirements for graduation. (P, B, R)

2. If the country is in a state of anarchy, it cannot be reformed unless a charismatic leader appears. No charismatic leader can appear if the country is in a state of anarchy. The country surely is in a state of anarchy. Hence, it cannot be reformed. (A, R, C)

3. Either Michael will go to law school, or he will study forestry if he works as a park ranger. If I know him, he will not study forestry. Consequently, if he works as a park ranger, he will also go to law school. (L, F, R)

*4. Wilkins would have won the case if Jenkins turned state's evidence, provided that Jenkins could be located in time. Although Wilkins didn't win, Jenkins was found in time. Thus, Jenkins didn't turn state's evidence. (W, S, L)

5. Either the president is mistaken or the senator is telling the truth. If the senator is telling the truth, then either the president's press secretary is lying or the White House chief of staff is suppressing evidence. The president is not mistaken and the press secretary is not lying. Thus, the chief of staff is suppressing evidence. (M, T, L, S)

6. If the guerrillas' demands are met, then international terrorism will increase. On the other hand, if the guerrillas' demands are not met, innocent hostages will suffer. So either international terrorism will increase or innocent hostages will suffer. (D, T, H)

7. It's not the case both that the senator will be elected and that he will not campaign in New York State. If he campaigns in New York State, then he must campaign vigorously for both black and Jewish votes. He will not campaign vigorously for Jewish votes. Therefore, the senator will not be elected. (E, C, B, J)

*8. If it is the case that Edith either went to the Bar Association meeting in Boston or went to Cape Cod for the week, then she left the Brewster case unprepared. If she didn't finish her work on the Brewster case, then she didn't finish the Dillon case. But if she has left the latter case unprepared, she'll surely return on Saturday. Edith did go to the Bar Association meeting. So, she will return on Saturday. (M, C, B, D, S)

9. Either the Reagan administration won't discontinue welfare programs, or poor blacks will riot if big business prospers. If poor blacks do riot, then the Reagan administration won't cut welfare programs. But it won't happen that both big business will prosper and the Reagan administration won't cut welfare programs. Therefore, either big business won't prosper or poor blacks won't riot. (W, R, B)

10. If the United States increases defense spending, then American leaders won't be intimidated by the Soviet military buildup. But Soviet leaders will be intimidated if the United States increases defense spending. If the Soviet leaders are intimidated, they are sure to increase the deployment of Warsaw Pact troops in Eastern Europe and intimidate American leaders after all. Thus, increasing defense spending in the United States is a sufficient condition for the intimidation of American leaders. (D, I, S, W)

11. Either India will implement birth control programs and avert mass starvation, or birth control will be implemented and martial law will be declared. Mass starvation will not be averted; and if birth control is implemented, a popular uprising will occur. Thus, a popular uprising will occur. (I, A, M, P)

*12. If the Soviets are bargaining in good faith and they are not on the verge of a technological breakthrough, then a new treaty will be negotiated with them. If the Soviets are not on the verge of a technological breakthrough and United States intelligence is reliable, a new treaty will be negotiated, and then the United States will cut back on defense spending. The United States will not cut back on defense spending. Furthermore, either the Soviets are on the verge of a technological breakthrough or United States intelligence is unreliable, or the Soviets are not bargaining in good faith. Therefore, no new treaty will be negotiated with them. (S, V, T, I, D)

13. Either Hartley cheated on his logic exam, or he did not cheat and he failed. If he failed, he will be depressed. If he cheated, he will be depressed only if he is ashamed of himself. Hartley is not ashamed of himself, but he is depressed. Therefore, he failed and he did not cheat. (C, F, D, A)

14. If I do these logic deductions, then I won't have time left to read *Moby Dick*. I can get an A in English only if I read *Moby Dick*, and I'll be miserable unless I get an A in English. But if I don't finish these logic deductions, I'll be too distracted to concentrate on *Moby Dick*, and without concentration on *Moby Dick*, I can't get an A in English. Either I do these deductions or I do not. So I won't get an A in English. (*D, R, E, M, C*)

15. If God is omnipotent, then he can do anything. If he is omniscient, then he knows that evil exists. If he knows that evil exists and can do anything, then he would eradicate evil if he was also beneficient. But evil continues unabated in the world. Therefore, either God is not omniscient, or if he can do anything, he is not beneficient. (*Op, D, Os, K, E, B*)   ■

□ 8-4. INDIRECT PROOF, OR *REDUCTIO AD ABSURDUM*

If an argument is invalid, it will not be possible to construct a formal deduction that moves step-by-step from the premises to the conclusion. We must therefore *suspect* that an argument is invalid if we are unable to construct a deduction for it. However, failure to complete a deduction is not a *demonstration* of invalidity. The difficulty may simply be that the proper sequence of steps has not been found.

When there is difficulty in proceeding with a deduction as described in Section 8-3, an alternative approach that can be of help is the method of *indirect proof*, often called *reductio ad absurdum*:

> Indirect proof, or *reductio ad absurdum*, is a method of deductive reasoning in which a conclusion is defended by showing that its negation leads to a necessarily false statement.

To perform an indirect proof or *reductio*, one assumes the negation of the conclusion and then shows that this assumption leads to an absurdity—the assertion of a contradiction.

In the indirect method, the premises are listed, as before, and then the negation of the conclusion is given as an additional premise. One next proceeds to construct a deduction, attempting to derive a contradiction. This procedure can be illustrated by means of the sample argument that was used to demonstrate the introduction of a tautology into a deduction:

1. $J \equiv (L \lor M)$	Premise
2. $\sim(L \lor M)$	Premise
3. $M \supset (L \ \& \ K)$ /∴ $\sim(J \ \& \ K)$	Premise/Conclusion
4. $\sim[\sim(J \ \& \ K)]$	Negation of the conclusion
5. $J \ \& \ K$	From (4) by double negation

6. *J*   From (5) by conjunctive simplifi-
                                     cation
7. ~*J*   From (1) and (2) by biconditional
                                     argument
8. *J* & ~*J*   From (6) and (7) by adjunction

The premise added at line 4 is the negation of the conclusion, and the contradiction derived in line 8 shows that the three original premises and the negation of the conclusion cannot all be true. If the first three premises are true, then the fourth premise must be false. And because the fourth premise is the negation of the original conclusion, the original conclusion must be true. This establishes that the original argument is valid: if the premises are all true, the conclusion must also be true.

This indirect method for evaluating truth-functional arguments is usually no faster or easier than the direct method of deduction. Its usefulness lies in the possibility of deriving new lines when the negation of the conclusion is added as a premise.

■ **EXERCISE 8-4**

■ A. Using both the indirect method and the method of formal deduction, prove that each of the following arguments is valid. (Construct two proofs for each argument.)

1. *A* ⊃ *B*   *4. (~*A* ∨ ~*C*) ∨ *B*
   B ⊃ *C*   ~*C* ⊃ *D*
   D ∨ ~*C*   *E* ∨ ~*D*
   A   ~*E* & *A*
   ∴ *D*   ∴ *B*

2. *D* ⊃ *E*   5. *A* & (*B* ⊃ *C*)
   E ⊃ *F*   *C* ⊃ *D*
   F ⊃ *G*   ~(~*B* & *A*)
   ∴ *D* ⊃ *G*   ~*D* ∨ (~*E* ∨ *F*)
                                         ∴ *E* ⊃ *F*
3. ~*A* ∨ *B*
   ~(*B* & ~*C*)
   ~*C*
   ∴ ~*A*

■ B. Prove that each of the following arguments is valid by using the indirect method.

1. General George Custer was defeated at the Battle of Little Big Horn. But he was defeated at this battle if and only if he was in Montana. If General Custer was in Wyoming, he was not in Montana. Therefore, he was not in Wyoming. (*C, M, W*)

2. If interest rates on bank loans increase, then mortgage money will become tighter and there will be fewer housing starts. There will be fewer housing starts only if personal income does not increase. Hence, if interest rates on bank loans increase, personal income will fail to increase. (*I, M, H, P*)

3. If the professor is given tenure, then if his book is published and his teaching

improves he will either be promoted or he will be given sabbatical leave. He will not be promoted and he will not be given sabbatical leave unless his book is published. His book is not going to be published, although his teaching has improved. Thus, if he is given tenure, then neither will he be promoted nor will he be given sabbatical leave. (*T, B, I, P, S*)

*4. Either the assassination was the work of the mob, or else the crime was an inside job and the Secret Service is implicated. The mob could have committed the crime only if its assassins had precise information on the president's security. But the Secret Service is implicated if the mob had this information. Therefore, the Secret Service is definitely implicated. (*M, J, S, P*)

5. Either the coal strike will not be successful or coal miners' wages will rise. If wages do rise, then there will be an increase in the cost of making steel. It is not the case both that the cost of making steel will rise and the price of automobiles will not rise. If the price of automobiles does rise, then the cost-of-living index will rise. Therefore, if the coal strike is successful, the cost-of-living index will rise. (*C, W, S, A, I*) ■

☐ 8-5. PROVING INVALIDITY: ABBREVIATED TRUTH TABLES

Although formal deductions are superior to truth tables in proving the validity of long and complex arguments, the truth-table method is more effective than deduction in two important respects: (1) A truth table has a definite terminating point, and (2) the completed table is guaranteed to show whether the argument is valid or invalid. By contrast, a formal deduction can remain incomplete. And the fact that one is unable to complete a deduction does not *prove* that the argument is invalid; the proof may just be elusive.

Since formal deduction cannot be used to prove that an argument is invalid, one must resort to the truth-table method when it is necessary to demonstrate invalidity. Fortunately, it is possible to prove invalidity by taking shortcuts and constructing abbreviated truth tables.

The method consists in attempting, by trial and error, to assign truth values to the simple statements contained in the argument in a way that will create the equivalent of an invalidating row in a full-scale truth table. This involves finding at least one possible combination of truth values of the simple statements that would make all the premises of the argument true and its conclusion false. If such a combination of truth values can be found, the argument will be shown to be invalid without its being necessary to construct the entire truth table.

To see how this is done, consider the following argument:

(1) $R \supset S$
$\quad$ $W \supset U$
$\quad$ $\sim R \lor \sim W$
$\quad$ $\therefore \sim S \lor \sim U$

For the conclusion to be false, the disjunction "~S ∨ ~U" must be false as a whole. Thus, both "~S" and "~U" must be false—and these compounds will be false only if "S" is true and "U" is true. Having assigned the value T to both "S" and "U" in the conclusion, we assign the same value to "S" and "U" each time they occur in the premises. For the assignment of truth values must be *consistent*: the same value must be assigned to the same simple statement every time it occurs.

The argument is now rewritten showing these assignments. The truth value for each simple statement is placed under the letter for that statement, and the truth value for each compound is placed under its logical operator. The truth value for the conclusion as a whole is distinguished by placing it under the dominant operator and enclosing it in parentheses:

(1a)　1. R ⊃ S
　　　　　　　T
　　　2. W ⊃ U
　　　　　　　T
　　　3. ~R ∨ ~W　　　/∴ ~S ∨ ~U
　　　　　　　　　　　　　FT(F)FT

The next step is to try to assign truth values to the other simple statements so as to make all the premises come out true. Because "R ⊃ S" will be true whether "R" is T or F, and because "W ⊃ U" will be true whether "W" is T or F (because the consequent of each conditional is true), we allow their truth values to depend on the ones assigned to these letters in "~R ∨ ~W." This disjunction will be true when "~R" is true, when "~W" is true, or when both are true. And because the truth values of the components of the first two premises allow any or all of these conditions, we provisionally assign T to each negation and to the compound as a whole. Statements "R" and "W" in premises 1 and 2 now become false (given the truth of "~R" and "~W" in premise 3). Because "S" and "U" are known from premises 1 and 2 to be true, "~S" and "~U" in the conclusion must both be false. As a result, the disjunction "~S ∨ ~U" is false:

(1b)　1. R ⊃ S
　　　　　F(T) T
　　　2. W ⊃ U
　　　　　F(T) T
　　　3. ~R ∨ ~W
　　　　　TF(T)TF　　　/∴ ~S ∨ ~U
　　　　　　　　　　　　　FT(F)FT

As illustrated by (1b), an assignment of truth values can be found that will make the premises true and the conclusion false. On that assignment, "R" and

"W" are false, while "S" and "U" are true. Thus, the argument has been shown to be invalid.

The truth table for an invalid argument can have more than one invalidating row because there may be more than one assignment of truth values that will produce an invalidating combination. For example, consider the following argument:

(2) $A \lor B$
$\quad A \supset C$
$\quad B \supset C \qquad /\therefore C \& D$

Argument (2) can be shown to be invalid by assigning the truth values listed in either the left column or the right column below:

C, True	C, True
D, False	D, False
A, False	A, True
B, True	B, False

Just as there are often several assignments of truth values that will show a conclusion to be false, there can be assignments that will not produce invalidating combinations. While the abbreviated truth table saves time and energy, sometimes more than one attempt is required before an invalidating combination is found.

■ **EXERCISE 8-5**

Use the abbreviated truth-table method to prove that the following arguments are invalid.

1. $A \supset \sim B$
   $\sim A \equiv B$
   $\sim A$
   $\therefore \sim B$

2. $A \supset (B \lor C)$
   $B \supset (D \& E)$
   $D \supset (E \supset F)$
   $\sim(A \& F)$
   $\therefore A \equiv C$

3. $E \supset F$
   $F \supset G$
   $\therefore F \lor G$

*4. $P \supset (Q \lor R)$
   $(Q \& R) \supset \sim P$
   $\therefore \sim P$

5. $S \supset (T \lor U)$
   $(T \& U) \supset V$
   $\therefore S \& V$

6. $(S \& T) \supset U$
   $U \supset V$
   $(S \& V) \supset T$
   $\therefore \sim U \lor T$

7. $L \supset [(M \& N) \lor (O \& P)]$
   $M \supset \sim(O \& P)$
   $L \supset \sim(M \& N)$
   $\therefore (L \& O) \supset (P \supset M)$

*8. Either congressional leaders are mistaken or the president is not telling the truth. If the president is telling the truth, then either the secretary of defense is lying or the White House chief of staff is suppressing evidence. Congressional leaders are mistaken and the defense secretary is not lying. We may conclude, however, that the chief of staff is suppressing evidence. (M, T, L, S)

9. If a letter of acceptance has not arrived from Stanford University, then Lucinda will be depressed; and if Lucinda's depressed, her mother will be unhappy. Lucinda's father will refuse to pay for her college education unless she gets into Stanford. His otherwise refusing to pay for her college education will make Lucinda's mother unhappy. In fact, Lucinda's mother is quite unhappy. So, Lucinda did not get a letter of acceptance from Stanford. (L, D, M, R)

10. If sales of Japanese cars continue to decline, then General Motors sales will increase only if sales of European imports also decline. Sales of European imports will not decline if sales of Japanese cars continue to decline. Therefore, General Motors sales will not increase. (J, G, E)

11. If professors are patient and students are optimistic, then students will do logic exercises. If students are optimistic and do logic exercises, then the logic course will be worthwhile. Professors are certainly patient. Therefore, the logic course is worthwhile. (P, O, E, W)

*12. It is not the case that the company will both give salary raises to its employees and hire new workers. If sales double in the next quarter, then either employees will get raises or new workers will be hired. If new workers are hired, then employees will get better fringe benefits. New workers have been hired. Therefore, there will be better fringe benefits, and it is not the case either that sales doubled or that there will be salary raises. (R, H, S, F)

13. Either the president will brief the Senate Foreign Relations Committee about the Central Intelligence Agency's covert military activities, or his nominee for secretary of state is not telling the truth about the United States role in Central America. If the prospective secretary of state is not telling the truth, then either he or she will be exposed by an investigative reporter or will not be confirmed by the Senate. The president has decided to brief the Senate Foreign Relations Committee about the Central Intelligence Agency's covert military activities, and an investigative reporter has not exposed the president's nominee for secretary of state. Therefore, the Senate will confirm the president's nomination for secretary of state. (B, T, E, C)

14. Either the Atlanta Falcons will win the title in the Central Division, or Dallas will win the Eastern Division and the Falcons will be a wild-card team. If the Falcons win a wild-card berth, then either the Chicago Bears will be a wild-card team or the Redskins will. The Redskins will be a wild-card team only if Dallas loses the next game. But Dallas will win both the next game and the Eastern Division title. Therefore, the Falcons will be a wild-card team, and the Redskins will not go to the playoffs this year. (Let "A" stand for "Atlanta Falcons win the C.D. title," "D" for "Dallas wins the E.D. title," "F" for "The Falcons are a wild-card team," "B" for "The Chicago Bears are a wild-card team," "R" for "The Redskins are a wild-card team," and "L" for "Dallas loses the next game.") ■

CHAPTER NINE

Predicate logic

The categorical logic presented in Chapters 5 and 6 concerns the internal structure of simple statements—the logical relations between terms in these statements. Truth-functional logic, presented in Chapters 7 and 8, treats the internal structure of compound statements—the logical relations between the simple statements making up these compounds. Predicate logic—also known as *quantifier logic* or *quantification*—is concerned with the internal structures of both simple and compound statements.

> **Predicate logic is a system of deductive logic that combines the analysis of terms with the analysis of statements.**

Consequently, predicate logic makes it possible to prove the validity of many valid arguments that cannot be shown to be valid by the techniques of either categorical logic or truth-functional logic alone. Truth-functional logic, for example, is of no help in proving the validity of an argument that has a form as basic as the standard *AAA* syllogism:

All dogs are mammals.
Fido is a dog.
_____
Therefore, Fido is a mammal.

The key to the validity of this example lies in the presence of common terms in the premises and conclusion. But since each of the statements is a simple one, the syllogism would be symbolized in truth-functional logic as the invalid form

p
q
$\therefore r$

The methods of predicate logic enable one to prove the validity of any argument that can be shown to be valid by the methods of traditional categorical logic. In addition, by incorporating and extending the rules of inference and techniques of truth-functional logic, predicate logic permits the analysis of arguments that have internal structures more complicated than those of the arguments treated by categorical logic.

Here is an example of a valid argument that cannot be shown to be valid by either syllogistic or truth-functional methods:

> **All philosophers are both thoughtful and wise.**
> **Some philosophers are obscure.**
> **Therefore, some thoughtful persons are obscure.**

The system of logic explored in this chapter can be used to demonstrate the validity of the above argument and of a large number of others that also resist analysis by the methods discussed earlier.

☐ 9-1. BASIC CONCEPTS OF PREDICATE LOGIC

We begin our study of predicate logic by examining the internal structure of sentences expressing statements that are truth-functionally simple.

☐ *Predicates*

Consider these sentences:

> **1.** Prince Charles is wealthy.
> **2.** Prince Charles is older than Princess Diana.

The grammarian would divide (1) into the subject, *Prince Charles*, and the predicate, *is wealthy*. Thus, the predicate is everything in the sentence exclusive of the subject. For instance, in (2) the entire phrase *is older than Princess Diana* is the grammatical predicate.

The logician, however, considers the predicate of a sentence to be the *predicate term*:

> The predicate term is an expression that is taken to refer to some property or some relation.

In (1) *wealthy* is the predicate term, while *is* operates as a term indicating that the individual referred to by a given name (Prince Charles) has the property designated by the word *wealthy*.

The logician identifies the predicate term of (2) as the expression *older than*. This is a relational term because it refers to a characteristic shared by two or more objects or individuals—in this case, by Prince Charles and Princess Diana. Examples of other relational terms are *taller than* and *wiser than*.

The fundamental distinction in predicate logic is between terms designating *individuals*,[1] which have *properties* or *relations*, and terms specifying the properties or relations they have. Terms that grammarians identify as adjectives, nouns, verbs, and verb phrases may all be treated in logic as predicates, *as long as they can be construed as referring to a property or relationship that one or more individuals can have.* Thus, in (3) the noun *Englishman* is a predicate, while in (4) the verb *rules* is also a predicate.

3. Prince Charles is an Englishman.
4. Prince Charles rules.

For logical purposes, there is no significant difference between the sentences "Prince Charles rules" and "Prince Charles is a ruler" nor between the sentences "Prince Charles is English" and "Prince Charles is an Englishman."

Logicians also distinguish between *monadic* and *polyadic* predicates. A monadic predicate applies to only one individual. Thus, in "Prince Charles is wealthy," *wealthy* is a monadic predicate. On the other hand, a *polyadic* predicate requires two or more individuals if the sentence is to be meaningful. An example is the expression *older than* in (2).

We form a *predicate expression* by placing dots to signify that a term referring to some individual must be implicitly understood as replacing the dots if the predicate is to function in a meaningful sentence. Thus, . . . *is wealthy* is a *monadic predicate expression* that becomes a sentence with the addition of a term designating an individual. The predicate expression . . . *is older than* . . . requires two terms for individuals; one cannot say that a single individual has the property designated by *older than.* All relational predicate expressions are *polyadic predicate expressions.*

A polyadic predicate expression may require the addition of two, three, or more terms specifying individuals to become a complete sentence. When only two terms are needed, the expression is called *dyadic.* The predicate expression . . . *visited* . . . *in place of* . . . in (5) is *triadic* because it requires terms designating three individuals for its completion.

5. Prince Charles visited Canada in place of Queen Elizabeth.

There can also be *quadratic* predicate expressions:

6. Prince Charles rode his horse at the coronation parade beside Princess Diana.

Here . . . *rode* . . . *at* . . . *beside* . . . is the predicate expression, and *Prince Charles, his horse, the coronation parade,* and *Princess Diana* are the four terms

---

[1] Henceforth the term *individual* will be used to stand for any person, object, or entity—animate or inanimate—that can meaningfully be said to have a property or attribute.

that complete it. In this discussion, we shall be concerned only with monadic and dyadic predicate expressions, leaving the analysis of complex polyadic predicate expressions to more advanced courses in symbolic logic.

□ *Singular statements*

When a predicate expression is completed by a term or terms that designate specific individuals, the resulting sentence expresses a *singular statement*. This is the case whether the sentence has a monadic or a polyadic predicate. Thus, any sentence about one or more specific individuals expresses a singular statement.

Individuals are designated by many terms in addition to proper names such as *Prince Charles, Princess Diana,* and *Canada.* Other expressions used to designate specific individuals include the definite articles *this* and *that,* as in *this man* or *that car.* Individuals are also designated by possessive nouns and pronouns—*Mary's, student's, his, hers,* and so forth—and by definite descriptions such as *the first American president, the first woman in outer space,* and *the largest planet in the solar system.*

Sentences expressing singular statements are translated into the symbolic notation of predicate logic by using capital letters to represent the predicate terms and small, or lowercase, letters to represent the individuals designated. Returning to example (1), "Prince Charles is wealthy," and example (2), "Prince Charles is older than Princess Diana," and rewriting them as predicate expressions, we have:

1a. . . . . is wealthy
2a. . . . . is older than . . .

The capital letter assigned as the symbol for a predicate term is generally the first letter of a major word in the predicate. Thus, (1a) and (2a) become

1b. . . . W
2b. . . . O . . .

The lowercase letter that symbolizes a particular individual is called an *individual constant,* and the same letter is used to designate that individual throughout the context in which the name occurs. Again, the letter assigned is the first letter of a name or of some key word in a definite description—but with the letters w through z reserved for another purpose. The names *Prince Charles* and *Princess Diana* in the examples are symbolized as c and d.

We follow the further convention of always writing the capital letter for the predicate immediately to the left of a small letter referring to an individual. Thus, (1b) and (2b) become

1c. Wc.
2c. Ocd.

When the singular statement being symbolized contains a polyadic expression, the individual constants are written in an order that represents the relationship of the individuals in the original statement. So (2) cannot be correctly symbolized as "*Odc*" because the latter is equivalent to "Princess Diana is older than Prince Charles."

☐ *Propositional functions*

The attribute of wealth can be *predicated* of a number of individuals by saying, for example, "Prince Charles is wealthy," "Jacqueline Onassis is wealthy," "David Rockefeller is wealthy," and "Reggie Jackson is wealthy." These sentences are symbolized, respectively, as "*Wc*," "*Wo*," "*Wr*," and "*Wj*." All the expressions have a common pattern, which can be represented as "*W*___," with the line indicating that an individual constant is to be placed to the right of the predicate symbol to express a singular statement.

In logic, the standard way of symbolizing such a pattern is to use, instead of a line, one of the lowercase letters from *w* through *z* (individual constants having been selected from the letters *a* through *v*). Thus, the common pattern formed by asserting that an individual has the property of being wealthy is symbolized as "*Wx*." The letter *x*, called an *individual variable*, is a placeholder to indicate where individual constants can be inserted to express statements in the symbolic language.

The expression "*Wx*" does not represent any one sentence; instead, "*Wx*" is a *propositional function*:

> **A propositional function is an expression that contains one or more individual variables, such that when all its individual variables are replaced by individual constants, the result is a symbolized statement.**

Propositional functions are also called *open sentences* because they symbolize predicate expressions waiting to be ascribed to particular individuals.

When an individual constant is substituted for the individual variable in a propositional function, the result represents a singular statement. Every singular statement is called a *closed sentence* or a *substitution instance* of a propositional function.

Because they do not express statements, propositional functions are neither true nor false; but their substitution instances *are* either true or false. Ordinarily, a propositional function will have some true substitution instances and some false ones. For instance, when "*A*" symbolizes the predicate expression *an American*, the sentence "Davy Crockett was an American" expresses a true substitution instance of "*Ax*," while "Mao Zedong was an American" expresses a false substitution instance of "*Ax*."

When the replacement of a variable by a symbol for the individual's name expresses a true statement, we say that the individual constant *satisfies* the function. Thus, because "Davy Crockett was an American" expresses a true statement, the individual constant c (for *Davy Crockett*) satisfies the propositional function "Ax."

□ *General terms and quantifiers*

Unlike *Prince Charles* and *Princess Diana*, terms such as *wealthy* and *English* represent properties that a number of different individuals share (being wealthy, being English) and are therefore identified as predicates. Such expressions are also called *general terms*, because they characterize a general class of individuals—all those having the property in question. Thus, *English* can be used to describe numerous individuals: Henry VIII, Charles Dickens, Virginia Woolf, Margaret Thatcher, and so forth.

General terms can be nouns, verbs, or adjectives. For example, the general term *dancer* in "Baryshnikov is a dancer" is a noun. *Dancing* in "Baryshnikov is dancing" is a verb. And *dance* in "Baryshnikov is a dance master" is an adjective.

Although general terms apply to classes of individuals, they need not describe any actual individual. *Centaur* is a general term, for example, although the property of being a centaur is possessed by no creature that has ever lived.

In all the examples discussed so far—(1) through (6)—general terms occur as predicates in sentences that express singular statements. However, general terms also occur as predicates in sentences that do *not* ascribe properties to specifically designated individuals:

7. Someone is interesting.
8. Something is valuable.
9. Everyone is interesting.
10. Everything has value.

Sentences (7) and (8) assert only that some individual or other has a certain property; they do not say which specific individual has this property. Likewise, while (9) and (10) say that each and every individual has a certain property, no reference is made to a specific individual.

Note that sentences (7) through (10) all begin with an expression signifying a quantity—a word that tells how many or how much. Any simple sentence beginning with a quantity expression such as *some, every, all,* and *no* and containing one or more general terms expresses a *general statement*. General statements do not refer to any particular individual; they are not substitution instances of propositional functions. For instance, (7) and (9), unlike "Prince Charles is interesting," are not substitution instances of the proposition function "Ix." Instead, (7) and (9) are *quantifications* of the function "Ix."

The symbols that are used to represent quantifying expressions such as *someone* and *everyone* are called *quantifiers*. The *existential quantifier* is used to assert that *some* individual—that is, *at least one individual* and possibly more than one—has a given property. It is symbolized by a capital letter E

written backwards, followed by an individual variable (w, x, y, or z) with the whole enclosed in parentheses—for example, "$(\exists x)$," or "$(\exists y)$." The *universal quantifier* is symbolized by an individual variable enclosed in parentheses— "(x)," "(y)," and so forth—and is used to assert that *all* individuals have some property or properties.

The first step in symbolizing a general statement is to reword it to emphasize that it is an assertion about a quantity. Sentence (7), for example, becomes

7a. There is at least one individual who is interesting.

In (7a), the word *who* serves as a relative pronoun referring back to the word *individual*. Next, using the individual variable "x" in place of both the pronoun *who* and its antecedent, we write (7a) as

7b. There is at least one x such that x is interesting.

Now (7b) can be rewritten with the symbolization adopted earlier for predicate expressions:

7c. There is at least one x such that Ix.

Finally, the quantifying expression *there is at least one* x *such that* is replaced by the existential quantifier:

7d. $(\exists x)Ix$

Similarly, (8) can undergo transformations to become

8d. $(\exists x)Vx$

where "V" is taken to stand for the general, or predicate, term *valuable*.

All the following sentences express statements that are equivalent to the one expressed by (8), and they are all symbolized by (8d):

There is at least one valuable thing.
There are valuable things.
There are some valuable things.
Valuable things exist.

In symbolizing the universally quantified statement expressed by (9), we again rewrite the sentence in a logically equivalent manner as

9a. Given any individual whatever, he or she is interesting.

Sentence (9a) is rewritten as

9b. Given any x, x is interesting.

Next, (9b) becomes

9c. Given any x, Ix.

Finally, we replace the quantifying expression, *given any* x, with the universal quantifier:

9d. $(x)Ix$

Similarly, (10) can undergo transformations to become

10a. $(x)Vx$

where "V" is taken to stand for the general term *value*.

All the following sentences express statements that are equivalent to the one expressed by (10), and they are all symbolized by (10a):

All things have value.
Each thing has value.
Anything has value.

An existential quantification expresses a true statement if there is *at least one* individual constant that satisfies the quantified function. Thus, "$(\exists x)Ix$" will express a true statement if there is at least one substitution instance for this quantified function that is true: there must be at least one sentence of the form

x is interesting.

that expresses a true statement when the variable x is replaced by a term that designates an individual.

A universal quantification expresses a true statement if and only if *each* of its substitution instances expresses a true statement. It is false if there is even one substitution instance that does not satisfy the quantified function. Thus, "$(x)Ix$" is false if there is even one statement of the form

x is interesting.

that is false when the variable x is replaced by a term that designates an individual. The symbolization "$(x)Ix$" expresses a true statement only if all sentences of the form

x is interesting.

express true statements when the variable x is replaced by a term that designates an individual.

■ EXERCISE 9-1

■ A. Identify the predicates in the sentences listed below. Determine whether each predicate is monadic or polyadic, and if it is polyadic, state the number of places it has.
1. Mary is logical.
2. St. Louis is larger than Minneapolis and New Orleans.
3. The judge sentenced the convicted individual.
*4. The Boston Celtics defeated the Philadelphia 76ers.
5. Neither Betty nor Ruth loves Henry.
6. George loves God only if he has faith.
7. Cleveland is to the west of Pittsburgh, but not to the west of Indianapolis.
*8. Beckly loves Mozart and Beethoven.
9. Charles prefers Coke to Pepsi.
10. Harold breeds Airedales and salukis.

■ B. Which of the following sentences express singular statements, and which express general statements? For each sentence expressing a singular statement, write a propositional function for which that sentence is a substitution instance.
1. Flipper is a dolphin.
2. A dolphin is a mammal.
3. Hannibal's army attacked Rome.
*4. Hannibal's elephants crossed the Alps.
5. The planets are satellites.
6. The earth is a satellite of the sun.
7. A lawyer can help.
*8. The president is not infallible.
9. All professors are fallible.
10. John F. Kennedy and Lyndon B. Johnson were Democratic presidents.
11. There are pessimists and there are optimists.
*12. No one got everything right.
13. The chairperson reports to the faculty senate and not to the provost.
14. Men and women cannot really understand each other.
15. Vegetarianism is becoming more popular.

*16. God is omniscient and omnipotent.

17. The Beatles were knighted by Queen Elizabeth II.

18. If Socrates was right, then virtue is knowledge.

19. It's not the case that Caesar conquered both Gaul and Greece.

*20. It is not true that all Americans are energy-wasters. ■

□ 9-2. QUANTIFIERS AND TRUTH-FUNCTIONAL OPERATORS

As shown in Section 9-1, there are two ways to obtain a complete statement[2] from a propositional function. One way is to replace each occurrence of an individual variable with an individual constant. For example, from

1. *x* is human.

a *singular* statement can be obtained by replacing the variable "*x*" with an appropriate name—say, *Clark Kent*. This will yield the substitution instance

1a. Clark Kent is human.

The second way is to quantify the propositional function to produce a *general* statement. Thus, (1) can become

1b. Something is human.

This is symbolized as

1c. $(\exists x)Hx$

Both (1a) and (1b) are *simple statements*: neither contains a component that by itself could be regarded as a statement. However, all the logical operators introduced in Chapter 7 can be used to produce truth-functional compound statements from propositional functions. The components of these compound statements can be singular statements, general statements, or combinations of the two. For example, consider (2) through (4), each of which is followed by its translation:

2. Sylvia is fair and Sylvia is wise.
   Fs & *Ws*

---

[2] In the interest of economy of expression, the term *statement* will be used throughout the remainder of this chapter to mean both the statement, or proposition, and the sentence used to express it. The distinction between sentences and statements is discussed in Section 1-1.

3. Either everything is material or something is spiritual.
$(x)Mx \lor (\exists x)Sx$

4. If anything is omnipotent, then God is omnipotent.
$(x)Ox \supset Og$

Statement (2) is a conjunction with singular statements as its components; (3) is a disjunction of two general statements; and (4) is a conditional with a general statement as its antecedent and a singular statement as its consequent. All are truth-functional compound statements because they contain components that can be regarded as independent statements.

☐ *Compound propositional functions*

Compound statements such as (2) through (4) are distinguished from *compound propositional functions*, examples of which are

5. x is fair and x is wise.
$Fx \& Wx$

6. If x is fair, then Sylvia is wise.
$Fx \supset Ws$

7. Either everyone is honest or y is honest.
$(x)Hx \lor Hy$

Example (5) consists of two propositional functions connected by the ampersand, or sign of conjunction. In (6) we have a conditional formed with a propositional function as antecedent and a singular statement as consequent. And (7) illustrates a disjunction with a general statement as the first disjunct and a propositional function as the second disjunct. None of the three is a complete statement because each contains at least one unquantified individual variable.

A compound propositional function such as (5) can be quantified in the same way as the simple propositional function "x is fair." Recall that the latter is quantified by rewriting it as "There is some x such that x is fair," or "$(\exists x)Fx$." Similarly, (5) becomes quantified by rewriting it as "There is some x such that x is fair and x is wise," or

5a. $(\exists x)(Fx \& Wx)$

Although (5a) contains a logical operator (the ampersand, "&"), it is not a truth-functional compound. Because it does not have a component that can be regarded as an independent statement, it must be regarded as a *simple* general statement.

☐ *Logical operators in general statements*

In Chapter 7, logical operators were used only to combine simple statements into truth functions. Logical operators can also be used for this purpose in predicate logic, as illustrated by examples (2) through (4). However, predicate logic requires that we symbolize *internal* relations—those between the terms of a simple statement—as well as *external* relations—those between the simple statements that are combined into truth functions.

Consider the difference between the statement "Elsbeth is a cow" and statement (8).

8. Elsbeth is a brown cow.

The same symbolization could be used for both statements. That is, "C" could be made to stand either for *cow* or for *brown cow*, as in (8a).

8a. *Ce*

But, for the purposes of predicate logic, it is preferable to replace (8) with

8b. *Ce & Be*

In (8b), "C" stands for the quality involved in being a cow ("cowhood" or "cowness"), "B" stands for the property of brownness, and "*e*" designates Elsbeth.

Both (8a) and (8b) have exactly the same truth conditions and are therefore logically equivalent. However, (8b) makes explicit the logical relations between the terms in (8). And by translating statements as explicitly as possible, we will find it easier to check formal inferences involving relations between the terms.

Example (8) is a singular statement containing a predicate that designates *compound properties*. It is standard practice in predicate logic to translate a statement of this kind as a conjunction, each component of which contains a predicate term designating a simple property—as was done in (8b).[3]

Furthermore, every substitution instance of a simple propositional function containing a term or symbol for a compound property will be a substitution instance of the corresponding compound propositional function. The compound propositional function in this case will consist of a conjunction of predicate symbols with the same variable repeated in each conjunct. Thus, (8) is a substitution instance of both (8c) and the compound propositional function (8d).

8c. *x* is a brown cow.
8d. *x* is a cow and *x* is brown.

---

[3] Exceptions must sometimes be made when one predicate term is an adjective qualifying another predicate term. For example, "Smythe is an intellectual giant" is correctly translated as "*Is*," not as "*Is & Gs*." For to say that someone is an intellectual giant is not to say that the person is an intellectual and a giant.

Next consider the statement

9. Some cows are brown.

This statement is the quantification of the propositional functions in (8c) and (8d). It can be rephrased to read "There is at least one x such that x is a cow and x is brown" and symbolized as

9a. $(\exists x)(Cx\ \&\ Bx)$

Look now at

10. All cows are herbivorous.

This statement is the universal quantification of the propositional function "x is a herbivorous cow." Note that (10) could *not* be correctly symbolized as "$(x)(Cx\ \&\ Hx)$" because this is equivalent to "Given any x, x is a cow and x is herbivorous." Statement (10) asserts only that all *cows* are herbivorous—not that *everything* is both a cow and herbivorous. Rather, in asserting (10), we mean "whatever is a cow is herbivorous" or, more explicitly, "If anything is a cow, then it is herbivorous." Thus, (10) is translated as the quantification of a conditional:

10a. $(x)(Cx \supset Hx)$

General statements such as (9) and (10)—which were identified as *categorical statements* in Chapter 5—occur frequently in arguments and are therefore important in predicate logic. The role of such statements and their translation into the symbolic language of predicate logic are discussed at length in Section 9-3.

☐ *The scope of a quantifier*

When quantifying a compound propositional function, it is necessary to enclose the entire propositional function in parentheses. This makes it clear that all components of the compound propositional function fall within the *scope* of the quantifier:

> **The scope of a quantifier is the part of a quantified propositional function that is governed by the existential or universal quantifier preceding it.**

For example, the parentheses enclosing the conditional in (10a) indicate that the conditional is within the scope of the universal quantifier "(x)."
The variables of the expression "$Cx \supset Hx$" in (10a) refer to whatever is designated by the variable x that serves as the universal quantifier. Because

every occurrence of *x* refers back to that quantifier, *x* is called the *variable of quantification*. The variable *x* is also said to *range over* the conditional "*Cx* ⊃ *Hx*" since the parentheses show that it is attached to the whole of the expression.

In some kinds of statements, however, the quantifiers are not attached in this way. In examples (4) and (7), for instance—"(*x*)*Ox* ⊃ *Og*" and "(*x*)*Hx* ∨ *Hy*"—quantifiers are attached to only a portion of each expression. Here is a further example:

11. Either something is solid or everything is liquid.

When considered as a whole, this is not a quantified statement but instead a disjunction whose components are quantifications. It is expressed symbolically as

11a. (∃*x*)*Sx* ∨ (*x*)*Lx*

The scope of the existential quantifier, "(∃*x*)," is restricted to the first disjunct, and the scope of the universal quantifier, "(*x*)," to the second disjunct.

Any symbolized statement or propositional function is called a *formula*. Thus, expressions such as "*Sx*," "*Sx* ∨ *Px*," "(*x*)(*Sx* ⊃ *Px*)," and "(∃*x*)(*Sx* & *Px*)" are all formulae.

The portion of a formula that falls within the scope of a quantifier is said to be *bound* by that quantifier. So, in the quantified statement "(*x*)(*Sx* ⊃ *Px*)," "*Sx* ⊃ *Px*" is bound by the universal quantifier "(*x*)" and is called a *bound formula*. A formula that does not begin with a quantifier—in other words, a formula with an individual variable that is not under the scope of a quantifier— is a *free formula*. Examples of free formulae are "*Sx*" and "*Sx* ∨ *Px*."

The transformation rules that were introduced in Chapter 7 can be applied to both free and bound formulae. For example, since "*p* ⊃ *q*" is equivalent by conditional exchange to "~*p* ∨ *q*," then "*Sx* ⊃ *Px*"—whether it appears as a free or a bound formula—is also equivalent to "~*Sx* ∨ *Px*" by conditional exchange. Similarly, since "~(*p* & *q*)" is equivalent by De Morgan's laws to "~*p* ∨ ~*q*," "(∃*x*)~(*Sx* & *Px*)" is also equivalent by De Morgan's laws to "(∃*x*)(~*Sx* ∨ ~*Px*)."

□ *Summary: statements and functions in predicate logic*

Predicate logic makes use of a larger variety of expressions than any other deductive system. So far, we have considered singular statements, simple and compound propositional functions, general statements, and truth-functional compounds. All of these can be symbolized as formulae using the notation of predicate logic. Following is a summary of the different expressions, with examples of each.

☐ SINGULAR STATEMENTS

Statements that contain one or more predicate terms and one or more names designating specific individuals are singular statements. These may be simple (for example, "Sylvia is fair") or truth-functionally compound ("Sylvia is fair and Sylvia is wise").

☐ PROPOSITIONAL FUNCTIONS

Expressions that contain at least one free individual variable are propositional functions. They may either be simple ("x is fair") or compound ("x is fair and x is wise"), although they are not themselves statements.

☐ GENERAL, OR QUANTIFIED, STATEMENTS

Simple statements consisting of one or more predicate terms preceded by either an existential or a universal quantifier are general statements, also known as quantified statements. They can be obtained by quantifying a simple propositional function—for example, by quantifying "x is interesting" to obtain "$(x)Ix$." They are also obtained by quantifying compound propositional functions—for example, by obtaining "$(\exists x)(Fx \;\&\; Wx)$" from "x is fair and x is wise."

☐ TRUTH-FUNCTIONAL COMPOUNDS

Compound statements whose truth values are entirely determined by the truth values of the simple statements that form their component parts are truth-functional compounds. Both singular and general statements can be combined to form truth-functional compounds, as shown by these examples:

> "Sylvia is fair and Sylvia is honest." (Both components are singular statements.)
> "If anything is infinite, then God is infinite." (The first component is a general statement and the second one is a singular statement.)
> "Either everything is solid or something is liquid." (Both components are general statements.)

It is important to distinguish general statements obtained by quantifying compound propositional functions from truth-functional compounds. Consider the following:

12. Every human being is either male or female.

This is a general statement because none of its terms designates a particular individual. Furthermore, the word *every* indicates that the universal quantifier is appropriate for its translation. Thus, (12) is symbolized as

12a. $(x)[Hx \supset (Mx \lor Fx)]$

where "Hx" is substituted for "x is a human being," "Mx" for "x is male," and "Fx" for "x is female."

Now compare (12) and (12a) with (13) and its translation, (13a):

13. Either every human being is male or every human being is female.
13a. $(x)(Hx \supset Mx) \lor (x)(Hx \supset Fx)$

While (12) and (12a) are probably true, (13) and (13a) are certainly false. It is not the case that all human beings are male, and it is not the case that all human beings are female. Thus, although (12) and (13) at first *appear* to assert the same thing, they do not. Statement (12) is a simple general statement that requires the use of logical operators to symbolize the internal relationships between its terms. Statement (13) is a compound statement with general statements as its components.

■ **EXERCISE 9-2**

(a) Determine which of the following formulae express statements and which symbolize propositional functions. (b) For each formula expressing a statement, determine whether it expresses a simple statement or a truth-functionally compound statement. (c) For the formulae containing variables (x, y, or z), indicate whether the variables are free or bound.

1. $(x)(Fx \supset Ga)$
2. $Fa \lor {\sim}Fb$
3. $(x)Fx$
*4. $(\exists x)Sxy$
5. $(\exists x) {\sim}Fxa$
6. $Fx \supset Gb$
7. $(x)Fx \lor {\sim}(x)Fx$
*8. $(x)Fx \supset (y)Gx$
9. $(x)Fx \supset Gx$
10. $(\exists y)Fx \,\&\, Gy$
11. $(\exists y)(Fy \,\&\, Gy)$
*12. $(\exists z)(Fz \,\&\, Ga)$
13. $(x)[Sx \supset (Px \lor Tx)]$
14. $(x)(x$ is female $\lor x$ is male$)$
15. $(\exists y)(y$ is moral$) \,\&\, y$ is immoral
*16. $(\exists y)(y$ is moral$) \,\&\, z$ is immoral
17. $(z)(z$ is immoral $\supset y$ is moral$)$
18. $(x)\ x$ is a liquid $\&\ (\exists y)\ y$ is solid
19. $(\exists x)x$ is a gas $\&\ [(y)\ y$ is a solid $\supset (\exists z)z$ is a liquid$]$
*20. x is mortal $\lor (\exists z)z$ is immortal ■

☐ 9-3. QUANTIFYING CATEGORICAL STATEMENTS

When a general statement in English is transformed into one of the *standard categorical forms*—A, E, I, or O—it is given invariant features. In each case, the statement starts with a quantifier word: *all, no,* or *some.* The quantifier word is followed by a noun or noun phrase designating the *subject* (S) of the statement. The subject is followed by the *copula*—the word *are.* This is followed in turn by the *predicate* (P), which designates the attribute, or property, of the subject. The four standard forms for categorical statements are listed, for convenient reference, in Table 9-1.

Categorical forms are useful in predicate logic because *it is possible to give simple and exceptionless rules for translating standard categorical statements into the symbolic notation of predicate logic.* A general statement in English is more easily translated into a symbolized quantified statement if it is first put into standard categorical form. Thus, the translation is a two-step process.

The techniques for translating general statements in English into standard-form categoricals are presented in Section 5-1. The remainder of this section will focus on the second step: the translation of categorical statements into the language of predicate logic.

☐ *Symbolizing universal statements*

We shall begin by considering the universal categorical statement forms—the universal affirmative, A, and the universal negative, E. It might at first seem that the A-form statement in (1)

1. All S are P.

could be translated as in (1a), where "*a*" and "*b*" are names of individuals and the subscript "*n*" stands for any member of class S.

1a. $(Sa$ is $P)$ & $(Sb$ is $P)$ . . . & $(S_n$ is $P)$

TABLE 9-1 *The standard categorical forms*

FORM	EXAMPLE
A: All *S* are *P.*	All sophomores are undergraduates.
E: No *S* are *P.*	No juniors are seniors.
I: Some *S* are *P.*	Some humanists are professors.
O: Some *S* are not *P.*	Some scientists are not doctors.

But although (1) is the assertion that all individuals that are S are P, it is not a claim that there are any individuals in the class designated by "S." Suppose we doubt that anything can properly be described as an S or are uncertain about the existence of such individuals. Under either of these conditions, an assertion of the form exhibited in (1) should not be interpreted as declaring that anything is an S.

Logicians therefore treat all A-form statements as *generalized*, or *quantified, conditionals*—as assertions that *if* anything is an S, then that thing is also a P. To illustrate this point, consider the statement

2. All gnomes are cranky.

Because gnomes are inventions of the imagination, (2) can hardly be analyzed as the conjunction shown in (2a):

2a. (Ga is cranky) & (Gb is cranky) & . . . & (G_n is cranky).

Instead, (2) is treated as asserting (2b) and as an instantiation of the compound proposition function shown in (2c).

2b. If anything is a gnome, it is cranky.
2c. Given any x, if x is a gnome, then x is cranky.

There being no gnomes, (2) cannot be a statement describing or referring to such creatures. It is, rather, a statement about everything there is: the textbook you are now reading, the air you breathe, the clothes you wear, the corner mailbox, and so on. It says that if this textbook is a gnome, then it is cranky; and if the shoe on your left foot is a gnome, then it is cranky, too. But nothing is a gnome—and (2c), as a universal claim, does not assert that anything is a gnome.

A-form categorical statements are treated as quantified conditionals even when they are assertions about existing creatures. For example,

3. All palominos are horses.

amounts to the declaration that

3a. Given any x, if x is a palomino, then x is a horse.

This does *not* say that there are any palominos. Instead, (3a) represents such assertions as "If this animal is a palomino, it is a horse," and "If Trigger is a palomino, he is a horse."

The final translation of (2) is, then,

2d. $(x)(Gx \supset Cx)$

where "*Gx*" stands for "*x* is a gnome" and "*Cx*" stands for "*x* is cranky." And the final translation of (3) is

3b. (x)(Px ⊃ Hx)

where "*Px*" is taken to symbolize "*x* is a palomino" and "*Hx*," "*x* is a horse."

As shown in Section 9-1, singular statements, which in categorical logic are translated into *A* form, are not so translated in predicate logic. For example, in categorical logic, "Hector is a puppy" would be translated as "All things identical to Hector are puppies." However, in predicate logic, where a sharp distinction is maintained between singular and general statements, this statement would be translated as "*Ph*," with "*P*" standing for "puppy" and "*h*" for "Hector."

The same considerations that apply to *A*-form statements also apply to statements of the universal negative, *E* form:

4. No S are P.

These, too, are treated as quantified conditionals. Statement (4) is construed as declaring that if anything is an *S*, then that thing is *not* a *P*. Consider this example:

5. No sea serpents are mammals.

This does not mean that there are sea serpents that are not mammals. Rather, (5) asserts that if anything is a sea serpent, it is not a mammal. Thus, it must be analyzed as

5a. Given any x, if x is a sea serpent, ⊃ ~(x is a mammal).

When completely symbolized, with "*Sx*" taken to mean "*x* is a sea serpent" and "*Mx*" to mean "*x* is a mammal," (5) becomes

5b. (x)(Sx ⊃ ~Mx)

All *E*-form propositions are treated the same way. Thus, statement (6)

6. No beagles are dachshunds.

represents assertions such as "If this animal is a beagle, then it is not a dachshund"; "If this dog is a beagle, then it is not a dachshund"; "If Nutmeg is a beagle, then she is not a dachshund"; and so forth.

All *E*-form statements, like all *A*-form statements, are about everything there is. They are not construed as being about only the individuals allegedly described by the subject and predicate terms. The rules shown in the inset are therefore exceptionless rules.

Rule 1:   Statements in *A* form—All *S* are *P*—are always translated as $(x)(Sx \supset Px)$.

Rule 2:   Statements in *E* form—No *S* are *P*—are always translated as $(x)(Sx \supset {\sim}Px)$.

Translating all universal statements as universally quantified conditionals amounts to adopting what in Section 5-3 was called the "hypothetical viewpoint," or the "Boolean interpretation" of universal categorical statements. In categorical logic, determining the validity of certain categorical syllogisms depends on distinguishing between the hypothetical viewpoint and the existential viewpoint; some syllogisms valid from the existential viewpoint are not valid from the hypothetical viewpoint (see Sections 6-2 and 6-3). It may therefore seem surprising that in predicate logic all universal categorical statements *must* be considered hypothetical claims.

The decision to interpret universal statements as universally quantified conditionals is both *justified* and *necessary*, however. It is *justified* because it involves no loss of truth. As will be seen, the procedures for performing deductions in predicate logic make it possible to replace a quantified universal statement with substitution instances specifying appropriate individuals. Treating universal statements as conditionals even when the *S* and *P* terms describe real individuals or classes of individuals (as in "All residents of Kalamazoo are residents of Michigan") does not require us to abandon the view that these individuals exist. Predicate logic does not eliminate the existential viewpoint. Rather, it supersedes the distinction between the two viewpoints by insuring that statements that are true because they designate real individuals remain true within the system.

The interpretation of universal statements as universally quantified conditionals is *necessary* because the consistency of the deductive system requires it. In predicate logic, it must be possible to formulate arguments involving particular statements and arguments involving universal statements within a single formalized system. Given the proper translation of particular statements, discussed immediately below, the universal statements must be interpreted as quantified conditionals.

□ *Symbolizing particular statements*

Particular categorical statements—the *I* and *O* forms—are *not* translated as quantified conditionals but, rather, as *quantified conjunctions*. To understand why this translation is justified, consider the *I*-form statement (7) and the *O*-form statement (8).

7. Some *S* are *P*.
8. Some *S* are not *P*.

Unlike their universal counterparts, these assert the existence of some *S*, as shown by the alternative formulations (7a) and (8a).

7a. There is something that is S, and it is also P.

8a. There is something that is S, and it is not also P.

Thus, (7) and (8) are symbolized, respectively, as (7b) and (8b).

7b. $(\exists x)(Sx \,\&\, Px)$

8b. $(\exists x)(Sx \,\&\, {\sim}Px)$

The same analysis of particular statements is needed when the S and P terms describe imaginary or possibly nonexisting things. Statement (9) is therefore paraphrased as (9a) and symbolized as (9b).

9. Some unicorns are not wild.

9a. There is at least one x, such that x is a unicorn and x is not wild.

9b. $(\exists x)(Ux \,\&\, {\sim}Wx)$

The treatment of particular categorical statements is summarized in the exceptionless rules shown in the inset.

Rule 3:   Statements in *I* form—Some S are P—are always translated as $(\exists x)(Sx \,\&\, Px)$.

Rule 4:   Statements in *O* form—Some S are not P—are always translated as $(\exists x)(Sx \,\&\, {\sim}Px)$.

The reason for regarding "$(\exists x)(Sx \,\&\, {\sim}Px)$" as the correct translation of an O-form statement will become clear by considering a commonplace example:

10. Some athletes are not basketball players.

As this statement is understood in everyday language, it will be true if there is at least one athlete who is not a basketball player, and it will be false if all athletes are basketball players. If there were no athletes at all, (10) would also be false—because if there were no athletes whatsoever, there could not be any non–basketball-playing athletes. In other words, if the statement "There is at least one athlete" is false, the statement "There is at least one athlete, and that athlete is not a basketball player" must be false as well. And this conforms to the interpretation of (10) as the quantification of a conjunction:

10a. $(\exists x)(Ax \,\&\, {\sim}Bx)$

Because of the truth conditions for the conjunction, (10a) will be false if either "Ax" or "${\sim}Bx$" is false or if both are false.

Suppose (10) were translated, instead, as a quantified conditional: "$(\exists x)(Ax \supset {\sim}Bx)$." According to the truth conditions for the conditional, this formula will be *true* even if there are no athletes at all, for the conditional is true whenever its antecedent is false. But as noted above, such an interpretation is counter to the way the English sentence is understood. Furthermore, the quantified conditional "$(\exists x)(Ax \supset {\sim}Bx)$" will be *false* when there is at least one athlete who *is* a basketball player. But surely anyone who asserts (10) does not intend to rule out the possibility that at least one athlete is a basketball player.

In addition, because of the equivalence of the conditional "$Ax \supset {\sim}Bx$" to the disjunction "${\sim}Ax \lor {\sim}Bx$" (by the transformation rule "$p \supset q; {\sim}p \lor q$"), "$(\exists x)(Ax \supset {\sim}Bx)$" is equivalent to the statement "There is something such that either it is not an athlete, or it is not a basketball player." And this statement is *trivially* true: any number of individuals will satisfy this propositional function, including an orange, a fountain pen, and a skyscraper. It is unlikely that anyone who asserts (10) intends to make such a trivial statement. Thus, "$(\exists x)(Ax \;\&\; {\sim}Bx)$" is the only reasonable translation of (10).

The same considerations apply to particular statements about imaginary or possibly nonexisting individuals. If (9) were read as "$(\exists x)(Ux \supset {\sim}Wx)$," we would be forced, because of the truth conditions for the conditional, to accept it as true. And given the equivalence of "$Ux \supset {\sim}Wx$" and "${\sim}Ux \lor {\sim}Wx$," (9) would also be true because of its equivalence to the trivially true statement "There is something such that either it is not a unicorn, or it is not wild." But this interpretation is absurd. Statement (9) is false because there are no unicorns—and the paraphrase and symbolization in (9a) and (9b) permit this to be shown.

☐ *Predicates that designate compound properties*

After an English categorical statement has been paraphrased into standard form, the subject or predicate expression, or both, will often designate a compound property. To translate such statements completely into the symbolic notation of predicate logic, we must express them as quantifications of compound propositional functions. For instance, statement (11) could be translated as the quantification of a universal statement, as in (11a).

11. All Andean condors are endangered animals.

11a. $(x)(x$ is an Andean condor $\supset x$ is an endangered animal$)$.

But since both the S and P terms express compound predicates, (11) is more fully translated as

11b. $(x)[(x$ is Andean $\&\; x$ is a condor$) \supset (x$ is an animal $\&\; x$ is endangered$)]$.

Then, where "Ax" is written for "x is Andean," "Cx" for "x is a condor," "Nx" for "x is an animal," and "Ex" for "x is endangered," statement (11) is completely symbolized as

11c. $(x)[(Ax \text{ \& } Cx) \supset (Nx \text{ \& } Ex)]$

As a further example, consider (12), which is paraphrased in standard form as (12a).

12. Some bulls become angry if they are teased.
12a. Some bulls are things that become angry if teased.

Now statement (12a) can be treated as an *I*-form proposition with a compound predicate term and translated accordingly:

12b. $(\exists x)[x \text{ is a bull \& } (x \text{ is teased} \supset x \text{ becomes angry})]$.

Finally, with "*Bx*" written for "*x* is a bull," "*Tx*" for "*x* is teased," and "*Ax*" for "*x* becomes angry," (12) is completely symbolized as in (12c).

12c. $(\exists x)[Bx \text{ \& } (Tx \supset Ax)]$

□ *The word* and

The word *and* occurring as part of the subject term of a categorical statement in English can be problematical. When the statement is correctly paraphrased into A form, *and* is usually replaced by *or*. For example,

13. Strawberries and raspberries are delicious.

should be paraphrased as

13a. Anything that is either a strawberry or a raspberry is delicious.

and *not* as

13b. All strawberries and raspberries are delicious. (Wrong!)

The difference between (13a) and (13b) is more clearly revealed by symbolizing the statements. Version (13a) becomes "$(x)[(Sx \vee Rx) \supset Dx]$"—where "*Sx*" stands for "*x* is a strawberry," "*Rx*" for "*x* is a raspberry," and "*Dx*" for "*x* is delicious." However, (13b) becomes "$(x)[(Sx \text{ \& } Rx) \supset Dx]$"—which is *erroneous*, because nothing is both a strawberry *and* a raspberry.

Normally, the word *and* is also replaced by *or* when it is the dominant operator in a phrase beginning with the quantifier word *only*. For example, statement (14) is *not* correctly paraphrased as (14a), for the sense of (14a) is that *mad dogs* and *Englishmen* designate the same creatures.

14. Only mad dogs and Englishmen go out in the noonday sun.

14a. All those who go out in the noonday sun are mad dogs and Englishmen. (Wrong!)

The *correct* paraphrase of (14) is, rather, (14b).

14b. All those who go out in the noonday sun are either mad dogs or
Englishmen.

Note that (13) and (14) are not compound statements. They are categorical
statements—that is, simple general statements—with compound terms.

When *and* is not functioning as a logical operator, it *normally* behaves in
the way described above—as replaceable by *or*. But there are exceptions: sometimes in a phrase following *all* or *only*, the word *and* will remain through the
paraphrase into standard form. For instance, (15) is correctly rendered (at a
preliminary stage) as (15a), because there can be no doubt that the subject is
the musicals Richard Rogers and Oscar Hammerstein composed together.

15. Musicals by Rogers and Hammerstein are outstanding examples of
artistic collaboration.

15a. $(x)[(x$ is a musical by Rogers & x is a musical by Hammerstein$) \supset x$
is an outstanding example of artistic collaboration].

There are no grammatical clues indicating when *and* should become *or*
and when it should not. We must instead rely on our judgment of the *meaning*
of the statement as well as on common sense.

☐ *The expression* all and only

The quantifier expression *all and only* serves much the same function in predicate logic as the operator *if and only if* serves in truth-functional logic. Statements containing *all and only* may be handled in either of two ways. For
example, the statement

16. All and only residents are eligible to vote.

may be paraphrased as the conjunction of two A-form propositions: one with
all and the other with *only*. Thus, (16) can become (16a) and then (16b).

16a. All residents are eligible to vote & only residents are eligible to vote.

16b. All residents are eligible to vote & all persons eligible to vote are
residents.

Statement (16b) is translated as

16c. $(x)(Rx \supset Ex) \& (x)(Ex \supset Rx)$

Alternatively, (16) may be translated as a universally quantified biconditional—that is, as

16d. $(x)(Rx \equiv Ex)$

Statements (16) through (16d) are all logically equivalent.

☐ *Universal quantifiers masquerading as particular quantifiers*

The quantity terms *someone, somebody,* and *something* are generally replaced by existential quantifiers. There are exceptions, however, that must be noted. Consider, for example,

17. Something is good only if it is illegal, immoral, or fattening.

Presumably what is meant is *not* (17a).

17a. There is at least one x such that x is good, and either x is illegal, or x is immoral, or x is fattening. (Wrong!)

This is incorrect because (17) may still be true even if (17a) is false. Instead, (17) should be paraphrased as in (17b), which is symbolized in (17c).

17b. Given any x, if x is good, then either x is illegal, or x is immoral, or x is fattening.
17c. $(x)[Gx \supset (Ix \lor Mx \lor Fx)]$

Statement (18) is another example in which the universal quantifier is represented by the phrase *someone who* even though *someone* ordinarily serves as a particular quantifier.

18. Someone who weeps is forlorn.

This is correctly translated as

18a. $(x)(Wx \supset Fx)$

The best way to decide whether the universal or the existential quantifier applies is simply to (1) consider alternative paraphrases and translations and then (2) ask oneself which version is closest to what someone asserting the original English statement would most likely have intended.

■ **EXERCISE 9-3**

■ A. Translate each of the following into the symbolic notation of predicate logic, using the suggested predicate symbols.

   1. Everything is alive. (A)

   2. Something is round. (R)

   3. Each square is a rectangle. (S, R)

   *4. Every creature is mortal. (C, M)

   5. No students are morons. (S, M)

   6. Some metals are not expensive. (M, E)

   7. There are some ores that are iron. (O, I)

   *8. Some women are university trustees. (W, U)

   9. Some juveniles aren't delinquents. (J, D)

   10. Some politicians are not dishonest. (P, D)

   11. Someone insane is a world leader. (I, W)

   *12. The tiger is predacious. (T, P)

   13. Whatever is a platypus is oviparous. (P, O)

   14. If anything is a cetacean, then it is warm-blooded. (C, W)

   15. There is an informer who is a Soviet. (I, S)

   *16. Predacious apes exist. (P, A)

   17. Any black snake is not venomous. (S, B, V)

   18. At least one gorilla is a killer. (G, K)

   19. Everything edible is healthful. (E, H)

   *20. Something that is sweet is also unhealthful. (S, H)

   21. Every answer is wrong. (A, W)

   22. Some Indians are non-Buddhists. (I, B)

   23. No non-residents are voters. (R, V)

   *24. Only traitors are executed. (T, E)

   25. A few ministers are divorced. (M, D)

   26. Secretaries are not sex objects. (S, O)

   27. "Blessed are the meek." (B, M)

   *28. All that glitters is not gold. (G, O)

   29. He who hesitates is lost. (H, L)

   30. None but the worthy are saved. (W, S)

   31. All and only students are eligible contestants. (S, E)

   *32. If something is valuable then it is worth seeking. (V, W)

   33. Only clams and oysters are delectable mollusks. (C, O, D, M)

   34. There are some women who, if they are hard-working, will achieve greatness. (W, H, G)

   35. All professors are eligible if and only if they are not insurance risks. (P, E, I)

■ B. Translate each of the following, using the suggested notation.

1. Horses exist but unicorns do not. (*Hx*—*x* is a horse; *Ux*—*x* is a unicorn.)

2. None but the strong survive. (*Sx*—*x* is strong; *Vx*—*x* survives.)

3. He who laughs last, laughs best. (*Px*—*x* is a person; *Lx*—*x* laughs last; *Bx*—*x* laughs best.)

*****4.** Someone succeeds only if he or she is dedicated and self-confident. (*Sx*—*x* succeeds; *Dx*—*x* is dedicated; *Cx*—*x* is self-confident.)

5. All wine is either red or white. (*Wx*—*x* is wine; *Rx*—*x* is red; *Hx*—*x* is white.)

6. If all students are overachievers, then they are alert. (*Sy*—*y* is a student; *Oy*—*y* is an overachiever; *Ay*—*y* is alert.)

7. Every linebacker is aggressive and quick-tempered. (*Ly*—*y* is a linebacker; *Ay*—*y* is aggressive; *Qy*—*y* is quick-tempered.)

*****8.** Either some players have no talent or some coaches are incompetent. (*Py*—*y* is a player; *Ty*—*y* has talent; *Cy*—*y* is a coach; *Iy*—*y* is incompetent.)

9. It is false that all men are sexists. (*My*—*y* is a man; *Sy*—*y* is a sexist.)

10. It is not the case that no feminists are men. (*Fy*—*y* is a feminist; *My*—*y* is a man.)

11. Either some students are highly motivated or some professors are inspirational. (*Sz*—*z* is a student; *Hz*—*z* is highly motivated; *Pz*—*z* is a professor; *Iz*—*z* is inspirational.)

*****12.** Someone is happy, but it is not the case that everyone is happy. (*Hz*—*z* is happy.)

13. If all detectives are astute, then some safecrackers will be caught. (*Dz*—*z* is a detective; *Az*—*z* is astute; *Sz*—*z* is a safecracker; *Cz*—*z* will be caught.)

14. Philosophers exist who are logicians, but not every philosopher is a logician. (*Pz*—*z* is a philosopher; *Lz*—*z* is a logician.)

15. If some students are interested, and a professor is willing, then a new course will be offered. (*Sz*—*z* is a student; *Iz*—*z* is interested; *Pz*—*z* is a professor; *Wz*—*z* is willing; *Nx*—*x* is a new course; *Ox*—*x* will be offered.)

*****16.** Any valid argument that is not sound has a false premise. (*Vw*—*w* is a valid argument; *Sw*—*w* is sound; *Fw*—*w* has a false premise.)

17. If there is no possible answer, then there is no real question. (*Pw*—*w* is a possible answer; *Rw*—*w* is a real question.)

18. Some people are neither honest nor truthful. (*Pw*—*w* is a person; *Hw*—*w* is honest; *Tw*—*w* is truthful.)

19. No famous artists are unrecognized geniuses. (*Fw*—*w* is famous; *Aw*—*w* is an artist; *Rw*—*w* is recognized; *Gw*—*w* is a genius.)

*****20.** If any judge takes bribes, then that judge deserves to be impeached. (*Jw*—*w* is a judge; *Bw*—*w* takes bribes; *Dw*—*w* deserves to be impeached.)

21. If any taxpayer can take that deduction, then every taxpayer can. (*Tx*—*x* is a taxpayer; *Dx*—*x* can take the deduction.)

22. Economists are neither prophets nor wizards. (*Ex*—*x* is an economist; *Px*—*x* is a prophet; *Wx*—*x* is a wizard.)

23. All children need food, warmth, and shelter. (Cx—x is a child; Fx—x needs food; Wx—x needs warmth; Sx—x needs shelter.)

*24. No physicists who are scientific thinkers are astrologers. (Px—x is a physicist; Sx—x is a scientific thinker; Ax—x is an astrologer.)

25. No physicists are both scientific thinkers and astrologers. (Px—x is a physicist; Sx—x is a scientific thinker; Ax—x is an astrologer.) ■

☐ 9-4. QUANTIFIER NEGATION

Universal affirmative (A) and universal negative (E) categorical statements are, respectively, *contradictories* of particular negative (O) and particular affirmative (I) statements (see Section 5-3). In other words, the denial, or negation, of an A is an O; and the denial, or negation, of an E is an I. This means that a universal affirmative statement, "All S are P," can be expressed equivalently as

1. Given any x, if x is S, then x is P—symbolized as $(x)(Sx \supset Px)$.

1a. It is false that there is some x such that x is S and x is not P—symbolized as "$\sim(\exists x)(Sx \ \& \sim Px)$."

Likewise, "No S are P" can be expressed equivalently as

2. Given any x, if x is S, then x is not P—symbolized as $(x)(Sx \supset \sim Px)$.

2a. It is false that there is some x such that it is S and P—symbolized as "$\sim(\exists x)(Sx \ \& \ Px)$."

The universal and existential quantifiers are, then, connected in meaning through negation. The symbolic expression of A form shown in (1a) is equivalent to "Given any x, it is false that x is S and x is not P." Put another way, $\sim(\exists x)(Sx \ \& \sim Px)$ is equivalent to $(x)(Sx \supset Px)$.

To deny, or negate, any expression of the form "There is at least one x such that Sx—or "$(\exists x)Sx$"—is to say, "There is no x such that Sx"—or "$\sim(\exists x)Sx$." This is also the same as saying, "Nothing is S," or, "For any x, it is not Sx." Thus,

$\sim(\exists x)Sx$ is equivalent to $(x)\sim Sx$.[4]

---

[4] In predicate logic, as in truth-functional logic, parentheses and brackets serve as punctuation marks. Thus, for example, parentheses are used to show that for "$(\exists x)(Sx \ \& \ Px)$" the compound propositional function "Sx & Px" is within the scope of the quantifier "$(\exists x)$." The parentheses also prevent misinterpretation of the formula as "$(\exists x)(Sx) \ \& \ Px$," which is not a quantified statement but a truth function, one component of which is a quantified statement. However, where there is no danger of misunderstanding, the parentheses are unnecessary. Thus, instead of "$(\exists x)(Sx)$," we simply write "$(\exists x)Sx$," and instead of "$(x)(\sim Sx)$," we write "$(x)\sim Sx$."

Furthermore, the negation of "$(x)Sx$" is "It is false that everything is an S," which is to say, "It is false that for any x, x is S." This, in turn, is equivalent to "There is at least one x such that it is not S." Thus,

~$(x)Sx$ is equivalent to $(\exists x)$~Sx.

These equivalencies show that the combination of symbols "~$(\exists x)$" has the same meaning as "(x)~" and that the combination "~(x)" has the same meaning as "$(\exists x)$~." Two important transformation rules for predicate logic are based on this relationship between universal and existential quantifiers. The rules, which are shown in the accompanying box, are summarized informally by saying that a negation sign can be "pushed through" a quantifier, either to the right or to the left, provided that the type of quantifier is changed from universal to existential or vice versa.

Quantifier Negation (Q.N.) Transformation Rules

Q.N. Rule 1   A formula bound by the universal quantifier and immediately preceded by a negation sign is equivalent to the negation of the formula immediately preceded by the existential quantifier:

~$(x)Sx \equiv (\exists x)$~Sx

Q.N. Rule 2   A formula bound by the existential quantifier and immediately preceded by a negation sign is equivalent to the negation of the formula immediately preceded by the universal quantifier:

~$(\exists x)Sx \equiv (x)$~Sx

The transformation rules for quantifier negation differ from the transformation rules for truth-functional logic, which, as noted in Section 9-2, are also incorporated into predicate logic. Whereas the rules explained in Chapter 7 pertain to equivalencies both between truth-functional compounds and between quantified statements, Q.N. Rules 1 and 2 pertain only to quantified statements. In addition, Q.N. Rules 1 and 2 apply only to a bound formula or a bound formula immediately preceded by a negation sign, whereas the truth-functional equivalency principles also apply to free formulae.

To see how both kinds of rules can be employed in performing a deduction, consider the following examples:

~$(\exists x)$~Sx is equivalent to $(x)Sx$.
~(x)~Sx is equivalent to $(\exists x)Sx$.

TABLE 9-2 *Equivalencies in predicate logic*

A All *S* are *P*.	$(x)(Sx \supset Px)$	$(x)\sim(Sx \ \& \sim Px)$	$\sim(\exists x)(Sx \ \& \sim Px)$
E No *S* are *P*.	$(x)(Sx \supset \sim Px)$	$(x)\sim(Sx \ \& \sim\sim Px)$	$\sim(\exists x)(Sx \ \& \ Px)$
I Some *S* are *P*.	$(\exists x)(Sx \ \& \ Px)$	$(\exists x)\sim(Sx \supset \sim Px)$	$\sim(x)(Sx \supset \sim Px)$
O Some *S* are not *P*.	$(\exists x)(Sx \ \& \sim Px)$	$(\exists x)\sim(Sx \supset Px)$	$\sim(x)(Sx \supset Px)$

The first equivalency follows from the fact that "$\sim(\exists x)\sim Sx$" is equivalent to "$(x)\sim\sim Sx$" by Q.N. Rule 2 and to "$(x)Sx$" by double negation. Likewise, "$\sim(x)\sim Sx$" is equivalent to "$(\exists x)\sim\sim Sx$" by Q.N. Rule 1 and to "$(\exists x)Sx$" by double negation.

In applying either kind of transformation rule, care must be taken when using negation signs with quantifiers. While "$(\exists x)\sim\sim Sx$" is equivalent to "$(\exists x)Sx$" by double negation, "$\sim(\exists x)\sim Sx$" is *not* equivalent to "$(\exists x)Sx$" but rather to "$(x)Sx$." Whereas "$\sim(\exists x)\sim Sx$" says "Everything is *S*," or "Nothing is not *S*," "$(\exists x)Sx$" says "Something is *S*." Similarly, one must distinguish "$\sim(x)Sx$" from "$(x)\sim Sx$." The former asserts that something is not *S*, or not everything is *S*, whereas the latter asserts that everything is not *S*.

A tilde *after* the quantifier operates only on that part of the formula that follows it, but a tilde *in front* of a quantifier serves to negate the entire statement following it. Thus, "$\sim(x)Sx$" should be thought of as "$\sim[(x)Sx]$." And "$\sim(\exists x)\sim Sx$" should be thought of as "$\sim[(\exists x)\sim Sx]$."

The equivalencies discussed in this section are summarized in Table 9-2.

It should now be clear why the consistency of predicate logic requires the hypothetical, or Boolean, interpretation of universal categorical statements to the exclusion of the traditional existential interpretation. The negation of an O-form statement—"$\sim(\exists x)(Sx \ \& \sim Px)$"—is equivalent by Q.N. Rule 2 to "$(x)\sim(Sx \ \& \sim Px)$." The latter, by an application of conditional exchange, is equivalent to "$(x)(Sx \supset Px)$," which represents the translation we require for any A-form statement in predicate logic. Likewise, the negation of an I-form statement—"$\sim(\exists x)(Sx \ \& \ Px)$"—becomes by Q.N. Rule 2 "$(x)\sim(Sx \ \& \ Px)$." This is equivalent by De Morgan's laws to "$(x)(\sim Sx \lor \sim Px)$" and also, by conditional exchange, to "$(x)(Sx \supset \sim Px)$." Consequently, the decision to translate any E-form statement as the quantification of a conditional with a negative consequent rests upon the fact that the I- and E-form statements are contradictories. The logical relations between categorical statements when they are quantified in predicate logic necessitate the hypothetical interpretation of universal statements.

■ **EXERCISE 9-4**

For each of the following pairs of formulae, show how (a) can be transformed into (b).

1. (a) $(x) \sim(Fx \supset Gx)$
    (b) $\sim(\exists x) \sim(Fx \ \& \sim Gx)$

2. (a) $(\exists x)(Fx \ \& \ Gx)$
   (b) $\sim(x)(Fx \supset \sim Gx)$

3. (a) $(x)(Fx \supset Gx)$
   (b) $\sim(\exists x)\sim(\sim Gx \supset \sim Fx)$

*4. (a) $(x)(Fx \supset \sim Gx)$
   (b) $\sim(\exists x)\sim(\sim Fx \lor \sim Gx)$

5. (a) $\sim(\exists x)(Fx \lor Gx)$
   (b) $(x)(\sim Fx \ \& \ \sim Gx)$

6. (a) $(x)(Fx \supset Gx)$
   (b) $\sim(\exists x)(Fx \ \& \ \sim Gx)$

7. (a) $(x)[Fx \supset (Gx \lor Hx)]$
   (b) $\sim(\exists x)[Fx \ \& \ (\sim Gx \ \& \ \sim Hx)]$

*8. (a) $(x)(Fx \lor Gx) \supset (x)\sim(Gx \equiv Rx)$
   (b) $(\exists x)(\sim Fx \ \& \ \sim Gx) \lor \sim(\exists x)(Gx \equiv Rx)$

9. (a) $\sim(x)\sim Fx \lor \sim(x)\sim(Fx \ \& \ Gx)$
   (b) $(\exists x)Fx \lor (\exists x)(Fx \ \& \ Gx)$

10. (a) $\sim(x)Fx \lor \sim(x)(Gx \supset Rx)$
    (b) $(x)Fx \supset (\exists x)(Gx \ \& \ \sim Rx)$ ∎

□ 9-5. THE DOMAIN OF DISCOURSE AND TRUTH-FUNCTIONAL EXPANSION

A universally quantified statement tells something about each member of a domain of discourse.

The domain, or universe, of discourse is the set of individuals described by the general statements in an argument, or discourse.

The range of a quantifier can be restricted, however, to some set of individuals less than the total number in the domain. Restricting the domain of discourse simplifies translation, thereby making deductions involving quantified statements easier to manage.

□ *Restricted domains*

When a general statement is translated into symbolic notation, the domain is the set of individuals over which the variables range. For instance, suppose we take the quantified statement "$(x)Fx$" and limit the domain to a finite set of n individuals named "a_1," "a_2," . . . "a_n." Since "(x)" is a universal quantifier, it affirms the predicate "F" of all members of the set n, but its range is *restricted* to individuals in the set n. The quantification "$(x)Fx$" is false if any of the individuals specified in the domain is not F, but it is not false if some individual *outside* the domain is not F.

The domain of discourse is always relative to the particular argument, or discourse, being symbolized—that is, every argument concerns a certain individual or set of individuals. Statement (1), for example, is about all Greeks.

1. All Greeks are mortal.

Where the domain of discourse has not been restricted, this is symbolized as (1a).

1a. $(x)(Gx \supset Mx)$

Because (1) is an A-form categorical statement, the quantifier, (x), represents everyone and everything. The statement asserts that if anything is Greek, then it is mortal. But the translation of (1) can be simplified if the domain is restricted to Greeks. We can then substitute (1b) for (1a).

1b. $(x)Mx$

This is understood, within the restricted domain, as saying, "Given any Greek x, x is mortal."

Similarly, where the domain of (2) is unrestricted, the translation requires predicate symbols not only for "odd" and "even" but also for "positive integer"—as in (2a).

2. All positive integers are either odd or even.
2a. $(x)[Px \supset (Ox \lor Ex)]$

However, the translation of (2) can be simplified if the domain is restricted to the set of positive integers. In this case, (2) can be written simply as

2b. $(x)(Ox \lor Ex)$.

In light of the restricted domain, we read (2b) back into English as "Given any positive integer, either it is odd or it is even"—or, alternatively, "Given any positive integer x, either x is odd or x is even."

Restriction of the domain is indicated explicitly as part of the translation. It is conventional to use the capital letter D to stand for "domain" (being careful not to confuse it with a capital letter symbolizing a predicate) and to provide a translation guide, or *symbolization key*, next to the translation. For instance, with its symbolization key (2b) would appear as (2c).

2c. $(x)(Ox \lor Ex)$
   D—set of positive integers; Ox—x is odd; Ex—x is even.

☐ *Truth-functional expansions*

Any universal or existential quantification over a finite set of individuals can be expanded truth-functionally by dropping the initial quantifier and substituting an individual constant for the freed variable each time it occurs in the resulting free formula. Since a universally quantified statement says something about each member of the *domain*, it can be expressed as a conjunction: it says something about *this* individual, and *that* individual, and so on. Thus, for a finite set of n individuals, we can express (3) as the finite conjunction (3a).

3. $(x)Fx$
3a. Fa_1 & Fa_2 & . . . Fa_n

An existential quantification that ranges over a finite domain can be expressed as a truth-functional disjunction. It says something about this individual, *or* that individual, and so on. So, if the domain is restricted to n individuals, (4) can be expressed as (4a).

4. $(\exists x)Fx$
4a. $Fa_1 \lor Fa_2 \lor$ . . . Fa_n

Given the same restricted domain, formulae (3a) and (4a) are, respectively, *truth-functional expansions* of (3) and (4).

A truth-functional expansion is a finite conjunction or a finite disjunction of singular statements representing, respectively, restricted domains of universally quantified or existentially quantified general statements.

Truth-functional expansions of quantified statements for a finite domain provide us with a method by which to determine the possible truth values these statements have for the restricted domain.

The truth conditions for truth-functional expansions are determined by *interpretations*: the determination of the proper domain, the assignment of individual constants to particular individuals in the domain, and the interpretation of predicates relative to the domain. On a given interpretation, the same constant must always designate one and the same individual. In this regard, logic differs from English where, for example, the same individual may be referred to as "the author of *Lolita*" and as "Vladimir Nabokov" and where different individuals may be referred to as "the senator from Oregon."

The set of individuals that a predicate designates is the *extension* of the predicate for the interpretation in question. For instance, if we let our domain be the set of deciduous trees and decide to interpret "Mx" as "x is a maple," then on this interpretation the predicate "M" has as its extension—that is, it designates a property possessed by—all and only those deciduous trees that are maples. If we let the domain be the deciduous trees of Vermont, the "M" designates all the deciduous trees in Vermont that are maples; the extension of "M" is the set of Vermont maples. If we interpret "Sx" as "x is a spruce" for the domain of deciduous trees, then, on this interpretation, "S" designates nothing in the domain, because not a single deciduous tree is a spruce. The extension of "S," in this case, is an *empty set*.

For the purpose of illustrating expansions, assume a small artificial domain: one with three individuals—*a*, *b*, and *c*—and five properties—represented by the letters "*F*," "*G*," "*H*," "*J*," and "*K*." Whether a certain statement is true or false under this interpretation will depend on which individuals exhibit which properties. Suppose the properties are distributed in the following table, where "+" means that the individual has the property and "−" means that the person lacks it.

	F	G	H	J	K
a	+	−	+	−	−
b	−	+	+	−	+
c	+	+	+	−	−

According to the table, the following singular statements (among others) are true:

> *Fa*
> > ~*Ga*
>
> *Fb* ∨ *Hb*
> *Fa* & ~*Jc*.

But what of each of the following quantifications?

> (*x*)*Hx*
> (∃*x*)(*Gx*)
> (*x*)(*Jx* ⊃ *Kx*)
> (∃*x*)(*Jx* & *Kx*)

The propositional function "(*x*)*Hx*" is expanded for the domain as follows:

> *Ha* & *Hb* & *Hc*.

And as the table shows, "(*x*)*Hx*" will yield true substitution instances for any value of *x*. Whatever individual constant we substitute for the variable *x*, the result will be a true statement. Thus, the conjunction "*Ha* & *Hb* & *Hc*" is true for the interpretation given.

The propositional function, "(∃*x*)*Gx*" is expanded as follows:

> *Ga* ∨ *Gb* ∨ *Gc*.

And as the table shows, this disjunction is also true under the interpretation given. This follows from the facts that "*Gb*" and "*Gc*" are true substitution instances of the propositional function and that a disjunction is true if any one of its disjuncts is true.

The quantification "(*x*)(*Jx* ⊃ *Kx*)," after the universal quantifier is dropped and the resulting free variables are replaced with individual constants, becomes the following expansion:

(*Ja* ⊃ *Ka*) & (*Jb* ⊃ *Kb*) & (*Jc* ⊃ *Kc*).

By the truth conditions for the conditional, each conjunct of the resulting statement is true for the interpretation specified.

By contrast, the existential quantification "(∃*x*)(*Jx* & *Kx*)" will have no true substitution instances under this interpretation. This is because not one of the disjuncts of the expanded quantification that follows turns out to be true.

(*Ja* & *Ka*) ∨ (*Jb* & *Kb*) ∨ (*Jc* & *Kc*)

Note that in each of these examples, the conjunction or disjunction re-placing the free formula contains one conjunct or one disjunct for *each member* of the domain. When completing the truth-functional expansion of a universal quantification, replacing each occurrence of the variable freed as a result of dropping the initial quantifier with one of the individual constants produces a different *conjunct* for each of the individual constants. When completing the truth-functional expansion of an existential quantification, replacing each occurrence of the resulting free variable with one of the individual constants produces a different *disjunct* for each of the individual constants.

Because the truth-functional expansion of a formula in predicate logic always results in a truth-functional compound of simple statements (or in one simple statement for a simple formula with a domain of one member), a truth table can be constructed for such an expansion. Each simple constituent is treated as truth-functionally independent—that is, the truth value of one sim-ple component does not depend on the truth value of another. And as men-tioned earlier, each individual constant designates a different member of the domain. Otherwise, if *a* and *b* designated the same individual, then "*Fa*" and "*Fb*" would have the same truth value, as would "*Ga*" and "*Gb*," "*Ha*" and "*Hb*," and so forth.

Let us consider a truth table for the expansion of "(∃*x*)(~*Fx* & *Kx*)" for a domain of two individuals, *a* and *b*. (Reducing the number of individuals in the domain makes the construction of the truth table less tedious. A table for "(∃*x*)(~*Fx* & *Kx*)" for a three-member domain would require sixty-four rows.) The expansion is the following disjunction:

(~*Fa* & *Ka*) ∨ (~*Fb* & *Kb*)

Fa	Fb	Ka	Kb	~Fa	~Fb	(~Fa & Ka)	∨	(~Fb & Kb)
T	T	T	T	F	F	F	F	F
F	T	T	T	T	F	T	T	F
T	F	T	T	F	T	F	T	T
F	F	T	T	T	T	T	T	T
T	T	F	T	F	F	F	F	F
F	T	F	T	T	F	F	F	F
T	F	F	T	F	T	F	T	T
F	F	F	T	T	T	F	T	T
T	T	T	F	F	F	F	F	F
F	T	T	F	T	F	T	T	F
T	F	T	F	F	T	F	F	F
F	F	T	F	T	T	T	T	F
T	T	F	F	F	F	F	F	F
F	T	F	F	T	F	F	F	F
T	F	F	F	F	T	F	F	F
F	F	F	F	T	T	F	F	F

The truth table for its expansion shows that the quantified compound propositional function "$(\exists x)(\sim Fx \ \& \ Kx)$" is true on some interpretations with a two-member domain and false on some interpretations. That is, the expansion is true on some assignments of truth value to the simple components Fa, Fb, and so forth. It is true in seven of the sixteen rows (rows 2, 3, 4, 7, 8, 10, and 12) and false in the remaining nine rows. Row 4, for example, tells us that if we have an interpretation of the formula for a two-member domain in which both members are in the extension of the predicate "K" and neither member is in the extension of "F," then the expansion will be true on that interpretation.

Note that an abbreviated truth table can be used to show that the formula "$(\exists x)(\sim Fx \ \& \ Kx)$" is true on at least one interpretation with a two-member domain. This is done by showing that there is an assignment of truth values for which the expanded formula will be true. The following assignment, which duplicates row 2 of the complete truth table, will do:

Fa	Fb	Ka	Kb	~Fa	~Fb	(~Fa & Ka)	∨	(~Fb & Kb)
F	T	T	T	T	F	T	T	F

By employing the concept of an interpretation and the method of truth-functional expansion, logicians are able to specify the meanings in predicate logic of *logically true*, *logically false*, *logically contingent*, and *logically equivalent*.

A formula *P* in predicate logic is logically, or quantificationally, true if and only if substitution instances of *P* are true on every interpretation.

A formula *P* in predicate logic is logically, or quantificationally, false if and only if substitution instances of *P* are false on every interpretation.

A formula *P* in predicate logic is logically contingent, or quantificationally indeterminate, if and only if *P* is neither quantificationally true nor quantificationally false.

Two formulae *P* and *Q* in predicate logic are logically, or quantificationally, equivalent if and only if there is no interpretation on which *P* and *Q* have different truth values.

These definitions are the respective analogues of the definitions in truth-functional logic of *necessarily true, necessarily false, contingent,* and *logically equivalent.* It follows from the definition of a quantificationally true formula that any of its substitution instances is a necessarily true statement; and it follows from the definition of a quantificationally false formula that any of its substitution instances is a necessarily false statement. Furthermore, it follows from the definition of a quantificationally indeterminate formula that none of its substitution instances will be a necessary statement. Each and every formula of predicate logic will have one and only one of these three properties.

To demonstrate that a formula is quantificationally true, or quantificationally false, one would have to consider the truth values of its substitution instances on *every* interpretation. But this cannot be done because there are infinitely many possible interpretations. In truth-functional logic, a truth table will show, after a finite number of steps, whether a compound statement correctly formulated in symbolic language is necessarily true (a tautology), necessarily false (a contradiction), or contingent. Such a complete, effective, and mechanical decisionmaking procedure cannot be developed for determining the quantificational status of formulae in predicate logic, however. This is due largely to the fact that predicate logic allows us to symbolize the terms of general statements, and truth tables cannot be completed if they must include the simple components of general statements in an unrestricted domain.

In predicate logic, it is therefore necessary to adopt an indirect strategy in determining the logical status of a formula. Because no formula can be quantificationally true and have a false substitution instance, we can determine that a formula is *not* quantificationally *true* by showing that a substitution instance is false on at least one interpretation. And because no formula can be quantificationally false and have a true substitution instance, we can determine that a formula is *not* quantificationally *false* by showing that, under at least one interpretation, it has a true substitution instance.

Suppose, for example, that "$(x)(Fx \supset \sim Fx)$" is claimed to be quantificationally false. We can refute this claim by first constructing a truth-functional expansion of the formula for a two-member domain—say, "$(Fa \supset \sim Fa)$ & $(Fb \supset \sim Fb)$." We can then show, by means of an abbreviated truth table, that the expansion is true on one assignment of truth values—and, therefore, that the original formula cannot be quantificationally false:

Fa Fb	$\sim Fa$	$\sim Fb$	$(Fa \supset \sim Fa)$ & $(Fb \supset \sim Fb)$
F F	T	T	T T T

Although we cannot demonstrate that the formula "$(\exists x)(Fx \lor \sim Fx)$" is quantificationally true by going through each of the possible interpretations, we can assure ourselves that it is quantificationally true by the following reasoning: because this formula is existentially quantified, it will be true on an interpretation if at least one member of the domain is either in the extension of "F" or not in the extension of "F." Without knowing what the interpretation of "F" is, we know that *every* member of a domain will satisfy this condition, for every member is either in or not in the extension of "F." Furthermore, since every interpretation must have a nonempty set as a domain,[5] we know that the domain for any interpretation has at least one member—and, hence, at least one member that satisfies the free formula "$Fx \lor \sim Fx$." Therefore, "$(\exists x)(Fx \lor \sim Fx)$" is true on every interpretation.

All the statements examined in this section involve monadic—that is, one-place—predicates. Although truth-functional expansions can also be given for quantified statements with polyadic predicates, a discussion of polyadic predicates would take us beyond the limits of this introductory text. It is also possible to expand formulae containing more than one quantifier as well as formulae in which a quantifier falls within the scope of another quantifier. These procedures are also discussed in more advanced courses in symbolic logic.

■ EXERCISE 9-5

■ A. Using the artificial domain presented on page 304, determine which of the following statements are true and which are false.

    1. $(\exists x)(Hx \ \& \sim Gx)$

    2. $(\exists x)(Jx \ \& \sim Gx)$

    3. $(x)(Fx \supset Hx)$

  *4. $(x)(Gx \supset \sim Kx)$

    5. $(x)[(Gx \ \& \sim Fx) \supset Kx]$

    6. $(\exists x)[Fx \ \& (Gx \equiv Hx)]$

    7. $(Fb \lor Gc) \supset (\exists x) \sim Hx$

---

[5] While a predicate may have an empty set as an extension, we cannot have an empty set as a domain. To give an interpretation to a formula is just to assign individual constants to the variables and predicates to the predicate letters, and the domain is just the set of individuals designated by the constants. Thus, it is logically impossible for an interpreted formula to have an empty set as its domain.

*8. $(x)[(Fx \lor Kx) \supset (Hx \& Gx)]$

9. $(x)(\sim Kx \supset \sim Jx)$

10. $(\exists x)(Fx \& Kx)$

■ B. Assuming a finite domain of individuals, a, b, c, construct a truth-functional expansion of each of the following.

1. $(x)\sim Fx$

2. $\sim(\exists x)Fx$

3. $(x)Fx \supset (\exists x)Fx$

*4. $\sim(\exists x)Fx \lor (\exists x) \sim Fx$

5. $(x)Fx \supset Fa$

6. $(x)(Fx \equiv Gx)$

7. $\sim(x)(Fx \supset Gx)$

*8. $(\exists x)(Fx \& \sim Gx)$

9. $(\exists x) \sim(Fx \supset Gx)$

10. $(x)Gx \& (Fa \supset Fb)$

11. $(x)\sim(\sim Fx \& \sim Gx)$

*12. $(x)[Fx \supset (Gx \equiv Hx)]$

13. $(\exists x)Fx \& (x)Gx$

14. $(\exists x)Fx \lor (\exists x)Gx$

15. $(x)(Fx \equiv Gx) \& \sim(\exists x)Fx$ ■

□ 9-6. FORMAL DEDUCTIONS IN MONADIC PREDICATE LOGIC

Monadic predicate logic includes all and only those arguments that can be formalized using monadic predicates, and the rules to be discussed in this section constitute a *natural deduction* system for demonstrating the validity of such arguments,[6] just as the rules presented in Chapters 7 and 8 constitute a natural deduction system for truth-functional logic.

The deduction system presented is both *sound* and *complete* for monadic predicate logic. It is sound because in applying the rules, we will not validate an invalid monadic predicate argument. It is complete in that its rules are sufficient to show that any argument correctly symbolized in the language of monadic predicate logic is either valid or invalid.

The system makes use of two groups of rules. The first group consists of

---

[6] A system of the kind to be explored is called *natural deduction* for two reasons: (1) The deduction proceeds in a way that resembles everyday reasoning, and (2) such systems employ rules that are often used in everyday reasoning.

An alternative system of deduction for predicate logic is the method of *truth trees*. Some of the books listed in "Suggested Readings" discuss this method.

all the rules for truth-functional logic—the rules of inference and transformation rules introduced in Chapters 7 and 8.

The second group, which concerns the part played by the inner structure of simple statements in a valid argument, can itself be divided into two subgroups. One subgroup consists of rules presented earlier in this chapter: rules for translating categorical statements, which tell how to disclose the internal structure of statements; and rules for quantifier negation, which tell which formulae are equivalent.

The second subgroup consists of rules of inference presented for the first time in this section. These include rules that allow us either to drop, or discharge, quantifiers from formulae or to add quantifiers.

In predicate logic, once an argument has been symbolized, the next step in its evaluation is to apply rules that permit quantifiers to be dropped, or discharged, from the premises. When this has been done, deductions can be performed using other rules. In some arguments, the deduction is completed by using only the rules for truth-functional logic. In other deductions, it is necessary also to use the transformation rules for quantified statements—Q.N. Rule 1 and Q.N. Rule 2. Still other cases require the use of new rules that permit quantifiers to be added again once truth-functional rules have been applied.

☐ *Universal instantiation*

The first new rule to be considered allows us to discharge a universal quantifier and then to infer that what is true of each of a number of individuals is also true of one of these individuals. The rule, *universal instantiation* (U.I.), is as follows:

> **Rule U.I.: From a universally quantified statement, one can derive any of its substitution instances.**

A substitution instance of a universal generalization is obtained by dropping the quantifier and uniformly replacing all occurrences of the quantified variable with occurrences of any single individual constant within the domain. As an illustration, consider the general statement "$(x)(Fx \supset Gx)$," where the individual constants a and b designate individuals within the domain. The following are substitution instances of this statement:

1. $Fa \supset Ga$

   $Fb \supset Gb$

But the formulae in (2) are *not* substitution instances of this general statement.

2. $Fa \supset Gb$

   $Fx \supset Ga$

In (1), a single individual constant correctly replaced x in each of its occurrences after the quantifier, (x), was dropped. In (2), however, more than one individual constant was used in the first conditional, and a single constant did not replace each occurrence of the variable of quantification in the second conditional.

In providing a substitution instance of a quantified statement, we *instantiate* it by supplying an individual name appropriate to the domain of discourse and the meaning of the statement. The following deduction illustrates the application of U.I.

3. All senators are citizens.
   Thurmond is a senator.
   Therefore, Thurmond is a citizen.
   Key: Sx—x is a senator; Cx—x is a citizen; t—Thurmond

   1. (x)(Sx ⊃ Cx)   Premise
   2. St   /∴ Ct   Premise/Conclusion
   3. St ⊃ Ct   1, U.I.
   4. Ct   2, 3 M.P.

U.I. was properly applied to line 1, since line 3 is a substitution instance of that general statement. And the completed deduction establishes that argument (3) is valid.

For a somewhat more extensive deduction, consider example (4):

4. All librarians are Virgos.
   All Virgos are introverted.
   Alicia is a librarian.
   Therefore, Alicia is introverted.
   Key: Lx—x is a librarian; Vx—x is a Virgo; Ix—x is introverted; a—
        Alicia

   1. (x)(Lx ⊃ Vx)   Premise
   2. (x)(Vx ⊃ Ix)   Premise
   3. La   /∴ Ia   Premise/Conclusion
   4. La ⊃ Va   1, U.I.
   5. Va ⊃ Ia   2, U.I.
   6. La ⊃ Ia   4, 5 Chain
   7. Ia   3, 6 M.P.

Although U.I. is a simple, straightforward rule, it can be misapplied. One error is to produce lines—like those in example (2)—that are not true substitution instances of the general statement "(x)(Fx ⊃ Gx)" because not all occurrences have been replaced by a single individual constant.

A second error is to apply U.I. not to a universal generalization but to part of a compound that contains a universal generalization.

1. $\sim(x)Fx$ Premise
2. $\sim Fa$ 1, U.I.   (Wrong!)

The expression "$\sim(x)Fx$" is not a general statement but a truth-functional compound—the negation of a general statement, which, by Q.N. Rule 1, is equivalent to "$(\exists x)\sim Fx$." We can see this argument form is invalid by finding a counterexample: an argument of the same form that reaches a false conclusion from a true premise. The following interpretation will produce such a counterexample:

Domain—buildings in Manhattan;

Fx—x is a skyscraper;

a—the World Trade Center.

In the next example, U.I. is also applied erroneously to part of a truth-functional compound—the antecedent of a conditional statement.

1. $(x)Fx \supset Ga$ Premise
2. $Fa \supset Ga$ 1, U.I.   (Wrong!)

The following interpretation will produce a counterexample proving that the inference is invalid:

Domain—voters in the 1984 presidential election;

Fx—x voted for Walter Mondale;

Gx—x is elected; a—Walter Mondale.

Remember that *U.I. can be applied only to independent universal generalizations and not to existential generalizations or parts of truth-functional compounds.*

□ Existential generalization

The next new rule permits an existential quantifier to be added to a statement. From "Fa," we may validly infer "$(\exists x)Fx$" because what is true of a particular individual is true of some—that is, at least one—individual. This rule is called *existential generalization* (E.G.):

Rule E.G.: From a statement containing an individual constant, we may validly infer an existential quantification of that statement.

In applying E.G., we place an existential quantifier at the beginning of the statement and replace either *all* or *some* occurrences of the individual constant with the variable of quantification. Thus, for example, from (5) either (5a) or (5b) may be inferred.

5. *Fa & Ga*
5a. $(\exists x)(Fx \ \& \ Gx)$
5b. $(\exists x)(Fa \ \& \ Gx)$

The method of truth-functional expansion discussed in Section 9-5 insures the validity of both the inference from (5) to (5a) and the inference from (5) to (5b). For if *a* is known to be an individual in the domain and *n* represents any other individual, then

$$(Fa \ \& \ Ga) \vee \ldots \vee (F_n \ \& \ G_n)$$

correctly represents the expansion of both "$(\exists x)(Fx \ \& \ Gx)$" and "$(\exists x)(Fa \ \& \ Gx)$."

Applying E.G. along with U.I. allows us to demonstrate the validity of arguments such as the following:

6. Clark Kent is virtuous and influential.
Anyone who is either influential or charismatic is popular.
Therefore, someone is virtuous and popular.

To see how the rules can be combined, first consider (7):

7. Clark Kent is virtuous and influential.
Anyone who is either influential or charismatic, is popular.
Therefore, Clark Kent is virtuous and popular.

This can be shown to be valid by using only U.I., restricting the domain to persons:

1. *Vk & Ik*	Premise
2. $(x)[(Ix \vee Cx) \supset Px]$ /∴ *Vk & Pk*	Premise/Conclusion
3. $(Ik \vee Ck) \supset Pk$	2, U.I.
4. *Ik*	1, Conj. Simp.
5. *Ik* $\vee$ *Ck*	4, Disj. Add.
6. *Pk*	2, 5 M.P.
7. *Vk*	1, Conj. Simp.
8. *Vk & Pk*	7, 6 Adj.

Now, by using E.G., argument (6) can be shown to be valid as well. We add to the deduction above the additional step:

9. $(\exists x)(Vx \,\&\, Px)$ 8, E.G.

The deduction for (6) illustrates both uses of quantifier inference rules mentioned at the outset of this section. U.I. is applied at line 3 to drop the quantifier in premise 2, and E.G. is employed at line 9 to add the existential quantifier in the conclusion.

Note also that replacing the "x's" of line 2 with the individual constant k, rather than some other constant, is based on strategy. In applying U.I., it is permissible to use any individual constant. But by selecting k for line 3, we are able to derive line 8—from which, by E.G., the conclusion can be inferred. When U.I. and E.G. are applied in the same argument, one must choose the individual constant that will work in the deduction.

E.G. can be applied only to statements completely bound by the existential quantifier, just as U.I. can be applied only to statements completely bound by the universal quantifier. If E.G. were allowed to apply to part of a compound statement, the deduction system would not be sound. It would validate obviously fallacious inferences such as the following:

8. Charlie Brown is not Russian.

    Therefore, no one is Russian.

    1. $\sim Rb$ Premise

    2. $\sim(\exists x)Rx$ 1, E.G. (Wrong!)

    3. $(x)\sim Rx$ 2, Q.N. 2

□ *Existential instantiation*

Now consider a valid argument that cannot be demonstrated to be valid using only the rules introduced so far.

9. Every crime is punishable.

    Some things are crimes.

    Therefore, some things are punishable.

We begin a deduction as follows:

    1. $(x)(Cx \supset Px)$ Premise

    2. $(\exists x)Cx$ Premise

    3. $Ca \supset Pa$ 1, U.I.

But none of the rules now at our disposal helps us to proceed beyond line 3.

Suppose instead that we start over with line 3 as follows:

3. *Ca*   2, _____

the deduction then could be completed in the following manner:

4. *Ca ⊃ Pa*   1, U.I.
5. *Pa*   3, 4 M.P.
6. *(∃x)Px*   5, E.G.

What is needed, therefore, is a rule for *existential instantiation* that is analogous to U.I. Indeed, the justification for line 4 might be stated as,

> **Preliminary Rule E.I.: From an existentially quantified statement, one may validly infer any of its substitution instances.**

When stated in this preliminary way, however, the rule is too sweeping. For example, it would validate the following:

10. Someone is alive.
    Charles de Gaulle is dead.
    Therefore, someone is both alive and dead.

    1. *(∃x)Ax*   Premise
    2. *Dg*   Premise
    3. *Ag*   1, E.I.   (Wrong!)
    4. *Ag & Dg*   2, 3 Adj.
    5. *(∃x)(Ax & Dx)*   4, E.G.

To avert this kind of erroneous use of E.I., we specify that an individual constant already appearing in a premise of the argument may not be used again. Since *g* already appeared in premise 2, using it in line 3 is a violation of this restriction.

A second restriction will avert attempts to use E.I. to validate fallacious arguments such as the following:

11. Something is a penguin.
    Therefore, Ronald Reagan is a penguin.

    1. *(∃x)Px*   Premise
    2. *Pr*   1, E.I.   (Wrong!)

Here the problem is created by replacing the variable in line 1 with an individual constant, "*r*," that already appears in the conclusion of the argument. So we specify that an individual constant that appears in the conclusion may not be used in applying E.I.

A third restriction required to avert the misapplication of E.I. is illustrated by the erroneous deduction that follows.

12. Something is red.
    Something is not red.
    Therefore, something is red and not red.

1.	$(\exists x)Rx$	Premise
2.	$(\exists x) \sim Rx$	Premise
3.	Ra	1, E.I.
4.	$\sim Ra$	2, E.I. (Wrong!)
5.	$Ra \ \& \sim Ra$	3, 4 Adj.
6.	$(\exists x)(Rx \ \& \sim Rx)$	5, E.G.

In this case, the error occurs when an individual constant already introduced in line 3 is reintroduced in line 4. To prevent such false moves, we stipulate that an individual constant that has been introduced into a deduction by an earlier application of E.I. may not be used again in another application of the rule.

An existentially quantified statement such as "$(\exists x)(Fx \ \& \ Gx)$" is true for at least one and not necessarily all the individuals in the domain. Thus, when we derive a substitution instance from "$(\exists x)(Fx \ \& \ Gx)$," we must make sure that the singular statement replacing it has the name of whatever individual it is that makes the general statement true. We provide this assurance by making sure that the individual constant that replaces occurrences of x when the quantifier is dropped does not appear in the premises or conclusion or was not previously introduced by E.I.

The three restrictions on E.I. are covered by the following reformulation of the rule:

> **Rule E.I.: From an existentially quantified statement, one may validly infer any substitution instance of it, provided that the individual constant being introduced in the substitution instance does not occur in a premise, the conclusion, or a previous line of the deduction.**

☐ Universal generalization

The rules of inference for monadic predicate logic require only one addition: a rule that will permit a universal quantifier to be added to a formula. The deduction in (13) is invalid for the interpretation shown.

13. Fa
    ∴ $(x)Fx$ (Wrong!)
    Domain—persons; Fx—x is a movie star; a—John Travolta.

But there are cases in which one may validly infer from what is true of *a* to what is true of all individuals in the domain. Argument (14) illustrates such a case.

14. All panhandlers are offensive.
    Offensive people are depressing.
    Therefore, all panhandlers are depressing.

Because the premises of (14) are universal generalizations, a universal generalization will be valid for the conclusion. Where the domain is restricted to persons, the deduction proceeds as follows:

1. $(x)(Px \supset Ox)$ Premise
2. $(x)(Ox \supset Dx)$ Premise
3. $Pa \supset Oa$ 1, U.I.
4. $Oa \supset Da$ 2, U.I.
5. $Pa \supset Da$ 3, 4   Chain
6. $(x)(Px \supset Dx)$ 5, _____

Line 6 may be derived from 5 in the context of the argument, because what is true of *a* is true of all members of the domain. We can apply U.I. to 1 and 2 with respect not only to *a*, but to *b, c, d, . . . n*, where these are individuals in the domain.

The rule that will justify line 6 is called *universal generalization* (U.G.). It is stated in a preliminary way as follows:

Preliminary Rule U.G.: From a statement containing an individual constant, one may validly infer the universal generalization of that statement.

Let us understand the words "the universal generalization of that statement" to mean a general statement obtained by uniformly replacing *all* occurrences of the constant with occurrences of a variable *bound* by the universal quantifier. In other words, "$(x)(Px \supset Dx)$" is a universal generalization of "$Pa \supset Da$."

Neither of the following, however, is a universal generalization of "$Pa \supset Da$."

$(x)(Pa \supset Dx)$
$(y)Py \supset Dy$

In "$(x)(Pa \supset Dx)$," not all occurrences of *a* are replaced by the variable *x*. And in "$(y)Py \supset Dy$," while all occurrences of *a* are replaced by a variable, the consequent of the conditional is not within the scope of the quantifier—as indicated by the absence of parentheses. The quantifier binds "Py," but not "Dy."

To insure that U.G. will be sound two restrictions must be added:

Restriction 1: U.G. may not be used to infer a generalization of any statement containing an individual constant if that constant appeared in any premise.

Restriction 2: U.G. may not be used to infer the generalization of a statement containing an individual constant if that constant was introduced into the deduction by E.I.

The first restriction allows us to screen out invalid arguments such as those illustrated by (13) and the following:

15. Everyone is either a genius or not a genius.
    Joshua is a genius.
    Therefore, everyone is a genius.

1. $(x)(Gx \lor \sim Gx)$	Premise
2. Gj	Premise
3. $Gj \lor \sim Gj$	1, U.I.
4. Gj	2, 3 Disj. Arg.
5. $(x)Gx$	4, U.G. (Wrong!)

In example (15), line 3 is justified—for what must be true of any individual in the domain must be true of each, including Joshua. Line 5, however, is *not* justified. One cannot justifiably infer that what is true of a particular individual in the domain is true of any individual in the domain. We may not validly infer a universal generalization from "Gj" because j has already been used in premise 2, as part of a claim about a particular individual.

The second restriction bars fallacious inferences such as this:

16. Something is valuable.
    Therefore, everything is valuable.

1. $(\exists x)Vx$	Premise
2. Va	1, E.I.
3. $(x)Vx$	2, U.G. (Wrong!)

Since premise 1 is a claim about some individuals in the domain, line 2 is a valid inference only for some individuals. To derive line 3 by U.G. is, again, the erroneous inference that what is true of some must be true of all.

The two restrictions on U.G. are covered by the following reformulation of the rule:

Rule U.G.: From a statement containing an individual constant one may validly infer the universal quantification of the statement, provided that the individual constant did not appear in any premise and was not introduced into the deduction by E.I.

For convenient reference, all four of the new rules are restated in the accompanying box.

Quantifier Inference Rules for Monadic Predicate Logic

Universal Instantiation (U.I.): One may validly infer any substitution instance of a universally quantified statement.

Existential Generalization (E.G.): One may validly infer an existential quantification of any statement containing an individual constant.

Existential Instantiation (E.I.): One may validly infer any substitution instance of an existentially quantified statement, provided that the individual constant being introduced in the substitution instance does not occur in a premise, the conclusion, or a previous line of the deduction.

Universal Generalization (U.G.): One may validly infer the universal quantification of a statement containing an individual constant, provided that the individual constant did not appear in any premise and was not introduced into the deduction by E.I.

■ **EXERCISE 9-6**

■ A. State the justification for each step that is not a premise in each of the following deductions. Indicate what principle is applied and which earlier lines, if any, are involved at each step.

(1) 1. $(z)(Sz \supset Pz)$ Premise
      2. $(\exists z)(Tz \ \& \ Sz)$ /∴ $(\exists z)(Pz \ \& \ Tz)$ Premise/Conclusion
      3. $Ta \ \& \ Sa$ _____
      4. $Sa \supset Pa$ _____
      5. Ta _____
      6. Sa _____
      7. Pa _____
      8. $Pa \ \& \ Ta$ _____
      9. $(\exists z)(Pz \ \& \ Tz)$ _____

(2) 1. $(x)(Jx \supset Kx)$ Premise
      2. $(x)(Kx \supset Lx)$ /∴ $(x)(Jx \supset Lx)$ Premise/Conclusion
      3. $Jb \supset Kb$ _____
      4. $Kb \supset Lb$ _____
      5. $Jb \supset Lb$ _____
      6. $(x)(Jx \supset Lx)$ _____

(3) 1. $Ha \ \& \ Fa$ Premise
      2. $(x)[(Fx \lor Gx) \supset Wx]$ /∴ $(\exists x)(Hx \ \& \ Wx)$ Premise/Conclusion

3. $(Fa \lor Ga) \supset Wa$ _____
4. Fa _____
5. $Fa \lor Ga$ _____
6. Wa _____
7. Ha _____
8. $Ha \& Wa$ _____
9. $(\exists x)(Hx \& Wx)$ _____

*(4) 1. $(y)(Cy \supset Ay)$ Premise
    2. $(\exists y)(Cy \& Fy)$ /∴ $(\exists y)(Fy \& Ay)$ Premise/Conclusion
    3. $Ca \& Fa$ _____
    4. Ca _____
    5. $Ca \supset Aa$ _____
    6. Aa _____
    7. $Fa \& Ca$ _____
    8. Fa _____
    9. $Fa \& Aa$ _____
  10. $(\exists y)(Fy \& Ay)$ _____

(5) 1. $(\exists w)(Fw \lor Gw)$ Premise
    2. $\sim(\exists w)Gw$ /∴ $(\exists w)Fw$ Premise/Conclusion
    3. $Fa \lor Ga$ _____
    4. $(w) \sim Gw$ _____
    5. $\sim Ga$ _____
    6. Fa _____
    7. $(\exists w)Fw$ _____

(6) 1. $[(x)(Mx \supset \sim Px) \& (\exists x)(Mx \& Sx)]$ Premise
      /∴ $(\exists x)(Sx \& \sim Px)$ Premise/Conclusion
    2. $(\exists x)(Mx \& Sx)$ _____
    3. $Ma \& Sa$ _____
    4. $(x)(Mx \supset \sim Px)$ _____
    5. $Ma \supset \sim Pa$ _____
    6. Ma _____
    7. $\sim Pa$ _____
    8. Sa _____
    9. $Sa \& \sim Pa$ _____
  10. $(\exists x)(Sx \& \sim Px)$ _____

(7) 1. $(\exists x)(Fx \& Gx) \supset (x)\sim(Jx \supset Kx)$ Premise
    2. $(\exists x)(Jx \supset Kx)$ /∴ $(x)(Fx \supset \sim Gx)$ Premise/Conclusion
    3. $(\exists x)(Fx \& Gx) \supset \sim(\exists x)(Jx \supset Kx)$ _____
    4. $\sim\sim(\exists x)(Jx \supset Kx)$ _____
    5. $\sim(\exists x)(Fx \& Gx)$ _____
    6. $(x)\sim(Fx \& Gx)$ _____
    7. $(x)(\sim Fx \lor \sim Gx)$ _____
    8. $(x)(Fx \supset \sim Gx)$ _____

*(8) 1. $(z)[Gz \supset (Fz \lor Hz)]$ Premise
    2. $(\exists z)(Gz \& \sim Hz)$ /∴ $(\exists z)(Fz \& \sim Hz)$ Premise/Conclusion
    3. $Ga \& \sim Ha$ _____
    4. $Ga \supset (Fa \lor Ha)$ _____
    5. Ga _____
    6. $Fa \lor Ha$ _____

      7. ~Ha   _____
      8. Fa   _____
      9. Fa & ~Ha   _____
     10. (∃z)(Fz & ~Hz)   _____
 (9) 1. ~(x)(Fx ∨ Gx)   Premise
      2. (y)[(~Gy ∨ Hy) ⊃ Ky]   /∴ (∃z)Kz   Premise/Conclusion
      3. (∃x) ~(Fx ∨ Gx)   _____
      4. ~(Fa ∨ Ga)   _____
      5. ~Fa & ~Ga   _____
      6. ~Ga   _____
      7. (~Ga ∨ Ha) ⊃ Ka   _____
      8. ~Ga ∨ Ha   _____
      9. Ka   _____
     10. (∃z)Kz   _____
(10) 1. (x)(Fx ⊃ Gx)   Premise
      2. (y)[Gy & (Hy ⊃ Jy)]   Premise
      3. ~(∃z) ~Fz   /∴ (x)(Hw ⊃ Jw)   Premise/Conclusion
      4. (z) ~~Fz   _____
      5. (z)Fz   _____
      6. Fa   _____
      7. Fa ⊃ Ga   _____
      8. Ga   _____
      9. Ga & (Ha ⊃ Ja)   _____
     10. Ha ⊃ Ja   _____
     11. (w)(Hw ⊃ Jw)   _____

■ B. Demonstrate the validity of each of the following arguments.

   1. All Zionists are Jewish, and no Moslems are Jewish. However, there are Moslems who are Israelis. Thus, some Israelis are not Zionists. (Zx—x is a Zionist; Jx—x is Jewish; Mx—x is a Moslem; Ix—x is an Israeli.)

   2. All screen stars are attractive. Some screen stars are feminists. All attractive persons are envied persons. Thus, some feminists are envied persons. (Sz—z is a screen star; Az—z is attractive; Fz—z is a feminist; Ez—z is envied.)

   3. Every Basque is either Spanish or French. There are non-Spanish Basques. Therefore, some Basques are French. (Bx—x is a Basque; Sx—x is Spanish; Fx—x is French.)

   *4. Any act of violence is either dangerous or foolhardy. Anything that is either dangerous or foolhardy is immoral. Thus, if anything is desirable, then if it is violent, it is immoral. (Vy—y is violent; Dy—y is dangerous; Fy—y is foolhardy; Iy—y is immoral; Sy—y is desirable.)

   5. If Alex passes, then everybody will; but if Alex doesn't pass, then neither will Brett. Brett will pass, so everybody will. (Px—x will pass; a—Alex; b—Brett.)

   6. "All babies are illogical. No one is despised who can manage a crocodile. Illogical persons are despised. Therefore, no baby can manage a crocodile."—Lewis Carroll, *Symbolic Logic* (Bx—x is a baby; Ix—x is illogical; Mx—x can manage a crocodile; Dx—x is despised.)

   7. Not all of the rebels were unsuccessful. None but the unsuccessful were martyrs. The only rebels were new converts. Consequently, at least some of the new con-

verts weren't martyred. (Rz—z is a rebel; Sz—z is successful; Mz—z is a martyr; Cz—z is a new convert.)

*8. There are souls or there are minds only if everything is spiritual. But since some things are not spiritual, it follows that there are things that are not souls and not minds. (Sx—x is a soul; Mx—x is a mind; Px—x is spiritual.)

9. Standard IQ tests are culturally biased. Anything culturally biased is discriminatory. But whatever is constitutional to use in public schools is nondiscriminatory. So standard IQ tests are not constitutional to use in public schools. (Sw—w is a standard IQ test; Cw—w is culturally biased; Dw—w is discriminatory; Uw—w is constitutional to use in public schools.)

10. If and only if a woman's potentialities are fulfilled, is her life a success. Hence, if either her potentialities are fulfilled or her life is a success, then both her potentialities are fulfilled and her life is a success. (Domain—Women; Px—x has fulfilled potentiality; Sx—x has a successful life.) *Hint*: $(p \equiv q)$ is equivalent to $(p \& q) \lor (\sim p \& \sim q)$. ∎

☐ 9-7. PROVING INVALIDITY

Just as a truth-functional argument is valid or invalid in virtue of its *form*, an argument that is quantificationally valid is valid because of its form. And just as a truth-functionally valid argument is valid no matter what statements are symbolized by its variables, a quantificationally valid argument is valid no matter what predicates are symbolized by the predicate letters. Also just as in truth-functional logic, we can demonstrate that an argument in predicate logic is invalid by showing that an argument of that form can have a conclusion that is false with premises that are true.

☐ *Invalidating natural interpretations*

Two procedures allow us to carry out such demonstrations in predicate logic, and both are analogous to methods of demonstrating invalidity employed in truth-functional logic. One method, introduced during the discussion of quantifier inference rules in Section 9-6, consists of discovering a counterexample: an interpretation of the argument that will make the premises all true and the conclusion false. Such an interpretation is called an *invalidating natural interpretation*.

To supply an invalidating natural interpretation, we assign meaning to the predicate letters and individual constants so that the formalized premises and conclusion are replaced by statements that are true or false of the universe we inhabit. Any assignment can be used, as long as it is *consistent*—that is, a predicate letter must be replaced by the same predicate expression each time the letter occurs, and the same individual constant must be replaced by the same name throughout the whole argument. Such an interpretation is said to be natural because the point of giving it is to show that the premises of the argument are, *as a matter of fact*, true while the conclusion is, *as a matter of fact*, false.

This method of proving invalidity requires an interpretation that is unmistakably invalidating. As an illustration, we can show that any argument of form (1) below is invalid by providing the natural interpretation shown in (1a).

1. $(x)(Fx \supset Gx)$
   $(x)(Hx \supset Gx)$
   $\therefore (x)(Hx \supset Fx)$

1a. All dogs are mammals.
   All cats are mammals.
   Therefore, all cats are dogs.

When an invalidating interpretation is challenged because there is doubt that a premise is true or that the conclusion is false, it should be replaced with an interpretation that is obviously invalidating. For example, (2a) might not be considered a conclusive demonstration that (2) is an invalid argument form because the truth or falsity of the conclusion and premises might not be known. In that case, (2b), which has the same form, could be used.

2. $(x)(Fx \supset Gx)$
   $(x)(Fx \supset Hx)$
   $\therefore (x)(Gx \supset Hx)$

2a. All logicians are philosophers.
   All logicians are professors.
   Therefore, all philosophers are professors.

2b. All cows are mammals.
   All cows are herbivorous.
   Therefore, all mammals are herbivorous.

Producing an invalidating interpretation of an argument form shows that any argument of that form is invalid.

The advantage of this first method of proving invalidity is that for a large number of arguments it is easy to employ. The primary disadvantage is that there are no rules to follow for discovering an invalidating interpretation. As a result, a conclusively invalidating natural interpretation cannot always be found.

☐ *Model universes and abbreviated truth tables*

The second method of proving invalidity builds upon the truth-functional expansions of quantifications discussed in Section 9-5. Universally and existentially quantified statements are expanded for a *model universe* consisting of a finite and small set of individuals. Selecting such a model universe makes it possible to use an *abbreviated truth table* (discussed in Section 9-5) to present an invalidating assignment of truth values.

Without assuming a model universe, it would be impossible to set up an abbreviated truth table. The truth-functional expansion of a quantified statement about the actual universe would have as many conjuncts or disjuncts as there are individuals in the universe, and the corresponding truth table would have as large a number of base columns. Therefore, to make the expansion and truth table manageable, we imagine a universe that consists of a limited number of individuals.

To illustrate this process, let us test example (1) by means of the simplest model possible—a universe consisting of a single individual, *a*.

1. $(x)(Fx \supset Gx)$
    $(x)(Hx \supset Gx)$
    $\therefore (x)(Hx \supset Fx)$

On this model the expansions of the premises and conclusion are as follows:

$Fa \supset Ga$

$Ha \supset Ga$

$Ha \supset Fa$

And the following abbreviated truth table shows that there is an assignment of truth values that will make the premises of (1) true and the conclusion false.

Fa	Ga	Ha	PREMISE $Fa \supset Ga$	PREMISE $Ha \supset Ga$	CONCLUSION $Ha \supset Fa$
F	T	T	T	T	F

If it seems strange that the truth values of statements about an imaginary model universe can be the basis for an evaluation of statements about the actual universe, remember that validity concerns argument form. An argument is valid if it would be impossible for an argument of that form to have true premises and a false conclusion. The validity of an argument will not be affected by empirical matters of fact—by what the actual universe happens to be like. Thus, if it can be shown that there is a model universe in which a particular argument would be invalid—a model universe in which it *could* have all true premises and a false conclusion—that will suffice to show that the argument form is invalid.

Since the actual inventory of the universe is irrelevant to the validity or invalidity of an argument, we need not be concerned about the kind of individual in the model universe. In fact, constants are usually listed as *a*, *b*, *c*, and so forth, without imagining them to designate any specific kind of individual.

The size of the model universe must be taken into consideration, however.

For example, there must be at least one thing in the universe, because certain valid arguments—such as "$(x)Fx$; therefore, $(\exists x)Fx$"—would be invalid if the universe were empty.

And many invalid arguments cannot be shown to be invalid for universes below a certain size because within these universes it would be impossible for the premises to be true and the conclusion false. For example, consider invalid argument (3) and its symbolized form, (3a):

> 3. All tigers are striped.
>   Some tigers are tame.
>   Therefore, all tame things are striped.

3a. $(x)(Fx \supset Gx)$
    $(\exists x)(Fx \ \& \ Hx)$
    $\therefore (x)(Hx \supset Gx)$

If we select a model with only one member, a, we cannot find an assignment of truth values that will prove the argument invalid. For as the truth table shows, one premise will be false under any assignment that makes the conclusion false.

			PREMISE	PREMISE	CONCLUSION
Fa	Ga	Ha	$Fa \supset Ga$	$Fa \ \& \ Ha$	$Ha \supset Ga$
T	F	T	F	T	F
F	F	T	T	F	F

However, if we use a model universe of two individuals, a and b, the argument is shown to be invalid under this assignment:

						PREMISE	PREMISE	CONCLUSION
Fa	Fb	Ga	Gb	Ha	Hb	$(Fa \supset Ga) \ \& \ (Fb \supset Gb)$	$(Fa \ \& \ Ha) \lor (Fb \ \& \ Hb)$	$(Ha \supset Ga) \ \& \ (Hb \supset Gb)$
T	F	T	F	T	T	T	T	F

It is always advisable to start with a universe having the same number of members as there are existentially quantified premises in the argument. If the argument contains fewer than two premises beginning with an existential quantifier, start with a two-member universe. An argument that is demonstrated to be invalid within a given model universe will be invalid within all larger ones.

The disadvantage of the model-universe method is that it is often impossible to know how large a model must be to yield an invalidating assignment of truth values. If an interpretation fails to produce such an assignment, one may *not* conclude that the argument is valid. An argument that has not been shown to be invalid for a model universe of a certain size will not be invalid for a model of a *smaller* size. But an interpretation for a *larger* universe might prove the argument invalid.

There is an upper limit to the size of the model universe we must consider before concluding that an argument in monadic predicate logic must be valid for every model universe, however. Where n is the number of different predicate letters, and where all predicates in the argument are monadic, the largest universe needed for that argument will be one of 2^n members.[7]

■ **EXERCISE 9-7**

Use either (a) an invalidating natural interpretation, or (b) a model universe and an abbreviated truth table to prove that each of the following arguments is invalid.

1. $(x)(Fx \supset Gx)$
   $(\exists x)Fx$
   $\therefore (x)Gx$

2. $(\exists x)(Fx \,\&\, {\sim}Gx)$
   $(\exists x)(Gx \,\&\, {\sim}Kx)$
   $\therefore (\exists x)(Fx \,\&\, {\sim}Kx)$

3. $(\exists y)(Fy \,\&\, Gy)$
   $(\exists y)(Gy \,\&\, Hy)$
   $\therefore (\exists y)(Fy \,\&\, Hy)$

*4. $(x)(Fx \supset {\sim}Gx)$
   $(x)(Gx \supset {\sim}Hx)$
   $\therefore (x)(Fx \supset {\sim}Hx)$

5. $(z)(Fz \supset {\sim}Gz)$
   $(\exists z)(Hz \,\&\, Gz)$
   $\therefore (z)(Fz \supset {\sim}Hz)$

6. $(\exists x)(Px \,\&\, (\exists x)Rx \,\&\, (\exists x)Sx$
   $\therefore (\exists x)(Px \,\&\, Rx \,\&\, Sx)$

7. $(z)[(Fz \,\&\, Gz) \supset Hz]$
   $(z)(Hz \supset Jz)$
   $\therefore (z)(Fz \supset Jz)$

*8. $(\exists x)(Ax \,\&\, Bx)$
   $(\exists x)(Ax \lor {\sim}Bx)$
   $\therefore (\exists x)(Ax \,\&\, {\sim}Bx)$

9. $(y)(Py \supset Ry)$
   $(\exists y)(Sy \,\&\, Ry)$
   $(\exists y)(Sy \,\&\, {\sim}Ry)$
   $\therefore (y)(Py \supset Sy)$

10. $(y)[Ay \supset (By \supset Cy)]$
    $(y)({\sim}Dy \supset {\sim}Cy)$
    $\therefore (y)[{\sim}Dy \supset (Ay \lor By)]$

---

[7] There is *no* upper limit to the size of the model universes for many arguments in polyadic predicate logic. See Bangs L. Tapscott, *Elementary Applied Symbolic Logic* (Englewood Cliffs, New Jersey: Prentice-Hall, 1976), p. 270.

□ *Part three*

INDUCTIVE REASONING

CHAPTER TEN

Generalization, analogy, and probability

Two types of inductive argument are not only common in daily experience but also constitute the primary means by which we increase our store of knowledge about the world. These are arguments by generalization and arguments by analogy.

Because inductive arguments differ significantly from deductive arguments, their evaluation requires different criteria. And instead of being judged in terms of validity and soundness, they are assessed as having "reliable" premises and "probable" conclusions. Their evaluation therefore raises questions that involve the theory of probability.

☐ 10-1. ARGUING TO PROBABLE CONCLUSIONS

Since only deductive arguments can have logical forms such that if their premises are all true, their conclusions must be true as well (see Sections 2-1 and 2-2), strictly speaking, only deductive arguments can be *valid*. But although an inductive argument cannot be valid, neither should it be characterized as invalid. An inductive argument should not be interpreted as a weak or inadequate deduction, but rather as a different kind of argument: one that attempts to extend knowledge beyond what is known to what could become known through future experience.

The objective of inductive reasoning is to present evidence in the premises that is of sufficient weight and relevance to make the conclusion *probable*. While the relation between premises and conclusion is never one of logical implication, as it is in deductive reasoning, the premises of an inductive argument support, warrant, or corroborate the conclusion. To claim, for instance, that a conclusion is "highly probable" or "almost certain" is to take the position that the evidence cited is sufficient to support the truth of the conclusion to a high degree. In effect, the claim is made that, given the truth of the premises, it is *highly unlikely* that the conclusion will turn out to be false. In evaluating such an argument, one must therefore judge whether the premises do provide enough evidence to support the conclusion so that, *if they were true*, they would warrant the claim that the conclusion is probably true as well.

> **A reliable inductive argument is an inductive argument in which the premises, when assumed to be true, would make the conclusion probable to the degree claimed for it.**

An inductive argument can be reliable—that is, the inference may be good—even when its premises are false. And because true premises can never *guarantee* the truth of the conclusion of an inductive argument, it is also possible that, although the inference is good and the premises are true, the conclusion is false. So in inductive reasoning we can never be absolutely sure that we will avoid error.

Because the conclusion of an inductive argument may be false even when the premises make its truth probable, the reliability of an inductive argument is never a consequence of the form of the argument. Two inductive arguments may have the same form although one may be reliable and the other unreliable.

The elements crucial to evaluating the reliability of an inductive argument are the amount of evidence provided by the premises, the relevance of this evidence to the conclusion as stated, and the degree of probability claimed for the conclusion. We can often estimate the sufficiency of the evidence—regarding both quantity and relevance—without knowing whether the premises are true or false.

The degree of probability claimed for the conclusion may range from quite weak to very strong, depending on the arguer's estimate. The conclusion will often contain a *modal quantifier*—a word such as *possibly*, *probably*, or *highly likely*—that signifies the degree of probability of truth claimed for the conclusion. In some cases, a numerical value or percentage—say, *a 70-percent chance*—may be attached to the conclusion as a specific measure of the degree to which the speaker believes we can accept or rely upon the conclusion. Whether the probability of the conclusion is presented as specific (*a 70-percent chance*) or as an estimate (for example, as *likely*), however, the important question is whether the evidence stated in the premises supports the conclusion to *that* extent. It would be unfair to attack an argument for failing to make the conclusion almost certainly true when all that was claimed, given the premises, was that the conclusion was more probably true than false.

The conclusions of inductive arguments are subject to revision in light of new evidence, and the same statement takes on different degrees of probability relative to different amounts of information. For example, if all we know about Diane is that she is a physically healthy twenty-year-old, the conjecture that she will live to see her twenty-first birthday is highly probable. However, if we learn that Diane is a skydiving enthusiast and jumps at least once every Saturday, the probability that she will be alive next year must be considered reduced. Furthermore, if we now learn that Diane has just made a jump and that her parachute has failed to open, the probability of our original conjecture concerning her longevity is low indeed. But its degree of probability is raised again when we learn with relief that Diane was able to cling to another skydiver whose parachute brought them both to earth without serious injury.

In evaluating the reliability of the inference made in any particular argument, we estimate the strength and relevance of the premises, as actually presented, to the conclusion, as actually stated. Although additional information, including future observations or experiments, may increase or decrease the probability of the conclusion, one's task in analyzing an argument is to judge the probability of the conclusion in relation to the *stated* premises—not in relation to all the information that might have a bearing on its truth or falsity.

☐ *Probability as rational credibility*

Three senses of *probability* are relevant to inductive reasoning. The word may be used, as in the example regarding Diane, to signify the *rational credibility* of the argument—that is, the degree to which it is reasonable to believe the conclusion. In this sense, the term always refers to the relationship between the conclusion and premises of an argument, and it involves an estimate—even if only a rough one—of the degree to which the premises make the conclusion probable.

☐ *Probability as relative frequency*

The term *probability* is also used in connection with numerical measures of the likelihood of certain events. When a statistician refers to the probability of lung cancer in a population of smokers or an insurance company estimates the probability of theft of new luxury cars in a metropolitan area, the word refers to the *relative frequency* with which an event occurs. And this judgment, in turn, is based on the percentage—or proportion—of the time an event of the same kind has occurred in the past.

Suppose, for example, that Mrs. Harper lives in a suburb and commutes to work by train and that each weekday evening her husband drives to the station to pick her up on his way home from his job as manager of a hardware store. Today, the phone rings as Mr. Harper is heading for the door. "I'll answer it," he tells the clerk who works for him. "The train is probably late anyway."

In this case, Mr. Harper is reasoning inductively from past experience: he has met his wife at the station for the past three years, and as he remembers it, the train has been late more often than not. In fact, he might justify his conclusion that the train will probably be late by pointing to records showing that it has been late in sixty-eight of the eighty-five times he has met his wife during the last four months—or 80 percent of the time. He might therefore say that there is an 80-percent chance that the train will be late again.

□ *Probability as mathematical odds*

"Classical," or mathematical probability, refers to *mathematically determined odds* that an event will occur. In contrast to statistical probability, which is based on past occurrences, mathematical probability is determined prior to and independently of the examination of test data, by means of the *calculus of probability*. For example, the mathematical probability of rolling an ace with one throw of a die is defined as the ratio of the possible number of favorable outcomes to the total number of possible outcomes. Because a die has six sides and only one side has a single dot, the mathematical probability is one in six, or 1/6.

Determining mathematical probability always involves two assumptions: (1) that all possible outcomes are known, and (2) that the outcomes are all equally likely. The second assumption, which is called the *principle of indifference*, limits the application of mathematical probability to games of chance or situations in which we must make decisions under conditions of complete uncertainty. It would not be used to refer to the probability that it will snow in the second week of February, that a train will arrive on time, or that a middle-aged man with hypertension will have a heart attack.

The conclusion of any inductive argument can be evaluated in terms of rational credibility. However, because many inductive arguments are about events that can be estimated in terms of either relative frequency or mathematically determined odds, it is often possible to speak of the probability of a conclusion in numerical terms. Then the rational credibility of the conclusion is *based on* the mathematical or statistical probability.

■ **EXERCISE 10-1**

■ A. Read each of the statements numbered below, and determine whether it should be regarded as true or false. Give reasons for your answers.

   1. To say that an inductive argument is reliable is to say either that the premises entail the conclusion or that the conclusion is proved conclusively to be true.

   2. If the premises of an inductive argument are true but the conclusion is false, then the argument may be either reliable or unreliable, but not both.

   3. An inductive argument can have true premises and can be a reliable inference even though its conclusion is false.

   *4. Inductions, unlike deductions, cannot be appraised by virtue of their form.

   5. The reliability or unreliability of an inductive argument depends entirely upon the amount of evidence provided in the premises.

   6. Inductions as well as deductions are appraised by considering the strength of the relation between premises and conclusion.

   7. Inductive arguments can easily be identified because the conclusion of an inductive argument always contains a modal quantifier such as *possibly* or *probably*.

   *8. In evaluating an inductive argument, the logician examines the extent to which the premises make belief in the conclusion reasonable.

9. The probability of the conclusion of an inductive argument may increase or decrease depending upon the relevance of new evidence.

10. Valid deductions, unlike inductions, are "self-contained" in the sense that the premises, if true, provide all the evidence needed to establish the truth of the conclusion.

11. Reliable inductive arguments can be compared with each other as to their degrees of probability; but deductions cannot be, because the conclusion of a valid deductive argument is always certain with respect to its premises.

*12. In some inductions, the rational credibility of the conclusion can be represented quantitatively, or numerically.

13. To talk about the probability of a statement is to talk about the degree to which it is "probably true"; thus, a statement that is "highly probable" cannot turn out to be false.

14. Rational credibility can never be understood in terms of relative frequency, because the latter sense of probability refers to the frequency with which events occur and the former sense of probability refers to the reasonableness of statements.

15. The mathematical probability of a certain outcome, such as drawing the queen of hearts from a deck of cards, can be determined only when each possible outcome is equally likely.

■ B. Determine which of the following probability statements should be understood in terms of relative frequency, which in terms of mathematical probability, and which can be understood only in terms of rational credibility.

1. The probability of snow tomorrow is 40 percent.

2. The probability that a human birth will be a male birth equals .51.

3. The quantum theory is probably true.

*4. The probability of getting a five with one roll of an honest die is 1/6.

5. The Highlanders will probably beat the Stingers at soccer this afternoon.

6. The probability that a given American male will die of lung cancer in the next year is 8/1,000.

7. There is probably no life on any planet in Andromeda Galaxy.

*8. The theory of determinism in the psychology of B. F. Skinner is probably false.

9. The probability of death among American males in their thirty-ninth year is .012.

10. As Pascal said, if there is any probability that God exists, you should believe that he does.

11. The probability that you hold the winning ticket in this lottery is 1/850.

*12. The evidence shows that increased coffee consumption probably leads to increased risks of pancreatic cancer.

13. The rookie's batting average is .325, so the odds are that he will get a hit about once in every three times at bat.

14. The likelihood of getting heads on 30 tosses of a coin is 15/30, or 1/2.

15. Human beings are probably not instinctively aggressive animals. ■

☐ 10-2. INDUCTIVE GENERALIZATION

The rational credibility of a conclusion—the probability that it is true—must often be estimated on the basis of criteria that cannot be quantified or precisely measured. Indeed, perhaps most of the inductive arguments encountered in daily life cannot be evaluated in terms of the numerical probabilities of specific outcomes. Many *arguments by generalization* are of this kind.

> An argument by generalization is an argument in which statements about observed individuals or instances are used as the bases for a conclusion about unobserved individuals or instances.

☐ *Kinds of generalization*

There are two types of arguments by generalization: *enumerative inductions* and *statistical inductions.*

☐ ENUMERATIVE INDUCTION

In a typical enumerative induction, the premises list the observed individuals, and the conclusion makes a claim about all individuals of the same type or class. It is characteristic of such arguments that if a single premise is false, the conclusion is false as well. For example, the conclusion "All robins' eggs are pale blue," reached by generalizing from observations of robins' eggs, must be false if a single egg known to be a robin's is observed to be a color other than blue. The argument to the conclusion about the color of robins' eggs has this form:

1. a_1 has been observed to be S and has P.
   a_2 has been observed to be S and has P.

   .

   .

   .

   a_n has been observed to be S and has P.
   Therefore, probably all S have P.

In argument form (1), we take $a_1, a_2, \ldots a_n$ to stand for different observed individuals (eggs), S to stand for the class to which all of the observed individuals belong (eggs from robins), and P to stand for the characteristic, or property, each individual in the sample has been observed to have (blueness).

An alternative way to formulate this same argument would be to include all the enumerated instances in a single premise and add, as a premise, the statement that we have not observed a counterexample:

2. $a_1, a_2, \ldots a_n$ each has been observed to be S and P.
   No S has been observed to be non-P.
   Therefore, probably all S are P.

Another variation of inductive enumeration occurs where the conclusion is not about the whole class but about the next new member we will encounter.

3. a_1 has been observed to be S and has P.
   a_2 has been observed to be S and has P.

   .

   .

   .

   a_n has been observed to be S and has P.
   Therefore, the next S we observe ($a_n + 1$) will probably have P.

The conclusion of an argument of this form would be supported by the same premises that supported the conclusions in arguments of types (1) and (2). If the premises support a claim about all members of a class (all robins' eggs), then they certainly support a claim about a single member of the class (the next robin's egg).

Claims about a single member do not support claims about all members, however. Premises adequate to support the claim in (3) that the next S we observe will probably have P may not present enough evidence to support the claim that all S are P. For example, after having enjoyed a number of business trips to New Orleans, a business executive might reasonably conclude that the very next visit to the city will be enjoyable. But this person would be incautious to conclude that all future trips to New Orleans will be enjoyable. A visit might be marred by losing a briefcase, by a hotel employees' strike, or by catastrophic weather conditions—to mention only a few hazards of travel.

☐ STATISTICAL INDUCTION

Statistical induction is an inference from the evidence that some proportion or percentage of observed S's have P to the conclusion that the same proportion or percentage holds for all S's, both those observed and those unobserved. An argument of this kind takes the following form.

4. *n* percent of a_1 . . . a_n have been observed to be S and have P.
   Therefore, probably *n* percent of all S have P.

☐ *Evaluating arguments by generalization*

A clear counterexample refutes an argument by generalization. The conclusion of an inductive enumeration is false if we find one S that does not have P, and the conclusion of a statistical induction is false if it can be shown that some percentage other than *n* percent of S have P.

A way is needed, though, to estimate the rational credibility of a conclusion when all the available evidence tends to support it. We must be able to decide *how much* evidence is enough and how to judge the *relevance* of the evidence to the claim made by the conclusion in question. Although there are no mechanical procedures by which to test the reliability of inductive inferences, criteria for judging them have been developed.

☐ REPRESENTATIVENESS OF THE SAMPLE

The premises of an argument by generalization are about a group of individuals—a_1, a_2, . . . a_n—observed to have a common characteristic—P. This group is called a *sample*, for it is from observations of these individuals that we reason to the conclusion that a certain larger group, or *population*—S—has the characteristic P. The reliability of the inference depends on the extent to which individuals in the sample are typical, or *representative*, of the population about which the inference is being made.

The individuals in the sample should, then, be chosen from among the entire population that the argument concerns. For example, a reporter preparing a story on student reaction to an administration's plan to discontinue intercollegiate competition in football should interview students throughout the campus. If only students in the gymnasium or at sports events were interviewed, the sample would undoubtedly be biased, or unrepresentative. And if all the students interviewed were on athletic scholarships and played football in high school, the sample would be even less representative. When the interviewees share special interests and backgrounds, the chances are poor that their views represent those of the entire population.

The more alike the characteristics of the sample—other than their all being an S—the greater its *positive analogy*; and the greater the differences between individuals in the sample, while still having P, the greater its *negative analogy*. If the reporter's sample consisted entirely of football enthusiasts, the positive analogy would be too great for the findings of the survey to be reliable. The individuals sampled would probably have characteristic P (opposition to the university's plan) in common because of other shared characteristics. A large negative analogy among observed individuals—as would be the case in a campuswide survey—increases the reliability of the survey findings.

Checking positive and negative analogy in a sample is therefore one important way to evaluate the reliability of an argument by generalization:

> The greater the negative analogy among the observed individuals in the sample, the more probable the conclusion, and the greater the positive analogy among the observed individuals in the sample, the less probable the conclusion.

☐ SAMPLE SIZE

The size of the sample is important because a large sample is likely to be more representative of the population than a small one.

> Generally speaking, the larger the number of observed individuals, the greater the reliability of the conclusion.

However, negative analogy does not automatically increase with an increase in sample size; thus, large size does not assure reliability. And small size does not preclude reliability: a sample can be quite small relative to the population under study and yet be representative of the larger group.

Whether a sample is sufficient in size depends on the population the generalization concerns and on the method of sampling. In the case of a presidential election poll, for example, all classes of voters are relevant: men, women; blacks, whites, Hispanics, Asian-Americans; city dwellers and country dwellers; Protestants, Catholics, Jews; blue-collar and white-collar workers; Democrats, Republicans, Independents; and so forth. To avoid bias, the sample must be selected at *random*—that is, in such a way that only chance determines which individuals are selected—from among the entire voting-age population. But because of the great diversity of American voters, a merely random sample would have to be extremely large before one could be confident that it was completely representative. A sample could consist of millions of people without including a single Hispanic or a single Jew.

A large population can be reliably represented by a relatively small sample if individuals are chosen through *stratified random sampling*. Under this method, a statistician identifies both the relevant strata—or subgroups—in the population and the number of individuals in each stratum. A random sample is then selected from each stratum in a number proportionate to the number of individuals in that stratum. The relevant strata for a survey determining television-show ratings, for example, would be groupings of people according to characteristics—such as age, sex, geographical region, and educational attainment—that could influence their preferences in programs.

In predictive polls, such as those used to predict the outcomes of presidential elections, the reliability of generalizations from the sample is increased by a further technique called *time-lapse sampling*. Two or more surveys are made, using different samples and allowing a significant lapse of time between the surveys. The results are then compared for consistency. The method thus detects changes in the relevant characteristics of the population, such as shifts in party allegiance and changes of opinion on certain issues. A dramatic illustration of the importance of time-lapse sampling was provided by the presidential election of 1948, when pollsters stopped taking samples in midsummer and failed to detect a shift of sentiment late in the campaign that produced a sweeping victory for Harry S Truman over Thomas E. Dewey.

By the methods of stratified random sampling and time-lapse sampling, the major national public opinion polls such as those of Gallup, Harris, and Roper have been able to get by quite reliably on sample sizes as small as 1,500 to 3,000. But recognizing that there is a statistical probability that their sample is in error, reputable pollsters usually do not claim that their polls support conclusions such as "49 percent of voters prefer X." Instead, results are phrased in some such way as "Our sample shows that in all probability between 47.5 percent and 51 percent of voters prefer X."

□ RELEVANCE OF *P* TO *S*

A generalization based on evidence that there is a uniform connection between being a certain kind of individual and having a certain property, *P*, must be evaluated partly on the basis of the importance of that quality to a definition of S. The possibility must be considered that the observed individuals all happened by coincidence to have the given quality and that other individuals of the same kind do not share that property:

> **The greater the relevance of having property *P* to being an *S*, the more probable the conclusion; and as the relevance of *P* to *S* decreases, so does the probability of the conclusion.**

In eighteenth-century logic textbooks, the standard example of a reliable generalization was the argument supporting the conclusion that all mature swans are white. This conclusion was well supported by a large number of observations—for wherever Europeans had gone throughout the world, adult swans were seen to be white. In addition, the negative analogy among observed swans was quite high: females as well as males had been observed, as had swans in captivity and in the wild, swans in various kinds of natural habitats, and so forth.

In the nineteenth century, though, settlers in Australia discovered birds that were exactly like swans in all ways but one: instead of being white, they were completely black except for having white wing tips. This raised the question, "How relevant is being white to being a swan?"

Prior to the discovery of the Australian swans, it was reasonable to suppose that being white was relevant to being an adult swan. This quality was shared by all observed swans, and we know from observation that birds of the same species usually have the same coloring. So although the conclusion of the argument by generalization concerning the whiteness of swans turned out to be false, the generalization was a good inductive argument just the same.

☐ HOW MUCH THE CONCLUSION SAYS

The statement "All swans are white" is more sweeping than "All European swans are nonblack." So even before settlement of Australia led to the discovery of black swans, the second statement was more probable than the first: in general, the less specific the subject term *S* and the more specific the term *P*, designating the property, the more sweeping the generalization—that is, the stronger the claim it makes.

> **The more sweeping the conclusion, relative to the evidence stated in the premises, the less its probability; and the less sweeping the conclusion relative to the same evidence, the greater its probability.**

Statistical as well as enumerative inductions can differ in the strength of the claims they make. For example, suppose we are trying to guess how many students in professor Higley's astronomy class are likely to receive an A this semester. We know that eight out of thirty-two, or 25 percent, of Higley's astronomy students received an A last semester and that the same percentage received A's in the two preceding semesters as well. This information could be used as the basis for either of the following conclusions:

1. Twenty-five percent of Professor Higley's students will receive an *A* this semester.
2. Twenty-five percent of Professor Higley's astronomy students will receive an *A* this semester.

Statement (1) is more sweeping relative to the available information and therefore less reliable. For Professor Higley may teach other courses with different distributions of grades. The following conclusions could also be drawn:

3. Exactly 25 percent of the students in Professor Higley's astronomy class this semester will receive an *A*.
4. At least 25 percent of the students in Professor Higley's astronomy class this semester will receive an *A*.
5. Twenty-five percent of the students in Professor Higley's astronomy class this semester will receive a *B* or better.

Here, although the subject term of (3)—"exactly 25 percent"—is more specific than "at least 25 percent," (3) is stronger than (4). It encompasses only one possibility, whereas (4) will be true if either that percentage or more receive *A*'s. Statement (3) is also stronger than (5), because the predicate term of the latter—"a *B* or better"—is less specific than "*A*," the predicate term of (3).

As these examples show, special considerations apply in evaluating the conclusion of a statistical induction. The proportion or percentage of the population claimed in the conclusion to have a certain property should not be greater than the proportion or percentage of the sample observed to have this property. And if the conclusion becomes too specific, the rational credibility of the conclusion relative to the evidence may decrease.

Summary of Criteria for Reliable Generalizations
The sample must be representative of the population as a whole.
The size of the sample must be sufficiently large.
The property, *P*, attributed to a group of . . . individuals, *S*, must be relevant to the definition of *S*.
The scope, or sweep, of the conclusion should be related to the scope of the evidence on which it is based.

The extent to which a generalization satisfies the criteria just summarized is a matter of degree, with considerable variation among the arguments to be tested. Whether failure to meet one of the "tests" destroys reliability in a given case is a matter of judgment about which there can be reasonable disagreement. And it may be difficult to estimate the rational credibility of a conclusion reached by means of an argument that is weak on a number of criteria but not glaringly weak on any single one.

But the criteria serve as guides in identifying clearly defective arguments and in strengthening weak ones. We would not conclude that a generalization is reliable if it is known that the sample is unrepresentative, if there are good reasons for believing that P is not relevant to S, or if the conclusion is far too sweeping. And thinking of arguments in terms of the criteria helps us decide where to look for further evidence that could make a conclusion more convincing.

□ *The fallacy of hasty generalizations*

Jumping to conclusions seldom leads to happy landings.
STEVE SIPORIN

Any enumerative or statistical induction that fails to meet one or more of the criteria discussed above is defective to a degree. Some patterns of inductive reasoning, however, are so notoriously flawed that they deserve to be separately identified. Collectively, these can be considered *hasty generalizations*: attempts to reach a conclusion without adequate evidence.

A classic case of hasty generalization, or "jumping to a conclusion," is the move from observation of a small and unrepresentative group of individuals to a generalization about the class these individuals supposedly represent. The following are examples of this kind of fallacious reasoning:

Left-handed people have natural artistic abilities—Leonardo da Vinci and Pablo Picasso were left-handed.

I can't consider a college dropout for this job because they are all immature and unreliable. The one I hired last year quit in the middle of the Christmas rush.

Newspapers today are filled with nothing but sensationalistic journalism. Just look at the paper I'm holding in my hand: five front-page stories are about sex and crime.

The judgment that a generalization is hasty is based upon the evidence cited *in* the argument. Even though evidence for the conclusion may exist— for example, in a published report—the argument is defective if it does not *itself* either supply information based on the arguer's observations or cite the source of such information.

A generalization based on insufficient evidence is illustrated by remarks that were made in an interview for a *Washington Post* story about the employment of skilled blacks in the construction trades in Washington, D.C.[1] A

---

[1] "Ten-Year Effort Fails to Alter Racial Ratio in the Trades," *The Washington Post,* March 10, 1981.

vice-president of one of the largest contractors in the area was quoted as saying, "We've tried hard to find minorities, but there are tremendous problems in this city. . . . You can't keep 'em once you make a hire. You have to hire ten to get three because they just won't stay on the job. You can't run a business like that." Because the speaker neither presented evidence for the claim that blacks wouldn't stay on the job nor alluded to such evidence (presuming that the *Post* story was fair to the speaker), the comment must be regarded as a hasty generalization.

Another kind of hasty generalization occurs when someone fails to see that the observed characteristics of the sample are irrelevant to the conclusion based on the observations. Here is an example:

> Lois is of English ancestry and reads Shakespeare beautifully.
> David and Loren are of English descent and read Shakespeare beautifully.
> Melissa is also of English ancestry.
> Therefore, Melissa probably reads Shakespeare beautifully.

This argument is fallacious because being of English ancestry is irrelevant to one's ability to read Shakespeare with artistic sensitivity.

In the next example, the fallacy lies in attempting to establish a general rule from exceptional situations.

> American television and radio announcers are not permitted to broadcast obscene messages.
> Americans are not permitted to slander their neighbors.
> No citizen is permitted to yell "Fire!" in a crowded theater.
> Therefore, American citizens are not free to speak as they wish.

Obscene broadcasts and slander—not to mention yelling "Fire!" in crowded places—do not provide normal, or typical, tests of a society's dedication to freedom of speech.

When the selection of a sample is "loaded," or biased, because of failure to consider contrary but readily available evidence that would cast doubt on the conclusion, the resulting hasty generalization can be considered a *forgetful induction*. In his *Novum Organum*, the seventeenth-century philosopher Francis Bacon (1561–1626) called the tendency to ignore evidence that does not suit our purposes an "Idol of the Tribe," by which he meant a faulty habit of thinking common to the human race.

Aphorism 45

And therefore it was a good answer that was made by one who, when they showed him hanging in a temple a picture of those who had paid their vows and then escaped shipwreck, and would have him say whether he did not now acknowledge the power of the gods—"Aye," asked he, "but where are they painted that were drowned after their vows?" And such is the way of all superstitions, whether in astrology, dreams, omens, divine judgments, or the like; wherein men, having a delight in such vanities mark the events where they are fulfilled, but where they fail, though this happens much oftener, neglect and pass them by.

Inductive fallacies arising from unrepresentative samples can all be called instances of forgetful induction, even when the selection of the sample is more than a case of innocent forgetfulness. Each of the following cases involves forgetful induction:

A representative of Sun-Up Cola surprises patrons of a supermarket by telling them that they are being filmed for a television commercial and then asks them what they think of Sun-Up Cola. Under such circumstances, approval of the product would be far more likely than disapproval.

A marketing surveyor, wanting to measure the number of customers who might patronize a store at a potential site, conducts a streetcorner survey mid-morning on a weekday. The chances are that fewer potential customers will be identified than if the survey were taken during the evening rush hour.

A member of the student-government association wishes to survey student opinion on increasing college scholarship aid, but the student only remembers to collect opinions when studying in the library. A sample consisting of students encountered in the library can be expected to be biased in favor of an expenditure that favors scholarship.

■ **EXERCISE 10-2**

■ A. The Corleones' neighbors, the McGuires, purchased a Kitchen Magician dishwasher three years ago and have received excellent service from it. The Franklins have never had a problem with their Kitchen Magician dishwasher in the two years since they bought it. And both the Peppers and the Goldsteins purchased Kitchen Magician dishwashers a year ago and have had excellent service. The Corleones conclude that they will probably receive excellent service from the Kitchen Magician dishwasher they have just bought.

(a) Determine whether this inference would be made stronger or weaker by each of the following alterations. (Each alteration should be considered separately.) Answer *stronger, weaker,* or *neither* in each case. (b) State a *brief* reason for each response (e.g., *increases negative analogy*).

1. The McGuires, Franklins, Peppers, and Goldsteins all live in a large city in the Midwest.

2. The McGuires and Franklins use Snow Brite, the soap powder recommended by the manufacturer, whereas the Peppers and Goldsteins use the least expensive brand of soap on the market.

3. The Findlay and Lopez families have both purchased Kitchen Magician dishwashers in the last three years and have received excellent service.

*4. The Franklins and Peppers enjoy cooking and always prefer eating at home, whereas the Goldsteins often eat at restaurants and the McGuires eat at home only rarely.

5. The Corleones conclude that their new dishwasher will probably give them excellent service for at least three years.

6. The McGuires and Franklins purchased their dishwashers from a major ap-

pliance store, the Peppers purchased theirs from a department store, and the Goldsteins got theirs with the purchase of a new home.

7. The price of shares in Zephyr Appliances, the manufacturer of the Kitchen Magician, has risen steadily over the last three years on the New York Stock Exchange.

*8. The McGuires, Franklins, Peppers, and Goldsteins all purchased their dishwashers from an appliance dealer who has a reputation for excellent service.

9. The Corleones conclude that their new dishwasher will give them excellent service for at least the next year.

10. The Corleones conclude that their new dishwasher will give them better-than-average service for the next one to three years.

■ B. Suppose that on a visit to a small Greek island in the Aegean Sea called Samos, you notice that the first ten Samians you meet are all farmers who drink a wine called *retsina* when they eat feta cheese. You therefore conclude that probably all Samian farmers drink retsina when they eat feta cheese. (a) Explain whether this inference would be made stronger or weaker by each of the following alterations. (Consider each alteration separately.) Answer *stronger, weaker,* or *neither* in each case. (b) State a brief reason for each response (e.g., "increases negative analogy").

1. The ten Samians you observe are adult men who have worked in grain fields for many years.

2. The ten Samians are all members of Samos's championship soccer team.

3. Three of the ten Samians had visited Athens in the last year, four had never left the island, one had traveled to the Turkish mainland, and two had visited Cyprus.

*4. None of the ten Samians can speak English.

5. You observe thirty-two additional Samians drinking retsina while eating feta cheese.

6. You remember seeing many Greeks on other islands and on the mainland drinking retsina and eating feta cheese.

7. The ten Samians are all observed on the same day of the week.

*8. The ten Samians include two who own the grain fields plus four laborers from the local village; and, in another part of the island, an older man, his son, and two grown daughters.

9. You change the conclusion to read, "All Greek farmers drink retsina when they eat feta cheese."

10. The ten Samians are observed on different days of the week, sometimes in the evening and sometimes at noon.

11. The ten Samians have only three different surnames among them.

*12. A group of five Samians is observed sitting down to a lunch of bread, black olives, and feta cheese; but none of the five touches the cheese until a sixth Samian arrives with retsina and pours it.

13. One of the Samians tells you that eating feta cheese on a warm day will make him ill unless he drinks lots of retsina with it.

14. You change the conclusion to read, "Samian farmers eat feta cheese only when they have retsina to drink with it."

15. You change the conclusion to read, "Samian farmers prefer to have retsina to drink when they eat feta cheese."

■ C. Read each of the following arguments, and explain why it is fallacious.

1. "What do you mean 'not all garage mechanics are crooks'? When was the last time you weren't overcharged for a repair job on your car?"

2. "Because a check revealed that every tenth bottle coming off the conveyer belt was properly sealed, there's essentially no chance that every bottle didn't get sealed."

3. "There is probably great public support for increasing the tax levy for the schools because every member of the PTA favors such a proposal."

*4. "I won't shop at Gaylord's Department Store because the employees there are discourteous. I found that out when I was treated rather abruptly in the store during the Christmas shopping season."

5. "I would say that about 80 percent of single males residing in San Francisco are homosexual, and my evidence for this conclusion is based on the frequency of homosexuality among male patients who come to my office."

6. A smoker said he was skeptical about the claim that smoking causes lung cancer. Despite the mass of data purporting to establish this causal connection, the smoker responded, "No one has proved that there could not be some as yet unknown 'third factor' that causes people to smoke more and also causes them to suffer more lung cancer. This would mean that smoking and cancer are not causally connected but are, rather, both effects of some undiscovered cause. It might be some hidden genetic factor."

7. "Being a college professor at a small college in a rural area has tremendous drawbacks—low salaries, oversized classes, poor research facilities and assistants, and inadequate libraries, as well as the lack of intellectual stimulation found at major universities. Nevertheless, America's country Ph.D.'s seem content with their lot. According to a survey taken by *The New Academy*, a full 50 percent wrote back that they 'basically like teaching at a small college.' Only 1 in 15 regretted that he or she was not at a research institution in a major city, and only 1 in 30 would 'choose some other line of work altogether.'"

*8. "Jane did lie to her husband when he asked her how she liked his new haircut, but the lie was justified, because she didn't want to hurt his feelings. She was also justified in lying to that man when she said the seat next to her was taken because she thought he was rude and offensive. And she did lie to her niece, but it was for the little girl's own good. So, I'm sure Jane will have right on her side, even if she does lie to her professor about her term paper."

9. "I'm sure Morris, your blind date, will turn out to be a gentleman. Why, in all my years, I've never met a man with that name who has not been polite and kind."

10. "Here comes Elbert 'Bull' Ripple to the plate. Old 'Bull' is hitting better than .380 this season against right-handed pitchers, so he is sure to get a hit off this right-hander." ■

□ 10-3. INDUCTIVE ANALOGY

Callahan Makes Up His Mind

Probably the strangest of [the] strange breed was a tough-looking boy named Callahan, who appeared out of nowhere one afternoon [at "Diamond Lew" Bailey's "Bucket of Blood" in Miami]. A preliminary boxer had been taken suddenly ill, and Lew needed someone to take his place. He offered the new-comer five dollars.

"I don't know," the boy hesitated. "I'll be back by six o'clock and let you know."

The ex-barber was in no hurry. Callahan departed. Promptly at six he thrust a battered nose through the door, and accepted the afternoon's offer.

"What in hell took you so long to make up your mind?" asked "Diamond Lew."

The boy shrugged. "Well," he said, "I ain't never been in the ring, and wasn't sure how I'd do. So I went around to diff'rent saloons and picked fights with the toughest guys I could find. I licked 'em all, so I guess I'll do okay."

JACK KOFOED, MOON OVER MIAMI (NEW YORK: RANDOM HOUSE, 1955), p. 161.

We make use of *analogy* when we characterize something by indicating in what ways it is similar to something else with which we are familiar. An analogy is thus a relation of likeness between two or more things. Similes and metaphors, which were discussed in Section 3-2, are figurative uses of analogy. Even extended analogies are often merely descriptive and intended to be used as illustrations.

An analogy can also serve as the basis of an argument, however. In such an argument, one claims that because certain things are similar in some respects, they are likely to be similar in another respect as well.

Arguments by *inductive analogy* generally display one of the following patterns:

Individual c has properties P_1, P_2, P_3, P_4.
d has properties P_1, P_2, P_3.
Therefore, probably d has property P_4.

Individuals a, b, and c all have properties P_1, P_2, P_3, P_4.
d has properties P_1, P_2, P_3.
Therefore, probably d has property P_4.

Arguing by analogy may also involve the use of statistics. A *statistical analogy* has the following form:

n percent of the individuals having properties P_1, P_2, P_3 also have property P_4.
d has properties P_1, P_2, P_3.
Therefore, the probability is n percent that d has P_4.

Inductive analogies and inductive generalizations are similar in some respects. Both require an inference from observed individuals to something unobserved. Both may be based upon the same evidence. In addition, many of the conclusions that result from generalization could also result from reasoning by analogy. For example, from past experience in having taken the 8:10 train, I can infer that probably the 8:10 train will be late today—and I can do so either by generalization based on observation *or* by drawing an analogy between the present case and past instances when the train has been late.

The anecdote "Callahan Makes Up His Mind" can be seen to illustrate either generalization or analogy. Callahan's reasoning can be considered an inductive enumeration from the instances of saloon fights he won to the conclusion that he will probably win any fight he is in. Alternatively, he could be said to be reasoning by inductive analogy—inferring that because he was good in saloon fights, he will probably be good in a boxing match. For, although boxing matches differ from saloon brawls in certain respects, they are like them in other respects.

Despite the similarities between inductive generalization and inductive analogy, there are important differences between these two patterns of reasoning. First, the conclusion of a generalization is usually about a whole class. (In the case of statistical induction, for instance, this conclusion states that the class as a whole has a certain percentage of members with a certain property.) By contrast, the conclusion of an analogy is a singular statement about just one individual or instance.

Second, in making generalizations, we treat the observed individuals a, b, and c as a sample of a class to which they belong, while the observed individuals in analogies are not, strictly speaking, a sample. Arguments by generalization depend upon the size and representativeness of the sample. But inductive analogies are based upon the degree of similarity between the observed individuals, on the one hand, and the new individual, d, on the other hand.

Third, we ordinarily would not accept an inference from one observed individual to a whole class as a reliable generalization, but a reliable inductive analogy may be based on one observed instance. In such an analogy, though, the observed individual and the new individual must have many relevant properties in common. This last point is illustrated by the following example:

> Ida Labelle, a Democratic congresswoman from an urban district in the Northeast, voted to cut military expenditures for nerve gas. She opposed the MX missile and the deployment of cruise missiles in Europe. She has also opposed the development of antisatellite weapons.
>
> Hans Bier is a Democratic congressman from an urban district in the Northeast. He also voted to cut military spending on nerve gas and opposed both the MX and cruise missiles.
>
> Therefore, Congressman Bier will probably oppose the development of antisatellite weapons.

□ Criteria for reliability

The reliability of an inductive analogy is estimated by using certain criteria to judge the strength of the connection between the premises and conclusion.

One of the most important criteria for such a judgment is the *degree of similarity* between the observed individual or group and the new individual mentioned in the conclusion.

☐ DEGREE OF SIMILARITY

If it is known that the previously observed individual c or the group a, b, and c possesses properties that d lacks, or that d possesses certain properties that c lacks, then the analogy is weakened. The reliability of the argument that Congressman Bier will probably oppose antisatellite weapons is related to the number of national defense and nuclear deterrence issues on which he and Congresswoman Labelle agree. The inference would be weakened by the discovery that Labelle also opposed deployment of the Trident submarine and the development of the B-1 bomber while Bier did not. The inference would be weakened still further if it were learned that Bier argues for laser beam and particle beam ballistic missile defenses and that Labelle opposes these policies.

☐ RELEVANCE OF THE PROPERTIES

A second criterion of major importance is the *relevance of the observed similarities* on which the analogy is based. Suppose the observed individual c has qualities P_1, P_2, P_3, and P_4 and that the new individual, d, has P_1, P_2, and P_3. We must then decide whether it is reasonable to suppose that anything that has P_1, P_2, and P_3 will also have P_4, or whether P_4 is a characteristic an individual can have by chance.

The next example involves a weak inference because of the irrelevance to the conclusion of the properties identified in the premises.

> The introductory logic course at Babson College presents inductive and deductive logic, uses the textbook by Palmer, and has three hourly exams and a large B curve.
>
> The introductory logic course at this college also presents inductive as well as deductive logic, uses the Palmer text, and has three hourly exams.
>
> Therefore, the introductory logic course at this college will probably have a large B curve.

Although there are close similarities between the logic courses at the different colleges, these properties are not relevant to the grading policy and, therefore, do not make the inference regarding the B curve reliable.

☐ POSITIVE AND NEGATIVE ANALOGY

When the inductive analogy is based on observation of several individuals— a, b, and c—it is possible to employ the criteria concerning positive and negative analogy introduced in the discussion of generalization (Section 10-2). In inductive analogy, the positive and negative analogy pertain to the degree of similarity among the *observed* individuals.

If the positive analogy among the observed individuals increases—that is, if they are discovered to be alike in more and more ways while the total number of similarities between these individuals and the one about whom the conclusion is being drawn remains the same—the probability of the conclusion decreases. A very high positive analogy among the observed individuals suggests that they are alike because they belong to the same class. And the fewer the qualities they share with the new individual, d, the less likely it is that d belongs to the same class. This, in turn, increases the likelihood that the similarities that do exist between the observed individuals and d are merely coincidental.

An increasing negative analogy, however, dispels this notion. If the negative analogy among the observed individuals increases—if they are found to differ in more and more ways—while the total number of similarities between them and the new individual d remains the same, then the reliability of the conclusion about d increases.

The role of positive and negative analogies is illustrated by the way physicians often reason in diagnosing illness. Suppose a patient has symptoms—S_1, S_2, and S_3—that are unlike any the doctor has seen before. Initial laboratory tests are inconclusive but suggest that the patient suffers from a new viral infection. Sometime later, the doctor, seeing another patient with what appear to be the same symptoms, reasons that the second patient may be suffering from the same viral infection. With each subsequent case presenting similar symptoms, the doctor will reason by analogy that the same virus must be at work. And confidence that the cause of illness is a virus will increase if, aside from sharing the same symptoms, the patients differ in significant ways— for example, by race, sex, age, occupation, medical history, and life-style.

If, however, a high positive analogy is discovered among the patients, the doctor will lose confidence in the inference that the illness is due to the same virus. For instance, if the patients are all blood relatives, the doctor cannot rule out the possibility that the exotic illness has a genetic cause. Likewise, if the patients are all employed in a large industrial plant, the possibility arises that the illness may be due to environmental pollution. Now a new individual, d, who manifests similar symptoms but does not share other characteristics with the previous patients, is less likely to be seen as suffering from the same illness.

This example shows the close connection between inductive analogy and inductive generalization. For as both the number of patients with similar symptoms grows and the negative analogy increases, the physician acquires a sample from which it is possible to reason by generalization that patients with symptoms S_1, S_2, and S_3 are suffering from the same viral infection.

☐ HOW MUCH THE CONCLUSION SAYS

Finally, as with reliable generalizations, the conclusion of a reliable inductive analogy must not be stronger than the premises warrant. The more sweeping the conclusion relative to the evidence stated in the premises, the less reliable it is. And the less sweeping the conclusion, relative to the evidence, the greater the probability of its being correct.

Summary of Criteria for Judging Analogies

The greater the number of similarities between the observed individual or group and the new individual, the more reliable the analogy.

The similarities between the observed individual or group and the new individual must be relevant to the inference being based on these similarities.

If an increased number of similarities are discovered among the observed individuals while those between them and the new individual remain the same, the reliability of the inference is decreased.

If the number of differences among the observed individuals is found to increase while the total number of similarities between them and the new individual remains the same, the reliability of the inference is increased.

The more sweeping the conclusion relative to the evidence presented, the less reliable the inference.

The less sweeping the conclusion relative to the evidence presented, the more reliable the inference.

☐ *Faulty analogies*

As with arguments by generalization, there is no mechanical way of deciding how completely an inductive analogy must meet the criteria before it can be judged reliable. Whether an argument is unacceptably weak is, again, a matter over which reasonable people may disagree. But we would not want to consider an inductive analogy reliable if we had serious doubts about the similarities between the observed individuals and the new individual or about the relevance of the property in question. Nor would we consider the argument reliable if it scored poorly against the full range of criteria.

Any unreliable inductive analogy is a fallacious argument. However, the name *fallacy of faulty analogy* should be reserved for the more blatant fallacies—arguments involving the mistaken inference that because two or more things share some superficial similarities, they will be alike in significant and relevant respects. By focusing on superficial similarities and ignoring important differences, fallacies of faulty analogy distort the facts. Here are two examples:

> If a child gets a new toy, he or she will want to play with it. If a woman gets a new dress, she will want to wear it. Therefore, if a nation gets a new weapon, it will want to use it.

> Surely you agree that it would be justified to use force to prevent delirious persons from leaping over the edge of a cliff and harming themselves. Thus, it is also permissible to use force to prevent people from smoking marijuana, for they just don't know how they are harming themselves.

"Do you think," said Candide, "that men have always massacred each other, as they do today, that they have always been false, cozening, faithless, ungrateful, thieving, weak, inconstant, mean-spirited, envious, greedy, drunken, miserly, ambitious, bloody, slanderous, debauched, fanatic, hypocritical, and stupid?"

"Do you think," said Martin, "that hawks have always eaten pigeons when they could find them?"

"Of course I do," said Candide.

"Well," said Martin, "if hawks have always had the same character, why should you suppose that men have changed theirs?"

VOLTAIRE, *CANDIDE*

■ EXERCISE 10-3

■ A. On the last three occasions when you took your Japanese car to the Sun Auto Clinic, the repair work on the car was excellent. You therefore conclude that you will get excellent repair work if you take your car to the Sun Auto Clinic today. (a) Determine whether this inference would be strengthened, weakened, or unaffected by each of the statements that follow. (Each statement is to be considered independently of the others.) (b) Give a reason for each answer.

1. You previously had engine work done on your car at the clinic, but this time you plan to have work done on the car body.

2. There is a new manager at the clinic who claims that the policies of the previous management will continue.

3. You have brought your car to the clinic on eight different occasions, and the repair work has always been excellent.

*4. Repair work in the past has included work on the brakes, the air conditioner, the electrical system, the drive shaft, and the carburetor.

5. The Sun Auto Clinic has many more cars to service now than it had in the past.

6. The last time the car came to the clinic it had been driven 32,000 miles, and it now has been driven an additional 12,000 miles.

7. All the repairs in the past were to an older car that you have since sold, whereas the repair work on this occasion will be on a car that you just recently purchased.

*8. Keiko, the mechanic who serviced your car in the past, is now on vacation.

9. The repair work on your car was performed by a different mechanic each time it was brought to the Sun Auto Clinic.

10. You change the conclusion to read, "Any repair work on my present car will probably be as good as the repair work on the cars I have owned in the past."

■ B. Lucy Daze has received grades between 85 and 95 on every homework assignment, quiz, and hour exam in introductory psychology during the semester. Her average going into the final exam is 90. Therefore, Lucy reasons that she can expect at least 90 on the final exam. (a) Indicate whether Lucy's inference would be strengthened, weakened, or left unchanged by each of the following considerations. (Consider each statement independently of the others.) (b) Give a reason for each answer.

1. Lucy was in a section that had six one-hour examinations during the semester instead of the usual three.

2. Most of Lucy's psychology grades were on homework assignments, and they were consistently better than her grades on quizzes and hour exams.

3. Lucy studied very hard for the hour exams but only moderately hard for the final exam.

*4. Lucy's psychology grades during the semester were all either 85 or 95, rather than being distributed between 85 and 95.

5. All the one-hour exams were made up by Lucy's instructor, whereas only one-fifth of the final exam will be made up by her instructor.

6. Each of the hour exams had been made up by a different instructor.

7. Lucy expects to score at least 92 on the final exam.

*8. Lucy expects a score of 88 on the final exam.

9. Before the previous exams and quizzes, Lucy felt calm and confident, but now she feels nervous and unsettled.

10. Lucy knows that Joe, a classmate she would like to impress, has an average of 93 going into the final exam.

■ C. For the past three semesters, Professor Grotley has consistently given A's to the top 40 percent of his astronomy class. Your friend Alphonse, a science major with a grade-point average of 3.5, has signed up for Professor Grotley's astronomy class next semester. You infer that Alphonse will probably get an A in the course. (a) Indicate whether this inference would be strengthened, weakened, or left unchanged by each of the following considerations. (Consider each statement independently of the others.) (b) Give a reason for each answer.

1. The grade-point averages of the students who received A's in the past ranged from 2.8 to 3.8.

2. Seventy-five percent of the science majors with a grade-point average of 3.4 or better have received A's in the past.

3. Next semester's class, like last semester's classes, will meet in the same room and at the same time.

*4. Professor Grotley has just received tenure.

5. In past classes, Professor Grotley assigned take-home exams, but next semester Professor Grotley will be requiring in-class exams.

6. In the past, the students with grade-point averages of 3.5 or above who did not receive A's were not science majors.

7. Unlike the majority of students in past classes, the majority in next semester's class will not be premed.

*8. Professor Grotley has used a different text and has changed his examination questions each time he has taught the astronomy class.

9. Next semester's class will contain twelve students, whereas previous classes have contained between twenty and twenty-eight students.

10. All of the students in the last class who received A's were in at least one class with Alphonse in the past, and in each class Alphonse scored as high or higher than each of the students.

■ D. Discuss the strengths and weaknesses of each of the following attempts to establish a conclusion by inductive analogy. Which arguments, if any, should be regarded as fallacies of faulty analogy? Select the three most plausible arguments, and explain what changes should be made to strengthen them.

1. Young people must prepare for marriage in the same way that they prepare to drive and to swim. Learning to swim and learning to drive require practice. No one can learn to drive unless he or she gets behind the wheel, and no one can learn to swim unless he or she gets into the water. Thus, the only way men and women can prepare for marriage is to live together and try it out.

2. What is taught at this university should depend entirely upon the interests of the students. Teachers "profess" their beliefs, and that is nothing but selling ideas. If nothing is learned, then nothing is taught, just as when nothing is bought, nothing is sold. So, just as buyers determine what is to be sold, students should determine what is to be taught.

3. Everyone expects students to do their best on examinations, just as we all expect doctors to do their best for their patients and lawyers to do their best for their clients. But when physicians encounter difficult problems, they consult other doctors and look up cases in their medical books. Likewise, lawyers consult their colleagues and look up cases in their law books. Therefore, when students take difficult exams, they should be allowed to consult with their classmates and look up answers in their textbooks.

*4. "The argument is advanced that guns cause accidental deaths and wounding in private homes. This is, of course, true.

"So also do stairways, defective flooring, the edges of carpeting, power tools, lawn mowers, gas stoves, axes, heating plants, and medicine cabinets. Do you want some civil servant inspecting yours?

"It seems to me that persons who wish to assume the risk of having guns in their homes ought to be permitted to do so. Else, why not ban fast cars, skiing, swimming, ocean sailing, and other activities which produce a certain amount of injury and death every year?"—David B. Wilson, *The Boston Globe*, February 19, 1974

5. "Look round the world, contemplate the whole and every part of it: you will find it to be nothing but one great machine. . . . The curious adapting of means to ends, throughout all nature, resembles exactly, though it much exceeds, the productions of human contrivance—of human design, thought, wisdom and intelligence. Since therefore the effects resemble each other, we are led to infer, by all the rules of analogy, that the causes also resemble and that the author of nature is somewhat similar to the mind of man, though possessed of much larger faculties. . . ."—David Hume, *Dialogues Concerning Natural Religion* [speech by Cleanthes]

6. "Often in assessing beliefs we do best to assess several in combination. A very accomplished mechanic might be able to tell something about an automobile's engine by examining its parts one by one, each in complete isolation from the others, but it would surely serve his purpose better to see the engine as a whole with all the parts functioning together. So with what we believe. It is in the light of the full body of our beliefs that candidates gain acceptance or rejection. . . ."—W. V. Quine and J. S. Ullian, *The Web of Belief*

7. The competition in the development of nuclear arms between the United States and the Soviet Union is like a track meet between two teams. In a track meet, there are many different events; a team may do well in some, may do poorly in some, and may not even bother to compete in others. The teams may also decide to exclude certain competitions. The situation is the same with respect to nuclear arms: there are many different weapons systems; the United States leads in the development of some and lags behind the Soviets in the development of others. Furthermore, each side has developed some weapons the other side has not tried to match, and both sides have agreed to ban certain weapons—as witnessed by the SALT I accord. Now in a track meet there may not be a clear winner; overall standings depend upon a purely arbitrary allocation of points to different competitions and different performances. And this shows that there may be no clear winner in the nuclear arms competition between the great powers. Only arbitrary ways of "keeping score" make it look as if one side or the other is emerging victorious.

*8. "The claim can be made of course that if an individual sacrifices sex without love *now* he will experience more pleasure by having sex with love in the future. This is an interesting claim; but I find no empirical evidence to sustain it. In fact, on theoretical grounds it seems most unlikely that it will be sustained. It is akin to the claim that if an individual starves himself for several days in a row he will greatly enjoy eating a meal at the end of a week or a month. I am sure he will—provided that he is not too sick or debilitated to enjoy anything."—Albert Ellis, "Sex Without Guilt"

9. "All voting is a sort of gaming, like chequers or backgammon, with a slight moral tinge to it, a playing with right and wrong, with moral questions; and betting naturally accompanies it. The character of the voters is not staked. I cast my vote, perchance, as I think right; but I am not vitally concerned that that right should prevail. I am willing to leave it to the majority. Its obligation, therefore, never exceeds that of expediency. Even voting *for the right* is *doing* nothing for it. It is only expressing to men feebly your desire that it should prevail. A wise man will not leave the right to the mercy of chance, nor wish it to prevail through the power of the majority."—Henry David Thoreau, "On the Duty of Civil Disobedience"

10. We all agree that it is legitimate for the state to quarantine someone who has a highly infectious and dangerous disease. But if it is legitimate to quarantine such an individual, then the preventive detention of individuals prone to crime and deemed dangerous to society is also legitimate. The two situations are alike in all relevant respects: individuals are quarantined not for their own good, nor because they have done something wrong, but to avoid harm to others; the quarantine lasts only as long as authorities judge them to be capable of infecting others; and finally, the quarantine is carried out and enforced by the state. All this is equally true of preventive detention: individuals are detained not for their own good, nor because of past crimes, but because they pose a high risk to other members of society; their detention lasts only as long as the authorities judge them to pose a threat to society; and, in addition, the detention is enforced by the state. Because the practice of quarantining individuals with serious contagious diseases is so widely accepted, how could anyone find preventive detention of potential criminals morally objectionable? ■

□ 10-4. NUMERICAL PROBABILITIES

The race is not always to the swift, nor the battle to the strong—but that's the way to bet.
DAMON RUNYON

"If you had it all to do over, would you change anything?"
  "Yes, I wish I had played the black instead of the red at Cannes and Monte Carlo."
QUESTION ADDRESSED TO WINSTON CHURCHILL, AND HIS RESPONSE.

The discussion so far has been concerned mainly with probability as rational credibility—the extent to which it is reasonable to believe a conclusion, given the evidence expressed in the premises. Because they are matters of judgment, estimates of the rational credibility of a conclusion usually are not numerically precise. In some cases, however, it is possible to assess the rational credibility of a conclusion by calculating the *numerical probability* of an outcome.

□ *Relative frequency*

The evidence on which a statement is considered probable can often be stated in terms of *relative frequencies*, or *statistical evidence*. For example, we think it highly probable that twenty-year-old Margaret will live until her next birthday because past experience has shown that the life expectancy of twenty-year-olds is considerably more than a year. An examination of data on the class of twenty-year-olds would reveal that the frequency with which members of this class survive until their twenty-first birthday is far greater than the frequency with which they do not.

Thus, we can analyze the rational credibility of the claim that it is highly probable that Margaret will live until her next birthday in terms of the statistical evidence that, say, 980 out of 1,000 twenty-year-olds—or 98 percent—have lived until their twenty-first birthdays. The probability of the event "Margaret-living-to-be-twenty-one" is .98, which permits us to say that the rational credibility of the conclusion "Margaret will live to be twenty-one" is .98. To put it another way, there are only 2 chances out of 100 that the conclusion will be false.

□ *Mathematical odds*

In other cases, the primary evidence for or against a conclusion is based on the *mathematical chances*, or *odds*, of a certain outcome. Such odds are determined by means of a mathematical theory of probability.

For instance, consider the following problem. Suppose you set out to flip a coin a hundred times. By a rare but possible chance, you get heads on all of the first 20 tosses. A friend points out that since the "law of averages" says you should get about 50 heads in any 100 trials, you can expect only about 30 heads to 50 tails in the remaining 80 tosses. Is your friend right, or should you expect that the actual outcome after 100 trials will be closer to 60 heads and 40 tails?

The evidence in this case consists of the actual outcomes on 20 tosses *plus* the mathematical probability of getting heads on the toss of a coin; and as it turns out, your friend is wrong. When a coin falls, one of two sides— either heads or tails—must face upward (assuming we do not count as a "toss" a trial in which the coin lands on its edge). As long as the coin is not a trick coin, both possible outcomes are *equally likely*. The mathematical probability of getting heads on any one toss is therefore 1/2, or .50. Thus, out of 100 trials, one would reasonably expect approximately 50 heads and 50 tails. But if, in fact, you got heads on each of the first 20 tosses, it is reasonable to predict that a total run of 100 tosses will yield approximately 60 heads. Because the possibility of heads or tails remains equally likely for the remaining 80 trials, you should expect approximately 40 more heads to add to the 20 that came up in the first 20 throws.

Note that the computation of numerical probabilities involves deduc- tion—as does all mathematical reasoning. From statistics about the life ex- pectancy of twenty-year-olds, we deduce a mortality rate for that population. Likewise, from the mathematical probability of getting heads on a single toss of a coin, we deduce that the probability of getting heads on a run of 100 trials will be 1/2, or 50 percent. In each case, the reasoning concludes with a cal- culation of probability for a certain *type* of event.

It may therefore seem paradoxical that conclusions stated in terms of the statistical or mathematical probability of outcomes can be the conclusions of *inductive* arguments. But such arguments, while supported by calculations of probability, *go beyond* the statistical or mathematical evidence they offer. For example, we reason inductively when we conclude that Margaret's chances of living to be twenty-one are 98 out of 100. The statistical calculations upon which we base this judgment cannot *guarantee* that Margaret will live to be twenty-one—nor can they guarantee that 98 percent of all the twenty-year- olds alive today will live to be twenty-one. Likewise, we can reasonably expect that 100 trials of a coin toss will produce approximately 50 heads and 50 tails, but that result cannot be guaranteed for any actual trial. Whenever reasoning concludes with a judgment about the probability of *some actual outcome for which we lack complete evidence*—either because it is a future event or because information about the past is incomplete—the reasoning is inductive.

☐ *The probability calculus*

Whether a numerical induction concerns the likelihood that a given twenty- year-old will live to be twenty-one—where relative frequency, or statistical probability, applies—or the outcome of a coin toss—where mathematical, or classical, probability applies—the argument will contain three elements: it will make reference to a *population* (such as twenty-year-olds or a trial of 100 coin tosses), a *property* (living to be twenty-one or getting a certain number of heads), and a *fraction* or *percentage* (the percentage of those living to be twenty-one or the percentage of coin tosses that yield heads).

A probability statement tells what proportion or percentage of a population has the property in question.

Both kinds of numerical probability are also calculated mathematically in the same way. The sum of the probabilities of the outcomes must always equal 100 percent or, when expressed as a fraction or a decimal, the whole number 1. Thus, in the case of a coin toss, the probability of heads and the probability of tails are both 50 percent, or .50, and the probability that one or the other will turn up is 100 percent, or 1. If the weather forecaster says that the probability of rain on a given day is .30, this means that on past days like this it has rained 30 percent of the time. Therefore, on days like this it will probably rain 30 percent of the time and will probably not rain 70 percent of the time; the probability of rain and the probability of nonrain = .30 + .70 = 1.

If it is known that an event must occur or that it cannot possibly occur, a probability of either 1 or 0 is assigned. For example, the probability that a trick, two-headed coin will land heads up is 100 percent, or 1. The probability that the same coin will land tails up is zero percent, or 0.

The probability of a compound event—for example, the probability of getting heads on three consecutive tosses of a coin or of Margaret's living to be twenty-one and being involved in a nonfatal automobile accident—can be determined by means of a set of simple mathematical rules. These axioms, or postulates, are called the *probability calculus*. Given the probability of the occurrence of each of several simple events, or initial possibilities, the probability calculus enables one to calculate the probability of their occurring in various combinations.

The probability calculus is most easily explained in terms of the mathematical, or classical, theory. So the examples in this discussion will involve outcomes from rolling dice, flipping coins, card games, and games of chance such as roulette. However, because essentially the same probability calculus is used to calculate statistical probabilities we could, with slight reinterpretation, describe these results in terms of relative frequencies.

Let us start by determining the probability of a simple event: having a total of 7 dots turn up on a single roll of a pair of regular dice ("regular" meaning that each die has 6 different faces and that the dice are not weighted, or "loaded," so as to favor particular faces). The various faces of each die will come up about equally often in the long run, although the sequence will be unpredictable. Thus, each die represents 6 different alternatives that are equally reasonable to expect, and each of these outcomes must therefore be assigned a probability of 1/6. To determine the probability of getting a total of

TABLE 10-1 *The possible outcomes of one roll of a pair of dice*

1–1	1–2	1–3	1–4	1–5	1–6
2–1	2–2	2–3	2–4	2–5	2–6
3–1	3–2	3–3	3–4	3–5	3–6
4–1	4–2	4–3	4–4	4–5	4–6
5–1	5–2	5–3	5–4	5–5	5–6
6–1	6–2	6–3	6–4	6–5	6–6

seven dots with a throw of two dice, we reason as follows: because each die can land in one of six equally probable ways, there are 36 equally probable outcomes for two dice. These possibilities are shown in Table 10-1, where the first number of each pair represents die 1 and the second number die 2.

Of the 36 possible outcomes, 6 show a total of 7 dots (6–1, 5–2, 4–3, 3–4, 2–5, and 1–6). Thus, the probability of rolling a 7 with two dice equals 6 divided by 36, or 1/6:[2]

In general, the initial probability of an event can be determined by dividing the number of outcomes favorable to that event by the total number of possible outcomes.

This is expressed by the following formula, where $Pr(E)$ stands for the initial probability of an event, f for favorable outcomes, and n for the total number of possible outcomes.

$$Pr(E) = \frac{f}{n}$$

The ratio of the number of favorable possibilities to the number of unfavorable possibilities is called the *odds of success*. In the example, the *odds against* obtaining a 7 on a single roll of two dice are expressed as the ratio 36:6, or 6:1. The *odds in favor* of obtaining any number except 7—that is, 2 through 12—are 30:36, or 5:6.

Because the total number—or 100 percent—of the outcomes are equivalent in decimals or fractions to the whole number 1, the probabilities together equal 1. This means that the probability of *not* getting a 7 on one roll of the

[2] On the theory of relative frequency, the initial probability of obtaining a 7 on rolling the dice once would be determined by observing a large sample of trials and dividing the number of observed favorable outcomes by the total number of outcomes. After a sufficiently long run of trials, the probability values for such events as determined by the relative frequency method are usually fairly close to those for the same events as determined by the classical method.

dice is equal to 1 minus the probability of that outcome relative to the 36 possible outcomes, or $1 - 1/6 = 5/6$. This calculation is an illustration of the *law of negation*:

$$Pr(\sim E) = 1 - Pr(E)$$

In interpreting the formula for this law, note that the tilde on the left-hand side of the equal sign and the minus sign on the right-hand side serve different purposes. Mathematical symbols ($-$, $+$, and so forth) are used to indicate operations involving numbers, whereas the tilde is used to express the negation of a statement about an event.

Now let us consider the probability of a *compound, or complex, event*. Such an event can be thought of as a whole made up of parts, each of which is itself an event. For example, getting 7s on two successive rolls of the dice is a complex event that has as its component events getting a 7 on each throw. And getting a total greater than 4 and less than 7 on a single throw is a complex event that has as its components getting a total greater than 4 and getting a total less than 7. Even though the dice are thrown only once in the second example, the outcomes are separate events, for one can occur without the other.

In calculating the probability of a complex event, one must consider whether the parts of the complex whole are *independent* of one another or *dependent* on one another. Two events are considered *independent* if the occurrence or nonoccurrence of either one has no effect on the occurrence or nonoccurrence of the other. For example, getting a 7 on a single roll of the dice is independent of getting a 7 on a second roll.

Events are *dependent* if one event affects the circumstances of a second event in such a way that the probability of the second is no longer what it would have been if the first event had not occurred. Getting a total greater than 4 and less than 7 on a single roll of the dice is a complex event that is the product of two dependent events.

To calculate the probability of such a complex event, one first determines the probability of one component and then, based on that, the probability of the combined components. As Table 10-1 shows, the probability of getting a total greater than 4 is 30/36, or 5/6, because 30 possible outcomes of the total of 36 are favorable. In calculating the probability of getting less than 7, we now count the number of favorable outcomes out of 30 possibilities—6 of the original 36 outcomes having been ruled out because the combined dots are equal to or less than four. The table indicates 9 favorable outcomes where the total is greater than 4 dots but less than 7 dots (1–4, 1–5, 2–3, 2–4, 3–2, 3–3, 4–1, 4–2, and 5–1). Thus, the probability of getting dots totaling less than 7 and more than 4 is 9/30. The combined probability of the two dependent events is then obtained by multiplying the probability of one times the probability of the second: 30/36 times 9/30, or 1/4.

Note that the probability of getting less than 7, when calculated as an independent event, is not 9/30 but 15/36. In other words, the odds in favor of throwing less than a 7 are 5 to 12—much higher than the 3-to-10 odds in favor of that outcome when it is dependent on the other event.

The procedure followed in calculating the probability of a joint occurrence of simple dependent events is based on the *law of conjunction*:

$$Pr(E_1 + E_2) = Pr(E_1) \times Pr(E_2 \text{ given } E_1)$$

Expressed in terms of this formula, the information from the previous example is as follows:

Pr (total greater than 4 + total less than 7)

= *Pr* (total greater than 4)

$\times$ *Pr* (total less than 7, given that it will be greater than 4), or 30/36 $\times$ 9/30 = 9/36 = 1/4

Where the conjoint occurrences are *independent* events, that is, where the probability of E_2 is unaltered by the assumption that E_1 has occurred, the probability of the complex event ($E_1 + E_2$) is determined in a simpler way. To calculate the probability of getting 7s on two successive rolls of the dice, for example, we multiply the probability of getting 7 on the first roll (which is 6/36, or 1/6) times the probability of getting 7 on the second roll (which is again 1/6). The probability of the conjoint occurrences is, then, 1/6 $\times$ 1/6, or 1/36. Because the conjoint events are independent of each other, this method is called the *law of restricted conjunction*:

$$Pr(E_1 + E_2) = Pr(E_1) \times Pr(E_2)$$

A different method is needed for determining the probability that one of two or more exclusive events will occur. Suppose, for example, that we wish to calculate the probability of drawing the one red ball out of an urn containing ten differently colored balls on two tries. The probability of getting the red ball on the first try is 1/10, and if we succeed we stop. However, if on the first trial we do not get the red ball, we try again, without returning the non-red ball to the urn. The probability of getting the red ball on the second try is now 1/9. It might at first seem that the two tries taken together are conjoint occurrences of dependent events. In that case, we would apply the law of conjunction:

Pr(red ball on first try + red ball on second try)

= *Pr*(red ball on first try)

$\times$ *Pr*(red ball on second try, adjusted to number of balls remaining)

But this produces the following absurd result:

$$Pr(E_1 + E_2) = 1/10 \times 1/9 = 1/90$$

According to this calculation, the odds are only 1 out of 90 in favor of getting the red ball on two tries combined, whereas the odds are 1 out of 10 on the first try *alone* and 1 out of 9 on the second try *alone*.

In fact, getting the red ball on two tries is a *disjunction* of events. We want to know the probability of getting the red ball on *either* the first *or* the second try.

In addition, the outcomes are *mutually exclusive*, since we cannot get the red ball on both the first and second tries: the probability of getting the red ball in two tries is therefore calculated by applying the *law of exclusive disjunction*:

$$Pr(E_1 \lor E_2) = Pr(E_1) + Pr(E_2)$$

Thus,

Pr(red ball on first try $\lor$ red ball on second try)

$= Pr$(red ball on first try) $+ Pr$(red ball on second try),

or $Pr(E_1 \lor E_2)$

$= 1/10 + 1/9$

$= 9/90 + 10/90 = 19/90$

This gives us odds slightly less favorable than 1 out of 5.

Two events are mutually exclusive if and only if it is impossible for both to occur at the same time.

To calculate the probability of complex events made up of simple events that can occur at the same time, a different method is needed. For example, suppose we wish to calculate the probability of getting heads at least once when two coins are tossed. The probability of getting heads with the first coin is 1/2, and the probability of getting heads with the second coin is also 1/2. But we cannot add these separate probabilities to get an answer, for this would give a total of 1, or 100 percent, and it is not certain that we will get heads at least once because both coins may yield tails. On the other hand, the answer "1/2" is also incorrect, because the events are not exclusive: both coins may land heads up. In fact, there are four possible outcomes, and three of these will yield heads at least once.

H–H T–H
H–T T–T

Thus, the probability of this outcome equals the probability that each coin will land heads up *minus* the probability that both coins will land heads up.

This requires application of the *law of nonexclusive disjunction*:

$$Pr(E_1 \lor E_2) = Pr(E_1) + Pr(E_2) - Pr(E_1 + E_2)$$

The calculations are as follows:

Pr(heads first coin $\lor$ heads second coin)

$= Pr$(heads first coin) $+ Pr$(heads second coin)

$- Pr$(heads first coin $+$ heads second coin)

More fully symbolized, this becomes

$$Pr(H_1 \lor H_2) = Pr(H_1) + Pr(H_2) - Pr(H_1 + H_2)$$

or,

$$Pr(H_1 \lor H_2) = 1/2 + 1/2 - (1/2 \times 1/2) = 1 - 1/4 = 3/4$$

THE PROBABILITY CALCULUS

Formula for Probability of a Simple Event: $Pr(E) = f/n$

Law of Negation: $Pr(\sim E) = 1 - Pr(E)$

Law of Conjunction: $Pr(E_1 + E_2) = Pr(E_1) \times Pr(E_2 \text{ given } E_1)$

Law of Restricted Conjunction:
$Pr(E_1 + E_2) = Pr(E_1) \times Pr(E_2)$

Law of Exclusive Disjunction:
$Pr(E_1 \lor E_2) = Pr(E_1) + Pr(E_2)$

Law of Nonexclusive Disjunction:
$Pr(E_1 \lor E_2) = Pr(E_1) + Pr(E_2) - Pr(E_1 + E_2)$

☐ Reasoning about probabilities

The rules of probability provide reasonable grounds for making certain kinds of decisions. To make effective use of the rules, however, one must follow several guidelines. One is that all the possible outcomes of a situation must be identified.

☐ NOTING ALL THE POSSIBILITIES

The total number of possible outcomes of an event is often large. Suppose, for example, one wanted to determine the probability that a certain combination of dessert and beverage would be ordered at a restaurant that offers cheese cake, apple pie, chocolate ice cream, egg custard, or fruit for dessert, and that serves coffee, tea, or milk. In this case, there are 5 × 3, or 15, possible orders.

A reliable way to keep track of all the possibilities is to construct a *tree diagram* like the one in Figure 10-1. In a tree diagram, the event is divided into "steps"—which here represent successive coin tosses. These are separated by broken vertical lines, with straight lines indicating the possible outcomes at each step. As the diagram shows, the probability of getting heads at least once is 1/2 on one toss of a coin, 3/4 on two tosses, 7/8 on three tosses, and 15/16 on four tosses.

□ COMBINING THE RULES OF PROBABILITY

Determining the probability of complex events sometimes requires the use of both conjunction and disjunction rules. The complex event in the following

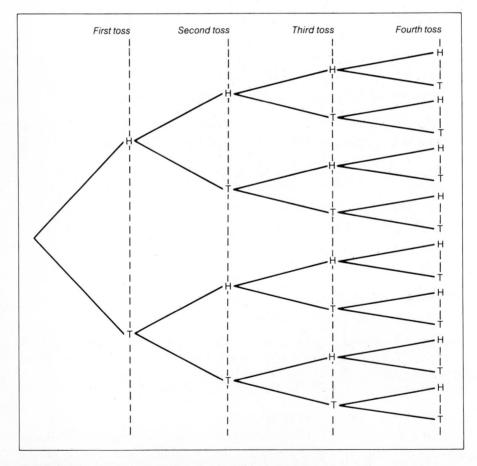

FIGURE 10-1

Tree diagram showing possible outcomes of four successive tosses of a coin

problem, for example, has as its components events that are themselves complex:

Calculate the probability of getting either three 2s or three 3s on a single throw of three dice.

Because the occurrence will be either one of two events—getting either 3 sides with 2 dots each or getting 3 sides with 3 dots each—it is a disjunction. And because the component events are mutually exclusive, the law of exclusive disjunction applies:

$$Pr(E_1 \lor E_2) = Pr(E_1) + Pr(E_2)$$

Pr(getting three 2s $\lor$ getting three 3s)
= Pr(getting three 2s) + Pr(getting three 3s).

Before the formula will give the answer, however, the initial probabilities of E_1 (getting 2 dots on each of 3 different die) and E_2 (getting 3 dots on each of 3 different die) must be determined. Because the components of these complex events are independent events, the probabilities E_1 and E_2 can be determined by applying the law of restricted conjunction. The following formulae represent the calculations, where C_{1a}, C_{2a}, and C_{3a} stand for the component events of E_1 and C_{1b}, C_{2b}, and C_{3b} stand for the component events of E_2:

$$Pr(E_1) = Pr(C_{1a} + C_{2a} + C_{3a}) = Pr(C_{1a}) \times Pr(C_{2a}) \times Pr(C_{3a})$$
$$Pr(E_2) = Pr(C_{1b} + C_{2b} + C_{3b}) = Pr(C_{1b}) \times Pr(C_{2b}) \times Pr(C_{3b})$$

Calculations show that the probabilities of E_1 and E_2 are identical. Since each die has 6 sides and only 1 side of each die has 2 dots, the probability of getting 2 dots on the first die is 1/6, of getting 2 dots on the second die is 1/6, and of getting 2 dots on the third die is 1/6. Thus, the probability of getting three 2s is

$$1/6 \times 1/6 \times 1/6 = 1/216$$

Since each die has 3 dots on only one side, the probability of getting 3 dots on the first die is also 1/6, as are the probabilities of getting 3 dots on the second and on the third die. The probability of getting three 3s is, therefore

$$1/6 \times 1/6 \times 1/6 = 1/216$$

Having made these calculations, we can determine the probability of the disjunction (either E_1 or E_2):

$$Pr(E_1 \lor E_2) = Pr(E_1) + Pr(E_2) = 1/216 + 1/216 = 2/216 = 1/108$$

The calculation is based on two applications of the law of restricted conjunction and one application of the law of exclusive disjunction.

☐ MATHEMATICAL EXPECTATION

The cost of taking a chance—such as spending $1 to buy a raffle ticket for a prize worth $500 where 1,000 raffle tickets will be sold—can be calculated as the *mathematical expectation*, or "expected value," of a gain or loss. Whether it would be *reasonable* for a given individual to spend $1 for a ticket depends partly upon the *utility* to the person of having the cash on hand. And measuring utility, in turn, depends on factors that vary among individuals and that must often be subjectively weighed. But an *objective* measure of the cost of a risk can be determined mathematically.

Mathematical expectation is calculated by multiplying the probability of a favorable outcome times the amount to be won or gained. Thus, because in our example there are 1,000 raffle tickets sold, the probability of holding the winning ticket is 1/1,000 for each ticket purchased, and the mathematical expectation of a person who holds one of these raffle tickets is 1/1,000 × $500 = $0.50. A *fair price* for the ticket, therefore, where "fair" means that the amount paid roughly equals the mathematical expectation of winning, would be $0.50. But here, again, the objective measure may not be the sole important consideration. If $1 would decrease the wealth of 1,000 persons by a minuscule amount and enrich a charity by $500, then it may be a fair price to ask, even if the mathematical expectation is only $0.50.

☐ FALLACIES IN ESTIMATING PROBABILITIES

A discussion of numerical probability is not complete without a consideration of the most common fallacies related to the subject. One such error involves a *failure to understand a law of probability*. Suppose, for example, that you may either draw once for the single lucky ticket in a box of 10 or draw 10 times for the lucky ticket in a box of 100, replacing the ticket each time before drawing again. In any group of people, some are sure to prefer one method over the other. But there is really no reason to do so, because the mathematical chances are identical: 1/10.

Another kind of error is to *confuse the addition of probabilities with the multiplication of probabilities*. Imagine a game show in which a contestant must choose either (1) to answer one question where there is 1 chance in 10 of getting the right answer and winning a $1,000 prize or (2) to answer three questions where in each case there is 1 chance in 3 of getting the right answer and where all three must be answered correctly to win the $1,000. In such a situation, many people would choose the latter, although their chances of winning the $1,000 would be the product of three fractions (1/3 × 1/3 × 1/3), or a slim 1 chance in 27. By contrast, the former alternative offers the contestant 1 chance in 10 to win the $1,000.

Betting on the Fish

The story . . . started with a poker game in Havana, in which our hero [W. T. (Fatty) Anderson], because of the mistaken assumption that three queens was the high hand, came out into the cold gray light of morning with several hundred miles of water and a five-dollar bill between him and his homeland.

On the way to his hotel he met a man carrying a large fish.

"What kind of fish is that?" he asked.

"Red snapper," said the fisherman.

"For five dollars it's not," said Anderson.

It developed that the fish was on the way to be sold and it was agreed that the decision of the fishmonger would be final.

"What kind of fish is this?" said the fisherman, tossing it down on a block.

"No jokes in the morning," said the buyer. "You've been fishing these waters for years and you ought to know. Get on with you."

"Never mind that," said the fisherman. "To decide a bet, what kind of fish is it?"

"It's a red snapper," said the merchant. "You know cursed well it is."

Anderson handed over the five-dollar bill.

"You win," he said, "but it was still a good bet. I had every other kind of fish in the ocean running for me."

JOE H. PALMER, IN *THIS WAS RACING,* ED. RED SMITH (SAN DIEGO: A. S. BARNES AND CO., 1953), P. 60.

One error could be called the *fallacy of unequal chances* because it always involves a failure to see that some possible outcomes are far more likely or unlikely than others. Anderson, in the anecdote "Betting on the Fish," thinks he made a good bet because he had "every other kind of fish in the ocean running for me." But of course he should have realized that because the fish had already been caught, each of these outcomes was not equally likely.

A fallacy also occurs when one *fails to see that some possible outcomes are equally likely.* During World War II, for example, soldiers under bombardment would sometimes leave the foxholes they had dug as cover against artillery and go instead into fresh shell holes on the assumption that it was unlikely for two shells to hit any given spot on the same day. But although the *mathematical* probability that two shells would land in the same place might be small, a spot that has been hit is actually just as likely as any other to take the next shell.

This failure to see that possible outcomes are equally probable has been called the *gambler's fallacy* and the *Monte Carlo fallacy* after an unusual event in the casino at Monte Carlo. On August 18, 1913, the roulette wheel stopped on a black number a record twenty-six times in succession.[3] Casinos have "house limits" on the amount of money that can be won, but if Monte Carlo had suspended the limit on that occasion, a player betting consistently on black all twenty-six times could have made millions of dollars. What actually happened, however, was a near-panicky rush to bet on red, beginning about the time black had come up a phenomenal fifteen times. Players betting on red doubled and tripled their stakes, reasoning that after black came up the twen-

---

[3] Darrell Huff, *How to Take a Chance* (New York: W. W. Norton & Co., 1959), p. 29.

tieth time, there was not a chance in a million of another repeat. These players failed to remember that after each outcome, there was a 50–50 chance that the next outcome would also be black. A roulette wheel has no memory, and its future behavior is not affected by what has happened in the past. So in the end, the unusual run on black enriched the casino by millions of dollars.

The players who switched to betting on red numbers might have argued that such a long run of black was inconsistent with the law of large numbers (often referred to as "the law of averages"). Indeed, a successive run of twenty-six black in roulette is extraordinarily unlikely—$(18/37)^{26}$. But the law of large numbers tells us simply that outcomes with coins, dice, and roulette wheels will tend to be equal after a *very large number* of trials. The law does not rule out the possibility of lopsided outcomes in any particular segment of trials. And that which is highly unlikely sometimes does occur.

The tendency of large numbers to swallow up disparities tempts one to think that coins, dice, or roulette tables obey something like a "law of atonement." If a coin tossed 20 times "misbehaves" by falling heads-up only 6 times, it may seem to be trying to "catch up" by later falling heads-up more often than tails-up. When a coin produces only 6 heads in 20 tosses, the disparity does seem large, but if for the next 480 tosses heads and tails come out equally, the total result will be 246 heads and 254 tails—at which point the disparity seems small. After another 500 tosses, the number of heads might be even closer to the number of tails—perhaps 498 to 502. But this result, which is consistent with the law of large numbers, would not warrant the conclusion that in any segment of trials—say, 20, 30, or 50 tosses—heads would come up more often than tails. The probability of heads on any given toss is no more nor less than 1/2.

■ EXERCISE 10-4

Questions 1–7 involve possible outcomes.

1. (a) If a college schedules four lecture sections and eight laboratory sections for first-year chemistry, then in how many different ways can a student sign up for one of each? (b) How many of these possibilities are left if a student finds that two of the lecture sections and three of the laboratory sections are already filled?

2. In a student government election, Baker, Mishkin, and Matthews are running for president, while Schultz, Mason, and Perkins are running for vice-president. Assuming that each candidate will be elected separately, construct a tree diagram showing the nine possible outcomes of this election. Use the diagram to determine the number of ways in which these students can be elected so that (a) both of their names begin with the letter *M*, and (b) neither of their names begins with the letter *M*.

3. (a) Is it more likely that the next birthday of a person chosen at random will fall on a Monday or that the birthdays of two persons chosen at random will fall on the same day of the week? (b) Is it as likely that one could choose a person at random whose birthday was on a given day of the year—say, March 12—as it would be that someone could choose two persons at random whose birthdays were on the same day of the year?

*4. In a traffic court, violators are classified according to whether or not they are properly licensed, whether their violations are major or minor, and whether or not they have committed any other violations in the preceding twelve months. (a) Construct a tree diagram to show the various ways in which this traffic court classifies violators. (b) If there are ten violators in each of the categories listed in the diagram and the judge gives each violator who is not properly licensed a stern lecture, how many of the violators will receive a stern lecture? (c) If, furthermore, the judge imposes a $50 fine on everybody who either has committed a major violation, has committed another violation in the preceding twelve months, or both, how many of the violators will receive a $50 fine? (d) How many of the violators will receive a stern lecture from the judge as well as a $50 fine?

5. A student can study either zero, one, or two hours for an economics exam on any given night. Construct a tree diagram to show that there are ten different ways in which the student can study altogether six hours for the examination on four consecutive nights.

6. There are four different trails to the top of a certain mountain. In how many different ways can a person hike up and down the mountain if (a) he or she must take the same trail both ways; (b) he or she can, but need not, take the same trail both ways; (c) he or she does not want to take the same trail both ways?

7. If the combination of a lock is REX, or some other group of three letters, how many possible combinations might be used?

Questions 8–19 involve the probability of a favorable outcome.

*8. What are the probabilities of getting, on a single roll of a die, (a) either 1 or 3 and (b) an even number?

9. When one card is drawn from a well-shuffled deck of 52 playing cards, what are the probabilities of getting (a) a red king; (b) a jack, queen, king, or ace; (c) a card that is neither a jack nor a queen; and (d) either a spade or a diamond?

10. If H stands for "heads" and T for "tails," the eight possible outcomes for three flips of a coin are HHH, HHT, HTH, THH, HTT, THT, TTH, and TTT. Assuming these eight possibilities are equally likely, what are the respective probabilities of getting zero, one, two, and three heads?

11. If a pitcher pitches a complete, nine-inning baseball game and walks no one, what are the pitcher's odds of pitching a perfect no-hit game?

*12. A bowl contains 12 black jelly beans, 10 red jelly beans, 25 yellow jelly beans, and 3 green jelly beans. If 1 jelly bean is drawn at random, what is the probability that it will be (a) yellow, (b) black or red, and (c) green or black?

13. Four men agree to rent four hotel rooms. Each draws a key at random from a box containing only the four keys for the four hotel rooms, and each goes to a different room to determine whether he has the proper key. (a) What is the probability that the youngest man has the right key? (b) What is the probability that each man goes successively to the room that his key opens?

14. What is the probability of getting (a) two heads in three tosses of a coin; (b) at least two heads in three tosses; (c) heads on both of the first two tosses out of three; and (d) three heads in three tosses?

15. Suppose you draw two cards from a standard deck without replacing the first

one before drawing the second. What is the probability that you will get (a) two aces, (b) at least one ace, (c) two spades, and (d) two black aces?

*16. Half of the philosophy professors at Ionia State University are existentialists, and one-fourth of them are logicians. What is the probability that a philosophy professor picked at random from Ionia State University is either an existentialist or a logician?

17. John and Jane are studying for final exams. The odds are 1 out of 2 that John will pass the logic exam, and 4 out of 5 that he will pass biology. The odds are 7 to 9 that Jane will pass economics and 3 to 5 that she will pass logic. What is the probability that (a) both students will pass logic; (b) John will pass both exams; (c) either student will pass logic; (d) both John and Jane will pass all of their exams; (e) either John will fail one exam or Jane will fail one exam; (f) either John will fail both exams or Jane will fail both exams; and (g) either John or Jane will pass both exams.

18. In your pocket or coin purse you have two dimes and three nickels. If you reach in to get money for a candy bar, what is the probability that (a) the first two coins you draw out will add up to 15 cents; (b) the first two coins you draw out will add up to 20 cents; (c) the first three coins you draw out will add up to 15 cents; and (d) you will get 20 cents on either the first two or the first three draws?

19. You have 24 friends who give parties on their birthdays. You can attend only one party on any day. What would you calculate the chance to be that you will have to miss a party because more than one falls on the same day of the year?

Questions 20–21 involve mathematical expectation.

*20. If a service club sells 500 raffle tickets for a color television set worth $420, what is the mathematical expectation of a person who buys one of these tickets?

21. To introduce a new car to the public, a dealer offers a drawing for a car worth $6,520 to a lucky person chosen at random from among those who come to the showroom, inspect the new models, and write their names on a special card. If 10,000 persons come to the dealer's showroom, inspect new models, and sign such cards, what is each entrant's mathematical expectation? Would it be worthwhile to spend $0.82 on gasoline to drive to the dealer's showroom just to have a chance to win the car?

Discuss the soundness of the reasoning involved in questions 22 to 30.

22. "I'll tell you my strategy for winning on a coin toss. Let the other fellow make the call, because seven out of ten people will call 'heads,' but heads will turn up only five times out of ten on the average. So if you let your opponent call, you have the greater probability of winning."

23. "If you ask someone to think of a number from one to ten, what's the probability that she'll name any given number? You'd expect it to be one in ten. But on the basis of my research, people are most likely to name three or seven. This result shows that the concept of probability as mathematical odds is mistaken."

*24. The *Wall Street Journal* reported on July 14, 1977, that billionaire H. L. Hunt gave this advice to one of his sons: "It's all right to gamble, but don't ever try to get even. You lose what you can afford to and then leave the table. But you can lose it all trying to play double and catch up."

25. A logic student was overheard telling his friends that he had never been in an automobile accident and that he therefore assumed his chances of being involved

in an accident increased each time he got behind the wheel. He also said that since he had flown on airplanes five times without a mishap, there was a greater chance of a crash on his next airplane trip than there had been on his first airplane trip.

26. "You have been having a run of good luck lately, so you had better watch out. Bad luck is waiting right around the corner."

27. "When I asked the doctor what chance Aunt Sophie had of pulling through the operation, the doctor said that she had a good chance. The doctor pointed out that although statistics show that only 1 out of 3 come through this operation successfully, so far this year out of 25 patients who had such operations, 15 had survived. So the chances of survival for this next one are better than 50–50."

*28. "I know I should study harder in my courses, but I only need to pass two of my four courses to graduate from college, and I figure that I have a 50–50 chance of passing in each course. Thus, I'm sure to pass in at least two of my four courses."

29. A card player shows you three cards. One is white on both sides. One is red on both sides. The third is white on one side and red on the other. The card player mixes the cards in a hat and lets you take one and place it flat on the table while the card player looks away. The upper side of the card you picked turns out to be white. "It's obvious," says the card player, "that this is not the red-red card. It must be one of the other two, so the reverse side can be either red or white. Even so, I'll be generous. I'll bet you a dollar against 75 cents that the other side is also white." Is this a fair bet? Does it actually favor you?—Adapted from Darrell Huff, *How to Take a Chance*

30. During the years when young men were being drafted to fight the war in Vietnam, four college seniors gloomily discussed their future. One had joined the national guard and was dreading the basic training he would have to undergo that summer. Another hoped to get into an ROTC program while he was in graduate school, while a third said he was appealing for a deferment as a conscientious objector. The fourth student said that, as a gambling man, he'd take his chances. "Well," he said, "I always figure I've got two chances: I might get drafted, and I might not. And even if I'm drafted, I still have two chances: I might pass the physical, and I might not. And if I pass, I still have two chances: I might go to 'Nam, and I might not. And even if I go to 'Nam, I still have two chances: I might get shot, and I might not. And even if I get shot, I still have two chances: I might die, and I might not. And even if I die, I still have two chances!"

CHAPTER ELEVEN

Hypotheses and causal relations

The goal of the physical and social sciences is to increase understanding of the *factual* nature of the world we inhabit. This means that no new statement may be added to the body of scientific knowledge unless it can be verified through observation. Whether a contingent statement is accepted as true or rejected as false depends upon the quantity and relevance of the empirical evidence available to support it. Prior to the evaluation of such evidence, all statements advanced as scientific explanations are treated as *hypotheses*:

> **A hypothesis is a tentative statement, subject to investigation, that is advanced to explain an event or relate facts in a given context.**

The progress of science is based on the successful investigation of hypotheses. Isaac Newton's law of gravitation was first put forward as a hypothesis. The germ theory of disease was developed from Louis Pasteur's hypothesis about the role of invisible microorganisms in the spread of contagion. Quantum mechanics received considerable support from the verification, in 1905, of Albert Einstein's hypothesis that light is composed of individual particles, or grains of energy, called photons.

If you spend any time spinning hypotheses, checking to see whether they make sense, whether they conform to what else we know, thinking of tests you can pose to substantiate or deflate your hypotheses, you will find yourself doing science.
CARL SAGAN, *BROCA'S BRAIN*

Logic plays a vitally important role in the formulation and testing of hypotheses. Investigators develop a hypothesis in response to a puzzling event, or problem, and hypothetical reasoning about the implications of the hypothesis can lead them to its solution. Logic is used in evaluating arguments that are put forward to justify the claim that a hypothesis is a satisfactory explanation of an event. Logic is used in designing controlled experiments and in judging the extent to which favorable experimental results increase the probability that a hypothesis is correct. Finally, through methods developed by the nineteenth-century philosopher and logician John Stuart Mill, logic provides a means for testing hypotheses that concern relationships of cause and effect.

☐ 11-1. HYPOTHETICAL REASONING

It is a popular belief that scientific investigation begins with an unprejudiced "gathering of the facts," which is followed by inductive generalization based on observed instances. But without a hypothesis as a guide, the scientist would not know what facts needed to be gathered. One cannot collect relevant evidence before identifying a puzzle and formulating a tentative hypothesis to explain it. Thus, observation and the formulation of hypotheses are interdependent.

"Cheshire Puss," she began, rather timidly, . . . "Would you tell me, please, which way I ought to go from here?"

"That depends a good deal on where you want to get to," said the Cat.

"I don't much care where—" said Alice.

"Then it doesn't matter which way you go," said the Cat.

LEWIS CARROLL, *ALICE'S ADVENTURES IN WONDERLAND*

New scientific theories and the conceptual changes they introduce play an important role in suggesting these initial hypotheses—or conjectures, as they are often called. For instance, Einstein's hypothesis that light consists of photons was suggested to him by Max Planck's discovery that radiant energy given off by heated bodies is emitted not in an unbroken stream, but as discontinuous bits, or particles, termed *quanta*. So Einstein's challenge to the then-prevailing theory that light travels in waves fitted into the emerging theory that all forms of radiant energy—including heat, radio, and X-rays—travel through space in separate and discontinuous quanta. His hypothesis was part of a theoretical reorientation toward the behavior of subatomic particles.

The initial hypotheses used to direct observation and experimentation are not always derived from theories or suggested by background knowledge. The history of science shows that many fruitful hypotheses were the result of insight and imagination, an example being Friedrich Kekulé's discovery of the structural formula for the benzene molecule. Or they may result from lucky accidents—as did Alexander Fleming's discovery of the mold, penicillin, which was later to have widespread application as an antibiotic.

Whatever the sources of hypotheses, the study of the ways they originate falls outside the scope of logic. Sudden insights and chance occurrences do not lend themselves to logical analysis. Nor can logic explain why a person or community regards a certain situation as a puzzle to be solved. Exploring this question belongs to the fields of psychology, sociology, and history.

Once an investigator has an initial hypothesis, however, evaluating the hypothesis involves a pattern of inference. Whether the field is biomedical engineering, plasma physics, experimental psychology, or any other area, scientists are concerned with the *justification* of the hypothesis: determining how well it solves a problem. And rigorous standards have been developed for judging the inferences drawn from the results of testing hypotheses. The logic involved in applying these standards is called *hypothetical reasoning*:

Hypothetical reasoning is the process of inferring certain implications from a hypothesis and then making observations or conducting experiments to determine whether these implications are true.

An illustration of the use of hypothetical reasoning in scientific inquiry is the discovery by Ignaz Semmelweis (1818–1865) of the cause of childbed fever.[1] Semmelweis, a young physician of Hungarian birth, was employed as an assistant in one of the maternity divisions of the Vienna General Hospital from 1844 to 1848. For approximately twenty years before he began his internship, the hospital had a reputation for a high mortality rate among maternity cases. A large percentage of the women who gave birth there contracted a serious, often fatal illness known as puerperal, or childbed, fever. Semmelweis was puzzled by the fact that mortality rates for the First Maternity Division—the one to which he had been assigned—were much higher than they were in the Second Maternity Division. In 1844, as many as 260 out of 3,157 mothers in the First Division, or 8.2 percent, died of the disease; for 1845, the death rate was 6.8 percent, and for 1846, it was 11.4 percent. By contrast, in the adjacent Second Division the death toll from the disease was much lower: 2.3, 2.0, and 2.7 percent, respectively, for those years.

Semmelweis was determined to discover the cause of childbed fever, but he initially defined his problem more narrowly. Why should the mortality rate in the First Division be almost three times as high as the rate in the Second Division?[2]

---

[1] This account is based upon Paul de Gruif, *Men Against Death* (New York: Harcourt, Brace and World, 1932), and Sir William J. Sinclair, *Semmelweis, His Life and His Doctrine* (Manchester, England: Manchester University Press, 1909).

[2] Semmelweis did not distinguish between the rates of mortality (death) and morbidity (infection). Although there could have been two sets of causal factors, he assumed only one set—probably because so many of the patients who became infected subsequently died.

Several explanations already existed. One widely accepted view attributed the fever to "epidemic influences," which were vaguely described as "atmospheric-cosmic-telluric changes." But why would epidemic influences plague the First Division so much more severely than the Second Division? In addition, how could this view be reconciled with the fact that while the fever was raging in the hospital, hardly a case occurred elsewhere in the city of Vienna or in its surroundings? Semmelweis reasoned that a genuine epidemic, such as cholera, would not be so selective.

Another hypothesis, which Semmelweis rejected, maintained that overcrowding was a cause of mortality in the First Division. He pointed out that, in fact, the crowding was greater in the Second Division—partly because of the desperate efforts of patients to avoid assignment to the notorious First Division.

The arrangement of the maternity wards of the hospital into two similar divisions provided a number of constant factors: characteristics of the population served, ventilation, diet, and general care of the patients. These similarities led Semmelweis to believe that the factor responsible for the high mortality rate in the First Division had to be due to some still-unobserved difference.

One possibly significant difference between the First and Second Divisions was the psychological factor of fear. The First Division was so arranged that a priest bearing the last sacrament to a dying woman had to pass through five wards before reaching the sickroom beyond. In 1846, of approximately 4,000 lying-in women, there were 459 deaths; thus, the priest came on the average of once every 19 hours throughout the year. The appearance of the priest, preceded by an attendant ringing a bell, was held to have a terrifying and debilitating effect on the patients, predisposing them to infection. In the Second Division, this adverse condition was absent, since the priest had direct access to the sickroom.

To test this conjecture, Semmelweis persuaded the priest to come by a roundabout route and without the ringing of the bell, thereby reaching the sickroom silently and unobserved. But this change had no effect on the mortality rate.

In 1846, a commission appointed to investigate the matter drew attention to another difference between the two divisions. The First Division served as a clinic for training medical students, while the Second served as a clinic for training midwives. The commission attributed the prevalence of illness in the First Division to injuries resulting from rough examinations by the medical students. Semmelweis rejected this difference as superficial, because (a) the injuries resulting naturally from the process of birth are much more extensive than those that might be caused by rough examination, and (b) the midwives who received their training in the Second Division examined their patients in much the same way as the medical students did. Nevertheless, in response to the commission's report, the number of medical students was halved, and their examinations of the women were reduced to a minimum. However, after a brief decline, the mortality rate rose to higher levels than ever before.

Finally, "like a drowning man clutching at a straw," Semmelweis decided to test a second difference between the two divisions. In the First Division the women were delivered lying on their backs; in the Second Division, on their sides. Although he thought it would produce no significant change, Semmelweis introduced the use of the lateral position in the First Division. But the mortality rate remained unaffected.

Semmelweis's investigation up to this point illustrates the salient features of hypothetical reasoning—the four steps, or phases, shown in Figure 11-1. He proceeded in the same way with each investigation.

First, he formulated a *tentative hypothesis*. Sometimes, the hypothesis was proposed by other investigators. Sometimes, it was suggested by Semmelweis's own definition of the problem as the need to explain the difference in the mortality rates between the two maternity divisions.

Second, *he elaborated the implications of the tentative hypothesis*. He reasoned that *if* "epidemic influences" were the cause of childbed fever, *then* the incidence of disease should be the same in both divisions, as well as within the rest of the hospital and elsewhere in Vienna. He next reasoned that *if* overcrowding were the cause of the illness, *then* the rate of mortality should be greater in the more crowded division. He reasoned further that *if* the presence of the priest were the cause of the illness, *then* the absence of the priest should reduce the rate of infection. Finally, he reasoned that *if* either the method of examination or the position during delivery were the cause of the fever, *then* a change in both these procedures would produce a corresponding change in the incidence of the disease.

Third, he conducted a test to determine whether the implications of each hypothesis were supported by the facts. This involved comparing mortality rates in the hospital with those in the rest of the city. It also meant changing hospital routines and medical procedures to observe the results.

Step 1: Formulate a tentative hypothesis.

Step 2: Elaborate the implications of the hypothesis (make predictions).

Step 3: Test the hypothesis.

Step 4: Accept or reject the hypothesis.

FIGURE 11-1
Hypothetical reasoning

In the fourth phase of reasoning about each hypothesis, Semmelweis concluded that it was false. His reasoning at this stage is represented as the following argument:

> **If the tentative hypothesis, *H*, is true, then certain observable events, *P*, should occur under specified circumstances.**
>
> **These observable events *P* did *not* occur under the specified circumstances.**
>
> **Therefore, the tentative hypothesis *H* is false.**

Or, expressed symbolically:

> **If *H*, then *P*.**
> **Not-*P*.**
> **Therefore, not-*H*.**

If, for example, *H* is taken to stand for the tentative hypothesis that the position of the women during delivery is the cause of childbed fever and *P* for the test implication of *H*—the *prediction*, or statement, that given a change in the position at delivery, the mortality rate will decline—the failure of *P* to occur disproves the hypothesis.[3]

Any argument of this form—*modus tollens*—is deductively valid: if the premises are true, the conclusion *must* also be true (see Section 8-1).

The argument form is therefore an infallible means of *disconfirming* and refuting a hypothesis—provided that the premises have been established as true.

To utilize this form of argument, one must be justified in believing that the hypothesis could not be true and the prediction false. The truth conditions for the conditional statement (see Section 7-1) must apply to the first premise, which means that it must be possible by deduction to infer the test implication, *P*, from *H*. In addition, the evidence must reliably show the prediction to have been false: premise 2 must be true. If these conditions are satisfied, one can be confident that the hypothesis has been disconfirmed. Its rejection then leads to the formulation of another tentative hypothesis—as represented by the "feedback loop" in Figure 11-1.

While a hypothesis can thus be conclusively *disconfirmed* by a deductive argument, it cannot be proved, or *confirmed*, by deductive argument. This point is crucial in understanding the arguments scientists present to justify a hypothesis. To see this as concretely as possible, let us return to Semmelweis's investigation and his discovery, at long last, of a hypothesis that he could accept as explaining the cause of puerperal fever.

---

[3] "Prediction" can be used to refer either to the possible physical event that has been predicted or to the *statement* that describes this possible event. In this chapter, the term is used to refer to the statement.

Early in 1847, an accident gave Semmelweis a decisive clue. While Professor Kolletschka, a teacher of anatomy, was performing an autopsy, he received a puncture wound in the finger from the scalpel of a student assistant. Kolletschka died after an agonizing illness, during which he exhibited the same symptoms that Semmelweis had observed in the victims of childbed fever.

Reasoning by analogy from Kolletschka's case to those of the lying-in women, Semmelweis proposed the hypothesis that "cadaveric matter" introduced into the body was the cause of infection. Although the role of microorganisms in disease had not yet been recognized, Semmelweis had grasped the tragic truth: the doctors and medical students were the carriers of infection, for they came to the First Division and examined women in labor directly after performing dissections in the autopsy room. He noted that the midwives, who performed the examinations in the Second Division, did not perform dissections of cadavers as part of their instruction in anatomy.

Although the doctors and students washed thoroughly with soap after dissecting cadavers, Semmelweis reasoned that they still introduced the infection. So in May 1847, he introduced washing with chlorinated lime as a way of chemically destroying the infectious material adhering to the hands of staff members. The mortality rate from childbed fever promptly began to decrease, and for the year 1848, it fell to 1.27 percent in the First Division, compared to 1.33 percent in the Second.

While Semmelweis's explanation of the cause of puerperal fever seems obvious today, it was not at all obvious in the middle of the nineteenth century. His work was the first to establish a link between decaying organic matter and disease. Nevertheless, it would be erroneous to say that his investigation *confirmed* the hypothesis that the higher mortality rate in the First Division was due to contamination from the hands of physicians and medical students.

Semmelweis's argument in favor of his final hypothesis, *Hs*, can be represented as follows:

> **If *Hs* is true, then the destruction of cadaveric matter by washing hands in a solution of chlorinated lime will greatly reduce the incidence of childbed fever in the First Division.**
>
> **Washing with a solution of chlorinated lime does greatly reduce the incidence of childbed fever in the First Division.**
>
> **Therefore, *Hs* is true.**

Because it is *inductive*, this argument at most increases the probability that *Hs* is true. If the argument were regarded as a deductive inference, it would illustrate the *fallacy of affirming the consequent* (see Section 8-1). It is deductively invalid, which means that its conclusion can be false even if its premises are true.

Even if many predictions have been successful, such a hypothesis can still be false. Consider the argument

> **If *H* is true, then $P_1, P_2, P_3, \ldots P_n$ are true.**
>
> **$P_1, P_2, P_3, \ldots P_n$ are all true.**
>
> **H is true.**

The set of favorable results obtained by testing different implications—or predictions P_1, P_2, P_3, . . . P_n—does show that *as far as past experience goes*, the hypothesis has been borne out. These results, especially if they follow a range of precise predictions, can make the truth of the hypothesis highly probable. For this reason, scientists speak of a hypothesis as being *corroborated* by successful predictions. But it always remains possible that a new prediction that is inferred from the hypothesis will turn out to be false. The correct hypothesis cannot be corroborated with the same certainty with which rival hypotheses are disconfirmed.

Figure 11-1 represents the *logic* of scientific reasoning. To evaluate a hypothesis, a scientist deduces a test implication, or prediction, from it: a statement of some phenomenon or event that must be true if the hypothesis is true. The scientist then conducts an experiment and observes the results, or otherwise collects data to determine the truth or falsity of the prediction. The corroboration or disconfirmation of the hypothesis then depends on the strength of arguments that connect a successful or failed prediction to the hypothesis.

■ EXERCISE 11-1

Below are ten brief descriptions of scientific experiments. For each case study, (a) identify the hypothesis or hypotheses being tested and the test implication(s) or prediction(s). (b) Tell whether the results of the experiment tend to corroborate or to disconfirm the hypothesis. Explain your answers.

  1. It was not until the careful experimental tests of Louis Pasteur in the 1870s that the idea that many infections and contagious diseases were spread by microorganisms became widely accepted. In the early part of the nineteenth century, one leading hypothesis maintained that diseases were due to the presence of evil humours in the body, and that there could be recovery by purging the blood of these humours. Bloodletting was a widely accepted procedure, and failure to let blood in a serious illness almost constituted professional negligence. In 1828, the French physician Pierre Charles Alexandre Louis began to test this hypothesis quantitatively and found that, in patients suffering from pneumonia, the hypothesis was wrong. For patients bled in the first three days after the onset of pneumonia, the mortality rate was 50 percent, while for those bled only after seven to nine days had elapsed from the onset, the mortality rate was only 16 percent.

  2. One hypothesis about the origin of the moon claims that the moon was pulled or thrown out from what is now the basin of the Pacific Ocean. To test this hypothesis, it was necessary to determine the geological ages of the Pacific Ocean basin and the rocks of which the moon is made. With the availability of moon rocks for detailed study, it has now been conclusively demonstrated that the moon is made of very old rock— about as old as the earth, and orders of magnitude older than the Pacific Ocean basin.

  3. In 1851, by experimenting with a pendulum, the French physicist Jean-Bernard-Léon Foucault corroborated the hypothesis that the earth spins on its axis. The pendulum, consisting of a heavy weight suspended from the ceiling of a high building, was set swinging freely along a line marked on the ground. The pendulum appeared to twist slowly in a clockwise direction relative to the line on the ground, but Foucault reasoned that the pendulum had continued to swing in the same direction whereas the

line fixed on the surface of the earth had twisted in a counterclockwise direction. On the hypothesis that the earth was rotating on its axis once every 24 hours, Foucault calculated from the latitude of Paris (where the experiment was conducted) a predicted pendulum swing through 360 degrees in 31.9 hours. The experimental result of 32 hours was in close agreement with the prediction.

*4. In about 240 B.C., the ancient scientist Eratosthenes demonstrated the curvature of the earth and calculated the earth's circumference. He studied the curvature of the earth by considering the different angles of the noon sun at Syene (near Aswan) in Egypt, and at Alexandria, 480 miles to the north. At noon, the midsummer sun at Alexandria was 7.2 degrees away from the vertical, as deduced from the length of the shadow of a pillar. Eratosthenes therefore concluded that the circumference of the world, assuming it to be spherical, is 480 × 360/7.2 miles, i.e., 24,000 miles. This figure is remarkably close to the modern figure of 24,860 miles.

5. In 1842, Charles Darwin presented a hypothesis about the formation of coral barrier reefs and atolls. He proposed that the coral organisms built up the reefs from mountains that had once had their peaks far above the surface of the ocean, but that had gradually subsided. According to this hypothesis, a deep bore made on the atoll should reveal a thick cap of limestone formed from dead coral organisms. Furthermore, since coral cannot live at depths greater than about 120 feet, a very deep limestone cap would corroborate the hypothesis that slow subsidence of mountain peaks had occurred. In 1952, at Eniwetok atoll, two borings were made to the great depths of 4,222 and 4,530 feet. The limestone from the dead coral persisted down to nearly the bottom of each bore—only close to the bottom was volcanic basalt rock encountered. The rock was the summit of an extinct and very old volcano that still rose two miles above the ocean floor.

6. Sir Isaac Newton's corpuscular theory of the refraction of light (published in 1704) postulated that rays of light were composed of minute particles traveling at high velocity and emitted from shining substances. In a homogeneous medium, these corpuscles traveled in straight lines; but on entering a denser medium—e.g., on passing from air to water—the corpuscles were supposed to undergo an additional attraction perpendicular to the surface, accelerating them and so deflecting them toward the perpendicular in the denser medium. This theory was preferred through the eighteenth century to the rival "wave theory" proposed by Christiaan Huygens in 1690, but Newton's theory was finally refuted in 1850 by Foucault's direct measurement of the velocity of light, which showed that light actually travels more slowly in a dense medium, in contrast to the prediction of Newton's theory that it is accelerated.

7. A great many ornithologists had insisted that homing birds depended entirely on eyesight to return "home," flying search patterns until they picked up a familiar landmark. Others, pointing out that a few birds get lost and do not return to their lofts, suggested that homing is nothing but a matter of chance—released birds fly every which way, and only those that happen to get within sight of their lofts or nearby landmarks make it back. In 1951 and 1952, Geoffrey Matthews of the University of Cambridge experimented with both pigeons and Manx shearwaters, the latter being homing shore birds native to the British Isles. Matthews released a number of banded Manx shearwaters from various points around the British Isles. He dispatched twenty from a ship in the Atlantic Ocean and even sent one by airplane to Boston, Massachusetts, where it was released by a colleague. That bird, identified by its band AX6587, was back in its burrow on the island of Skokholm off the coast of Wales twelve-and-a-half days later, beating by ten hours a letter announcing that it had been released on the other side

of the Atlantic. When this and other shearwaters made their way home across thousands of miles of land and ocean, Matthews pronounced that the explanation of homing in terms of chance and the hypothesis that the birds navigated by eyesight had been disproved.

*8. In the nineteenth century, the English sociologist Francis Galton investigated the effectiveness of prayer. He was not attempting to investigate the value of prayer to the person praying; rather, he was interested in determining whether prayer was effective as a means of achieving what was prayed for.

Galton reasoned that if prayer were effective, then something regularly prayed for would probably come about. He knew that in the nineteenth century, when people went regularly to church, there would be many people praying each Sunday for the good health and longevity of the queen and members of the royal family. Galton observed the recorded and well-established facts of the ages attained by royalty at death, and he compared these with the equally well-established facts of the age at death of the members of the higher social classes. He noted that royalty did not live longer, on the average, than the others.

In addition, Galton studied the efficacy of the prayers of the clergy for their own babies. He decided to see whether stillbirths were less frequent among the clergy than among the professional classes generally. Galton examined the announcements of births and stillbirths in the *Record*, a clerical newspaper, and in *The Times*. He found that there were the same proportions of stillbirths to live births for clerical families as there were for others.

9. Einstein's relativity theory implies that a strong gravitational field affects light or radar signals by retarding them as well as deflecting them. In 1967, I. Shapiro at the Massachusetts Institute of Technology succeeded in reflecting radar signals (which travel at the speed of light) off the planet Mercury, when the latter was nearly behind the sun. Relativity theory predicts that the very strong gravitational attraction of the sun will slow down the radar signals, lengthening their 23-minute round-trip to Mercury by a predicted 0.0002 seconds. As Mercury began to move behind the sun, the reflected radar signals were carefully timed, and a measurable delay was indeed observed. This delay increased to approximately 0.0002 seconds just before Mercury passed behind the sun.

Similar tests have since been carried out with radio signals beamed to the Mariner spacecraft. When the signals reached the craft, they were automatically amplified and transmitted back to earth. The round trip time was 43 minutes and the retardation predicted by relativity theory was calculated to be 0.0002001 seconds, as the radio beam was bent by passing through the sun's gravitational field. After exercising immense care and precision, investigators obtained a measured retardation of the radio signal by 0.000204 seconds.

10. Giant figures of animals and geometric designs were engraved and carved on the barren Nazca plains of southern Peru as early as 400 B.C. Many of the giant patterns are miles long—so large, in fact, that they can be discerned only from the air and thus were not discovered until modern men and women flew over them. How did the ancient Peruvians create these giant figures?

According to one hypothesis, the Indian artists of southern Peru first sketched the drawings on small plots of land and then used their knowledge of geometry and a complex system of rock piles and rock walls to enlarge the figures. Others have insisted that the figures could have been constructed only if the Nazcas had an elevated vantage point. Because there are no nearby mountains, some speculate that the construction was supervised by extraterrestrial visitors in spacecraft who relayed instructions to workers on the plain below. But members of the International Explorers' Society, influenced by what appears to be a picture of a hot-air balloon on an ancient Nazca ceramic pot, propose that Nazca observers directed the gigantic projects from balloons. In November 1976, IES members attempted to support their view by constructing a crude balloon, called the *Condor I*, and flying it over the Nazca plains.

The *Condor I* had an 88-foot-high air bag made from a fabric similar to the close-woven cotton textiles discovered at Nazca gravesites. The balloon's lines and fastenings were made from native plant fibers, and the boat-shaped gondola was woven from totora reeds native to Lake Titicaca in Peru.

On its maiden flight, *Condor I* quickly rose to 600 feet with two passengers, but was driven back to earth by brisk winds. It rose without passengers to about 1,200 feet, flew for about two miles, and then gently landed. IES director Michael DeBakey was enthusiastic about the results: "We set out to prove that the Nazcas had the skill, the materials and the need for flight," he said. "I think we have succeeded." (*Science/Nature Annual*, 1977, 173.) ■

☐ 11-2. JUSTIFYING HYPOTHESES

A hypothesis can be conclusively proved unreliable because an argument disconfirming it can be expressed in the deductively valid form known as *modus tollens*. But an argument supporting a hypothesis is always inductive and therefore can only express the *probability* that the hypothesis is true. This gives rise to the question, When are arguments *for* hypotheses *reliable*? That is, when scientists accept a hypothesis as probably true—as the correct explanation for an event—what arguments do they present to justify this decision?

An argument of the form shown in (1) cannot be depended on to be a reliable inductive argument.

1. If hypothesis *H* is true, then prediction *P* must be true.
   P is true.
   Therefore, probably *H*.

Scientists do accept the results of Semmelweis's experiment with a disinfectant of chlorinated lime as significantly increasing the probability that his hypothesis was true. And his argument was in the same form as (1). What more is needed to justify the view that these results did corroborate Semmelweis's hypothesis? Scientists must depend upon more than the fact that the second premise affirms the consequent of the first premise. The *justification* of a hypothesis as the correct explanation of a puzzling phenomenon involves complex arguments that take account of the amount of *corroboration*, the *explanatory range* of the hypothesis, and the *results of controlled experimentation*.

□ Repeated corroboration

Scientists reason by generalization from the results of repeated tests. As the hypothesis continues to be corroborated by the replication of the experiment and the observations of other investigators, the sample of favorable instances increases. In other words, while an argument of form (1) does not justify a hypothesis, scientists can use the conclusions of a number of these arguments as the premises in an argument by generalization (see Section 10-2). Each premise of the generalization will be a report of the corroboration of the hypothesis in a different experimental test.

Moreover, the hypothesis is subjected to a variety of tests. This is illustrated by the experiments that served to corroborate Einstein's hypothesis that time is relative to gravitational force. Einstein had predicted that clocks on the surface of the earth would be found to run more slowly than clocks that were far from the earth and other massive bodies. This prediction has now been verified by means of experiments using various kinds of atomic clocks, which, because atoms absorb and emit light rays at precisely defined frequencies, are the most reliable timepieces available for scientific research. The experiments involved (a) taking portable cesium clocks around the world in passenger jets and comparing them with atomic clocks at the U.S. Naval Observatory; (b) having United States Navy aircraft carry cesium and rubidium clocks in five 15-hour flights, making 20-mile loops over Chesapeake Bay at an altitude of 30,000 feet; and (c) having radio signals from a hydrogen-maser atomic clock carried 6,000 miles away from the earth by a Scout rocket fired from Wallops Island, Virginia.

The diversity of successful experimental tests increases the negative analogy among the observed instances, thereby increasing the probability of the hypothesis. The greater the variety of experiments, the greater the chance of finding an unfavorable instance if the hypothesis should be false. Thus, to the extent that an unfavorable instance is *not* found and the hypothesis is *not* refuted, scientists are justified in accepting it as probable.

□ Explanatory range

The *explanatory range, or power,* of a hypothesis is the completeness with which it accounts for the puzzling facts surrounding the initial problem. Statements of these explained facts are said to *converge* on the hypothesis and support it:

> **A converging statement is one that increases the probability of a hypothesis by affirming a consequence that would be expected to be true if the hypothesis were true.**

The explanatory range of a hypothesis increases with the number and variety of converging statements in support of it. And the reliability of the hypothesis increases with its explanatory range.

All of the following can be counted as converging statements for Semmelweis's hypothesis:

In the Second Division, prenatal examinations were performed by midwives who did not receive training in anatomy by dissecting cadavers.

Medical students and doctors performing examinations in the First Division usually moved systematically through the wards from one bed to the next, and the outbreak of the disease, one row after another, seemed to follow the same pattern.

The incidence of disease was lower in patients who had had "street births" before arrival at the hospital and had not undergone prenatal examinations at the hospital.

The incidence of disease was highest among patients who endured long labors in the First Division and who had undergone several examinations.

The instances of fever among newborn babies were all among babies whose mothers had contracted the disease during labor; when the mother's infection followed the birth, the child was less likely to become infected.

Each statement would be expected to be true if the hypothesis was correct. In other words, the truth of the hypothesis explains why each of these converging statements is true. And the reliability of Semmelweis's hypothesis was greatly enhanced by the fact that it alone, among the hypotheses considered, explained why all of these converging statements were true.

□ Controlled experimentation

Confidence that Semmelweis had indeed found the cause of childbed fever also depends upon the extent to which he was able to control other factors that might have contributed to the disease. Because he was in charge of arrangements for the Maternity Division, he could think of the patients in the Second Division, where the mortality rate was lower, as a *control group.*

A control group is a collection of individuals who differ from the group being studied only in that they are not subjected to the particular treatment being given as a test to the other group.

This situation allowed Semmelweis finally to infer that the only significant difference between the two divisions concerned patient examinations.

If Semmelweis had not been able to control conditions, washing with chlorinated lime might not have reduced the mortality rate, even though he was right about the cause of the disease. For example, the laundry service, knowing that disinfectant was being used in the hospital, might have become careless and inadequately washed bed linen. Or due to a labor shortage, orderlies who were assigned to clean the dissection rooms might also have been required to work in the kitchen, handling utensils used by patients in the First Division.

Semmelweis's ability to control against unanticipated factors leads us to conclude that the predicted result was unlikely to have come about unless the hypothesis that the cause of the higher mortality rate in the First Division was infection from cadaveric matter, was true. It is reasonable to suppose that if his hypothesis had been wrong, the incidence of childbed fever would not have decreased. And if the use of the disinfectant had had no effect on the mortality rate, it would have been an odd coincidence that the incidence declined precipitously at exactly the time chlorinated lime was employed.

Whenever possible, scientists test a hypothesis by arranging conditions to produce a specified and measurable outcome. The experiment is performed for the sole purpose of obtaining information about the truth or falsity of the hypothesis, and the outcome may be one that would not normally occur outside the controlled context. The investigator designs the experiment so that the *initial conditions* can be completely specified and all *auxiliary assumptions* are identified.

The *initial conditions* involve the procedures by which the expected outcome is produced, the conditions under which observations are recorded, and the properties of the scientific instruments used to measure the effect. Semmelweis controlled the initial conditions by changing the approach of the priest, by reducing the number of examinations by medical students, and by changing the positions of women during delivery. Because he was concerned with human subjects, however, he was not able to establish a completely controlled experiment. To rule out the possibility of other causes, Semmelweis could have compared the mortality rate for a control group of women, who received examinations as usual, against the mortality rate for those who were examined only after the use of disinfectant. But this would have been unethical treatment of the control group. He did conduct controlled experiments on animals, finding that the introduction of cadaveric matter into pregnant rabbits was always a sufficient cause of a higher rate of infection. (See the discussion of sufficient cause in Section 11-3.)

The *auxiliary assumptions* consist of claims about the extent to which extraneous factors have been eliminated, the expected effects of factors that cannot be entirely eliminated by the investigator, and the margin of acceptable experimental error.

Scientists generally do not regard a hypothesis as adequately tested until it has been corroborated by controlled experimentation. Successful results in such tests provide the strongest support for the claim that a hypothesis is correct. Therefore, designing a way to subject a hypothesis to a good experimental test is often a major challenge faced by an investigator.[4]

---

[4] The remainder of this section is indebted to the excellent account of testing hypotheses in Chapter 6 of Ronald N. Giere, *Understanding Scientific Reasoning* (New York: Holt, Rinehart & Winston, 1979).

□ SHOWING THAT THE PREDICTION FOLLOWS FROM THE HYPOTHESIS

In a good experimental test, the investigator tries to show that the prediction follows from the hypothesis, *H*, in conjunction with statements of the initial conditions, *IC*, and the auxiliary assumptions, *AA*. In other words, the investigator tries to demonstrate the truth of the following conditional:

If [*H* and *IC* and *AA*], then *P*.

If the prediction does not follow from *H* plus *IC* and *AA*, a failure of the prediction cannot disconfirm the hypothesis. And it is crucial that a failure of the prediction disconfirm the hypothesis.

The investigator therefore attempts to design the experiment so that no questions about the truth of *IC* and *AA* arise. The only statement in doubt is the hypothesis itself—and its probable truth directly depends on the success or failure of the prediction.

To appreciate this, consider the form an argument designed to refute a hypothesis must take:

If [*H* and *IC* and *AA*], then *P*.
Not-*P*
Therefore, not [*H* and *IC* and *AA*].

The conclusion follows from the premises by *modus tollens*. But the conclusion itself is equivalent, by De Morgan's laws, to

Not-*H* or not-*IC* or not-*AA*.

This raises the question whether *IC*, *AA*, or both could be false, rather than *H*. To offset this doubt, the experiment is designed so that *IC* and *AA* are known to be true. The investigator can thus reason, by conjunctive argument, as follows:

Not-[*H* and *IC* and *AA*].
But *IC* and *AA* are true.
Therefore, not-*H*.

On the other hand, if the prediction succeeds—if *P* turns out to be true—then *H* is probably true, because the investigator knows that *IC* and *AA* do not entail *P* on their own.

Paradoxically, a true prediction (a favorable outcome) significantly increases the probability of a hypothesis only if the falsity of the same prediction (an unfavorable outcome) would refute it. Logicians often follow the philosopher of science Karl Popper in speaking of a hypothesis as *falsifiable* when this condition has been satisfied.

☐ SHOWING THAT THE PREDICTION WOULD NOT FOLLOW FROM ANOTHER HYPOTHESIS

Scientists attempt to meet a second condition in a controlled experiment: *precision*. The prediction must be sufficiently specific so that it is very unlikely to be derived from any other hypothesis. If a prediction is too vague or too general, it may be deducible from more than one hypothesis even when the initial conditions and auxiliary assumptions remain the same.

The more probable of two or more rival hypotheses is therefore the one that generates a prediction that cannot be deduced from any other hypothesis. For example, the laws of gravitation of both Einstein and Isaac Newton yield the same correct predictions concerning many mechanical and astronomical phenomena. Both theories predict (what Galileo Galilei had earlier discovered) that, if air resistance is discounted, bodies of different mass in free fall will accelerate at exactly the same speed.

But Einstein's theory also predicts effects that are unaccounted for in Newtonian theory—for instance, the eccentric behavior of the planet Mercury. Instead of revolving in its elliptical orbit with the regularity of the other planets, Mercury deviates from its course each year by a slight but persistent degree. Mercury is small, travels with great speed, and lies closest to the sun of all the planets—factors that under Newtonian laws would not account for the difference between its motions and those of the other planets. But according to Einstein's laws, the intensity of the sun's gravitational field and Mercury's enormous speed cause the whole ellipse of Mercury's orbit to revolve slowly about the sun, accounting for the observed deviation.

It is important that the same initial conditions and auxiliary assumptions would yield a decidedly different prediction with any other hypothesis. This means that if *IC* and *AA* are true but *H* is false, the prediction is probably false as well:

If [not-*H* and *IC* and *AA*], then very probably not-*P*.

If this conditional statement can be accepted as true, and the prediction turns out to be true, we can then reliably infer that *H* is probably true as well. The inference can be represented by the following argument:

1. If [not-*H* and *IC* and *AA*], then very probably not-*P*.	Premise
2. *P* is true.	Premise
3. *IC* and *AA* are true.	Premise
4. Very probably not [not-*H* and *IC* and *AA*].	From 1 and 2 by *modus tollens*
5. Very probably not[not-*H*].	From 3 and 4 by disjunctive argument
6. Very probably *H*.	From 5 by double negation

That the form of the argument is deductively valid insures that nothing is wrong with the inference from the premises to the conclusion. But note that the conclusion states "very probably *H*." The argument establishes not the certainty of *H* but its high probability, because one of the premises itself is a probability statement. The claim in the consequent of the first premise is only "very probably not-*P*." Because of this element of probability, it is still possible that *P* is true and *H* is false. But the argument provides strong support for the truth of *H*.

A famous experiment concerning Einstein's hypothesis about the effects of gravitation on light illustrates the importance of precise prediction. The evidence supporting the prediction warrants the claim that it very likely could not have been made if the hypothesis in question were not true.

From purely theoretical considerations, Einstein concluded that because light is a form of energy, it has mass, and thus it will therefore be affected by a gravitational field. Hence, he hypothesized that light travels in a curve when passing through the gravitational field of a massive body. Einstein suggested that his hypothesis could be put to the test by seeing whether and by how much the light of distant stars would bend when it passes close to the sun. Since the sun and stars are visible together in the sky only during an eclipse of the sun, Einstein proposed that photographs be taken of the fixed stars immediately bordering the darkened face of the sun during an eclipse. If his hypothesis were correct, the light from these stars would be bent inward, toward the sun, causing them to appear to observers on the earth to be shifted outward from their usual positions in the sky. Einstein expected there to be a discrepancy between the known positions of these stars and their apparent positions as calculated from photographs taken during the eclipse. The discrepancy could be checked by photographing the same stars at night and measuring the distances revealed by the two photographs. Einstein calculated the degree of deflection that should be observed and predicted that for the stars closest to the sun the deviation should be about 1.75 seconds of an arc.

The component parts of the experimental test of Einstein's hypothesis— leaving aside technical details related to mathematical calculations—are as follows:

Hypothesis: The gravitational field of the sun bends starlight passing close to the sun.

Prediction: During an eclipse of the sun, the stars closest to the sun would appear to be approximately 1.75 seconds of an arc farther away from the sun than they were known to be.

Initial Conditions:

The identification of the stars that would be seen as closest to the sun during the eclipse.

The calculation of the positions of the stars based on independent astronomical data (such as photographs of the constellations taken at night).

Knowledge of the speed of light and the gravitational field of the sun.

The time of the total eclipse and the locations on earth from which it could be seen.

The known properties and effects of photography.

Auxiliary Assumptions:

There would be no other major object with a gravitational field sufficient to deflect the starlight to a significant degree.

The photographs would accurately represent the images of the identified stars during the total eclipse.

Differences in the locations from which the stars were photographed would not significantly affect the outcome.

Einstein's hypothesis was tested during a total eclipse of the sun that occurred on May 29, 1919. The eclipse, which was not visible from Europe or America, was photographed by two groups of astronomers—one in Sobral, Brazil, and the other on the island of Príncipe, off the coast of West Africa. When the two sets of photographs were examined, they showed that the deflection of the starlight in the gravitational field of the sun averaged 1.64 seconds of an arc. This figure was as close to perfect agreement with Einstein's prediction as the accuracy of instruments at that time allowed.

Scientists, then, have three major ways of arguing that a hypothesis is correct:

1. They may argue by inductive generalization from a series of tests, each of which corroborates the hypothesis.

2. They may argue that the explanatory range of the hypothesis exceeds its rivals, citing the number and variety of statements converging on the hypothesis.

3. When controlled experimentation is possible, they argue that favorable results show both that it is reasonable to believe the prediction is true because the hypothesis is true and that it is improbable the prediction would have been true if the hypothesis had been false.

Any one of these methods may be enough to establish a hypothesis as the best current explanation for an event. But a hypothesis is usually not accepted as *the* explanation for an event until persuasive arguments of all three types have been made for it.

■ **EXERCISE 11-2**

Below are three case histories of scientific investigation and experimentation. Read each case history carefully, section-by-section, and answer the questions after each section.

I. The Discovery of Atmospheric Pressure

As was known in Galileo's time, a simple suction pump, which draws water from a well by means of a piston that can be raised in the pump barrel, will lift water no higher than 34 feet above the surface of the well. Galileo's student Evangelista Torricelli was struck by this and advanced a new explanation. He argued that the earth is surrounded by a sea of air, which by reason of its weight exerts pressure upon the surface below, and that this pressure upon the surface of the well forces water up the pump barrel when the piston is raised. The maximum length of 34 feet for the water column in the barrel thus simply reflects the total pressure of the atmosphere upon the surface of the well.

Torricelli reasoned that if his conjecture were true, it could be deduced that mercury, which is 14 times heavier than water, can be made to rise in a tube only about thirty inches. Around 1643, Torricelli performed an experiment that verified this prediction. He took a glass tube over thirty inches long that was closed at one end, filled it with mercury, placed his finger over the opening, inverted the tube, submerged the open end in a dish of mercury, and removed his finger. The mercury dropped until the column was about 30 inches high—just as predicted. In effect, Torricelli had invented the mercury barometer.

1. What was the initial phenomenon Torricelli wished to explain?
2. What new view or theory about air did Torricelli propose?
3. State the hypothesis Torricelli formulated to test this theory.
*4. State the prediction Torricelli made.
5. Write a conditional statement indicating the relationship between the test hypothesis, the initial conditions involved, and the prediction.

Blaise Pascal, who read about Torricelli's experiment, reasoned that if we live in a sea of air that exerts pressure, then the pressure should diminish as we rise to the "surface" of this "sea." If the pressure so diminishes, then the height of a mercury column should decrease as the column is carried up a tall mountain. In 1648, Pascal had his brother-in-law, Floriu Perier, measure the length of the column in a Torricelli barometer at the foot of the Puy de Dome, a mountain some 4,800 feet high, and then carefully carry this apparatus to the top and repeat the measurement there while a control barometer was left at the bottom under the supervision of an assistant. Perier found the mercury column at the top of the mountain more than three inches shorter than that at the bottom, whereas the length of the column in the control barometer had remained unchanged. Pascal and Perier repeated the experiment five different times, obtaining the same result each time.

6. State the specific prediction made by Pascal.
7. By what process of reasoning did Pascal arrive at the belief that the atmospheric pressure at the top of the Puy de Dome would be less than it was at the bottom of the mountain?
*8. Was the test of Torricelli's hypothesis that Pascal and Perier devised a controlled experiment? Why, or why not?
9. State two auxiliary assumptions for the Pascal-Perier experiment.

II. Halley's Comet

Edmund Halley was a young scientist in 1695 when he first began to wonder whether Newton's theory of gravitation (published in 1687) could explain the motions of comets. Halley began investigating a comet he himself had observed in 1682. Using data recorded on the path and motion of this comet, Halley inferred that, due to the gravitational attraction of the sun, the comet should be traveling around the sun in a large and elongated elliptical orbit that took about seventy-five years to complete. He realized that there must be some effect of the gravitation of other planets upon the comet, especially Jupiter, but he ignored these influences as being relatively small and too difficult to calculate.

Halley also concluded that this comet must have been around many times before, and he was able to show that there had been comets reported at roughly seventy-five-year intervals going back to 1305. Halley claimed that these were all sightings of the same comet whose orbit he had deduced from Newtonian theory. In addition, Halley calculated the probable time of its next return and predicted that it would again be sighted in December 1758.

Halley published his work on comets in 1705 and died in 1743, fifteen years before the predicted return of the comet. The comet, which was subsequently to bear Halley's name, reappeared on Christmas Day in 1758, following the trajectory described by Halley.

1. Identify Halley's hypothesis.
2. Cite two different statements that converge on Halley's hypothesis.
3. State a major auxiliary assumption made by Halley.
*4. Identify the initial conditions with which Halley worked.
5. Did the result, as predicted by Halley, constitute a good test of Halley's hypothesis? Why, or why not?

III. Lavoisier's Experiments on Oxygen and Phlogiston

In 1775, Antoine-Laurent Lavoisier attempted to convince fellow chemists of the importance of oxygen in combustion. Lavoisier took a measured amount of mercury and carefully enclosed it in a container with a known amount of air. As Lavoisier heated the mercury, a red oxide (called a *calx* by chemists of the eighteenth century) was formed. The red oxide weighed more than the metal from which it had been formed. In addition, about one-fifth of the air in the closed container had disappeared. Lavoisier thus claimed that something had disappeared from the air and combined with the metal to produce the oxide.

Lavoisier next heated the red oxide in an enclosed space with the sun's rays brought to a focus by a large lens or "burning glass," thus evolving a new gas (oxygen) and regenerating the metal. Lavoisier reasoned that this oxygen was the same as the "something" that had disappeared from the original air, for the quantity was the same, and the oxide had lost weight in the right amount. Furthermore, the oxygen, when mixed with the residue from the first stage of the experiment, was shown to yield a mixture identical to common air.

1. State the hypothesis Lavoisier was testing.
2. State the specific prediction or predictions made by Lavoisier.

3. Was the test Lavoisier devised for his hypothesis a good controlled experiment? Why, or why not?

*4. Write out a conditional statement relating Lavoisier's hypothesis to the predicted result of heating mercury in a closed container of air.

5. For the second part of Lavoisier's experiment write out a conditional statement asserting that the predicted results would be very unlikely unless Lavoisier's hypothesis were true.

Lavoisier's experiment was a crucial step in changing our understanding of the process of combustion. In particular, his experiment dealt a death blow to the phlogiston theory, although many chemists in his own day were reluctant to accept this result.

Phlogiston had been regarded as an element or substance inherent in any material capable of undergoing combustion. Materials that burned easily, such as charcoal, were believed to be phlogiston-rich; and it was assumed that when charcoal (or any combustible material) was heated, the phlogiston left the charcoal and combined with the air, leaving only ashes behind. Most of Lavoisier's contemporaries explained the formation of metallic oxide or calx as the removal of phlogiston from the metal. The formation of the metal from its oxide was explained as the addition of phlogiston.

The presence or absence of phlogiston was also said to explain other facts about combustion. For example, when a bell jar is placed over a lighted candle, the candle will soon go out. According to modern chemistry, the reason is that the oxygen in the jar has been used up. But according to the phlogiston theory, the air has been saturated with phlogiston and hence can hold no more.

6. What would an adherent of the phlogiston theory hypothesize about the heating of mercury?

7. What would an adherent of the phlogiston theory predict as an outcome of the heating of mercury in air?

*8. Cite one outcome that would be predicted from both Lavoisier's hypothesis and the phlogiston hypothesis.

9. Did Lavoisier's experiment constitute a good controlled experimental test for the phlogiston hypothesis?

10. Present a brief argument that reaches the conclusion that the phlogiston hypothesis is false. ■

☐ 11-3. CAUSAL RELATIONS AND MILL'S METHODS

One major use of hypotheses in science is to provide causal explanations of events—claims such as the following:

Cigarette smoking causes lung cancer.

Streptococcol bacteria cause scarlet fever.

Gravitational attraction causes the earth to orbit the sun.

Vitamin C increases one's resistance to colds.

Special methods for testing causal hypotheses were advocated by the philosopher-logician, John Stuart Mill (1806–1873) and are therefore known as

"Mill's methods of experimental inquiry." Mill's methods simplify the development of experimental tests by extending the procedures involved in inductive reasoning by analogy (discussed in Section 10-3).

☐ *The concept of causation*

Causal hypotheses are claims about universal regularities, or uniform connections between different factors. Consequently, when a causal hypothesis is corroborated, it provides evidence for some underlying scientific law—an invariant association between the set of conditions that make up the cause and those that constitute the effect. A particular event—a case of sickness, an individual's death, or a chemical reaction, for instance—can then be explained as an instance of these general underlying regularities. Causal hypotheses, when well corroborated, are thus rich in explanatory power: they enable scientists to understand and predict a great number of particular events.

The objective of causal investigation in the sciences is to discover a set of conditions such that in their presence, a specific effect occurs and in their absence the effect does not occur. That is, scientists seek a set of causal conditions that are *necessary* and *sufficient* for the effect in question. Suppose, for example, that after years of research, physicians determine that patients can be cured of a serious disease by a certain treatment, or set of conditions, H. For H to be *necessary* for the cure, it must be the case that each patient known to be afflicted by the disease could not have recovered without H. For H to be *sufficient* for the cure, it must have been all that was required to insure the patients' recovery. Each case of recovery is an instance of some general regularity such that any future patient whose case is similar will also be cured by H.

> A necessary condition, *N*, for a specified effect, *E*, is a condition without which *E* cannot occur.

This definition can be expressed in the following conditional statement:

If not-N, then not-E.

In truth-functional symbolism, this becomes

$\sim N \supset \sim E$

Another way of stating this connection is to say that if *E* occurs, then *N* has to have occurred.[5] This can be expressed as the contrapositive of the previous

---

[5] We are accustomed to thinking of the cause coming *before* the effect, and this familiar sense of temporal sequence will be preserved as much as possible in the language of this chapter. However, the temporal priority of the cause is not a *logical* requirement. There is nothing logically inconsistent in supposing that the cause and effect occur simultaneously.

conditional, or

$E \supset N$

According to the truth conditions for a conditional statement, E cannot be true while N is false; and this is what is meant by saying that N is a necessary condition for E. Thus, knowing that some event N is necessary for a specified effect E allows us to infer both that E will not occur unless N is present and that if E has occurred, then N must have been present.

However, we are *not* entitled to infer that, if N is present, then E must occur. Whereas one or more conditions may be necessary for a given effect to occur, no one of these necessary conditions may be sufficient on its own. For instance, if a car is to run, it must have fuel, but the presence of fuel alone is not sufficient; the ignition switch must also be turned on.

> A sufficient condition, S, for the occurrence of a specified effect, E, is a condition such that if S occurs, then E must also occur.

This definition can also be expressed as a truth-functional conditional:

$S \supset E$

Thus, if we know S has occurred, we can infer that E must occur too. And if we know E has not occurred, then we can infer that S has not occurred:

$\sim E \supset \sim S$

But we are *not* entitled to infer from the occurrence of E that S has occurred. A given effect may have a number of different sufficient causes, no one of which is necessary. For instance, a mechanical failure may be a sufficient condition for an automobile accident, but not a necessary condition because accidents also result from reckless driving and hazardous road conditions.

Finding the necessary and sufficient conditions for a specified effect represents an *ideal* of science. It is often extremely difficult to specify all the conditions that are jointly necessary and sufficient for an effect. Furthermore, either to produce a desirable outcome or prevent an undesirable one, we may not need to know all of the necessary and sufficient conditions for that effect.

In general, what an investigator regards as *the* cause of an event is a function of our efforts to control—that is, either to prevent or to bring about—the event. This is why a coroner, asked to determine the cause of death when a man has been shot, is likely to report that the victim died because a bullet penetrated his heart, rather than that he died because his heart stopped beating, his blood stopped circulating, and his brain ceased to receive oxygen. Each event might be sufficient on its own, and the entire chain is necessary before the victim dies. But the shooting itself is the event upon which attention should be focused to prevent other deaths of this kind.

Whether scientists look for the necessary or sufficient condition or conditions in investigating the cause of an effect often depends on the practical aim. Usually, when they are trying to *prevent* a certain occurrence, they need only find the necessary condition whose removal will make that occurrence impossible. For instance, physicians and public health officials may prevent a disease by finding a single condition necessary for the growth of a bacillus and eliminating that condition. Thus, it is usually a necessary condition that is regarded as "the cause" in taking preventive action.

Conversely, in the endeavor to *produce* an effect, "the cause" is usually a sufficient condition—one in the presence of which the effect is sure to take place. For example, a wire made of copper metal is sufficient to conduct electricity—but not necessary, since aluminum, lead, niobium, and silver also conduct electricity. So any one of these substances could serve the purpose.

When scientists search for a sufficient condition, they often simply assume that other conditions necessary for the effect—the normal or expected circumstances—are present and operating. Their approach can be likened to a search for the cause of a forest fire. We normally would not consider oxygen and conifer trees to be causes because oxygen and combustible material are present whether a forest burns or not. We would try to find some difference— some intervening factor that triggered the fire. Did lightning strike a stand of trees? Did a careless camper leave a camp fire unattended? Did someone throw a lighted cigarette into the underbrush?

□ Causal claims about populations

Statistical studies show that there is a significant positive correlation between heavy smoking and lung cancer—that is, a high percentage of the people who develop the disease are heavy smokers. And careful and extensive research conducted over decades has established that cigarette smoking is indeed a cause of lung cancer.

But for any particular smoker chosen at random, smoking may be neither a necessary nor a sufficient condition for lung cancer. Whereas some causal connections always hold between events of a certain kind—a magnet always attracts iron filings, and acid will always turn litmus paper red—smoking and lung cancer are not always connected in individual cases. We cannot claim that smoking is a necessary condition for, say, Arthur's developing lung cancer, since there are cases of lung cancer in nonsmokers. Even if Arthur does not smoke, he might contract the disease because of exposure to asbestos, radioactive materials, or X rays. Nor can we claim that smoking is a sufficient condition for Arthur's developing lung cancer because some heavy smokers do not contract it.

The statement that smoking causes lung cancer must therefore be understood as a causal claim about the statistical probability of lung cancer for a *specified population*, or group of people—smokers. It is a claim that the percentage of the population who smoke and develop lung cancer is greater than the percentage of the population who do not smoke and contract it. Thus, we infer the probability that a particular smoker, Arthur, will develop lung cancer from the facts we have about that individual and about the difference between the cancer rates for smokers and nonsmokers.

When understood in connection with the statistical probability of an outcome in a population, smoking can be seen to be both a necessary and sufficient condition for the *higher rate of lung cancer among smokers.* Smoking is necessary for the present rate to be as high as it is because, as statistics show, it is highly probable that the percentage of lung cancer cases will drop if smoking decreases appreciably. And smoking is sufficient to increase the rate of lung cancer because, as statistics show, it is highly probable that increased smoking will bring about a rise in the percentage of lung cancer cases. (For statistical evidence that smoking causes lung cancer, see Table 11-4.)

☐ *Mill's methods*

It is possible to test causal hypotheses by comparing and contrasting particular cases to develop arguments by analogy. In his book *A System of Logic* (1843), Mill calls these procedures the *method of agreement* and the *method of difference.* Although Mill did not make a formal distinction between necessary and sufficient conditions, his method of agreement is basically a means of testing a hypothesis that a certain factor is a necessary condition for a certain effect and his method of difference a means for testing a hypothesis that a certain factor is a sufficient condition for a certain effect.

☐ THE METHOD OF AGREEMENT

The method of agreement is based on the principle that nothing that is absent when an event occurs can be a necessary condition for the event. The method requires us to collect and compare as many positive instances as practicable—that is, instances that all contain the same effect, E. Although these instances are all positive, they must differ from each other as much as possible in other regards. The objective is to show that all the instances share one factor in addition to E—namely, the condition being tested to determine whether it is necessary.

We set up the test by listing a number of instances where the effect E is present, along with other characteristics that are observed in each case. For the example shown in Table 11-1, the only factor that is common to all the instances other than E is N. No single one of the group of factors L, M, O, P, Q, and R can be a necessary condition for the effect, since each factor is absent in at least one instance in which E occurs. It is therefore highly probable that N is a necessary condition.[6]

---

[6] Because the argument is *inductive*, we cannot be certain that N is a necessary condition. We may yet find a positive instance in which N is absent. However, the hypothesis that N is a necessary condition continues to be corroborated by each successive discovery that a positive instance has N.

TABLE 11-1 *The method of agreement*

POSITIVE INSTANCE CONTAINING *E*	FACTORS OTHER THAN *E*
Instance 1	*L M N O*
Instance 2	*L M N P*
Instance 3	*M N P Q*
Instance 4	*N P Q R*

Thus, the method involves an argument by analogy: the probability that the one factor in which all the positive instances agree is a necessary condition increases as the negative analogy among the observed instances increases. With every increase in the number of factors—such as L, M, O, P, Q, and R—that are ruled out, the possibility that the cause of E is some condition other than N decreases. Thus, confidence in N increases as other conditions are successively eliminated.

The method of agreement is routinely employed in the experimental sciences. The experimenter begins with a number of instances in which the effect E has been observed in connection with different factors—L, M, N, O, P, Q, R, and so forth. Experiments are then planned in which various factors are eliminated, to test whether E will still occur. Suppose, for example, that L is eliminated but that E still occurs; then R and M are eliminated but E continues to occur. Because E still occurs, some or all of the remaining factors must constitute the necessary condition, but at least three possible factors have been eliminated.

☐ **THE METHOD OF DIFFERENCE**

To use Mill's methods to test the claim that a single factor is a sufficient condition, we must employ the method of difference. This method is based on the principle that nothing that was present when an event failed to occur can be a sufficient condition for the event. The method involves taking *one* positive instance and comparing it with others that are as like it as possible except that they are negative instances—instances in which the effect E does not occur. The objective is to show that the difference between the positive instance and the negative instances can be explained only by the presence of one other factor in the positive instance—the sufficient condition being sought.

The test is set up by listing the positive instance with its other characteristics, followed by the negative instances with their observed characteristics—as in Table 11-2. Any factor that appears in a negative instance cannot be a sufficient condition for E. So negative instances are selected in a way that will successively eliminate possible sufficient conditions. The example in the table

TABLE 11-2 *The method of difference*

INSTANCE	FACTORS OTHER THAN E
Positive Instance (containing *E*)	*P Q R S*
Negative Instance 1 (not containing *E*)	*P R T U*
Negative Instance 2	*P R T U*
Negative Instance 3	*P Q T U*

corroborates the hypothesis that *S* is a sufficient condition for *E* because *E* occurs only when *S* is present and does not occur when *S* is absent.

The method of difference has been used extensively to test the hypothesis—based on research showing that the tar from tobacco contains carcinogens—that cigarette smoking causes lung cancer. Because this is a causal claim about the difference between the rate of lung cancer for smokers and the rate of lung cancer for nonsmokers, the positive and negative instances must consist of *groups* rather than particular individuals. The positive instance must consist of a group of smokers with a certain incidence of lung cancer. The rate of lung cancer among members of this group must be compared with the incidence of the disease among groups of nonsmokers who are otherwise as like the first group as possible. Suppose, for example, that the positive instance consists of a group of male smokers, fifty to sixty-nine years of age, who live in small towns, and who are all white-collar professionals. Each of the negative instances would be a group with a significantly lower rate of lung cancer. The first negative instance would consist of a group with a lower rate of lung cancer who are as like the first group as possible except that they do not smoke. The second negative instance will vary by one other factor—say, age. The third and fourth groups would also differ by one factor each—say, place of residence and occupation. Each subsequent instance of a group of nonsmokers would also differ by one factor until all possible relevant factors had been considered.

Studies of this kind do show that smoking is a sufficient condition for lung cancer: the incidence among smokers is greater than the incidence among nonsmokers even if the groups are the same with respect to all other relevant characteristics. It does not show that smoking is the *only* sufficient condition for lung cancer; an effect may have more than one sufficient cause. But this does not undermine the evidence against smoking.

☐ THE JOINT METHOD OF AGREEMENT AND DIFFERENCE

A condition that is both necessary and sufficient can be identified by jointly applying the method of agreement and the method of difference. For example, Semmelweis's investigation, although it was not described in Section 11-2 in terms of Mill's methods, can be seen to conform to a joint use of the two methods. The method of agreement would show that examinations performed by medical students with contaminated hands was a necessary condition for the higher death rate. The positive instances all have this factor in common. The method of difference would show that the necessary condition was also a sufficient condition—that is, after the medical students were required to wash their hands in chlorinated lime, the death rate was lowered, and this was the only relevant change in the circumstances.

☐ THE METHOD OF CONCOMITANT VARIATION

Mill intended the method of concomitant variation to be used in circumstances in which the process of elimination employed by the preceding methods is of no avail. Mill's own example concerned the hypothesis that the gravitational attraction of the moon causes the rise and fall of the tides. He pointed out that the method of agreement cannot be used because the proximity of the moon at high tide is not the only circumstance present in all cases of high tide; the fixed stars are also present and cannot be eliminated. And the method of difference cannot be used because we cannot eliminate the moon from the heavens. Mill noted, however, that a different method can be employed: "When we find that all the variations in the *position* of the moon are followed by corresponding variations in the time and place of high water, the place being always either the part of the earth which is nearest to, or that which is most remote from, the moon, we have ample evidence that the moon is, wholly or partially, the cause which determines the tides."[7]

Thus, the method of concomitant variation can be used when it is not possible to find instances that are similar or that differ by only one factor. But it can be used only when the intensity of the effect can be positively correlated with the intensity of a single factor. If a factor is present in all cases in which a certain effect is observed, then the more closely its variations in degree are correlated with the variations in the degree of the effect, the greater is the probability that this factor is a cause of the effect.

Use of this method is illustrated in Table 11-3, where plus and minus signs

TABLE 11-3 *The method of concomitant variation*

INSTANCE	DEGREE OF EFFECT E	FACTORS OTHER THAN E
Instance 1	E	$S\ T\ U\ V$
Instance 2	E^+	$S\ T\ U\ V^+$
Instance 3	E^-	$S\ T\ U\ V^-$

[7] *A System of Logic*, Book III, Chapter 8, Section 6.

TABLE 11-4   *Application of the method of concomitant variation*

INSTANCE	DEGREE OF EFFECT E: LUNG CANCER DEATH RATE PER 100,000 MEN PER YEAR	FACTORS OTHER THAN E: QUANTITY OF CIGARETTES SMOKED DAILY
1	3.4	None
2	51.4	Less than one-half pack
3	59.3	One-half to one pack
4	143.9	One to two packs
5	217.3	More than two packs

Source: E. C. Hammond and D. Horn, "Smoking and Death Rates," *Journal of the American Medical Association* 166 (1958).

indicate the greater or lesser degree to which a varying phenomenon is present in a given situation.

Because the evidence shows that the factor represented by V varies directly with variations in the effect E, we can accept the evidence as corroborating the hypothesis that factor V is a cause of E. But the method of concomitant variation cannot tell whether V is a necessary or a sufficient condition, or both, for E. Its usefulness resides in allowing us to test causal hypotheses when the method of agreement and the method of difference cannot be used.

The method of concomitant variation can also be used as an additional test for hypotheses that can be tested by the other methods. For example, the incidence of lung cancer has been found to vary according to the number of cigarettes smoked. This evidence is presented in Table 11-4.

☐ **THE METHOD OF RESIDUES**

Mill also proposed a fourth method, which he called the method of residues. However, this does not comprise an independent *test* for causal hypotheses. Instead, the method should be thought of as a way of organizing evidence in order to discover or formulate hypotheses to be tested. In brief, the method of residues states that if known factors cause only part of an effect, then that part of the effect left over—the residue—is to be accounted for by an additional factor that was not previously considered.

☐ **IDENTIFYING RELEVANT FACTORS**

Before either the method of agreement or the method of difference can be effective, there must be reason to assume that one and only one of the possible causal factors listed as L, M, N, O, P, Q, R, and so forth is the cause of the effect in question. The method of agreement requires that the instances observed have only one relevant factor in common. The method of differences requires the instances to differ by only one relevant factor.

These requirements, in turn, make it necessary to identify relevant factors with care. In studying the effects of cigarette smoking, for example, researchers do not take account of educational attainment, national origin, or height and weight because the background information about cancer suggests that these factors are not related to the disease, whereas other factors are. In addition, the choice of factors to examine is determined by the analysis of the problem at hand. Semmelweis, by defining the problem as the cause of the higher rate of childbed fever in the First Division, was able to rule out such factors as general medical care, diet, and "epidemic influences." He knew that the sufficient condition for the higher rate of childbed fever in the First Division must be a factor that was not present among the Second Division cases. Finally, he was guided by the death of his colleague to the hypothesis that contamination from cadaveric matter was not only a relevant factor but a necessary condition for the higher death rate. Thus, Mill's methods can be successfully employed only when background information or tentative hypotheses indicate which factors are to be treated as relevant to a specified effect.

As a practical matter, we should ask ourselves two questions whenever we want to employ Mill's methods:

1. *Have we correctly identified all of the relevant factors?* An example of the failure to identify all the relevant factors is provided by a professor's conclusion—based on the method of agreement—that studying calculus causes students to perform better in other subjects. The professor had noticed that a consistently high proportion of the A students in the department's introductory courses either had studied calculus or were studying it during the current semester. A high percentage of A students in introductory courses given by colleagues in other departments were also found to have studied calculus. But the professor did not consider two factors, either of which could be the real cause of the higher academic performance: students who take calculus and compete for As may be more highly motivated as a group, or many of them may have entered college with higher SAT scores.

2. *Have we correctly analyzed the situation into a set of distinct causal factors?* A failure to distinguish between possible causal factors was involved in a controversy over the so-called XYY syndrome. Investigations conducted in maximum-security prisons revealed that 3.5 percent of the prisoners who had committed crimes of violence had a genetic abnormality known as the XYY chromosome. This was held to be a statistically significant proportion of the criminal population, since the incidence of the genetic abnormality in the general noncriminal population is roughly 0.1 percent. Some behavioral scientists went on to claim that the extra Y chromosome in these males was a cause of the violence for which they had been incarcerated.

Most social behaviorists now believe that in making this assessment, the antecedent circumstances had not been adequately analyzed, because there are other differences between normal XY males and XYY males. The latter group is less intelligent, on the average, and they share physical features—such as large size and severe acne—that frequently create an unattractive appearance. It therefore seems more probable that the cause of antisocial behavior in these individuals is not the extra Y chromosome but *society's re-*

sponse to the physical characteristics associated with this genetic anomaly. As one social scientist put it, "Under the pressures of unfavorable social conditions, as juveniles, adolescents, or adults, such males may find themselves selectively nurtured in environments encouraging physical aggression as a means of adaptation."[8]

□ *Causal fallacies*

Two patterns of fallacious reasoning about causal connections are so common that they require special attention. They are the *post hoc fallacy* and the *fallacy of confusing causes and correlations*.

The Quaker's Coat

[A] Quaker . . . shipowner, being disturbed by the profanity of one of his workmen, said to him one day, "Jack, I think if thee should wear my coat for a week, thee might cure thyself of the habit of swearing." Jack agreed to try it, and on returning the coat at the end of the week, the Quaker asked, "Well, Friend Jack, did thee have any inclination to swear while thee was wearing my coat?" "No," said Jack, "but I did have a terrible hankerin' to lie."

WILLIAM F. MACY, *The Nantucket Scrap Basket* (New York: Houghton Mifflin, 1930), p. 33.

□ THE POST HOC FALLACY

The *post hoc* fallacy derives its name from the Latin phrase, *post hoc, ergo propter hoc*, which means, "after this, therefore because of this." The fallacy is the assumption that because event B happened after event A, it must have happened as the effect of event A—that the sequence of events by itself establishes a causal relationship.

Many superstitious beliefs are based on the *post hoc* fallacy. Accidents are attributed to having broken a mirror, or having walked under a ladder, or having had a black cat cross one's path. A basketball team breaks a losing streak after the players start to wear new uniforms, and a sports commentator on the evening news says "there must be some magic in those new uniforms they're wearing."

---

[8] Ashley Montagu, *The Nature of Human Aggression* (New York: Oxford University Press, 1976), pp. 220–221. See also John L. Hamerton and Park S. Gerald, "Studies Cast More Doubt on 'Criminal Gene' Idea," *Journal of the American Medical Association* 230 (1974): 655–658.

The *post hoc* fallacy is common in political rhetoric as well. During the 1976 presidential campaign, for example, Gerald Ford, who was running for reelection, declared, "Since I came to office the inflation rate has dropped to 6 percent." "Since Gerald Ford took office," countered challenger Jimmy Carter, "the unemployment rate has risen 50 percent."

☐ CONFUSING CAUSES AND CORRELATIONS

Two factors can be regularly correlated—one factor may vary directly or inversely with another—without a causal relation holding between them. For example, nearly perfect correlations exist between the death rate in Hyderabad, India, from 1911 to 1919 and variations in the membership of the International Association of Machinists during the same period, but no one would consider these correlations to be anything more than a coincidence.[9] If X and Y occur together regularly, a number of possible hypotheses may explain the correlation: X may be the cause of Y, Y may be the cause of X, Z may be the cause of both X and Y, or there may merely be a coincidence between the occurrence of X and Y.

Some persons have attributed significance to the fact that since 1840, every American president elected in a year ending in zero has died in office—William Henry Harrison (1840), Abraham Lincoln (1860), James A. Garfield (1880), William McKinley (1900), Warren G. Harding (1920), Franklin D. Roosevelt (1940) and John F. Kennedy (1960). But this, too, is an example of mistakenly assuming that a correlation necessarily involves a causal connection. Given the great differences among the instances—ranging from the health of the president to the circumstances of death—it seems highly unlikely that there is a single underlying cause to be implicated in each case.

Dr. Lewis Thomas, president of Memorial Sloan-Kettering Cancer Center in New York City, commented on an interpretation of research data that seemed to involve the mistaking of correlations for causes.[10] In the late 1970s, Blue Cross placed prominent advertisements in major newspapers informing readers that they could add as many as eleven years to their life spans by adopting seven healthy habits:

1. Eating breakfast.
2. Exercising regularly.
3. Maintaining normal weight.
4. Not smoking cigarettes.
5. Not drinking excessively.
6. Sleeping eight hours each night.
7. Not eating between meals.

[9] Harold Larrabee, *Reliable Knowledge* (Boston: Houghton Mifflin, 1954), p. 368.
[10] See *The Medusa and the Snail: More Notes of a Biology Watcher* (New York: Viking Press, 1979), pp. 22–26.

The recommendations were based on an extensive study conducted by epidemiologists in California. The researchers had conducted a questionnaire survey about life-styles, gathering information from some 7,000 people. Five years later, county death certificates were obtained for those among the 7,000 who had died, and the answers given on the questionnaires of these 371 persons were then checked. The investigators found that there were many deaths among heavy smokers and heavy drinkers. They also found surprisingly high mortality rates among those who said they did not eat breakfast; those who slept poorly; those who were underweight; and those who took no exercise at all—not even by going off in the family car for weekend picnics.

Given the known incidence of lung cancer in smokers and of both cirrhosis of the liver and auto accidents among heavy drinkers, it is reasonable to assume a causal connection between high mortality rates and either heavy smoking or heavy drinking. But, as Dr. Thomas points out, it is hard to imagine that going without breakfast, sleeping poorly, being underweight, and failing to exercise could be *causes* of higher mortality rates. In fact, it is more likely these factors were the *effects* of illness or disease.

Among the 7,000 who answered that they did not eat breakfast, slept poorly, were underweight, and did not go off on picnics, some must already have been ill when they filled out their questionnaires. Hypertension, undetected cancer, early kidney failure, and other organic diseases could explain the symptoms they described. The researchers did not ascertain the cause of death in the group of 371, and the questionnaire had no way of detecting undiagnosed diseases. Yet, just a few deaths from undetected disorders would have made a significant statistical impact on the results. While those who had conducted the research were careful to note alternative explanations for these correlations, the Blue Cross advertisements treated the "seven health habits" as if they were *causes* of longer life.

■ **EXERCISE 11-3**

■ A. Answer each of the following questions, assuming ordinary circumstances. Explain your answers.

    1. Are clouds a necessary condition for rain? A sufficient condition for rain?

    2. Is oxygen a necessary condition for life? A sufficient condition for life?

    3. Are worn tire treads a necessary condition for a car's skidding? A sufficient condition?

    *4. Is oxygen a necessary condition for lighting a match? A sufficient condition?

    5. Is being a male a sufficient condition for being a hemophiliac? A necessary condition?

    6. Are streptococcal bacteria a necessary condition for scarlet fever? A sufficient condition?

    7. Is being shot in the heart a necessary condition for death? A sufficient condition?

*8. Is being a woman a sufficient condition for bearing a child? A necessary condition?

9. Is desiring to see a movie a sufficient condition for seeing one? A necessary condition?

10. Is making a higher income a sufficient condition for paying more taxes? A necessary condition?

■ B. For each of the following passages (a) identify the causal hypothesis being tested and (b) indicate which of Mill's methods is being used. (Choices: agreement, difference, concomitant variation, and both agreement and difference)

1. After visiting East Africa and observing the herbal remedies of medicine men, a chemist from the University of California has isolated a promising antibiotic from an African plant. Dr. Isao Kubo visited a number of rural villages in East Africa and saw entire tribes line up to drink a tea to ward off cholera. The tea was made from the fruit of the *Maesa lanceolata* bush, and Dr. Kubo judged from the low rate of cholera in the villages that it probably worked.

Back in his laboratory in Berkeley, Dr. Kubo discovered that the active ingredient was a chemical named maesanin. He gave it to mice who were then exposed to a normally lethal strain of bacteria. The mice survived with no sign of infection. Dr. Kubo believes that after further tests, maesanin can be used to combat cholera, urinary-tract infections, and other bacterial diseases.—*Science* 83 4 (June 1983)

2. Medical researchers at Harvard University and Tufts University have discovered that stress depletes a person's immune system. Researchers, led by psychologist John B. Jemmott, measured the production of an immunoglobulin in sixty-four dental students during the first year of an accelerated three-year curriculum. Immunoglobulin-A or IgA is an enzyme in saliva that fends off viruses such as those that cause colds.

The level of IgA dropped in all of the students during the academic year, and reached a low in April when they had a particularly difficult exam on crowns and bridges. The researchers also discovered that the students who were least satisfied with their work, even though they did as well or better than others, had the lowest amounts of IgA. By contrast, students with close personal relationships had consistently higher IgA levels, and those who were most relaxed about the challenges of the curriculum had the highest IgA levels.—*Science* 83 4 (September 1983)

3. At an automobile assembly plant, an outbreak of food poisoning occurred among employees who had eaten at the company cafeteria. All the ill employees said that they had first noticed symptoms several hours after lunch on Monday. The director of the plant's health clinic announced that the probable cause of the food poisoning had been the beef stew served Monday at the lunch hour. The director supported this claim by interviewing four employees suffering from the malady. The first worker had eaten vegetable soup, salad, beef stew, and apple pie. The second employee had consumed chocolate milk, beef stew, and fruit. The third had eaten cottage cheese, lima beans, beef stew, and ice cream; and the fourth had eaten vegetable soup, beef stew, iced tea, and apple pie.

*4. Scientists have identified heredity, diet, smoking, and stress as factors increasing the likelihood of heart disease. Some Norwegian scientists screened ten thousand fellow Norwegians who had heart attacks between 1971 and 1975. They found that seventy-eight individuals in this group had a living identical twin sibling who had not suffered a heart attack. They undertook an intensive study of the social environment, life-styles, and physical conditions of these twins. In an initial report on about one-half of the group, they found that the primary difference between those who had had heart attacks and the twins who had not suffered one was the degree of stress in the life-styles of the heart victims.—*Science News* 112 (September 10, 1977).

5. Does formal reasoning describe natural adult reasoning, or is it a special set of skills that are acquired from formal education? The psychologist Jean Piaget believed that formal reasoning was a universal outgrowth of everyday life experiences. However, researchers are finding increasing evidence that people in preliterate cultures are not inclined to follow the rules of formal logic.

Preliterate peoples in the cultures studied do only slightly better than chance in their answers to questions about the validity of simple syllogisms. By contrast, the great majority of literate people in Western cultures answer correctly. Researchers in Liberia and the Yucatan found that as little as two years of schooling produces a sharp rise in the ability of people to give correct answers to syllogisms. The more schooling people have had, the better they are at it, and those who have gone as far as high school in each culture answer correctly in the majority of cases.

For instance, psychologist Sylvia Scribner puts this syllogism to Vai villagers in Liberia: "All people who own houses pay a house tax; Boima does not pay a house tax; does Boima own a house?" Those Vai who had gone to school gave logical answers such as, "If you say Boima does not pay a house tax, he cannot own a house." But illiterate villagers were more apt to suppose that Boima did own a house and to look for ways to maintain this stance. "Boima does not have the money to pay a house tax," one said, while another made up a justification: "Boima has a house, but the government appointed Boima to collect the house tax so they exempted him from paying the house tax."

From evidence such as this, Scribner and her colleagues conclude that formal education increases one's ability to give correct answers to syllogisms. Schooling disciplines people to accept the ground rules of logic, especially the rule that says: base your answer on the terms defined by the questioner. Nonschooled people, not having been trained in this special way, rely on personal knowledge that they insist on adding to the premises given them. Preliterate people also reject syllogisms with premises they find unreasonable, or find rationales to help them reach a conclusion they consider sensible.—Morton Hunt, *The Universe Within: A New Science Explores the Human Mind* (New York: Simon and Schuster, 1982).

6. The low incidence of heart-disease deaths among Japanese men—only 92 per 100,000—compared with 378 per 100,000 in the United States, has long been attributed to the low-fat, fish-and-rice Japanese diet. However, researchers at the University of California at Berkeley now believe that stress is probably the cause of the difference.

In a ten-year study, 3,809 Japanese-American men living in the San Francisco Bay area were given a twenty-four-page questionnaire dealing with their backgrounds and life-styles. They were asked about the number of years they had spent in Japan, whether they had attended Japanese or American schools, and the religion they practiced. They also described their diet, exercise, and smoking habits. Finally, they received physical examinations.

When the data were analyzed, it was found that the men who maintained traditional Japanese cultural behavior—staying in a close-knit group, leading quiet lives, and being noncompetitive—had by far the lowest number of coronaries. Even the traditionalists who had adopted high-fat diets seemed to fare well. But those who had opted for the more aggressive and competitive American way of life had paid the price.

The study concluded that Japanese-Americans who made a moderate transition to Western ways suffered two-and-a-half times as many heart attacks as the traditionalists. Among those who had become fully "Americanized," the rate was five times as high.—*Nature/Science Annual*, Jane D. Alexander, ed. (New York: Time-Life Books, 1977), p. 177.

7. The male hormone testosterone, long a suspected factor in heart attacks and strokes, was implicated further by researchers at Georgetown University. They reported in June 1976 on tests in which they first induced blood clots—the actual cause of strokes and many heart attacks—in rats' arteries by inserting plastic loops into them.

Both the size of the blood clots and the rate of death from them were greater for young male rats than for young females but about the same for older rats of both sexes— a situation that is roughly parallel with the effects of blood clots in humans. In the next step, the researchers injected male hormones into one group of rats, female hormones into another, and then induced clots in these two groups and in a control group that had received no injections.

Both the female rats and the male rats in the group that received the male hormone grew larger clots and suffered a fourfold increase over the control group in the death rate. However, there was no increase in death rate in the group given female hormones, and an actual decrease in clot size among the males in the latter group. When an agent that inactivates male hormones was administered to another group of rats that had been injected with testosterone, their death rate was cut in half.—*Nature/Science Annual*, Jane D. Alexander, ed., (Alexandria, Virginia: Time-Life Books, 1978), p. 180.

*8. You can prove that the tightness of a violin string is the cause of the higher pitch it makes when it is vibrated, for the more tightly you draw the string on the violin, the higher is the pitch when the string is played.

9. Psychiatric researchers have found that the drug, Vasopressin, now in use for a number of ailments, can also improve memory. In experiments conducted at the National Institutes of Mental Health, eighteen college students were found to improve their memory on tests involving unrelated words when they were given Vasopressin. The students improved their performance by an average of 20 percent after they had taken the drug.

The researchers also tested four patients suffering from depression. Their before-test memory scores were lower than average for persons of their age. After being given Vasopressin, they improved 50 percent on words in one category and almost 100 percent on a third word-recall test. In addition, the drug was given to three patients about to undergo electroshock therapy. All three improved their recall of words by 300 percent, with a higher-than-usual statistical reliability. (Note: The drug is prescribed to constrict blood vessels or help the kidneys retain water. It is considered to have dangerous effects on healthy individuals.)—*The Washington Post*, January 31, 1981.

10. The inhabitants of Utah are among the healthiest in the United States while the residents of Nevada are at the opposite end of the spectrum. Infant mortality is about 40 percent higher in Nevada. What's more, the mortality rate in Nevada exceeds the mortality rate in Utah by a significant percentage for every age level. (For example, the differential in the age group twenty to thirty-nine is 44 percent for males and 42 percent for females; and in the age group forty to forty-nine, it is 54 percent for males and 69 percent for females.) However, the two states are very much alike with respect to income, schooling, degree of urbanization, climate, and many other variables. The number of physicians and of hospital beds per capita are also similar in the two states.

One explanation for the large difference in death rates has to do with differences in life-styles of the residents of the two states. Utah is inhabited primarily by Mormons, whose influence is strongly felt throughout the state. Devout Mormons do not use tobacco or alcohol and, in general, lead stable, quiet lives. Nevada, on the other hand, is a state with high rates of cigarette and alcohol consumption and very high indexes of marital and geographical instability. The contrast with Utah in these respects is extraordinary.—Victor R. Fuchs, *Who Shall Live?*

11. For an eight-year period, from 1948 to 1955, a careful study was made of the incidence of leukemia among the survivors of the atomic bombs dropped on Hiroshima and Nagasaki. These survivors were divided into four groups based on their distance from the hypocenter (the point on the surface of the earth directly below the bomb when it exploded). The first group, A, consisted of a very few survivors who were within 1 kilometer of the hypocenter. The second group, B, consisted of 13,730 survivors between 1.0 and 1.5 kilometers from the hypocenter; the third, C, of 23,060 between 1.5 and 2.0 kilometers; and the fourth, D, of the 156,400 over 2.0 kilometers from the hypocenter. During the eight-year study, the survivors in groups A, B, and C had been dying of leukemia at an average rate of 9 per year, and many more cases of leukemia occurred in the 15,600 survivors of groups A and B than in the 156,400 survivors of group D, who received much less radiation. The survivors of group A received an estimated average of 650 roentgens, those of group B, 250; those of group C, 25, and of group D, 2.5. The incidence of leukemia in the three populations A, B, and C was proportional to the estimated dose of radiation. The researchers thus attributed the increased incidence of leukemia to the exposure to radiation.—Linus Pauling, *No More War* (New York: Dodd, Mead & Company, 1983), pp. 97–98.

*12. A researcher at the University of Minnesota Medical School has suggested that eating black tree fungus—an ingredient of Chinese cooking—may be one reason why people in China have far less heart disease than do Westerners. Dr. Hammerschmidt believes that the flat, dark food somehow slows the natural tendency of the blood to form clots. The ingredient, known as *mo-er* to the Chinese, is often used in Szechuan and Mandarin dishes such as mooshi pork and hot-and-sour soup.

Dr. Hammerschmidt was intrigued to find that blood samples from a man participating in a medical experiment suddenly failed to clot normally. The subject's last meal had been a plate of Szechuan hot bean curd. Working on a hunch, Dr. Hammerschmidt contacted the chef who prepared the dish and asked the chef to prepare more hot bean curd for the original customer and three lab assistants. For the sake of comparison, four other people ate sweet-and-sour pork. Just as the doctor hoped, the blood of those who had eaten bean curd was very slow to clot, while the people who had eaten pork showed no change.

However, Dr. Hammerschmidt still was not sure whether the important ingredient was black tree fungus or a radishlike vegetable called *sar qort.* He therefore had his subjects eat the two ingredients straight, and the fungus turned out to be responsible.—*The Washington Post,* May 22, 1980.

13. An experiment was designed by psychologists to study the relation of stress to behavior. Students were divided into two groups. Group 1 was to complete twenty-six shopping tasks within a half-hour in a shopping center. Group 2 was to complete twice as many tasks within the same time. These two groups were then subdivided so that groups 1a and 2a were to complete their tasks during periods of crowded shopping conditions. But groups 1b and 2b were to complete their tasks during periods of low congestion in the shopping mall.

Each student was to begin the tasks at different times, and after completing the tasks, each student was to meet with an interviewer in a dimly lighted and deserted hallway in the mall. Upon arriving at the hallway, the student encountered a planted person who claimed to be searching for a lost contact lens. The design of the study was to determine how many students from each group would assist in searching for the lens.

No one from group 2a, with the greater number of shopping tasks to complete during crowded conditions, stopped to help look for the lens. About one-third of the students from groups 1a and 2b helped to look for the lens. But 80 percent of the students from group 1b, who completed fewer tasks during uncrowded conditions, helped to look for the lens.—*Science News* 112 (September 10, 1977).

14. Researchers studying the possible connection between XYY males—those possessing an extra Y chromosome—and men imprisoned for violent crimes, found an XYY rate of roughly 1 percent for inmates of several large penitentiaries. This is a statistically significant proportion of the criminal population, since the incidence of the abnormality in the noncriminal population is 0.1 percent, or one-tenth of the rate for the criminal population. However, the researchers also noted that XYY males tend to be taller and stronger, but less intelligent, than genetically normal males. They reasoned that larger suspects are more likely to be involved in violent acts just because they are more powerful, and less intelligent suspects are more likely to be caught and imprisoned. This suggested controlling for the variables of size and intelligence—studying men over six feet tall with IQs of less than 100. When this is done, the percentage of XYYs in the criminal group remains about 1 percent, but that in the noncriminal group increases to roughly 0.8 percent. This difference is not statistically significant.—*Science* 193 (August 13, 1976).

■ C. Read each of the following passages, and discuss the extent to which it reports a causal fallacy. Identify any fallacy committed, and briefly explain how it has come about.

1. When the treasure-laden tomb of the Egyptian pharaoh Tutankhamen was unearthed in 1922, some of the Egyptian natives warned of a 3,000-year-old curse: "Death shall come on swift wings to he who toucheth the tomb of a Pharaoh!" And the records show that the curse worked, for by 1929, twenty-two people associated with the opening of the tomb had perished.

2. A study of medical statistics shows that marriage is good for your health. The statistics show that death rates from all causes are lower among married persons than among the unmarried. In heart disease, lung cancer, and almost all other diseases, mortality rates are consistently highest among the divorced, next highest among single persons, and lowest among the married.

3. "Sex educators loudly proclaim that there is no relationship between their methods and promiscuity. Yet the facts are disheartening, to say the least. At a time when youngsters know more about sex than any preceding generation, we have more venereal disease, more teenage prostitution, more rape and generally, more sex-related problems than at any other time in history. If the advocates of sex education as now taught consider this an endorsement of their approach, then I think they're more in need of 'instruction' than their childish charges."—Donna W. Cross, *Word Abuse*, pp. 200–201.

*4. Researchers at the University of Ottawa sought to corroborate the hypothesis that the dreaming associated with rapid eye movement (REM) during sleep is essential to learning and long-term memory. The researchers found that among students who were enrolled in an intensive language course, those who were learning had an increase in REM sleep. Poor learners experienced no increase. One investigator concluded that students who stay up all night cramming for an examination are only hurting their chances of passing, since staying awake prevents learning.—*Nature/Science Annual*, Jane D. Alexander, ed., (Alexandria, Virginia: Time-Life Books, 1978), p. 169.

5. A major study reported by the Distilled Spirits Council of the United States concludes that a little alcohol may lead to safer driving. While the council certainly does not advocate drinking before driving, it nevertheless released statistics showing that accident rates among very light drinkers were "about 10 percent" lower than those among abstainers. The results were obtained by a research team which studied drivers' drinking habits by stopping, interviewing, and breath-testing nearly eight thousand drivers at accident-prone locations in Grand Rapids, Michigan. Researchers then went to accidents and hospitals to take breath tests on more than seven thousand drivers, both drinkers and nondrinkers, after crashes.—*The Washington Post*, March 7, 1981.

6. When Roger Babson was a young man, he contracted tuberculosis and was advised by his doctor to remain in the West, where he had gone to convalesce. He chose instead to return to his home in Wellesley Hills, Massachusetts. To insure an abundance of fresh air, he refused to close any of his windows. It is reported that during the freezing winter, he wore a coat with an electric heating pad attached to the back, and his secretary is said to have done her typing by wearing mittens and hitting the typewriter keys with rubber hammers. After his recovery, Babson became a fanatic on the subject of the medicinal value of fresh air. He advocated the early training of children to enjoy chilling air, and the construction of buildings with special designs, such as slightly sloping floors, to improve their ventilation and airflow.—Martin Gardner, *Fads and Fallacies in the Name of Science* (New York: Dover Publications, 1957)

7. Antoine Bechamp, a French chemist and contemporary of Pasteur, rejected the theory that many diseases are caused by bacteria. He contended that disease is not the result of the invasion of the body by harmful microbes. Rather, these microbes are the product of the disease. They develop within ailing body cells, but once sufficiently developed, they can be infectious.—Martin Gardner, *Fads and Fallacies in the Name of Science* (New York: Dover Publications, 1957)

*8. In the late 1950s, John T. Molloy, an instructor in a New England prep school, began to observe the connection between the kind of shoes a teacher wore and student performance. He noticed that an instructor who wore laced shoes seemed to get consistently better results than one who wore penny-loafers. Intrigued by this apparent connection, Molloy began to construct a number of experiments. He found that secretaries follow the directions of people whose dress and manner suggest position and authority more willingly than they do those of people with a shabby appearance. These observations are reported to have enabled Molloy to build a very successful wardrobe engineering consulting business.—*Time*, September 4, 1972 ■

☐ *Part four*

PRACTICAL REASONING

CHAPTER TWELVE

Fallacious reasoning

Although fallacious reasoning has been discussed earlier, the subject is such an important part of logic that it merits separate treatment. Being able to recognize fallacies and explain why they are fallacies is essential to forming intelligent judgments in everyday life. This skill also makes it possible to present one's own ideas effectively.

As noted earlier, the word *fallacy* in logic refers only to faulty argumentation:

A fallacy is any argument rendered defective by an error in reasoning.

It don't even make good nonsense.
DAVY CROCKETT
(remarking on a statement by President Andrew Jackson)

The identification and diagnosis of fallacious reasoning is a practical application of logic. Though a firm understanding of the principles of sound deduction and reliable inference can make one aware that an argument is flawed, it does not suffice for analyzing its defects. In fact, many fallacies are called *informal fallacies* because they cannot be detected through the use of formal rules and mechanical procedures.

Recognizing patterns of reasoning that habitually lead people astray calls for skills like those involved in recognizing arguments: the ability to make mature judgments, drawing on our awareness of language usage; the ability to fit an argument into context; and sensitivity to the arguer's intention or purpose. Studying fallacies is an investigation of the boundary between the legitimate and illegitimate use of argument.

Not only are there many kinds of fallacies but—as noted in earlier chapters—some have been recognized by so many generations of philosophers that

TABLE 12-1   *Categories of Fallacies*

CONDITION FOR A SOUND OR RELIABLE ARGUMENT	ARGUMENTS THAT FAIL TO MEET THESE CONDITIONS
It must be logically possible for the premises and the conclusion all to be true.	Fallacies of Inconsistency
It must be logically possible for the premises to be true independently of the conclusion.	Fallacies of Begging the Question
The link between premises and conclusion must be sufficient to support the conclusion to the required degree.	Fallacies of *Non Sequitur*

they have acquired specific names. The first great logician, Aristotle (374–322 B.C.), lists thirteen types of fallacies in his *Sophistical Refutations.* In recent decades, the list has been greatly expanded, and one book distinguishes fifty-one fallacies by name.[1]

There is little agreement among logicians as to how fallacies should be grouped, or classified. This is partly because of the inventiveness with which some people mislead themselves and others, and partly because a particular argument can often be defective in more than one way. Thus, any scheme for classifying fallacies must be flexible, allowing some fallacies to be placed in more than one category.

We will organize fallacies into three groups that indicate major ways in which an argument can be faulty.[2] Each group represents arguments that fail to meet one of three general conditions that must be satisfied if premises are to provide justification for a conclusion:

1. It must be logically possible for the premises and the conclusion all to be true—that is, they must not be contradictory or inconsistent.

2. It must be possible for the premises to be true independently of the conclusion—that is, the premises must provide one-directional support for the conclusion.

3. The connection between the premises and conclusion must be sufficient—that is, the premises must support the conclusion to the required degree.

Table 12-1 lists the three major groups of fallacies that result from violating these three conditions.

[1] Ward Fearnside and William B. Holther, *Fallacy: The Counterfeit of Argument* (Englewood Cliffs, N.J.: Prentice-Hall, 1959).
[2] This classification follows that given by Stephen F. Barker, *The Elements of Logic,* 2d ed. (New York: McGraw-Hill, 1980), p. 194.

□ 12-1. FALLACIES OF INCONSISTENCY

An argument is inconsistent if it contains statements that are logically related in such a way that they cannot all be true:

A fallacy of inconsistency is an argument in which either the premises or a premise and the conclusion contradict each other, or the premises are inconsistent.

Note that the term applies to *arguments*, and not to necessarily false, or self-contradictory, statements (discussed in Section 2-3). An example of a self-contradictory statement is the reply given by Napoleon the pig, in George Orwell's *Animal Farm*, to a question about why the pigs in the animals' new egalitarian society are living better than the other animals: "We are all of us equal, but some are more equal than others."

Neither does the term *fallacy of inconsistency* apply when a speaker or writer asserts one thing at one time and place and then speaks or acts in a way that contradicts it at another time and place. For example, while campaigning for Republican candidates in 1966, Richard Nixon said that President Johnson owed it to the American people to "come clean" and tell them exactly what his plans were for ending the Vietnam War: "The people should be told now, and not after the elections." But as a presidential candidate in 1968, Nixon declared that he had a "secret plan" to end the war and that "No one with this responsibility who is seeking office should give away any of his bargaining position in advance. . . . Under no circumstances should any man say what he would do next January."[3] Although these two viewpoints contradict each other, they are not presented within a single argument and consequently do not fit the definition of a fallacy.

An example of a fallacy of inconsistency—an argument in which the conclusion contradicts the premises—is this opening sentence of an essay on knowledge: "We cannot know anything, because we know that our senses are not reliable." Here the premise asserts that we can know something, which the conclusion denies.

Most fallacies of inconsistency are more complicated, however. The difficulty may involve a logical inconsistency between the premises that is not apparent on a first reading or hearing. Premises can be logically inconsistent without being flatly contradictory. *The stated premises are inconsistent if they imply pairs of consequences that are contradictories.*

The following is an example.

When it is passed, the Equal Rights Amendment will forbid anyone, whether in the government or private institutions, to allocate money and resources on

---

[3] Quoted by William G. Effros, *Quotations: Vietnam 1945–1970* (New York: Random House, 1970).

the basis of sex classification. Of course, the ERA will also require fair and equal treatment of the sexes in educational athletic programs. The ERA will require that athletic facilities and programs for women be brought up to par with those currently available for men. Thus, the ERA will bring to an end sex discrimination in athletics.

If the first premise is true (the ERA will forbid allocations of money and resources on the basis of sex classification), then it must also be true that equal expenditures will be made in educational and athletic programs for both sexes. (In the second sentence, it is asserted that the ERA requirements will apply specifically to education and athletics.) But if what is asserted in the third sentence is true (the ERA will require facilities and programs for women to be brought up to par with those existing for men), then it must also be true that greater expenditures will have to be made for women's facilities and programs—because they are not now on a par with those for men. Thus, the stated premises imply the contradictory pair of consequences that equal ex-

---

Socrates' Exchange with Thrasymachus

Listen then, said he. I say that the just is nothing else than the advantage of the stronger. . . .

I would first understand your meaning, said I, for I do not know it yet. You say that the advantage of the stronger is just. What do you mean, Thrasymachus? . . .

Do you not know, he said, that some cities are ruled by a despot, others by the people, and others again by the aristocracy? . . . and each government makes laws to its own advantage . . . and when they have made these laws they declare this to be just for their subjects, that is, their own advantage, and they punish him who transgresses the laws as lawless and unjust. This then, my good man, is what I say justice is, the same in all cities, the advantage of the established government, . . .

Now I see what you mean, I said. . . . Obviously, we must investigate whether what you say is true. . . .

Well, go on looking, he said.

We will do so, said I. Tell me, do you also agree that obedience to the rulers is just?

I do.

And are the rulers in all cities infallible, or are they liable to error?

No doubt they are liable to error.

When they undertake to make laws, therefore, they make some correctly and others incorrectly?

penditures will be made on athletics for both sexes and that equal expenditures will not be made on athletics for both sexes.

According to his famous pupil Plato, the philosopher Socrates (470?–399 B.C.) was expert at exposing inconsistencies in the beliefs of others. The quotation in the accompanying box is Plato's account—from *The Republic*—of Socrates' exchange of views about justice with the sophist Thrasymachus. Thrasymachus, who has been maintaining the thesis that "might makes right," asserts that justice is what is in the interest of the rulers. Socrates leads Thrasymachus to admit that it is always right for subjects to obey the strong individuals who rule them. He next has Thrasymachus concede that rulers are fallible; those in power may make mistakes—for example, they may lay down a law that does not really serve their interests. Now Socrates has Thrasymachus in a snare; the premises imply a pair of consequences that are contradictories: it is always right to do what is in the rulers' interest, and it is sometimes right not to do what is in the rulers' interest. Thrasymachus has committed a fallacy of inconsistency.

I think so.

"Correctly" means that they make laws to their own advantage, and "incorrectly" not to their own advantage. Or how would you put it?

As you do.

And whatever laws they make must be obeyed by their subjects, and this is just?

Of course.

Then, according to your argument, it is just to do not only what is to the advantage of the stronger, but also the opposite, what is not to their advantage.

What is that you are saying? he asked.

The same as you, I think, but let us examine it more fully. Have we not agreed that, in giving orders to their subjects, the rulers are sometimes in error as to what is best for themselves, yet it is just for their subjects to do whatever their rulers order. Is that much agreed?

I think so.

Think then also, said I, that you have agreed that it is just to do what is to the disadvantage of the rulers and the stronger whenever they unintentionally give orders which are bad for themselves, and you say it is just for the others to obey their given orders. Does it not of necessity follow, my wise Thrasymachus, that it is just to do the opposite of what you said? The weaker are then ordered to do what is to the disadvantage of the stronger.

Plato, The Republic, bk. 1, 338c–340, trans. G. M. A. Grube (Indianapolis: Hackett Publishing Company, 1974), pp. 12–14. Reprinted by permission of Hackett Publishing Company, Inc.

It was Socrates' conviction that a search for knowledge could not begin in earnest until one had sorted through one's beliefs to see if any of them were inconsistent or implied contradictory propositions. If two beliefs are contradictory, we know that one must be false—even if we do not know which one. It does not merely *happen* that contradictory statements cannot both be true; they *necessarily* cannot both be true. As noted in the discussion of paradoxes of entailment (Section 8-2), any statement whatsoever may be derived from a set of inconsistent premises. Thus, fallacies of inconsistency are not *deductively* invalid. But premises that can be used to support any conclusion whatsoever cannot serve as reasons for accepting any particular conclusion. Arguments with inconsistent premises do not provide grounds for affirming the *truth* of a conclusion.

■ **EXERCISE 12-1**

Decide whether each of the following passages contains a fallacy of inconsistency. For each fallacy, what inconsistency has occurred?

1. I'll give you two reasons why we shouldn't allow more Asian and Latin American refugees into the United States. In the first place, these refugees are taking away the declining number of unskilled jobs from native-born Americans. On top of that, we have to extend welfare and unemployment benefits to virtually all of them, and these benefits come from nowhere else but tax dollars earned by native-born citizens.

2. It's always socialistic for government to take over any job from free, private enterprise; to do so stifles people's initiative and forces everyone down to a stagnant level. Now, I'm not talking about things like education—we couldn't leave that to private enterprise, because many poorer kids couldn't get adequate schooling and grow up to become enterprising business and professional people if there were no state-supported schools. But I do say that socialism of any form is always harmful, and that's why government must leave medicine entirely in private hands.

3. In January 1977, the printers' union of the London *Times* went on strike for one day, making it impossible for the *Times* to publish. The underlying problem was that the union refused to set the type for an article the newspaper's editors wanted to carry in that issue. The members of the union refused to set a story that claimed that the printers' union practiced censorship.

*4. The descendants of the white races of Northern Europe have buit a society that is still economically sound and politically stable for all citizens of the United States. Now unemployed members of minority groups have become so numerous that they threaten to riot in our major cities. Thus, to keep what our forefathers have built, we must attempt to silence the malcontents through police power.

5. As a representative of the nuclear power industry, I want to assure you that problems at the Three Mile Island nuclear reactor were wildly exaggerated. The possibility of a catastrophic reactor incident is so slight that it should not worry reasonable men and women. Now, in answer to your question, it's true that the manufacturers of nuclear equipment would not build plants until the Price-Anderson Act of 1957 became law. So what? It was only wise and prudent for officials of these companies to wait for the law to take effect, because the law limits liability in a single nuclear accident to $560 million.

   6. A historian writes that President George Washington rejected a request from the House of Representatives that he turn over copies of instructions and other papers relating to the Jay Treaty of 1796. The historian explains that although Washington based his refusal on the ground that the House was not involved in the treaty-making process and that all the papers affecting the negotiations with Britain had already been laid before the Senate, Washington established a larger precedent that later presidents have used to deny information to the Senate as well as the House.

   7. "[Teachers should] show students that all knowledge is based on challengeable assumptions. (A mathematical proof has been developed that shows that it is impossible to develop a structure of knowledge that does not contain at least one unprovable first assumption.) Few students are aware of this harsh reality; most leave college believing that what they have learned in economics, sociology, political science, and psychology rests on some rational theoretical base, rather than in a nineteenth-century set of assumptions that have long ago been shown to be special cases."—Robert Theobald, *Beyond Despair*

   *8. In 1978, the United States Senate debated and then ratified the Panama Canal Treaty, which returns control of the canal to Panama and reverts complete ownership of the canal back to Panama by the year 2000. Before ratifying the treaty, however, the Senate adopted several amendments and reservations to it. One amendment stated that the United States has the right to take whatever action is necessary to keep the canal open but does not have the right to intervene in the internal affairs of Panama.

   9. God is the perfect being. This means that he is omniscient—he knows from all eternity everything that happens. He is beneficent, or all-good, and he is also omnipotent, or all-powerful. Now, I admit, as you say, that evil is an indisputable fact of life. But you must realize that God neither knows about nor can prevent this evil. God wills only good for humanity. But individuals choose to perform evil acts as well as good acts. Thus, humanity and never God is responsible for any evil that exists.

   10. Some people have been puzzled by the paintings of the great Spanish painter El Greco. The human figures he painted seem strangely distorted and unnaturally elongated and thin. One explanation has been that El Greco was strongly influenced by a school of painters called the Mannerists, who tended to render the human figure as elongated and distorted. However, a professor of art history argued against this hypothesis. He said that El Greco suffered from astigmatism, which caused him to see things in this strangely distorted manner. Thus, the professor concluded that El Greco was no Mannerist. Rather, he was a "realist" who painted things as he saw them. ∎

☐ 12-2. BEGGING THE QUESTION

I, a learned scholar
Am asked the cause and
   reason why

Opium puts me to sleep.
To which I reply:
Because it possesses
A dormitive power
Whose nature it is
To make the senses drowsy.
MOLIÈRE, *LE MALADE IMAGINAIRE*

Begging the question violates the second rule of sound argumentation—
that it must be possible for the premises to be true independently of the conclusion. The premises must establish the probability of the conclusion, rather
than deriving their own plausibility from it.

**The fallacy of begging the question is an attempt to use the conclusion as part
of the evidence used to support that very same conclusion.**

In a fallacious argument of this sort, one is invited to assume that something has been *con*firmed when in fact it has only been *re*affirmed. The reader
or listener is in effect "begged" to accept the point in question—hence the
name, which is a translation of the Latin phrase *petitio principii*.

☐ *Circular reasoning*

A common version of the question-begging fallacy is *circular reasoning*. This
fallacy consists in either explicitly or implicitly asserting in one of the premises
of an argument what is asserted in its conclusion.

The fallacy is easy to detect when the argument contains only one premise,
but otherwise recognition can be difficult. When the conclusion appears as a
premise, it is usually disguised through a change of words. Sometimes, the
flawed premise is suppressed. Or there may be a number of steps between the
conclusion and the premise that lists the conclusion as its own reason.

A circular argument generally has the following form, although the length
of the chain can vary.

p is true because *q* is true.
q is true because *r* is true.
r is true because *p* is true.

Note that arguments that exemplify these fallacies are *formally* valid. It is
impossible for all the premises to be true and the conclusion false because the
conclusion *is* one of the premises (see Section 8-1). As indicated above, *p* is
both the conclusion and a premise.

Here are some examples of circular reasoning:

1.   Free trade will be good for this country. The reason is patently clear. Isn't it obvious that unrestricted commercial relations will bestow on all sections of this country the benefits that result when there is an unimpeded flow of goods between countries?

This argument is circular because *free trade, unrestricted commercial relations,* and *unimpeded flow of goods* all have the same meaning. A paraphrase of the reasoning would be "Free trade will bestow the benefits of free trade; therefore, free trade will be beneficial."

2.   The ancient philosopher Sextus Empiricus had an argument for the existence of the gods. He argued that you do not serve the centaurs because the centaurs are nonexistent. However, you do serve the gods. Thus, the gods certainly exist, or else you could not serve them.[4]

Argument (2) contains two subarguments. One is about centaurs: "Centaurs do not exist; therefore, one does not serve them." The second subargument, about the gods, is an enthymeme (see Section 1-4). The missing premise, "If you can serve something, that thing must exist," must be supplied to make it plausible. But this is precisely what Sextus Empiricus needs to prove.

3.   Cheating on exams is wrong. Why? Because anything that violates the moral code is wrong, and cheating violates the moral code. The moral code? That is what tells you what is right and wrong.

Argument (3) is an extended version of a circular argument. In it, the conclusion is reintroduced as a reason for accepting a statement that, in turn, had been offered as a reason for the conclusion. Paraphrased, the argument is "Cheating is wrong because it violates the code that tells us that cheating is wrong."

□ *Question-begging expressions*

Question-begging expressions are terms or phrases that appear merely descriptive but actually imply a position on the very question at issue. Such an expression occurs in the following argument presented by a lawyer to a jury:

You cannot let this man go free, because your sister, or daughter, may be his next victim.

By using the phrase *his next victim,* the lawyer assumes that the defendant is in fact a criminal—which is precisely what must be proved.

Often a question-begging expression does not occur in an explicit argu-

---

[4] Adapted from W. Fearnside and W. Holther, *Fallacy: The Counterfeit of Argument,* p. 166.

ment but takes the form of an *epithet*:

> An epithet is a descriptive word or phrase used to characterize a person, a thing, or an idea.

The listener is "begged" to infer a particular conclusion, although no reasons are presented for doing so. Instead, slanted language is used to present an opinion, value judgment, or attitude as if it were a matter of established fact. In the following examples, the epithets are in italics:

> QUESTION: Can Willard be depended on?
> WILLARD: You mean *old reliable* me?
> No *right-thinking* American could support this measure.
> The governor's *shocking* proposal is calculated to subvert the *just aspirations* of hard-working men and women.

The earlier discussions of emotive meaning (Section 3-2) and the pitfalls of language (Section 3-3) provide details of how linguistic devices such as question-begging epithets work and why people are sometimes influenced by them.

□ *Complex questions*

Sometimes known as a "loaded" question, a *complex question* is formulated so as to create the impression that a prior question has already been answered. It begs the question because it attempts to force a respondent to grant an assumption that is itself in need of proof. For example, asking "Have you given up your vicious habits?" conveys the impression that the person addressed has previously acknowledged such habits.

Because a complex question consists of two or more questions disguised as one, it cannot be properly answered by a simple "yes" or "no." Here are additional examples:

> Why are the students in this class more intelligent than other students in the university?
> What are your views on the token efforts made by the administration to respond to the demand that a student be elected to the board of trustees?
> Did you cheat by copying from your neighbor or by smuggling in your notes?

Anyone confronted with a complex question should point out that an assumption is embedded in it and should insist that its parts be distinguished and each part addressed separately.

A *leading question* is a special case of complex question. In addition to being "loaded" with a presumed answer, it also suggests, or "plants," a proposed response. Leading questions often take the form of a declarative sentence with

"Shoe" by Jeff MacNelly. © Jefferson Communications, Inc., 1980. Reprinted by permission.

a query tacked onto the end:

You didn't really intend to hurt that litte boy, did you?

Judges often rule such questions out of order when attorneys use them in examining witnesses. A defense lawyer might address a defendant in the following manner: "You were told that the car you drove across town belonged to your friend, were you not?" Here the attorney is assuming a position on the very question at issue—namely, whether the defendant (1) was an accessory to theft by receiving a stolen automobile or (2) innocently borrowed an automobile that was thought to belong to an acquaintance. The prosecuting attorney is likely to protest to the judge that the defense attorney is "leading the witness."

☐ Invincible ignorance

The *fallacy of invincible ignorance* occurs when someone argues that new evidence need not be considered because he or she knows in advance that it is irrelevant to the truth or falsity of a belief. The arguer is convinced, *prior* to investigation, that the truth of a certain belief is established. And any counterevidence that might be offered is explained in a way that preserves the belief.

Fallacies of invincible ignorance are forms of begging the question because, like circular arguments, they fail to provide support for the conclusion. The premises merely assert that the conclusion is true beyond doubt.

Some cases of invincible ignorance involve circular definitions (see Section 4-5). The arguer attempts to make the claim at issue "true by definition" and thereby to settle what is really an empirical issue. It is reported, for example, that in 1951 Red China's General Wu appeared before the Assembly of the United Nations to deny that China was an aggressor in Korea. "It cannot possibly be so," he said. "Why not?" he was asked. "Because my government, *by definition*, is a peace-loving nation."[5]

A seventeenth-century example of this fallacy was the reaction of Galileo's

[5] Stuart Chase, *Guides to Straight Thinking* (New York: Harper & Row, 1956), p. 127.

colleagues at the University of Padua to his discovery, using the newly invented telescope, that the planet Jupiter has satellites. The discovery challenged the dominant astronomical theory that the earth was the center of the solar system. When invited by Galileo to look through the telescope and see the satellites for themselves, his colleagues refused. They *knew* that Jupiter could not have satellites; hence, the images he reportedly saw must have been caused by an imperfection in the lens of the telescope or by witchcraft or trickery. They argued that the whole universe illustrates the importance God attaches to the number seven. It was therefore sacrilegious and against all reason to suppose that there could be more than seven heavenly bodies:

> There are seven windows given to animals in the domicile of the head. . . . From this and many other similarities in nature, such as the seven metals, etc., which it were tedious to enumerate, we gather that the number of the planets is necessarily seven. Moreover, these [alleged] satellites of Jupiter are invisible to the naked eye, and therefore can exercise no influence on the earth, and therefore would be useless, and therefore do not exist. Besides, [from the earliest times, men] have adopted the division of the week into seven days, and have named them after the seven planets. Now, if we increase the number of the planets, this whole and beautiful system falls to the ground.[6]

☐ INVINCIBLE IGNORANCE AND SCIENTIFIC HYPOTHESES

Subtler versions of the fallacy of invincible ignorance sometimes occur in debates over scientific hypotheses. The fallacy can take either of two forms. In one form, a key concept is defined so broadly or ambiguously that even contrary evidence can be said to be covered by its meaning, creating what is called an *irrefutable hypothesis*. In the second form, an attempt is made to salvage a hypothesis by rationalizing, or "explaining away," a failed prediction—which is known as the sobriquet *ad hoc rescue*.

An irrefutable hypothesis appears to occur in the argument made by Robert Ardrey in his book *The Territorial Imperative*. Ardrey attempts to explain human warfare and aggression by arguing that human beings have an innate compulsion to gain and defend territory. This "territorial imperative" is said to be no different from the territorial instincts that motivate other animals. Early in his book, Ardrey makes it clear that he accepts the general scientific consensus that an instinct is a fixed-action pattern that causes an organism to react to a given stimulus with a predetermined behavior; it is "the genetically determined pattern which informs an animal how to act in a given situation."[7]

As Ardrey's argument unfolds, he must continually face adverse evidence. Two kinds of data are most damaging to his theory. Many studies suggest that aggression is often an adaptation to specific environmental stimuli and not an

---

[6] W. T. Sedgwick and H. W. Tyler, *A Short History of Science* (New York: Macmillan, 1917), pp. 222–223.
[7] Robert Ardrey, *The Territorial Imperative* (New York: Atheneum, 1966), p. 29.

instinctive reaction. Other research indicates that territorial behavior, at least in the "higher" animals, is not instinctive, but is rather learned social behavior.

To accommodate this unfavorable evidence, Ardrey redefines his concept of instinct. The fixed-action patterns of organisms are now described as "closed instincts," while "open instincts" are characterized as those that complete their innate patterns only by gaining information from individual experience. By thus reworking the concept of instinct, Ardrey is able to explain human behavior as diverse as war, patriotism, international politics and diplomacy, labor confrontations, debates, street fights, and athletic competitions. But explaining all these unstructured activities as instinctive is inconsistent with the generally accepted definition of an instinct as a fixed-action pattern.[8]

Ad hoc rescue involves the invention of an assumption to explain why a prediction has failed. Instead of concluding on the basis of the failure that the hypothesis is probably false, the investigator maintains that it is true and that the original set of auxiliary assumptions was at fault. (See Section 11-2 for a discussion of auxiliary assumptions.) In scientific research, revising auxiliary assumptions is acceptable up to a point. Before conducting an experiment, a scientist cannot always be expected to identify all the factors that may affect the outcome. But when revisions are consistently used to discredit evidence that would otherwise refute the hypothesis, it is reasonable to suspect that the investigator is simply refusing to acknowledge the weight of contrary evidence.

An example of the *ad hoc* rescue is provided by the research of the nineteenth-century scientist Paul Broca (1824–1880). Broca made a number of lasting contributions to both medicine and anthropology, but he was also the leading European exponent of a theory about the relationship between brain size and intelligence that was subsequently discarded. He maintained that higher intelligence was the consequence of having a larger brain, as indicated by the size and shape of the skull. And he argued that the mental capacities of races and individuals could be determined by measuring their skulls. Broca predicted that members of the white race would be found to have larger brains than members of other races, that men would have larger brains than women, that the intellectually and culturally distinguished would have larger brains than those less distinguished, and that middle-class people would have larger brains than members of the lower classes.

The evidence showed that there was no positive correlation between brain size and intellectual development or accomplishment and that there were no differences in brain sizes among races, sexes, or classes that were not simply the result of differences in body size. Broca responded with a series of *ad hoc* explanations. For example, when investigators showed him evidence that some very eminent professors had small brains, he changed an auxiliary assumption by introducing corrections for age and postulated disease. He then decided that a "professional robe" was not a mark of intellectual distinction after all. Finally, when confronted with cranial measurements placing blacks higher

[8] This discussion is based on that of Ashley Montagu, *The Nature of Human Aggression* (New York: Oxford University Press, 1976), p. 257.

than whites, he decided that those measurements were not of scientific interest after all.[9]

■ EXERCISE 12-2

Explain why each of the following passages should be regarded as an example of begging the question. Assign the name that best describes the version of the fallacy that is involved.

1. How much longer are you going to waste your time in graduate school when you might be giving better care to your young daughter and be more supportive of your spouse? If you had a stronger sense of responsibility, you would quit school immediately.

2. Art and music are a waste of time. Why? Because they don't make any money. But, you ask, aren't there other values than those of money-making? Those other values are worth nothing because they are a waste of time.

3. My reason for opposing capital punishment is perfectly clear, for capital punishment is nothing more than legalized killing.

*4. Did your grades improve as a result of copying the work of your roommates? You answer the question by saying "No." So you admit that you copied their work. Don't you know that this academic dishonesty could lead to your expulsion?

5. "What a brain! And you know how to prove things, like the big shots?

"Yeah, I have a special method for that. Ask me to prove something for you, something real hard."

"All right, prove to me that giraffes go up in elevators."

"Let's see. Giraffes go up in elevators . . . because they go up in elevators."

"God, that was great! . . . Suppose I asked you to prove giraffes *don't* go up in elevators."

"That's easy. I just prove the same thing, but the other way around."—Fernando Arrabal, *The Automobile Graveyard*

6. "There isn't any mincing, lackadaisical, pink-pantied gigolo going to dethrone John L. in his own convention!"—Labor leader John L. Lewis, *Time*, September 25, 1944

7. Because democracy is the best form of government, it should be preserved. To preserve it, we must be prepared to fight for such principles as freedom of speech and freedom of worship. Because such freedoms are worth fighting for, it is evident that democracy is the best form of government.

*8. When two self-styled flying-saucer "experts" were asked why there was no detection by radar of the flying saucers they had sighted, they replied that flying saucers were made of a metal that radar could not detect.

9. The attorney brought out the fact that the woman had worked in numerous bars and had several after-hours jobs. The attorney then asked the question, "Didn't you ever think of becoming a respectable woman and quitting these jobs?"

10. Ruth's attitude of superiority regarding her friends arises from an inferiority complex, for all such attitudes of superiority arise from this source, as Ruth's case proves.

---

[9] Broca's research is critically analyzed in Stephen Jay Gould, *The Mismeasure of Man* (New York: W. W. Norton, 1981).

11. We are going to debate the issue of whether abortion is right or wrong in class today. It will be interesting to see whether anyone believes that murdering unborn children can be justified.

*__12.__ The twins would never harm anyone. I know my own children. They were always polite and thoughtful. We raised them right. They went to church with us every Sunday. No matter what evidence they cook up against the twins, I know they didn't attack anyone.

13. The dean of Buchanan College told a professor, Charles Smith, that a male student had requested permission to drop the course because of Smith's prejudiced attitude toward the student. Smith said he was astonished to hear this news because he had spoken to the student only twice—once to ask whether he was one of those students who was going to be habitually late for class and once, after the student had volunteered a comment in class, to ask why it was that some students were intent on challenging his authority. Smith ended his conversation with the dean by asking when the college intended to increase the staff at the student psychiatric counseling center.

14. Allowing people to compete among themselves is a necessary condition for great social achievement. The technical and economic progress of our free enterprise system is unique in the history of the world, and it would not be possible without the advances motivated by competition.

15. What is the correct explanation for mental telepathy?

*__16.__ President Richard Nixon's speechwriter Patrick Buchanan wrote a piece for the op-ed page of the *New York Times* on June 12, 1974, asserting that the Washington, D.C., grand jurors who voted to name the president an unindicted co-conspirator in the Watergate break-in were from "the most anti-Nixon city in the United States."

17. You don't want to continue with this irrelevant line of questioning, do you?

18. "How can we explain why the universe conforms to our intellectual desires?"— Norman Campbell

19. "Materialism cannot be true, for it is impossible to conceive the existence of matter if there is no mind to picture it."—T. H. Huxley

*__20.__ The world was not created by God; for matter has always existed and, there-fore, the world must have always existed.

21. "Miserable man and worm upon the earth that you are, ashes and food for worms, how can you confront the eternal wisdom with your unspeakable blasphemy? What foundation have you for this rash, insane, deplorable, accursed doctrine?"— Letter received by the philosopher Benedict Spinoza

22. Mary Jones, a lie-detector expert, announced the hypothesis that plants react to the thoughts of human beings in their vicinity. She claimed that these reactions can be registered on a device similar to a lie detector and attached to the plants. She also claimed that she had conducted many tests that confirmed this hypothesis. However, when the tests were repeated for a well-known plant physiologist, no such responses were observed. The lie-detector expert explained that nothing registered because the plants had "fainted," fearing that the plant physiologist might harm them. She pointed out that the plant physiologist was known to dissect and incinerate plants when doing experimental work.

23. Lying is morally wrong because it is unconditionally bad to state that which is not the truth.

*__24.__ During the Third Reich, German pseudo-anthropology and genetics made

much of the concept of race, and particularly the "Aryan race." According to Alfred Rosenberg, a leading philosopher of Nazism and the author of *The Myth of the Twentieth Century*, everything good about civilization was due to Aryan influence. Jesus Christ was even said to be an Aryan, although his views were supposedly corrupted by Jewish influences. When the Japanese became allies of Germany, they too were declared Aryan. A prominent Nazi journalist was discovered to have a grandmother who was a Sioux Indian. But after much anthropological deliberation, the Chamber of the Press ruled that Sioux Indians were officially Aryan.—Adapted from Martin Gardner, *Fads and Fallacies in the Name of Science* (New York: Dover Publications, 1957).

25. Everybody knows that it is the environment that turns some people into criminals. In the first place, individuals don't choose to pursue a life of crime; they are determined to do so by the slums and poverty in which they are conditioned. Second, it is clear that there is no inherited propensity to commit criminal acts.

26. "Dear Friend: I don't hate the homosexuals! But as a mother I must protect my children from their evil influence."—Opening of a fund-raising letter from Anita Bryant, 1980

27. Paul Broca, professor of clinical surgery at the Faculty of Medicine in Paris and the founder of craniology, argued that women were generally inferior in intelligence to men because, on the average, they had smaller brains than men. From 292 autopsies performed on males in four Parisian hospitals, Broca calculated an average weight of 1,325 grams for the male brain. From 140 autopsies on females, Broca calculated that the average female brain weighed 1,144 grams, lighter than the male brains by about 14 percent. Broca understood, of course, that part (if not all) of this difference might be attributed to the greater size and height, on the average, of males. Yet, he made no attempt to measure the effect of size, and he actually stated that it cannot account for the entire difference because we know that women are not as intelligent as men.—Adapted from Stephen Jay Gould, *The Panda's Thumb: More Reflections in Natural History*

*28. The historian Herbert Aptheker, in *American Negro Slave Revolts*, meant to prove that there were many revolts by slaves in the United States. At the outset of his study, Aptheker defined a revolt as something involving "a minimum of ten slaves" with "freedom as its object." He concluded his study by claiming that there had been some 250 slave revolts in the United States in less than 200 years. However, as Professor Aptheker proceeded, he included events involving fewer than ten people, uprisings not directed toward freedom, revolts in French and Spanish colonies, conspiracies, and even alleged conspiracies. In terms of his initial understanding of slave revolts, the total number shrinks to about fifteen or twenty.—Adapted from David H. Fischer, *Historians' Fallacies* (New York: Harper & Row, 1970).

29. Astrologers maintain that the personality of an individual is shaped by the positions of the sun, the moon, and the planets in relation to various constellations of stars at the instant of birth. Furthermore, over the years, the individual's particular nature will be affected in predictable ways by the constantly changing configurations of the heavens. But how can very distant celestial bodies influence particular individuals in the manner predicted by astrologers? Because of the great distances involved, gravitational, magnetic, and radioactive forces from celestial bodies are exceptionally weak. In fact, the gravitational forces at birth produced by the doctor and nurse and by the equipment in the delivery room far outweigh these celestial forces. Nevertheless, some astrologers attempt to get around this problem by proposing that each planet gives off a unique and still undetected radiation, or "vibration."—Adapted from *1977 Nature/ Science Annual*

30. According to some interpretations of Genesis, the earth was created in six days in about 4,000 B.C. However, in the eighteenth and nineteenth centuries, the study of fossils and the dating of rock formations supported an entirely different account of the creation of the earth and its flora and fauna. Many books published in the nineteenth century attempted to harmonize geology and Genesis. In a work called *Omphalos* (Greek for "navel"), the English zoologist Philip Gosse insisted that the earth had been created in six days in or around 4,000 B.C. exactly as the Bible said. However, Gosse also accepted the geological evidence that plants and animals had flourished long before the time of Adam. Gosse explained this apparent inconsistency by arguing that, just as Adam had been created with a navel, the relic of a birth that never occurred, so the entire earth was created with all the fossil records of a past that had no existence. Thus, the remains of extinct volcanoes, glacier scratchings upon rock and limestone mountains formed by the remains of marine life, as well as millions of fossils, were not evidence of the great geological age of the earth. These had all been created in the six-day period that also brought about Adam.—Adapted from Martin Gardner, *Fads and Fallacies* ■

☐ 12-3. *NON SEQUITURS:* UNWARRANTED ASSUMPTIONS

A *non sequitur*, which in Latin means "It does not follow," is reasoning that is fallacious because the connection between the premises and the conclusion is so weak that the premises fail to provide sufficient reason for accepting the conclusion. These fallacies make up a large group that can be divided into many smaller groups (see Table 12-2).

Several kinds of *non sequiturs* were discussed earlier:

Fallacies of linguistic confusion, discussed in Sections 4-1 and 4-2, result from the use of ambiguous or vague words or phrases that obscure the failure of premises to support the conclusion.

Formal fallacies are arguments that lack a valid form or that become defective because of the misapplication of a specific logical principle. Because the ability to recognize and avoid such fallacies is best cultivated by attention to the rules for valid deductive inference, they were discussed, where appropriate, in Chapters 6, 8, and 9 and in Section 10-4. (Fallacies of estimating probabilities are classified as formal because errors involving the laws of probability are similar to those involving deductive rules of inference.)

Hasty generalization, forgetful induction, and *fallacies of causal reasoning* are inductive arguments in which the evidence presented in the premises is insufficient to make the conclusion probable to the degree claimed for it. These arguments were discussed in Sections 10-2, 10-3, and 11-3.

Two other groups of *non sequiturs* will be considered in this chapter:

Fallacies of irrelevance, discussed in Section 12-4, are arguments in which the premises make irrelevant appeals to emotion or to popular prejudice.

TABLE 12-2 *Classification of Non Sequiturs*

GENERAL CATEGORY	SUBCATEGORY	SOME SPECIFIC FORMS
Fallacies of Linguistic Confusion	Fallacies of Ambiguity	Amphiboly Accent Equivocation
	Exploiting Vagueness	Slippery Slope
Formal Fallacies	Formal Fallacies in Deduction	Undistributed Middle Illicit Distribution Faulty Exclusion Unwarranted Existential Assertion Affirming the Consequent Denying the Antecedent
	Fallacies of Estimating Probabilities	Unequal Chances Gambler's Fallacy
Inductive Fallacies	Hasty Generalization Forgetful Induction Faulty Analogy *Post Hoc* Argument	
Fallacies of Irrelevance	Personal Attacks	Abusive Circumstantial *Tu quoque*
	Appeals to Emotion	Appeal to Fear Appeal to Pity Appeal to the Gallery
	Appeals to Authority or Tradition	Appeal to Tradition Appeal to Inexpert Authority
	Prejudicing the Issue	Genetic Fallacy Poisoning the Well
Fallacies of Unwarranted Assumption	False Alternatives Moralism and Wishful Thinking Negative Proof	

Fallacies of unwarranted assumption—the subject of this section—are arguments containing unreliable statements.

A fallacy of unwarranted assumption is an argument in which the premises are at present unsupported by evidence and have been shown by experience to be generally unsupportable.

Three types of argument involve unwarranted assumptions: those that rely on *false alternatives*, on *moralism* and *wishful thinking*, and on *negative proof*. Unfounded assumptions are embedded in the fallacies of false alternatives and moralism as suppressed premises. Without unacknowledged reliance on these assumptions, the argument would not appear coherent. In the case of negative proof, the unwarranted assumption is not unacknowledged or suppressed. Rather, one who reasons in this way mistakenly assumes that the premises present evidence needed to support the conclusion when in fact they do not.

□ *False alternatives*

Reasoning that incorporates false alternatives has many names—among them, *bifurcation* (from the Latin word for "two-pronged"), *the black-and-white fallacy*, and *false dilemma*. Whatever the name, the flaw remains essentially the same:

A fallacy of false alternatives is any argument that presumes a distinction to be exclusive and exhaustive when other, unmentioned alternatives are plausible.

Note that the unwarranted assumption in a fallacy of false alternatives has two parts: It is assumed *both* that there are too few alternatives (usually just two) *and* that one of the designated alternatives must be true. But few

"*Which are you—a victim of society or a crook?*"

Ed Arno. © The New Yorker Magazine, 1979. *Reprinted by permission.*

situations actually present exclusively either-or alternatives, and both of the choices offered may be wrong.

Unwarranted assumptions are embedded in a wide range of political slogans and clichés. For example, during the cold war of the 1950s, one often heard the chant, "Better dead than Red!" while others shouted back, "Better Red than dead!" Both groups failed to acknowledge the alternative of peaceful coexistence. And here are two examples drawn from everyday conversation:

> "If you're so smart, why aren't you rich?"
> "If you're not for me, you must be against me."

The following argument is fallacious because it employs false alternatives:

> As I see it, we have a choice between giving in to student demands and teaching what students want, and standing firm and teaching what needs to be taught. Why did we spend so many years earning advanced degrees and doing research? So that we'd know what knowledge must be passed on to new generations. Our only choice, therefore, is to resist the students' demands.

The arguer assumes that only two alternatives are available and that one of the two must be correct. Ignored is the possibility that a compromise between the two positions might be found and that neither of the alternatives presented is desirable.

Often the fallacy of false alternatives is a result of failure to differentiate properly between *contraries* and *contradictories* (see Section 5-3). Two statements are said to be contraries when it is impossible for both of them to be true but possible for both to be false. "Sarah is rich" and "Sarah is poor," for example, are contraries. Sarah cannot be both rich and poor at the same time, but she may be neither. Contraries also allow for gradations between their extremes: *hot* and *cold* (*lukewarm*), *moral* and *immoral* (*amoral*), *love* and *hate* (*indifference*), and so forth.

If two statements are contradictories, however, they are exactly opposite in truth value. If one is true, then the other is false and vice versa. "Either Sarah is rich or Sarah is not rich" and "Either Paris is the capital of France or Paris is not the capital of France" are pairs of contradictories.

Consider the following argument:

> Either the people of China are free or they are enslaved. Now it is obvious that they are not free to choose their own jobs, to live where they want, or to read and say what they please. Since it is false that the Chinese are free, it follows that the Chinese are all slaves of the Communist state.

It is certainly true that the people of China are not free in the same sense as are citizens of the Unites States—for example, they lack the political freedoms protected by the Bill of Rights. But they do possess privileges and rights that slaves have traditionally lacked—such as being permitted to marry partners of their own choice and to purchase goods with wages they have earned. So "the people of China are free" and "the people of China are slaves" are contraries; both are false. The argument erroneously presents them as contradictory alternatives.

□ *Moralism and wishful thinking*

All Nature is but Art, unknown to thee:
All chance, direction which thou canst not see;
All discord, harmony not understood;
All partial evil, universal good;
And, spite of Pride, in erring Reason's spite,
One truth is clear, Whatever is, is right.
ALEXANDER POPE

The *fallacy of moralism* is also known as the *is-ought fallacy*. It involves the unwarranted assumption that simply because something *is* the case, it *ought* to be the case or that because something *is not* the case, it *ought not* to be the case.

Thus, the fallacy is often used in attempts to establish that a particular behavior is right on the basis of its being exhibited by a large number of people. An example of this use is the following argument.

I'm convinced from my study of anthropology and psychology that people always act to advance their own long-range interests. Even cases of so-called "personal sacrifice" can be explained—through identification with others— as self-interested action. Human beings are natural egoists. Thus, it is quite clear that it is right for everyone to pursue their own exclusive interests.

Attempting to justify a situation by pointing out that it represents the status quo is another version of this fallacy:

The best argument against the claim that we ought to permit a student to sit on the board of trustees is the fact that students are not now included on the board of any major college or university in the state. Students have petitioned many times to be included in these governing bodies. They would not have been excluded unless there were good reasons for it. And I'm not going to second-guess those eminent business leaders.

Although there may be good reasons for accepting a practice, the fallacious argument does not present them. The premises do not justify the conclusion, and the reasoning should be rejected.

The fallacy of moralism can be detected in some of the arguments that have been advanced in favor of *ethical relativism*—the theory that what we believe to be good and right can be understood to be good and right only in the context of our own society. This viewpoint drew support from the findings of pioneer sociologists and anthropologists that the ideals of one society may be diametrically opposed to those of another society. In *Patterns of Culture,* for example, anthropologist Ruth Benedict reports that Navajo Indians value cooperation and refuse to assert themselves as individuals, while the Kwakiutl Indians strongly encourage competition and self-assertiveness.

Many people believe that their views about right and wrong are culturally determined. It is argued that Americans value the freedoms guaranteed by the Bill of Rights only because they happen to have been brought up in the United States. Someone who had been reared in a totalitarian state—the argument goes—or who had been born a slave in ancient Rome would not value personal liberty so highly. And we oppose polygamy, it is argued, because our society has declared it to be wrong. But polygamy is not considered wrong in every society.

The crucial flaw of some arguments for ethical relativism is the assumption that "whatever a society *believes* is good, is *good* for them." But it does not follow from the fact that different societies have different institutions and beliefs that all beliefs are equally worthy and that *no* moral principles are universal. Thus, a person who argues that it is pointless to apply moral principles to the behavior of persons in other societies—for the reason that people in these societies do not observe the principles—commits the fallacy of moralism.

Closely related to moralism is a kind of fallacious reasoning called *wishful thinking.* This occurs when one attempts to draw the conclusion that something *is* the case from premises that express wishes, hopes, desires, and beliefs about right and wrong.

> **He will recover from cancer, because he is a good man and good men deserve to live a lot longer than he has lived.**
> **I know that I didn't fail that exam. It just would not be fair, after I've worked so hard.**

Wishful thinking, like moralism, becomes fallacious reasoning only when it is presented as the justification for a conclusion.

☐ Negative proof

The *fallacy of negative proof* is also called *ad ignorantiam,* which is Latin for "appeal to ignorance." It involves the assumption that the inability to demonstrate that a statement is true constitutes proof that the statement's contradictory is true.

Such arguments are fallacious because the fact that a statement has not been conclusively established to be true or false usually proves only that one is unable—at least, at present—to confirm or disconfirm it. And such reasoning is unfair, because it shifts the burden of proof from the arguer to anyone who might be skeptical of the claim.

The fallacious argument will have one of the following forms:

1. There is no proof (or you have not proved) that p is true. Therefore, p is false.

2. There is no proof (or you have not proved) that p is false. Therefore, p is true.

Argument (1*a*) is an example of the first form.

1a. No one has demonstrated beyond doubt that God exists. Therefore, we are justified in believing that God does not exist.

The response of the late Senator Joseph McCarthy to a question about his claim that someone in the State Department had Communist affiliations illustrates argument form (2):

2a. "I do not have much information on this except the general statement of the agency that there is nothing in the files to disprove his Communist connections."[10]

The fallacy often takes the form of an assertion that the situation of a group of people is satisfactory because no complaints have been expressed:

1b. There have been no student complaints about the length of the reading assignment I gave the class last week. This shows that the assignment was fair.

Fallacies of negative proof sometimes occur when scientists appraise rival hypotheses. Suppose, for instance, that three hypotheses—H_1, H_2, and H_3—all purport to explain some puzzling phenomenon. Suppose, further, that an investigator claims to *prove* that H_3 is true by eliminating rivals H_1 and H_2. The argument presented is that because H_1 and H_2 are refuted by the evidence, we can by disjunctive argument conclude "therefore H_3":

$H_1 \lor H_2 \lor H_3$

$\sim H_1 \ \& \ \sim H_2$

$\therefore H_3$

[10] Richard H. Rovere, *Senator Joe McCarthy* (New York: World Publishing Co., 1959), p. 132.

Although the conclusion is validly derived from the premises, it cannot be accepted as true. We cannot safely assume that the first premise—"$H_1 \lor H_2 \lor H_3$"—is true because all three rival hypotheses may be false. Indeed, we are not justified in assuming that the hypotheses tested are *all* the possible explanations of the phenomenon. At most, the elimination of rival hypotheses increases the inductive probability of the remaining hypothesis. (See Section 11-2 for a discussion of justifying hypotheses.) Thus, an investigator who assumes that the refutation of rival hypotheses counts as proof that the favored hypothesis is true commits the fallacy of negative proof.

Arguments based on negative proof are legitimate under some circumstances—notably, in courts of law. In the absence of evidence to the contrary, every accused person is presumed to be innocent before the law. This reasoning is not fallacious because the legal system of the United States intentionally imposes a heavy burden of proof on the prosecution. "Due process of law" requires that we not deprive a person of liberty or property unless guilt has been established beyond "reasonable doubt." From the point of view of those who enforce the law, an "innocent person" is, by definition, one who has not been *proven* guilty. But in this context, the word *innocent* is ambiguous. A person may be innocent of having committed the crime or—having committed it—innocent in the legal sense that the prosecution lacks sufficient evidence of the deed.

■ **EXERCISE 12-3**

Decide for each of the following arguments whether it is a fallacy of false alternatives, moralism, or negative proof.

1. We must either deny freedom of speech to all critics of government or give the Communists a free hand in destroying the government. Because the latter course is unthinkable, we must pursue the former.

2. The Soviet invasion of Afghanistan is merely an affirmation of a historical truth that was known to American leaders as early as the end of World War II. We must either resist Soviet expansionist tendencies with force or appease the Soviets. Again, because history shows that appeasement fails, we have no choice but to resist militarily.

3. Voters of Massachusetts, we have charged my opponent with dishonesty in public office. We have offered my opponent numerous chances to come forward and rebut our charges. My opponent has not done so, Therefore, citizens of this just state, do you wish to reelect a dishonest individual?

*4. Despite wild speculation to the contrary, the white supremacist government of the Republic of South Africa does not have atomic weapons. If it did, the CIA and United States defense intelligence agencies would certainly know about it. And so far, these intelligence agencies have not concluded that the South Africans have tested atomic devices.

5. No responsible scientist has proved that saccharin causes cancer in humans. Therefore, we can disregard the alarmists and continue to consume foods and soft drinks artificially sweetened with saccharin.

6. If abortion were to be made illegal in the United States, hundreds of thousands of women would obtain them illegally. If necessary, some might travel as far as Mexico or Sweden. The situation would be similar to the way it was in the United States before abortion was legalized in the 1970s. It follows, therefore, that it would be morally wrong to prohibit abortion.

7. Professor Derek is certainly fair in assigning grades to students. Why, there has never been so much as a murmur of protest against the professor.

*8. As you know, an unusually high proportion of AIDS—acquired immune deficiency syndrome—victims are homosexuals. Those afflicted by AIDS usually do not recover. These facts show that homosexuality is unnatural and, thus, that it is morally wrong to have sexual relations with members of your own sex.

9. We must accept the fact that extrasensory perception exists because many people have claimed to have this ability, and no one has ever disproved that these people have the psychic powers they claim to have.

10. When campus activists present their demands to college officials, the way the officials respond can make all the difference. When the officials give in and grant what is demanded, they encourage the activists. If only they would have the wisdom and courage to resist, the activists would be defeated and campuses would remain peaceful.

11. "Mr. [John] Sparkman and Mr. [Adlai] Stevenson should come before the American people, as I have, and make a complete financial statement as to their financial history and if they don't, it will be an admission that they have something to hide."—Richard Nixon in a 1956 campaign speech

*12. "Every simple idea must be copied from a preceding impression; for there is no proof of any other origin of such ideas."—David Hume

13. "You cannot eliminate one basic assumption, one substantial part of this philosophy of Marxism . . . without abandoning truth, without falling into the arms of bourgeois-reactionary falsehood."—V. I. Lenin

14. "Former Treasury Secretary and Chairman of Democrats-for-Nixon, John Connolly, looks on the bright side. After his acquittal on bribery charges Connolly allowed that he might still be able to run for national political office. If the IRS, FBI, and special Watergate prosecutors couldn't find anything on him following 18 months of investigation, Connolly argued, he must be the most innocent politician in America."—Peter Passell, *How To*

15. "Concession is surrender. White South Africans faced a simple choice between survival and downfall, and they would defend themselves in all ways, even with the rifle if it could not be otherwise."—South African Prime Minister Hendrik F. Verwoerd, 1963 ■

□ 12-4. *NON SEQUITURS:* FALLACIES OF IRRELEVANCE

In *fallacies of irrelevance*, the premises fail to provide proper support for the conclusion because they are irrelevant to the issue being considered:

> **A fallacy of irrelevance is an argument based on a feature of the context in which the argument occurs that has no bearing on whether the conclusion is true or false.**

These arguments can be divided into four groups: *personal attacks, appeals to emotion, appeals to authority or tradition,* and *prejudicing the issue.*

☐ *Personal attacks,* or ad hominem *fallacies*

The *personal attack,* or argument *ad hominem* (Latin for "against the person"), attempts to undercut a claim by drawing unfavorable attention to the person making it. Invective as such is not an instance of this fallacy; the *ad hominem* fallacy is always an argument. An opponent's thesis is asserted to be wrong or unworthy of attention because of the opponent's character or situation. Such reasoning is fallacious because it does not address the truth or falsity of the proposition itself.

Logicians have identified three specific kinds of *ad hominem* fallacy: the *abusive,* the *circumstantial,* and the one best known by the Latin name *tu quoque.*

☐ ABUSIVE *AD HOMINEM*

An abusive *ad hominem* argument involves an attack on someone's character or ability. It has the general form, "A is defective in some respect, so whatever A says on this issue is defective." Resort to such reasoning is illustrated by the anecdote quoted in the accompanying box and by the following example:

> You can disregard the Fergusons' views on school-board policy. What can individuals know about high-school education when their own high-school grades were so low that they could not be admitted to college?

Lincoln's Fallacy

In a case where Judge [Stephen T.] Logan—always earnest and grave—opposed him, Lincoln created no little merriment by his reference to Logan's style of dress. He carried the surprise in store for the latter, till he reached his turn before the jury. Addressing them, he said: "Gentlemen, you must be careful not to permit yourselves to be overcome by the eloquence of counsel for the defense. Judge Logan, I know, is an effective lawyer. I have met him too often to doubt that; but shrewd and careful though he may be, still he is sometimes wrong. Since this trial has begun I have discovered that, with all his caution and fastidiousness, he hasn't knowledge enough to put his shirt on right." Logan turned red as crimson, but sure enough, Lincoln was correct, for the former had donned a new shirt, and by mistake had drawn it over his head with the pleated bosom behind. The general laugh which followed destroyed the effect of Logan's eloquence over the jury— the very point at which Lincoln aimed.

William H. Herndon, Herndon's Life of Lincoln, *introduction and notes by Paul M. Angle (New York: World Publishing Co., 1965), p. 288.*

Another kind of abusive *ad hominem* argument is the suggestion of guilt by association. In this case, the undesirable aspect exploited is the person's relationship with others who are the subject of criticism.

☐ CIRCUMSTANTIAL *AD HOMINEM*

In circumstantial *ad hominem*, the opponent's personal situation is cited as a reason why the opponent might be expected to accept the conclusion in dispute. By suggesting that the opponent's attitude is self-serving, the arguer attempts to undercut the position:

> Of course you oppose student participation on the board of trustees, Dean Kelso. Your reasons are perfectly transparent. You're bound to oppose any institutional change that would dilute the power of your office.

☐ *TU QUOQUE*

In *tu quoque*, which in Latin means "you're another," the arguer does not address an issue raised by an opponent but instead calls attention to an alleged weakness or wrongdoing of the opponent. The following anecdote contains an example:

> Stuart Chase relates the story of an American tourist who was invited to inspect a Russian subway station when the Moscow underground was first opened to visitors in the 1930s. He was shown the self-registering turnstiles and the spotless washrooms. "Fine," he said, "how about the trains?" They showed him the safety devices and the excellent tile frescoes on the tunnel walls. He was again impressed, but continued to look anxiously down the tracks. "How about the trains?" he asked again. "How about the trains?" snapped his guide. "How about the sharecroppers in Alabama?"[11]

Not every use of *ad hominem* reasoning is fallacious. It is considered legitimate in a court of law, for example, to introduce information about a witness's character in order to weaken his or her credibility. In a general election, it is appropriate to consider the character of a candidate—assuming that the favorable or unfavorable traits being considered are relevant to the duties of the office.

☐ *Appeals to emotion*

In an *appeal to emotion*, the arguer, instead of presenting evidence for a conclusion, attempts to win approval for it by playing upon the feelings of those to whom the argument is addressed. Fallacies of irrelevance in this group can be subdivided according to the predominant emotion to which the appeal is made: *fear, pity,* or *sympathy.*

---

[11] Stuart Chase, *Guides to Straight Thinking* (New York: Harper, 1956), p. 65.

☐ APPEALS TO FEAR

The king to Oxford sent a troop of horse
For Tories own no argument but force:
With equal skill to Cambridge books he sent,
For Whigs admit no force but argument.
SIR WILLIAM BROWNE (1692–1774)

Traditionally known as *argumentum ad baculum*, which in Latin literally means "argument toward the stick," the *appeal to fear* is an attempt to intimidate an opponent into acquiescence:

SUPERVISOR: Your idea has some interesting points. Other employees have expressed interest in it.

EMPLOYEE: Thank you. I plan to submit it to the board of directors, and I hope it is accepted.

SUPERVISOR: Personally, I don't think your proposal is as good as Joe Johnson's.

EMPLOYEE: Perhaps not, but I think the board should be the judge of that.

SUPERVISOR: I'm not sure you should submit your proposal. If you do submit it, Johnson will have to criticize it in defense of his own idea. You know Johnson has more experience here than you do, and I'd hate to see him embarrass you in front of the other employees.

☐ APPEALS TO PITY

Professor Stepanovich Receives a Student

"Sit down," I tell my visitor. "Now, what can I do for you?"

"Sorry to disturb you, Professor," he begins haltingly, not looking me in the eye. "I wouldn't venture to bother you if—er . . . I've taken your examination five times now and—er, have failed. I beg you, please pass me because . . . , er—"

All idlers defend themselves with the same argument. They have passed with distinction in all other subjects, they have only failed mine—which is all the more amazing because they've always studied my subject so industriously, and know it inside out. Their failure is due to some mysterious misunderstanding.

"I'm sorry, friend," I tell my visitor, "but I can't pass you. Go and read your lecture notes again, then come back—and, we shall see about it."

From Anton Chekhov, "A Dreary Story," The Oxford Chekhov, Vol. V, trans. and ed. by Ronald Hingley (London: Oxford University Press, 1970), p. 44.

The *appeal to pity* (in Latin *argumentum ad misericordiam*) introduces an emotional dimension into what should be reasoned discourse. The student in the excerpt from a story by Anton Chekhov (see accompanying box) attempts to influence the professor with such an appeal.

☐ APPEALS TO SYMPATHY, OR APPEALS TO THE GALLERY

The *appeal to sympathy* is often called an "appeal to the gallery" because it is widely used by speakers to persuade audiences to respond favorably to them. In making such an appeal, the speaker frequently uses expressions familiar to the audience in an effort to be perceived as an "insider"—someone who belongs to the group.

An example of an appeal to the gallery is the following excerpt from a closing argument to a jury made by the famous lawyer Clarence Darrow:

> You folks think we city people are all crooked, but we city people think you farmers are all crooked. There isn't one of you I'd trust in a horse trade, because you'd be sure to skin me. But when it comes to having sympathy with a person in trouble, I'd sooner trust you folks than city folks, because you come to know people better and get to be closer friends.[12]

Darrow cleverly mixes apparent openness about his suspicion of country farmers with indirect praise for their shrewdness in making business deals. All this has the effect of saying, "I know you're suspicious of me, and I'm suspicious of you too because you're shrewd in your own way, but. . . ." Then comes another appeal to their pride and self-respect at being unpretentious, friendly, and warm-hearted people.

Achieving a sense of a common bond with an audience is a valuable skill, but one that can easily be abused. A fallacious appeal to the gallery occurs when shared beliefs or moral evaluations are offered in place of reasons relevant to accepting a conclusion. No matter how sympathetic an audience may feel toward a speaker, such a feeling is not sufficient for accepting a conclusion as true.

☐ *Fallacious and other appeals to authority*

Arguments containing *fallacious appeals to authority* can be subdivided into two types: *appeals to inexpert authority* and *appeals to tradition*, or *ad verecundiam* fallacies. Both types capitalize on common psychological factors: that we feel secure in situations with which we are familiar; that we often lack confidence in our own judgment and are eager to rely on the opinion of someone who seems more qualified; and that we often feel uncomfortable if we take a position that differs from that of our family, friends, or associates. All such fallacies involve the assumption that simply because someone, A, believes or asserts some proposition, "*p*," there is good reason for accepting "*p*."

---

[12] Quoted by Irving Stone, *Clarence Darrow for the Defense* (Garden City, New York: Garden City Publishing Co., 1941).

Not all apeals to authority are fallacious. If the premises present evidence to the effect that A is a reliable authority on a subject, S, and "*p*" is a statement about S, the result is a nonfallacious inductive argument of the following form:

A says that *p*.
A is a reliable authority on subject S.
p is a statement about S.
Therefore, probably *p*.

This type of argument is inductive because the truth of the premises cannot guarantee the truth of the conclusion: even the foremost authority on a subject can be in error. The crucial premise, "A is a reliable authority on subject S," is usually supported by generalization from A's success in the past or by analogy between S and subjects known to be within the range of A's expertise. (For a discussion of generalization and analogy, see Chapter 10.)

☐ **APPEALS TO INEXPERT AUTHORITY**

In *fallacies of inexpert authority*, the opinion of the person cited is not relevant to the truth of the conclusion. Numerous examples can be found, including advertisements that take the form, "So-and-so superstar endorses such-and-such. Therefore, such-and-such is a good product for you." Closely related are endorsements of political candidates by popular entertainers.

Here are two examples of fallacies of inexpert authority:

We have nothing to fear from death, for if death were terrible then Socrates, the wisest of all men, would have known it to be so. But Socrates faced his own death with equanimity.

This idea of supporting research on dolphins is ridiculous. We shouldn't be throwing thousands of dollars away on studies of the intelligence of these animals. We were discussing it today at lunch, and the treasurer, sales manager, and personnel manager of the company all agreed it was a colossal waste.

To determine whether an argument is fallacious, one must distinguish between cases when one is justified in asserting the premise "A is a reliable authority concerning S" and cases when one is not so justified. The following criteria serve as guides in evaluating the relevancy of an authority's opinion— and in judging the strength of the key premise.[13]

1. The individual must be known as an authority on the subject under consideration. An expert in one field is not necessarily knowledgeable about another field.

---

[13] The criteria are suggested by Howard Kahane, *Logic and Contemporary Rhetoric*, 2d ed. (Belmont, Calif.: Wadsworth Publishing Co., 1976), pp. 7–8.

2. There should be a limited amount of disagreement over the proposition among experts in the field. The greater the degree of controversy among more-or-less equally qualified experts, the less reliable the judgment of any particular expert.

3. The expert should present the evidence on which the judgment is based. In other words, the expert should present an argument, rather than merely expressing an opinion.

4. If the subject is in a new field about which there is little accepted knowledge, the expert consulted should have a reputation for having made successful predictions or accurate appraisals in the past.

☐ *Appeals to tradition, or* ad verecundiam *fallacies*

The *fallacy of appeal to tradition*—in Latin, *ad verecundiam*—is an argument in which rituals or customs of the past are offered to justify claims about what should or should not be done in the present. Precedent is substituted for reason. These arguments are likely to include remarks such as, "Let's stick to tried and true methods," "That's just the way the system works," and "We like to do things by the book."

The fallacy is illustrated by the following comment by Senator Sam Ervin of North Carolina about the Equal Rights Amendment: "Why Ladies, any bill that lies around here for 47 years without getting any more support than this one has got in the past obviously shouldn't be passed at all. Why, I think that affords most conclusive proof that it is unworthy of consideration."[14]

Often, the authoritative appeal is to sheer numbers, as if quantity alone were enough to constitute authority. Here is an example of the *fallacy of numbers*:

> Flying saucers from outer space must exist, because otherwise so many thousands of people would not have claimed to have seen them, and newspaper and magazine editors would never have taken such an interest in them. Thousands of eyewitness accounts cannot be all wrong.

In some versions of the *ad verecundiam* argument, the beliefs or actions of the crowd serve as justification. Reference is made to what "everyone does" or what "everyone believes." This is called the *appeal to common practice*:

> Human beings must have free will. Otherwise, we wouldn't think and act the way we do. We all expect people to make the right decisions, and we blame them when they err. We wouldn't do any of this if free will did not exist.

Appeals to common practice can involve moral issues. They sometimes attempt to exploit the false notion that if everyone does or would do something,

---

[14] *The New York Times Magazine*, September 20, 1970.

then it must be all right to do it. Or they include one or both of the related notions that two wrongs make a right and turnabout is fair play: "You cheated on me, and besides, most of our friends cheat from time to time, so I don't see why you think what I did was so wrong." Such appeals to common practice resemble the *tu quoque* fallacy, discussed earlier.

☐ Prejudicing the issue

Prejudicing the issue is an attempt to discredit a position by claiming that its source is for some reason unacceptable. By appealing to irrelevant background and contextual features of the viewpoint in question, the arguer seeks to deny it a hearing. Such arguments usually take one of two forms: the *genetic fallacy* or *poisoning the well*.

☐ THE GENETIC FALLACY

To explain something genetically is to describe its origin—to give a kind of historical account of how it came to be. The genetic fallacy occurs when the arguer disparages the way in which a viewpoint developed or was acquired, rather than the view itself. Such critical explanations are usually employed in a diagnostic manner, as if the speaker were discussing the case history of a disease:

> It is curious to observe how the theory of what is called the Christian Church, sprung out of the tail of the heathen mythology. A direct incorporation took place in the first instance, by making the reputed founder to be celestially begotten. The trinity of gods that then followed was no other than a reduction of the former plurality, which was about twenty or thirty thousand. The statue of Mary succeeded the statue of Diana of Ephesus. The deification of heroes changed into the canonization of saints. The Mythologists had gods for everything; the Christian Mythologists had saints for everything. The church became as crowded with the one, as the pantheon had been with the other; and Rome was the place of both. The Christian theory is little else than the idolatry of the ancient Mythologists, accommodated to the purposes of power and revenue; and it yet remains to reason and philosophy to abolish the amphibious fraud.[15]

Logicians sometimes classify the genetic fallacy with the *ad hominem* fallacy because both commonly trace an idea to the attributes of a particular person. The similarity of the fallacies can be seen in the following comment about the nineteenth-century philosopher Arthur Schopenhauer: "How should a man avoid pessimism who has lived almost all his life in a boarding house? And who abandoned his only child to illegitimate anonymity? At the bottom of Schopenhauer's unhappiness was his rejection of the normal life—his rejection of women and marriage and children."[16] By tracing Schopenhauer's doc-

---

[15] Thomas Paine, *The Age of Reason*, from Howard Fast, ed., *The Selected Works of Tom Paine* (New York: The Modern Library, 1945), p. 288.

[16] Will Durant, *The Story of Philosophy* (New York: Simon and Schuster, 1926), p. 378.

trine that pessimism is an appropriate outlook on life to Schopenhauer's personal experiences, the writer diminishes Schopenhauer's contribution to philosophy. The passage can be seen as illustrating the genetic fallacy, or the *ad hominem* fallacy, or both.

Genetic explanations can be illuminating: they can tell much about why an idea has assumed its present form and acquired its present following. But they are fallacious when offered as reasons for accepting or rejecting the conclusion of an argument. The origin of a premise is *not* relevant to the credibility of the argument that employs it.

☐ POISONING THE WELL

Poisoning the well is an attempt to structure a controversy so that any response by the opponent can be regarded as untrue, disingenuous, or misguided. In effect, the opponent's statements are cited as evidence of bad faith or delusion. A first-rate example comes from the pen of philosopher Friedrich Nietzsche: "Those who disagree with me when I say that mankind is corrupt prove that they are already corrupted."

This fallacy received its name in the nineteenth century as the result of a controversy between John Cardinal Newman, a British churchman, and the novelist Charles Kingsley. During their dispute, Kingsley suggested that Newman, as a Roman Catholic priest, did not place the highest value on truth. Newman protested that Kingsley had "poisoned the well" because the accusation made it impossible for Newman, or any other Catholic, to defend his religious beliefs. Truth is the ultimate criterion for the worth of a proposition—it is the "well" from which we all must "drink." If Kingsley assumed from the start that Newman would use fraudulent tactics to win the dispute, then anything Newman might say to support his case would be automatically disregarded.

Poisoning the well is illustrated by a letter to the editor of the *New York Times* on the subject of a Supreme Court ruling on obscenity and pornography. The Court ruled that local community standards would prevail in judging whether printed or filmed material was obscene or had "socially redeeming" value. Some authors and film producers, noting that standards of decency varied greatly throughout the United States, expressed fear that the decision

Momma

By Mell Lazarus

"Momma" by Mell Lazarus. © Field Enterprises, Inc., 1979. Reprinted by permission.

would make it impossible for them to estimate whether their work would be subject to legal prosecution. The letter to the *Times* commented, in part, as follows: "Motion picture producers, writers and artists with high moral standards do not fear the new [Supreme Court] decision simply because they would never stoop to the depths of degeneracy. It is only those who are morally deficient who fear the decision."[17]

■ EXERCISE 12-4

■ A. Identify and explain the fallacies of irrelevance in the following arguments. Examples include appeals to fear, appeals to pity, and appeals to the gallery and abusive, circumstantial, and *tu quoque* personal attacks.

1. If you do not agree with me that merging our businesses would be mutually profitable, then you may find yourself in a price war. Such competition would be inevitable, I'm afraid, and I'm sure we would both regret its occurrence.

2. You can't possibly accept his views that the employees need a raise. After all, he is the executive secretary of the labor union, and he is paid to make such statements.

3. JUNIOR: My Uncle Scruggs, who is now in prison, used to preach to us kids about self-control. But I can't see any value in his ideas if he can't live up to them himself.

*4. What right do you have to advise me that cigarette smoking is bad for my health? Didn't you smoke for many years?

5. My opponent maintains that the legislation I introduced in the House is unfair to working people. To refute that claim, I need only point out that my opponent has sponsored legislation that would eliminate cost-of-living increases for those on social security.

6. Ladies and gentlemen, the rent-control bill proposed by Mrs. Williams and her associates is unjust and must therefore be rejected by the city council. Mrs. Williams and all those who have joined her in sponsoring the bill are tenants and renters. There isn't a single property-owner in the group.

7. St. Anselm's rational proofs for the existence of God can be rejected as fallacious. Anselm had already accepted the existence of God on the basis of faith, so he was only trying to add philosophical respectability to beliefs he held without rational proof.

*8. If you think your family can do without this important protection, please read this. . . .

"Perhaps you're not going to take advantage of this opportunity. This concerns me. Maybe it shouldn't. Maybe you've already updated your insurance protection to keep up with inflation. If you have, I'm glad. But if you're like most people, you don't have enough life insurance to protect your family during these times of rising costs. Wouldn't it be hard enough for them if they lost you . . . without having to lose some of the things you provide? Please don't be underinsured. Fill out your application and mail it to us today!"—Letter from W. R. Mullens, President, J. C. Penney Life

9. "In origin, Socrates belonged to the lowest class: Socrates was plebs. We know,

[17] The *New York Times*, September 9, 1973.

we can still see for ourselves how ugly he was. But ugliness, in itself an objection, is among the Greeks almost a refutation. Was Socrates a Greek at all?"—Friedrich Nietzsche, "The Problem of Socrates," *Twilight of the Idols* (1888).

10. "I testify unto every man that heareth the words of the prophecy of this book. If any man shall add unto these things, God shall add unto him the plagues that are written in this book: And if any man shall take away from the words of the book of this prophecy, God shall take away his part out of the book of life, and out of the holy city, and *from* the things which are written in this book."—Revelation 22:18–19.

11. "I described to him an impudent fellow from Scotland, who . . . maintained that there was no distinction between virtue and vice. JOHNSON. 'Why, Sir, if the fellow does not think as he speaks, he is lying; and I see not what honor he can propose to himself from having the character of a lyar. But if he does really think that there is not distinction between virtue and vice, why, Sir, when he leaves our house let us count our spoons.'"—James Boswell, *The Life of Samuel Johnson*

*****12.** Writing in *The Village Voice* on November 17, 1975, Ken Auletta defended the Speaker of the New York State Assembly against the charge of illegally promising an appointment in return for a campaign contribution. "There probably aren't two politicians in New York who couldn't be indicted for a similar crime. . . . Might we also indict presidential candidates who promise cabinet or ambassadorial posts in exchange for convention support? . . . Is a mayor [guilty] when he makes a generous settlement with a municipal union which then endorses his reelection?"

13. "Thirty-eight states are needed to enact the anti-abortion constitutional amendment into law. Polls show that if such an amendment were passed in Congress today, 19 states would endorse it immediately. That means *the anti-abortionists are halfway to victory right now*—halfway to hurtling us back to the dark, dangerous, and degrading days of back-alley abortionists, days that left too many young women dead, maimed, or mentally scarred for life."—Letter from Robin C. Duke, President, National Abortion Rights Action League

14. Clarence Darrow, defending Thomas I. Kidd, an officer of the Amalgamated Woodworkers Union who had been charged with criminal conspiracy, addressed the jury as follows: "I appeal to you not for Thomas Kidd, but I appeal to you for the long line—the long, long line reaching back through the ages and forward to the years to come—the long line of despoiled and downtrodden people of the earth. I appeal to you for those men who rise in the morning before daylight comes and who go home at dark when the light has faded from the sky and give their life, their strength, their toil to make others rich and great. I appeal to you in the name of those women who are offering up their lives to this modern god of gold, and I appeal to you in the name of those little children, the living and the unborn."—Quoted by Irving Stone in *Clarence Darrow for the Defense*

15. "Nixon said that he knew that surreptitious entries and wiretaps—after all, that was what Watergate was all about, wasn't it?—were a way of life in the Kennedy and Johnson administrations. 'I know this has been going on for 20 years. It is the worst kind of hypocrisy for the Democrats to make so much of it.'. . . What he did should be measured against the record of prior administrations."—Bob Woodward and Carl Bernstein, *The Final Days*

*****16.** Francine du Plessix Gray, in an interview with Tim Galloway, the author of *Inner Tennis*, asked the tennis pro how he had come to believe Maharaj Ji was God. Galloway responded, "When I first heard him my only approach was to say to myself,

'He's either the real thing or a con artist.' Well, the first time I saw him he just did too bad a job as a con artist. A good con artist wouldn't wear a gold wristwatch or give such stupid answers. When I was staying with him in India I once asked him how much time I should spend on work and how much on meditation and he just said get up an hour earlier and go to bed an hour later, hardly a profound answer. I decided that if he was doing such a bad job of being a holy man he simply had to be genuine."

"Did it ever occur to you that he might be a bad con man?" Gray asked.

"Then how could he have six million followers?" Galloway replied.—From "Blissing Out in Houston," *The New York Review of Books*, December 13, 1973

17. Jay Gourley, reporter for the *National Enquirer*, responded as follows to the charge that he invaded the privacy of Henry Kissinger when he examined and reported on the contents of garbage taken from the Kissinger residence: "Of all the printed commentary . . . only a few editorial writers thought to express the obvious point that when it comes to invasion of privacy, the man who as National Security Advisor helped to bug the home phones of his own staff members is one of our nation's leading practitioners."—*Washington Monthly*, October 1975

18. "Well, here we go again with another round of that all-time favorite American game of 'Don't do as I do—do as I say.'

"In this case we have a woman (Marabel Morgan) telling other women how to be happy with a housewife's career, while she is out making a cool $1.5 million plus on the lecture circuit as a writer of popular literature."—*Time*, April 4, 1977

19. In his book, *Worlds in Collision*, Immanuel Velikovsky argues that a giant comet once erupted from the planet Jupiter, passed close to the earth on two occasions, then settled down as Venus. Velikovsky's theory was widely criticized by scientists, and on one occasion, Velikovsky remarked, "If I had not been psychoanalytically trained I would have had some harsh words to say to my critics."—Quoted in *The New York Times Book Review*, April 2, 1950

*20. A female opponent of the Equal Rights Amendment recently stated that she was against it because "the women who support it are either fanatics or lesbians or frustrated old maids."

21. Former President Richard Nixon wrote a book called *The Real War* in which he criticized American foreign policy under the Carter administration and discussed alternative ways of responding to terrorist activities. However, we cannot take Nixon's views seriously, because he resigned the presidency rather than face impeachment charges. Haven't you heard that expression, "Don't buy books by crooks?"

22. "So what you do is just reach up there and get that lever and just say, 'All the way with LBJ.'"

"Your mammas and your papas and your grandpas, some of them are going to forget this. But I am depending on you young folks who are going to have to fight our wars, and who are going to have to defend this country, and who are going to get blown up if we have a nuclear holocaust—I am depending on you to have enough interest in your future and what is ahead of you to get up and prod mamma and papa and make them get up early and vote."—President Lyndon Johnson, October 31, 1964

23. During hearings by the District of Columbia City Council, U.S. Attorney Charles F. C. Ruff presented the following argument against establishing mandatory sentences for certain crimes: "I oppose the institution of mandatory minimums. . . . Picture the case of your mother or sister who is charged with an offense. Don't you want the prosecutor to have the discretion to say your sister is a special person, and this is a one-time offense?"—Quoted by *The Washington Post*, March 13, 1981

*24. A woman argued as follows before a committee convened by a state constitutional convention to consider a right-to-die amendment: "I maintain that to give to people facing certain death . . . the right to die quickly, easily, and in peace when they want to do so, is being compassionate, intelligent, and humane. And I affirm that it is an act that God, who gave us all life, would approve of."

Poignantly describing the lingering death of her 86-year-old father, she continued:

"He was compassionate and merciful. He asked for the same mercy for himself.

"For eight weeks he died, little by little, minute by minute, day by day. . . . He was just denied a release from the suffering and torture which he knew, and we knew, and the doctor knew he faced.

"Have you wiped the eyes that will not close and that look as though they had never closed in over 85 years since they opened on the world? Have you struggled with your own breathing, trying unconsciously to help his labored gasps which came nearly as fast as your own pulse beats? . . . And have you, then, rebelled at a system where this barbaric suffering was called necessary because unfeeling and unimaginative men declare that God willed it?"

25. "We know that [Benjamin] Franklin, who as a boy stranded in London had published an atheistical work, later repented of that act of youthful braggadocio and dismissed the whole stupendous question by the casual remark that while a mechanical theory of the universe might be true it was 'not very useful'; certainly not very useful to him, a respectable printer and politician living in Philadelphia. . . ."—Carl C. Becker, *The Heavenly City of the Eighteenth Century Philosophers*

■ B. In the following arguments, identify and explain the fallacies of irrelevance. Examples include genetic fallacies, poisoning the well, appeals to inexpert authority, and *ad verecundiam* fallacies.

1. Because of alleged inaccuracies in discussions of animal behavior, some parents in Montgomery County objected to the use in county public schools of the book *Animals Everywhere*, by Ingri and Edgar Pasin d'Aulaire. Mrs. Dean, the head of a book-evaluation committee, wrote Doubleday, the publisher, stating the committee's objections. She got an answer from a sales manager, who noted that in the twenty-one years the book had sold more than 150,000 copies and that it was issued in paperback three years ago. "He said nothing about our objections, so I guess they don't plan to make any changes," Mrs. Dean said.—The *Washington Star*, June 6, 1977

2. ". . . a powerful measure of desire for aggression has to be reckoned as part of man's instinctual endowment. . . . *Homo homini lupus*; who has the courage to dispute it in the face of all the evidence in his own life and history?"—Sigmund Freud, *Civilization and Its Discontents*

3. The phenomena reported by this group of mystics is certainly startling; they speak of cases of prophecy, revelation, and the gift of tongues. These events are so unusual that we would need extremely good evidence before we could believe them. But it is impossible to obtain the required evidence because we cannot trust people who claim to be mystics or who believe that such events occur.

*4. "[President Jimmy] Carter refused to debate [Senator Edward] Kennedy. What happened next is in dispute. According to Kennedy's account, which White House aides emphatically denied, Carter said: 'No incumbent President has ever debated a member of his own party.' Kennedy retorted that last November, when the polls showed him far ahead of the President, 'you were eager to debate.' Carter did not respond."— *Time*, June 16, 1980

5. During the period just before the revolutionary war, Thomas Paine was a bitter opponent of reconciliation between the colonies and England. Writing in *Common Sense*, Paine said, "Though I would carefully avoid giving unnecessary offense, yet I am inclined to believe that all those who espouse the doctrine of reconciliation may be included within the following descriptions.

"Interested men, who are not to be trusted, weak men who *cannot* see, prejudiced men who will not see, and a certain set of moderate men who think better of the European world than it deserves; and this last class, by an ill-judged deliberation, will be the cause of more calamities to this Continent than all the other three."

6. TEACHER: You got number six wrong.

STUDENT: I just don't understand why my answer is wrong.

TEACHER: If you weren't so stubborn you'd see that your answer is wrong.

STUDENT: I don't regard supporting my view as stubborn.

TEACHER: Anyone who sticks to an idea like yours has got to be stubborn.

7. Civil disobedience must be justified because none other than Dr. Spock, the well-known authority on child growth and development, was an advocate of civil disobedience during the era of protest against the war in Vietnam.

*8. If your idea were any good, then someone would have thought of it already.

9. The concept of alienation can have no place in the philosophy of one who genuinely advocates freedom and individual autonomy. Why, the concept of alienation, although suggested by the philosopher, Hegel, first took shape in the hands of Karl Marx.

10. "Dear Abby: Your outdated advice to the woman whose husband wanted her to have sex with other men really irked me. . . . Did you ever stop to think that maybe the husband enjoyed her so much in bed that he wanted to show others what a great wife he has? Or it's possible that his sexual enjoyment may really be heightened if she has sex with other men?

"Please don't call this perverted, or say that this man needs a psychiatrist. He doesn't need one. Read the sex manuals. This is an accepted sex practice and it's widely accepted nowadays. [signed] SEE THE LIGHT."—From a letter to "Dear Abby"

11. "I have never had any doubt about it [the Bible] being of divine origin. And to those who . . . doubt it, I would like to have them point out to me any similar collection of writings that have lasted for so many thousands of years and is still the best seller worldwide. It had to be of divine origin."—President Ronald Reagan, as quoted by Lee Edwards, *Ronald Reagan: A Political Biography*

*12. Noam Chomsky commented on the view expressed by B. F. Skinner in *Beyond Freedom and Dignity* that we act as we do because our behavior is determined: "At this point an annoying, though obvious, question intrudes. If Skinner's thesis is false, then there is no point in his having written the book or our reading it. But if his thesis is true, then there is also no point in his having written the book or our reading it."— *New York Review of Books*, December 30, 1971

13. I can't possibly support the construction of a nuclear-powered electricity-generating plant in this state. I saw *The China Syndrome*, I read about the near-disaster at Three Mile Island in *Newsweek*, and I know that Governor Jerry Brown of California was opposed to the construction of nuclear power plants in California.

14. "The religions of mankind must be classed among the mass delusions of this kind. No one, needless to say, who shares a delusion ever recognizes it as such."—Sigmund Freud, *Civilization and Its Discontents*

15. "Since the end of the draft, a lot of young people are discovering a good place to invest their time. The Army. They've come, over 250,000 strong. Join the people who've joined the Army."—United States Army recruitment advertisement ■

☐ 12-5. AVOIDING FALLACIES AND PLAYING FAIR

Each and every fallacy falls under one of the three general types shown in Table 12-1: inconsistency, begging the question, or *non sequitur*. But it would be impossible to identify every specific way in which arguments can be fallacious. Even the extensive list of *non sequiturs* in Table 12-2 does not include all the specific forms of that group. So instead of continually subdividing the classification, it often makes more sense simply to describe an argument as, say, a fallacy of irrelevance.

In addition, remember that a given argument may contain more than one kind of fallacy; the premises may be irrelevant to the conclusion in more than one way. Or an extended argument may contain several types of fallacies.

Improving one's ability to recognize faulty reasoning requires constant practice, careful attention to the meaning of what is written or spoken, and an organized approach. The procedures set out below also incorporate some ethical considerations relevant to diagnosing fallacies. Together, they constitute an answer to the question, How should one respond when one encounters an argument that appears to be fallacious?

1. *Determine whether the comments constitute an explicit argument or contain statements supporting a conclusion that is not expressed.* If the material is neither an argument nor part of an argument, it is not a logical fallacy. The remarks may, though, be unacceptable for some other reason—because they contain a false accusation or inflammatory language, for example.

2. *Where possible, consider the speaker or writer's intentions and the context in which the discourse occurs.* Details about the suffering of a terminally ill patient, if presented as reasons for passing a constitutional amendment granting such patients the right to be removed from life-support systems, would constitute an appeal to pity and hence be fallacious. But if the speaker or writer is merely providing *evidence*—say, to a legislative committee appointed to gather information and draft a model bill—the remarks should not be judged by the criteria applied to arguments.

3. *Once it has been decided that the discourse is or could be used as an argument, determine how the reasoning goes astray.* First, decide on the category of fallacious thinking to which it belongs: inconsistency, begging the question, or *non sequitur*. Then try to determine its specific difficulty.

4. *Determine your own attitude with respect to the intended conclusion.* Knowing whether you are inclined to support the conclusion or to challenge it will help you decide how to respond to the fallacy. If you accept the conclusion, you may want to show the arguer how the defect can be repaired— for example, by suggesting deletion of a premise that contains an abusive *ad hominem* appeal.

If you reject the conclusion, you must decide how best to inform your adversary that the argument is unacceptable. In this case, remember three rules: (a) *The person presenting the argument must demonstrate why the conclusion is justified.* It is not your responsibility to show why the conclusion is unacceptable. (b) *Avoid committing a fallacy of negative proof.* Do not suppose that because a fallacious attempt has been made to support a conclusion, the conclusion has thereby been *disproved.* Other, more plausible, reasons may be presented for the proposition in question. (c) Do *not* consider someone who commits a fallacy to be so discredited as to be incapable of making any relevant and valuable remarks. Everyone errs from time to time.

5. *Regard reasoning as a cooperative enterprise, not as competition.* A balanced attitude involves a willingness to recognize good reasoning by an opponent; logical criticism is not all negative.

Unfortunately, some individuals have the mistaken impression that the whole point of logic is to score debating victories. When confronted by an argument, they immediately set out to convince the arguer that it represents one form of fallacy or another.

Fair and constructive criticism requires that one exercise care in charging another with fallacious reasoning. Undiscriminating judgments impede the discussion process. To misrepresent an argument by mistakenly claiming it to be fallacious is like setting up a *straw man* (Section 2-4) that one then proceeds to kick around as if drubbing the opponent. The destructive effect of carelessly labeling reasoning as fallacious has led some logicians to identify a further fallacy— "the false charge of fallacy."

6. *Expose a fallacious argument if the opportunity arises.* When the fallacy is a *formal* fallacy, the most effective way of exposing its defect is by means of a *counterexample.* This consists of presenting an argument of exactly the same *form* that reaches an absurd or plainly false conclusion—a conclusion your opponent will recognize as unjustified (see Sections 2-2, 8-5, and 9-7).

In the case of an *informal fallacy,* a more direct approach is needed. Simply say that the argument is unacceptable and, as clearly as possible, explain why. Be as exact as possible without going into needless detail. Divide a complex argument into different parts, and focus on what is questionable. Ask your opponent, for instance, "Do you mean to conclude that X by using Y as a reason?" If possible, indicate what you would regard as an acceptable reason in support of the conclusion your opponent is advocating—or at least what sort of premises might place the argument on the right track.

Consider one of your objectives to be preparing your opponent to engage in reasoned argument with you on future occasions. It may be advisable to avoid flatly stating that the argument is fallacious because the other person may not understand by *argument* the linking of premises and conclusion and may think you are trying to prejudice the issue. It may also be better to use the English rather than the Latin names for the fallacies, so as not to appear condescending.

Fallacies occur today with depressing regularity in articles and editorials and in the pronouncements of political figures. To be a responsible judge of a proposed remedy for a social, political, or moral issue, one must be able to recognize and avoid fallacious thinking. Logic provides the means for developing this ability.

■ **EXERCISE 12-5**

For each of the following discourses, decide (a) what conclusion or point of view is being advocated (if the passage makes it clear) and (b) what fallacy or fallacies (if any) have been committed and by whom.

1. "Black leaders echoing their pleas of the riot-punctuated 1960s are asking once again: Do we have to burn our neighborhoods in order to be heard?"—*Time,* June 16, 1980

2. "The blood-bespattered, slaughter-gutted archives of human history from the earliest Egyptian and Sumerian records to the most recent atrocities of the Second World War accord with early universal cannibalism, with animal and human sacrificial practices or their substitutes in formalized religions, and with the world-wide scalping, head-hunting, body-mutilating and necrophiliac practices of mankind in proclaiming this common bloodlust differentiation, this predaceous habit, this mark of Cain that separates man dietically from his anthropoidal relatives and allies him rather with the deadliest carnivora."—Raymond Dart, *International Anthropology and Linguistic Review*

3. "The Rev. James Robinson holds up a slick white bumper sticker with the word 'vote' emblazoned in bright blue. The television audience quickly realizes that this is not your typical League of Women Voters appeal. The 't' is elongated and highlighted to resemble a cross.

"'We have made a god out of our government, and it has placed us in bondage,' says Robinson in a $1.3 million, hour-long television special entitled, 'Wake Up America, We Are All Hostages.'

"'We either bind the government or the government surely will bind us,' he warns. 'That's why the vote is important.'"—*The Washington Post,* July 1, 1980

*4. "[On one occasion, Bryant Gumbel, co-host of NBC's *Today*] interrupted a man who was talking about drugs to ask, 'Why should we care what you say—you're a junkie, right?'"—*Washington Post,* January 4, 1982

5. "Dear Friend:
I think you will appreciate, more than most Americans, what I am sending you.
"I have enclosed two flags: the red, white, and blue of Old Glory—and the white flag of surrender.
"I want to show you by these two flags, what is at stake for America under the Salt II Treaty with Russia. . . . You and I must choose—and the Senate must decide—whether we will personally accept the White Flag of Surrender as America's banner."—Opening of a letter from the Conservative Caucus, signed by Howard Phillips

6. "The questions you must ask yourself are these: Are you going to allow the 'Moral Majority' to pervert the Constitution in order to take control of your life . . . take away your personal liberty, your freedom of choice, your right to plan your own family, your right to control your own destiny?"—Letter from Faye Wattleton, President, Planned Parenthood Federation of America

7. "To the Editor: Your disgusting editorial in support of freedom of pornography versus the Supreme Court decision benumbs the Spiritual sensibilities of all right-thinking people who are concerned about the morals of young Americans."—Letter to the *Washington Evening Star*, reprinted in *The Capitol Voice*, Dale Crowley, editor

*8. "My answer to genocide, quite simply, is eight black kids—and another baby on the way.

"I guess it is just that 'slave master' complex white folks have. For years they told me where to sit, where to eat, and where to live. Now they want to dictate our bedroom habits. First the white man tells me to sit in the back of the bus. Now it looks like he wants me to sleep under the bed. Back in the days of slavery, black folks couldn't grow kids fast enough for white folks to harvest. Now that we've got a little taste of power, white folks want us to call a moratorium on having babies.

"Of course, I could never participate in birth control, because I'm against doing anything that goes against Nature. That's why I've changed my eating habits so drastically over the years and have become a vegetarian. And birth control is definitely against Nature. Can you believe that human beings are the only creatures who would ever consider developing birth control pills? You mention contraception to a gorilla and he will tear your head off."—Dick Gregory, "My Answer to Genocide," *Ebony*, October 1971

9. HE: I don't think I really matter to you.

SHE: Now why are you saying that?

HE: I just feel taken for granted. . . .

SHE: Far from it, just tell me what I can say or do to please you.

HE: See, this is proof of what I just said. I don't really matter to you. If I did, you wouldn't have to ask me what you should be doing.

10. "If we are going to rear and kill animals for our food, I think we have a moral obligation to spare them pain and terror in both processes, simply because they are sentient. I can't *prove* they are sentient; but then I have no proof *you* are. Even though you are articulate, whereas an animal can only scream or struggle, I have no assurance that your 'It hurts' expresses anything like the intolerable sensations I experience in pain. I know, however, that when I visit my dentist and say 'It hurts,' I am grateful that he gives me the benefit of the doubt.

"I don't myself believe that, even when we fulfill our minimum obligations not to cause pain, we have the right to kill animals. I know I would have no right to kill you, however painlessly, just because I liked your flavour, and I am not in a position to judge that your life is worth more to you than the animal's to it. . . ."—Brigid Brophy, writing in the *Sunday Times* (London), October 10, 1965

11. George Latimer was Lieutenant William Calley's defense attorney at the latter's court martial for premeditated murder at My Lai in Vietnam. At one point, Latimer pleaded with the jury of career officers to consider the army itself. "I'm proud of the United States Army," he told them. "It grieves me to see it being pulled apart from

within. . . . An acquittal will help the Army. It will show the judicial process protects a man who makes an error in judgment. . . ." Six days later, Latimer pleaded for his client's life: "Lieutenant Calley, outside of a normal traffic ticket, was a good boy. . . . He stayed that way until he got in that Oriental environment. . . . Maybe you can say he used bad judgment and became too aggressive and went too far. . . . But who taught him to kill, kill, kill?"—*The Washington Post*, April 11, 1974

*12. "Sen. William Scott (R–Va.) denied yesterday that he was 'the dumbest' member of Congress, as *New Times* magazine said he was, but, he added, he was in a quandary whether it would be wise to take the matter to court. . . . He hasn't decided yet whether to file a libel suit against *New Times*, Scott said, because in libel suits the element of malice, a crucial point, is very hard to prove. 'I don't want to bring a suit that I don't win, because somebody might think the article is true if I don't win,' he said."—"Sen. Scott Won't Test His Intelligence," *Miami News*, May 24, 1974

13. "I believe I have omitted mentioning that in my first voyage from Boston to Philadelphia, being becalmed off Block Island, our crew employed themselves catching cod and hauled up a great number. 'Till then I had stuck to my resolution to eat nothing that had had life; and on this occasion I considered, according to my Master Tyron, the taking every fish as a kind of unprovoked murder, since none of them had or ever could do us any injury that might justify this massacre. All this seemed very reasonable. But I had formerly been a great lover of fish, and when this came hot out of the frying pan, it smelled admirably well. I balanced sometime between principle and inclination till I remembered that when the fish were opened, I saw smaller fish taken out of their stomachs. 'Then,' thought I, 'if you eat one another, I don't see why we mayn't eat you.' So I dined upon cod very heartily and have since continued to eat as other people, returning only now and then occasionally to a vegetarian diet. So convenient a thing it is to be a *reasonable creature*, since it enables one to find or make a reason for everything one has a mind to do."—From *The Autobiography of Benjamin Franklin*

14. "Throughout history, presidents, senators and representatives, seizing upon short-run political or popular opposition, have attempted to negotiate unpopular constitutional decisions through the action of mere legislative majorities: by impeaching Justices, by packing the Court or by curtailing its jurisdiction. Always in the past, despite their discontent with particular decisions, the American people and the Congress have rejected the backdoor assaults upon the Constitution as dangerously unprincipled.

"They should be rejected again today."—Archibald Cox, "Don't Overrule the Court," *Newsweek*, September 28, 1981

15. "In our system of government, judges have the legal authority to review the constitutionality of legislation and executive action. Thus, the law is what the judges say it is."

*16. "The board of trustees of Bob Jones University is made up of 50 godly men and women from all sections of the United States. They are *unanimous* in their conviction that Bob Jones University should not enroll Negro students.

College years are the time when young people make their life contacts, fall in love, and get married; and we do not believe intermarriage of the races is Scriptural. That such is the purpose of the whole present emphasis is apparent from a statement from one of the leaders of the NAACP who said, 'The racial problem will not be settled in the courtroom but in the bedroom.'"—Statement from the president, Bob Jones University, *The Citizen*, February 1971

17. "Parapsychologists claim that the existence of psi [defined as 'extrasensorimotor exchange with the environment'] is testable. They conduct a series of tests or

runs in which the subject tries to guess unseen targets (clairvoyance) or future targets (precognition) or tries to influence which target will turn up (psychokinesis). If the results of the experiments are significantly above the level expected by chance, that shows psi was in operation. If the subject gets a score significantly *below* chance expectation, that shows the existence of psi as well. The term for it is *psi-missing*, which is defined as 'the exercise of psi ability in a way that avoids the target the subject is attempting to hit.'"—Daisie Radner and Michael Radner, *Science and Unreason*

18. "Bernard Brodie, a political scientist who was among the first writers to consider critically what the advent of nuclear weapons implied for world politics and military strategy, has more recently taken to task certain of the foremost American hard-liners, who use the argument that the Russians believe they can win a nuclear war in order to promote the complementary view that America could. He cites Professor Pipes, a professor of Russian History at Harvard University, and well-known for his belligerent attitude, as one of the main protagonists of this view. . . . Brodie refers to a recent article by Professor Pipes entitled 'Why the Soviet Union thinks it could fight and win a nuclear war,' and then goes on to say, 'The "why" in the title of Mr. Pipes' article preempts the prior question *whether* some entity called the Soviet Union thinks as he says it does. The appropriate question is: *Who* in the Soviet Union thinks they can fight and win a nuclear war? The article tells us that it is some Soviet generals who think so, not a single political leader being mentioned.'"—Solly Zuckerman, *Nuclear Illusion and Reality*

19. Researcher George Stone believes he has found the explanation for two successive harsh winters in North America. He believes that the abnormally cold weather was probably caused by the Soviet Cosmos satellite that crashed in northern Canada early in 1975. In *The Skeptical Inquirer* (Fall 1978), he was quoted as claiming, "The satellite that crashed in Canada in January was in just the right position to control our weather all along the East Coast, where the snowstorms hit. . . . I admit I have no hard evidence, but then there is no negative evidence either."

*20. "Suppose death puts an end to all care. Suppose that it cuts it off together with the senses of the body. This is another problem to be solved. . . .

"But it is unthinkable that this could be true. It is not for nothing, not mere chance, that the towering authority of the Christian faith has spread throughout the world. God would never have done so much, such wonderful things for us, if the life of the soul came to an end with the death of the body."—St. Augustine, *Confessions* ∎

CHAPTER THIRTEEN

Legal reasoning

The decisions made by judges, especially those in appellate courts, vitally affect all members of society. To settle disputes effectively, judges must persuade educated citizens, as well as trained lawyers, that their decisions are reasonable. Thus, it is in written judicial opinions—the finished and public records of the appellate courts—that legal reasoning is most highly developed and the standards for argumentation are most rigorous.

Logicians are concerned with the structure of the arguments presented in legal reasoning and the criteria for distinguishing good arguments from weak ones. Therefore, evaluating an argument in this context differs little from evaluating an argument for a scientific hypothesis or for a conclusion in any other area of human activity. In each instance, the logician appraises the logical strength of the reasoning involved and considers neither the subject matter of particular arguments nor the psychological processes of thought.

But unlike deduction, and unlike induction as it is employed in science, legal reasoning cannot be abstracted from the operations of the system in which it occurs. Legal procedures established for the resolution of disputes greatly influence the arguments judges make to explain and justify their decisions. Thus, the study of legal reasoning is, at the same time, an analysis of *practical reasoning*—a study of the way logical principles and methods have been adapted to meet the requirements of problem solving imposed upon the courts.

□ 13-1. LAW AS A FORUM FOR ARGUMENT

Whoever hath an absolute authority to interpret any written or spoken laws, it is he who is truly the lawgiver, to all intents and purposes, and not the person who first spoke and wrote them.
BISHOP HOADLEY

The law is best understood as a problem-solving process rather than a collection of rules or a set of institutions made up of courthouses, prisons, and police stations. Lawyers and judges are primarily problem solvers.

Contrary to the impression created by television drama, with its emphasis on courtroom battles, most legal decisions are not made in courts at all. They are made by professional lawyers, experienced officials, and even legally knowledgeable laypersons who reason about the probable outcome of a dispute by considering the decisions set forth in earlier court cases. If it were not possible to settle most disputes outside the courthouse, the demands made on the courts would paralyze them. The courts are able to handle only a very small percentage of all the legal problems that arise at any given time.

Glossary of Legal Terms

APPELLANT.   The party who appeals to a higher court because of dissatisfaction with the decision of the lower court.

APPELLATE COURT.   A court that hears appeals regarding the judgments of a lower court and either affirms, reverses, or modifies the judgments. Each state in the United State has a hierarchy of courts—including trial courts, appeals courts, and a final, or "supreme," court. (In New York State, the final appeals court is called the New York Court of Appeals; and the trial courts are called "supreme courts" to distinguish them from lower, petty courts such as traffic and small-claims courts.) In the federal court system, the trial courts are called district courts, and there are eleven appeals courts, each receiving appeals from several district courts that fall within its area, or circuit. Finally, the highest appellate court of the land is the United States Supreme Court, which reviews cases decided in the federal courts of appeal. It also reviews any cases from a highest state court in which a federal statute has been held invalid or in which a state statute has been upheld against attack on federal grounds.

COMMON LAW.   The body of judicial decisions, first developed in England but accepted and expanded in the United States, that is applied in various areas—including disputes over property, torts, and contracts. In modern times, it has been largely supplanted by statutory law.

DISSENT, OR DISSENTING OPINION.   A written statement in which an appellate-court judge gives reasons for disagreeing with the majority decision.

DONEE.   A recipient of a gift.

JURISDICTION.   The extent of the authority of a given court.

PETITIONER.   One who submits a formal, written application asking a court for a specific judicial action. The petitioner thus initiates the action. When reporting cases, the name of the original petitioner is always given first, even though in an appellate case, the petitioner may be either the plaintiff or the defendant of the trial case.

Lawyers generally practice a sort of "preventive law," providing assistance designed to reduce the chance that conflict will occur. Among many other activities, they help people to write valid wills, dissolve unhappy marriages, select insurance policies, and negotiate bank loans. Of course, sometimes clients do not follow a lawyer's advice, and sometimes conflicts—auto collision, a physician's mistake, or the angry firing of an employee, for example—begin without lawyers. When lawyers are unable to negotiate a compromise, the opponents are likely to go to court and ask a judge to settle their differences.

What sets lawyers and judges apart from other problem solvers—such as accountants, engineers, physicians, educators, and city planners—is the *kind* of problem on which they work. Legal issues are defined in terms of rules that

PLAINTIFF. The party who brings suit against another in a trial court.

PRECEDENT. A principle, doctrine, or rule that governed the decision in a given case and that is deemed to be a controlling authority in similar situations coming before later courts. The term may also refer to the earlier case from which the principle, doctrine, or rule is taken.

PROBATE. The proof that a written statement is the last will and testament of a deceased person.

REMAND. To send a case back to a lower court with instructions about further proceedings.

RESPONDENT. The party contending against an appeal from a lower court to a higher court.

STANDING. The legal ability to sue in a court of law. In a federal court, a person instituting a suit must meet several requirements: the plaintiff must have a personal stake in the outcome of the controversy, one that warrants the request that a federal court assume jurisdiction and that justifies use of the court's remedies. In addition, the plaintiff must be shown to be injured—economically or in some other way—by the challenged action of the defendant.

STARE DECISIS (Latin, "Let the decision stand"). The principle of following precedent in deciding new cases.

SYLLABUS. A short report immediately preceding the statement of the majority opinion in an appellate-court decision. It contains a summary of the facts as found by the lower court and a statement of the lower court's ruling.

TESTATOR. One who has made a valid will. Such a person is said to have died *testate*. One who has not made a valid will is said to have died *in testate*.

TORT. The term (from the Latin *tortum*, meaning "twisted") applied to a miscellaneous group of civil wrongs, other than breach of contract, for which a court may afford a remedy in the form of an action for damages. The law of tort is concerned with compensation for losses suffered by private individuals through the unreasonable conduct of others.

TRIAL COURT. The court of original jurisdiction, where a case is first heard.

officials and agencies of the government have established and are willing—
and expected—to enforce. So to study the use of logic in law is to study, first
and foremost, how judges justify the choices they must make between alternative solutions to problems involving *rules*.

☐ Sources of law

The rules that define legal conflicts are of four different kinds:

1. Regulations of administrative bodies such as the Food and Drug Administration and the Internal Revenue Service
2. Articles and clauses of state constitutions and the United States Constitution
3. The common law
4. Statutes or enactments of legislative bodies

This discussion will concern primarily common-law rules and legislative enactments.

The *common law* consists of a large body of rules that are applied in the
courts but that have never been enacted as regulations, statutes, or ordinances
by administrative or legislative bodies. Its roots go back hundreds of years to
customs that the royal courts of England adopted and attempted to apply
uniformly, thereby making them *common* to all the king's land. Today, the
common law provides judges with a great number of precedents—drawn from
thousands of reported cases—that can be used to solve problems in the absence
of formal rules. The common law is divided into branches concerning such
areas of dispute as property, contracts, and torts.[1]

Statutes and ordinances result from legislative efforts to address public
problems, set priorities, and make public policy. They are the means by which
legislators make their decisions legally binding. Such enactments instruct the
public to cope with a problem in a certain way—for instance, by paying taxes,
registering for the draft, and operating automobiles in a reasonable and prudent
manner. Someone who does not comply may be prosecuted by the government
or sued by individuals seeking compensation for losses they suffered as a result
of the noncompliance. Then statutes, like all other legal rules, serve as *instructions* to judges to settle the conflict in one way rather than another.

☐ Questions of fact and questions of law

When a legal problem becomes a court case, the proceedings must follow a
standard sequence of steps and must satisfy the necessary conditions of orderly
procedure, or *due process*. In fact, failure to follow the proper sequence can

---

[1] For the legal meaning of this term and others that occur throughout the chapter,
see the "Glossary of Legal Terms" in the box on pp. 456–457.

be an effective ground for appeal: a "formally defective" legal proceeding can be declared void by a higher court. Ensuring the ritual formality of court proceedings is a precaution intended to give fair and equitable protection to the contesting parties.

The proceedings terminate when, after going through each stage of the process, the court presents a verdict: rather than working out a "settlement" agreeable to both parties, the court must decide for, or *rule for*, one or the other of the two adversaries. If a compromise could have been reached, the issue would presumably have been dealt with earlier, without the need for a judicial hearing.

In the trial court—or court of original jurisdiction—where the case is first heard, the dispute usually turns on *questions of fact*. The two sides present rival accounts of the same episode, and the task of the judge—or the jury, if it is a jury trial—is to determine what the facts are. This part of the legal process involves a kind of historical research: Did the deceased man pull a knife on the defendant before the defendant shot him, or didn't he? Is the signature on the will a forgery, as the disinherited daughter claims, or is it the deceased's "very own," as the will's beneficiary maintains?

Over the years, elaborate rules of evidence have been developed to control what judges and juries may rely on in rendering a verdict. The evidence is carefully sifted to eliminate irrelevant information apt to draw attention from the questions immediately at issue and to insure that only information deemed authentic enters the court record.

While fact-finding can be dramatic, court trials that seek primarily to answer these historical questions do not involve extensive legal reasoning. This is probably why the public feels confident about letting such research be conducted by a single judge or by a group of amateur historians—ordinary citizens in the jury box.

Legal reasoning mainly concerns *questions of law*. It consists not in determining what happened but in deciding how to interpret the facts once they are known, in analyzing the rules claimed to be relevant to the facts, and in deciding how these rules apply.

The appellate-court judge, who hears appeals from trial courts, is concerned primarily with questions of law—whether the trial judge applied the proper rule to the facts. Here, the facts in a case are learned by reading the trial transcript—the record of testimony presented and conclusions reached by the lower court. The judge usually assumes the facts to be those accepted by the judge or jury in the lower court, although a case will be returned, or *remanded*, to the lower court for retrial if the judge believes an error in fact-finding has occurred.

The appellate judges, in reviewing questions of law, write opinions explaining their conclusions. The judges or their law clerks search the records of precedent cases for statements of the rules of law inherent in them. These rules of law, in the form of quotations taken from the opinions of the courts that decided the precedent cases, are entered into the written opinions of the appellate-court judges. Thus, the masses of legal precedents that fill the shelves of law libraries emerge from the appellate process. And because appellate judges review trial judges' interpretations of all kinds of law, appellate opinions interpret and apply all kinds of law.

Because the decision of the highest appellate court in a jurisdiction represents the final stage of the legal process, the appellate judge's decision is decisive. If the judge of a lower court believes that a court higher in the judicial hierarchy has created a governing precedent, that judge cannot ignore it even if he or she believes the precedent is unwise and should be discarded. For lower courts in the same jurisdiction, that precedent is a rule that binds them as surely as the Constitution.

Judges of state supreme courts and the United States Supreme Court have considerably more discretion than lower-court judges in selecting precedents that seem apt. They may refer to earlier decisions by courts in different jurisdictions. And they may "overrule" themselves by rejecting precedents they themselves generated.

☐ The central role of the appellate courts

Just as the lower courts look to the appellate courts for direction, lawyers also base recommendations to their clients on these appellate decisions. Indeed, in estimating the chance that a suit will have an outcome favorable to a client, a lawyer reasons about precedents in much the same way as the judge. Thus, the reasoned decisions of judges at the appellate level form the very backbone of the legal process.

By making the courts the last resort in dispute-settling, the legal system gives judges the last word on the law. An aphorism often heard in legal circles— "The law is what the judges say it is"—underlines the importance of their interpretations of the rules. A lawyer suggesting a way for a client to prevent or resolve a conflict, a legislator wording a proposed bill, an administrative officer designing a new regulation—all must try to anticipate how the courts will react to their efforts. If they estimate incorrectly, if the courts interpret and apply a rule in an unexpected way, they fail to achieve their purposes.

☐ The effects of the adversary process on legal reasoning

Legal reasoning is strongly influenced by the adversary proceedings in the courtroom. Its distinctive features result from the way clashing interests are accommodated in the "law forum."

In the first place, judges must decide concrete cases. A judge may not make general pronouncements on broad aspects of the law but must focus on the narrow issues presented by the specific conflict. And unlike the legislative and administrative organs of government, which formulate broad social policies, the courts must deal with the elements of social conflict—such as conflicting interests and values—as they are represented by the parties' opposed claims in a particular case.

It cannot be expected that in deciding a difficult case, a judge will discover the one right solution that everyone believes is best. But the judge's "audience"—the public—expects the legal process to show that divergent facts, general rules, pressing social conditions, and competing moral values can somehow be reconciled or harmonized. The judicial process therefore plays a major role in preserving the public's confidence that even the gravest problems can be resolved *within* the community by an exercise of reason.

The adversary nature of courtroom proceedings also *shapes the arguments judges develop to justify their decisions.* By pitting the plaintiff and defendant against each other, the law forum requires attorneys to proceed as competitors. Both attorneys will press upon the judge examples of prior cases, arguably relevant to the facts of the present case and representing outcomes favorable to their client's interests. The judge must select, from among the facts in the present case, those that resemble facts in previous cases urged as precedents, as well as facts that differ from those of prior cases.

Attorneys expect a judge to justify a decision by explaining why one set of analogies—between the case at hand and a given line of precedents—is more appropriate than another set. They expect the judge's opinion to reflect careful consideration of the distinctions between one example and the next. This reasoning by analogy—or "reasoning by example," as it is often called—is prominent in the judicial opinions written by judges of appellate courts.

Appellate judges write opinions explaining their decisions to meet requirements of reasonableness. A questionable justification in an opinion provokes dissents by other judges of the same court; spurs criticism from legal scholars as expressed in bar-association speeches and articles in law reviews; and undermines public confidence. Even the members of a lay audience can often distinguish between their personal hopes regarding an outcome—that "their side" should win—and their expectations of impartiality, deliberate care, and fairness on the part of the judge. It is the deliberate, articulate, and public quality of the judge's reasoning that surpasses the coercive power of the state and gives a court ruling its authority and its quality as law.[2]

■ **EXERCISE 13-1**

■ A. Discussion questions

1. In terms of the law as a forum for argument, what is the difference between questions of fact and questions of law? How are arguments concerning facts likely to differ from arguments concerning law? Why are the trial courts primarily concerned with questions of fact?

2. Why do the judges of appellate courts have a crucial role in determining what the law requires? In "making law," how does the role of the appellate courts differ from the role of the legislature? How do practicing attorneys contribute to the development of the law? How do private citizens contribute to the development of the law?

---

[2] This point is made by Leif H. Carter in his book *Reason in Law* (Boston: Little, Brown, 1979), pp. 231–232.

3. Explain the apparent anomaly that while most appellate cases raise difficult and unsettling choices for judges, most law is generally clear and stable.

*4. There seems to be a paradox: unless courts do their work well, lawyers will not be able to settle most legal disputes outside of court; and unless lawyers settle most legal disputes outside of court, the courts will not be able to work well. Is this really a paradox? Explain.

5. When the law is understood as a problem-solving process, it is easy to see that it has many different functions. Give a specific example of the kind of problem the law "solves" in fulfilling each of the functions listed below:

a. Dispute-settling between private parties

b. Maintaining order

c. Securing efficiency, harmony, and balance in the operation of the government

d. Protecting citizens from excessive and unfair government power

e. Dispute-settling between states and nations

f. Providing a framework in which private citizens can have confidence in their ability to plan for the future

g. Protecting the health and safety of citizens

h. Promoting broad social objectives

i. Providing a framework in which certain common expectations about the transactions and accidents of daily life can be met

■ **B.** The following are "exploratory problems" designed to help you think provocatively about the questions raised in this introductory section and anticipate the topics addressed in subsequent sections.

1. A legal rule of the community in which you live prohibits citizens from taking a vehicle into the public park. As the local magistrate, you must decide in each of the following cases whether the rule has been violated. Present your reasons for each decision. (Try to rule so that at least some of the circumstances will not constitute violations of the rule.)

a. A group of youths are arrested after driving a car through the park late at night.

b. A man under psychiatric care becomes temporarily disoriented and drives his car fifty to seventy feet into the park to get it off the highway.

c. Elderly citizens complain that their safety is endangered by youths who ride their bicycles down the walkways.

d. Two men and a woman have been apprehended using the service drive through the park as a shortcut during rush-hour traffic.

e. A police patrol car enters the park to investigate a suspicious activity.

f. Some citizens complain that they are annoyed by the odors from a cart wheeled into the park by a hot-dog vendor.

g. After a large number of skateboard injuries in the park, the park service bans skateboards. A group of angry citizens protests this restriction.

h. The city council approves a petition of the VFW to erect in the park an armored personnel carrier mounted on a large pedestal.

2. A statute says, "It shall be a misdemeanor to sleep at a railway station." Does the word "at" include those comfortably asleep in their upper berth while their train rests at the station? Does "at" include a hobo asleep on the sidewalk ten yards from the station? Is the tired commuter dozing upright while waiting for the delayed train "asleep"? Should the law apply to someone sprawled on a bench in a drunken stupor?— Adapted from Leif H. Carter, *Reason in Law*, p. 63.

What sort of problem or problems do you think the statute was intended to solve? If it were your responsibility to enforce the statute, would you apply it with a view toward the purposes you believe it was intended to serve, or strictly on the basis of its literal meaning?

3. Discuss the distinction between the concept of doing something by *mistake* and doing something by *accident*. Use the following tale to help you: "You have a donkey, so have I, and they graze in the same field. The day comes when I conceive a dislike for mine. I go to shoot it, draw a bead on it, fire: the brute falls in its tracks. I inspect the victim, and find to my horror that it is *your* donkey. I appear on your doorstep with the remains and say—what? 'I say, old sport, I'm awfully sorry, etc., I've shot your donkey *by accident*'? Or '*by mistake*'? Then again, I go to shoot my donkey as before, draw a bead on it, fire—but as I do so, the beasts move, and to my horror yours falls. Again the scene at the doorstep—what do I say? 'By mistake'? Or 'by accident'?—J. L. Austin, "A Plea for Excuses," *Proceedings of the Aristotelian Society*, 1956–1957

Discuss the situations in which the distinction between accidents and mistakes may be fairly insignificant. Present hypothetical situations in which the distinction is important (where a rule says, for example, that harm unintentionally produced by accident but not by mistake is excusable).

*4. While eating a piece of "homemade" fruit pie in the Stardust Restaurant, Ms. Wright ingests a small metal tack concealed in the pie filling. The tack must be surgically removed. Ms. Wright recovers for damages from the restaurant. Soon afterward, Mr. Gotwals ingests a small tack while eating a piece of "homemade" fruit pie in Samantha's Restaurant. The tack is surgically removed, and Mr. Gotwals recovers for damages. Later, Ms. Capezio ingests a small tack while eating "homemade" pie at the Wagon Wheel Restaurant.

(a) As the attorney for Ms. Capezio, how would you advise your client? As the attorney for the Wagon Wheel Restaurant, how would you advise your client? (b) Do you think the lawyers' advice would help Ms. Capezio and the Wagon Wheel Restaurant to settle their differences outside of court? Why or why not?

5. Imagine that there is a student-faculty panel, the honor commission, in your college or university. It is the responsibility of the commission to hear charges against students involving a wide range of rule violations—including plagiarism, cheating, disorderly conduct in the residence halls, vandalism, and illegal parking. For some time, the commission has been careless about the manner in which it has made decisions in these cases. Often, decisions seem to be arbitrary, biased, or based on intuition.

Discuss the probable effects on the decision making of the honor commission of the following changes:

a. In the future, all members of the commission must be nominated by the president of the student government organization and appointed by the president of the university. Each nominee must also demonstrate, in oral examination, a thorough knowledge of the university regulations.

b. Students will now be allowed to appear before the commission and present their side of the controversy.

c. Decisions of the commission must now be explained in writing as well as announced.

d. The opinions of the commission begin to appear in print as a regular feature of the student newspaper (although the names of those charged with violations are not printed).

e. The commission now elects one of its members to serve as a recording secretary whose responsibility is to maintain a file of cases, including summaries of the facts and records of the decisions reached.

f. After stormy debates in the faculty senate and the student government organization, it is decided that the files of the commission shall be open to inspection by any member of the university community.

g. It is decided by the board of trustees that decisions of the commission will be subject to review by a review board on appeal. ∎

☐ 13-2. LOGIC AND LEGAL REASONING

The life of the law has not been logic; it has been experience.
JUSTICE OLIVER WENDELL HOLMES

Holmes did not tell us that logic is to be ignored when experience is silent.
JUSTICE BENJAMIN N. CARDOZO

Judges in appellate courts are strongly influenced by contesting attorneys—each arguing to "win" the case. For this reason, some observers believe that judicial decision making does not involve logic. A group of critics, sometimes called "legal realists," have asserted that logical analysis reveals little about the way judges make decisions.

☐ *The view of the legal realists*

On first impression, it seems that judges must offer demonstrative arguments for their decisions. They do not say, "On the basis of the evidence, the defendant was probably acting legally," nor that "the defendant's claim is more probable than the plaintiff's claim." Rather, because judges are required to render verdicts, their decisions must be final and decisive. A formal, deductive mode of reasoning therefore seems appropriate to achieve the level of certainty and finality judicial decision making requires.

According to the legal realists, however, the appearance that judicial reasoning is primarily deductive is deceptive. Writing in *The Common Law*, Justice

Oliver Wendell Holmes said, "The life of the law has not been logic: it has been experience. The felt necessities of the time, the prevalent moral and political theories, intuitions of public policy, avowed or unconscious, even the prejudices which judges share with their fellowmen, have had a good deal more to do than the syllogism in determining the rules by which we should be governed."[3]

The view that the judicial decision process is not primarily logical was shared by Justice Jerome Frank. In his book *Law and the Modern Mind*, Frank observed that "in theory, the judge begins with some rule or principle of law as his premise, applies the premise to the facts, and thus arrives at his decision." But this theory, Frank contended, does not accord with the facts: "Since the judge is a human being and since no human being in the normal thinking process arrives at decisions (except in dealing with a limited number of simple situations) by the route of any such syllogistic reasoning, it is fair to assume that the judges, merely by putting on the judicial ermine, will not acquire so artificial a method of reasoning. Judicial judgments, like other judgments, doubtless, in most cases, are worked out backward from conclusions tentatively formulated."[4] In other words, Frank believed that the judge usually begins with what seems like the proper conclusion and then attempts to explain this result by showing how it is necessarily derived from the relevant legal rule. But the justification is a mere rationalization—a self-satisfying but incorrect explanation. The decision process employed in any particular case can be correctly described only by reference to what Justice Frank described as the "peculiarly individual traits of the persons whose inferences and opinions are to be explained." The personality of the judge is, consequently, the key to understanding the way in which cases have been decided.

Other legal realists assert that a hunch, or intuition, regarding what is the just solution to a particular case is the crucial factor in the decision process, or even that the judge's emotional reaction to the facts of the case determines the outcome. But all agree that irrational factors are the primary influences on the judge and that the judge only makes it *appear* that the decision was dictated by prior rules applied in accordance with the canons of formal logic.

Judges must say what the law "is" to resolve the disputes before them. A judge cannot hear a case and then refuse to render a decision because the legal answer cannot be determined. Nor can a judge say, "Maybe the law is X. Maybe the law is Y. I'll guess Y. You lose!" Consequently, to render justice in our society, *judges must often make certain that which is inherently uncertain*. They must sometimes state how the law applies to a case when, up until the point of decision, it is unclear whether and how the law does apply. Therefore, the legal realists contended it should not be surprising that judges cling to the illusion that their decisions deductively follow from clear and settled rules of law.

---

[3] Oliver Wendell Holmes, *The Common Law* (Boston: Little, Brown, 1881), pp. 1–2.
[4] Jerome Frank, *Law and the Modern Mind*, 6th ed. (New York: Coward McCann, 1949), p. 101.

□ *Uncertainty and judicial choice*

It might be thought that if we allowed a statement of a statute or some other rule of law to serve as one premise and a statement of the facts of a given case to serve as another premise, the rules of logic would dictate the proper decision as a valid and necessary inference from these premises. The task of the court would be simply to find the correct rule and put it into the syllogism as a premise.

But as the realists have pointed out, each dispute differs from every other in some respect, and many disputes introduce principles that conflict. This means that in many cases—and especially the controversial ones that reach the appellate courts—judges cannot simply apply rules of law to the facts. They must choose between competing principles, or rules, in settling a dispute. And sometimes they must choose between different interpretations of the same rule, sifting through the facts of a case and selecting those that allow it to be classified under that rule.

□ COMPETING PRINCIPLES

The task faced by Judge Robert Earl, when the case of *Riggs* v. *Palmer*[5] reached the New York Court of Appeals in 1889, illustrates judicial choice between competing principles.

In 1880, Francis B. Palmer made a will, leaving small legacies to his two daughters, Mrs. Riggs and Mrs. Preston, and the bulk of his estate to his grandson, Elmer Palmer. But in 1882, Francis Palmer married a second time, and he began to consider changing the provisions of his will that were in Elmer's favor. The changes were never made, however, because Elmer murdered his grandfather—a crime for which he was duly convicted and sentenced to prison. Mrs. Riggs and Mrs. Preston sought to have the will, so far as it bequeathed property to Elmer, annulled. But from behind prison bars, Elmer claimed his property, and he won against his aunts' challenge—at least in the lower court.

A Note on Finding Cases

In citations to law reports and periodicals, the volume number precedes the name of the series. For example, the Supreme Court case *United States* v. *Nixon*, 418 U.S. 683 (1974), can be found in volume 418 of *United States Reports*, the official reports of the Supreme Court (abbreviated as "U.S."), beginning on page 683. A similar system is followed in reporting decisions of the federal circuit courts and the state appeals courts. For instance, "22 N.E." refers to the twenty-second volume of *North Eastern Reporter*, and "F. 2d" refers to *Federal Reporter*, second series.

---

[5] *Riggs* v. *Palmer*, 22 N.E. 188 (1889). For an explanation of the method of case citation see the box, "A Note on Finding Cases."

The only question for decision before the New York Court of Appeals was whether Elmer could have the property. On Elmer's behalf, it was argued that the will had been made out in proper form, that it had been probated, and that "it must have effect according to the letter of the law." Nothing in the law, Elmer's lawyer argued, requires a will to be annulled if the legatee murders the testator to prevent the person from making proposed changes in it. It was argued, too, that by depriving the murderer of his inheritance, the court would be unjustly enhancing "the pains, penalties and forfeitures provided by law for the punishment of crime."

On the basis of the principles argued by counsel for Elmer, the court of appeals could have affirmed the decision of the lower court. Judge Earl admitted that statutes regulating the making, proof, and effect of wills and the handing down of property, if literally construed, would leave Francis Palmer's estate securely in the hands of the murderer. The purpose of these statutes was to enable the maker of a will to decide how to dispose of an estate and to be assured that the donees would receive the property left to them. By invalidating a technically sound will, the court ran the risk of frustrating this purpose.

Other principles influenced the court's thinking, however. Earl cited two principles of long standing in common law. One is that "all laws as well as all contracts may be controlled in their operation and effect by general, fundamental maxims of the common law." The other, as stated by Earl, is that "No one shall be permitted to profit by his own fraud, or to take advantage of his own wrong, or to found any claim upon his own iniquity, or to acquire property by his own crime." This latter principle was followed by the court. The lower court's ruling upholding the will was reversed by a five-to-two decision of the court of appeals.

By taking as a premise the statement, "No one shall be permitted to acquire property by his own crime," and by adding as a further premise that Elmer killed his grandfather to inherit property, one could deduce the conclusion that Elmer should not be granted the inheritance. But it would be just as easy to deduce the conclusion that Elmer should be allowed to inherit from the premise that the grandfather's will was valid as written and, as a second premise, the principle that a will "must have effect according to the letter of the law." So Judge Earl could not simply apply a rule to the facts; he first had to find the *right* rule and then give his reasons for imposing it.

The crucial question had to do with why one principle was selected in preference to the other or, in the words of Justice Benjamin N. Cardozo, with "why and how the choice was made between one logic and another."[6] In his comments on the Riggs case, Cardozo said, "analogies and precedents and the principles behind them were brought together as rivals for precedence; in the end, the principle that was thought to be most fundamental, to represent the larger and deeper social interest, put its competitors to flight." He points out that the murderer lost the legacy because, in controversies over inheritance, the social interest served by refusing to permit the criminal to profit by his

[6] Benjamin N. Cardozo, *The Nature of the Judicial Process* (New Haven: Yale University Press, 1928), p. 41.

crime is greater than that secured by the enforcement of the legal rights of ownership.

The general prohibition in the common law against unjust enrichment had not previously been applied to problems of inheritance, so Earl did not cite precedents in which this principle controlled the result. But following his decision, the principle, "No one shall be permitted to inherit by his own crime," became a rule in the law regarding wills.

☐ ALTERNATIVE INTERPRETATIONS OF A RULE

Examples of judicial choice among alternative interpretations of a single rule are found in cases concerning the Nationality Act of 1940, which provided that an alien seeking to become a citizen must have been a person of "good moral character" for the five years preceding the date of application. One notable test of this act was the case of Louis Repouille.

Repouille, an alien residing in New York, filed a petition for citizenship on September 22, 1944, while on probation for the crime of putting his thirteen-year-old son to death on October 12, 1939. Repouille was the sole support of a family that included five children—one of whom, a congenital idiot, was blind, mute, deformed, and incapable of taking care of himself in any way. The father chloroformed this child because the care of the four normal children was jeopardized by the burden imposed upon him by the fifth. Indicted for manslaughter in the first degree, Repouille was tried and found guilty of manslaughter in the second degree—the jury recommending the "utmost clemency." He received a suspended sentence, was immediately placed on probation, and was discharged from probation in December 1945.

Repouille's petition was denied by the Immigration and Naturalization Service but granted, on appeal, by the district court. The district attorney, on behalf of the Immigration and Naturalization Service, then appealed to the circuit court of appeals for a reversal of the order, on the ground that Repouille had suffered a "moral lapse" during the five-year period.

The question before the circuit court of appeals in *Repouille* v. *United States* was whether the applicant for citizenship had revealed lack of "good moral character" in taking his child's life. If the meaning of the Nationality Act had been clear, the judges might have had little difficulty in applying it. As it turned out, however, the act did not define the phrase *good moral character.*

Three judges on the court of appeals heard the Repouille case. All three knew the law, were acquainted with the facts, had read the lawyers' written statements, and had heard the same oral arguments. Yet they were not able to agree on a decision: two voted to reverse the ruling of the district court and deny Repouille's petition, and one voted to remand the case to the district court. It is reasonable to suppose that the three judges would have agreed in recognizing an extreme example of bad moral character. A molester of children, an arsonist, or a purveyor of drugs to adolescents would probably have been unanimously disqualified for citizenship. But it was unclear how the test should be applied to Repouille. All the judges agreed that except for one possible lapse, he was a person of good moral character.

In his written statement of the majority opinion, Judge Learned Hand observed:

> It is reasonably clear that the jury which tried Repouille did not feel any moral repulsion at his crime. Although it was inescapably murder in the first degree, not only did they bring in a verdict that was flatly in the face of the facts and utterly absurd—for manslaughter in the second degree presupposes that the killing had not been deliberate—but they coupled even that with a recommendation which showed that in substance they wished to exculpate the offender. Moreover, it is also plain from the sentence which he imposed, that the judge could not have seriously disagreed with their recommendations.[7]

Judge Hand noted further that many people of "unimpeachable virtue" think it morally justifiable to put an end to a life "so inexorably destined to be a burden to others, and . . . condemned to a brutish existence, lower indeed than all but the lowest forms of sentient life." He admitted as well that many people—probably most people—do not equate legal rules with moral principles, and that many conscientious persons will defy a law that is repugnant to their deepest moral convictions. In effect, Hand was suggesting that a definition of *good moral character* could be found in the generally accepted moral conventions of the time.

But this raised the problem of how to define the generally accepted moral conventions of the time. Although the jury that convicted Repouille of manslaughter in the second degree had not felt "repulsion" at his crime, this did not mean that they regarded his action as morally acceptable. And noting that a similar offender had been imprisoned for life in Massachusetts, Hand expressed skepticism about the degree to which jury opinions were representative of public morality. Indeed, he believed that it would be difficult to apply any test of public morality in the absence of some "national inquisition" such as a Gallup poll. "Left at large as we are," said Hand, "without means of verifying our conclusion, and without authority to substitute our individual beliefs, the outcome must needs be tentative." Nevertheless, he felt reasonably secure in holding that the moral conventions of the time did not permit an individual to play the role of God, as Repouille had done, and decide when another's life should end.

Judge Hand's colleague Jerome Frank agreed that *good moral character* should be measured by "the generally accepted moral conventions at the time" but, in a dissenting opinion, he expressed the view that these conventions were to be found in "the attitude of our ethical leaders," not in popular moral attitudes. He argued that the case should have been remanded to the district court with instructions that the district judge secure reliable information on the subject to "reconsider his decision and arrive at a conclusion." Frank seemed to believe that a survey of the attitudes of the nation's ethical leaders might reveal that Repouille's act was not immoral at all.

But Judge Frank's proposed solution presented new difficulties. For the

[7] *Repouille v. United States*, 165 F. 2d 153 (1947).

problem of defining *good moral character,* Frank substituted the problems of identifying ethical leaders and reconciling the inevitably divergent opinions of any such group.

Unhappily for Judge Hand and the circuit court of appeals over which he presided, cases requiring a definition of *good moral character* continued to arise under the Nationality Act. Such cases often involved illicit sexual behavior on the part of the petitioner. Consistent with his decision in the Repouille case, Hand maintained that a definition had to be based on moral feelings prevalent in this country. Thus, in *Schmidt v. United States,* he reasoned that in public opinion there was enough difference between fornication and adultery to allow the petition of an admitted fornicator but to deny that of an adulterer. He was ready to admit, however, that another judge, operating with a different "test" of public morality, might not have noticed the distinction.

In *Johnson v. United States* (1951), the Court of Appeals reversed the district court that had granted a petition for naturalization. Simeon Johnson, the petitioner, had left his wife and son. And although he had been ordered to pay for their support, he rarely did so; he found it difficult to keep a job. In addition, Johnson admitted that he had lived "in illicit relations" with a woman within the probationary five-year period. A portion of Judge Hand's opinion is worth quoting, not only because of its response to the opposing view of Judge Frank—that the moral conventions of the time might be elicited from the nation's ethical leaders—but also because of the candor with which it faces uncertainty in judicial decision making:

> We must own that the statute imposes upon courts a task impossible of assured execution; people differ as much about moral conduct as they do about beauty. There is not the slightest doubt that to many thousands of our citizens nothing will excuse any sexual irregularity; for some indeed this extends even to the subsequent marriage of an innocent divorced spouse. On the other hand there are many thousands who look with a complaisant eye upon putting an easy end to one union and taking on another. Our duty in such cases, as we understand it, is to divine what the "common conscience" prevalent at the time demands; and it is impossible in practice to ascertain what in a given instance it does demand. We should have no warrant for assuming that it means the judgment of some ethical elite, even if any criterion were available to select them. Nor is it possible to make use of general principles, for almost every moral situation is unique; and no one could be sure how far the distinguishing features of each case would be morally relevant to one person and not to another. Theoretically, perhaps we might take as the test whether those who would approve the specific conduct would outnumber those who would disapprove; but it would be fantastically absurd to try to apply it. So it seems to us that we are confined to the best guess one can make of how such a poll would result.[8]

Learned Hand's travail illustrates the difficulties encountered by judges

[8] *Johnson v. United States,* 186 F. 2d 589–590 (1951).

in applying ambiguous or vague rules. In the naturalization cases, the decision to affirm a petition for naturalization, deny it, or remand the case to a lower court depended on how the facts of each case were interpreted in relation to the legal rule concerning the good moral character of the petitioner. Judge Hand and Judge Frank agreed that this rule was to be understood in the light of the prevailing morality of the community. But in the absence of a reliable test of public morality, they could not agree on an assessment of what facts were relevant as evidence that a petitioner was a person of good moral character.

The cases of *Riggs* v. *Palmer*—which illustrates a conflict between different rules—and *Repouille*—which represents differing interpretations of a single rule—show why a simple deductive model of judicial decision making is impractical. The rules of deductive logic cannot tell judges which principles to select as premises of arguments nor which facts to count as decisive in justifying a decision.

☐ *The role of logic in law*

Thanks to the legal realists, few people today believe that the techniques of formal logic alone can adequately account for the arguments involved in legal decision making. But this does not mean that legal reasoning has no use for rigorous standards. Nor does it mean that legal reasoning is nonlogical and that therefore there is no point in trying to evaluate the inferences found in judicial opinions. The realists' theory of the judicial process does not adequately account for the regularity and predictability of the judicial process. Nor can it explain why judicial decisions are usually accepted by society as legitimate and authoritative.

While searching for the psychological processes through which judges reach decisions, the realists lost sight of the role of *justification* in legal argument. Questions about the manner in which a decision or conclusion is reached are not identical to questions about the reasons for that decision or conclusion. Sir Isaac Newton's demonstration of the principle of gravitation would not be less convincing if it were to be proved that he had been struck by a falling apple before the idea of gravitation first entered his head. Why, then, be concerned about whether Judge Earl may have had an intuition about the right outcome of *Riggs* v. *Palmer* before he had worked through the case to reach a reasoned conclusion?

As with scientific reasoning, the logical analysis of legal reasoning is concerned with *arguments*. These arguments can be studied independently of both the judge's motives for advancing them and psychological accounts of their formation in the judge's mind. The logician is concerned with whether the reasons put forward for a decision are adequate justification for it. The opinion is a sham or rationalization only if weak and irrelevant reasons are made to seem *as if* they are strong and relevant.

It does not follow from the fact that an argument is not *formally* valid that there are no good reasons for accepting its conclusion. By ignoring nondeductive arguments, the realists supposed that there were no logical criteria for judicial decision making. But as justifications for decisions, the written opinions of appellate judges are arguments, and it *is* possible to appraise the inferences found in these arguments.

Legal reasoning can be said to have a logic of its own. Deductive and inductive inference are both involved, but its basic character is the special kind of reasoning by analogy, or reasoning by example, mentioned earlier. This pattern represents the adaptation of reasoning to the problem-solving tasks of the courts and to the demands made on judges to assess present problems in terms of the analogies urged by both sides in a controversy.

■ EXERCISE 13-2

1. Why have those, like Oliver Wendell Holmes and Jerome Frank, who criticize the view that legal reasoning is logical, been called *legal realists*?

2. What problem for judicial decision making is illustrated by *Riggs* v. *Palmer*? How is it related to the legal realists' position?

3. What problem for judicial decision making is illustrated by *Repouille* v. *United States*? How is it related to the legal realists' position?

*4. (a) What is the difference between *rationalizing* and *reasoning*? (b) Is there any way of telling when a person is rationalizing rather than basing a decision on reasons duly considered and weighed? (c) Why did the legal realists believe that judicial opinions are often mere rationalizations? (d) What features of the court system, if any, might operate to check or otherwise deter judges from offering rationalizations rather than arguments for their decisions?

5. If a simple deductive, or "mechanical," model is inadequate as a description of judicial decision making, what contribution can logic make to the understanding and evaluation of legal reasoning?

6. Discuss the following comment: "Each discipline faces two kinds of problems: technical ones, which can be dealt with on the basis of what is already known or assumed in the discipline; and fundamental ones, which challenge the very roots of the discipline and test its outer limits."

Considering the specialized training of lawyers and judges to be a discipline, present examples of technical problems that arise within the law. Present examples of fundamental problems concerning the law.

7. By what criteria do the people whom you work with or know make decisions? Does actual decision making match the expectations of those influenced by the decisions? Does actual decision making in groups (for example, in clubs, college organizations, churches, and offices) match the officially prescribed ways that decisions are to be made?

*8. In his book *Law and the Modern Mind*, Jerome Frank considers the testimony of Judge Hutcheson to the effect that [in Judge Hutcheson's words], "the judge really decides by feeling and not by judgment, by hunching and not by ratiocination, such ratiocination appearing only in the opinion. The vital motivating impulse for the decision is an intuitive sense of what is right or wrong in the particular case." Jerome Frank goes on to argue, "If the law consists of the decisions of the judges and if those decisions are based on the judge's hunches, then the way in which the judge gets his hunches is the key to the judicial process. Whatever produces the judge's hunches makes the law."—Cited in J. Bonsignore et al., eds., *Before the Law*, 2d ed. (Houghton Mifflin, 1979), p. 91

Evaluate Jerome Frank's argument.

a. Do you believe, or are you inclined to believe, that Frank is right? If so, how would you attempt to defend his view?

b. How would the argument be criticized on the basis of the discussion of legal reasoning in this section?

c. Can it be true that "the law consists of the decision of the judges" and false that "whatever produces the judge's hunches makes the law"? Explain.

d. Can it be both true that "the vital motivating impulse for the decision is an intuitive sense of what is right or wrong in the particular case" (as Hutcheson says) and false that "whatever produces the judge's hunches makes the law"? (Allow *intuitive sense* to be synonymous with *hunches*.) Explain.

9. (a) An advertisement says, "Mohawk Motors' cars over the last five years have needed fewer repairs than Apache Motors' cars." Some consumers induced by this advertisement to purchase a Mohawk car have been disappointed with the mechanical performances of their cars. They have taken their complaints to an agency charged with enforcing a truth-in-advertising law. The law simply states that anyone selling goods or services to the public shall be subject to a penalty for making a false claim about the product or service in question.—Adapted from Leif H. Carter, *Reason in Law*, p. 62

One consumer testifies that the ad made him believe that all Mohawk cars performed more reliably than all Apache cars, and he found this to be false. Another consumer complains that the ad led him to believe that Mohawk's bottom-line models performed more reliably than Apache's bottom-line models, but found this to be false.

Is there evidence that Mohawk Motors made a false statement in advertising? Why, or why not?

(b) Apache Motors runs an advertisement stating, "Bigger cars are safer than little cars, and the Apache Brave-SX is bigger than the Mohawk Chief-LD. Go Apache!" Mohawk Motors files a complaint against Apache Motors for false advertising.

Is Apache Motors guilty of false advertising if the evidence shows that

1. the Brave-SX is 512 pounds heavier than the Chief-LD, but 6 inches shorter?

2. the Brave-SX is 13 inches longer than the Chief-LD, but 103 pounds lighter?

3. the Chief-LD is 23 inches longer than the Brave-SX and 11 inches wider, but 871 pounds lighter?

4. the Brave-SX and the Chief-LD have the same weight and size, but National Highway Safety Administration collision test results show that the Brave-SX sustains less damage than the Chief-LD in collisions at speeds up to 45 miles per hour?

5. the Brave-SX is longer, wider, and heavier than the Chief-LD, but NHSA collision-test results show that the Chief-LD does just as well as the Brave-SX in protecting passengers from serious injury?

10. Addressing his remarks to law-school students, Karl N. Llewellyn said:

Above all, as you turn this information to your own training you will, I hope, come to see that in most doubtful cases the precedents *must* speak ambiguously until the court has made up its mind whether each one of them is welcome or unwelcome. And that the job of persuasion which falls upon you will call, therefore, not only for providing a technical ladder to reach on authority the result that you contend for, but even more, if you are to have *your* use of the precedents made as *you* propose it, the job calls for you, on the facts, to persuade the court your case is sound.

People—and they are curiously many—who think that precedent produces or ever did produce a certainty that did not involve matters of judgment and persuasion, or who think that what I have described involves improper equivocation by the courts or departures from the court-ways of some golden age—such people simply do not know our system of precedent in which they live.—*The Bramble Bush* (Oceana Press, 1951), p. 69

a. Why do you suppose Llewellyn says that in doubtful cases the precedents are ambiguous?

b. Does Llewellyn's view suggest that lawyers have more influence on judicial decision making than they should have? If so, in what ways?

c. How do you think Llewellyn would respond to the criticism that his view of the ambiguity of precedent would undercut the stability and predictability of the law? ■

☐ 13-3. REASONING BY EXAMPLE

[Be it] regarded hereafter as the law of this court, that its opinion upon the construction of the Constitution is always open to discussion when it is supposed to have been founded in error, and that its judicial authority should hereafter depend altogether on the force of the reasoning by which it is supported.

CHIEF JUSTICE ROGER B. TANEY

The model of judicial decision making presented in this section is an ideal, or theoretical, reconstruction of the way in which appellate judges develop and assemble reasons for their decisions. While the model concerns the process of justification, it does not describe either the judge's psychological process or means of organizing an inquiry and apportioning time and attention. Nevertheless, many written opinions presenting reasons for a judicial decision can be represented as arguments conforming to this model.

The model applies to all types of legal conflict at the appellate level, whether they concern administrative regulations, statutes, provisions of common law, or constitutional issues. In addition, the model divides judicial decision making into four steps, or stages:

1. Classifying the present case on the basis of analogies between it and prior cases introduced as precedents

2. Finding the significant facts of the case

3. Announcing the rule inherent in the precedents

4. Applying the rule to the present case

☐ *Classifying the case*

The reasoning involved when classifying a case is best explained by means of a hypothetical example:

A young woman, entranced by the freedom of flight, removes a Cessna from an airstrip in Delaware and manages to survive a landing in a Maryland tobacco field. In addition to being charged with grand larceny, she is prosecuted under the National Motor Vehicle Theft Act, which prohibits transportation "in interstate or foreign commerce [of] a motor vehicle, knowing the same to have been stolen." The statute defines *motor vehicle* to "include an automobile, automobile truck, automobile wagon, motorcycle, or any other self-propelled vehicle not designed for running on rails."

The case gives rise to two main questions: (1) Does the young woman's brief and unauthorized flight amount to transportation of the plane "in interstate . . . commerce"? (2) Is an airplane a motor vehicle within the meaning of the act?

Now suppose that the amateur aviator has been convicted in the trial court of violating the National Motor Vehicle Theft Act, and you, as her lawyer, are arguing in a court of appeals that the lower court's judgment should be reversed. In preparing your argument, you discover the 1931 case *McBoyle v. United States*, in which the United States Supreme Court held that the phrase *motor vehicle* in the statute did not include airplanes. The Court had reasoned in 1931 that when the National Motor Vehicle Theft Act was passed, air travel, being in its infancy, was intentionally excluded by Congress from the act. You could therefore point out *McBoyle* to the appellate court. The judges would presumably see the similarity, articulate the ruling in the McBoyle case, and reverse the conviction.

In classifying this case, it might be tempting to suppose that it turns on a *verbal dispute* (see Section 4-3). Someone could try to dismiss the problem by saying, "Well, it's just a matter of definition. If by *motor vehicle* you mean 'any self-propelled machine designed to transport goods or people,' then this amateur aviator has violated the federal law. If you don't include that in your definition, then she hasn't violated the law." But the issue cannot be settled by merely expanding or contracting the definition of *motor vehicle*. Central to the dispute is the question whether an airplane should be considered a motor vehicle for the *purposes of the law*. And the dispute is therefore about the *reasons* for regarding the young woman's act as a violation of the law versus the *reasons* for deciding not to do so.

One might also attempt to reason deductively about this legal problem. Suppose an attorney were to argue as follows:

> All acts of transporting stolen vehicles across state boundaries are violations of the National Motor Vehicle Theft Act.
>
> All acts of transporting stolen airplanes across state boundaries are acts of transporting stolen vehicles across state boundaries.
>
> Therefore, all acts of transporting stolen airplanes across state boundaries are violations of the National Motor Vehicle Theft Act.

This is a valid deductive argument. But it is not helpful because the second premise presupposes exactly what needs to be decided in the first place: whether a stolen airplane that moves across states lines is a stolen vehicle for the purposes of the act. In fact, because at this stage the second premise is just as controversial as the conclusion, the deduction is an example of the fallacy of begging the question (see Section 12-2).

The process of reasoning called for by this problem is *analogical*. As the amateur aviator's attorney, you attempt to place the case in a category favorable to your client by drawing on similarities between it and *McBoyle,* in which the Supreme Court said that airplanes do not fall within the meaning of *motor vehicle.* And you can expect the prosecutor either to look for other cases in which courts held that airplanes are motor vehicles or to call attention to differences between the present case and the facts of the *McBoyle* case— differences that would make it reasonable for the court to decide that your client has violated the act. Since the classifications of both sides cannot be accepted, the judge must find reasons for rejecting one set of analogies and accepting the other set.

Suppose that to the misfortune of your client, federal prosecutors have found two cases between 1931 and the present in which circuit courts of appeals had decided that the act did apply to airplanes. In one case where the act had been found to apply, the stolen airplane was subsequently sold. In the other case, an airplane was stolen to transport contraband goods from one state to another. In both cases, the United States Supreme Court had denied review, allowing the convictions to stand.

Your case would still be far from hopeless. You could distinguish it by pointing out that in the precedents cited by the prosecution, the defendants had intended to use the stolen planes for commercial purposes. But your client had no premeditated plan. Although she did know that the plane belonged to someone else, she was carried away by excitement and was oblivious to the fact that she had strayed across the state boundary. Perhaps you have even found a case somewhere in which a young man, having stolen a car and driven it about the state on a joyride, suddenly comes to his senses, realizes his crime, and in attempting to return the car, takes a wrong turn and unintentionally crosses into another state. This young fellow was not convicted of violating the act. Your client, too, realized the nature of her impulsive action soon after takeoff, you argue, and would have returned the airplane immediately to the airstrip from which she had taken it, except for her inexperience.

Note that, unlike deductive reasoning, neither your reasoning nor the prosecutor's can claim to be demonstrative. In each case, the truth of the premises at best presents strong reasons for accepting the conclusion (either that the amateur aviator is guilty of violating a federal statute or that she is not).

But this sort of reasoning also differs from induction. Inductive inferences move from premises about individuals or events that have been observed to conclusions about what has not been observed. For this reason, the conclusion of an inductive argument by analogy can be regarded as a *prediction*, and the truth or falsity of the conclusion depends upon what continued observation or future experience reveals. The point of an inductive argument—in supporting a conclusion that goes beyond experience—is to add to our store of information.

By contrast, in concluding that transporting a stolen airplane across state boundaries is or is not a violation of the National Motor Vehicle Theft Act, one is not making a factual claim that goes beyond present experience. The conclusion cannot be verified by future experience and is not intended to increase our factual information. By determining the proper classification of an action or event, the judge decides how to respond to it.

Because reasoning by example in the law is neither deductive nor strictly inductive, it is best described as *noninductive reasoning by analogy*:

Noninductive reasoning by analogy is a process by which reasons are developed for classifying a new case through a careful weighing of the similarities and differences between the new case and past cases that represent distinct categories.

As shown by the hypothetical case of the stolen airplane, analogical reasoning can be complex. The example involved several analogies and disanalogies: the analogy with *McBoyle*; the prosecutor's analogies with cases in which an airplane was ruled to be a vehicle; your argument that, in the absence of an economic motivation for the crime, the new case was unlike those others; and your likening of your client's action to other criminal acts of impulsiveness. How complex the analogies become depends on the vagueness or generality of a rule, the number and variety of previous cases, and the ingenuity and experience of the attorneys.

In general, an analogical argument is considered to be strong when the facts of the precedent cases are very much like those of the present one. But sometimes certain aspects of a case closely resemble facts cited in precedent cases while other aspects are quite different. In these situations, judges must not only determine how much the facts of a new case resemble those of the precedent cases but also whether these similarities are sufficiently important to classify the case in the same way.

□ *Finding the significant facts*

The appellate judge usually accepts the facts of a case as they are presented in the syllabus of the trial court. Provided that due process has ensured an unbiased and accurate gathering of facts in the lower court, no new historical search is initiated. The judge will also follow precedent, rather than making up a special rule to resolve the present difficulty. And by choosing the most relevant precedent from among the sets of analogies presented by the competing attorneys, the judge decides which facts are to be regarded as decisive. This feature of judicial choice has been called the *fact freedom* of the judge.[9]

The fact freedom of the judge tends to increase the difference between analogical reasoning in the law and the use of inductive analogy in science. In deciding, for example, whether an animal observed in an unusual habitat is a member of a known species, one bases an estimate of the similarity between the new animal and known members of the species on fixed characteristics exhibited by every individual of that species. But if one is reasoning about the similarities between the theft of an airplane and violations of the National Motor Vehicle Theft Act, the category—stolen vehicles transported across state boundaries—is itself subject to interpretation. Thus, judgments regarding the strength of the analogy between the present case and a category of past cases cannot be so easily based on estimates of the degree of similarity between objective characteristics.

According to the prevailing popular theory, facts are "out there" in nature and absolutely rigid, while principles are somewhere "in the mind" under our scalps and changeable at will. . . . Actually, however, what we call facts are not so rigid and theory not so flexible; and when the two do not fit, the process of adaptation is a bilateral one. When new facts come up inconsistent with previous theories, we do not give up the latter, but modify both the theory and our view of the facts by the introduction of new distinctions or hypothetical elements.
MORRIS R. COHEN, *LAW AND THE SOCIAL ORDER*

Because analogies used in the law are based on facts chosen for their significance, judgments about them are often affected by forces extraneous to the case itself. Fact freedom often means that what facts are found to be significant depends upon the questions the judge asks about the intentions of

[9] Carter, *Reason in Law*, p. 32.

the legislators who wrote and passed a statute, abut the purposes served by enforcing a rule, or about the social implications of the case.

☐ INTENTIONS OF THE LEGISLATORS

To illustrate the effect of trying to determine the legislators' *intentions*, let us return to the problem created by the amateur aviator who flies a "borrowed" Cessna into an adjacent state. The imagined facts of this hypothetical case were suggested by the actual 1931 Supreme Court case *McBoyle v. United States*.[10] We can imagine McBoyle's lawyer arguing that when the act was passed, Congress did not intend to include airplanes within the meaning of *motor vehicle*. "Certainly airplanes are very different from automobiles," he might have said, "even though both are used to transport goods and people. Airplanes are far more conspicuous: they move more quickly and make more noise. And because they require airstrips, they cannot be moved about as easily as automobiles. These obvious differences make it highly unlikely that the omission of the word *airplanes* from the act was unintentional. And because Congress did not intend to make the transportation of a stolen airplane across state lines a federal crime, my client cannot be convicted for this offense." If the Supreme Court justices were to focus on the intentions of Congress in passing the legislation, they might well accept the lawyer's argument.

☐ PURPOSES OF THE LEGISLATION

But if the justices were instead to consider the *purposes* of the act—if they were to ask what kind of criminal offenses require the law-enforcement assistance this act provides, they might find the lawyer's argument unconvincing. The purpose of the act could be related to the fact that movement from state to state makes it difficult for the states—which have primary responsibility for apprehending and prosecuting criminals—to detect violations and enforce the law. Police may have trouble tracking a stolen car that has been driven to another state; furthermore, police and prosecutors in one jurisdiction do not have authority in another. Thus, the fact that *physical movement* creates difficulties for law enforcers makes taking a stolen airplane into another state much like taking a stolen automobile into another state.

Rarely do appeals to purpose settle difficulties, however. Suppose that McBoyle's lawyer had also argued as follows: "The purpose of this act is to provide federal assistance to the states in finding stolen vehicles, to be sure. But the assistance is needed not so much because the vehicles are easily moved, but because they are so easily hidden and disguised. One black Ford may look like a thousand other black Fords almost anywhere, but airplanes are fewer in number and more distinctive in shape and size. In addition, while easily moved, airplanes are really like trains—which the act expressly excludes—

---

[10] *McBoyle v. United States*, 283 U.S. 25 (1931). The following account of hypothetical reasoning concerning the facts of the *McBoyle* case is based upon the discussion in Carter, *Reason in the Law*, pp. 80–84.

because they are tied to places where they cannot be hidden. Just as trains must run on rails, airplanes must land on airfields. Therefore, because Congress intended to assist the states only in locating easily hidden vehicles, not all movable vehicles, this act does not cover airplanes."

The hypothetical arguments suggested by *McBoyle* illustrate the extent to which judgments about the significance of certain facts depend on different interpretations of a rule. The facts that airplanes are larger than automobiles and must land on airfields, just as trains must run on rails, are significant or trivial depending on what one considers to be the purpose of the act. These facts are important if the act was intended to provide federal assistance to the states in locating only stolen vehicles that are easily disguised and hidden. They are less significant if its purpose was to provide federal law-enforcement assistance whenever the rapid physical movement of a stolen vehicle would compound the difficulty of apprehending the offender.

The actual *McBoyle* case was the first one to involve a stolen airplane and was thus a *case of first impression*—one presenting circumstances new enough to make even the closest precedents seem dubious. And whatever the attorneys may have argued before the Supreme Court, a majority of the justices decided that the defendant's conviction should be overturned. Writing for the majority, Justice Holmes reasoned that because the act made the transportation of stolen vehicles a federal offense, it was the responsibility of the legislature to give citizens "fair warning" by indicating exactly which actions would lead to prosecution under it. The omission of airplanes from the act meant that this warning had not been given concerning the conduct for which McBoyle was convicted. Here Holmes reverted to another principle of traditional jurisprudence: he pointed out that an important purpose of the criminal law is to facilitate rational planning—to help citizens clearly perceive the distinction between legal conduct and illegal behavior, and to be able to act with assurance that conduct found legal today will still be legal tomorrow.

☐ SOCIAL IMPLICATIONS

When the judge decides that certain facts are significant based on an interpretation of how the law best promotes important *social policy*, differences that seem slight to the layperson may be used to distinguish one case from another. This is illustrated by the distinction the New York Court of Appeals made between two cases concerning workers who suffered accidents on the way to and from their jobs. The first was that of William Littler.

Littler was a bricklayer working for the Fuller Company, which was constructing a residence in Great Neck, Long Island. The job site was some two miles from the railroad station, and the men who commuted to Great Neck by train had refused to work unless Fuller furnished them with free transportation from the railway station and back again at the end of the day. The employer hired a truck to transport workers, and Littler was injured when the truck turned over in a ditch. Littler sued the Fuller Company for damages, alleging negligence on the part of his employer.[11]

The legal issue was whether Littler was entitled to seek relief from the Fuller Company for negligence, or whether his compensation was limited to that provided under the Workmen's Compensation Law as a consequence of an injury resulting from an accident "arising out of and in the course of his employment." Although the trial court agreed with Littler that the injury did not arise out of or in the course of the employment, the court of appeals thought otherwise. Said Judge Cuthbert Pound,

> **The vehicle was provided by the employer for the specific purpose of carrying the workmen to and from the place of employment and in order to secure their services. The place of injury was brought within the scope of the employment because Littler, when he was impaired, was on his way . . . from his duty within the precincts of the company. . . . The day's work began when he entered the automobile truck in the morning and ended when he left it in the evening.[12]**

Pound thus ruled that Littler's compensation would be limited to what the Workmen's Compensation Law awarded.

The second case occurred just a few years later. James Tallon, who had been employed as a guard on the trains of the Interborough Rapid Transit Company in New York, was killed in a train collision. His wife sued the transit company for damages, alleging negligence and arguing that at the time of the accident, her husband was a passenger on one of the defendant's trains and not an employee within the meaning of the Workmen's Compensation Law. The facts were that Tallon, who lived at 146th Street, was required to report for duty each morning at the company's 177th Street station. He was provided by the company with a pass that allowed him free passage to and from work. On the morning of the fatal collision, Tallon was on his way to work and wearing his guard's uniform.[13]

The issues were the same as those that had been raised in *Littler*. At the trial, the attorney for the transit company, no doubt relying on the *Littler* verdict, argued that Tallon's death had occurred under the conditions of his employment. This argument lost in the trial court but won in the appellate division—which ruled that the only relief to be afforded Mrs. Tallon was that provided for under the Workmen's Compensation Law. The court of appeals, however, reversed the ruling of the appellate division and affirmed the judgment of the trial court. Judge Frederick Crane, speaking for the majority of the court of appeals, distinguished the *Littler* case from "the matter at hand":

> **The cardinal underlying fact is that Tallon's employment did not actually begin**

[11] *Matter of Littler* v. *Fuller Co.*, 223 N.Y. 369, 371 (1918).
[12] Ibid.
[13] *Tallon* v. *Interborough Rapid Transit Co.*

until he reported for work at One Hundred and Seventy-seventh Street and Third Avenue. He had to get there, and get there on time, and to facilitate his arriving on time the defendant gave him the right to ride in his passenger trains free of charge, but I cannot see how this in any way changes the reality, the existing fact, that the employment commenced at One Hundred and Seventy-seventh Street and Third Avenue at the time of reporting. It would cause no such change, had Tallon paid his fare on defendant's train or had ridden in another conveyance, the defendant paying his fare.[14]

Judge Crane added:

Now this case differs materially from those cases where the employer in order to get his employees to and from work, provides conveyances exclusively for their use which in no sense are public conveyances and in which the employees undertake to ride as part of their contract of employment in going to and from work. Such a case was *Matter of Littler* v. *Fuller Co.*[15]

By thus distinguishing the *Littler* case, Judge Crane and the majority of the court of appeals allowed Mrs. Tallon to recover damages from the wealthy transit company, whereas Mr. Littler had to accept an award limited by the Workmen's Compensation Law.

But Crane's colleague Judge Chester McLaughlin could not see the sense of the distinction. In a dissent supporting the judgment of the intermediate court, McLaughlin wrote,

[A]t the time of the collision Tallon occupied the status of an employee and, therefore, relief should have been sought under the Workmen's Compensation Law. At the time of the accident he was riding on a pass which entitled him to free transportation to and from work. Such transportation was an incident of the employment. It was a part of the contract of employment and enforceable by him as such. The facts bring the case directly within the principle laid down in *Matter of Littler* v. *Fuller Co.*[16]

Whether the differences between the two cases were sufficiently great to justify applying different rules depends upon one's perspective. McLaughlin thought not; he was persuaded by the analogy between the *Littler* and *Tallon* cases because he saw the transit company's offer of transportation to Tallon as an "incident of employment" like the transportation afforded to Littler by the Fuller Company. In Crane's view, what had been involved in the employment contract differed significantly in the two cases. Note that Fuller provided transportation to Littler and his coworkers *after* they had indicated that free transportation was a condition of their continued service at the con-

---

[14] *Tallon* v. *Interborough*, 413–414.
[15] *Tallon* v. *Interborough*, 414.
[16] *Tallon* v. *Interborough*, 415.

struction site. Thus, unlike the transportation offered to Tallon, the transportation furnished by the Fuller Company to its workers could be characterized as a concession won by labor through bargaining.

The *Tallon* case was decided in 1922, during a decade of great union organization in the United States. Judge Crane may well have believed that the courts had to go further than Judge McLaughlin was willing to go in helping company managers, labor officials, and lawyers more clearly define the liabilities of employers.[17]

This discussion of the *Tallon* and *Littler* cases illustrates noninductive reasoning by analogy, for the crucial issue raised by the Tallon case was whether compensation for Mrs. Tallon should be limited, as it had been in the *Littler* case, by the Workmen's Compensation Law. But the discussion also shows that the strength of analogical arguments in the law depends on *judgments* about the significance of facts. In Judge McLaughlin's view, Tallon's train trips, like Littler's truck rides, were part of the "contract of employment." In Judge Crane's view, however, the role of the workers in the *Littler* case—in bargaining for transportation—established a significant disanalogy between the *Tallon* and *Littler* cases.

☐ Announcing the rule inherent in the precedents

After identifying the significant facts of a case and the precedents that fit them, a judge announces the rule of law that will be applied in rendering a decision. Sometimes, the record of a precedent case contains an explicit statement of a rule or principle—called a *ratio decidendi*—that justifies the decision. The judge then simply restates the rule and announces that it controls the present verdict.

At other times, however, no precise statement of the rule is found in the precedents. The judge must then abstract a general rule from the reasons given by previous judges.

The following imaginary case illustrates this process of abstraction. "In the 1790s the driver of a wagon loaded with buckskin goods stops for the night at an inn in Massachusetts. He is received as a guest, and the innkeeper takes charge of his property. During the night a fire breaks out, and the wagon and goods are destroyed. The owner of the property sues the innkeeper for damages."[18]

The case is the first of its kind to come before an American court, so the judge looks to the English common law. In the 1584 case *Cross v. Andrews*, the liability of innkeepers was expressed as follows: "The defendant, if he will keep an inn, ought at his peril, to keep safely his guests' goods." And another early case, *Coyle's Case*, contains the statement, "If one brings a bag or chest, etc. of evidences into the inn as obligations, deeds, or other specialties, and

---

[17] See G. Gordan Post, *An Introduction to the Law* (Englewood Cliffs, N.J.: Prentice-Hall, 1963), pp. 85–86.
[18] This example is taken from Post, *An Introduction to the Law*, pp. 81–82.

by default of the innkeeper they are taken away, the innkeeper shall answer for them." Similar statements are found in other cases involving the destruction of a guest's goods in an inn. But the judge also sees that courts have found for the defendant innkeeper in the following situations: where the guest left property in the courtyard without informing the innkeeper, and the property was subsequently destroyed by rain and hail; where the guest had conspired with a third party to make a pretense of stealing the goods; where the loss of property was caused by a fire resulting from lightning; and where the goods were carried off by an unruly mob that ransacked the inn.

Having reviewed all the cases and the reasons set forth for the judgments rendered, the judge now formulates the rule needed for the present situation: "An innkeeper is responsible for the safekeeping of property committed to his custody by a guest. He is an insurer against loss, unless the loss was caused by the negligence or fraud of the guest, by an act of God, or by the public enemy." The judge has thus found in *Cross* v. *Andrews*, *Coyle's Case*, and the other precedents on innkeepers' liabilities the appropriate rule to apply to the present case. But what the rule actually says must be understood in light of the present problem.

Rules embedded in precedent are often reworked by the accretion of new cases and by drawing new analogies between cases. Consider, for example, how the use of the *Littler* case as a precedent was narrowed by the decision in *Tallon* and how the National Motor Vehicle Theft Act was interpreted differently before and after the *McBoyle* case. In separating what is relevant from what is not, a judge must mentally arrange precedents in order of increasing similarity with the present case. This casts the precedents in a new light, with factual situations that previously seemed insignificant often taking on new significance. And the precedents thus reorganized may suggest a new interpretation of a rule. Sometimes, the rule changes in one or more details; sometimes, it is changed so that its effects become quite different; and sometimes, it is declared invalid—as when a court reverses or overrules a previous decision.

☐ REWORKING A RULE

An example of the reworking of a rule is to be found in Justice Benjamin N. Cardozo's reasoning in *MacPherson* v. *Buick Motor Co.*,[19] a landmark case on the manufacturer's reponsibility to consumers. Donald MacPherson had just purchased a new Buick from a dealer in Schenectady, New York. While he was driving the automobile, the spokes of the rear wheel collapsed and he was thrown into a ditch and injured. MacPherson brought suit, not against the dealer with whom he had entered into a contract for the purchase of the car, but against the Buick Motor Company, with which he had no contractual relationship. The issue raised by MacPherson's suit was thus whether Buick, as the major manufacturer, was liable for negligence to a third party with whom

---

[19] *MacPherson* v. *Buick Motor Co.*, 217 N.Y. 386 (1916).

it had no contractual relationship. Buick itself had purchased the wheel from a subcontractor, the Imperial Wheel Company.

At the time, the general rule for such cases of negligence was that "a contractor, manufacturer, vendor, or furnisher of an article is not liable to third parties who have no contractual relations with him for negligence in the construction, manufacture, or sale of such article." The only exceptions to the general rule recognized in New York were cases in which the article sold "was of such a character that danger to life or limb was involved in the ordinary use thereof"—in other words, where the article sold was said to be "inherently dangerous." The New York courts considered loaded guns, poisons, and explosives to be "inherently dangerous" commodities. But in a long line of cases involving defective carts, coaches, and carriages, the courts had steadfastly refused to view vehicles used in transportation as likely to impose danger to life and limb through their ordinary use. With the dawn of the automobile era, it appeared that motorized vehicles, like coaches and carriages, would not be considered "inherently dangerous." Indeed, in a 1915 case very much like *MacPherson*, the court had been persuaded by the obvious similarities between automobiles and carriages and had not allowed the petitioner, a Mr. Johnson, to receive compensation from the Cadillac Motor Company.

Things worked out differently in MacPherson's case, however. The trial judge instructed the jury that an automobile was not an inherently dangerous vehicle but that it could become one if equipped with a defective wheel. The jury returned a verdict granting the plaintiff $5,025.

The Buick Company then appealed to the appellate division, but Judge John Kellogg affirmed the decision of the lower court. He was not impressed by the analogies between automobiles and coaches or carriages. Instead, he noted some significant differences that made the distinction reasonable. In the first place, a motorcar is capable of much greater speed; it is likely to do more serious damage if an accident results from a defect and more likely than a coach or carriage to cause injury to people other than those using it. Furthermore, an automobile is more complicated in its design and operation. While a coach or carriage can be fairly easily examined by a potential purchaser, the ordinary purchaser is far less qualified to make an examination of an automobile and judge its safety.

The Buick Company next appealed to the highest state court, the New York Court of Appeals. The sole question to be determined was "whether the defendant owed a duty of care and vigilance to anyone but the immediate purchaser"—that is, the retail dealer. If the article was "inherently dangerous," then the manufacturer would be liable to third parties; if it was not, then the manufacturer would not be liable to third parties. Counsel for the Buick Company argued strenuously to persuade the court that things inherently dangerous to life were poisons, explosives, and deadly weapons and that the automobile was not like any of these. But the attorney for MacPherson argued that an automobile "propelled by explosive gases" and capable of "a speed of 50 miles an hour" is an inherently dangerous machine.

The court of appeals affirmed the judgment of the appellate division in a decision formulated by Justice Cardozo. Cardozo "found" the rule by examining three precedents:

1. In an 1853 case, *Thomas* v. *Winchester,* a druggist had purchased a bottle of what was supposedly extract of dandelion from Winchester, who operated a pharmaceutical business. The bottle actually contained belladonna, a poison, and had been incorrectly labeled through the negligence of one of Winchester's employees. A Mr. Thomas bought a small quantity of this liquid from the druggist for his wife, who, after taking a few spoonfuls, became violently ill. Mrs. Thomas sued Winchester, not the druggist, and recovered damages. The court found that the poison was the sort of thing that posed a grave danger to human life through its ordinary use. "The defendant's negligence," said the court in the Thomas decision, "put human life in imminent danger." Cardozo selected the *Thomas* case as a precedent because it offered an analogy between a poison that had been mislabeled and an automobile with a defective wheel: whatever other similarities or differences there are between these commodities, they both create dangers that can be foreseen by the manufacturer but that are difficult for an untrained consumer to detect.

2. In the case of *Devlin* v. *Smith* in 1882, the defendant contracted to build a scaffold for a painter. The painter's workmen were injured when the scaffold collapsed, and the contractor was held liable although there was no contract between him and the workmen. Commenting on *Devlin,* Cardozo said the defendant "knew that the scaffold, if improperly constructed, was a most dangerous trap. He knew that it was to be used by the workmen. . . . Building it for their use, he owed them a duty, irrespective of his contract with their master, to build it with care."

3. In *Statler* v. *Ray Manufacturing Company* in 1909, the manufacturer of a coffee urn was held liable when one of the urns, installed in a restaurant, exploded and injured the plaintiff. In this case, the judge had followed *Thomas* in allowing the plaintiff to collect damages from the manufacturer of the urn. But his understanding of the Thomas rule was questionable: an urn, unlike poison, is not dangerous in its ordinary use but only if it is defectively made. However, the Statler decision might have deviated from the ordinary understanding of the rule concerning inherently dangerous commodities, it gave the interpretation Cardozo wanted.

Together, the *Statler* and *Devlin* cases reflected a greater concern with the danger a defective product poses to third parties than with the risks involved in its ordinary use. These precedents thus allowed Cardozo to read the *Thomas* rule in a new light: "Whatever the rule in *Thomas* v. *Winchester* may once have been, it has no longer that restricted meaning. A scaffold . . . is not inherently a destructive instrument. It becomes destructive only if imperfectly constructed. A large coffee urn . . . may have within itself, if negligently made, a potency of danger, yet no one thinks of it as an implement whose normal function is destruction." This means that an automobile, too, could be considered inherently dangerous. The rule of *Thomas,* Cardozo declared, was no longer limited to "poisons, explosives and things of like nature."

This brief history of the way Justice Cardozo arrived at his interpretation of the "inherently dangerous commodity" rule illustrates the first three steps involved in legal reasoning: classifying the case by means of analogy; discovering the significant facts; and stating, or announcing, the appropriate rule. In particular, this history shows how the third step—announcing the rule of law—often involves noninductive reasoning by analogy. Justice Cardozo reformulated the "inherently dangerous commodity" rule by a process of reclassification. By redrawing analogies between precedent cases, he developed a new category of inherently dangerous commodities—one that included mislabeled poison, improperly constructed scaffolds, defective coffee urns, and defective automobiles.

□ *Applying the rule to the present case*

The last step in the decision-making process—applying the rule—is purely deductive. Once the rule has been articulated, the facts of the case are subsumed under it. This step poses no new problems of analysis. Any errors made in imposing the rule result from weakness of the analogies presented, from faulty selection of significant facts, or from misinterpretation of the rules stated in earlier cases.

Note that the process of legal reasoning has been broken up into four steps only for the purposes of explanation. Although the *model* of such reasoning has four steps, the actual thinking of the judge may not follow this course. In fact, it is unlikely that judges reach decisions by first finding precedents, next looking for the significant facts, and only then announcing and applying a rule. Most likely, the judge's thoughts continually go back and forth from one aspect of the problem to another. The reconstruction of the process represented by the model is an attempt to make each facet of the deliberation subject to rational analysis and criticism.

■ EXERCISE 13-3

■ A. Below you will find summaries of two cases and a legal rule derived from them. Read the case summaries and the rule carefully; then proceed as directed.

In *Erickson* v. *Dilgard*, a competent, conscious adult patient was admitted to a county hospital suffering from intestinal bleeding. Doctors concluded that a blood transfusion was necessary, because the patient would have little chance of survival without additional blood. When the patient refused this treatment, the superintendent of the hospital went to court seeking an order to compel the transfusion. However, the court refused to compel the patient to accept the transfusion, declaring that the individual undergoing the medical treatment should have the final say.

In *Plainfield County Hospital* v. *Brooks*, Ms. Brooks had repeatedly informed the physician who was treating her for a peptic ulcer that her "religious and medical convictions" prevented her from receiving blood transfusions. However, when she was admitted to the hospital in critical condition, the hospital petitioned the court for permission to give blood transfusions. The court refused, declaring that Ms. Brooks's exercise of her religious beliefs in refusing medical treatment did not endanger the public health or welfare. In addition, although Ms. Brooks was disoriented when she entered the hospital, the court concluded that she had been fully competent when she originally refused treatment and that her prior refusal continued to the point where the situation became urgent.

On the basis of these and similar cases, the court announced the following rule in *Brooks*: when no circumstances establish that preserving the life of a competent adult patient is necessary for the welfare and safety of others, a court will not invade either the patient's religious conscience or the patient's right to determine what should be done with his or her own body by compelling submission to medical treatment—even though the patient is in imminent danger of death and the lifesaving treatment is relatively simple and safe.

1. For each of the three cases summarized below: (a) Indicate whether the court's decision is consistent or inconsistent with the *Brooks* rule and the precedent cases. (The cases occur in the order given so that each case serves as a precedent for the cases that follow.) (b) Justify your decisions by indicating the crucial similarities and differences between each new case and the relevant precedents.

Georgetown University Hospital v. *Jones*: Ms. Jones, a twenty-five-year-old woman, was brought to the hospital in imminent danger of death from the loss of two-thirds of her body blood due to a ruptured ulcer. Ms. Jones was the mother of a seven-month-old child. Although largely disoriented and incoherent, Ms. Jones, when told she would die without the blood, responded that the transfusions were against her will. The court declared that the hospital could proceed with the treatment.

United States v. *George*: A thirty-nine-year-old Jehovah's Witness, the father of four, refused blood transfusions for religious reasons while lucid but in a physically critical condition from a bleeding ulcer. The court ordered transfusions.

Jacobson v. *Massachusetts*: Mr. Jacobson had been convicted under a state statute authorizing the fining of an adult who "refuses or neglects" to be vaccinated as required by the statute. The vaccination had been intended to protect inhabitants of the state from a dangerous, contagious disease. In appealing his case to a higher court, Jacobson claimed the "inherent right of every free man to care for his own body." The higher court upheld Jacobson's conviction.

2. Answer the questions that follow the case summaries below.

John F. Kennedy Memorial Hospital v. *Heston*: Delores Heston, aged twenty-three and unmarried, was severely injured in an automobile accident. She was taken to the hospital, where it was determined that surgery and a blood transfusion were needed to save her life. She was disoriented and incoherent, but her mother informed the hospital that the patient and family, as Jehovah's Witnesses, were opposed to the transfusion.

a. As an attorney for the hospital, how would you argue before a judge? (You are arguing that the hospital should be permitted to administer blood to Ms. Heston.)

b. As an attorney for Ms. Heston, how would you argue?

Hillside Medical Center v. *Levitt*: An eighty-four-year-old man was admitted to the hospital with a gangrenous leg that, if not amputated, would cause his death. He was a good surgical risk, but because he was acutely ill with blood poisoning, he had been unable for about two weeks to respond coherently to questions about his health. Evidence showed that prior to this period of mental incompetence, the patient had told a doctor that "I would rather die than live like that" and "I came into life with two legs and I'm going out with two legs."

c. Assuming that the judge allowed the hospital to proceed in the *Heston* case, argue that the hospital should be permitted to proceed in this case as well.

Palm Springs General Hospital v. *Martinez:* Seventy-two-year-old Ms. Martinez suffered from terminal hemolytic anemia. Death was certain without treatment. However, she refused transfusions and the removal of her spleen, begging her family not to "torture me further with surgery."

d. What analogies do these facts suggest with the precedent cases? What disanalogies are suggested?

e. As a judge, what additional questions of fact would you want resolved before making a decision in this case?

■ B. On June 25, 1910, the Mann Act, passed by the United States Congress, went into effect. The act proclaims that it "shall be known and referred to as the 'White Slave Traffic Act.'" The act states (in part): "Any person who shall knowingly transport or cause to be transported, or aid or assist in obtaining transportation for, or in transporting, in interstate or foreign commerce or in any territory or in the District of Columbia, any woman or girl for the purpose of prostitution or debauchery, or any other immoral purpose, or with the intent and purpose to induce, entice, or compel such woman or girl to become a prostitute, or to give herself up to debauchery, or to engage in any other immoral practice . . . shall be deemed guilty of a felony."

The Mann Act was passed during a period when many large cities had "red-light" districts. Women were believed to be procured for houses of prostitution by "white slavers" who operated throughout the United States as well as in foreign countries. Many of the women who were forced or lured into the business were thought to be quite young. And once captured, each was taken from her own community and became, as the House Report said, "practically a slave in the true sense of the word."

1. Read the summaries of the cases below and answer the questions that follow.

Hoke and Economides v. *United States,* 227 U.S. 308 (1913): Hoke and Economides had been indicted for inducing a woman "to go in interstate commerce . . . for the purpose of prostitution." In upholding their conviction, the appeals court emphasized the involuntary nature of the woman's conduct, the "system" involved (presumably referring to some form of organization), the interstate transportation involved, and the belief that many of the women connected with the defendants' business were minors. Hoke and Economides appealed their conviction to the United States Supreme Court.

Athanasaw v. *United States,* 227 U.S. 326 (1913): Athanasaw had been convicted under the Mann Act for having caused a young woman to be transported from Georgia to Florida for the ostensible purpose of appearing as a chorus girl in a theater operated by the defendant. In upholding the conviction, the appeals court cited evidence of improper advances made to the "girl" upon her arrival, advances that were related to her membership in the theater group organized by Athanasaw. Athanasaw appealed his conviction to the United State Supreme Court.

a. What purpose do you think the Mann Act was intended to serve (based upon the portion of the text and the brief history given above)?

b. Discuss whether you believe the convictions under the Mann Act in the *Hoke* and *Athanasaw* cases should be upheld by the Supreme Court. (Base your decision upon the information presented in these exercises.)

c. What are the similarities between the *Hoke* case and the *Athanasaw* case? What are the differences between these two cases? What differences, if any, in the factual situations of the two cases seem significant to you?

2. The Supreme Court upheld the convictions of both Hoke and Economides and of Athanasaw. Petitioners in these cases, as well as those that follow, raised questions about the constitutionality of the Mann Act that we do not need to consider.

Read summaries of the next three cases, and answer the questions that follow. Answer each question *before* going on to the next one.

United States v. *Holte*, 236 U.S. 140 (1915): Holte, a woman, had been convicted by a trial court for a "conspiracy" in violation of the Mann Act. The conspiracy charged was between the defendant, Holte, and one Laudenschlager that the latter should "cause the defendant to be transported from Illinois to Wisconsin for the purpose of prostitution." The evidence showed that Holte had willingly consented to the business arrangement. The appeals court reversed Holte's conviction, and federal prosecutors appealed to the Supreme Court.

Caminetti v. *United States*, 242 U.S. 470 (1917): Several cases involving conviction under the Mann Act were reported under the heading of *Caminetti*. The indictments involved the transportation of women for the purpose of paid cohabitation or for the purpose of having them become mistresses and concubines. The indictments did not involve commercialization and organized vice. In addition, the women were not inexperienced victims. One case was fairly representative of the group. In this case, the woman in question was a prostitute and made no pretense of virtue. One Mr. Hays happened to meet her in Oklahoma City while attending a cattleman's convention there. After Hays's return to his home, another woman telegraphed the Oklahoma woman to come to Kansas, sending her the money with which to buy the ticket. In response to this message, the woman went from Oklahoma City to Wichita, where she met and entertained Hays. The appeals court upheld the conviction of Hays and the others whose indictments were reported in *Caminetti*. The defendants petitioned the Supreme Court for review.

Gebardi v. *United States*, 287 U.S. 112 (1932): The appeals court upheld Gebardi's conviction under the Mann Act, although it had been argued in his defense that Congress had not passed the act to deal with cases that involve the woman's consent and agreement to the forbidden transportation.

a. Discuss the similarities and differences between each of the cases summarized above and the *Hoke* and *Athanasaw* precedents.

b. Using the *Hoke* and *Athanasaw* precedents, decide which, if any, of the appeals-court decisions discussed in the three cases above should be reversed by the Supreme Court. Which decisions should be upheld by the Supreme Court? Construct brief arguments for your decisions.

c. As it turned out, the Supreme Court reversed the appeals court in *Holte* and sustained the appeals court in *Caminetti* and *Gebardi*. Restate the "rule" of the Mann Act in your own words to cover the factual situations of *Holte*, *Caminetti*, and *Gebardi*. Restate the "rule" of the Mann Act to cover the *Hoke* and *Athanasaw* cases but *not* the last three cases.

3. Considering all the cases discussed so far as precedents for further review of convictions under the Mann Act, answer the questions that follow the next three case summaries.

Mortensen v. *United States*, 322 U.S. 369 (1944): The petitioners, a husband and wife named Mortensen, operated a house of prostitution in Grand Island, Nebraska. In 1940, they planned an automobile trip to Salt Lake City, Utah, to visit Mrs. Mortensen's parents. Two "girls" who were employed by the Mortensens as prostitutes asked to be taken along for a vacation, and the Mortensens agreed to their request. They motored to Yellowstone National Park and then on to Salt Lake City, where they all stayed at a tourist camp for four or five days. They then visited Mrs. Mortensen's parents and returned by automobile to Grand Island to the "house of ill fame," where the prostitutes retired to their respective rooms. From the time they left Grand Island until their return, the two prostitutes had not engaged in any activities related to prostitution or sexual promiscuity. The appeals court upheld the Mortensens' conviction.

United States v. *Beach*, 324 U.S. 193 (1945): The defendant, Ms. Beach, operated a dress shop in the District of Columbia and employed a young woman who lived with her as her assistant. On the suggestion of the defendant that she could earn more money by "selling herself," the young woman agreed to work for the defendant as a prostitute. The trip cited in the indictment was a four-block taxicab ride within the District of Columbia from the home of the defendant to the Hotel Hamilton. The taxicab ride was taken for the purpose of prostitution and was paid for by the defendant. The appeals court reversed Beach's conviction.

Cleveland v. *United States*, 329 U.S. 14 (1946): The defendants were all Mormons, members of a religious sect, who believed in and practiced polygamy. They had transported plural wives across state lines. The appeals court upheld their conviction under the Mann Act.

    a. Present a brief argument for the prosecution that the facts of *Mortensen* are sufficiently like the facts of the Mann Act precedents to justify upholding the Mortensens' conviction. Present a brief argument for the defense.

    b. Do the same for the *Beach* and *Cleveland* cases.

    c. The Supreme Court overturned the conviction of the Mortensens. In doing so, did the Supreme Court refuse to follow the precedent set by *Caminetti*? Why or why not?

    d. The Supreme Court reinstated the lower-court conviction in the *Beach* case. Are the differences between *Beach* and *Mortensen* sufficient, in your opinion, to justify distinguishing the cases? The Supreme Court upheld the conviction of the Mormons in *Cleveland*. To which of the precedents is *Cleveland* closest? How does it differ from every other case described so far? ■

☐ 13-4. EVALUATING JUDICIAL DECISIONS

It is of course dangerous that judges be philosophers—almost as dangerous as if they were not.
PAUL FREUND

[R]eason, our reason, can give us the confidence to assert that some judicial choices are better than others.
LIEF H. CARTER

Judges in the United States operate within a system that is designed to preserve stability while allowing courts to respond creatively to new social problems. Thus, reasoning by example, discussed in Section 13-3, is a mode of problem solving: it serves as a mechanism by which the court fulfills its role of reconciling facts, rules, and social interests. And just as the logic of "reasoning by example" is largely a product of the adversary nature of courtroom proceedings, the adversary process also encourages the judge to see the problem before the court in terms of competing social interests.

□ *The values of stability and progress*

In presenting the client's side of a controversy, each attorney points out precedents favorable to the client's interest. And if precedent more clearly supports one side of the controversy, a decision favoring it will almost inevitably be seen as representing the value of stability.

The attorney whose case is weak regarding precedent is likely to appeal, in the name of progress, to conceptions of justice or considerations of social policy. For example, in the *Riggs* case (Section 13-2), Elmer Palmer had precedent on his side insofar as the law of wills was concerned. But the opposing attorney could easily argue that progress toward the fair and equitable administration of the law of wills required that he be denied the inheritance.

Stare decisis, which means "let the decision stand," is the major force for stability in the legal system. This policy impels judges to apply precedents, thus solving new problems by using the solutions to similar problems reached by judges in the past. The consequent predictability in judicial decision making increases the number of legal problems that can be solved outside the courts. The ability of lawyers to anticipate rulings and inform clients of their options ultimately depends upon the extent to which the law can be "known." When past decisions make the interpretation of rules clear, and when everyone is convinced of the way a case will turn out, the disputants usually do not go to court in the first place.

But citizens as well as litigants expect judges to be responsive to the demands of justice. Thus, when new problems arise or when citizens question the fairness of a rule, the law takes on a dynamic quality as judges mold old rules to meet the challenges of new and complex problems. It is this ability of the courts to adapt old solutions to serve changing needs and purposes that makes recourse to the courts to settle human disputes a constant possibility. In the words of Justice Cardozo, "If we figure stability and progress as opposite poles, then at one pole we have the maxim of *stare decisis* . . . at the other we have the method which subordinates origins to ends. The one emphasizes considerations of uniformity and symmetry. . . . The other gives freer play to considerations of equity and justice, and the value to society of the interests affected."[20]

[20] Benjamin N. Cardozo, *The Paradoxes of Legal Science* (New York: Columbia University Press, 1928), p. 8.

Reasoning by example protects the interests of individuals and the social interests with which their claims become identified by assuring that competing analogies are brought before the court. The arguments of the attorneys for the opposed parties present the common ideas of society. Thus, different ways of viewing the facts all have their "day in court," which contributes to the sense that the judicial hearing has been fair.

Since no two cases ever present identical facts, the legal forum must treat different cases *as if* they were the same—and must do so in a way that litigants accept as fair. Because the trial proceeds as a contest, each side can hope to persuade the judge that a certain interpretation of the conflict is correct. When the judge finally determines that the similarities of the present case to a given precedent case justify applying a rule from that case, the losing side has had an opportunity to try to persuade the judge that the present case *ought* to be classified differently. By thus facilitating careful exploration of opposing viewpoints, the system acts as a stabilizing social force.

Reasoning by example is an incremental process in which, case by case, new facts and new arguments pro and con repeatedly come before the courts. The process allows judges to remain close to the certainty of the past while allowing the law to change and adjust to new social conditions. It also allows lawyers to persuade judges to interpret precedents, statutes, and constitutions to meet changing beliefs about right and wrong. In the long run, however, much of the law remains the same, with innovation occurring at certain points: new doctrines develop slowly by the accretion of cases; and a change can be treated by judges in subsequent cases as an aberration.

Edward H. Levi, a former attorney general of the United States, has called reasoning by example a "moving classification system." As he explains the process,

> **Reasoning by example shows the decisive role which the common ideas of the society and the distinctions made by experts can have in shaping the law. The movement of common or expert concepts into the law may be followed. The concept is suggested in arguing a difference or similarity in a brief; but it has no approval from the court. The idea achieves standing in the society. It is suggested again to a court. The court this time reinterprets the prior case and in doing so adopts the rejected idea. In subsequent cases the idea is given further definition and is tied to other ideas which have been accepted by courts. It is now no longer the idea which was commonly held in the society. It becomes modified in subsequent cases. Ideas first rejected but which gradually have won acceptance now push what has become a legal category out of the system or convert it into something which may be its opposite. The process is one in which the ideas of the community and of the social sciences, . . . as they win acceptance in the community, control legal decisions.[21]**

---

[21] Levi, *An Introduction to Legal Reasoning* (Chicago: University of Chicago Press, 1949), pp. 5–6.

Levi adds that vagueness or ambiguity in a legal rule can also contribute to a reconciliation of social tensions while allowing for change:

> In an important sense legal rules are unclear, and, if a rule had to be clear before it could be imposed, society would be impossible. The mechanism accepts the differences of view and ambiguities of words. It provides for the participation of the community in resolving the ambiguity by providing a forum for the discussion of policy in the gap of ambiguity. On serious controversial questions, it makes it possible to take the first step in the direction of what otherwise would be forbidden ends. The mechanism is indispensable to peace in a community.[22]

Legal reasoning is, then, a consequence of the kind of problem solving required of courts in our society. Judges must find just solutions to particular conflicts, but their problem solving must also serve social interests by furthering both stability and progress.

☐ Prescriptive uses of the model of legal reasoning

The model of legal reasoning presented in Section 13-3 is *descriptive*. Whether it can also be used *prescriptively*—as a guide in arriving at or identifying a good judicial decision—depends upon what *good judicial decision* is taken to mean. If it means a *reasonable* decision—one based on careful argument— then the model can serve as a standard. It shows that judges must classify cases on the basis of examples and according to factual similarities; that the important facts of a case are chosen on the basis of judgments about their meaning and significance; and that legal rules undergo change as cases are read and compared. Thus, insofar as the model outlines the way reasoning is shaped by the legal process, it tells what a judge must attempt to do to reach a well-reasoned and justified decision.

But the model cannot specify the *results* of legal reasoning. It cannot tell judges which choices to make and which decisions to reach. The "rightness" of the judicial decision is based upon the nature of the specific conflict, the reliance and expectations of the parties, and the social and moral issues involved. These substantive concerns are not part of the reasoning process but, instead, provide the subject matter *about which* the reasoning is exercised. Thus, the model can help judges to develop defensible arguments for their decisions, and it can help others to appraise the strength of the reasoning found in judicial opinions. But it cannot lead judges to just decisions.

To guide judges to choices that are morally correct and that maximize social values, an analysis of legal reasoning would have to be supplemented with a theory of the proper role of the judiciary in American government. *Theories of judicial function* attempt to define this role by asking whether

---

[22] Levi, *An Introduction to Legal Reasoning*, p. 1.

judicial decisions help to reinforce basic values or to achieve social objectives. According to such theories, correct, or just, decisions are those in which judges either assign significance to facts or select from among competing rules in ways that promote the values recognized as fundamental by the theory.

Controversy rages in the literature of jurisprudence and the philosophy of law over which theory of judicial function the courts should follow. There is disagreement, first, over the choice and ranking of basic values and objectives. And even when a consensus on fundamental values and objectives emerges, there is disagreement about how the courts can act to support or achieve them.

The debate has divided into two basic "camps." The *judicial activists* assign a major role to the appellate courts in protecting the rights of individuals and advancing public policy. The advocates of *judicial restraint* believe that democratic principles require the courts to accept a minimal role in public policy and, whenever possible, to follow the problem-solving initiatives of legislative bodies and executives.

Because theories of the judicial function attempt to identify substantively correct judicial decisions, they go well beyond a logical analysis of legal reasoning. Logic alone cannot tell judges how to use their knowledge and freedom of choice. Even the most completely developed logical systems cannot determine the *content* of arguments. Deductive logic, for example, can be used to determine whether many different arguments are valid or invalid, but it cannot supply premises. And except when statements are *necessarily* true or *necessarily* false (see Sections 2-3 and 8-2), deductive logic cannot establish whether premises are true. In inductive logic as well, the criteria for generalizations and inductive analogies can help us decide what arguments are reasonable, but they cannot tell us what evidence to seek in the first place.

The logic of legal reasoning, then, can tell judges that answers to questions about facts are judgments rather than mere reports of what was seen, heard, or read. *But it cannot tell judges when they have completed the task of "finding" the facts or whether they have "found" the facts that are significant.* The model can tell judges that they must compare the present case for similarities and differences with other cases, *but it cannot tell judges which similarities to emphasize and which to ignore.* And the model can tell judges that the rules undergo change as reasoning progresses, *but it cannot tell judges which rules to impose.*

The objective in studying reasoning is to help us not only to find right answers but also to *know* when we have—or probably have—done so by being able to supply reasons for the result. So, too, we expect of judges, first, that they attempt to justify their decisions and, second, that they attempt through their written opinions to convince us that they have done so. The discussion of legal reasoning in this chapter provides a basis for evaluating the *reasonableness* with which appellate judges defend their verdicts. Being reasonable can never guarantee being right. But in law, as elsewhere in human experience, being reasonable increases the probability of arriving at the best solution to a problem.

■ **EXERCISE 13-4**

1. Why is *stare decisis* an important doctrine in the law? If judges respect the importance of *stare decisis*, then how can legal reasoning contribute to the ability of the law to change and solve new problems?

2. The terms *stability* and *progress*, as used in this section, both signify a cluster of related values and interests. For example, social interest in stability permits citizens to rely on rules as they have traditionally been understood, makes for efficiency in judicial administration, assures similar treatment of persons similarly situated, and promotes public confidence in the courts. Present some examples of the way these factors contribute to stability in public life.

What are some of the interests the law promotes that contribute to progress? Which interests, in your view, involve issues of justice?

3. Explain what Edward Levi means by calling reasoning by example a "moving classification system." Levi also suggests that vagueness and ambiguity in the law can serve a positive social function. How is this possible?

*4. Discuss the following comments:

a. It is of the greatest importance that those trained in the law should develop a theory of the logic of legal reasoning. Only such a theory can provide judges with a decision-making procedure that will lead to just decisions in particular cases.

b. If a logical analysis of legal reasoning cannot be used as a decision-making procedure enabling judges to get results guaranteed to be just, then such an analysis is an empty intellectual exercise of very little value.

c. I've read that when it comes to a judge's decision making, "being reasonable can never guarantee being right." This apparently means that a judge can justify a decision as reasonable even though it cannot be shown to be just according to some ultimate standard of justice. But this assertion must be incoherent, for what could it mean to say that a judicial decision is "just," except that it is "reasonable"? A just decision is, by definition, the most reasonable decision a judge could make in a particular case.

5. A young New York woman supports her drug addiction by working as a prostitute in an environment of crime and corruption. After serving a brief jail sentence, she travels to California, determined to begin her life anew. She marries a respectable young man, becomes a leader in civic and church affairs, and raises a large and happy family. But twenty years after her arrival in town, a neurotically jealous neighbor learns of her past and publishes a lurid and accurate account of it for the whole community to read. As a consequence, her associates snub her; she is asked to resign her post as a church leader; gossipmongers prattle ceaselessly about her; and obscene inscriptions appear on her property and in her mail.

The injured party sues her neighbor for malicious defamation of character. Her suit is successful in the lower court, but an appeals court reverses the judgment, stating that "even when defamation has been proved, the defamer may yet escape liability by establishing that the utterance or publication was in fact true, however malicious the intent."—Adapted from Joel Feinberg, "Limits to the Free Expression of Opinion," in Joel Feinberg and Hyman Gross, eds., *The Philosophy of Law*, 2d ed. (Belmont, Calif.: Wadsworth, 1980), p. 194.

Discuss the appeals court's decision.

a. Do you think the social interest in the truth is important enough to override a private person's interest in his or her reputation?

b. Are there circumstances in which the public welfare is served by the utterance and publication of "malicious truths"? If so, what would be an example of such a situation? ■

CHAPTER FOURTEEN

The practice of analyzing arguments

The method of argument evaluation presented in this chapter combines the skills that were developed earlier into a systematic procedure. Presenting each critical activity as a separate step (see the accompanying box) serves two purposes: First, the steps together provide a framework for efficient and thorough analysis. Second, following the steps enables one to weigh each criticism judiciously before judging the overall success or failure of the argument.

The Six Steps of Argument Analysis

1. Identify the main conclusion.
2. Clarify meaning and formulate tacit assumptions.
3. Portray the structure.
4. Assess the premises.
5. Evaluate the inferences.
6. Make an overall assessment.

☐ 14-1. THE SIX STEPS OF ARGUMENT ANALYSIS

The six steps of argument analysis are presented in the order in which they should be performed. One can go back to a step that was previously considered or temporarily skip a step. But by following this sequence of steps, one faces the easier problems early on and also answers questions that must be answered to complete the later, crucial steps of the evaluation.

Because each step involves a survey of the entire argument, the procedure is useful mainly for evaluating written material. It could be applied to spoken comments, though, if they were brief or if one had time to take detailed notes.

☐ *Step one: Identify the main conclusion*

To identify the conclusion, one must have an overall understanding of the material and must have determined that it indeed presents an argument. So you must first read the entire passage to develop a sense of the discourse as a whole. If you decide that the material before you is argumentative, then try to find the *main conclusion*—a sentence or a group of sentences that expresses the major point the author wishes to make. Set this off from the rest of the text by circling or underlining it and labeling it "MC."

Even if the passage is an argument, the main conclusion may be unstated. The author may be trying to make a point without actually spelling it out. Or sometimes a text contains two or more premises that, when combined, lead to a conclusion that is not explicitly drawn. In such cases, you have to "read into" the text and write down what you take to be the conclusion. This conclusion will be subject to revision as your understanding of the whole argument—and the author's probable intentions—increases.

Often a passage contains more than one argument. If the author jumps from one issue to another, presenting arguments that are independent of one another, they must be evaluated separately. But if they are connected—if there is one major conclusion supported by subsidiary arguments—then the entire passage can be treated as an *extended argument*.

> An extended argument is a complex argument consisting of one main conclusion supported by premises that are the conclusions of subarguments.

If the passage contains multiple arguments, list each conclusion. For an extended argument, write down only the main conclusion.

☐ *Step two: Clarify meaning and formulate tacit assumptions*

The primary objective at the second stage is to understand every statement that plays an integral role in the argument. This involves three operations: reducing ambiguity and vagueness, standardizing statements, and formulating tacit assumptions.

☐ REDUCING AMBIGUITY AND VAGUENESS

To begin, refer to a dictionary and replace all unfamiliar terms with familiar synonyms. Next, look for any faulty or unusual grammatical constructions that interfere with understanding, and reformulate the sentence to reveal what you think is the author's intended meaning. Also identify any significant terms that are ambiguous or vague, and be mindful of how such expressions can be used to mislead (see Sections 4-1 and 4-2).

☐ STANDARDIZING STATEMENTS

Because only statements integral to the argument are to be considered, cross out whatever is repetitious or nonessential. If the author has made the same point in a number of different ways, retain the clearest expression of it and disregard the other versions. Delete digressions, examples, personal recollections, exclamations, and phrases such as "on the other hand" and "as a matter of fact." Remember, though, that the meaning of a sentence does not depend on its grammatical form but on the way it functions in the passage. As noted in Section 1-1, even an exclamatory sentence can be used to express a statement.

Be careful when an author makes a general statement and then proceeds to qualify it by considering counterexamples. When this occurs, only the modified version should be identified as the author's claim, and the initial generalization—along with the qualifying remarks—can be dropped.

Unless you remember how inflammatory language and extraneous emotional appeals can be used to sway opinion (Section 3-3), you may mistake for a premise a sentence that only serves to deflect attention from the real issue. But if a sentence that you have positively identified as expressing a premise contains words or phrases with distracting emotive effects, "desensitize" the language by substituting neutral terms.

Finally, identify *suppositions* and treat sentences that express them as conditionals. The first sentence of the following example is a supposition:

> 1. **Suppose you cheated on the next exam. In that case you would feel that the university rules against dishonesty didn't apply to you. And you would have to admit that anyone else in your shoes should feel and act the same way. But you wouldn't accept everyone's doing the same thing, so you shouldn't cheat yourself.**

A supposition works like a premise, but unlike a premise, it is not affirmed as true by the arguer. It is only assumed hypothetically to show that certain consequences follow from it. Interpreting the supposition in (1) as the antecedent of a conditional statement permits the example to be rewritten as follows:

> 1a. **If you cheated on the next exam, then you would feel that the university rules against dishonesty didn't apply to you.**
>
> **If you felt that the university rules against dishonesty didn't apply to you, then you would have to admit that anyone else in your shoes should feel and act the same way.**
>
> **But it's not the case that you would admit this. Therefore, you shouldn't cheat on the next exam.**

□ FORMULATING TACIT ASSUMPTIONS

Once all the explicit statements have been identified, add any unstated assumptions. These are premises that are *implicit* in the argument—tacitly indicated by the context, by other sentences, or even by certain uses of language.

Adding such premises requires caution. They must be statements that it is reasonable to believe the arguer would accept, they must be consistent with the original premises, and there must be good reason to believe they are true. If the added premises were false or implausible, the arguer would be justified in protesting that you had set up a straw-man argument (see Section 12-6).

The following example contains two tacit assumptions:

> 2. Homosexuality has in fact formally had an outlaw status in this country for years, and laws against homosexuality, however unevenly enforced, are currently on the books of all but one of the United States. These laws are barbarous, not to say illogical: when committed by consenting adults, homosexuality is a crime without a victim, and for this reason alone the onus of criminality ought to be lifted.[1]

The conclusion of (2) is explicit and can be paraphrased as, "acts of homosexuality ought not to be regarded as criminal." But the sentence "When committed by consenting adults, homosexuality is a crime without a victim" involves two implicit premises. The argument can be reconstructed as follows:

> 2a. The only acts that ought to be regarded as criminal are those that involve a victim.
>
> Homosexual acts between consenting adults have no victims.
>
> Therefore, such acts ought not to be regarded as criminal.

Example (3) contains a tacit conclusion as well as two tacit assumptions as premises:

> 3. To return to our discussion of legislating against abortion, pornography, and other so-called sex crimes, what of Jerry Falwell and his Moral Majority? They're neither moral nor a majority!

The premises, contained in the concluding exclamatory sentence, can be spelled out as follows:

> Jerry Falwell's Moral Majority does not constitute a real democratic majority of voters.
>
> The opinions of Jerry Falwell's Moral Majority are not authoritative on moral matters.

The conclusion can be interpreted as follows:

> Legislators have no obligation to heed the recommendations of Falwell's Moral Majority.

---

[1] Joseph Epstein, "Homo/Hetero: The Struggle for Sexual Identity," *Harper's Magazine,* September 1970, p. 50.

Note that how forcefully we state the conclusion depends on the forcefulness of the premises. The arguer in (3) may believe that legislators *should not* pay attention to the Moral Majority because the arguer believes this lobbying group makes *immoral* recommendations. But such an interpretation is probably too strong.

☐ *Step three: Portray the structure*

In step 3, how to portray the structure—the relationship between the support claims and the main conclusion—depends on the complexity of the argument. A simple structure can be shown by circling the conclusion and putting brackets around each of the premises. But the greater the complexity, the more helpful it is to remove the argument from its grammatical context. Arguments to which unstated conclusions or tacit premises have been added should be fully rewritten, as was done with examples (2) and (3).

In a lengthy extended argument, the conclusion of each subargument will itself be a premise, either for the main conclusion or for another subargument. To represent the relations between the premises and the main conclusion, you should use a *tree diagram*. How to do this is explained in Section 14-2.

Whatever method is used, remember three important points: First, include all the premises—even those that seem to be irrelevant to the claim they are intended to support (see *non sequiturs*, Sections 12-3 and 12-4). Second, make a mental or marginal note of any gaps you find in the argument, but do not attempt to fix a flawed argument by adding premises that are not implicit. Third, identify any premise or subargument that gives little or no support to the main conclusion. Such material can be set aside later—at step 6—without weakening the overall argument.

☐ *Step four: Assess the premises*

Assessing the plausibility of all statements that function as premises is the fourth stage of the evaluation procedure. Although you may lack sufficient information to evaluate all or even most of the claims, you may be able to detect weak claims. In addition, it should be possible to decide what kind of information is needed to verify that a claim is true.

Because that which is examined—factual evidence, logical form, or the meanings of words—and the tests used to examine it will depend on the statement's logical status, each premise should be identified as either necessary or empirical (Section 2-3). Consequently, you must ask yourself two questions: Does the arguer appear to consider the claim to be necessarily true or based on empirical findings? How would ordinary users of the language understand the claim in typical contexts?

☐ NECESSARY STATEMENTS

If the statement is intended to be necessarily true, ask *why* it should be so regarded—what led the author to believe that all possible counterexamples had been ruled out? If the premise is supposed to be true by definition—if the author attempts either to state the meaning of a particular word or phrase or

to give an analysis of a concept—apply the appropriate techniques for criticizing definitions (Sections 4-4 through 4-7).

If the claim rests on the logical form of the statement, try to think of
possible counterexamples: statements of the same form that are clearly *not*
necessarily true. For instance, consider (4):

4. Every card-carrying Communist is a Communist.

This statement is necessarily true because of the meaning of *card-carrying
Communist*, but *not* because of its logical form. Its form is *not* "Every A that
is a B is an A," but "Every BA is an A," and here are some counterexamples:
"Every imaginary Communist is a Communist," "Every suspected kidnapper
is a kidnapper," and "Every aspiring aviator is an aviator."

If a premise is necessarily *false*—that is, flatly self-contradictory—point
this out. But first, make sure that you have not misinterpreted it. Charity
requires that the claim be given as plausible a reading as possible, even if the
writer has expressed it carelessly. (The same approach should be followed when
premises are jointly inconsistent. In this event, look for readings of one or
more of the premises that will allow them to be consistent.)

☐ EMPIRICAL STATEMENTS

If a premise is an empirical statement, determine what sort of evidence would
make it true or false. If the claim is a simple predication ("S has P"), a statistical
generalization ("70 percent of S are P"), or a relational statement ("A is to the
left of B"), it must be based on reliable reports of observations.

If the claim is a universal generalization ("All S are P" or "No S are P"),
then it can be tested by trying to find counterexamples. To test "All S are P,"
try to think of an indubitable case of S that is definitely not P. Similarly, to
test "No S are P," find an indubitable instance of S that is P.

☐ MORAL JUDGMENTS

Some claims that are presented as if they were empirical turn out to be *moral
judgments*: assertions about what *ought* to be the case rather than what *is* the
case. For instance, suppose someone states that homosexuality is unnatural.
This appears to be an empirical claim that homosexual activity is foreign to
human nature. But when it is pointed out that almost every human society
has a certain amount of homosexuality and that it is possible for a majority of
a society's members to practice both homosexual and heterosexual activity (as
seems to have been the case in ancient Greece), the speaker replies that this
does not disprove the assertion that the practice is unnatural. At this point,
one must explore the possibility that the speaker means by *unnatural* something different from "foreign to human nature"—perhaps that procreation is
the only natural purpose of sexual activity. Then, biological and psychological
evidence might be presented to support the view that sexual activity is in itself
a natural source of pleasure and an expression of love. But if the speaker's
assertion is really a moral judgment, no amount of evidence can disprove it.
For it is perfectly consistent to maintain that what does happen *ought not* to

happen. Indeed, because moral judgments don't even attempt to say what *is* the case, they cannot be refuted by factual claims.

This does not mean that moral judgments are impervious to criticism. Like other claims, they can be *rationally* defended or opposed by enlisting reasons that support or discredit them. In most cases, defense or criticism will require that attention be directed toward the underlying *moral standard* from which the judgment is derived. Moral reasoning will therefore be examined in Section 14-3 in conjunction with a discussion of some of these standards.

☐ THE RELIABILITY OF EVIDENCE

Premises often consist of claims that are based on "plain facts," or direct evidence. In these cases, whether it is reasonable to doubt the premises depends not only on the nature of the evidence but also on what is at stake. Where the consequences of accepting or rejecting the argument would be serious, it is reasonable to examine claims that seem obvious at first sight. The extent to which one can challenge factual claims without having special knowledge of the subject matter is extremely limited. Nevertheless, logical analysis suggests two critical questions to raise before concluding that the evidence is unassailable:

1. *Are the "facts" direct observations, or are they inferences based on reports of what was observed?* For instance, what historians usually call facts include inferences about complex events. An example is the "fact" that General Robert E. Lee's defeat at the Battle of Gettysburg was due to the failure of Pickett's Charge. Although the role of inference may be hidden, it should be brought out and challenged.

2. *Is the statement or historical record the best explanation of the evidence cited?* Treat each factual claim as a hypothetical account of what it reports. Then develop rival hypotheses, and rank them in the order of their plausibility. Finally, decide how the arguer's claim ranks against the most plausible of these alternatives.

Even the most straightforward of historical records and documents—such as transcripts of oral testimony, photographs, and eyewitness drawings—must be approached as a hypothetical account of the event recorded. For instance, as the historians James W. Davidson and Mark H. Lytle point out regarding eyewitness drawings, the historian should ask, "Is the fact that the artist witnessed this event the best explanation for what the drawing depicts?"

> [t]he apparent directness of pictorial communication is often deceptive. Eyewitness drawings no more necessarily record an event "as it really happened" than do written eyewitness accounts. In evaluating pictorial evidence, historians must establish the historical context of a painting just as they would establish the context of any document. They must be sensitive to the artistic conventions that shape or even distort a painting's subject matter. And they must be prepared to acknowledge that some paintings provide more information about their creator than about the subject being portrayed.[2]

[2] James West Davidson and Mark Hamilton Lytle, *After the Fact: The Art of Historical Detection* (New York: Alfred A. Knopf, 1982), p. 136.

All statements of fact, including the verbal reports of eyewitnesses, must therefore be critically evaluated. Such testimony expresses the witness's confident belief that an event occurred. So one should also treat this confidence as something requiring explanation and should ask, "Is the hypothesis that the belief is true the best account of the witness's confidence?" Rival hypotheses regarding this confidence would include the possibilities of honest mistake, perceptual unreliability, and self-interest on the part of the witness.

It is important to distinguish the *evidence* for a belief from the *causes* of a belief, for only some causes of belief can be counted as reasons for accepting it. In the best of cases, what causes, or motivates, one to accept "*p*" is the truth or reliability of the premises stating evidence for "*p*." We might also be caused to believe "*p*" in many other ways, however, including a subconscious association of ideas, a catchy advertising jingle, a misunderstanding of someone's words, or an offhand remark by an unqualified "expert."

The purpose of challenging testimony is not to challenge directly the truth of the report but to undermine confidence in its plausibility by attacking the basis of its support. In arguing that the testimony is weak, one is arguing that accepting *that the witness so testifies* as a reason for believing the report is unwarranted. This is different from arguing that "*p*" is false because X acquired belief in "*p*" in an unusual manner or because it is in X's interest to have "*p*" accepted. Such an argument would be a fallacy of personal attack, or an *ad hominem* argument (Section 12-5).

☐ PROVISIONAL ACCEPTANCE

An argument containing a questionable premise must be considered flawed, even if the inference is valid or inductively reliable. But when the premise occurs in a deductively valid argument, one can accept such an argument *provisionally*, on the condition that the questionable premise is true. If the premise indeed turns out to be true, then the conclusion is true. Should it turn out to be false, however, the conclusion remains doubtful.

The provisional acceptance of an argument is expressed by weakening the original argument. Its conclusion is converted into a conditional statement with the questionable premise as the antecedent and the conclusion as the consequent. For example, where P_4 is questionable, we convert argument (5), in which it occurs, into argument (5a):

5. P_1 5a. P_1
    P_2 P_2
    P_3 P_3
    P_4

    $\overline{}$ $\overline{}$
    C $P_4 \supset C$

The conclusion of the new argument asserts that *if* P_4 is true, then the original conclusion, C, will be true.

This procedure has the advantage of showing the conditions under which an argument like (5) would be valid when we are not in a position to determine the truth of the questionable premise on independent grounds. It avoids the necessity of going beyond the scope of the original argument for new information and thus allows the process of evaluation to continue.

☐ *Step five: Evaluate the inference*

The inferences evaluated at the fifth stage are those that were actually present in the original argument and those that resulted when implicit premises were made explicit in step 3. Because judgment of the strength of an inference depends on whether it is taken to be inductive or deductive, one must decide for the argument as a whole—and for each subargument of an extended argument—how it is to be treated. Bear in mind, though, that in special contexts—particularly, in legal reasoning (Section 13-4)—arguments can be both noninductive and nondeductive.

If the passage is an extended argument, begin by identifying the *leading argument*:

> **The leading argument is the part of an extended argument that consists of the main conclusion and the premises that directly support it.**

Where a premise of the leading argument is the conclusion of a subargument, decide whether the subargument is inductive or deductive, and then evaluate it accordingly.

If the leading argument is recognized as deductive, do not assume that all the subarguments will therefore be deductive. Unless an extended argument is addressed to a specialized audience (such as logicians or mathematicians), it is unlikely to be entirely deductive. The further the reach into background knowledge for support and the greater the variety of sources of support, the greater the likelihood that some subarguments will be inductive.

☐ INDUCTIVE INFERENCE

The claim of any inductive argument is that the conclusion is the best explanation for the evidence cited in the premises. The conclusion of such an argument can therefore be considered a hypothesis among rival hypotheses and tested by asking, "Given the supporting statements, is this conclusion the best of the rival hypotheses?" You then try to think of a rival hypothesis that is at least as plausible as the given conclusion. In the case of an argument by analogy, for instance, this test can result in a counteranalogy: a demonstration that the available evidence permits the construction of another argument by analogy that is no weaker and that produces an alternative conclusion.

The discovery of such a rival hypothesis would then require followup. You would need to point out the specific way in which the argument went wrong: that the conclusion of a generalization tries to encompass a whole class, for example, while the premises refer only to members with particular characteristics; that an analogical argument focuses on superficial similarities; or that someone using the method of difference has failed to isolate different causal factors. Inductive generalizations, analogies, causal arguments, and arguments for hypotheses can all be evaluated using the techniques presented in Chapters 10 and 11.

□ DEDUCTIVE INFERENCE

Any deductive inference is susceptible to disproof by means of a counterexample. To employ this method, construct an argument of the same logical form as the argument you wish to criticize, but one with premises that are obviously true and a conclusion that is obviously false.

   An illustration is the counterexample offered by Jay F. Rosenberg to the following assertion made by seventeenth-century philosopher René Descartes:

6. My senses sometimes deceive me.

Therefore, it could be the case that my senses always deceive me.

This exemplifies the pattern of reasoning shown in (6a).

6a. *X* is sometimes *F*.

Therefore, it could be the case that *X* is always *F*.

Rosenberg shows that (6a) is an invalid form by means of the following substitution instance, where *paintings* replaces X and *forgeries* replaces F:

6b. Paintings are sometimes forgeries.

Therefore, it could be the case that paintings are always forgeries.[3]

The premise of the substitution instance is true as a matter of fact, but the conclusion is false. It could not be the case that *all* paintings are forgeries, for a forgery is a *copy* of some original. If all paintings were copies, no paintings would be originals, and there would be nothing for the supposed copies to be copies of. Because the form of the argument is invalid, Descartes's argument (if correctly interpreted) is also invalid. It is possible to accept the premise but reject the conclusion. Thus, while Descartes's conclusion may be true after all, the argument does not establish that it is.

   Where many intermediate steps are involved and where truth-functional compounds and quantificational functions are extensively used, it may be difficult to think of appropriate counterexamples. The argument will then have to be checked by some other method. You may be able to determine that the argument is valid by constructing a derivation and applying the rules for natural deduction. But inability to deduce the conclusion does not *prove* that the

[3] Jay F. Rosenberg, *The Practice of Philosophy* (Englewood Cliffs, N.J.: Prentice-Hall, 1978), pp. 17–20. The argument Rosenberg analyzes comes from René Descartes, *Meditations on First Philosophy*, trans. Laurence T. Lafleur (Indianapolis: Bobbs-Merrill, 1960), p. 18.

argument is invalid. To do this, you must use one of the other methods for testing deductive arguments: Venn diagrams or the rules for syllogisms (Sections 6-2 and 6-3), abbreviated truth tables for truth-functional logic (Section 8-5), or truth-functional expansions for predicate logic (Section 9-7).

Although the methods of predicate logic are powerful enough to demonstrate the validity of most of the valid deductive arguments presented in this text, it does not follow that they should be the first employed. On the contrary, the more complex the technique and the greater the subtleties of analysis, the greater the risk of error. Employing the most elementary method suitable to the argument usually reduces the amount of work and minimizes the chance of error. And when formalizing an argument, you should use the fewest symbols needed to reveal its logical structure.

If the leading argument is deductive, it might be tempting to assert that it can be valid only if each subargument is valid. This would seem to follow from the fact that a valid deductive argument is a "truth transmitter," and any invalid subargument breaks a link in the chain between the premises and the main conclusion. But this assertion assumes that the main conclusion requires all the support claims offered for it, when actually it might follow deductively from a smaller set of claims. An extended argument can often be improved— and shown to be valid—by deleting an unneeded and invalid subargument.

☐ IDENTIFYING INFORMAL FALLACIES

Watch for any informal fallacy that may occur either in the leading argument or in a subargument. Identify the kind of error it involves, and treat it according to the recommendations in Sections 12-3 through 12-5. Always present your reasons for charging an author with a fallacy.

☐ *Step six: Make an overall assessment*

After completing steps 1 through 5, you are prepared to make a judgment about the argument as a whole, or about the leading argument of the extended argument. In doing so, consider the truth of the premises separately from the strength of the inference so you will know precisely where any difficulties are located. This will involve estimating the success of the argument when a false or obviously implausible premise has been removed or, in the case of an extended argument, when a subargument with an invalid or inductively unreliable inference has been deleted.

☐ SUCCESSFUL ARGUMENTS

When an argument has succeeded—that is, when analysis supports the judgment that it is strong—you must finally make your *own* decision about the subject debated. The conclusion of the argument is a statement of a thesis. Whatever the issue—abortion, pornography, sexual morality, gun control, the rationality of nuclear deterrence, or anything else—you have to decide for yourself what you think about it. And while a single argument cannot settle the issue, the justified judgment that an argument is strong provides a starting point.

Discovering that a particular argument is reasonable does not mean that there are no reasonable opposing arguments. The argument you have analyzed may or may not be better than its competitors. So try to step back and adopt a perspective on the issue and on what the argument has taught you about it. In making this final assessment, consider the following points:

1. Whether you know of other arguments on the same issue that support the opposite or different conclusions.

2. Whether you know of other arguments that support the same conclusion.

3. Whether you know of any new or previously unnoticed evidence that has a bearing on the issue and, if so, whether it gives support to this argument or to competing arguments.

☐ PRESUPPOSING AN ARGUMENT

When an argument has failed, it can still be instructive to presuppose, or hypothetically entertain, it. Doing so does not commit you to its conclusion; there is no inconsistency in advocating a view "for the sake of argument" while rejecting the position. But by seeing an argument from the "inside," you see the world from the point of view of someone who wants the conclusion to be true. And by thinking about what the argument could have accomplished had it been changed in certain ways, you further develop your own skill in argumentation.

Presupposing an argument involves one or more of three operations: *drawing new conclusions from given premises, reconstructing an invalid argument by adding validating premises, and reconstructing an invalid deductive argument as an inductive argument.* The result is a "made-over" argument that may diverge drastically from that of the original author.

The first step in presupposing an argument is to salvage as many claims as possible from the original argument. This operation involves *drawing new conclusions from given premises.* To illustrate the procedure, suppose that the argument has been shown to consist of several apparently unconnected claims. As far as the evidence goes, these claims are not obviously false—but you do not know whether to believe them. You might then do the following:

1. Determine whether the claims are consistent—whether it is possible for all of them to be true. If they are inconsistent, you will be able to deduce a contradiction from them.

2. If the claims are consistent, check the possibility that some can be deduced from others. Because the deduced claim will be true if its premises are true, this procedure will reduce the number of claims that need to be checked.

3. If the claims are consistent, think of other statements that can be deduced from the set. One of the things that will help you decide whether to accept a set of claims—say "A," "B," and "C"—are the implications of the set.

If you can show that other statements—say, "X," "Y," and "Z"—are validly deduced from set "A," "B," "C," and you find that "X," "Y," and "Z" disagree with evidence you possess on independent grounds, then you can infer that at least one of the claims in set "A," "B," "C" is false. But even if "X," "Y," and "Z" are known to be true on the basis of independent evidence, and even though set "A," "B," "C" implies "X," "Y," and "Z," set "A," "B," "C" need not be true. It is possible to have a valid inference, a true conclusion, and false premises. So this operation can show that one or more premises are false but not that they are true.

Reconstructing an invalid argument by adding validating premises consists of providing a link between the stated premises and the conclusion that is not an implicit part of the original argument. To do this, consider what needs to be added to the premises to make it impossible for an opponent consistently to accept the premises but deny the conclusion.

Adding validating premises may sacrifice plausibility. This will occur when the only premises that would make the argument valid are false, unreasonable, or highly controversial. To see this, consider the following invalid argument:

> **The minimum drinking age should be raised. For statistics have shown that when the drinking age is lowered, traffic fatalities go up, and when the drinking age is raised, traffic fatalities go down.**[4]

Even if the premises are accepted as true, they provide no support for the conclusion—"The minimum drinking age should be raised"—unless we assume that something *ought* to be done to reduce traffic fatalities. But although this can be considered an implicit premise, the argument remains invalid. Something stronger is needed—a premise, like P_3 in the reconstruction below:

P_1 When the drinking age is lowered, traffic fatalities go up.
P_2 When the drinking age is raised, traffic fatalities go down.
P_3 The number of lives saved by raising the drinking age fully justifies the loss of liberty imposed on young people.
    Therefore, the minimum drinking age should be raised.

With P_3 added, the argument becomes valid. It is not possible to deny the conclusion while maintaining that traffic fatalities vary with drinking age (P_1 and P_2) and that the restriction on liberty is justified by saving lives. But the argument has become valid at the expense of plausibility: premise P_3 is a claim that some parties to the debate over the drinking age would surely deny.

---

[4] This example and the subsequent reconstruction come from Steven M. Cahn, Patricia Kilcher, and George Sher, eds., *Reason at Work: Introductory Readings in Philosophy* (New York: Harcourt Brace Jovanovich, 1984), pp. 18–19.

Adding validating premises serves the following purposes:

1. By filling in details and showing how the argument *would* fit together, the reconstruction completely displays the interrelationship between the support claims and the conclusion.

2. By making explicit every bit of information and every definition needed to make the conclusion follow deductively, the reconstruction may uncover sources of disagreement that cannot be overcome and that would continue to make the argument unacceptable.

3. By showing the ramifications of certain premises, the reconstruction identifies other claims that the author would have to accept to maintain that the conclusion is implied by these premises.

Reconstructing an invalid deductive argument as inductive can usually be done if the argument concerns substantive matters. The invalid argument can be converted into an inductive one by replacing the general statements that are necessary for deductive validity with statements that provide specific evidence for the general statements. "All tree toads are brown," for example, might be changed to "Naturalists report that all observed tree toads have been brown." In some cases, the new premises, as factual reports, will support the same conclusion. In other cases, the conclusion will have to be weakened by making it more specific—"in 30 percent of cases"—or by inserting qualifiers such as *probably, generally, roughly speaking.*

Recasting the argument as inductive serves two purposes:

1. It replaces an argument that completely failed to establish its conclusion with one that provides some reason for accepting the conclusion or a modified version of it.

2. By shifting attention from the form of the argument to the evidence available for the conclusion, it shows the amount and kind of evidence that would increase the probability of the conclusion—and the acceptability of the argument.

■ **EXERCISE 14-1**

■ A. Answer the following questions in your own words.
   1. Why should the analysis of an argument always begin with the identification of the main conclusion?
   2. How is a long passage to be analyzed if it contains argumentation but no single point as a main conclusion?
   3. What is the difference between an extended argument and the leading argument in the same passage?
   *4. How does standardizing statements contribute to clarification of the meaning of an argument?

5. What is a tacit assumption, and how do tacit assumptions differ from validating premises?

6. How do tacit assumptions differ from suppositions, and how are suppositions expressed when an argument is reconstructed?

7. How is our understanding of an argument increased by portraying its structure?

*8. Why is it important to determine the logical status of a premise?

9. How do moral judgments differ from ordinary empirical statements?

10. What is a counterexample, and what different uses do counterexamples have in argument analysis?

11. What is the purpose of treating an empirical statement or the conclusion of an inductive argument as an explanatory hypothesis?

*12. What does it mean to accept an argument provisionally?

13. Why should premises and inferences be assessed separately when arguments are evaluated?

14. Why should we distinguish between deductive and inductive reasoning when inferences are evaluated?

15. Why is it helpful to evaluate the subarguments of an extended argument as if they were independent arguments?

*16. What does it mean to presuppose an argument?

17. Why does adding validating premises to an invalid argument often decrease the plausibility of the reconstructed argument?

18. How will deducing new implications from a set of claims help us determine whether these claims are true?

19. What is the procedure for reconstructing an invalid deductive argument as an inductive argument?

*20. What is the major objective of the overall assessment of an argument?

■ B. The following arguments are presented for practice in applying the six steps of argument analysis. Identify the main conclusion of each, and clarify the meaning by formulating any tacit assumptions.

1. "The decision to use the atomic bomb against Japan, for example, judged by the knowledge we have today of Japan's military potential in the summer of 1945, was probably a mistake. But even if the employment of the bomb spared the Allies an invasion and a bloody campaign in the main island of Japan, a country claiming to defend the cause of freedom and the ultimate dignity of the individual human being cannot justify such a step on the grounds of military strategy only. One cannot accept the argument that the shortening of a war is the supreme end without at the same time abandoning all moral restraints on the conduct of hostilities. This line of reasoning would justify not only the use of nuclear weapons but also the resort to poison gas, the dissemination of deadly germs, the torturing of prisoners, and mass killings of innocents by any other conceivable invention as long as strategists suppose they will be able to avoid the enemy's retaliation in kind."—Guenter Lewy, "Superior Orders, Nuclear Warfare, and the Dictates of Conscience," *The American Political Science Review* 55 (1961)

2. "The only proof capable of being given that an object is visible, is that people actually see it; the only proof that a sound is audible, is that people hear it: and so of

the other sources of our experience. In like manner, I apprehend, the sole evidence it is possible to produce that any thing is desirable, is that people do actually desire it. If the end which the utilitarian doctrine proposes to itself were not, in theory and in practice, acknowledged to be an end, nothing could ever convince any person that it was so. No reason can be given why the general happiness is desirable, except that each person, so far as he believes it to be attainable, desires his own happiness. This, however, being a fact, we have not only all the proof which the case admits of, but all which it is possible to require, that happiness is a good; that each person's happiness is a good to that person; and the general happiness, therefore, a good to the aggregate of all persons. Happiness has made out its title as *one* of the ends of conduct, and consequently one of the criteria of morality."—John Stuart Mill, *Utilitarianism* (first published in 1861)

3. "You all know, of course, that there used to be in the old days three intellectual arguments for the existence of God, all of which were disposed of by Immanuel Kant in the *Critique of Pure Reason*; but no sooner had he disposed of those arguments than he invented a new one, a moral argument, and that quite convinced him. He was like many people: In intellectual matters he was skeptical, but in moral matters he believed implicitly in the maxims that he had imbibed at his mother's knee. That illustrates what the psychoanalysts so much emphasize—the immensely stronger hold upon us that our very early associations have than those of later times.

"Kant, as I say, invented a new moral argument for the existence of God, and that in varying forms was extremely popular during the nineteenth century. It has all sorts of forms. One form is to say that there would be no right or wrong unless God existed. I am not for the moment concerned with whether there is a difference between right and wrong, or whether there is not: That is another question. The point I am concerned with is that, if you are quite sure there is a difference between right and wrong, you are then in this situation: Is that difference due to God's fiat or is it not? If it is due to God's fiat, then for God himself there is no difference between right and wrong, and it is no longer a significant statement to say that God is good. If you are going to say, as theologians do, that God is good, you must then say that right and wrong have some meaning which is independent of God's fiat, because God's fiats are good and not bad independently of the mere fact that He made them. If you are going to say that, you will then have to say that it is not only through God that right and wrong come into being, but that they are in their essence logically anterior to God. You could, of course, if you liked, say that there was a superior deity who gave orders to the God who made this world, or could take up the line that some of the gnostics took up—a line which I often thought was a very plausible one—that as a matter of fact this world that we know was made by the devil at a moment when God was not looking. There is a good deal to be said for that, and I am not concerned to refute it."—Bertrand Russell, "Why I Am Not a Christian," in *Philosophy: The Basic Issues,* ed. E. D. Klemke et al. (New York: St. Martin's Press, 1982), pp. 283–284.

*4. "Under certain conditions it is rational for an individual to agree that others should force him to act in ways which, at the time of the action, the individual may not see as desirable. If, for example, a man knows that he is subject to breaking his resolves when temptation is present, he may ask a friend to refuse to entertain his requests at some later stage.

"A classical example is given in the Odyssey when Odysseus commands his men to tie him to the mast and refuse all future orders to be set free, because he knows the power of the Sirens to enchant men with their songs. Here we are on relatively sound ground in later refusing Odysseus' requests to be set free. He may even claim to have changed his mind but, since it is *just* such changes that he wished to guard against, we are entitled to ignore them.

"A process analogous to this may take place on a social rather than an individual basis. An electorate may mandate its representatives to pass legislation which when it comes time to 'pay the price' may be unpalatable. I may believe that a tax increase is necessary to halt inflation though I resent the lower pay check each month. However in both this case and that of Odysseus, the measure to be enforced is specifically requested by the party involved and at some point in time there is genuine consent and agreement on the part of those persons whose liberty is infringed. Such is not the case for the paternalistic measure we have been speaking about. What must be involved here is not consent to specific measures but rather consent to a system of government, run by elected representatives, with an understanding that they may act to safeguard our interests in certain limited ways.

"I suggest that since we are all aware of our irrational propensities, deficiencies in cognitive and emotional capacities, and avoidable and unavoidable ignorance, it is rational and prudent for us to in effect take out 'social insurance policies.' We may argue for and against proposed paternalistic measures in terms of what fully rational individuals would accept as forms of protection."—Gerald Dworkin, "Paternalism," in *Morality and the Law*, ed. Richard A. Wasserstrom (Belmont, Calif.: Wadsworth, 1971)

5. "It is sometimes held that if there are innate psychological differences between females and males, sex roles are inevitable. The point of this argument is not, of course, to urge that there should be sex roles, but rather to show that the normative question is out of place, that there will be sex roles, whatever we decide. The argument assumes first that the alleged natural differences between the sexes are inevitable; but if such differences are inevitable, differences in behavior are inevitable; and if differences in behavior are inevitable, society will inevitably be structured so as to enforce role differences according to sex. Thus, sex roles are inevitable.

"For the purpose of this discussion, let us accept the claim that natural psychological differences are inevitable. We assume that there are such differences and ignore the possibility of their being altered, for example, by evolutionary change or direct biological intervention. Let us also accept the second claim, that behavioral differences are inevitable. Behavioral differences could perhaps be eliminated even given the assumption of natural differences in disposition (for example, those with no natural inclination to a certain kind of behavior might nevertheless learn it), but let us waive this point. We assume then that behavioral differences, and hence also role differences, between the sexes are inevitable. Does it follow that there must be sex roles, that is, that the institutions and practices of society must enforce correlations between roles and sex?

"Surely not. Indeed, such sanctions would be pointless. Why bother to direct women into some roles and men into others if the pattern occurs regardless of the nature of society? Mill makes the point elegantly in *The Subjection of Women*: 'The anxiety of mankind to interfere in behalf of nature, for fear lest nature should not succeed in effecting its purpose, is an altogether unnecessary solicitude.'"—Joyce Trebilcot, "Sex Roles: The Argument from Nature," *Ethics* 85 (April 1975) ■

□ 14-2. TREE DIAGRAMS FOR EXTENDED ARGUMENTS

Most of the arguments discussed in this book have been simple ones: however many premises they have had, there has been only one conclusion. Often, though, you will come across a complex or extended argument—one in which the main conclusion is supported by premises that are themselves the conclusions of subarguments. Portraying the structure of such an argument, as required by step 3 of the process outlined in Section 14-1, involves analyzing the role of each and every statement that is integral to it. The easiest way to do this is by means of a *tree diagram*:

> **A tree diagram is a drawing that shows the logical relationship between the main conclusion and every other statement integral to an argument.**

Applying the technique to the brief argument in example (1) will provide a quick understanding of how it works. First, the main conclusion is underlined and labeled "*MC*," as shown:

> **1. If a being is conceived by human parents and thereby has a human genetic code, then that being is a *human* being. Conception is the point at which nonhuman elements acquire a human genetic code. Thus, abortion involves the killing of a human being. And because it involves the taking of human life, (*MC*) abortion must be judged morally wrong, except in those rare cases where the mother's life is in danger.**

The next task is to identify every statement that serves as a direct premise for MC. These support claims are enclosed in brackets and labeled "*P*":

> **1a. If a being is conceived by human parents and thereby has a human genetic code, then that being is a *human* being. Conception is the point at which nonhuman elements acquire a human genetic code. Thus, (*P*) [abortion involves the killing of a human being]. And because it involves the taking of human life, (*MC*) abortion must be judged morally wrong, except in those rare cases where the mother's life is in danger.**

Depending on the length and complexity of the argument, there may be more than one premise and several "tiers" of *secondary premises*: the premises of one subargument may themselves be conclusions of still other subarguments. Then premises (*P*) must be distinguished from secondary premises (*SP*) and different premises identified by assigning arabic numerals as subscripts: P_1, P_2, and so forth for premises of the main argument and SP_1 and SP_2 for secondary premises.

> **1b. (*SP_1*) (If a being is conceived by human parents and thereby has a human genetic code, then that being is a *human* being.) (*SP_2*) (Conception is the point at which nonhuman elements acquire a human genetic code.) Thus, (*P*) [abortion involves the killing of a human being]. And because it involves the taking of human life, (*MC*) abortion must be judged morally wrong, except in those rare cases where the mother's life is in danger.**

All statements integral to the argument are identified and labeled in (1b). Note that the statement "because it involves the taking of human life" has not been labeled because it is simply a repetition of P.

The objective of diagramming is to represent the premises of the argument as the branches of a tree. The main conclusion is shown as the *base* of the tree. All other integral statements are represented in the diagram by *nodes*, which show where premises or secondary premises fit into the overall argument and thus are joined to the tree. The nodes directly aligned with the base indicate direct support claims for the main conclusion; all other nodes indicate secondary premises.

A *branch* consists of a single continuous line connecting a node or series of nodes with the main conclusion. As these lines descend through the tree, they converge on the main conclusion, thus depicting the general relation of support or implication from claims higher up in the tree down to the base itself.

The diagram for example (1) is shown in (1c). Circles designate both the base and the nodes. And the labels "MC," "P," "SP_1," and "SP_2" designate the statements that were identified as the main conclusion, the premise, and the secondary premises.

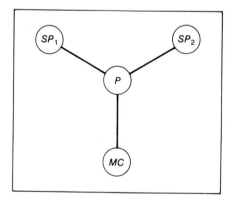

Although the tree diagram differs from trees in nature in that its branches support its base, it is constructed from the base upward. The main conclusion is shown first, as the base. Next, each of the direct premises is shown as a node connecting with the conclusion. After this, any secondary premises for these claims are shown as nodes connected with them—and so on, until the top of the tree has been formed.

A tree diagram can be used to portray the structure of simple arguments as well as extended ones. It can be applied to both deductive and inductive arguments. Even an extended argument that contains both deductive and inductive reasoning in different subarguments can be diagrammed as a single tree. Indeed, any argument can be diagrammed provided that five simple rules are consistently followed.

□ *Rule 1: Grouping*

Each premise supporting a single conclusion is connected to the base or the node it supports by a straight line.

Applications of the Rule of Grouping are illustrated by the diagrams for (1) and for the following example, which contains two premises in support of the main conclusion:

> 2. (*MC*) <u>Voluntary euthanasia should be legalized</u>; and here are the reasons in a nutshell. (*P₁*) [It is simply cruel to refuse an agonized and incurably ill person's request for "merciful release."] In addition, (*P₂*) [there is no demonstrable social interest sufficient to warrant the infringement of the patient's liberty caused by prohibiting voluntary euthanasia].

2a.

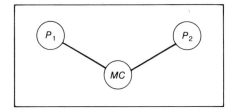

□ *Rule 2: Direction*

Each tree diagram has only one terminus, or base, and branching occurs only in an upward direction.

Under the Rule of Direction, if the same secondary premise supports the conclusions of two or more subarguments, it is represented by a corresponding number of nodes. As an example, consider argument (3):

> 3. (*P₁*) [There should be no legal interference with the access of consenting adults to pornographic material.] (*P₂*) [There should be no legal interference with homosexuality among consenting adults.] (*SP*) (A government can rightfully legislate against the private activity of consenting adults only on the grounds that such activity is harmful to other, nonconsenting persons.) Therefore, (*MC*) <u>don't give your support to the Moral Majority's protests against "victimless crimes."</u>

The main conclusion, expressed in the last sentence, is supported by two premises—bracketed and labeled "*P₁*" and "*P₂*." Both premises are, in turn, supported by the statement in parentheses that is labeled "*SP*": "A government can rightfully. . . ." By following the Rule of Direction, we construct the diagram shown in (3a). Because *SP* is used twice, it occupies two different nodes in the tree.

3a.

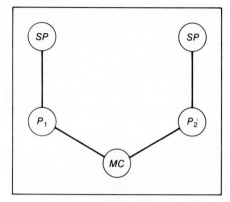

An alternative way to diagram this argument is to treat P_1 and P_2 as a conjunction. This would result in a diagram with SP occupying only one node:

3b.

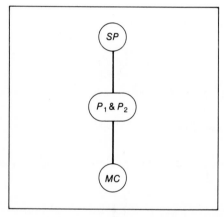

It would be incorrect, however, to diagram example (3) as follows:

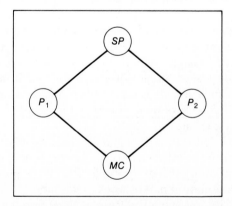

This tree branches downward (from SP to P_1 and P_2) as well as upward (from MC to P_1 and P_2) and thus violates Rule 2. Such a diagram does not clearly show that the main conclusion draws support from the premises while the premises support—but do not draw support from—the conclusion.

The only exception to Rule 2 occurs when circular, or question-begging, arguments are diagrammed (see Section 12-2). In this event, the diagram exposes the fallacy by showing that the support for the main conclusion is inadequate because the conclusion has been smuggled in as a premise. Example (4) is such an argument.

> 4. **The Holy Book must be obeyed** because (*P*) [it is the word of the Almighty One]. We know this to be true because (*SP₁*) (the prophet Althazar has proclaimed it). (*SP₂*) (That Althazar is the prophet of the Almighty One we know by decree of the Holy Book itself.) And what Althazar says must therefore be accepted, because (*MC*) <u>the eternal truth of the Holy Book must be obeyed</u>.

The arrows in (4a) indicate the circularity of the reasoning.

 4a.

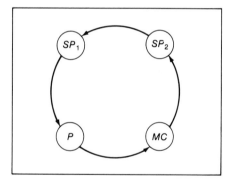

Because according to Rule 2 a tree may have only one main conclusion, each diagram represents a single argument, whether it is simple or extended. Thus, when two or more arguments with different main conclusions occur in the same passage, they must have separate diagrams even if the same premise is used in each.

Example (5) contains two distinct arguments, as shown by the independent conclusions.

> 5. As for laws prohibiting the sale of pornography, I say (*MC₁*) <u>it is wrong to legislate against this so-called "immorality."</u> So what if a self-styled Moral Majority is opposed to pornography? (*P₁*) [To enforce their moral views against the interests of individuals would create a tyranny of the majority.] And what of the legal prohibitions against casual sex between unmarried partners? (*MC₂*) <u>We shouldn't condemn sex without love,</u> (*P₂*) for [a repressive attitude would needlessly deprive many people of an effective channel of satisfaction or cause them to feel needless guilt].

Because P_1 and P_2 both function as premises for both MC_1 and MC_2, they appear in the diagram for each argument:

5a.

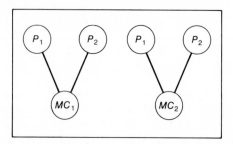

We must also distinguish between premises that support the conclusion independently and those that support the conclusion only in conjunction with other premises. Although the plausibility of any conclusion depends upon the *whole set* of premises offered for it, each premise on its own usually presents a separate reason for the conclusion. It sometimes happens, however, that statements are not relevant to a conclusion unless they are taken together. In this case, each premise supports the conclusion through the mediation of the other. Where this occurs, we follow the Rule of Dependence.

□ *Rule 3: Dependence*

A statement that counts as a premise only in conjunction with another statement is joined to the other by a brace in the tree diagram.

In example (6), P_1 and P_2 when taken together serve as reasons for the main conclusion—that there can be legal justification for prohibiting certain displays of obscene material.

6. (*MC*) There are some cases in which the law may legitimately prohibit offensive material, such as obscene displays on billboards and in store windows. (P_1) [In some cases, the reaction of any observer chosen at random can reasonably be expected to be one of revulsion, disgust, and avoidance.] (P_2) [When material which is universally offensive in this way is also displayed in such a manner that people cannot avoid it without unreasonable effort and inconvenience, the obscene material may be prohibited.]

Statement P_1 alone does not justify legal prohibition of even material that would offend almost everybody as long as those who do not wish to be exposed to it can avoid exposure. Statement P_2 alone is not a reason for MC because the law does impose some inconveniences and costs on all citizens—such as taxes, driver-licensing requirements, and regulations pertaining to affirmative action—that are supposedly justified by the benefits they promote. So although P_1 and P_2 are independent statements whose truth values could be independently established, their roles in argument (6) make them dependent on each other in that context. This is illustrated by the diagram:

6a.

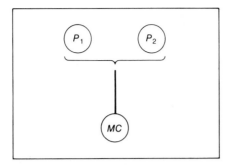

The Rules of Grouping, Direction, and Dependence are sufficient to portray the structure of most extended arguments. By adding two further rules, however, we greatly enhance the analytical usefulness of tree diagrams. These rules—the *Rule of Addition* and the *Rule of Divergence*—allow other important features of the structure of certain arguments to be represented.

Step 2 in the procedure for argument evaluation (Section 14-1) often reveals that significant but unstated assumptions have been made by the author. Two of the examples in this section rely on such assumptions. Example (1) tacitly assumes that it is morally wrong to kill innocent human beings. Example (3) has two suppressed premises, both related to the intended meaning of the term *victimless crime*: "The private use of pornographic material by adults causes no harm," and "Private homosexual relations among consenting adults are not harmful."

The Rule of Addition allows the roles of such important but unstated assumptions to be portrayed. For each suppressed premise, a circled asterisk is shown as a node of the tree.

☐ *Rule 4: Addition*

An implicit premise can be designated by an asterisk and added to any part of the tree diagram above the base.

Applying this rule to example (1) produces the following diagram:

1d.

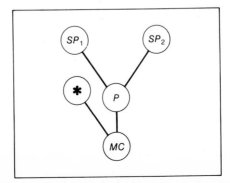

The most reasonable way to represent the role of the unstated assumptions in argument (3) is to join them to the secondary premises by applying the Rule of Dependence:

3c.

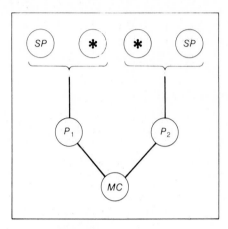

This makes clear why the author accepts SP as a reason for both premise 1 and premise 2. But there is no indication that the author woud accept these assumptions on their own as relevant reasons for P_1 and P_2.

An extended argument sometimes contains a statement that *does not support* but rather *weakens* a premise or even a whole subargument. If the author indicates how this negative consideration qualifies some other point, then all we need to represent in the diagram is the qualified statement. Otherwise, the weakening statement can be included by employing the Rule of Divergence.

☐ *Rule 5: Divergence*

A statement that weakens or diverges from another claim is attached by a broken line to the node representing the statement it affects.

In example (7), the main conclusion—"Sex discrimination is then unjustified"—is supported by P_1. But premise P_1 is weakened by the statement labeled "D," which alleges that the antecedent of P_1 may not be true, or at least not of all women.

7. (P_1) [If there are no psychological differences between the sexes, then sex is irrelevant to the capacity of an individual to perform a certain task.] And (*MC*) sex discrimination is then unjustified. (*D*) (Some studies do suggest that, due to hormonal differences, women are on the average more passive and submissive than men.) (P_2) [But even if there are psychological differences between the sexes, society does not have the right to systematically deny the same roles to all women simply because some women are incapable of fulfilling them.] (*SP*) (Each individual is entitled to be judged simply

on the basis of individual merit and not on the basis of the "average" psychological makeup of that individual's sexual group.)

The relationship between P_1 and D is indicated by the broken line in diagram (7a).

7a.

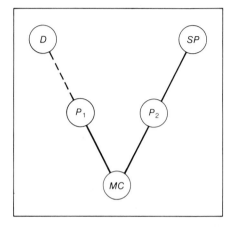

As the examples in this section show, tree diagrams are extremely useful in laying bare the logical structure of an argument. They are a valuable tool of analysis whenever careful criticism of an argument is required. But they are also valuable aids in *constructing* arguments. A full demonstration of this use of tree diagrams cannot be provided here, but the procedure can be briefly outlined as follows:

1. Write down the main conclusion that the argument will support, and label it "MC."

2. Make a numbered list of all the considerations that come to mind in support of the main conclusion.

3. Employ the rules for diagramming, showing how each of the numbered claims relates to the main conclusion.

4. As the tree is constructed, sort out important premises from irrelevant considerations, construct subarguments, and discover any gaps that require the addition of further premises.

■ **EXERCISE 14-2**

■ A. Identify the main conclusion, the direct premises, and the secondary premises for each of the following arguments. Complete a tree diagram for each argument.

1. Voluntary euthanasia ought not to be legalized. In the first place, it is difficult to ascertain whether the consent of the patient is really voluntary. Thus, there is substantial danger that the law will be abused. Second, the judgment that a person is incurably ill may be wrong on two counts: the diagnostic judgment may be in error, and the judgment that no cure will be available within the life expectancy of the patient may be in error. Thus, there is substantial risk that some will die unnecessarily. Finally, to legalize voluntary euthanasia is to accept the "thin edge of the wedge," thus preparing the way for the legalization of involuntary euthanasia.

2. The death penalty by its very nature is a cruel and unusual punishment and is thus in violation of the Eighth Amendment of the Constitution. The death penalty is excessive and unnecessary. In addition, it is abhorrent to currently existing moral values. For these two reasons, the death penalty is within the meaning of "cruel and unusual punishment" as established by previous decisions of the Supreme Court.

3. The principle I wish to attack is this: There is no natural difference between the sexes that makes the male-dominated society inevitable. There is such a difference. Owing to hormonal differences, males are inherently more aggressive than females. This greater aggressiveness assures male domination of the high-status roles in society.

Moreover, if society does not socialize women to reject competing with men, then most women will be condemned to failure and unhappiness. Given the innate aggression advantage of men over women, consider what would happen if society did not socialize women to reject competing with men for society's high-status positions. Some women would be aggressive enough to succeed. The vast majority would be failures, however—socialized to desire high-status positions but incapable of attaining them.

*4. Once we understand more clearly what *human* means, we can see that the view that abortion is wrong because it involves the killing of a human being is a mistaken view. A fetus is human only in the same sense that it is a member of the biological species *Homo sapiens*. But it is not as a biological organism that humans have a right to life. Rather, humans possess full and equal moral rights only as persons—that is, as members of the moral community. A fetus is so unlike a person that it has no significant right to life. It follows, therefore, that a woman's right to obtain an abortion is absolute. Abortion is morally justified at any stage of fetal development.

5. A stable family life is absolutely essential for the proper rearing of children and the consequent welfare of society as a whole. But the limitation of sex to marriage is a necessary condition of forming and maintaining stable family units. The availability of sex within marriage will reinforce the loving relationship between husband and wife, the *exclusive* availability of sex within marrriage will lead most people to get married and to stay married, and the unavailability of sex outside of marriage will keep the marriage strong. Therefore, the convention that sex is permissible only within the bounds of marriage is solidly based on considerations of social utility.

6. While I reject the traditional view that sex outside of marriage is not permissible, I certainly do not endorse promiscuity. Promiscuity reduces a humanly significant activity to a merely mechanical performance that is valued only for the transitory pleasures it produces. This in turn leads to the demeaning of human sensitivities, the loss of respect for members of the opposite sex, and even the disintegration of the human personality. Sex outside of marriage is permissible only when there is genuine love felt for the sex partner. But sexual expression ought to be limited only by the condition that sexual partners have love and affection for each other.

7. "It is a curious fact of our society that today television is the dominant producer of cultural symbolism. Previously, symbols were often fused into a hierarchy of significance by a well-defined code such as Christianity or Communism, or by a great poet or writer who created an organically consistent symbolic world, but television symbolism is fragmented and contradictory. Nonetheless, it can be argued that television symbolism currently provides the most significant model of behavior and norms of action. Television's imagery is thus prescriptive as well as descriptive, prescribing the proper attitudes toward the police, the property system, and consumer society. Television images assume a normative status: They not only reveal what is happening in the society but also show how one adjusts to the social order. Furthermore, television demonstrates the pain and punishment that result from not adjusting, as well as the machinations of power and authority. Television imagery thus contains a picture of the world and an ethics. It shows us that we should drive a car, have a nice house, wear fashionable clothes, drink, smoke, keep a pretty smile, avoid body odor, and stay in line. The endless repetition of the same images produces a television world where the conventional is the norm and conformity the rule."—Douglas Kellner, "T.V., Technology, and Ideology," in *Technology and Human Affairs*, ed. L. Hickman and A. Al-Hibri (St. Louis: C. V. Mosby, 1981).

*8. "Sex affords us a paradigm of pleasure, but not a cornerstone of value. For most of us it is not only a needed outlet for desire but also the most enjoyable form of recreation we know. Its value is nevertheless easily mistaken by being confused with that of love, when it is taken as essentially an expression of that emotion. Although intense, the pleasures of sex are brief and repetitive rather than cumulative. They give value to the specific acts which generate them, but not the lasting kind of values which enhances one's whole life. The briefness of these pleasures contributes to their intensity (or perhaps their intensity makes them necessarily brief), but it also relegates them to the periphery of most rational plans for the good life.

"By contrast, love typically develops over a long term relation; while its pleasures may be less intense and physical, they are of more cumulative value. The importance of love to the individual may well be central in a rational system of value. And it has perhaps an even deeper moral significance relating to the identification with the interests of another person, which broadens one's possible relationships with others as well. . . . Sexual desire, by contrast, is desire for another which is nevertheless essentially self-regarding. Sexual pleasure is certainly a good for the individual, and for many it may be necessary in order for them to function in a reasonably cheerful way. But it bears little relation to those other values just discussed, to which some analyses falsely suggest a conceptual connection."—Alan H. Goldman, "Plain Sex," *Philosophy and Public Affairs* 6 (Spring 1977).

9. "It was urged on behalf of the defendants that a fundamental principle of all law—international and domestic—is that there can be no punishment of crime without a pre-existing law. 'Nullum crimen sine lege, nulla poena sine lege.' It was submitted that *ex post facto* punishment is abhorrent to the law of all civilized nations, that no sovereign power had made aggressive war a crime at the time the alleged criminal acts were committed, that no statute had defined aggressive war, that no penalty had been fixed for its commission, and no court had been created to try and punish offenders.

"In the first place, it is to be observed that the maxim *nullum crimen sine lege* is not a limitation of sovereignty, but is in general a principle of justice. To assert that it is unjust to punish those who in defiance of treaties and assurances have attacked neighboring states without warning is obviously untrue, for in such circumstances the attacker must know what he is doing. . . . Occupying the positions they did in the government of Germany, the defendants . . . must have known of the treaties signed by Germany, outlawing the recourse to war for the settlement of international disputes. . . . On this view of the case alone, it would appear that the maxim has no application to the present facts.

"This view is strongly reinforced by a consideration of the state of law in 1939 so far as aggressive war is concerned. The General Treaty of the Renunciation of War of August 27, 1928, more specifically known as the Pact of Paris or the Kellogg-Briand Pact, was binding on 63 nations, including Germany, Italy, and Japan at the outbreak of war in 1939."—*The Judgment of the International Tribunal at Nuremberg,* Washington, D.C.: United States Government Printing Office, 1947.

10. "With Israel poised to attack West Beirut, the United States seems close to achieving some major Middle East goals but is on the verge of compromising its long-term national interests and those of its moderate Arab friends.

"Western diplomats and Arab analysts suggest that unless a way out is found for Yasir Arafat and his Palestine Liberation Organization—which seems increasingly unlikely—and unless a way is found to save West Beirut from Israeli ground attack, then the U.S. and its moderate allies will end up paying the heaviest part of the bill in the aftermath.

"If Arafat feels obliged to die fighting to keep the Palestinian cause alive for the future, the Arab world seems sure to seize upon his martyrdom as a perfidy specifically committed by the Americans in arming and encouraging the Israelis.

"Palestinian terrorism, whose destruction the Israelis have invoked as a goal to justify the invasion, is then likely to blossom as never before, uncontrolled and uncontrollable against American as well as Israeli targets. Palestinian moderates say an indiscriminate assault on West Beirut would result in everybody but the terrorists being killed.

"And if the Israelis destroyed a good part of West Beirut in their assault—a plausible assumption in light of the massive firepower they employed against Tyre, Sidon, and Damour—the number of civilian casualties, already very high, could easily double. . . . The probability . . . is that the guerrillas would keep on shooting, and the Israelis would use planes, artillery, and tanks to dislodge them block by block, street by street.

"Responsible Lebanese politicians believe that reconstructing this tormented country, a major aim proclaimed by Israel and the U.S. in this war, would be impossible for years to come in the wake of more Moslem dead and the Christian Phalangist militia's de facto alliance with Israel. And the U.S. would be tagged with responsibility for that aspect of the invasion."—Jonathan C. Randal, "Mideast Paradox," *The Washington Post,* June 24, 1982.

■ B. Use the rules for tree diagrams to construct an argument either pro or con for each of the issues below. Begin by establishing your main conclusion. Then use the "reasons" listed as separate premises. Use your own judgment in deciding whether to add implicit assumptions or validating premises. (Indicate, where appropriate, those premises that are accepted as true or probably true and those that are only presumed to be true for the sake of argument.)

    1. **Issue:** "Is marijuana, as presently used in the United States, good or bad?"

        (a) **Pro:**

            1. When properly smoked, marijuana produces a very pleasant experience for most people.

            2. Smoking marijuana is one very effective way of obtaining release from the tensions of modern living.

            3. The use of marijuana increases communication between human beings.

            4. Marijuana makes the user more responsive to the immediate environment by sharpening all the senses, including smell and taste.

    5. Marijuana increases fantasizing and thereby stimulates the imagination of the user.

  (b) **Con:**

    1. Marijuana impairs judgment, and the user therefore cannot estimate speed or distance accurately.

    2. There is a high correlation between urban crime and the use of marijuana.

    3. Because smoking marijuana reduces drive, induces lethargy, and increases fantasizing, it makes the user irresponsible and unfit for modern society.

    4. Marijuana is a stepping-stone to more dangerous drugs.

    5. Possession and use of marijuana exposes a person to severe penalties.

2. Issue: "Is civil disobedience ever right in a democracy?"

  (a) **Pro:**

    1. To obey an unjust law or to allow an immoral policy to go unchallenged is to assent to and even participate in moral wrong.

    2. The conscientious citizen has a moral obligation to remedy injustice or evil.

    3. Civil disobedience is sometimes the most effective technique for calling public attention to a social injustice.

    4. Civil disobedience is justified when there is no practicable alternative either because normal legal channels would take too long or because the legal procedures provided in a democracy are effectively denied to certain groups.

    5. Sometimes the government exceeds its authority, either because it enacts some law that goes beyond the limits of the authority granted to it by the Constitution, or because it infringes upon the inalienable rights of the citizens.

  (b) **Con:**

    1. By definition, civil disobedience is a violation of the law of the land.

    2. Civil disobedience violates the fundamental principle of majority rule.

    3. By stimulating further lawlessness, acts of civil disobedience weaken respect for the law.

    4. Acts of civil disobedience are unnecessary in a democracy because there are other, less objectionable ways to remedy social evils.

    5. The consequences of civil disobedience are often worse than the evil being protested.

    6. "Suppose everyone did the same": if every person in similar circumstances engaged in the same kind of action, a system of law and order would be impossible. ■

☐ 14-3. ANALYZING MORAL ARGUMENTS

In its broadest sense, ethics, or moral philosophy, is concerned with beliefs about right and wrong human conduct. These *normative* beliefs are expressed through such general terms as *good, bad, virtue, vice, praiseworthy, blameworthy, ought,* and *ought not.* When the belief is expressed as a decision, verdict, or conclusion, it is said to be a *moral judgment:*

A moral judgment is an assertion either that an action is right or wrong, or ought or ought not to be taken; or that either a person or some trait of a person, or an object or some quality of an object, is good or bad.

A moral judgment can be about a particular case (for example, "You ought not to lie about the money") or about classes of actions or things ("Lying out of self-interest is always wrong"). When they concern classes, moral judgments are also known as *moral rules* or *moral principles*.

Sentences that express moral judgments are of a type identified in Chapter 3 as *evaluative*. These sentences perform a variety of functions, depending upon the context of the discourse and the purpose of the speaker or author. As indicated in Section 3-2, they can be used to make claims about the qualities of actions or the attributes of persons or things, just as if they were factual statements; they can function as directives or prescriptions by expressing moral rules; and they can be used to express emotion or to influence the feelings or attitudes of others.

There has been considerable debate among philosophers about which of these functions of moral judgments is predominant. Some theorists maintain that, for the standard cases in which they occur, moral judgments must be understood as expressing statements, or propositions. Other theorists maintain that moral judgments must be understood as making recommendations, or issuing prescriptions. It has been argued by still other philosophers, known as the Emotivists, that moral judgments do not express statements, but are expressions of emotion.

□ *The role of logic in moral disputes*

While moral judgments may be used in some contexts to express emotion or to make recommendations, their function is not *exclusively* emotive or prescriptive, however. Indeed, if the Emotivist interpretation were correct—if it were true that moral judgments *never* expressed statements—there would be no role for logic in moral discourse.

But insofar as moral judgments are incorporated in moral *reasoning*, they are used to express statements. They can occur as either explicit or implicit premises and as either an explicit or an unstated conclusion. In Section 14-1, for example, argument (2) contains two moral judgments: an implicit premise, made explicit in (2a)—"The only acts that ought to be regarded as criminal are those that involve a victim"—and the conclusion—"Therefore, such [homosexual] acts ought not to be regarded as criminal."

Where efforts are made to *justify* moral judgments, the moral reasoning involved is a matter for logical scrutiny and evaluation. To support a moral judgment—for example, "You ought to tell the truth about what happened"— we provide reasons in a way very similar to our offering premises for conclusions to any other sort of argument. We cite evidence, invoke shared beliefs, point out the consequences of actions, and appeal to appropriate standards. In addition, we can agree that some efforts to justify moral judgments make more sense than others—that some are strong whereas others are weak. Our ability to evaluate these justifications in the same way that we evaluate other kinds of reasoning indicates that they are bona fide arguments, after all. So anyone who maintains that a moral judgment can be justified must concede (1) that it is appropriate for others to expect reasons for the judgment, and (2) that a judgment of the form "X is good"(or "A ought to do X") is the contradictory of a judgment of the form "X is not good" (or "A ought not to do X").

☐ Sources of disagreement

For the most part, arguments containing moral judgments can be analyzed in the same way as other kinds of arguments. When a moral judgment occurs as a conclusion, it must be supported by reasons that show it to be justified, just as does any other conclusion. Where such judgments occur as premises, they are subject to the examination described as step 4 of the argument-evaluation procedure.

As noted in Section 14-1, however, moral arguments are based—either explicitly or implicitly—on *evaluative standards*. Any argument with a moral judgment as its conclusion must contain at least one other moral judgment as a premise. This premise serves as the evaluative standard, giving the argument its moral dimension. This dimension can best be understood by considering the different ways in which people can disagree over the reasons given in support of a moral judgment.

☐ FACTUAL MATTERS

Nonmoral elements are often central to moral disputes. Such disputes can be at least partially resolved by obtaining critical factual information on the issues involved. Controversies over nuclear power plants and the disposal of nuclear wastes, toxic substances in the workplace, the use of marijuana and cocaine, research on recombinant DNA, and the disclosure of confidential information by government employees are among the many topics in which facts as well as values are at issue.

☐ DEFINITIONAL OR CONCEPTUAL MATTERS

Moral disputes can result from disagreement over the way language is used by the contending parties. In a controversy over the morality of euthanasia, for example, one party might define *euthanasia* as "voluntarily elected natural death" and another party might understand the word to mean "mercy killing." Before progress could be made, it would then be necessary to identify the arguers' positions as exactly as possible by distinguishing between voluntary and involuntary euthanasia (based on the presence or absence of the patient's wish for life to be terminated) and between active and passive euthanasia (based on the difference between active intervention to bring about the patient's death and letting the patient die by the withholding of lifesaving treatment).

Some moral controversies cannot be as easily traced to disputes over the meanings of certain terms but instead concern different views on what a concept should include. For instance, in a dispute over abortion, both parties may agree that it is morally wrong to kill innocent persons. However, one party may insist that a human fetus is not a person in the sense of having rights, even if it is admitted that the fetus is a human being. The other party may take the opposed view that the fetus's status as a human being and its potential for meaningful human interaction and personal development automatically qualify it for personhood.

□ EVALUATIVE STANDARDS

Moral disputes can also be based on controversies over the application of moral standards.

1. *There may be a disagreement over which moral principle is applicable.* This could occur, for example, in a debate over the desirability of an affirmative action—or "reverse discrimination"—program that gives preference in hiring and job training to women and members of racial minorities. One party might defend the program by claiming that *justice* requires compensatory measures to be taken on behalf of victims of past injustice. A second party might disapprove of the program on the grounds that absolute *equality* requires applicants to be considered on the basis of their individual qualifications for the job. A third party might maintain either that the *welfare of society* requires the most highly qualified people to be selected for training or that the *welfare of society* requires an increase in the opportunities of previously disadvantaged groups.

2. *There may be a dispute over the proper interpretation of a particular principle.* As an illustration, suppose the students enrolled in a difficult philosophy course find that outside the classroom, the professor is rarely accessible to those doing well in the course. The professor's office hours are used almost exclusively to give assistance to students who are doing poorly. In discussing this situation, everyone agrees that the professor should treat all the students equally; but there is disagreement over what this "equal treatment" entails. Some students maintain that the professor should try to give the same amount of time and attention to each student who comes to the office. Others point out that this plan could actually increase the discrepancy between those doing well and those falling to the bottom of the class. They argue that all the students should be given an equal opportunity to benefit from the course and that the professor is therefore justified in giving greater assistance to those having difficulty with it.

3. *There may be disagreement over which of several moral principles should be given precedence.* If two or more moral principles conflict, one party may believe that one particular principle should be given precedence over all others, while another party may argue that a different principle should be given precedence. Such disputes might involve conflict between one's duty to be honest and one's duty to help family members; one's duty to be fair and the obligation to be kind or charitable; or one's responsibilities as a citizen and the dictates of one's conscience.

When analyzing a moral controversy, one should always consider the types of issues involved—whether they are factual or empirical matters; the understanding of a definition or concept; or the application of a moral principle. It may be that only one kind of issue is basic to the disagreement. It may also turn out, however, that issues overlap and become entangled.

Rarely do moral disagreements turn solely on questions about evaluative standards, for one's view of the appropriate moral principle to apply to a problem usually depends in part upon one's understanding of the facts of the case. Equally important is the connection between one's view of the relevant moral principles and the definitions or conceptual distinctions that must be drawn in considering the matter at hand. When a factual issue or a verbal dispute can be identified as the source of disagreement and separated from questions about evaluative standards, the competing arguments can be analyzed by applying the six-step procedure outlined in Section 14-1. But *the assessment of evaluative standards presents a new challenge.*

□ Ought statements

A judgment about a particular action—such as telling a lie—can be expressed in various ways.[5] One might claim that the action does or does not possess a certain moral quality; that it is or is not morally appropriate; that it is or is not consistent with a moral principle; or that it is required, prohibited, or permissible. Among the terms used to describe actions in these ways are *good, bad, right, wrong, fair, unfair, just,* and *unjust.*

Moral judgments can also take the form of directives, prescriptions, or recommendations. For example, we say that someone was *obligated* to perform an action; had a *duty* to do it; or had a *right* to do or not to do it. Judgments of these kinds are also expressed by such remarks as "You ought to visit your sick aunt" and "You ought not say you are going unless you really intend to go." All these moral judgments have a common feature: they either employ the term *ought* or they employ words—*should, must,* and so forth—that can be translated without significant loss of meaning into *ought* expressions. For this reason, philosophers refer to such judgments as expressing moral *ought* statements.

Not every statement that contains *ought* or that can be rephrased using *ought* is a moral judgment. So to evaluate an argument containing such an expression, one must first discover the point of view of the arguer and his or her *reasons* for making the assertion.

[5] For the sake of convenience, the remainder of this discussion will be confined to standards that can be used to prescribe and evaluate actions. We will not be concerned with standards used to evaluate morally the people who perform these actions. This distinction significantly narrows the scope of our discussion. For while we do judge persons to be virtuous or vicious and praiseworthy or blameworthy, such judgments involve considerations that differ from or go beyond those needed to evaluate actions.

Consider, for example, this sentence:

1. You ought to return the correct change.

Different persons might use sentence (1) to express different statements. One speaker's reason for the assertion might concern the law; another speaker might be recommending prudent business practice; still a third might be thinking about the immorality of shortchanging innocent customers such as small children who wouldn't know the difference.

There *is* a common element of meaning in all three uses of (1): *ought* always indicates that the recommendation following the word is based on a relevant standard or is supported by compelling reasons. It is therefore crucial when evaluating a particular *ought* statement to determine the standards or reasons underlying its use, whether moral; legal; medical; aesthetic; customary; ceremonial (related to ritual, etiquette, or protocol); political; religious; or prudential, or practical.

Because not all *ought* statements are supported by principles or standards belonging to morality, there is sometimes no *real* disagreement between *ought* statements that appear to be contradictory. Where the standards relevant to "You ought to do X" are different from those relevant to "You ought not to do X," the statements can be consistent with each other. For instance, A, who says "You ought to register for the draft," is not contradicting B, who says "You ought not to register for the draft," if A is using *ought* in a legal sense and B is using *ought* in a moral sense. Even if—as A points out—you are legally obliged to register, the question of whether there are compelling *moral* reasons for doing so is an independent one. When the *ought* statements are understood unambiguously as being on either the legal or the moral plane, however, "You ought to do X" and "You ought not to do X" are contradictories.

If one person is basing the use of *ought* on a moral standard or reason and the other is using *ought* in a different sense, their disagreement is a *verbal dispute* (see Section 4-3). The controversy can often be resolved by pointing this out. For example, in the argument about registering for the draft, B might well agree that *if only legal reasons are to count*, then one ought to register. But if A and B fail to recognize that they are using *ought* statements in different ways, they are talking past each other.

Sometimes a disputant declares that an *ought* statement is based on a specific principle or standard and maintains that this standard *ought* to be decisive. For example, B may admit that, according to certain viewpoints, it makes sense to say, "You ought to register for the draft," but may believe that moral reasons override legal or other considerations. In that case, the argument between A and B is not a verbal dispute. Instead, B's position must be understood as involving the claim that "*All things considered*, you ought not to register for the draft"—a claim that should be treated as a moral *ought* statement. In effect, B is taking the position that when nonmoral standards conflict with moral standards, the moral standards should be given precedence—which can be defended only by taking the position that moral standards are of a higher order than all other standards.

Moral standards are ordinarily thought to be overriding and to be more widely applicable than other sorts of rules, or principles. Thus, when moral standards and other standards collide, we should expect to hear arguments that in the "final analysis" the action one "really ought" to take is the one that is supported by moral reasons.

Once someone's reasons for asserting an *ought* statement have been revealed, it is often possible to tell whether *ought* is being used in a moral or nonmoral sense. But it is sometimes difficult to distinguish between moral *ought* statements and other uses of *ought*. Some *ought* statements are supported by both moral and nonmoral standards, which can make identification difficult. And there may even be disagreement over whether a principle offered to support an *ought* statement is itself moral. For example, philosophers have long debated whether the following standard associated with a position known as Ethical Egoism counts as a *moral* standard: "Each person ought to act to maximize his or her own best long-term interests."

Nevertheless, certain considerations are relevant to the distinction between moral and nonmoral standards. In general, a principle being invoked as a *moral* standard can be expected to meet all or most of the following criteria:[6]

1. The standard has a peremptory character: it is supremely authoritative and overrides any nonmoral standards that conflict with it.

2. The standard applies to the whole range of human activity, rather than to a specific segment of it, such as the rules of order in legislative debates, the rules of games, or the canons of professional ethics.

3. The standard takes a *prescriptive form*: it is primarily intended to guide action and not to describe states of affairs.

4. The standard is concerned with human well-being; it thus makes direct reference to the welfare of persons or, at the very least, is concerned with harm and benefit to them, including the arguer.

5. The standard can be universalized; it can be applied in a similar way to all people situated in relevantly similar circumstances.

☐ RECONSTRUCTING MORAL ARGUMENTS

If the inference in a moral argument is to be valid, the premises must always contain a moral judgment as a reason for the conclusion, for the prescriptive element—the moral *ought* of the conclusion—cannot be derived from factual statements alone. One cannot move from so-called *is* statements to an *ought*

---

[6] Tom L. Beauchamp, *Philosophical Ethics* (New York: McGraw-Hill, 1982), pp. 11–14.

statement without relying upon an explicit or implicit statement of a moral rule.[7]

Thus, constructing moral arguments often involves rendering implicit standards explicit. And because the conclusion of a moral argument can often be justified on the basis of more than one moral standard, more than one premise can sometimes be considered implicit and added to the argument. If the premises fail to specify any standards and no implicit standards can be detected from the author's allusions to background material, then one must simply add whatever standard or standards seem plausible.

In most moral arguments, at least one premise will describe the factual situation to which the moral standard is held to apply and at least one other premise will present the relevant moral standard or standards. The reconstructed argument will have the following form:

> Premise or premises describing the factual situation
> Premise or premises presenting the relevant moral standard or standards
> Conclusion—the *ought* statement about what one should do in this particular situation or in this kind of situation

□ Assessing moral standards

Listed in the accompanying box are a number of standards that have been advanced by moral theorists and that are frequently relied on in controversies over moral issues. As noted in the discussion of step 5 in Section 14-1, moral judgments possess a sort of immunity to direct factual confrontation. Because they purport to say what *ought* to be the case and not what *is* the case, they cannot be refuted by ordinary counterevidence. The challenges that can be made to moral standards can also be applied to nonmoral statements, but they are most effective against statements that resist factual refutation. Five challenges will be considered here.

1. *One might attack the vagueness or generality of the standard.* Most moral standards are open to interpretation; their wording is usually so general that reasonable persons can reasonably disagree over their meaning and application. The advantage of this broad wording is that it gives the rule versatility. Wording that is specific drastically narrows the range of application. The disadvantage of such general wording is that the standard relied on may be too vague to yield a clear-cut *ought* in a given situation.

The extreme generality of several of the standards cited in the accompanying box would permit them to be invoked to support almost any moral judgment. Critics have made this complaint about the Natural Law standard, and it could also be made about the Subjectivist and Divine Command standards.

[7] This entailment gap between *is* and *ought* statements was first critically discussed by the Scottish philosopher David Hume in A *Treatise of Human Nature* (first published in 1739–1742) bk. III, pt. I, sec. I.

Standards for Judging the Morality of Actions

NATURAL LAW STANDARD: Moral actions are those that are in harmony with nature or with universal laws of nature.

DIVINE COMMAND STANDARD: Moral actions are those commanded by God.

SUBJECTIVIST STANDARD: Moral actions are those one personally likes or approves of or that make one feel good or happy.

EGOISTIC STANDARD: Moral actions are those that maximize the individual's own long-term interests or well-being.

RELATIVIST STANDARD: Moral actions for a given society are those that a majority of the members of that society accept as right or obligatory.

INTUITIONIST STANDARD: Moral actions are those that are consistent with the individual's conscience or that the individual intuits as a duty or obligation.

ACT-UTILITARIAN STANDARD: Moral actions are those that produce the greatest amount of happiness or well-being for the greatest number of people.

RULE-UTILITARIAN STANDARD: Moral actions are actions consistent with rules that maximize the overall happiness or well-being of those to whom the rules apply.

KANTIAN STANDARD: Moral actions are those for which the maxim, or rule, governing the individual's action could be willed to become a universal law for all rational beings.

A moral judgment often involves different "levels of justification." For example, if a judge orders a reporter to turn over notes for the judge's inspection, the reporter might refuse, maintaining that the social welfare is maximized when rules concerning the freedom of the press—such as a reporter's right to the confidentiality of sources—are consistently upheld. Here the reporter's ultimate justification (at the highest "level") might be a version of the Rule-Utilitarian standard. But arguments in defense of the refusal to submit to the judge's order involve other levels of justification. The refusal might first be defended by appealing to the narrower principle that confidentiality of information is required by freedom of the press. Freedom of the press might be justified, in turn, by appealing to the broader principle that the public in a democracy has a right to be informed—a right that can be maintained only by a corps of journalists willing to protect their sources. This broader principle also applies to nonjournalistic contexts—for example, it can be used to justify a freedom of information act that permits citizens to obtain confidential information about themselves that has been collected by government agencies and to justify the right of a defendant to a public trial.

However many levels of justification a moral argument may involve, it is open to the criticism of vagueness or generality at each junction between a moral judgment and a "higher" standard. One should ask whether the relevant standard is sufficiently clear and specific so that—in connection with correct and relevant factual premises—it would imply the moral judgment.

2. *One might consider whether the moral standard is internally inconsistent.* A moral standard is said to be internally inconsistent if its application would result in the justification of contradictory moral judgments. If a standard supports the judgment "You ought to do X," then it cannot consistently support the judgment "You ought not to do X"—provided that "X" has the same meaning in both instances and that *ought* is understood to be a moral *ought*.

Some commentators have maintained that most or all versions of the Egoistic standard involve inconsistency. To understand this criticism, suppose that two contestants, Jones and Smith, are in a struggle for very important stakes. Only one can win, although it is in the interest of each to do so. It would be in Jones's interest but not Smith's if Jones wins. Similarly, it would be in Smith's interests, but not in Jones's, if Jones were injured and had to drop out of the competition.

The Egoistic standard can be interpreted to mean that Smith ought to do everything possible to incapacitate Jones and eliminate him from competition, as long as he can do so without having himself disqualified. Likewise, Jones, knowing that his own injury is in Smith's interests, ought to take steps to protect himself and foil Smith's plans; indeed, it would be wrong for Jones not to do so. It therefore follows that if Jones prevents Smith from incapacitating him, his act—as judged by the Egoistic standard—is both wrong and not wrong. It is wrong because it is the prevention of what Smith ought to do and not wrong because it is what Jones ought to do.[8]

3. *One might challenge the adequacy or relevance of the evaluative standard as a justification for the moral judgment in question.* When employing this approach, the challenger attempts to show that resort to a certain kind of standard either defeats efforts to provide a *rational* defense of a moral judgment or defeats the claim that the evaluative standard is a *moral* standard. This is done by pointing out one or more of the following difficulties:

> Appeal to this standard makes rational debate over the moral judgment impossible or useless.
>
> Appeal to this standard supplies no reason for the moral judgment because it is question begging.
>
> The moral standard is one that cannot itself be justified by appeal to moral reasons.

Many commentators have held that most, if not all, versions of the Subjectivist standard make rational debate over moral judgments pointless. The basis of their criticism is that if the standard of moral evaluation is one's own *personal preference*, everyone's moral standard is subjectively determined. Thus, if Helen says "Execution of a convicted murderer is wrong" and Jason

---

[8] This example is adapted from Kurt Baier, *The Moral Point of View* (Ithaca, New York: Cornell University Press, 1958), p. 95.

says "Execution of a convicted murderer is never wrong," Jason—according to the theory—is not denying what Helen affirms. This follows from the fact that, according to the theory, Helen is saying something like "I never approve of the execution of a murderer," while Jason's remark is roughly equivalent to "I always approve of the execution of a murderer." And it is perfectly consistent for Jason to approve of an action and for Helen to disapprove of it; they are not *contradicting* each other by expressing different preferences.

Someone who says "Execution of a convicted murderer is always wrong" and means it to be the conclusion of an argument, however, is *denying* the affirmation that "Executing a convicted murderer is never wrong." In that case, it would be appropriate to ask for reasons why the judgment should be accepted as correct. Moral judgments require reasons in their support, whereas personal preferences do not.

Arguments based on the Relativist standard have been criticized as begging the question (see Section 12-2). The Relativist attempts to justify a moral judgment by saying that it concurs with a belief about right and wrong that is held by a group identified as socially relevant. But this is very much like saying, "Doing X is wrong for members of group A because all or most members of A believe it is wrong." And if the members of group A were to say to one another, "You ought not to do X because everyone, or almost everyone, says a person ought not to do it," the argument would be plainly circular. (See also the fallacy of moralism, Section 12-3, and the appeal to authority, Section 12-4.)

While it may be a truism that there is strength in numbers, there is no necessary connection between numbers and truth. Public-opinion polls can tell what most people believe and how they feel about an issue, but such polls cannot determine whether what people think or feel is warranted. The advance of scientific knowledge has repeatedly shown that false hypotheses can have large popular followings. There is no reason to think moral beliefs differ in this respect. Thus, "Because people believe it is right" never adequately answers the question, "Why ought I to do X?" when this question employs *ought* in the moral sense. The answer attempted by the Relativist always leaves room for the further questions "What reason is there for believing that those who say I ought to do X are right?" and "How do I know that what most people say and do is moral?"

The Divine Command standard has sometimes been criticized as one that cannot itself be justified by further moral reasons. Let us suppose that there is a Supreme Being who is never mistaken about moral questions, the critic says, and that this Supreme Being has supplied us with the necessary prescriptions for a moral life. But there is a distinction between obeying God's commands because God wills them and obeying God's commands because God commands what is moral. It seems plausible to say that God commands something *because it is right*, rather than that it is right *because God commands it*. There must be reasons why God commands certain actions and prohibits others, and it is these reasons that supply the *moral* justification for an action. If this were the case, however, what God commanded would be moral whether

God commanded it or not. Thus, the critic concludes, the appeal to Divine Command is an attempt to supplant reason with authority; but the fiat of an authority, even a divine authority, is not the same as moral justification for a judgment.

4. *One might check to see whether the argument from the evaluative standard to the moral judgment involves equivocation.* If equivocation (Section 4-1) occurs, it will involve a shift from a moral *ought* to an *ought* of some other kind. So a charge of equivocation is likely to be directed at the inference rather than a specific evaluative standard.

The moral *ought* might be contained either in the conclusion or in a premise. One might argue, for instance, that adultery and fornication are sinful and that legislators should therefore attach legal penalties to them, without considering reasons why these activities are matters for public concern. Likewise, one might argue that the possession of marijuana is a felony in some states and a misdemeanor in all other states—and that it is therefore immoral to smoke marijuana—without considering reasons why what is illegal should also be regarded as immoral.

5. *One might use an actual or hypothetical counterexample to show that in certain situations the standard prescribes an action or course of action that is at odds with our moral intuitions.* An actual or hypothetical counterexample can produce counterintuitive results in three ways:

1. The standard prescribes that an action X is wrong, while the critic and others feel intuitively certain that X is right, or vice versa.

2. The standard prescribes that X is obligatory, while the critic and others feel intuitively certain that X is prohibited, or vice versa.

3. The standard prescribes that X is morally permissible, while the critic and others feel intuitively certain either that X is morally prohibited or that X is obligatory, or vice versa.

The justification for using this method is that a moral standard should apply to all situations that are relevantly similar to the problem for which it is invoked. It is therefore perfectly legitimate to test the standard against hypothetical as well as actual cases.

The critic who uses this method is not claiming that the counterexample shows the standard to be false, in the way that a counterexample shows an empirical generalization to be false. Rather, the method illustrates that reliance upon the standard can lead to undesirable consequences. The counterintuitive result shows that the standard is inconsistent with other aspects of a more inclusive moral position. And by producing results that we find intuitively troublesome, the test also raises questions about the consistency of the whole set of moral beliefs and principles we tacitly accept.

Testing a moral standard against our intuitions is not the same as choosing the Intuitionist standard over other possible standards. The use of counterintuitive tests differs from Intuitionism in two ways: First, the counterexample is not thought of as providing a conclusive reason for rejecting a moral standard. The claim is much more modest: that one has *some* reason for rejecting a standard that prescribes an action clearly contrary to what one believes on the basis of established intuitions to be correct. And what counts is not so much the intuitive sense that the standard is wrong but what our intuitions help us see about the coherence of our overall moral point of view.

The second difference is that by using the "counterintuitive" method, we are not assuming, as the Intuitionist does, that one's conscience and intuitions are reliable guides in moral matters. Those who embrace the Intuitionist standard generally want to use it as a way of validating a moral judgment. They take the view that a moral judgment is justified if it is in accord with one's intuitions and not out of harmony with one's conscience. But even if the counterexample test shows that a standard agrees with intuition in that a counterintuitive example cannot be found, it does not follow that the standard is correct. Rather, intuitive beliefs and feelings are consulted for the more limited purpose of exploring the possibility of inconsistency with—and within—a moral system as a whole.

In this section we have been concerned with only two objectives of logical analysis: (1) identifying the constituents of moral arguments and determining how these arguments differ from other kinds of inferences, and (2) considering how critical questions can be raised about the moral standards embedded in moral arguments.

The criticism of certain moral standards was intended only to illustrate methods of analyzing moral arguments—not as a complete evaluation of the standards discussed. And the analysis has not given much attention to what most philosophers regard as the more important moral standards—the Act-Utilitarian, Rule-Utilitarian, and Kantian standards. Indeed, in moral philosophy today, the major rivalry is between those who espouse some version of a Utilitarian—or Consequentialist—standard and those who espouse some version of a Deontological standard—of which the one developed by Immanual Kant (1724–1804) is generally regarded as the most impressive example. An examination of this rivalry and a thorough assessment of the various ethical theories that have been discussed belong to the study of ethics. The works listed in the bibliography for Part IV can be profitably consulted by those wishing to pursue this area of philosophy.

■ **EXERCISE 14-3**

■ A. Rephrase each of the following sentences to make explicit the type of *ought* statement it expresses—for example, moral, legal, aesthetic, ceremonial, or prudential. There may be more than one plausible interpretation for some examples.

    1. You ought to tell children the truth.

    2. You ought to learn to appreciate music.

    3. If you want to stay out of trouble, you ought to follow her advice.

    *4. You ought to see your dentist at least twice a year.

5. If you are planning to sell souvenirs on the city streets, you ought to apply for a vendor's license.

6. If you are planning to sell souvenirs on the city streets, you ought to consider whether demand will justify one more vendor.

7. You shouldn't drive your competitors out of business.

*8. If you are planning to sell souvenirs on the city streets, you ought to give the students you'll employ a decent hourly wage.

9. If you know she's cheating, you ought to tell her to stop.

10. You ought to use a knife and fork when you eat with guests.

11. You ought to attend Harvard.

*12. You ought to let the school immunize your children against this disease.

13. If you know in advance that you will have to miss a class, you ought to inform your instructor.

14. You ought to say you're sorry.

15. You ought to pay your sister back for all the help she has given you.

*16. You ought to pay this library fine on time.

17. You ought to give the lead in the play to Amelia.

18. You ought to thank God for your many blessings.

19. You ought to pay more attention to your father.

*20. You ought to throw away that pornographic magazine.

■ B. Indicate the moral standard that is most likely being expressed or referred to by each of the following remarks.

1. By saying it is right, you are only expressing your own opinion; and your opinion is no better than anyone else's.

2. There are no ethical rules; each of us just "sees" what is right and what is wrong.

3. The end does justify the means.

*4. Before you can tell whether an act is moral or immoral, you have to ask, "What if everyone did the same thing?"

5. It is right to keep promises; because experience shows that in the long run, keeping promises produces the best consequences.

6. Follow your conscience, for, in the final analysis, there is no other guide.

7. It must be immoral if it is unnatural or regarded with repugnance by almost all men and women in the world.

*8. If God did not exist, then anything would be permissible.

9. Polygamy was morally permissible in Abraham's time, but it is immoral today.

10. What is wrong is what harms society; it is really that simple.

■ C. Treat each of the following claims as a moral judgment, and identify at least one moral standard that could be cited in an argument *for* that judgment. Identify at least one moral standard that could be cited in an argument *against* that judgment.

1. You ought to disobey a law you sincerely believe to be unjust.

2. Because all human beings have essentially the same basic physical and psychological needs, they should all be treated as equals.

3. It was right, as the Bible says, for Abraham to have prepared his son, Isaac, for sacrifice.

*__*4.__ The use of addicting narcotics is always wrong, despite the intense sensations of pleasure they produce.

5. You should keep your promises even if you believe better consequences would come from breaking them.

6. Abortion on demand is immoral, even if a majority of Americans now think it is legitimate.

7. Homosexuality is unnatural and prohibited by God.

*__*8.__ It's not wrong to steal from a large impersonal institution, like the university bookstore, as long as you don't get caught and you don't take too much.

9. There is nothing wrong with premarital sex as long as both you and your partner really want it.

10. It is wrong to report a friend whom you have seen cheating.

*■ D. The next exercise involves alternative ways of criticizing a moral standard. The Act-Utilitarian standard has been selected for this purpose. Following a brief description of Act-Utilitarianism are two criticisms of efforts to employ this standard. Explain what each criticism is intended to show, employing the methods for criticizing moral standards discussed in this section.

"Act utilitarianism essentially says that everyone should perform that act which will bring about the greatest good over bad for everyone affected. Its advocates do not believe in setting up rules for action, because each situation is different and each person is different. Each individual, then, must assess the situation he or she is involved in and try to figure out which act would bring about the greatest good consequences with the least amount of bad consequences, not just for himself or herself . . . but for everyone involved in the situation."—Jacques P. Thiroux, *Ethics: Theory and Practice* (Encino, Calif.: Glencoe Press, 1977), pp. 28–29.

Criticism 1: ". . . there is a certain impracticality in having to begin anew with each situation. . . . The time factor in moral decision making is an important one; a person does not have the time to constantly start from scratch with each new moral problem. In fact, having to constantly begin anew may result in the noncommission of a moral act in time.

"The act-utilitarian would answer that after experiencing many situations, one learns to apply his experience to the new situation readily and with a minimum of time wasting so that he is really not starting from scratch each time. But if he is calling on past experience and acting consistently in accordance with it, isn't he really acting on unstated rules?"—Thiroux, *Ethics: Theory and Practice*, pp. 29–30.

Criticism 2: "Imagine a town in which the young daughter of a prominent family had recently been kidnapped in broad daylight, then raped, and brutally murdered. The police are completely baffled and among the citizenry, aroused by the local newspaper, there is growing contempt for the police. It is becoming harder for the police to control the youth of the town, crime is on the increase, and fear is widespread. It seems that something should be done to restore confidence in law and the police. At this point the chief of police decides to find someone who can be accused of the crimes and brought to a speedy and decisive trial. The first hobo off the next through train is apprehended, and with planted witnesses and carefully chosen jurists quickly condemned to death. The town breathes easier, the police are prasied, happiness and tranquility are restored—except for one police patrolman who knew that the executed man was not guilty. But he is quickly reassured by the police chief who, not previously known for his morality, gives him a quick course in utilitarianism and then shows how the overall happiness has been maximized."—James W. Cornman, Keither Lahrer, and George S. Pappas, *Philosophical Problems and Arguments: An Introduction*, 3d ed. (New York: Macmillan, 1982), pp. 304–305. ∎

SUGGESTED READINGS

PART ONE: LOGIC AND ARGUMENT

Alston, William P. *The Philosophy of Language*. Englewood Cliffs, New Jersey: Prentice-Hall, 1973.

Anderson, Wallace L., and Norman C. Stageberg, eds., *Introductory Readings on Language*. New York: Holt, Rinehart and Winston, 1966.

Barry, Vincent E. *Invitation to Critical Thinking*. New York: Holt, Rinehart and Winston, 1984.

Chase, Stuart. *The Tyranny of Words*. New York: Harcourt, Brace and World, 1938.

Cross, Donna Woolfolk. *Word Abuse: How the Words We Use Use Us*. New York: Coward, McCann and Geoghegan, 1979.

Eschholz, Paul, Alfred Rosa, and Virgina Clark, eds., *Language Awareness*. 2d ed. New York: St. Martin's Press, 1978.

Fogelin, Robert J. *Understanding Arguments*. 2d ed. New York: Harcourt Brace Jovanovich, 1982.

Fowler, Roger. *Language as Ideology*. Boston: Routledge and Kegan Paul, 1977.

Govier, Trudy. *A Practical Study of Argument*. Belmont, Calif.: Wadsworth, 1985.

Hayakawa, S. I. *Language, Thought and Culture*. 3d ed. New York: Harcourt Brace Jovanovich, 1972.

Scriven, Michael. *Reasoning*. New York: McGraw-Hill, 1976.

Thomas, Stephen N. *Practical Reasoning in Natural Language*. Englewood Cliffs, New Jersey: Prentice-Hall, 1977.

Toulmin, Stephen, Richard Rieke, and Allan Janik. *An Introduction to Reasoning*. 2d ed. New York: Macmillan, 1984.

Vetterling-Bouggin, Mary, ed. *Sexist Language*. Totowa, New Jersey: Rowman and Littlefield, 1980.

Whorf, Benjamin. *Language, Thought, and Reality*. Edited by J. B. Carroll. Cambridge, Mass.: M.I.T. Press, 1964.

PART TWO: DEDUCTIVE REASONING

Berger, Fred R. *Studying Deductive Logic*. Englewood Cliffs, New Jersey: Prentice-Hall, 1977.

Bergmann, Merrie, James Moor, and Jack Nelson. *The Logic Book*. New York: Random House, 1980.

Copi, Irving M. *Symbolic Logic*. 4th ed. New York: Macmillan, 1973.

Copi, Irving M., and James A. Gould, eds. *Readings on Logic*. 2d ed. New York: Macmillan, 1972.

————. *Contemporary Philosophical Logic*. New York: St. Martin's Press, 1978.

Kahane, Howard. *Logic and Philosophy: A Modern Introduction*. 3d ed. Belmont, Calif.: Wadsworth, 1978.

Kapp, Ernst. *Greek Foundations of Traditional Logic*. New York: A.M.S. Press, 1967.

Klenk, Virginia. *Understanding Symbolic Logic*. Englewood Cliffs, New Jersey: Prentice-Hall, 1983.

Kneale, William, and Martha Kneale. *The Development of Logic*. Oxford: The Clarendon Press, 1962.

Lemmon, E. J. *Beginning Logic*. Indianapolis: Hackett, 1978.

Manicas, Peter T., ed. *Logic as Philosophy: An Introductory Anthology*. New York: Van Nostrand Reinhold, 1971.

Mates, Benson. *Elementary Logic*. 2d ed. New York: Oxford University Press, 1972.

Mitchell, David. *An Introduction to Logic*. Garden City, New York: Doubleday, 1970.

Pospesel, Howard, and David Marans. *Arguments: Deductive Logic Exercises.* 2d ed. Englewood Cliffs, New Jersey: Prentice-Hall, 1978.

Purtill, Richard L. *Logic for Philosophers*. New York: Harper & Row, 1971.

Quine, W. V. *Methods of Logic*. 3d ed. New York: Holt, Rinehart and Winston, 1972.

————. *Philosophy of Logic*. Englewood Cliffs, New Jersey: Prentice-Hall, 1970.

Standley, Gerald B. *New Methods in Symbolic Logic*. Boston: Houghton Mifflin, 1971.

Strawson, Peter F., ed. *Philosophical Logic*. London: Oxford University Press, 1962.

Tapscott, Bangs L. *Elementary Applied Symbolic Logic*. Englewood Cliffs, New Jersey: Prentice-Hall, 1970.

PART THREE: **INDUCTIVE REASONING**

Barker, Stephen F. *Induction and Hypothesis: A Study of the Logic of Confirmation*. Ithaca, New York: Cornell University Press, 1962.

Conant, James B. *Harvard Case Histories in Experimental Science*. Cambridge, Mass.: Harvard University Press, 1957.

Freund, John E. *Introduction to Probability*. Encino, Calif.: Dickenson, 1973.

Giere, Ronald N. *Understanding Scientific Reasoning*. 2d ed. New York: Holt, Rinehart and Winston, 1984.

Hempel, Carl G. *Philosophy of Natural Science*. Englewood Cliffs, New Jersey: Prentice-Hall, 1966.

Huff, Darrell. *How to Take a Chance*. New York: W. W. Norton, 1959.

Michalos, Alex C., ed. *Philosophical Problems of Science and Technology*. Boston: Allyn and Bacon, 1974.

Mill, John Stuart. *Philosophy of Scientific Method*, selections from A *System of Logic* (1872). Edited by Ernest Nagel. New York: Hafner, 1950.

Nagel, Ernest. *The Structure of Science*. New York: Harcourt, Brace and World, 1961.

Popper, Karl R. *The Logic of Scientific Discovery*. rev. ed. New York: Harper & Row, 1968.

Quine, M. V., and J. S. Ullian. *The Web of Belief*. 2d ed. New York: Random House, 1978.

Skryms, Brian. *Choice and Chance*. Belmont, Calif.: Dickenson 1966.

Swinburne, Richard, ed. *The Justification of Induction*. London: Oxford University Press, 1974.

Trusted, Jennifer. *The Logic of Scientific Inference: An Introduction.* London: Macmillan, 1979.

Wright, Larry. *Better Reasoning: Techniques for Handling Argument, Evidence, and Abstraction.* New York: Holt, Rinehart and Winston, 1982.

PART FOUR: **PRACTICAL REASONING**

A. *Fallacious reasoning*

Engel, S. Morris. *With Good Reason: An Introduction to Informal Fallacies.* 2d ed. New York: St. Martin's Press, 1982.

Fearnside, W. Ward, and William B. Holther. *Fallacy: The Counterfeit of Argument.* Englewood Cliffs, New Jersey: Prentice-Hall, 1959.

Fisher, David Hackett. *Historians' Fallacies: Toward a Logic of Historical Thought.* New York: Harper & Row, 1970.

Gardner, Martin. *Fads and Fallacies in the Name of Science.* New York: Dover, 1957.

——————. *Science: Good, Bad and Bogus.* Buffalo, New York: Prometheus, 1981.

Kahane, Howard. *Logic and Contemporary Rhetoric.* 4th ed. Belmont, Calif.: Wadsworth, 1984.

Radner, Dasie, and Michael Radner. *Science and Unreason.* Belmont, Calif.: Wadsworth, 1982.

B. *Legal reasoning*

Carter, Leif H. *Reason in Law.* Boston: Little, Brown, 1979.

Golding, Martin P. *Legal Reasoning. Essays and Materials in Law and Philosophy.* New York: Random House, 1980.

Horowitz, Joseph. *Law and Logic: A Critical Account of Legal Argument.* New York: Springer-Verlag, 1972.

Jensen, O. C. *The Nature of Legal Argument.* London: Basil Blackwell, 1957.

Levi, Edward H. *An Introduction to Legal Reasoning.* Chicago: University of Chicago Press, 1949.

Mermin, Samuel. *Law and the Legal System.* Boston: Little, Brown, 1973.

Post, C. Gordon. *An Introduction to the Law.* Englewood Cliffs, New Jersey: Prentice-Hall, 1963.

Wasserstrom, Richard. *The Judicial Decision.* Stanford, Calif.: Stanford University Press, 1961.

C. *The practice of analyzing arguments*

Beauchamp, Tom L. *Philosophical Ethics.* New York: McGraw-Hill, 1982.

Brody, Baruch A. *Logic: Theoretical and Applied.* Englewood Cliffs, New Jersey, Prentice-Hall, 1973.

Cornman, James W., Keith Lehrer, and George S. Pappas. *Philosophical Problems and Arguments: An Introduction.* 3d ed. New York: Macmillan, 1982.

Davidson, James West, and Mark Hamilton Lytle. *After the Fact: The Art of Historical Detection.* New York: Alfred A. Knopf, 1982.

Frankena, William K. *Ethics.* 2d ed. Englewood Cliffs, New Jersey: Prentice-Hall, 1970.

——————. *Thinking About Morality.* Ann Arbor: University of Michigan Press, 1980.

Gorovitz, Samuel, Merrill Hintikka, Donald Provence, and Ron G. Williams. *Philosophical Analysis: An Introduction to Its Language and Techniques.* 3d ed. New York: Random House, 1979.

MacIntyre, Alasdaire. *A Short History of Ethics.* New York: Macmillan, 1966.

Nosich, Gerald M. *Reasons and Argu-*

ments. Belmont, Calif.: Wadsworth, 1982.

Regan, Tom. *Understanding Philosophy.* Encino, Calif.: Dickensen, 1974.

Rosenberg, Jay. *The Practice of Philos-* *ophy.* Englewood Cliffs, New Jersey: Prentice-Hall, 1978.

Toulmin, Stephen. *The Uses of Argument.* London: Cambridge University Press, 1958.

SOLUTIONS TO SELECTED EXERCISES

CHAPTER 1

EXERCISE 1-1

■ *Section A*

4. Directive
8. Informative
12. Informative
16. Emotive
20. Ceremonial
24. Informative (as a report of the jury's decision), but it also functions as a directive because it informs the court that the defendant must now be sentenced.

■ *Section B*

4. Ceremonial expression, although it could express a statement depending upon contextual clues.
8. Most probably an emotive expression.
12. No doubt Cardinal Newman regarded this sentence as expressing a truth, but it might best be regarded as an emotive expression (e.g. "How great Thou art!").
16. Best treated as either an emotive or evaluative expression.
20. Directive
24. There are similar proverbs in French, Italian, German, and English. Serves an emotive and evaluative function (e.g., Spanish is the most romantic of all the languages).

28. Statement (may also be an evaluative expression)
32. It looks like a statement, but it is probably a subtle emotive expression (of jealousy, envy, anger, etc.).

EXERCISE 1-2

4. Argument. Conclusion: It seems highly improbable that Hamilton ever held any considerable sum in securities.
8. Argument. Conclusion: Nothing is worth (i.e., as valuable as) my life.
12. Not an argument.
16. Argument. Conclusion (paraphrased): Dave Lowry is probably not a hardened killer.
20. Argument. The conclusion is expressed in the first sentence.
24. Argument. Conclusion (paraphrased): Soldiers are responsible for killing innocent civilians. Or: The fact that soldiers are forced to fight does not give them an excuse to kill innocent civilians.

EXERCISE 1-3

4. P: Opinion and protest are the life breath of democracy. . . .
   C: No American . . . must ever be denied the right to dissent.
   (The statement "No minority must be muzzled" may be regarded as implicit in the conclusion. It neces-

sarily would be true if the conclusion is true.)

8. Not an argument. (This is a string of conditionals: no argument is asserted. It could become an argument by adding as a conclusion: "Therefore, if there be righteousness in the heart, there will be peace in the world.")

12. P: (Paraphrased) The electric power failure that affected 80,000 square miles in the U.S. and Canada was a total surprise.
P: For hours engineers and power officials were unable to turn the lights on again.
P: No one can promise that it won't happen again.
C: The age of innocent faith in science and technology may be over.

EXERCISE 1-4

4. Suppressed Premise (SP): There is a human nature only if God conceives of it.
SP: If there is no human nature, then man is only what he wills himself to be.

8. SP: The finer and more philosophical a subject, the more it expresses universal principles.

12. SP: If I'm gloomy or feverish, then I'm not tranquil.
SP: Either I am unoccupied (not busy) or I am occupied.

16. SP: Whatever goes beyond mere (surface) evidence reaches a richer vein of truth.

20. Unstated Conclusion: No valid conclusions about the behavior of animals were drawn by the scientists of Freud's day.

EXERCISE 1-5

■ *Section A*

4. No argument. It is asserted that King Charles's refusal to conciliate

was the cause of his being overthrown.

8. No argument. Conditional

12. No argument.

■ *Section B*

4. Willard Gaylin's argument can be represented as follows:
1st argument
P: Heroism implies choice and action.
P: (Paraphrase): The American hostages in Iran didn't have any choice; instead they experienced humiliation, impotence, and abandonment of responsibility.
C: (Paraphrase): The American hostages in Iran were not heroes.
P: (conclusion of first argument.)
2nd argument
P: (Suppressed): To hear themselves called heroes is to remind the hostages of their humiliation, etc.
P: It is wrong to make people feel humiliated for that which they could not prevent.
C: (Paraphrase): Calling the hostages heroes places an unfair burden on them.

■ *Section C*

4. Borderline. This can be treated as an argument to the conclusion that man is more a political animal than are other social animals. But it seems more likely that Aristotle is offering an explanation.

8. Argument. The speaker concludes that what he heard was not a spirit.

12. Argument. The conclusion is expressed in the first sentence.

16. Borderline. Lilienthal's thought is expressed in a single conditional that itself is not an argument. However, it can serve as an enthymeme

for an audience acquainted with the peril of nuclear proliferation. In this case, the conditional expresses the conclusion of an argument with the following suppressed premises: If a great number of countries come to have an arsenal of nuclear weapons, then a nuclear war is almost certain in the future. If a nuclear war in the future is almost certain, then those living at the time must expect a horrible death. If humans alive at the time must expect a horrible death, then I'm glad it won't be me . . . etc.

20. Argument. Gorgias concludes that speech exercises power over the soul.

CHAPTER 2

EXERCISE 2-1

4. Inductive: note use of *probably*.
8. Deductive
12. Deductive
16. Deductive
20. Inductive

EXERCISE 2-2

■ *Section A*

4. Valid; unsound; one Premise is false, Conclusion false

EXERCISE 2-3

■ *Section A*

4. Empirical (E)
8. E. A short person can be an intellectual giant.
12. E
16. E
20. Necessary (N); True (T)
24. NT
28. E. He may be neither a friend or an enemy.
32. NT
36. E. John and Jake may not be related.

40. NF. Carnivores are meat eaters and ruminant animals do not eat meat.

■ *Section B*

4. (c) If every rule has an exception, then there cannot be a rule that everything good is fattening.
8. (a) This appears to be NF, but by *wrong* Merton is probably referring to something other than having wrong answers.
12. (b)
16. (c) Berra is saved from contradicting himself if we interpret him as saying, "Anyone who is popular is bound to be disliked by a few (envious) people."
20. (a)
24. (a) Epicurus is claiming that persons who are still unsatisfied after their basic needs and wants have been met are in fact insatiable.
28. (a) Valery is using a self-contradictory phrase—"the future is not what it used to be"—to make a point about the way we think or feel about the future (e.g., "The trouble with our time is that we have lost the faith in the future possessed by our ancestors").
32. (a)
36. (c) The Queen's claim is self-contradictory (although Alice's claim, "We can't believe impossible things," is necessarily true).

CHAPTER 3

EXERCISE 3-1

■ *Section A*

4. Abraham Maslow's point can be understood as a metaphor about language. If one takes the view that the only function of language is informative, one will end up mistakenly trying to treat emotive and ceremonial expressions as if they were intended to convey information.

8. Abraham Kaplan's remark emphasizes the extent to which the same or similar terms may have uniquely different associations and connotations. If our attention is drawn to one set of connotations, we may overlook other aspects of a term's meaning. This is especially true when some connotations of a term are emotive.

12. Richard Eder offers a colorful view of the close connection between language and thought. Insofar as much abstract thought is verbal, words do "bear" the mind about. However, words may lead the mind into marshes and mists as well as keep it out.

16. Arthur Berger's hypothesis is certainly possible. Indeed, much jargon and bureaucratise, as well as euphemism, seems to be motivated by a desire to make routine tasks and mundane objects appear more interesting and important.

■ *Section B*

4. This example offers evidence that the association between vulgar or obscene words and sexual activity, so pervasive in Western societies, is not universal. The connection between vulgar expressions and certain bodily functions may thus be a result of social convention.

EXERCISE 3-2

■ *Section A*

[No solutions provided due to the nature of the exercise.]

■ *Section B*

[Source: Harold Wentworth and Stuart B. Flexner, *Dictionary of American Slang* (New York, Thomas Y. Crowell, 1967).]
(d) *bird:* an odd or unusual person; a thin person who "pecks" at food; also, *bird-brained* connotes someone who is dull or scatterbrained.

(h) *lamb:* an innocent trusting person; an inexperienced or naive person who is easily fooled or cheated; a sweetheart.
(l) *kitten:* a person with a soft, passive disposition; a person one is fond of (especially said of a female by a male); a friendly, harmless person.
(p) *owl:* knowledgeable or wise individual (usually older); one who works or performs late at night ("night owl").
(t) *ape:* a foolish person; one who imitates styles and fashions with little discernment; a hoodlum or henchman or stooge; one who is frenzied, uncontrollable, and wild ("to go ape").

■ *Section C*

[Solutions not provided due to nature of exercise.]

■ *Section D*

cornball: one who likes or perpetuates sentimentality, banality, or outdated styles (*corny*); also associated with unsophisticated rural folk. *Condemnatory.* Its persistence may be due to some vague antipathy between some city dwellers and country dwellers.
green thumb: one who has an aptitude for getting plants to grow; also, one who has the ability to produce a success and make money. *Commendatory.* Its widespread use may be due partly to the contrast it makes with "I'm all thumbs," which connotes a lack of skill, and the many associations between *green* and money (e.g., *greenback*).
fair-haired boy: a youth or young man who is a favorite of those in power. Its use may be *commendatory*—there is often admiration for the fortunate, "chosen" one—but also *condemnatory*—*boy* connotes a sense of servitude and a lack of independence or responsibility. Its

popularity may be due partly to this double-edged meaning.

lone wolf: one who keeps apart from any social group, does not have close friends, and does not reveal personal activities. Its use is somewhat *condemnatory* because *wolf* connotes a predator—one who cannot be trusted. The persistence of the description may relate to a social group's sense of itself as a close "pack" and different from outsiders.

fair-weather friend: a person who is friendly to another only when it is enjoyable or advantageous to be a friend; such a person lets friends down in times of adversity. *Condemnatory.* Its widespread use may be due partly to associations with familiar contrasts between fair weather and foul weather.

EXERCISE 3-3

■ *Section A*

4. The need for precise language in professional practice can be carried too far. Edward Packard's humorous example illustrates slanting: Assuring and discounting remarks intended to create an impression that goes beyond the actual information conveyed by the sentences.

8. Frantz Fanon, as quoted by the authors, has hypostatized *violence.*

12. Edwin Newman presents a good example of doublespeak: words like *source, intelligence,* and *document* have greater emotional impact than their pedestrian synonyms.

16. This is a chilling example of doublespeak current during World War II. To describe a fatal casualty as "falling" masks the reality of death.

■ *Section B*

4. low-income
8. encore telecasts
12. sexual reassignment
16. overdependence on drugs
20. culturally deprived

24. *nom de plume*
28. downturn

■ *Section C*

4. No difference in information (unless Pam's date really was a deaf mute), but a difference in impression. The first sentence suggests that Pam's date was dumbstruck or intimidated.

8. No difference in information, but a difference in impression. The second sentence suggests that she'd prefer to keep her attendance at the meeting a secret.

■ *Section D*

[No solutions given due to the nature of the exercise.]

■ *Section E*

[No solutions given due to the nature of the exercise.]

CHAPTER 4

EXERCISE 4-1

■ *Section A*

4. (a) Do fruit growers make special efforts to prevent the mice from injuring the orchards, or to prevent the mice from being injured? (b) The reference of the pronoun *them* is ambiguous. (c) Each year at this time, fruit growers have to make special efforts to prevent mice from seriously injuring the orchards.

8. (a) Who doesn't eat for two months, the adult penguin or its young? (b) The sentence is elliptical: an additional pronoun referring to the adult penguin needs to be added. (c) The Emperor Penguin is about 4 feet tall, and during the 2 months of incubating its young, it does not eat.

12. (a) Do the children like him because he doesn't press the children to come to him, or because he

doesn't press his pants? (b) Careless construction of the passage has brought the description of clothes too close to the phrase in which *press* is used to refer to the man's relationship with the children. (c) The simplest solution is to replace *press* with a synonym such as *urge, compel, solicit,* or *entreat.*

■ *Section B*

4. The shift concerns *facts of life* understood as social and political reality versus *facts of life* understood as facts about human reproduction.

8. The shift concerns *freedom* understood as a political liberty enjoyed by responsible adults versus *freedom* understood as mere license to do as one wishes.

12. The shift is from the honorable connotations of *expert* to its less emotive meaning as one who is knowledgeable or practiced in a certain area.

EXERCISE 4-2

4. In this example, vagueness surrounds the quantity: it may not make much difference if most customers take only one sample, but it will make a difference if a large number of customers take two or more samples.

8. The speaker is exploiting the vague and indeterminate meaning of *refugee.* But the fact that there are no hard-and-fast criteria does not mean that we cannot make meaningful distinctions between people allowed to enter the country as refugees and others who may also request our aid.

12. The argument exploits two gray areas: (1) the vague distinction between threats made by other states that should be met with resistance and threats that do not require active resistance, and (2) the equally vague distinction between foreign aggression that will be perceived by the people as dangerous and requiring opposition and acts of aggression that will not be perceived by the populace as warranting active resistance.

EXERCISE 4-3

■ *Section A*

4. This is a factual dispute over the reliability of the witness's testimony.

■ *Section B*

4. This example involves both a factual dispute and a verbal dispute. The factual dispute concerns Mr. Chase's probable intentions as they can be inferred from his observed behavior. The verbal dispute concerns the proper definition of lying, and it is a symptom of an underlying disagreement in attitude.

■ *Section C*

4. This is a verbal dispute over the meaning of *good impression.* The dispute should be resolved once this difference in meaning has been revealed.

8. This is a verbal dispute over the meaning of *good teacher,* but there is also a disagreement in attitude underlying the verbal dispute. Gruff's negative view of Professor Towertop and the college ("this dump") indicates that Gruff finds Puff's criteria for good teaching unacceptable.

EXERCISE 4-4

4. This definition of *rationality* violates Rule 1. It is too broad because the definiens is expressed negatively. In addition, it violates Rule 2 because it fails to give the most important characteristics of ration-

ality. The following, written as an explicit definition, is a better attempt: *Rationality* means "a human mental capacity to exercise reason, sound judgment, or good sense."

8. This definition of *clock* violates Rule 1 because the genus is too broad. To rule out sundials, the definition must indicate that a clock is a mechanical device with moving hands or pointers; and to rule out wristwatches, the definition must indicate that, while they are portable, clocks are not worn on the wrist or carried in the pocket. The following is a better definition: *Clock* means "a mechanical instrument with moving hands or pointers used to keep or indicate time, and not carried on the person."

12. This definition of *bread* violates Rule 4 because the language of the definiens is obscure and figurative. The following is a better definition: *Bread* means "a staple food made from flour or grain meal mixed with a liquid, usually combined with a leavening agent, and kneaded, shaped into loaves, and baked."

16. By offering a mere synonym, this definition of *pusillanimous* is circular and violates Rule 3. Note also that definition by genus and species is used to define nouns; *pusillanimous* is an adjective. We should therefore define *pusillanimous person* as follows: in calling someone a *pusillanimous person*, we mean "a person who has a disposition to be cowardly or weak-willed, easily yielding to pressures from other persons."

20. This definition of *lie* violates Rule 4. A clearer definition is the following: *Lie* means "a false statement or incorrect piece of information known to be false or incorrect by the speaker or writer but deliberately presented as being true."

EXERCISE 4-5

4. Technical. Ricardo is clarifying the meaning of *capital* as it is to be understood in a specific subject—economics.

8. Technical. Aquinas's definition of *law* as a "rule and measure of acts" is intended to make law intelligible within a larger theory of rational and purposive human behavior. His definition needs to be understood in the context of his "natural law" social philosophy.

EXERCISE 4-6

■ *Section A*

4. Persuasive. This may appear to be a neutral definition, but it excludes some groups who may live together and form a household. See exercise no. 11 for contrast.

8. Persuasive. This humorous comment does make an emotive impact by associating marriage with a lost opportunity for happiness.

12. Revelatory. This is not an adequate definition of *conclusion* as a term designating part of an argument. At the same time, it does convey a valuable insight—the unfortunate tendency of some people to accept on a subject the opinions that they heard last, just before their study of the subject became tedious or tiresome.

■ *Section B*

4. Judith Stern's colorful metaphor is insightful: Many important events in life, for which we could use the knowledge gained from experience, are unrepeatable.

8. Almost every word of this definition conveys a strong image: *biodegradable* and *nonrecyclable*, terms usually used to describe consumer goods, remind us of our mortality and uniqueness as a species; the

conjunction of the phrase about *opposable thumbs* with *grasping at straws* suggests that our superiority to other species and our creative imagination (which moves us to try to transcend our physical limitations) may be due to a simple physical difference between ourselves and other species.

CHAPTER 5

EXERCISE 5-1

■ *Section A*

4. *I* S (apples) P (red things)
8. *I* S (the students) P (persons over twenty years of age)
12. *O* S (habits of thought) P (activities that improve decision making)
16. *E* S (athletes who receive payments for their performances) P (amateurs)
20. *I* S (women) P (persons sent into outer space)

■ *Section B*

4. No persons who come on time are persons who will be sent away empty-handed.
8. All persons who do not complete these exercises are inattentive students.

EXERCISE 5-2

■ *Section A*

4.

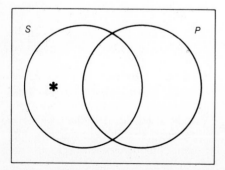

8.

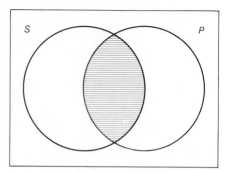

■ *Section B*

4. A form; S (rattlesnakes) distributed; P (pit vipers) undistributed
8. O form; S (ideals) undistributed; P (things realized in practice) distributed

EXERCISE 5-3

■ *Section A*

4. Undetermined, undetermined
8. False, true

■ *Section B*

4. (a) Contradiction; (b) it is false; (c) it is true
8. (a) Contrariety; (b) it is false; (c) nothing

■ *Section C*

4. Hypothetical (There may or may not be conscientious objectors now.)
8. Hypothetical (If a body is cooled to absolute zero, then it will conduct electricity.)

EXERCISE 5-4

■ *Section A*

4. Some nondrinkers are nonsmokers.
8. All belligerents are combatants.
12. Some basketball players are non-tall guards.
16. All nonpsychotics are nonschizophrenics.

20. Some intelligent beings are not humans.

■ *Section B*

4. Nothing. It is the converse of (d), but (d) is an A statement, and the conversion of A form does not produce an equivalent statement. Venn diagrams show that (4) and (d) are not equivalent.

(d)

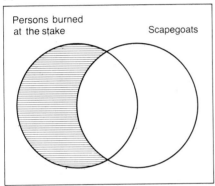

(4)

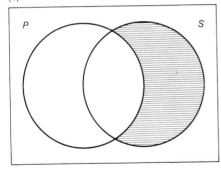

8. True. Conversion of (e).
12. Nothing. None of (a) through (e) has both *saints* and *puritans* or their class components as S and P terms.

EXERCISE 5-5

■ *Section A*

4. Sue's position is more reasonable. Lou fails to see that in obtaining the contrapositive of the A statement (paraphrased) "All persons who wait are persons who die," Fred failed to switch the subject and predicate terms. Fred invalidly inferred that "all persons who do not wait are persons who do not die." (The contrapositive of the first statement is "All persons who do not die are persons who do not wait.")

■ *Section B*

4. Some professors are not persons who wear beards.
8. All times when one is angry are times when one's adrenaline production increases.
12. All persons who survived are persons who were young children.
16. No nonboors are persons who would speak that way.
20. No persons who have not been told that they have a terminal illness are persons who can imagine how terrifying that news can be.
24. No Trinity graduates are persons who associate with thieves.

■ *Section C*

4. No tea lovers are coffee lovers.
   Some Americans are not tea lovers.
   _____
   Some Americans are coffee lovers.
8. All people who believe in astronaut-gods are gullible people.
   All fans of the book *Chariots of the Gods?* are gullible people.
   _____
   All fans of the book *Chariots of the Gods?* are people who believe in astronaut-gods.

CHAPTER 6

EXERCISE 6-1

4. All professional basketball players are people who are overpaid for their talents.
   Some people who are greatly admired are professional basketball players.
   _____
   Some people who are greatly ad-

mired are people who are overpaid for their talents.

8. All Christian Scientists are believers in the power of prayer.
Some social scientists are not believers in the power of prayer.

Some social scientists are not Christian Scientists.

EXERCISE 6-2

4.

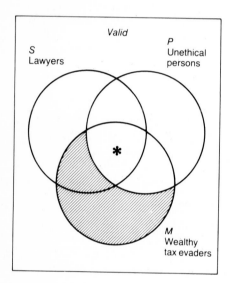

Valid
S
Lawyers
P
Unethical persons
M
Wealthy tax evaders

8.

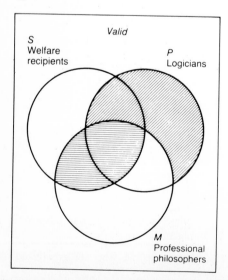

Valid
S
Welfare recipients
P
Logicians
M
Professional philosophers

12.

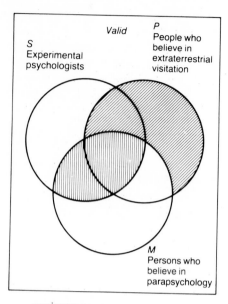

Valid
S
Experimental psychologists
P
People who believe in extraterrestrial visitation
M
Persons who believe in parapsychology

EXERCISE 6-3

■ *Section A*

4. All(mammals)are animals that have four-chambered hearts. (A)
Some animals found in Borneo are animals that have four-chambered hearts. (I)

Some animals found in Borneo are mammals. (I)

invalid—undistributed middle

8. All (Socialists) are advocates of Medicare. (A)
Some liberals are advocates of Medicare. (I)

Some liberals are Socialists. (I)

invalid—undistributed middle

12. No(pit vipers)are(household pets.) (E)

All(mambas)are(pit vipers.) (A)

No(mambas)are(household pets.) (E)

valid

16. No (common stocks) are (good investments.) (E)

All bonds are common stocks. (A)

Some bonds are good investments. (I)

invalid—faulty exclusion (One negative premise)

20. No (engineers) are (logicians.) (E)

No (lawyers) are (engineers.) (E)

All lawyers are logicians. (A)

invalid—faulty exclusion (Both premises are negative)

■ *Section B*

4. All (fans of *Chariots of the Gods?*) are gullible persons.

Some people impressed by *Worlds in Collision* are fans of *Chariots of the Gods?*

Some people impressed by *Worlds in Collision* are gullible persons.

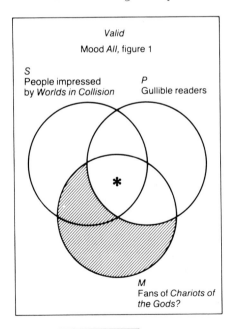

Valid

Mood *AII*, figure 1

S
People impressed
by *Worlds in Collision*

P
Gullible readers

M
Fans of *Chariots of the Gods?*

8. All (acts of gossiping) are irresponsible acts.

All (acts that reinforce prejudice) are acts of gossiping.

All (acts that reinforce prejudice) are irresponsible acts.

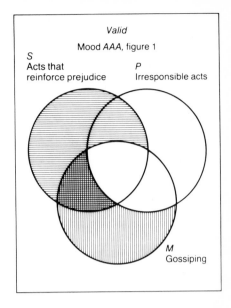

Valid

Mood *AAA*, figure 1

S
Acts that
reinforce prejudice

P
Irresponsible acts

M
Gossiping

12. All (biologists who believe in Darwinian evolution) are college graduates.

No (biologists who believe in Darwinian evolution) are (literal interpreters of Genesis.)

No (literal interpreters of Genesis) are (college graduates.)

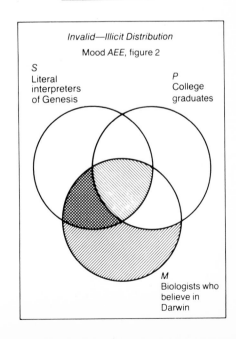

Invalid—Illicit Distribution

Mood *AEE*, figure 2

S
Literal
interpreters
of Genesis

P
College
graduates

M
Biologists who
believe in
Darwin

EXERCISE 6-4

■ *Section A*

4. Some honest persons are persons charged with cheating.
All cheaters are dishonest persons.

Some cheaters are not persons charged with cheating.

(Obvert minor premise)—No cheaters are honest persons.

The resulting syllogism will be invalid—fallacy of illicit distribution.

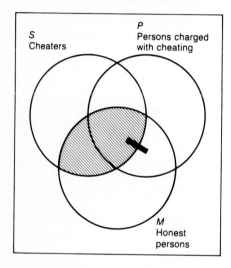

8. All survivors are victors in the struggle for life.

All strong individuals are victors in the struggle for life.

All survivors are strong individuals.

This syllogism is invalid—fallacy of undistributed middle.

(*Solution 8 continues at the top of the next column.*)

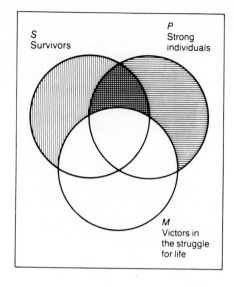

12. The business executive's argument can be paraphrased as follows:
"Those who can, do" → All persons who can succeed in business are persons in business.
"Those who can't, teach" → All persons who can't succeed in business are teachers.
"Teachers aren't doers" → No teachers are persons who can succeed in business.
(Contrapose major)—All persons who are not in business are persons who can't succeed in business.
(Obvert conclusion)—All teachers are persons who cannot succeed in business.
The result is the following syllogism:

All persons who are not in business are persons who can't succeed in business.

All persons who can't succeed in business are teachers.

All teachers are persons who cannot succeed in business.

The syllogism is invalid—fallacy of illicit distribution.

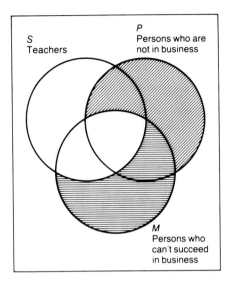

S
Teachers

P
Persons who are
not in business

M
Persons who
can't succeed
in business

■ *Section B*

[Missing premises and unstated conclusions are set off by parentheses]

4. (No freshmen are persons who can be expected to be good at calculus.)
All persons identical with him are freshmen.

No persons identical with him are persons who can be expected to be good at calculus.

valid

8. (Some acts of lying are acts most likely to sell products.)
All acts most likely to sell products are acts of salespeople.

Some acts of salespeople are acts of lying.

valid

12. (All acts opposed by a majority of Americans are acts that should be illegal.)
All acts of homosexuality are acts opposed by a majority of Americans.

All acts of homosexuality are acts that should be illegal.

valid

■ *Section C*

4. This argument seems to involve five different terms: (a) *laws supported by ethical women*, (b) *laws that discriminate against women*, (c) *laws inconsistent with ERA*, (d) *sexist laws*, and (e) *laws supported by moral women*. However, (a) and (e) can be treated as variants of the same term. And, in this context, (b) and (d) can be seen to mark out the same class. Thus, the argument can be handled as a syllogism:

All laws inconsistent with ERA are laws that discriminate against women.

No laws supported by ethical women are laws that discriminate against women.

No laws supported by ethical women are laws inconsistent with ERA.

valid

8. This argument can be treated as a sorites as indicated below. It is an invalid argument because both syllogisms commit fallacies of illicit distribution.

First syllogism { All Middle Eastern countries that approve of United States foreign policy are countries that will continue to supply the United States with crude oil.

No Middle Eastern countries influenced by Iran are Middle Eastern countries that approve of United States foreign policy.

Unstated conclusion { No Middle Eastern countries influenced by Iran are countries that will continue to supply the United States with crude oil.

Second syllogism $\Bigg\{$

All Middle Eastern countries that will continue to supply the United States with crude oil are countries that will become targets of increased Soviet hostility.

No Middle Eastern countries influenced by Iran are countries that will become targets of increased Soviet hostility.

CHAPTER 7

EXERCISE 7-1

■ *Section A*

4. $A \supset \sim(B \vee C)$
8. $A \vee [(B \supset \sim C) \equiv D]$

■ *Section B*

4. p
8. $\sim p \supset \sim q$
12. $(p \& q) \supset r$

■ *Section C*

4. (g)
8. (k)
12. (n)
16. (c)
20. (t)

■ *Section D*

4. T
8. T
12. T
16. T
20. F

EXERCISE 7-2

■ *Section A*

4.	p q r	$\sim r$	$(q \vee \sim r)$	$p \supset (q \vee \sim r)$
	T T T	F	T	T
	F T T	F	T	T
	T F T	F	F	F
	F F T	F	F	T
	T T F	T	T	T
	F T F	T	T	T
	T F F	T	T	T
	F F F	T	T	T

8.

p q r	~q	p & q	r ∨ ~q	(p & q) ⊃ (r ∨ ~q)
T T T	F	T	T	T
F T T	F	F	T	T
T F T	T	F	T	T
F F T	T	F	T	T
T T F	F	T	F	F
F T F	F	F	F	T
T F F	T	F	T	T
F F F	T	F	T	T

■ *Section B*

4. The compounds are not true under the same conditions: ("*q* ⊃ *p*" is true in rows 1, 3, and 4; "*q* ∨ ~*p*" is true in rows 1, 2, and 4).

p q	~p	q ⊃ p	q ∨ ~p
T T	F	T	T
F T	T	F	T
T F	F	T	F
F F	T	T	T

8. The compounds are not true under the same conditions: ("~(~*p* & ~*q*)" is true in rows 1, 2, and 3; "*p* & *q*" is true in row 1).

p q	~p	~q	p & q	~p & ~q	~(~p & ~q)
T T	F	F	T	F	T
F T	T	F	F	F	T
T F	F	T	F	F	T
F F	T	T	F	T	F

EXERCISE 7-3

■ *Section A*

4. ~(*p* & *q*), ~*p* ∨ ~*q*
8. *p* ∨ (*q* & *r*), (*p* ∨ *q*) & (*p* ∨ *r*)

■ *Section B*

4. A ⊃ B (conditional exchange)
8. B & (A ∨ C) (distribution)
12. ~S & ~R (De Morgan's laws)
16. ~(S & T) ∨ ~(S & R) (De Morgan's laws)
20. ~(S ∨ T) ∨ (A ⊃ B) (conditional exchange)

EXERCISE 7-4

■ *Section A*

4. *p* & ~*q*

8. Not a truth-functional compound; it is a subjunctive conditional.
12. Not a truth-functional compound; *as* expresses a temporal relationship.
16. *p* & *q*
20. Not a truth-functional compound; in this case *and* expresses a temporal relationship in the sense of *and then. . . .*
24. Not a truth-functional compound; the phrase *between a rock and a hard place* is used to connote a predicament. Thus, Perkins cannot be said to be at a specific location between a rock and some other place.
28. Not a truth-functional compound; *and* is not expressing the conjunction of two statements.

32. Not a truth-functional compound; in this case, *or* means "that is to say."
36. $p \ \& \ \sim q$
40. $p \supset p$

■ *Section B*

Let "A" stand for "Anna attends," and "S" for "Ivan will sing." We then need to know which compounds when symbolized are equivalent to "$A \supset S$"

4. Not equivalent (NE). ($S \supset A$)
8. E
12. E
16. NE ($S \supset A$)
20. NE ($S \ \& \ \sim A$)

CHAPTER 8

EXERCISE 8-1

■ *Section A*

4. $\sim(L \ \& \ S)$
   $\quad L$
   $\therefore \sim S$ *Valid.* Conjunctive argument.
8. $\quad C \supset S$
   $\quad S \supset E$
   $\therefore C \supset E$ *Valid.* Chain argument.
12. $\sim D \supset W$
   $\quad D$
   $\therefore \sim W$ *Invalid.* The form of this argument is:
   $\sim p \supset q$
   $\quad p$
   $\therefore \sim q$

This is the fallacy of denying the antecedent.

■ *Section B*

4. Let *p* replace "grade inflation is to cease," *q* replace "grade anxiety among students must decrease," and *r* replace "standardized test scores will become less important in law-school admissions."

$p \supset q$
$p \supset r$
$\therefore q \supset r$

Invalid

p	*q*	*r*	*p* $\supset$ *q*	*p* $\supset$ *r*	*q* $\supset$ *r*	
T	T	T	T	T	T	
F	T	T	T	T	T	
T	F	T	F	T	T	
F	F	T	T	T	T	
T	T	F	T	F	F	
F	T	F	T	T	F	—Invalidating Row
T	F	F	F	F	T	
F	F	F	T	T	T	

8. Let p replace "the economic theory of Adam Smith is sound," q replace "the economic theory of Thomas Malthus is sound," and r replace "the economic theory of David Ricardo is sound."

$\sim p \supset \sim q$ $q \supset p$
$\sim r \supset \sim p >$ Contraposition $< \quad p \supset r$
$\therefore q \supset r$ $\therefore q \supset r \quad$ *Valid*

p	q	r	$q \supset p$	$p \supset r$	$q \supset r$
T	T	T	T	T	T
F	T	T	F	T	T
T	F	T	T	T	T
F	F	T	T	T	T
T	T	F	T	F	F
F	T	F	F	T	F
T	F	F	T	F	T
F	F	F	T	T	T

12. Let p replace "Stephanie is a lawyer," and let q replace "she has been disbarred."

$p \supset \sim q$
$\sim(\sim q)$
$\therefore \sim p$

p	q	$\sim p$	$\sim q$	$\sim(\sim q)$	$p \supset \sim q$
T	T	F	F	T	F
F	T	T	F	T	T
T	F	F	T	F	T
F	F	T	T	F	T

Valid

■ Section C

4. $p \supset q$
   $r \& p$
   $\therefore q \lor r$

p	q	r	$p \supset q$	$r \& p$	$q \lor r$
T	T	T	T	T	T
F	T	T	T	F	T
T	F	T	F	T	T
F	F	T	T	F	T
T	T	F	T	F	T
F	T	F	T	F	T
T	F	F	F	F	F
F	F	F	T	F	F

Valid

8. $\sim p \lor q$
   $q \supset r$
   $\therefore \sim r \supset \sim p$

p	q	r	$\sim p$	$\sim r$	$\sim p \lor q$	$q \supset r$	$\sim r \supset \sim p$
T	T	T	F	F	T	T	T
F	T	T	T	F	T	T	T
T	F	T	F	F	F	T	T
F	F	T	T	F	T	T	T
T	T	F	F	T	T	F	F
F	T	F	T	T	T	F	T
T	F	F	F	T	F	T	F
F	F	F	T	T	T	T	T

Valid

12. $(p \supset q)$ & $(r \supset s)$
$\sim s \lor \sim q$
$\sim p$ *Invalid*
$\therefore \sim r$

Invalidating Row

p q r s	$\sim p$	$\sim q$	$\sim r$	$\sim s$	$p \supset q$	$r \supset s$	$(p \supset q)$ & $(r \supset s)$	$\sim s \lor \sim q$
T T T T	F	F	F	F	T	T	T	F
F T T T	T	F	F	F	T	T	T	F
T F T T	F	T	F	F	F	T	F	T
F F T T	T	T	F	F	T	T	T	T
T T F T	F	F	T	F	T	T	T	F
F T F T	T	F	T	F	T	T	T	F
T F F T	F	T	T	F	F	T	F	T
F F F T	T	T	T	F	T	T	T	T
T T T F	F	F	F	T	T	F	F	T
F T T F	T	F	F	T	T	F	F	T
T F T F	F	T	F	T	F	F	F	T
F F T F	T	T	F	T	T	F	F	T
T T F F	F	F	T	T	T	T	T	T
F T F F	T	F	T	T	T	T	T	T
T F F F	F	T	T	T	F	T	F	T
F F F F	T	T	T	T	T	T	T	T

EXERCISE 8-2

■ *Section A*

4. Equivalent

p q	$\sim p$	$\sim q$	$p \lor q$	$\sim q$ & $\sim p$	$\sim(\sim q$ & $\sim p)$
T T	F	F	T	F	T
F T	T	F	T	F	T
T F	F	T	T	F	T
F F	T	T	F	T	F

■ *Section B*

4. Contingent

p q	$\sim p$	$\sim q$	p & q	$\sim p$ & $\sim q$	$(p$ & $q) \lor (\sim p$ & $\sim q)$
T T	F	F	T	F	T
F T	T	F	F	F	F
T F	F	T	F	F	F
F F	T	T	F	T	T

8. Contingent

p	q	$p \vee q$	$p \& q$	$(p \vee q) \supset (p \& q)$
T T		T	T	T
F T		T	F	F
T F		T	F	F
F F		F	F	T

12. Tautology

p q r	$p \supset q$	$p \supset r$	$q \supset r$	$(p \supset q) \& (q \supset r)$	$[(p \supset q) \& (q \supset r)] \supset (p \supset r)$
T T T	T	T	T	T	T
F T T	T	T	T	T	T
T F T	F	T	T	F	T
F F T	T	T	T	T	T
T T F	T	F	F	F	T
F T F	T	T	F	F	T
T F F	F	F	T	F	T
F F F	T	T	T	T	T

■ *Section C*

4.

p q	$p \vee q$	$p \& q$	$p \& (p \vee q)$	$p \vee (p \& q)$	$[p \& (p \vee q)] \equiv [p \vee (p \& q)]$
T T	T	T	T	T	T
F T	T	F	F	F	T
T F	T	F	T	T	T
F F	F	F	F	F	T

■ *Section D*

4.

p q r	$p \vee q$	$p \supset r$	$q \supset r$	$(p \supset r) \& (q \supset r)$	$(p \vee q) \supset r$
T T T	T	T	T	T	T
F T T	T	T	T	T	T
T F T	T	T	T	T	T
F F T	F	T	T	T	T
T T F	T	F	F	F	F
F T F	T	T	F	F	F
T F F	T	F	T	F	F
F F F	F	T	T	T	T

EXERCISE 8-3

■ *Section A*

4. 3. 1, Con. Exch.
   4. 2, Con. Exch.
   5. 3, 4, Chain

8. 3. 2, Dist.
4. 3, Conj. Simp.
5. 4, Dup.
6. 1, Assoc.
7. 6, 5, Disj. Arg.
8. 7, Con. Exch.

■ *Section B*

4. 1. $(C \supset D) \& (F \supset G)$ Premise
2. $C \vee F$ Premise
3. $(D \vee G) \supset H$ $/\therefore H$ Premise/Conclusion
4. $C \supset D$ 1, Conj. Simp.
5. $F \supset G$ 1, Conj. Simp.
6. $D \vee G$ 4, 5, 2, C.D.
7. H 3, 6, M.P.

8. 1. $(A \supset B) \& (A \vee C)$ Premise
2. $(C \supset D) \& (C \vee A)$ $/\therefore B \vee D$ Premise/Conclusion
3. $A \supset B$ 1, Conj. Simp.
4. $C \supset D$ 2, Conj. Simp.
5. $A \vee C$ 1, Conj. Simp.
6. $B \vee D$ 3, 4, 5, C.D.

12. 1. $L \supset M$ Premise
2. $(N \vee O) \supset L$ Premise
3. $(\sim L \vee M) \supset O$ $/\therefore M$ Premise/Conclusion
4. $(L \supset M) \supset O$ 3, Con. Exch.
5. O 4, 1, M.P.
6. $O \vee N$ 5, Disj. Add.
7. $N \vee O$ 6, Com.
8. L 2, 7, M.P.
9. M 1, 8, M.P.

■ *Section C*

4. 1. $L \supset (S \supset W)$ Premise
2. $\sim W \& L$ $/\therefore \sim S$ Premise/Conclusion
3. L 2, Conj. Simp.
4. $S \supset W$ 1, 3, M.P.
5. $\sim W$ 2, Conj. Simp.
6. $\sim S$ 4, 5, M.T.

8. 1. $(M \vee C) \supset \sim B$ Premise
2. $\sim B \supset \sim D$ Premise
3. $\sim D \supset S$ Premise
4. M $/\therefore S$ Premise/Conclusion
5. $\sim B \supset S$ 2, 3, Chain
6. $(M \vee C) \supset S$ 1, 5, Chain
7. $\sim (M \vee C) \vee S$ 6, Con. Exch.
8. $(M \& \sim C) \vee S$ 7, De M.
9. $S \vee (\sim M \& \sim C)$ 8, Com.
10. $(S \vee \sim M) \& (S \vee \sim C)$ 9, Dist.
11. $S \vee \sim M$ 10, Conj. Simp.
12. S 11, 4 Disj. Arg.

12. 1. $(S \& \sim V) \supset T$ Premise
     2. $[(\sim V \& I) \supset T] \supset D$ Premise
     3. $\sim D$ Premise
     4. $(V \lor \sim I) \lor \sim S$ /∴ $\sim T$ Premise/Conclusion
     5. $\sim[(\sim V \& I) \supset T]$ 2, 3 M.T.
     6. $\sim[\sim(\sim V \& I) \lor T]$ 5, Con. Exch.
     7. $\sim[(\sim\sim V \lor \sim I) \lor T]$ 6, De M.
     8. $\sim[(V \lor \sim I) \lor T]$ 7, D.N.
     9. $\sim(V \lor \sim I) \& \sim T$ 8, De M.
     10. $\sim T$ 9, Conj. Simp.

EXERCISE 8-4

■ *Section A*

4. Indirect method:
     1. $(\sim A \lor \sim C) \lor B$ Premise
     2. $\sim C \supset D$ Premise
     3. $E \lor \sim D$ Premise
     4. $\sim E \& A$ /∴ B Premise/Conclusion
     5. $\sim B$ Negation of conclusion
     6. $\sim A \lor \sim C$ 1, 5, Disj. Arg.
     7. A 4, Conj. Simp.
     8. $\sim C$ 6, 7, Disj. Arg.
     9. D 2, 8, M.P.
     10. $\sim E$ 4, Conj. Simp.
     11. $\sim D$ 3, 10, Disj. Arg.
     12. $D \& \sim D$ 9, 11, Adj.

   Direct method:
     1. $(\sim A \lor \sim C) \lor B$ Premise
     2. $\sim C \supset D$ Premise
     3. $E \lor \sim D$ Premise
     4. $\sim E \& A$ /∴ B Premise/Conclusion
     5. $\sim E$ 4, Conj. Simp.
     6. $\sim D$ 3, 5, Disj. Arg.
     7. $\sim(\sim C)$ 2, 6, M.T.
     8. C 7, D.N.
     9. A 4, Conj. Simp.
     10. $\sim A \lor (\sim C \lor B)$ 1, Assoc.
     11. $\sim C \lor B$ 9, 10, Disj. Arg.
     12. B 11, 8, Disj. Arg.

■ *Section B*

4.   1. $M \lor (J \& S)$ Premise
     2. $M \supset P$ Premise
     3. $P \supset S$ /∴ S Premise/Conclusion
     4. $\sim S$ Negation of conclusion
     5. $\sim P$ 3, 4, M.T.
     6. $\sim M$ 2, 5, M.T.
     7. $J \& S$ 1, 6, Disj. Arg.
     8. S 7, Conj. Simp.
     9. $S \& \sim S$ 8, 4, Adj.

EXERCISE 8-5

4. $P \supset (Q \lor R)$
    T (T) T (T) F
    $(Q \ \& \ R) \supset \ \sim P$
    T (F) F (T) (F) T
    $\therefore \sim P$
    (F) T

                                               P—*T*
                                              Q—*T*
                                              R—*F*

8. $M \lor \ \sim T$
    T (T) (T) F

    $T \supset (L \lor S)$
    F (T) F (F) F
    $M \ \& \ \sim L$
    T (T) (T) F
    $\therefore S$
     F

                                               M—*T*
                                              T—*F*
                                            L—*F*
                                                S—*F*

12. $\sim (R \ \& \ H)$
    (T) F (F) T

    $S \supset (R \lor H)$
    T (T) F (T) T

    $H \supset F$
    T (T) T

    H
    T

    $\therefore F \ \& \ [\sim (S \lor R)]$
    T (F) (F) T (T) F

                                               F—*T*
                                             S—*T*
                                            R—*F*
                                              H—*T*

CHAPTER 9

EXERCISE 9-1

■ *Section A*

4. "Defeated": polyadic (two places).
8. Express the statement as a conjunction: "Becky loves Mozart, and Becky loves Beethoven." Then the predicate "loves" occurs as a polyadic, two-place predicate in each conjunct (*Lbm & Lbe*; where *L* replaces "loves," *b* replaces "Becky," *m* replaces "Mozart," and *e* replaces "Beethoven").

■ *Section B*

4. Singular: *Cxy*, where "*C*" replaces "crossed," "*x*" replaces "Hannibal's elephants," and "*y*" replaces "the Alps."
8. Negation of a singular statement: "~*Ix*," where "*I*" replaces "infallible" and "*x*" replaces "the president." An alternative is "~(~*Fx*)" where "*F*" replaces "fallible."
12. General.
16. Conjunction of two singular statements: "*Sx & Px*," where "*S*" replaces "omniscient," "*P*" replaces "omnipotent," and "*x*" replaces "God."
20. Negation of a general statement.

EXERCISE 9-2

4. (a) Propositional function. (b) Not applicable (NA). (c) *x* is bound; *y* is free.

8. (a) (Compound) propositional function. (b) NA. (c) x is bound in the antecedent; both variables are free in the consequent.
12. (a) Statement. (b) Simple, general statement. (c) z is bound.
16. (a) Propositional function (compound with a propositional function as the second conjunct). (b) NA. (c) y is bound in the first conjunct; z is free in the second conjunct.
20. (a) Propositional function. (b) NA. (c) x is free in the first disjunct; z is bound in the second disjunct.

EXERCISE 9-3

■ *Section A*

4. $(x)(Cx \supset Mx)$
8. $(\exists y)(Wy \& Uy)$
12. $(z)(Tz \supset Pz)$
16. $(\exists x)(Ax \& Px)$
20. $(\exists x)(Sx \& \sim Hx)$
24. $(y)(Ey \supset Ty)$
28. $(\exists z)(Gz \& \sim Oz)$
32. $(x)(Vx \supset Wx)$

■ *Section B*

4. $(x)[Sx \supset (Dx \& Cx)]$
8. $(\exists y)(Py \& \sim Ty) \lor (\exists y)(Cy \& \sim Iy)$
12. $(\exists z)Hz \& \sim(z)Hz$
16. $(w)[(Vw \& \sim Sw) \supset Fw]$
20. $(w)[(Jw \& Bw) \supset Dw]$
24. $(x)[Px \supset (Sx \supset \sim Ax)]$

EXERCISE 9-4

4. $(x) \sim\sim(Fx \supset \sim Gx)$, D.N.; $\sim(\exists x)\sim(Fx \supset \sim Gx)$, Q.N.2; $\sim(\exists x)\sim(\sim Fx \lor \sim Gx)$, Con. Exch.
8. $\sim[(x)(Fx \lor Gx)] \lor [(x)\sim(Gx \equiv Rx)]$, Con. Exch.; $[(\exists x)\sim(Fx \lor Gx)] \lor [(x)\sim(Gx \equiv Rx)]$, Q.N.1; $[(\exists x)\sim(Fx \lor Gx)] \lor [\sim(\exists x)(Gx \equiv Rx)]$, Q.N.2; $(\exists x)(\sim Fx \& \sim Gx) \lor \sim(\exists x)(Gx \equiv Rx)$, De M.

EXERCISE 9-5

■ *Section A*

4. False. Since Gb and Kb are both true, $Gb \supset \sim Kb$ will be false, and the conjunction resulting from the truth-functional expansion will also be false.
8. False. Since Fa and Ha are true, while Ka and Ga are false, the first conjunct of the truth-functional expansion will be false.

■ *Section B*

4. $[\sim Fa \lor (\sim Fa \lor \sim Fb \lor \sim Fc)] \&$ $[\sim Fb \lor (\sim Fa \lor \sim Fb \lor \sim Fc)] \&$ $[\sim Fc \lor (\sim Fa \lor \sim Fb \lor \sim Fc)]$
8. $(Fa \& \sim Ga) \lor (Fb \& \sim Gb) \lor (Fc \& \sim Gc)$
12. $[Fa \supset (Ga \equiv Ha)] \& [Fb \supset (Gb \equiv Hb)] \& [Fc \supset (Gc \equiv Hc)]$

EXERCISE 9-6

■ *Section A*

4. 3. 2, E.I.
   4. 3, Conj. Simp.
   5. 1, U.I.
   6. 4, 5 M.P.
   7. 3, Com.
   8. 7, Conj. Simp.
   9. 8, 6 Adj.
   10. 9, E.G.
8. 3. 2, E.I.
   4. 1, U.I.
   5. 3, Conj. Simp.
   6. 4, 5 M.P.
   7. 3, Conj. Simp.
   8. 7, 6 Disj. Arg.
   9. 8, 7 Adj.
   10. 9, E.G.

■ *Section B*

4.
1. $(y)[Vy \supset (Dy \lor Fy)]$ Premise
2. $(y)[(Dy \lor Fy) \supset Iy]$ $/\therefore (y)[Sy \supset (Vy \supset Iy)]$ Premise/Conclusion
3. $Va \supset (Da \lor Fa)$ 1, U.I.
4. $(Da \lor Fa) \supset Ia$ 2, U.I.
5. $Va \supset Ia$ 3, 4 Chain
6. $(Va \supset Ia) \lor \sim Sa$ 5, Disj. Arg.
7. $\sim Sa \lor (Va \supset Ia)$ 7, Com.
8. $Sa \supset (Va \supset Ia)$ 7, Con. Exch.
9. $(y)[Sy \supset (Vy \supset Iy)]$ 8, U.G.

8.
1. $(\exists x)(Sx \lor Mx) \supset (x)Px$ Premise
2. $(\exists x) \sim Px$ $/\therefore (\exists x)(\sim Sx \ \& \sim Mx)$ Premise/Conclusion
3. $\sim(x)Px$ 2, Q.N.2
4. $\sim(\exists x)(Sx \lor Mx)$ 1, 3 M.T.
5. $(x) \sim (Sx \lor Mx)$ 4, Q.N.2
6. $\sim(Sa \lor Ma)$ 5, U.I.
7. $\sim Sa \ \& \sim Ma$ 6, De M.
8. $(\exists x)(\sim Sx \ \& \sim Mx)$ 7, E.G.

EXERCISE 9-7

4. (a) Invalidating natural interpretation: Let "Fx" symbolize "x is a mother"; "Gx" symbolize "x is a bachelor"; and "Hx" symbolize "x is a woman."
(b) Model universe and abbreviated truth table: model universe with one member, a.

$Fa \supset \sim Ga$
$Ga \supset \sim Ha$
$Fa \supset \sim Ha$

Fa	Ga	Ha	$\sim Ga$	$\sim Ha$	$Fa \supset \sim Ga$	$Ga \supset \sim Ha$	$Fa \supset \sim Ha$
T	F	T	T	F	T	T	F

8. (a) Invalidating natural interpretation: Let "Ax" symbolize "x is an apple," and let "Bx" symbolize "x is a fruit."
(b) Model universe and abbreviated truth table: model universe with one member, c.

$Ac \ \& Bc$
$Ac \lor \sim Bc$
$Ac \ \& \sim Bc$

Ac	Bc	$\sim Bc$	$Ac \ \& Bc$	$Ac \lor \sim Bc$	$Ac \ \& \sim Bc$
T	T	F	T	T	F

CHAPTER 10

EXERCISE 10-1

■ *Section A*

4. True. Inductive arguments cannot be formally valid; nor is it correct to regard them as invalid.

8. True. The premises must contain sufficient evidence and be sufficiently relevant to the conclusion to make it probable to the degree claimed for it.

12. True. In some cases, the probability that the conclusion is true can be expressed numerically as relative

frequency—for example, "There is a 60-percent chance that it will rain tomorrow," or the probability that the conclusion is true can be expressed numerically as a mathematical calculation—for example, "The odds are one in two, or 1/2, that a coin will land tails up."

■ *Section B*

4. Mathematical probability.
8. Rational credibility.
12. Relative frequency (as a percentage of cancer cases for a population).

EXERCISE 10-2

■ *Section A*

4. (a) Stronger. (b) Increased negative analogy.
8. (a) Weaker. (b) Increased positive analogy.

■ *Section B*

4. (a) Weaker. (b) Increased positive analogy.
8. (a) Stronger. (b) Increased negative analogy.
12. (a) Stronger. (b) Both larger sample and greater relevance of P (drinking retsina when eating feta cheese) to S (Samian farmers).

■ *Section C*

4. Hasty generalization due to unrepresentative sample. (Employee attitudes during the rush of Christmas shopping are not representative of employee attitudes generally.)
8. Hasty generalization due to lack of a relevant connection between the sample and the conclusion it is intended to support. (The instances in which Jane's lying was justified are not relevant to the problem concerning her term paper.)

EXERCISE 10-3

■ *Section A*

4. (a) Strengthened. (b) Negative analogy increases.
8. (a) Weakened. (b) Degree of similarity decreases.

■ *Section B*

4. (a) Weakened. (b) Positive analogy increases.
8. (a) Strengthened. (b) Conclusion claims less.

■ *Section C*

4. (a) Weakened. (b) Degree of similarity decreases.
8. (a) Strengthened. (b) Increases negative analogy.

■ *Section D*

4. This passage actually contains two arguments by analogy. The unstated conclusion of the first is to the effect that "Civil servants should not inspect or regulate guns." A suppressed premise is "Civil servants do not inspect stairways, etc." The second inductive analogy occurs in the last paragraph, and its conclusion is expressed in the first sentence of that paragraph. The second sentence expresses two premises: "By not banning fast cars, etc., we allow individuals to assume risks of injury and death," and "Guns are like fast cars, etc., in terms of the risks of injury and death they create."

Both analogies are weak. In assessing the first argument, one must question the *relevance* of the properties (P) of stairways, defective flooring, etc., to governmental regulation (S). There is some possibility of injury connected with everything we use, but the probability of injury from everyday objects is low. By contrast, since guns are *designed* to inflict injury, accidents involving them are more likely to cause injury. Guns also pose a greater risk of more serious injury. These differences suggest that regulation may be relevant to guns but not to the other objects mentioned.

The major difficulty with the second argument concerns the low degree of similarity between having a gun and the other activities cited. Those at risk from driving fast cars, skiing, swimming, etc., are primarily the persons who choose to engage in these activities, whereas guns pose a risk primarily for persons *other than* the gun owner or gun user. Furthermore, guns are often used as instruments of crime, whereas other sporting equipment is far less conducive to violent crime.

8. This passage involves a fallacy of faulty analogy. The similarities between depriving oneself of casual sexual relations (sex without love) and depriving oneself of food are superficial. Starvation is a cause of poor health; but there is no evidence that depriving oneself of casual sex results in poor health.

EXERCISE 10-4

4. (a)

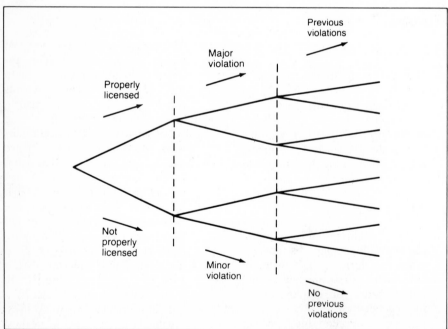

(b) 40, (c) 60, (d) 30.

8. (a) Employing the law of disjunction: $1/6 + 1/6 = 2/6 = 1/3$; (b) $3/6 = 1/2$.

12. (a) $25/50 = 1/2$; (b) $22/50 = 11/25$; (c) $15/50 = 3/10$.

16. Assuming independent events (i.e., no professor is both an existentialist and a logician): $1/2 + 1/4 = 3/4$. As-suming dependent events, the law of nonexclusive disjunction applies: $1/2 + 1/4 - (1/2 \times 1/4) = 3/4 - 1/8 = 5/8$.

20. $.84
24. This is sound advice if you want to gamble. It is based on recognition of the gambler's fallacy: that the "law of averages" does not make an "overdue" outcome more probable, (as long as each possible outcome remains equally probable).
28. If the student has only a 50–50 chance of passing each course, the chances of passing two courses are $1/2 \times 1/2$, or only one out of four. The student has confused the mul-tiplication of probabilities with the addition of probabilities.

CHAPTER 11

EXERCISE 11-1

4. (a) *Hypothesis:* The surface of the earth curves like the surface of a spherical object. (Eratosthenes for-mulates an additional hypothesis, which he does not test: the circum-ference of the world is approxi-mately 24,000 miles.) *Prediction:* At the same time of day the angle of sunlight at Syene should be mea-surably different from the angle of sunlight at Alexandria. (b) The re-sults corroborate the hypothesis. If the surface of the earth is flat and not curved, then we would expect the angle of sunlight to be the same at both Syene and Alexandria.
8. (a) *Hypothesis:* Something regu-larly prayed for will probably come about. (The hypothesis can be stated more precisely as follows: a result that is desired and for which there is prayer is more likely to occur than a result that is desired

but for which there is no prayer or less prayer.) *Predictions:* 1. The good health and longevity of royalty will be greater than the good health and longevity of members of the higher social classes generally. 2. The rate of stillbirths among the clergy will be lower than the rate of stillbirths among the professional classes generally. (b) The results certainly do not corroborate the hy-pothesis; they appear to disconfirm it. But whether all investigators ac-cept the evidence as disconfirming the hypothesis depends upon the probable truth of the conditional statements Galton forms (If *H* then *P*). Questions readily arise concern-ing these conditionals—for in-stance, is Galton warranted in as-suming that the clergy pray more frequently or more sincerely for their babies than do other members of the professional classes?

EXERCISE 11-2

■ *Section A*

4. Mercury, in a tube constructed to resemble the barrel of a pump, will rise to a height of 30 inches when the open end of the tube is sub-merged in a dish of mercury.
8. Yes. In the first place, they used two barometers—one remaining at the foot of Puy de Dôme. This ruled out the possibility that the atmospheric pressure changed at the foot of the mountain during the ascent. Sec-ondly, the column of mercury in the barometer carried up the moun-tainside was measured both at the base of the mountain and at its sum-mit. The reading at the base of the mountain was the same as the read-ing on the control barometer, thus ruling out the possibility that the barometer was defective.

■ *Section B*

4. The initial conditions consisted of data on the respective positions and velocity of the comet from observations made in 1682, the estimated gravitational attraction of the sun based on Newton's theory, and mathematical calculations of the comet's period and elliptical orbit (based on new mathematical developments such as infinitesimal calculus).

■ *Section C*

4. If [(*hypothesis*) oxygen combines with mercury when mercury is heated in a closed container of air], then [(*predictions*) the resulting calx, or red metallic oxide, will be heavier than the initial mercury and the volume of air in the container will have decreased].

8. When a bell jar is placed over a lighted candle, the candle will soon go out.

EXERCISE 11-3

■ *Section A*

4. A necessary condition, not a sufficient condition.
8. A necessary condition, not a sufficient condition.

■ *Section B*

4. (a) Stress is a sufficient cause of a higher rate of heart disease. (b) Difference.
8. (a) Tightening a violin string is a sufficient cause of the higher pitch it makes when vibrated. (b) Concomitant Variation.
12. (a) *First hypothesis:* Eating Szechuan hot bean curd is a sufficient condition for slowing the process of blood clotting. *Second hypothesis:* Eating black tree fungus is a sufficient condition for slowing the process of blood clotting. (b) *Test of first hypothesis:* Agreement and difference. *Test of second hypothesis:* Difference.

■ *Section C*

4. Unless these researchers have stronger evidence for the causal claim than that reported here, they have committed the causal fallacy of confusing causes with correlations. A positive correlation between an increase in REM sleep and learning is reported, but the evidence does not support the claim that the increase in REM sleep, *caused* the increase in learning. In fact, the reverse may be true: Success in learning may lead to greater personal satisfaction and, hence, to an enhanced ability to relax and sleep more deeply.

8. It is unclear from the *Time* report exactly what Molloy is claiming. If he is claiming only that certain clothes create the appearance of influence and authority, then he is hardly offering new advice. If he is making the more interesting claim that manner of dress *causes* greater personal influence and authority, then Molloy appears to have committed a causal fallacy by confusing a cause with a correlation. Certain styles and tastes in dress may be positively correlated with personal influence, but this may be because *both* dress and influence are caused by other factors. To show that clothes cause personal influence, Molloy needs to design experiments in which he could employ the method of difference to rule out other factors.

CHAPTER 12

EXERCISE 12-1

4. *This argument commits a fallacy of inconsistency:* From the second statement (about widespread unemployment and rioting), it would follow that the society is not economically sound and politically stable for all citizens. And this consequence contradicts the premise expressed in the first sentence.

8. *Not a fallacy of inconsistency: Because this passage does not present an argument, it is not a fallacy.* However, if what is claimed in the last sentence is correct, then one of the amendments to the Panama Canal Treaty is self-contradictory (at least in its wording).

EXERCISE 12-2

4. This passage contains an example of a fallacious argument resulting from a *complex question.*

8. This example suggests *invincible ignorance* on the part of the flying-saucer "experts." They seem to be attempting an *ad hoc rescue* for their hypothesis that flying saucers exist.

12. If taken as an argument for the conclusion that the twins did not attack anyone, this would be an example of *invincible ignorance* since the speaker's mind was made up before considering the evidence.

16. Patrick Buchanan used a *question-begging expression* to make it seem that the grand jurors were already prejudiced against President Nixon.

20. *Circular reasoning* occurs in this passage. That matter has always existed is presented as a reason why the world has always existed. But because we would normally understand the world to consist of matter, the speaker has not offered a reason independent of the conclusion.

24. This is an example of the variety of *invincible ignorance* known as *irrefutable hypothesis.* The concept of "Aryan race" turns out to be remarkably malleable and is hence pointless.

28. This can be seen as an instance of *invincible ignorance* of the type known as *irrefutable hypothesis.* The author continually revises his definition of "slave revolt" to insure that the evidence will not refute his hypothesis that the number of revolts was considerable.

EXERCISE 12-3

4. This is an example of the fallacy of *negative proof.* The government of South Africa may have atomic weapons, even though United States intelligence agencies have not acquired evidence to this effect.

8. This is an example of *moralism.* It attempts to conclude that homosexual relations are "unnatural" and immoral from statistical facts about the incidence of a disease in the homosexual population.

12. *Negative proof.* An alternative explanation may be true although there is no evidence at present for it.

EXERCISE 12-4

■ *Section A*

4. *Personal attack* of the *tu quoque* form. The charge "you smoke too" is irrelevant to the merits of the claim that smoking is hazardous to the smoker's health.

8. *Appeal to fear.* The appeal is irrelevant to either of the two issues raised by the letter: the adequacy of the insurance protection, and the value of the company's policies in meeting a family's insurance needs.

12. Ken Auletta is making a *personal attack* of the *tu quoque* form. His charge that the speaker's critics are probably guilty of similar infractions is irrelevant to his defense of the speaker's conduct. (In addition, by placing the speaker's conduct in the context of "politics as usual," the author can be said to be making an *appeal to tradition* known as the *appeal to common practice*.)

16. Tennis pro Tim Galloway offers an *appeal to the gallery* as his reason for believing in the divinity of Maharaj Ji. Galloway is playing on our sympathy for the guileless Maharaj Ji, who couldn't possibly pass as a con man. Galloway is also relying on an assumption he shares with his audience: we can all tell the difference between a con artist and an honest individual. (Note that this passage also contains two other fallacies. Galloway's initial reasoning about the divinity of Maharaj Ji suggests *false alternatives*: "He's either the real thing or a con artist." Furthermore, in responding to Ms. Gray's suggestion that Maharaj Ji was a bad con man, Galloway commits the *fallacy of numbers*, a specific version of the *appeal to tradition*.)

20. This is an example of an *abusive personal attack*. The opponent of the ERA tries to cast its supporters in a bad light without giving a cogent reason why the amendment is unacceptable.

24. This is an example of an *appeal to pity*. The emotional response the speaker wishes to evoke is irrelevant to the merits of the proposed right-to-die amendment. (However, the speaker's claim in the first paragraph that it is "compassionate, intelligent, and humane" to give people the "right to die" is not fallacious in itself.)

■ *Section B*

4. If President Carter responded as Senator Kennedy claimed, then his response, by appealing to the practice of past incumbents, is an *ad verecundiam* fallacy.

8. This statement can be interpreted as a premise in an implicit argument to the conclusion that the idea is of no value. As such, it is a case of *poisoning the well*, tantamount to the suggestion that the person in question is incapable of worthwhile notion.

12. Noam Chomsky poses a dilemma, the conclusion of which is, "there is no point in reading the book." Hence, he is *poisoning the well*.

EXERCISE 12-5

4. (a) It cannot be determined what conclusion either Bryant Gumbel or the other speaker advocated. (b) Bryant Gumbel poisoned the well.

8. (a) Dick Gregory is opposed, first of all, to birth control, and second, to what he calls "genocide"—presumably the attempt by organizations with predominantly white members to encourage black Americans to practice birth control. (b) Gregory commits the fallacy of moralism, arguing that birth control is wrong because it is not practiced by animals under natural conditions. Gregory's position also involves false alternatives: Either accept birth control *and* genocide, or reject birth control altogether.

12. (a) Senator William Scott wants to prove that *New Times*'s claim is libelous. (b) *New Times* seems to have committed an abusive personal attack on Senator Scott. However, the Senator's reasoning is also fallacious insofar as it involves false alternatives. He reasons that

either he will win the lawsuit and people will think he is intelligent, or he will lose the lawsuit and people will think *New Times* was right. But what people think of his intelligence may have nothing to do with his success in the courts.

16. (a) The president of Bob Jones University seeks to justify his university's refusal to admit black Americans. (b) The argument involves a hasty generalization: from a single statement made by a single leader of a civil-rights group, the president concludes that integrationists seek racial intermarriage. In addition, by suggesting to university students and their parents that the goal of racial integration must lead to racial intermarriage, the letter constitutes an appeal to fear. And, by trading on the assumption that the unanimity of the board's decision increases its justification, the writer introduces an *ad verecundiam* fallacy into the judgment. (A question could also be raised about the use of the NAACP leader's statement out of context. If its meaning has been distorted, the president has set up a straw man.)

20. (a) St. Augustine wishes to support the proposition that the soul is immortal, continuing with its cares after the death of the body. (b) In this passage, St. Augustine is recounting some of his reflections as a young man and, therefore, it may not be correct to treat it as argumentative discourse. However, if it is considered an argument, it is fallacious for two reasons: (1) Since the Christian faith proclaims the immortality of the soul and is now appealed to as a reason for accepting that proclamation, the position is circular, and (2) reliance on the authority of the Church makes it an *ad verecundiam* fallacy.

CHAPTER 13

EXERCISE 13-1

■ *Section A*

4. There is no real paradox. The legal system can operate effectively only if the vast majority of disputes can be settled out of court; otherwise the courts would be overburdened. In addition, a relatively small number of the cases heard in court raise new or difficult issues of law. And when issues of law do reach the appellate courts, judicial decisions, when they are supported by clear and relevant reasons, increase the ability of lawyers to settle similar problems arising in the future.

■ *Section B*

4. (a) *Attorney for Ms. Capezio:* If the foreign object in the pie has resulted in a health hazard requiring surgical expenses or in some other costly disability, then it is advisable to seek recovery from the restaurant for these expenses. It is probable that the Wagon Wheel will be willing to settle out of court.

    Attorney for the Wagon Wheel Restaurant: In view of the similarity between Ms. Capezio's accident and previous cases that have been decided in the plaintiff's favor, my recommendation would be to seek settlement out of court—unless Ms. Capezio's demands are unreasonable.

    (b) Yes. The lawyers' ability to "engineer" a solution to this problem is based on their knowledge of what the court is likely to decide, given the relevant precedents.

EXERCISE 13-2

4. (a) Reasoning involves making inferences: supporting a conclusion

by supplying the strongest available reasons. By contrast, rationalization is an attempt to create the appearance that a decision is reasonable, even though it was not reached by means of a logical process. (b) Ordinarily, someone who makes a rational decision can supply reasons that are both consistent and relevant to the conclusion they are intended to support. Someone offering a rationalization for a decision would be less able to present a clear, step-by-step, argument. (c) The legal realists appear to have believed that logical reasoning is always deductive. When judges make decisions that cannot be deduced from rules and statements of fact, they supposedly have no other pattern of reasoning upon which to rely and must therefore resort to such nonrational approaches as following "hunches." (d) Among these features are the following: (1) the expectation of lawyers that the judge's opinion will be responsive to the arguments made by counsel in the courtroom; (2) petitioner's and defendant's expectations that the judge's decision will conform to fundamental principles of justice, such as the principle that "like cases should be treated alike"; (3) legal training and experience, which will have made the attorneys familiar with a large number of previous cases; (4) the judge's awareness that the decision might be overturned by a superior court; (5) the judge's awareness that the decision might be scrutinized and criticized in law journals or other publications; (6) the judge's knowledge that the court's record will be published and that lawyers and judges in other cases may look to the decision for guidance.

8. (a) If Jerome Frank is correct, then we would expect his position to be supportable by evidence drawn from the behavior of judges. Judges with different backgrounds, political views, and personal tastes should have different feelings and should therefore reach different decisions. In addition, instead of giving so much attention to judicial opinions in past cases when preparing their arguments, lawyers should be more concerned to study the personality and personal history of the judge who will hear the case. (b) First, Frank and Hutcheson may have confused the psychological process by which a decision is made with the logic of making inferences. Hutcheson's claim that "decisions are based on the judge's hunches" is ambiguous, since *based on* in this context can mean either "motivated by" or "justified by." It is possible that many judges find hunches and intuitive sense useful in bringing the relevant facts and rules into view but do not consider these feelings legitimate reasons for a decision. (c) Yes. If law is understood as a problem-solving process, as suggested in Section 13-1, then decisions made by judges in appellate courts constitute the law. Such decisions are important in determining how rules made or enforced by the government can be used to solve specific problems. And what the judge decides about the meaning of a rule in a concrete case may be the conclusion of an argument, rather than the product of a nonrational intuition, or hunch. (d) Yes, just as it can be true that "the vital motivating impulse for the correct solution to a logic problem is the student's desire for a high grade" and false that "whatever pro-

duces the student's motivation makes the student's solution to the problem correct."

EXERCISE 13-3

[Because of the nature of these exercises, no solutions are provided.]

EXERCISE 13-4

4. (a) This comment confuses two different prescriptive uses of a model of legal reasoning. Such a model might improve the quality of argumentation and make judicial opinions more reasonable in the sense of logically stronger. But a logical model cannot be a decision-making procedure that tells judges which decisions are morally correct or just. (b) This attitude ignores the value of improving one's ability to solve problems reasonably. Experience shows that the more reasonable one is in facing most problems, the better the results tend to be, at least in the long run. (c) This position arises out of a verbal dispute over the meaning of the term *just*. The arguer believes that *just decision* simply means "reasonable decision," a belief that might be explained in either of two ways: (1) The arguer may be skeptical that moral standards apply to judicial decisions—although no reasons are presented for such skepticism. (2) The arguer may be failing to distinguish between procedural justice and substantive justice. Procedural safeguards—provisions generally referred to as "due process of law"—are intended to insure minimal levels of fair treatment. But assuring that proper procedures are followed does not exhaust the meaning of *justice*. There are also substantive principles to be considered.

CHAPTER 14

EXERCISE 14-1

■ *Section A*

4. Standardizing statements clarifies the meaning of an argument in several ways: (a) All sentences and expressions that do not function as statements in the argument are deleted. (b) Redundant assertions are removed. (c) Claims that are qualified are identified and rewritten as qualified. (d) Terms that have an emotive as well as a cognitive function are "desensitized" by the substitution of emotively neutral synonyms. (e) Suppositions, when they occur, are rephrased as antecedents of conditional statements.

8. The proper method of assessing the plausibility of a premise is most efficiently found by first deciding whether it is more reasonable to treat the premise as an empirical statement or as a necessary statement.

12. To accept an argument provisionally means that because the inference is deductively valid and all premises but one are acceptable, one will also accept the conclusion *on condition* that the questionable premise can also be shown to be true.

16. In presupposing an argument, one entertains the arguer's point of view and one attempts to determine what new insight or information could correct or improve the argument so that it would support its conclusion.

20. The major objective is to decide what position to take on the issue addressed by the argument.

■   *Section B*

4. (a) *Finding the main conclusion.*
On careful reading of this passage
from Dworkin's article, we find two
principles for which he offers support. One is expressed in the very
first sentence. The other occurs in
the last paragraph: ". . . it is rational
and prudent for us to . . . take out
'social insurance policies.'" But
which is the main conclusion? The
author is concerned more with paternalism as a social or political
measure than with privately arranged paternalistic relationships.
Thus, if we understand *social insurance policies* to be a system of
government that permits legislators
to make paternalistic laws on occasion, the sentence identified in
the last paragraph expresses the
main conclusion. (b) *Clarifying
meaning.* Careful scrutiny of the argument reveals four trouble spots:
(1) Because the whole argument involves the justification of paternalistic measures, we need to establish
a clear understanding of paternalism: paternalism occurs when an individual (e.g., a parent) or an organized group (e.g., the legislature)
decides that something must be
done to promote the welfare of another, even if this individual does
not agree that the action is in his or
her best interests. For example, a
state legislature acts paternalisti-
cally when it requires that motor-
cyclists must protect themselves by
wearing crash helmets. (2) The
meaning of *social insurance policies*
must be determined. It can be
understood as indicated in the preceding discussion of finding the
main conclusion. (3) How should
we understand the examples occurring in the first and second para-
graphs? The second paragraph can

be discarded; it *is* an example of the
situation described by the second
sentence of the entire passage. But
although that sentence begins with
"If, for example, . . ." it should not
be discarded. The sentence describes a condition under which it
is rational for an individual to accept paternalistic constraints.
Thus, it is a premise for the statement expressed in the first sentence
and, as such, is integral to the argument. (4) What are we to make
of the first sentence of the third paragraph? If it expresses a premise,
then what does it support? In fact,
it is not a premise but an indication
that the author is reasoning by analogy. The same point needs to be
made about the sentence toward
the end of the paragraph: "Such is
not the case for the paternalistic
measures we have been speaking
about." Here is an indication that
the author is now making a distinction between specific paternalistic
measures and a paternalistic system
of government. Both remarks are
thus clues to the structure of the argument but are not integral statements *in* the argument.

As shown by this discussion of
the overall structure of the extended argument, the basic pattern
of reasoning is by analogy. Paternalistic measures are most justifiable when the coercion or constraint
of an individual was (as in the case
of Odysseus) specifically requested
by that individual at some other
time. Specific paternalistic social
measures can be justified to the extent that they approximate this
model. Finally, a paternalistic "system of government" may be justified to the extent that its requirements would be desired or accepted
as forms of protection by fully rational individuals.

EXERCISE 14-2

■ *Section A*

4. The integral statements explicit in the argument (with some rephrasing) are as follows:

   MC: A woman's right to obtain an abortion is absolute.

   P_1: The view that abortion is wrong because it involves the killing of a human being is mistaken.

   P_2: A fetus does not have a moral right to life.

   SP_1: Only human beings that are also persons—members of the moral community—have a moral right to life.

   SP_2: A fetus is very unlike a person.

   D: Both fetuses and persons are biologically human.

   Tree Diagram

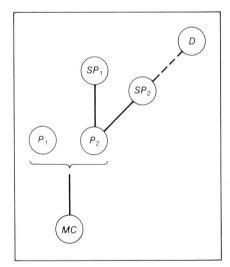

8. The integral statements:

   MC: Sex is not to be confused with love; only the latter is a cornerstone of lasting value.

   P_1: Sex is valuable as a source of pleasure and an occasional expres-

sion of love, but it is not a cornerstone or foundation for greater and more lasting values.

P_2: Love typically develops over a long-term relation: its pleasures are cumulative in value.

P_3: Love may well be central in an individual's rational system of values.

P_4: Love may have a deep moral significance relating to the identification of one's interests with those of another person.

SP_1: Sexual pleasure is good for the individual.

SP_2: Sexual pleasure may be necessary for many persons to function in a reasonably cheerful way.

SP_3: Sexual pleasure is essentially self-regarding.

SP_4: (Implicit) Sex is sometimes the expression of love.

SP_5: Sex does not create the lasting kind of value that enhances one's whole life.

SP_{11}: Sex is a needed outlet for desire.

SP_{12}: Sex is the most enjoyable form of recreation.

SP_{51}: The pleasures of sex are brief and repetitive rather than cumulative.

(The tree diagram for this exercise is shown on p. 582.)

EXERCISE 14-3

■ *Section A*

4. Prudential: To avoid serious dental problems, you ought to see your dentist at least twice a year.
   Moral: Because it is good to have healthy teeth and wrong to let them

Tree Diagram

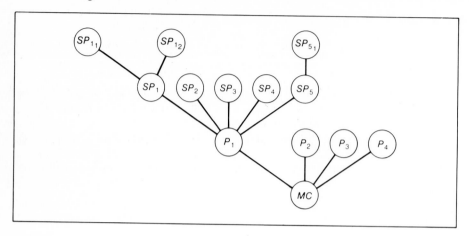

decay, you ought to see your dentist at least twice a year.

8. Moral: If you are planning to sell souvenirs on the city streets, you ought to be fair to the students you'll employ and give them an hourly wage they'll deserve for that tiring work.

12. Legal: Since the state legislature requires this program, you ought to let the school immunize your children.

   Prudential: Because it will cost you nothing in time or money and it protects your children's health, you'd be foolish not to let the school immunize your children.

   Moral: It is only right to let the school immunize your children so they won't become ill and suffer and perhaps spread the disease to others.

16. Ceremonial: The polite thing to do is to pay up whenever you are fined.

   Legal or prudential: You ought to pay the fine and avoid the risk of greater penalties.

   Moral: Because you promised to return the book on time and didn't do so, you ought to pay the fine.

20. Moral or aesthetic: You ought to throw away that magazine because it is ugly trash.

   Ceremonial: You should get rid of that pornographic magazine because it might embarrass your guests.

   Moral: You ought to throw the magazine away because it's wrong to entertain yourself with material that debases women.

■ *Section B*

4. Deontological, or Kantian standard.

8. Divine Command standard.

■ *Section C*

4. For: Several standards: Natural Law, Divine Command, Intuitionist, Egoistic (as contrary to one's long-term interests); Relativist (if the practice is generally condemned in society); Rule-Utilitarian, and Deontological, or Kantian (as against a duty or obligation to oneself or others).

   Against: Subjectivist or.Egoistic (if it is argued that it does not run contrary to one's best interests); Relativist (if it is argued that the action is generally accepted by society); Act-Utilitarian (if it is argued that the pleasure produced for the individual outweighs any harm and that other members of society are not adversely affected).

8. For: Subjectivist, Egoistic, Relativist (if pilfering and petty larceny or shoplifting are generally condoned in society); Act-Utilitarian (if it is argued that the good to the individual outweighs harm caused for all others).

Against: Divine Command; Deontological, or Kantian; Rule-Utilitarian (if it is argued that society is better off, on the whole, when its members obey rules against stealing and shoplifting); Intuitionist (if one's conscience says it is wrong); Relativist (if it is generally condemned by society).

■ *Section D*

Criticism 1: This criticism is intended to show that if one tries to use the Act-Utilitarian standard as a consistent guide to action, one will really end up employing the Rule-Utilitarian standard instead.

The criticism is implicitly directed at the vagueness of the Act-Utilitarian standard. On the one hand, it is too general to be applied to concrete problems because it does not specify which particular actions maximize happiness. On the other hand, if one relies on guidelines abstracted from experience, then one is acting on the basis of rules and not trying to calculate the maximum happiness in each case.

Criticism 2: The critics are presenting a hypothetical case to show that the Act-Utilitarian standard would justify an action that most people would find morally repugnant.

This is an example of an effort to attack a moral standard by showing that, under certain circumstances, the standard would prescribe an action that we find intuitively wrong. It attempts to show that application of the standard would be inconsistent with other strong moral beliefs. Presumably we should trust these strongly felt intuitions more than the standard in question.

INDEX